REGIMENTAL RECORDS OF THE ROYAL WELCH
FUSILIERS 1918–1945

VOLUME V
PART ONE, NOVEMBER 1918–MAY 1940

The Colours of the 1st Battalion in service between
1918 and 1945.

His Majesty King George V, Colonel-in-Chief of the Royal
Welch Fusiliers, 1902–1936. (R.W.F. Mus)

Regimental Records of the Royal Welch Fusiliers 1918–1945

Volume V: Part One, November 1918–May 1940

Compiled by
Lieutenant General Jonathon Riley CB DSO PhD MA FRHistS FRGS
Lieutenant Colonel Peter Crocker
the late Lieutenant Colonel Richard Sinnett

Helion & Company

Helion & Company Limited
Unit 8 Amherst Business Centre
Budbrooke Road
Warwick
CV34 5WE
England
Tel. 01926 499 619
Fax 0121 711 4075
Email: info@helion.co.uk
Website: www.helion.co.uk
Twitter: @helionbooks
Visit our blog http://blog.helion.co.uk/

Published by Helion & Company 2019
Designed and typeset by Mach 3 Solutions Ltd (www.mach3solutions.co.uk)
Cover designed by Paul Hewitt, Battlefield Design (www.battlefield-design.co.uk)
Printed by Short Run Press, Exeter, Devon

Text © Trustees of the Royal Welch Fusiliers Museum 2018
Photographs © as individually credited
Maps © Steve Waites 2018 except where otherwise credited

Cover images: © Trustees of the Royal Welch Fusiliers Museum 2018

ISBN 978-1-912390-76-2

British Library Cataloguing-in-Publication Data.
A catalogue record for this book is available from the British Library.

For details of other military history titles published by Helion & Company Limited contact the above
address, or visit our website: http://www.helion.co.uk.

We always welcome receiving book proposals from prospective authors.

Contents

List of Illustrations

List of Maps

Author's Preface
by Lieutenant General J.P. Riley

This is a Regimental Record, not a Regimental History – the two are different. A Regimental History will tend to present a narrative which highlights certain aspects of the Regiment's life, usually war service, and will tend to dwell on the more creditable actions during the period it covers. It will not, therefore, be comprehensive but rather selective: *The Red Dragon*, the Royal Welch Fusiliers' short history of the period from 1919 to 1945, is an excellent example. A Regimental Record, however, is just that. It is, as far as is possible, a comprehensive review of all the units within a Regiment's compass and all that took place, for good or ill. It will also record as far as possible the details of those who served.

Because of the comprehensive nature of Regimental Records, they tend to be lengthy. Volumes III and IV of our Records, for example, span only four years, 1914 to 1918, and yet fills two books. This Volume, V, fills the gap between the end of Volume IV in November 1918 and the beginning of Volume VI in late 1945 – and there is some overlap at both ends. During the Great War, the Regiment fielded a total of forty-five battalions, if the five battalions of the Volunteer Force are included. This is the fourth highest total of any Regiment on the Army List during those years, and remarkable given the relative paucity of population in Wales, compared with the great urban centres of England. During the Second World War, and without double-counting those units which changed their title, the Regiment fielded three Regular battalions, including a parachute battalion, seven Territorial battalions, six service battalions, two independent companies, three anti-tank companies or batteries, five artillery regiments and two independent H.G. troops, twenty-eight Home Guard battalions and three M.T. Companies – a total of fifty-one battalion-equivalent units. A summary is as follows:

Unit	Remarks
Regular Battalions	
1st	N.W. Europe, U.K., India, Burma
2nd	India, U.K., Madagascar, Burma
6th (R.W.) Para	Converted from 10th Battalion; U.K., N. Africa, Italy, S. France, Greece
Territorial Battalions	
4th	U.K. incl N.I., N.W. Europe
5th	Converted to 60th (R.W.F.) A.T. Regiment R.A.
6th	U.K. incl N.I., N.W. Europe

Unit	Remarks
7th	U.K. incl N.I., N.W. Europe
8th	U.K.; formed from 4 R.W.F. as second-line unit
9th	U.K., incl N.I.; formed from 6 R.W.F. as second-line unit
10th	U.K. formed from 7 R.W.F. as second-line unit; became 6th (R.W.) Para
Independent Companies	
No 2	Norway, U.K.
No 9	U.K.
115 (R.W.F.) A.T. Coy	U.K.
158 (R.W.F.) A.T. Coy	U.K.
Service Battalions	
1/11th	U.K.; became 11th Battalion
2/11th	U.K.; became 14th Battalion
11th	U.K.; originally formed from four National Defence Companies, divided into 1/11th and 2/11th; re-emerged on re-designation of 1/11th. Later re-designated as 30th Battalion
12th	U.K.; became 116th L.A.A. Regiment R.A. (R.W.)
13th	U.K. incl N.I.; formed from 50th Holding Battalion
14th	U.K.; formed from 2/11th Battalion and later re-designated as 31st Battalion
30th	U.K.; previously 11th Battalion
31st	U.K.; previously 14th Battalion
50th Holding Battalion	U.K. Formed from 7th Infantry Holding Battalion; re-designated as 13th Battalion
70th (Young Soldiers) Battalion	U.K.
Artillery Regiments	
60th (R.W.F.) A.T. Regiment	U.K., N.W. Europe 1940, N. Africa, Italy. Formed from 5 R.W.F.; converted to 101st L.A.A. & A.T. Regiment; then re-designated 76th (R.W.F.) A.T. Regiment before final re-designation as 60th (R.W.F.) A.T. Regiment
70th (R.W.F.) A.T. Regiment	U.K. Formed from 60th (R.W.F.) A.T. Regiment as second-line unit
71st (R.W.F.) A.T. Regiment	U.K., N.W. Europe; formed from cadres of 70th (R.W.F.) A.T. Regiment
76th (R.W.F.) A.T. Regiment	U.K., N. Africa. Formed from R.W.F. batteries of 101st L.A.A. & A.T. Regiment; re-designated as 60th (R.W.F.) A.T. Regiment
101st L.A.A. & A.T. Regiment	U.K., N.W. Europe 1940. Formed from 60th (R.W.F.) A.T. Regiment; re-designated 76th (R.W.F.) A.T. Regiment
116th L.A.A. Regiment (R.W.)	Formed from the 12th Battalion

Unit	Remarks
237 (R.W.F.) Independent A.T. Battery	Italy
Home Guard Units	
1st, 2nd and 3rd Anglesey	U.K.
1st, 2nd, 3rd, 4th and 5th Carnarvonshire	U.K.
1st, 2nd, 6th, 8th, 9th, 10th, 11th and 12th Denbighshire	U.K.
3rd, 4th and 5th Flintshire	U.K.
7th Denbigh & Flint	U.K.
1st, 2nd and 4th Merioneth	U.K.
5th, 6th, 7th Montgomeryshire	U.K.
3rd Merioneth & Montgomeryshire	U.K.
A Tp 456 and A Tp 457 H.G. L.A.A. Batteries	U.K.
221, 222 and 224 H.G. M.T. Companies	U.K.

For this reason, Volume V has had to be divided into two parts. Part One covers the Regiment's service from November 1918 – including a wrap-up of Great War units left unfinished in Volume IV – to the Summer of 1940; Part Two covers Summer 1940 to late 1945. The division in the Summer of 1940 was chosen because at that point, the 1st Battalion, 101st L.A.A. & A.T. Regiment and the Independent Companies had all been evacuated from Europe; the 2nd Battalion was homeward bound from India; the three first-line T.A. battalions had embarked for Northern Ireland; the three second-line T.A. battalions had been fully embodied; the first tranche of service battalions had been formed; and the Local Defence Volunteers were being transformed into the Home Guard. This, to us, seemed more logical than a rather artificial division on 3 September 1939.

The emphasis of the volume is of course on the Second World War during which our battalions, independent companies and artillery regiments served in every major theatre and campaign, except Ethiopia and Syria. However the division into two parts has allowed a proper examination of the British Army between the wars and its deployments around the world. In addition to the Imperial garrisons and the experimentation programme at home, there were operations in north and south Russia, the Transcaucasus, Turkey, Germany, Cyprus, Palestine, Somalia, Eritrea, Egypt, Ireland, Afghanistan, the North-West Frontier of India and China. It was no long week-end.

It has taken a long time for this Volume to see the light of day, first because, oddly, the Regimental Committee decided after the War not to continue with the tradition of Regimental Records but instead to produce a short history. This, although admirable in its way, has severe limitations. It is very short, does not cover every unit, mentions few people by name and, because the War Diaries were not available, is frequently wrong in detail. In the late 1990s the Regimental Committee decided to reverse that decision and put in hand Volumes V and VI, which would cover 1919 to 2000. Volume VI soon became Volumes VI and VII, for the reasons already spelt out and they were published in 2001. While I, the then Brigadier J.P. Riley, was writing Volumes VI and VII, Lieutenant Colonels Peter Crocker and Richard Sinnett began work on Volume V. This work however stalled, not least because of Richard Sinnett's death, but also because of Peter Crocker's retirement and move of house. In 2015, the Trustees of the Regimental Museum (there being no longer a Regimental Committee) decided that the work had to be re-energised and asked me to pick it up. This I did. Fortunately Peter Crocker had done at least half of the work needed on the inter-war years, and some of the Annexes; and Richard Sinnett had compiled large amounts of data on various subjects. This work, along with my own researches during the writing of the biographies of Generals Stockwell and Farrar-Hockley, allowed me, with more help from Peter Crocker – who has proof-read, edited and corrected every draft – and others named in the acknowledgements below but especially Allan Poole, to finish the work in time for the centenary of the Versailles Treaty in 1919 and the eightieth anniversary of the outbreak of Second World War in 1939.

Acknowledgements

I would like to thank many people and institutions for their help, without which this volume could not have been written. first, all those whom I interviewed or helped me with interviews, for their time, their trouble and their memories: Paddy Deacon, Teddy Gueritz, Glyn Hughes, Cliff Meredith, W.H. Jones and Jack Ellis. Jonathan Ware for material on 101st A.A. & A.T. Regiment in 1940. Donald E. Graves and the family of the late Major Jon Latimer for material on 76th (R.W.F.) Anti-Tank Regiment in 1942; Allan Poole, Richard Ward, Andrew Newson and Anne Pedley for carrying out extensive and invaluable research and correcting the drafts. Next, Kevin Mason, Shirley Williams, Allan Poole (again), Karen Murdoch, Keith Jones and Kelly Davies at the Royal Welch Fusiliers Archives, Wrexham, Caernarfon Castle and Bodelwyddan Castle; the Trustees of the Royal Welch Fusiliers Museum for permission to use material from *The Red Dragon, The Royal Welch Fusiliers 1919–1945* as well as other material from the archives as noted in the bibliography and source notes; Chris Hughes for research on vehicles and uniforms; Mrs Libby Owen for material from her father, the late Major Artro Roberts of 4 R.W.F.; Major Dominic Spencer and his family for the use of the diary of Major Fleming-Jones, 6th (RW) Para; the staff at the Liddell-Hart Centre for Military History, King's College London; the staff at the Imperial War Museum photographic archive; Max Arthur for material from *Men of the Red Beret;* Francesco di Cinito for material on 2 Parachute Brigade in Italy; Major T.C.C. Dumas for material from his memoir *Lucky Tim;* Major N.P. Cutcliffe for his memoir of Normandy; the late Mrs Dilys R. Glover for permission to use material from the collection of her late father, Lieutenant Colonel H. Maldwyn Davies (5 R.W.F.); Major Miles Stockwell for material from his father's collections; the Minshull-Ford family for material from the collections of John and Francis Minshull-Ford; Mr William Fox for material on 2 R.W.F. between the wars; Mr Simon Lloyd-Morrison for material from the collections of Colonel James Ellis Evans; Victoria Hodgson for material from the collections of J.R. Gibbins; the *Victor* comic ©DC Thomson & Co Ltd, for images reproduced by courtesy of DC Thomson & Co Ltd; the estate of Sir Oswald Hornby Joseph Birley for the use of his portrait of King George VI as Colonel-in-Chief of the Regiment; last but by no means least, Steve Waites, who has drawn the maps for this book to such a high standard, as he has done for my last nine books.

In addition to all the above I would like to place on record the work of the reviewing and editing committee of the Board of Trustees, which has scrutinized and corrected the work, adding much valuable information and saving me from a multitude of serious blunders. They were Colonel J.C.W. Williams MC DL, the late Colonel Philip Eyton-Jones TD DL,* Mrs Anne Pedley, Mr Allan Poole, Colonel N.J. Lock OBE, the Rev Mr Clive Hughes and Dr Philip Abbott.

---

*   Colonel Eyton-Jones, who had been secretary to the Trustees for many years, died in 2018, before the work on the Volume was completed.

Note on the Index

The two parts of this volume are separately indexed, in order to avoid the inconvenience of having both parts open when searching for an entry, which is the case with Volume IV. Readers should note, however, that in both parts, the major indexes dealing with Honours and Awards, and the Roll of Honour, are not indexed. This is because these Annexes are for the most part alphabetical.

Chronology 1919–1940

1919

General

Aug	Depot resumed the training of recruits at Wrexham from the 3rd (SR) Battalion at Limerick; Lt Col E.R. Kearsley DSO in command

1st Battalion

31 Jan	Lt Col J.B. Cockburn DSO to command	RD/363
23 Feb	Cadre left Italy	RRIV/268; AB487
1 Mar	Cadre reached Wrexham	J/Mar 32/2
12 May	re-formed Park Hall Camp, Oswestry	RD/2; AB487
19 Oct	embarked at Liverpool on HT *Northumberland* for India	J/Mar 32/2 AB487 25 Oct
17 Nov	arrived Lucknow, India	AB487

2nd Battalion

24 May	Cadre departed Blangy, France	Dunn, p 580–584; AB487
29 May	sailed from Le Havre	as above
6 Jun	arrived Wrexham	as above
6 Aug	arrived Limerick, Ireland	AB487
21 Aug	Lt Col O. de L. Williams CMG DSO to command	RD/363

3rd (Special Reserve) Battalion

9 Aug	absorbed by 2nd Bn at Limerick	AB487
23 Aug	disembodied and returned in cadre form to Wrexham. Lt Col A.R.P. Macartney-Filgate CBE in command	AB487

4th (Denbighshire) Battalion (T.F.)

16 May	arrived Shoreham from Belgium	AB487
?	moved to Wrexham	AB487
11 Jun	demobilised	AB487

5th (Flintshire) Battalion (T.F.)

Mar	nationalist uprising in Egypt	Clayton p 112–117
Jul	reduced to Cadre in Egypt	AB487
2 Aug	arrived Wrexham	AB487

4 Aug	disembodied Rhyl	AB487

6th (Caernarvon & Anglesey) Battalion (T.F.)
4 Aug	Reduced to Cadre in Egypt; to Caernarfon 4 Aug and disembodied	

5th/6th Battalion (T.F.)
Jul Egypt. To Wrexham 2 Aug and disbanded

7th (Merioneth & Montgomery) Battalion (T.F.)
	in Egypt	AB487
Mar	nationalist uprising in Egypt	Clayton p 112–117

24th (Denbighshire Yeomanry) Battalion (T.F.)
23 May	arrived Catterick from France	AB487
28 May	disbanded	AB487

25th (Montgomeryshire & Welsh Horse Yeomanry) Battalion (T.F.)
21 Jun	arrived Welshpool from France	AB487
29 Jun	disbanded	AB487

8th (Service) Battalion
7 Apr	arrived India from Mesopotamia	AB487
?	reduced to Cadre in India	AB487
16 Aug	arrived Wrexham	AB487
21 Aug	disbanded	AB487

9th (Service) Battalion
25 May	arrived Sandling from France	AB487
2 Jun	disbanded	AB487

11th (Service) Battalion
14 Oct	disbanded in Macedonia	AB487

13th (Service) Battalion (1st North Wales)
23 May	arrived Newmarket from France	AB487
4 Jun	disbanded	AB487

14th (Service) Battalion
23 May	arrived Newmarket from France	AB487
4 Jun	disbanded	AB487

16th (Service) Battalion
23 May	arrived Newmarket from France	AB487
6 Jun	disbanded	AB487

17th (Service) Battalion (2nd North Wales)
25 May	arrived Newmarket from France	AB487
7 Jun	disbanded	AB487

23rd (Service) Battalion

23 Mar	disbanded in Norfolk	

26th (Service) Battalion (formerly 4th Garrison Battalion)

7 May	to U.K. on leave from Belgium	AB487
23 May	to Marseilles, France	AB487
28 May	embarked Marseilles	AB487
4 Jun	arrived Alexandria, Egypt	AB487
9 Jun	to Damanhur, south of Alexandria	AB487
Aug	to Tanta, south of Alexandria	AB487
Sep	draft to 7th Bn (T.F.) in Egypt	AB487
Sep	to Sidi Bishr	AB487

1st Garrison Battalion

4 Nov	arrived Crowborough from Gibraltar	AB487

2nd Garrison Battalion

Mar	nationalist uprising in Egypt	Clayton p 112–117
17 Sep	disbanded in Egypt	AB487

3rd (Reserve) Garrison Battalion

16 May	disbanded in Ireland	AB487

6th Garrison Battalion

24 Jun	Egypt, to UK in June and disbanded	AB487

3rd Reserve Battalion

16 May	disbanded in Britain	

1st, 2nd, 3rd, 4th and 5th (Volunteer) Battalions

Oct	disbanded in North Wales	

1920

General

Feb	spelling of 'Welch' in title approved	Army Order 56

1st Battalion

	remained at Lucknow in India	
12 May	Lt Col C.C. Norman CMG DSO to command vice Lt Col Cockburn DSO (ill-health)	RD/2, 363
Jun	assisted in suppression of mutiny by 1st Connaught Rangers at Solon, India	Clayton, p 510
Jul	mutiny by detachment at Ranikhet	R.W.F. Mus 4284/1; James, p 206

2nd Battalion

	remained at Limerick, Ireland	
15 May	Lt Col C.C. Norman CMG DSO to command	RD/4, 363

vice Lt Col O. de L. Williams CMG DSO (to command T.A. Bde)

7th (Merioneth & Montgomery) Battalion (T.F.)

23 Jan	reduced to Cadre in Egypt	AB487
2 Mar	arrived Newtown	AB487
12 Mar	disembodied and demobilised	AB487

26th (Service) Battalion

10 Jan	Cadre returned to U.K.	AB487
20 Jan	disbanded	AB487

1st Garrison Battalion

14 Feb	disbanded	AB487

4th (Denbighshire) Battalion (T.A.)

Feb	reconstituted as a T.A. bn	Skaife p65
Aug	Camp at Rhyl	

5th (Flintshire) Battalion (T.A.)

Feb	reconstituted as a T.A. bn	Westlake, p120
Aug	Camp at Rhyl	

6th (Carnarvonshire & Anglesey) Battalion (T.A.)

Feb	reconstituted as a T.A. bn	as above
Aug	Camp at Rhyl	

7th (Montgomeryshire) Battalion (T.A.)

Feb	reconstituted as a T.A. bn	mentioned in Skaife
Aug	Camp at Rhyl	

1921

General

9 Aug	Col of Regt, Gen Sir Francis Lloyd, presented silk Union Flags to 8th, 10th, 11th, 15th, & 19th (Service) Bns, and 1st, 2nd & 6th Garr Bns at Wrexham. Those of the 8th, 9th, 10th, 19th, 26th, & 1st & 2nd Garr Bns placed in Wrexham Parish Church	J/May 22/15

1st Battalion

	remained at Lucknow, India	
10 Sep	Lt Col C.S. Owen CMG DSO to command vice Lt Col C.C. Norman CMG DSO	RD/36
1 Dec	Bn Depot formed at Lucknow	J/May 23/122
2 Dec	left Lucknow by train for Waziristan via Bareilly, Amritsar & Lahore	
4 Dec	arrived Mari Indus	as above
7 Dec	complete at Tank	as above
8 Dec	arrived Manzai	as above
	Bn Depot to Kuldana, Murree Hills	J/May 23/122

9 Dec	arrived Jandola	J/May 22/7
10 Dec	arrived Kotkai	as above
11 Dec	arrived Sararogha	as above
	CSM C. Rush DCM (A Coy) killed by sniper	as above
12/13 Dec	arrived Ladha Camp. Joined 9 Indian Inf Bde	as above

2nd Battalion, I.R.A.

	remained at Limerick, Ireland	
18 Mar	Lt Col F.J. Walwyn DSO to command vice Lt Col C.C. Norman CMG DSO	RD/36
28 Apr	Maj G.L. Compton-Smith DSO shot by IRA whilst hostage in Ireland	Hansard 1 Jun 21
11 Jul	truce came into effect in Ireland	Clayton

T.A. Battalions

	T.A. battalions to carry all Regimental battle honours on Colours	AO 338
13 Jul	5 R.W.F. War Memorial unveiled at Rhyl	
Aug	4, 5, 7 R.W.F. Camp at Rhyl; 6 R.W.F. Camp at Blackpool	
Sep	6 R.W.F. War memorial unveiled at Caernarfon	

1922

General

May	Regimental Journal *Y Ddraig Goch* Series I first published	J/May 22
13 Jul	5th Bn War Memorial unveiled at the Drill Hall, Rhyl	J/Oct 22/61
Sep	Regimental Battle Honours Committee met in London	J/May 23/172

Depot

| 27 May | Maj H.V. Venables Kyrke DSO to command vice Lt Col E.R. Kearsley DSO | J/Oct 22/58 |
| 20 Sep | tablet to VC winners unveiled | |

1st Battalion

	remained at Ladha, Waziristan	
1 May	Bn Depot moved from Kuldana to Dalhousie, Punjab	J/May 22/123
10 May	Sgt Hanscombe killed by sniper at Prospect Picquet	WD
4 Jul	Goat died at Dalhousie	WD
16 Jul	Gen Sir Claude Jacob, Chief of the General Staff (India) visited Bn	WD
29 Jul	action at Windy Snip/Prospect Picquet, 3 soldiers killed & 3 wounded	J/Oct 22/42; WD
5 Oct	Maj E.O. Skaife OBE assumed command vice Lt Col C.S. Owen CMG DSO (leave U.K.)	WD
13 Oct	Maj Gen Sir Torquhil Matheson, G.O.C. Waziristan, visited Ladha	
1 Nov	Bn Depot arrived Multan from Dalhousie	J/May 23/123
6 Dec	earthquake, no casualties	WD
13 Dec	Gen Sir William Birdwood, G.O.C. Northern Command, visited Ladha	WD

2nd Battalion

	remained in Ireland	
21 Mar	arrived Ponsonby Bks, The Curragh, from Co Limerick	J/May 22/24; AB487
15 May	arrived Pheonix Park, Dublin	J/Jan 23/88; AB487
Jun	civil war in Ireland started	Clayton
Sep	moved to Royal Hibernian School, Dublin	J/Jan 23/88
16 Dec	arrived Pembroke Dock from Ireland	J/May 23/128; AB487

T.A. Battalions

	Proficiency pay and allowances cut	
Feb	4 R.W.F. won T.A. Football Challenge Cup	
Aug	53rd Division Camp at Aberystwyth	

1923

General

Jun	designation 'Fusilier' approved for private soldiers	Army Order 222

1st Battalion

1 Jan	new Goat on parade at Bn Depot	J/May 23/123
1 Feb	evacuated Ladha Camp and moved to Piazha Raghza in snowstorm	WD
3 Feb	moved to Marobi	WD
4 Feb	moved to Tauda China Camp	WD
4 Feb	Makin Column formed by 7th & 9th Indian Inf Bdes (incl 1 R.W.F.) under Maj Gen Sir Torquhil Matheson	Off Hist
5 Feb	action at Split Hill Picquet. 5 soldiers killed; Lt B.H. Hopkins & 8 soldiers wounded (1 later died); four MMs awarded.	
6 Feb	burial of dead at Tauda China	WD
6 Feb	destruction of Makin began	Off Hist
10 Feb	destruction of Tora Tizha & Dinaur villages	Off Hist; WD
12 Feb	destruction of Makin complete	Off Hist
22 Feb	Guard of Honour provided for Jirga at Tauda China	Off Hist;
23 Feb	Makin Column disbanded	Off Hist
11 Mar	Fus J. Freegrove killed by sniper	WD
23 Mar	Guard of Honour provided for Jirga at Tauda China	WD
27 Mar	evacuated Tauda China and moved to Piazha Raghza	WD
28 Mar	moved to Sorarogha	WD
29 Mar	moved to Kotkai	WD
30 Mar	arrived Wana Camp	WD
3 Apr	evacuated Wana and moved to Chagmalai	WD
4 Apr	moved to Haidari Kach	WD
5 Apr	moved to Sarwekai	WD
11 Apr	moved to Dargai Oba	WD
17 Apr	arrived Wana Column Camp	WD
18 Apr	farewell visit by Maj Gen Sir Torquhil Matheson	
22 Apr	entrained at Kalabagh	WD
25 Apr	Bn complete at Multan, Lahore District	J/May 24/223; WD

2nd Battalion
remained at Pembroke Dock

3rd (S.R.) Battalion

Oct	Transferred to the Supplementary Reserve and placed in suspended animation. Colours remained with the Depot

T.A. Battalions

Feb	7 R.W.F. runners-up in T.A. Football Challenge Cup
Aug	158 Brigade Camp at Porthcawl

1924

General

Jan	'Flash' authorised for all ranks in service dress	ACI 62/1924;
15 Nov	Regimental War Memorial unveiled in Wrexham	J/Jan 25

1st Battalion
remained Multan

2nd Battalion
remained Pembroke Dock

22 Jan	Goat died	J/May 24/234
1 Mar	first parade of new Goat	as above
12 May	Lt Col C.I. Stockwell CB CMG DSO to command vice	
	Lt Col C.C. Norman CMG DSO	J/Jan 25/300
		RD/363

T.A. Battalions

Aug	158 Brigade Camp at Llandudno

1925

General

Jun	*Regimental Journal* Series I ceased publication

1st Battalion

10 Sep	Lt Col H.V. Venables Kyrke DSO to command vice	
	Lt Col C.S. Owen CMG DSO	RD/363
27 Dec	arrived Nasirabad, Rajputana from Multan	J/Mar 32/3; AB487

2nd Battalion
remained Pembroke Dock

14 Jul	Pageant of Empire, Wembley	J/Jan 25/301
Aug	Public Duties, London	RD/4

Depot

27 May	Lt Col M.L. Lloyd-Mostyn in command

<u>T.A. Battalions</u>

Aug   53rd Division Camp at Ramsey, I.O.M.

1926

<u>General</u>

27 Feb   Lt Gen Sir Charles Dobell KCB CMG DSO appointed Colonel of the Regiment
           General Strike

<u>1st Battalion</u>

           remained Nasirabad
           won the All India Inter Unit Boxing   J/Mar 32/3

<u>2nd Battalion</u>

           duties related to the General Strike; otherwise remained
           Pembroke Dock
9/10 Nov   arrived Bingen, B.A.O.R. from Pembroke Dock   AB487; *Cologne*
                                                                                 Post 1926 p20

<u>T.A. Battalions</u>

           No official Camp (General Strike); 6th Bn local voluntary Camp.

1927

<u>General</u>

30 Apr   alliance with 1st Bn Australian Military Forces approved   AO 138
30 Jun   alliance with 12th Infantry (Pretoria Regiment) approved   AO 213
31 Jul   alliance with Royal 22ème Régiment of Canada approved   AO 265

<u>1st Battalion</u>

           remained Nasirabad

<u>2nd Battalion</u>

           remained Bingen, B.A.O.R.
26 Oct   Lt Col P.R. Butler DSO to command vice Lt Col C.I.
           Stockwell CB CMG DSO   RD/36

<u>T.A. Battalions</u>

Aug   158 Brigade Camp at Pwllheli; 6 R.W.F. Camp at Dyffryn

1928

<u>Depot</u>

27 May   Maj G.E.R. De Miremont DSO MC in command

<u>1st Battalion</u>

23 Jan   arrived Quetta from Nasirabad   AB487

<u>2nd Battalion</u>

Mar	moved from Bingen to Biebrich, Wiesbaden	AB 487

T.A. Battalions
158 Brigade Camp at Porthcawl ; 6 R.W.F. Camp at Pwllheli.

1929

Depot
21 Oct	Maj (Bt Lt Col) Ll. A.A. Alston DSO MC in command	

1st Battalion
	remained Quetta	
10 Sep	Lt Col E.O. Skaife OBE to command vice Lt Col H.V. Venables Kyrke DSO	RD/363

2nd Battalion
Apr	4 Officers and 88 O.R.s with Saar Railway Defence Force	AB487n
9 Oct	moved from B.A.O.R. to England	AB487; RD/4
13 Oct	arrived Tidworth	as above

T.A. Battalions
Aug	158 Brigade Camp at Porthcawl	

1930

General
25 Jun	Presentation of March 'The Royal Welch Fusiliers' by Lt Cdr J.P. Sousa to the Regiment at Tidworth	J/Mar 31/8

1st Battalion
	won India Infantry Polo Tournament	J/Mar 32/3
28 Nov	farewell parade in India at Quetta	J/Mar 31/6
9 Dec	left Quetta	J/Mar 32/3
11 Dec	sailed for Sudan	AB487
19 Dec	arrived Sudan. One coy to Cyprus	AB487

2nd Battalion
	remained Tidworth	
	Lt Col P.R. Butler DSO gave up command on account of ill health	J/Jun 32/38

T.A. Battalions
	M.G. Companies formed in place of 4th rifle company	
Feb	4 R.W.F. won T.A. Football Challenge Cup	
Aug	158 Brigade camp at Porthcawl	

1931

General

Mar	*Regimental Journal* (Series II) started publication	
5 Jul	representative detachment to Buckingham Palace	J/Sep 32/54

1st Battalion

Feb	coys at Khartoum (D[M.G.]), Atbara (B),Gebeit (A), Cyprus (C)	J/Sep 31/21
Jun	coys at Atbara (A), Khartoum (B), Gebeit (D); Cyprus (C) at Nicosia, Larnaca & Famagusta	J/Sep 31/45
21 Oct	nationalist uprising in Cyprus	AQ 33/268
Dec	coys at Khartoum (A), Gebeit (B), Atbara (D), Cyprus (C) in Nicosia	J/Mar 32/6

2nd Battalion

20 Jan	Lt Col C.C. Hewitt DSO MC to command vice Lt Col P.R. Butler DSO	RD/363
9 Oct	sailed from Southampton on HT *Neuralia*	J/Dec 31/75
13 Oct	arrived Gibraltar	J/Dec 31/75; AB 487
	lost in final of Army Inter Unit Boxing	RD/5

T.A. Battalions

	New Efficiency Decoration and Medal introduced
Feb	5 R.W.F. runners-up in T.A. Football Challenge Cup
Aug	158 Brigade Camp at Tenby

1932

General

mid Apr	1st & 2nd Battalions met at Gibraltar	J/Jun 32

Depot

21 Oct	Maj E. Wodehouse in command

1st Battalion

6 Apr	sailed from Port Sudan on HT *Dorsetshire*	J/Jun 32/33; AB 487
mid Apr	arrived Gibraltar. 237 O.R.s transferred to 2nd Bn	J/Jun 32/33
21 Apr	arrived Southampton. To Bhurtpore Bks, Tidworth	J/Jun 32/33
7 May	C Coy arrived Southampton from Cyprus on HT *Neuralia* via Gibraltar	J/Sep 32/53

2nd Battalion

remained at Gibraltar

T.A. Battalions

No Camp (austerity measure); 6 R.W.F. 1st in drill in PoW Shield

1933

1st Battalion

remained at Tidworth
Lt Col J.G. Bruxner-Randall to command vice Lt Col E.O.
Skaife OBE   RD/363

2nd Battalion

remained at Gibraltar

T.A. Battalions

Aug   158 Brigade Camp at Aberystwyth; 6 R.W.F. 1st in drill in PoW Shield

1934

1st Battalion

remained at Tidworth
first exchange of Offrs with R. 22ème R. of Canada   J/Dec 34/8

2nd Battalion

21 Oct   sailed from Gibraltar for Hong Kong   RD/3
21 Nov   arrived Hong Kong   AB 487

T.A. Battalions

Gresford Colliery Disaster (4 R.W.F.)
Aug   158 Brigade Camp at Porthcawl; 5 R.W.F. wins PoW Shield

1935

General

1, 4, 5, 6, 7 R.W.F. take part in Jubilee celebrations

Depot

1 Mar   Depot quarter guard resumed full dress for St David's Day
21 Oct   Maj A.M.G. Evans in command

1st Battalion

15 Nov   arrived Woking from Tidworth   J/Jan 36/5
               became a M.G. battalion   AB 487

2nd Battalion

remained Hong Kong
1 Jan   Lt Col R.E. Hindson to command vice Lt Col C.C.
               Hewitt DSO MC   RD/363

T.A. Battalions

Feb   7 R.W.F. runners-up in T.A. Football Challenge Cup
Jun   6 R.W.F. Camp at Porthcawl
Aug   158 Brigade Camp at Tenby; 5 R.W.F. wins PoW Shield

1936

General

Jan	death of H.M. King George V, Colonel-in-Chief; accession of H.M. King Edward VIII
Dec	abdication of H.M. King Edward VIII; accession of H.M. King George VI

Depot

1 Jul	first Depot 'At Home'
	Mobilisation of Class A reservists for Palestine

1st Battalion

remained at Woking

2nd Battalion

	remained in Hong Kong	
	Lt Col R.E. Hindson to U.K. (sick leave)	J/Jul 36/31; RD/5
1 Aug	Lt Col D.M. Barchard to command	RD/363

T.A. Battalions

Aug	4 and 5 R.W.F. Camp at Douglas, I.O.M.; 6 and 7 R.W.F. Camp at Kinmel; 5 R.W.F. wins PoW Shield

1937

General

	H.M. King George VI becomes Colonel-in-Chief
May 1, 4–7	R.W.F. take part in the Coronation in London

1st Battalion

18 May	Lt Col Ll. A.A. Alston DSO MC to command vice	
	Lt Col J.G. Bruxner-Randall	RD/363
15 Jul	Guard of Honour for George VI at Caernarfon	J/Oct 37/5
19 Oct	arrived Blackdown from Woking	AB 487

2nd Battalion

14 Aug	sailed from Kowloon for Shanghai on SS *Maron*	J/Oct 37/25
17 Aug	arrived Shanghai	RD/6
	operations in the International Zone	

T.A. Battalions

	6 R.W.F. re-titled 'Caernarvonshire & Anglesey'	AO 168
	7 R.W.F. re-titled 'Merioneth & Montgomeryshire'	AO 168
Feb	7 R.W.F. won T.A. Football Challenge Cup	
Jul	street-lining for Royal visits to Aberystwyth and Caernarfon	
Aug	158 Brigade Camp at Hereford; 6 R.W.F. 1st in L.M.G, 7 R.W.F. 1st in signals in PoW Shield	

1938

General

Sep	Munich Crisis
26 Oct	Maj Gen J.R. Minshull-Ford CB DSO MC appointed Colonel of the Regiment

Depot

Depot modernisation programme began
21 Oct Maj H.C. Watkins MC in command

1st Battalion

remained at Blackdown

2nd Battalion

end Jan	sailed from Shanghai on HMT *Dunera* for Aden via Hong Kong (5 days)	J/Sp 38/40; RD 6
3 Mar	arrived Sudan. Coys to Kartoum (A & C), Gebeit (B), Atbara (A)	J/Sp 38/24,29
Jul	coys changed stations	J/Aut 38/24
26 Nov	left by train for Port Sudan	J/W 38-39/33
	sailed (below strength) for India on HT *Somersetshire*	J/W 38-39/34; AB 487
5 Dec	arrived Bombay	as above
7 Dec	arrived Lucknow	as above

T.A. Battalions

	battalions re-organised on same lines as regulars with four rifle companies and H.Q. Company.	
Feb	7 R.W.F. won T.A. Football Challenge Cup	
Aug	158 Brigade Camp at Ramsey, I.O.M.; 4 R.W.F. wins P.o.W Shield, 5 R.W.F. 1st in drill	
26 Oct	5th Bn converted to 60th (R.W.F.) Anti-Tank Regt R.A. (T.A.)	RD/8

1939

General

Aug	250th Anniversary celebrations	RD/8
3 Sep	war declared	

Depot

1 Sep	mobilisation; Depot became 23 I.T.C.

1st Battalion

19 Jul	Lt Col H.F. Garnons-Williams to command vice Lt Col Ll. A.A. Alston DSO MC	RD/363
3 Sep	Blackdown – 6 Brigade, 2nd Division	
23 Sep	embarked Southampton on the HT *Manxman*	
24 Sep	sailed, and disembarked Cherbourg	
25–29 Sep	Arrived Parcé, near Noyon, 15 miles (25 km) north-east of Compiègne	
30 Sep	moved to Hendecourt-lès-Cagnicourt, 10 miles (15 km) south-east of Arras	
6 Oct	moved to Mouchin area. Bn H.Q. at Lannay	

2nd Battalion

Continued at Lucknow, India

4th Battalion

	Aug Camp at Porthcawl	
1 Sep	mobilisation	
2 Sep	embodied. In 158 Brigade, 53rd Division	
	Locations:	
	Bn H.Q., H.Q. Coy	Wrexham
	A Coy	Rhos
	B Coy	Llay
	C Coy	Acrefair
	D Coy	Denbigh
8 Sep	8th Battalion split from 4th	
22 Oct	entrained for Stranraer	
23 Oct	sailed on *Princess Margaret* for Larne, Northern Ireland. Arrived Lisburn.	
	In 158 Brigade, Northern Ireland District	
20 Dec	moved to Victoria Barracks, Belfast	

60th (R.W.F.) A.T. Regiment R.A. (5th Battalion)

Aug	Camp at Trawsfynydd
1 Sep	Mobilisation; 70th (R.W.F.) A.T. Regiment R.A. formed as second-line unit at Mold
3 Sep	Embodied with H.Q. at Flint, 237 Battery at Flint, 238 Battery at Rhyl, 239 Battery at Flint and 240 Battery at Hawarden
Oct	Moved to Lille Barracks, Aldershot

6th Battalion

Aug	received New Colours during 250th Anniversary celebrations; Camp at Porthcawl	
1 Sep	received orders to mobilise in Caernarvon. In 158 Brigade, 53rd Division.	
3 Sep	9th Bn split and moved to camp at Coed Helen, Caernarvon	
5 Sep	moved into billets in Old Colwyn	
23 Oct	embarked in SS *Duchess of Hamilton* at Stranraer	
24 Oct	arrived Lurgan, Northern Ireland. In 158 Brigade, Northern Ireland District. Locations:	
	Bn H.Q., A D Coy	Brownlow House
	B Coy	Parochial Buildings
	C Coy	Old School Hall, Castle St
	H.Q. Coy	Ross Factory
20 Dec	moved to Lisburn	

7th Battalion

Aug	Camp at Porthcawl	
1 Sep	mobilisation	
2 Sep	embodied. In 158 Brigade, 53rd Division. Locations:	
	Bn H.Q.	Newtown
	A Coy	Llanidloes
	B Coy	Llanfyllin
	C Coy	Welshpool
	D Coy	Machynlleth
	H.Q. Coy	Newtown

24 Oct	departed Newtown
25 Oct	arrived Portadown, Northern Ireland. In 158 Brigade, Northern Ireland District
17 Dec	arrived Ebrington Barracks, Londonderry

8th Battalion

1 Sep	ordered to mobilise in Wrexham. In 115 Brigade, 38th Division. This bn was a duplicate of 4 R.W.F.
2 Sep	advance party moved to Coed Helen Camp (tented) at Caernarvon
5 Sep	H.Q. closed at Wrexham
	bn established at Coed Helen Camp, Caernarvon
1 Oct	moved into billets at Llanberis. Locations:

Bn H.Q.	L.M.S. railway station
A Coy	Victoria Hotel
B Coy	Snowdon railway station
C Coy	Church House
D Coy	Four council houses
H.Q. Coy	Drill Hall [with A Coy 6 R.W.F.]
Offrs Mess	Victoria Hotel [Later to Padarn Villa Hotel]
Sgts Mess	Café
Cookhouse	Victoria Hotel

16 Dec	moved to barracks and billets in Colwyn Bay

9th Battalion

Aug	formed as a duplicate of 6 R.W.F. at Llandudno
1 Sep	ordered to mobilise at Llandudno. In 115 Brigade, 38th Division
3 Sep	moved to Coed Helen Camp (tented) at Caernarvon and from there to billets in Penmaenmawr.

10th Battalion

1 Sep	ordered to mobilise at Newtown. In 115 Brigade, 38th Division. This Bn was a duplicate of 7 R.W.F.
5 Sep	at Coed Helen Camp, Caernarvon (tented) by this date
4 Oct	moved to billets in Beaumaris. Bn H.Q. at Baron Hill
18 Oct	A and D Coys to Red Hill, Beaumaris

70th (R.W.F.) A.T. Regiment R.A.

1 Sep	ordered to mobilise as a duplicate of 60th (R.W.F.) A.T. Regiment R.A.
5 Sep	moved to billets in Holywell.
16 Sep	assigned to 38th (Welsh) Division.
10 Nov	moved to Pembroke Dock

71st (R.W.F.) A.T. Regiment R.A.

15 Sep	Ordered to form from 70th (R.W.F.) A.T. Regiment R.A.

11th (National Defence) Battalion[1]

1 Nov	formed from No. 105 Group of National Defence Companies. Bn had H.Q. and six companies, located at:

Bn H.Q.	Grey Friars Road, Shrewsbury
A – Anglesey	Menai Bridge

B – Flintshire   Rhyl
C – Denbighshire   Church House, Wrexham
D – Montgomeryshire
E – Shropshire   Riding School, Coleham, Shrewsbury
F – Herefordshire   Hereford
ACI 742 gives establishment etc. Bn dispersed in detachments guarding V.P.s in North
Wales, Shropshire, Herefordshire, and Montgomeryshire

1940

General
B.E.F in France and Belgium; Expeditionary Force to Norway

Depot
Depot Party continued at Hightown Barracks, Wrexham

23 I.T.C.
continued at Hightown Barracks, Wrexham

311 I.T.C.
Spring   formed at Saighton Camp, Chester for recruit training for R.W.F. and others
9 Sep   reduced to cadre
9 Oct   disbanded

1st Battalion
            continued in France
10 May   German advance into Belgium and Holland began
12–13 May   bn advanced as part of the 2nd Division, B.E.F., through Brussels to Tombeek-
            Ottenbourg area and occupied positions on River Dyle
16 May   Allied withdrawal began
20–21 May   Tournai area. Defence of the Escaut (19–22 May)
23 May   La Bassée
24–27 May   St-Venant, defence of the Dunkirk Perimeter; Bn suffered heavy casualties
31 May–
1 Jun   remnants embarked Dunkirk area
4 Jun   Bn H.Q. established at Special Constabulary H.Q., John William St, Huddersfield,
            Yorkshire
14 Jun   Bn H.Q. established Albany Hall, Clare Hill, Huddersfield
22 Jun   moved to Barmston and Atwick area on East Coast
24 Jun   Bn H.Q. established at Dringhoe Grange, Skipsea, Yorkshire
22 Oct   moved into winter quarters at Bridlington, Yorkshire. Bn H.Q. at 25 St Oswald's Road

2nd Battalion
            Lucknow, India
4 Jun   departed Lucknow
6 Jun   embarked Bombay on SS *Aska*
19–20 Jun   Durban, South Africa
23–24 Jun   Capetown
6 Jul   Freetown, Sierra Leone

16 Jul	arrived Liverpool
18 Jul	arrived Salamanca Barracks, Aldershot. Formed 29 Independent Brigade with 1 R. Scots Fus, 2 E. Lancs, and 2 S. Lancs
end Jul	billeted at Horsham and Bolney in Sussex
6 Nov	moved to Angmering, between Littlehampton and Worthing, Sussex
4 Dec	Locations:

Bn H.Q.	Colwood House, Bolney
A, B & C Coys	Horsham
D Coy	Newells
H.Q. Coy	Wykehurst Park

4th Battalion

Apr	158 Brigade reverted to under command 53rd Division
19 Jun	moved to Lurgan
26–27 Jun	moved to Downpatrick
15–16 Oct	moved to Killyleagh, Co Down

6th Battalion

3 Jul	moved to Ballynahinch. Bn H.Q. at Montalto House

7th Battalion

3 Apr	moved to Glen Barracks, Newtownards, Co Down
24 May– 22 Jun	in Belfast for I.S. duties.

8th Battalion

56 Apr	moved to Burnham-on-Sea, Somerset. Detachments guarding V.P.s
May	detachments to airfield defence.
7 Jul	complete at Bromborough, near Birkenhead, Cheshire
7–12 Oct	marched from Bromborough to Pilsworth Bleach Mills, Whitefield, near Manchester
29–30 Oct	moved to Haig Hutments, near Crookham, Hampshire

9th Battalion

Apr	moved to Andover, Hampshire
26 Jun	moved to Oulton Park, Winsford, Cheshire
Sep	moved to Tatton Hall Camp, Knutsford, Cheshire
18 Oct	moved to Vale Mill, Rochdale, Lancashire
31 Oct	moved to Haig Lines, Church Crookham, Aldershot, Hampshire

10th Battalion

10–11 Jan	bn (less D Coy) to Rhos-on-Sea. Bn H.Q. at Inishmore
5 Apr	bn to Plymouth and Falmouth. Bn H.Q. at Millbay Barracks. Coys dispersed in detachments
10 Apr	B Coy from Millbay to Marshmills Camp (tented)
18 May	C Coy to Corsham, Wiltshire as mobile company
28 May	bn, less C Coy, moved to Windmill Hill Camp (Site 6), Tidworth (tented)
6 Jun	bn, less C Coy, moved to Oulton Park Camp, Tarporley, Cheshire (under canvas)
28 Jun	C Coy rejoined from Corsham
15 Jul	moved to Hornby Mill, Blackburn, Lancashire. Locations:

B Coy	Lytham St Anne's, Lancs
D Coy	Myerscough House, Preston
5 Aug	moved to Witton Park Camp (tented), Blackburn, Lancashire. B and D Coys rejoined
23 Sep	moved to Hornby Mill, Blackburn, Lancashire
22 Oct	R (First Reinforcement) Company formed
28–30 Oct	moved from Blackburn into requisitioned houses at Fleet, Hampshire. Bn H.Q. at 138 Fleet Road

11th (National Defence) Battalion

17 Jan	Bn H.Q. moved to the Drill Hall, Shrewsbury	
Jun	Bn issued with W.D. transport, Bren guns and anti-tank rifles.	
	In addition to guarding V.P.s, the bn became responsible for	
	all airfields between Anglesey and Hereford	L/2655/325
19 & 25 Sep	Bn divided into three battalions, 1/11th, 2/11th and	
	70th (Y.S.) – see below[2]	L/2655/325

1/11th (Home Defence) Battalion

25 Sep	formed when 11th (H.D.) R.W.F. was divided into three battalions. This battalion covered the eastern part of the old battalion area. Bn H.Q. at the Drill Hall, Shrewsbury
24 Nov	reverted to old title of 11 R.W.F. on demise of 2/11th R.W.F.

2/11th (Home Defence) Battalion[3]

25 Sep	formed at Llandudno when 11 (H.D.) R.W.F. was divided into three battalions. Bn H.Q.
	and five companies located in the western part of the old battalion area at: WD
	A Menai Bridge
	D Llandudno
	G Tern Hill
	K Penrhos
	Z Broughton
	Bn H.Q. at Braeside, St Margaret's Drive, Llandudno
24 Nov	redesignated as 14th Bn The Royal Welch Fusiliers. See below

12th (Service) Battalion[4]

4 Jul	formed at Infantry Training Centre, Wrexham	WD, AG card
8 Jul	moved to holiday camp at Pensarn, Abergele	
28 Sep	moved to Hoylake, Cheshire. H.Q. at The Priory, Meols Drive,	
1 Oct	Company locations:	
	A and B Bidston	
	C West Kirby	
	H.Q. and D Hoylake	

13th (Service) Battalion[5]

9 Oct	formed from 50th (Holding) Bn R.W.F on the establishment of an Infantry (Rifle) Battalion. Bn H.Q. at Denbigh. Companies – see 50th R.W.F.
14–15 Oct	moved to Bangor, Co Down, Northern Ireland. In billets, strength 838. Bn H.Q. Regent Palace Hotel

14th (Home Defence) Battalion[6]

24 Nov   formed at Llandudno from 2/11th (H.D.) R.W.F. Locations:

A Coy	Menai Bridge	WD
B Coy (ex Z)	Broughton	
C Coy (ex G)	Tern Hill	
D Coy	Llandudno	
E Coy (ex K)	Penrhos	

7th I.H.B.

2 Jan   formed at Denbigh
7 Jun   became 50th (Holding) Battalion R.W.F.

50th (Holding) Battalion

28 May   formed from 7th Infantry Holding Bn.* Locations were:

Bn H.Q., H.Q. Coy	Denbigh
A Coy	Bolsover Camp, Rhyl
B Coy	Formed 26 August
C Coy	Denbigh
D Coy	St Asaph

9 Oct   bn ordered to re-form as an infantry service battalion, and become 13 R.W.F.

70th (Young Soldiers) Battalion

19 Sep   formed at Rhyl by transfer of young soldier companies (aged 18 to 19½) of:
             11th (H.D.) Bn The Royal Welch Fusiliers (361 O.R.s)
             16th (H.D.) Bn The Welch Regiment
             17th (H.D.) Bn The Welch Regiment
             strength six companies of six platoons each

60th (R.W.F.) A.T. Regiment R.A.

Feb   formed R.H.Q. and two A.T. batteries of 101st L.A.A. & A.T. Regiment R.A.; joined by
             two L.A.A. batteries.

70th (R.W.F.) A.T. Regiment R.A.

18 May   moved to Trearddur Bay, Anglesey
5 Jul   moved to Liverpool

---

*   7th Infantry Holding Battalion (I.H.B.) was not a Royal Welch unit, so is not listed separately. It
     was formed at Denbigh on or just before 2 January 1940 precise date not known under the authority
     of WO/L20/Infy/3114 (AG2a) dated 19 December 1939. It was a holding battalion for the
     following regiments, each having one company:

A Coy	King's Own Royal Regiment	Bolsover Camp, Rhyl
B Coy	Lancashire Fusiliers	Rhyl
C Coy	Royal Welch Fusiliers	Denbigh
D Coy	King's Shropshire Light Infantry	St Asaph

     The detailed manuscript war diary, covering the period 2 January to 6 June 1940, is in the R.W.F.
     archives (Mus 245). This is the only known copy. On 6 June 1940, 7 I.H.B., having posted all its men
     of the other regiments, became the 50th Battalion The Royal Welch Fusiliers, under the authority of
     WO/UPT 1/148/(AG2a) dated 27 May 1940.

15 Sep	ordered to form 71st (R.W.F.) A.T. Regiment with 278 and 279 Batteries; 277 and 280 Batteries retained and 281 and 282 Batteries formed
26 Sep	moved to Stockport
Oct	moved to Aldershot

71st (R.W.F.) A.T. Regiment R.A.

| 1 Nov | formed with 278 and 279 Batteries |

76th (R.W.F.) A.T. Regiment R.A.

| 8 May | formed at Godalming from R.H.Q., 237 (R.W.F.) and 239 (R.W.F.) Batteries, 101st L.A.A. & A.T. Regiment R.A. |

101st L.A.A. & A.T. Regiment

17 May	formed from R.H.Q., 237 (R.W.F.) and 239 (R.W.F.) Btys
24 May	60th R.W.F. A.T. Regiment; joined by 43 and 44 L.A.A. Batteries.
25 May	ordered to France with 1st Armoured Division Support Group
28 May	Regiment complete at Brest
30 May	deployed to guard bridge crossings over the Somme
7 Jun	withdrawn to Airaines
10 Jun	to Friecamps
11–12 Jun	to Croixdale
	239 Battery in action at Aumele
	237 and 239 Batteries in action
30 Jun	withdrawal to St-Valery. Some men evacuated, remainder captured with 51st (H) Division. B Echelon to Brest and evacuated
26 Jul	re-formed at Longbridge Deverell
1 Nov	moved to Aldershot
	moved to Bramley, Hants
	R.H.Q., 237 (R.W.F.) and 239 (R.W.F.) Batteries converted to 76th (R.W.F.) A.T. Regiment R.A.; 43 and 44 Batteries detached.

No 2 Independent Company

23 Apr	formed at Ballykinler, N.I., from 53rd (Welsh) Div under Maj H.C. Stockwell
8 May	to Glasgow then Leith
10 May	embarked for Norway on MV *Royal Ulsterman*
13 May	arrived Bodø and joined Scissorsforce for operations
22 May	by steamer to Rognan and then to Pothus
23 May	Stockforce formed
25–26 May	action at Pothus
26 May	fighting withdrawal to Rognan, then by boat to Fauske
30 May	evacuation from Norway to Leith
20 July	Capt T.H. Trevor *Welch* assumed command vice Maj H.C. Stockwell (to Group of Independent Companies in Devon and Cornwall)
17 Oct	remained in Scotland until absorbed into No 1 Commando

No 9 Independent Company

| 21 Apr | formed at Ross-on-Wye from 38th (Welsh) Div under Maj W. Siddons DCM |

27 Apr	2 Lt J.O.K. Purdey and 30 O.R.s of 10 R.W.F. joined. Moved to Leith and embarked for Norway, but orders rescinded
Jun	Maj W. Glendinning *Welch* to command, vice Maj W. Siddons DCM
14 Jul	moved to Cornwall to join No 1 Group of Independent Companies
21 Jul	moved to Isles of Scilly for anti-invasion duties
17 Oct	absorbed into No 1 Commando under Lt Col W. Glendinning *Welch*

Home Guard

14 May	L.D.V. formed
31 May	5 Carns Bn formed
1 Jun	1, 4, 5, 9 Denbigh Bns; 2, 4, 5 Merioneth Bns; 5, 6, 7 Montgomery Bns; and 3 Merioneth & Montgomery Bns all formed
17 Jul	4 Denbigh re-titled 6 Denbigh; 5 Denbigh re-titled 8 Denbigh; 7 Denflint Bn formed
23 July	L.D.V. renamed as Home Guard
Aug	1, 2, 3 Anglesey Bns; 1, 2, 3, 4 Carns Bns; 2 Denbigh Bn; 3, 4, 5 Flints Bns; formed

Key:

AB 487	Green Book, MOD Library, London
AG Card	Card Index of moves held by the Adjutant General's Department
RR	Regimental Records
RD/	*Red Dragon* History/page
J/	Regimental Journal *Y Ddraig Goch*/date & page
WD	War Diary

Notes

1   According to the CO (see L/2655/325), the battalion strength was some 80 Officers and 2,200 Other Ranks by about June 1940.
2   See 14 R.W.F. war diary for 2/11th R.W.F. from Sep to Nov 1940.
3   See *The Red Dragon*, Pages 356 for a short history of the battalion.
4   See *The Red Dragon*, pages 323 for a few references to the battalion.
5   The A.G. card index has Home Defence in the battalion's title. The war diary does not.

Glossary of Terms and Abbreviations

AA	Anti-Aircraft
AA & QMG	Assistant Adjutant and Quartermaster General. The senior administrative Staff Officer in a divisional H.Q.
AB	Army Book
ACI	Army Council Instruction
ADC	*Aide de Camp*, personal assistant to a General Officer
AEF	Allied Expeditionary Force
AGRA	Army Group Royal Artillery
ALC	Assault Landing Craft
ALFSEA	Allied Land Forces South East Asia
Aligator	An amphibious assault vehicle
AMPC	Auxiliary Military Pioneer Corps (later the Royal Pioneer Corps)
APC	Armoured Personnel Carrier
AT	Anti-Tank
ATS	Auxiliary Territorial Service. The forerunner of the Women's Royal Army Corps
AVRE	Armoured Vehicle Royal Engineers, carrying fascines, bridging, or armed with 290mm Petard spigot mortar, for destroying blockhouses etc.
BAOR	British Army of the Rhine
BC	Battery Commander
BEF	British Expeditionary Force
BGS	Brigadier General Staff
BLA	Burma Liberation Army; also British Liberation Army (N.W. Europe)
BM	Brigade Major
BNCO	British Non-Commissioned Officer
Bofors	37mm anti-aircraft gun
BPAFL	Burmese People's Anti-Fascist League
BQMS	Battery Quartermaster Sergeant
BSM	Battery Sergeant Major
Bt	Baronet
Buffalo	American tracked amphibious carrier – 30 men or 4 tons
C-in-C	Commander-in-Chief
CB	Companion of the Order of the Bath
CBE	Commander of the Order of the British Empire

CF	Chaplain to the Forces – usually a civilian accredited to the T.A.
CIGS	Chief of the Imperial General Staff
CMG	Companion of the Order of St Michael and St George
CO	Commanding Officer
COHQ	Combined Operations Headquarters
COS	Chief(s) of Staff
CP	Command Post
CPX	Command Post Exercise
CQMS	Company Quartermaster Sergeant
Crocodile	*Churchill* tank flame thrower, towing a 400 gallon 2-wheeled fuel trailer – range 120 yds
Cromwell	27-ton 'cruiser' tank with 74mm gun
CRA	Commander Royal Artillery
cwt	One hundredweight; one-twentieth of an imperial ton
DAA & QMG	Deputy Assistant Adjutant and Quartermaster General. The senior administrative Staff Officer in a brigade H.Q.
DCIGS	Deputy Chief of the Imperial General Staff
DCO	Director of Combined Operations
DDMS	Deputy Director Medical Services
DL	Deputy Lieutenant (of a county)
DSO	Companion of the Distinguished Service Order
DUKW	'Duck' – an American amphibious vehicle
DZ	Dropping Zone
EME	Electrical and Mechanical Engineer
Firefly	Sherman tank up-gunned with the very effective British 17 pdr anti-tank gun.
Flail tank	Sherman tank, equipped with a front mounted rotary flail, designed to explode mines. Also known as a Crab
FAA	Forward Assembly Area
FMA	Forward Maintenance Area
FOO	Forward Observation Officer
FUP	Forming Up Place (for an attack)
GCB	Knight Grand Cross of the Order of the Bath
GCMG	Knight Grand Cross of the Order of St Michael and St George
GCVO	Knight Grand Cross of the Royal Victorian Order
GHQ	General Headquarters
GOC	General Officer Commanding – the Major General commanding a division or district.
GOC-in-C	General Officer Commanding-in-Chief – Lieutenant General or General commanding a command or an army.
GSO 1	General Staff Officer First Grade – a Lieutenant Colonel
GSO 2	As above – Second Grade – a Major
GSO 3	As above – Third Grade – a Captain; the equivalent in A and Q staff branches was the Staff Captain
GTC	General Transit Centre (for D-Day)

HMS	His Majesty's Ship
HMT	His Majesty's Troopship
HT	Hired Transport (Ship)
Honey	The American *Stuart* light tank
HQ	Headquarters
IHB	Infantry Holding Battalion
INA	Indian National Army
IS	Internal Security
ITC	Infantry Training Centre
ITD	Infantry Training Depot
IWT	Inland Waterways Transport (Burma)
Kangaroo	Based on the *Ram*, the Canadian version of the Sherman tank, with the turret removed, it was probably the first purpose-built armoured personnel carrier used by the British
KBE	Knight Commander of the Order of the British Empire
KCB	Knight Commander of the Order of the Bath
KD	Khaki drill
kia	Killed in Action
KG	Knight of the Garter
LAA	Light Anti-Aircraft
LAD	Light Aid Detachment
LCS	Landing Craft (Support)
LIAP	Leave in Advance of *Python*
LILOP	Leave in Lieu of *Python*
LMG	Light Machine Gun
LO	Liaison Officer
MA	Military Assistant
MBE	Member of the Order of the British Empire
MC	Military Cross
MG	Machine Gun
MLC	Mechanised Landing Craft
MMG	Medium Machine Gun
MV	Motor vessel
NCAC	Northern Combat Area Command (China and Burma)
NCO	Non-Commissioned Officer
Nebelwerfer	Literally smoke projector, but in fact it fired rocket-propelled warheads in three calibres, up to a range of 8,600 yards; German
OBE	Officer of the Order of the British Empire
OCTU	Officer Cadet Training Unit
OP	Observation Post
ORQMS	Orderly Room Quarter Master Sergeant
ORS	Orderly Room Sergeant
PAD	Passive Air Defence precautions
Panzerfaust	German anti-tank rocket launcher, firing a hollow charge grenade from a tube

PoW	Prisoner of War
psc	Passed Staff College
PT	Physical Training
PTC	Primary Training Centre
PTW	Primary Training Wing
Python	British Army discharge scheme at the end of the Second World War
QM	Quartermaster
QMG	Quartermaster General
RA	Royal Artillery
RAC	Royal Armoured Corps
RCS	Royal Corps of Signals
Recce	Reconnaissance
RMC	Royal Military College (the title of Sandhurst up to 1939)
SNOL	Senior Naval Officer Landing
SS	Steam Ship
STC	Special Training Centre, Inverailort
Tac HQ	Tactical H.Q. The command post of a battalion, brigade or divisional commander
TCC	Traffic Control Centre
TCV	Troop Carrying Vehicle
TEWT	Tactical Exercise Without Troops
U-boat	*Unterseeboot*; German submarine
USAAF	United States Army Air Force
V Force	Burmese Irregular Force with British Officers, employed chiefly in intelligence gathering and scouting
VP	Vulnerable Point
Wasp	Carrier fitted with a flamethrower
Weasel	Small amphibious tracked vehicle
wia	Wounded in Action
WNEC	Welsh National Executive Council
WO	Warrant Officer; War Office
Y List	Soldiers medically downgraded and not able to be employed within a unit
Zero Hour	Time for the start of an attack or operation; also known as H-Hour

Section I

The British Army, 1919–1940

Chapter 1

The British Army and the Inter-War Years, 1918–1940

In 1918, the British Army was probably the best fighting force, on the battlefield, in the world, more than a match for the Germans, and was a force that had shown it could transform radically while fighting a titanic struggle. In the last hundred days of the war it led the Allied advance on the Western front, winning nine major battles and equalling the combined totals of its French, American and Belgian allies in German prisoners and guns taken. In the ten years that followed the Armistice, however, the British Army struggled to maintain its edge and in the main it returned to the pre-1914 issues centred on the Empire. The British Army might have seemed to be better than most in 1930, but in reality there were serious problems. When Britain next fought a major war, problems with equipment, education, manning, sustainment, doctrine and training led to a series of disasters in the early years and a slow recovery thereafter.[1]

A number of seemingly divergent but actually inter-connected factors contributed to this. First, there were international aspects: the general anti-war and particularly anti-army opinion from 1920 onwards; secondly, heavy cuts in funding and in the ability to recruit men; thirdly, there were extra commitments – for it was in 1922 that the British Empire, with the League of Nations mandates that further expanded it, reached its greatest extent: a quarter of the world's land surface – over thirteen million square miles – with 450 million inhabitants was under one of several forms of British rule.[2] These resource constraints deprived the Army of the ability to afford the numbers and types of modern vehicles, weapons and equipments for a large-scale war against a modern, European enemy, the Germans, or indeed, as it turned out, an Asian enemy, the Japanese.

There were also other factors which stopped the army from moving forward: a climate of reactionary thinking; lack of any real strategic or tactical doctrine; a return to pre-1914 organisations rather than the flexible, combined-arms structures of 1917–1918; and a lack of professional ethos in training and education.[3] Given what observers and participants like Tom Wintringham[4] and F.O. Miksche[5] wrote about the Spanish Civil War; and what Marshal Mikhail Tuckhachevsky[6] was writing from the Soviet Union, the direction and nature of the next war should have been clear even without the obvious preparations being laid by the German General Staff after 1933.

When the Armistice came into effect in November 1918, the British Army had grown in size and capabilities to an extent unheard-of since it was established in 1660. On the Western Front, the Army, including the Imperial components, had fielded 2 million men at the highest strength, in fifty-six infantry and three cavalry divisions, formed into nineteen corps which in turn were grouped in five armies; another twenty-two infantry and three cavalry divisions were serving in other theatres: Italy, Salonika, the Middle East, North Russia, Britain and Ireland, East and West Africa and India. One-and-a-half million more men were serving in the thirty-eight Imperial formations – chiefly Indians, but also East, West and South Africans; Australians and New Zealanders; Canadians and Newfoundlanders; West Indians; and Chinese, if the five further divisions of the Labour Corps are included. On top of that there were an additional ten division-equivalents if the separate artillery, engineer, Royal Flying Corps and Tank Corps are included. To field a force of this size throughout the war, the British Empire had mobilised just under 9 million men, of whom over 900,000 were killed and over 2 million wounded. The British Isles share was 723,000 killed or died of wounds, with twice as many wounded.[7] Hardly a family in the country was unaffected. By contrast, less than 1,500 civilians were killed by enemy action.

The Army's budget for the year ending 31 March 1919 totalled £824,259,300 – much greater than at any time previously.[8] Not surprisingly, the end of the war brought immediate demands to demobilize. There was certainly a need to get manpower back into manufacturing industry and construction; but there also seemed to be little need for a large army, as victory had brought with it the collapse of the four great empires of Central Europe. Germany, Austria-Hungary and the Ottoman Empire had all been defeated, and Russia was consumed by civil war so that there seemed to be no immediate threat close to home.

A major international factor was faith in the League of Nations. This body, it was hoped, would put an end to war, replacing battle with arbitration. Few people could imagine that any political leader would willingly start another war in Europe with the level of blood-letting that had gone on from 1914 to 1918. Such a sacrifice could simply not be tolerated again, even though Britain's losses were lower in absolute terms, and as a percentage of their deployed forces, than any other combatant nation. In this context, disarmament and collective security were to be the principles.[9]

The Versailles Treaty of 1919 set up the League of Nations, which depended upon collective action to stop aggression. It was assumed that the League's very existence would reduce British military commitments, even though the Army General Staff was doubtful.[10] The 1925 Locarno treaties, which guaranteed the Franco-German and Belgian-German borders, presented other quandaries for the Imperial General Staff, as Britain's role in the event of aggression would be to aid the injured party against the attacker.[11]

Politically, this requirement seemed better than a continued *entente*, which the French began seeking since late 1918. After 1919 the British slowly became suspicious of French policy towards Germany, and the British had no wish once again to be dragged into a war in support of France. The Locarno Pact seemed the perfect solution. The British never earmarked any resources in case they had to fulfil their promise, however, since no-one in the government or on the Imperial General Staff believed these would ever be needed. After all, the Locarno treaties also put the Germans under an obligation to settle any disputes it might have with other States by arbitration rather than invasion.[12] This view was strengthened by the Kellogg-Briand Pact, ratified by fifteen countries in 1928, which outlawed war other than in exceptional circumstances or in self-defence.

The anti-war outlook among many people after 1919 was accentuated when some of the more critical writings on the Great War began to appear after 1929: *All Quiet on the Western Front* in Germany; *Undertones of War, Sherston's Progress* and *Her Privates We*, among others, in Britain. These undoubtedly influenced policy, especially that of Ramsay Macdonald between 1924 and

1935. There was also of course the famous Oxford Union debate on the motion 'that this house will in no circumstances fight for its king and country' in 1933, which was carried by 275 to 153. Corelli Barnett summed this up by saying that: 'The strong tide of pacifism flowed not only against war itself, which was understandable ... but against soldiers... The nation's anti-war sentiment became also a strongly anti-armed forces sentiment.'[13]

In addition to its anti-war opinions after the War, Britain went through an acute economic crisis. The war had drained the nation's wealth to the extent that Britain, the world's largest economy in 1914, was now in debt overseas, especially to the U.S.A. This stood at more than £820 million – £34 billion at today's rates[14] – with additional debts of over £2 billion.[15] Pre-war customers, like Germany, Russia and Austria, were also lost or weakened. New York, not London, was the financial centre of the world – a reflection of the fact that America had grown rich lending money and supplying the war effort. Unemployment and industrial unrest, a serious and growing problem immediately before the war, were once more on the rise. As far as the government was concerned, the Army must return quickly to its 1914 size and budget.[16] This conflict of interests was implemented by a panicky programme of demobilisation and budget cuts rather than by a thought-out programme.

In response, the Army's senior Officers tried to keep a force large enough to secure the Empire. They succeeded, but only just. In late 1918, Field Marshal Sir Henry Wilson, the Chief of the Imperial General Staff (C.I.G.S.),* reminded everyone that the war was not actually over – an armistice had been signed, albeit on terms highly favourable to the Allies – but that if the peace negotiations failed, rapid demobilisation would leave the Army too weak to fight the Germans.[17] Both he and Winston Churchill, Secretary of State for War and Air, tried two different ways of solving the problem. First, they did their best to get the government to reduce overseas deployments and to avoid taking on any new ones. They had some success, as the Foreign Office dropped plans for the Caucasus and Turkey.[18] Secondly, they tried to increase resources: conscription was extended until 30 April 1920 in order to provide manpower and the age of enlistment was lowered from 19 to 18.[19] However, Canada, Australia, New Zealand, South Africa and India refused to commit their forces to imperial defence; and the government remained determined to cut the Army's size and budget.[20]

In August 1919 the Cabinet, in concert with the Committee of Imperial Defence, agreed new guiding principles for its policy. First, it would be assumed in the new Defence Estimates, that the British Empire would not be engaged in any great war during the next ten years, and that no Expeditionary Force would therefore be needed. Secondly, that the principal duties of the Army and the Royal Air Force would be to garrison India, Egypt, the new League of Nations'

---

*   Field Marshal Sir Henry Hughes Wilson, 1st Baronet GCB DSO (1864–1922) was Director of Military Operations at the War Office, in which post he drew up plans to deploy an Expeditionary Force to France in the event of war. As Sub Chief of Staff to the B.E.F., Wilson was Sir John French's most important advisor during the 1914 campaign, but his poor relations with Haig and Robertson saw him sidelined from top decision-making in the middle years of the war. In 1917 he was military advisor to the Prime Minister David Lloyd George, and then British Permanent Military Representative at the Supreme War Council at Versailles. He became C.I.G.S. in 1918. After retiring from the Army, he served briefly as a Member of Parliament, and also as security advisor to the Northern Ireland government. He was assassinated on his own doorstep by two I.R.A. gunmen in 1922.

Mandated Territories and all other territories (other than self-governing ones) under British rule; as well as to provide support to the civil authorities, local and national, at home.[21]

In accordance with this statement, which became infamous as 'the Ten Year Rule', the Cabinet set a defence budget limit of £120 million, £75 million of which would have to make do for both the Army and the Royal Air Force. It is true that Wilson had written to Churchill, saying that he saw no danger of a major war for some time, but, he also stated that the likelihood of having to send troops to some point in the Empire was now greater than it had ever been.[22] He also argued strongly that the calculation method was wrong: first it was necessary to determine the total force package required to meet Britain's commitments, and *then* decide on funding levels, rather than the other way around.

Of course, Wilson got precisely nowhere. With the Ten Year Rule in effect, the Army's manpower and budget continued to fall towards, and then below, their 1914 levels. The situation only improved as some of Britain's military commitments began to reduce. The last British troops left North Russia in the summer of 1920; South Russia, the Trans-Caucasus and Turkey in 1922 – the Soviet regime was officially recognised in 1924; Ireland in 1922; Silesia in 1921 and the rest of Germany in 1929. In other places, light mechanised forces and aircraft were brought into play for imperial policing. In Iraq, the Royal Air Force took over prime respon-sibility for security in 1921, using aircraft and a few armoured cars, thus releasing most of the Army units that had been serving there.[*] However, as the possibility of war with the Soviet Union over Afghanistan receded it was replaced by doubt about the reliability of the Indian Army because of the rise of nationalism. The Middle East became a source of difficulty from 1929 onwards, especially in Palestine where violence increased and the British found themselves unable to manage the struggles between Arabs and Jews. Jewish emigration from Germany after the Nazi takeover had increased rapidly and in 1936, when the Peel proposals resulted in the Arab Revolt,[†] the garrison increased from two infantry battalions, about 1,500 men, to a full division of more than 10,000 men.[‡]

On 2 August 1921, Lloyd George's Cabinet formed the Committee on National Expenditure, headed by Sir Eric Geddes. This committee delivered a report in July 1922, which became known as the 'Geddes Axe'.[§] The report stated that the pre-1914 requirement for six infantry divisions and a cavalry division for service abroad no longer applied, since under the Ten Year Rule there could be no major war in that time frame. Troops were only needed in Britain to provide drafts for garrisons overseas, for internal security, and to prepare for minor expeditions. New technologies like armoured cars, radio, tanks and aircraft would reduce the need for large numbers of infantry. The Geddes committee therefore recommended a cut of 50,000 men in the 1914 Army, resulting in the disbandment or amalgamation of eight cavalry regiments and twenty-eight infantry battalions, with other cuts in combat support and combat service support. The Army Estimates for 1922–1923 would be cut from around £75 million to £55 million.[23] In the end the Army was able to claw back some funds, as the budget fell only to £62 million; but twenty infantry battalions were disbanded, ten of them from the Irish Regiments lost following

---

[*]   Clayton, p. 79.
[†]   A Royal Commission under Lord Peel recommended in 1937 the partition of Palestine into an Arab state and a Jewish state.
[‡]   Bond, p. 88.
[§]   Megargee, p. 5

the creation of the Free State, and nine cavalry regiments.* The Army's budget continued thereafter to fall until 1932 and its strength declined from 231,000 in 1922 to 207,000 in 1931. Worse, by 1931 the Army had failed in its recruiting targets by 8,000 men, with enlistment down in spite of high levels of unemployment.[24]

Defence expenditure overall fell throughout the 1920s: by 1932 it accounted for only 2.5% of G.D.P., compared with 3.5% in 1913, when commitments had been fewer.[25] By then, however, the Ten Year Rule appeared more and more unsafe. The Cabinet had renewed it annually from 1924, and in 1928 Winston Churchill, the Chancellor of the Exchequer, adopted the Rule as a standing assumption until either the Services or the Foreign Office could offer grounds to change it.[26] By the early 1930s those grounds appeared to have arrived. In 1926, thirty-six infantry battalions had been needed during the General Strike; and the seventeen battalions sent to the Far East in January 1927 – to safeguard Shanghai and the 1842 Treaty Ports in China from the Japanese – left only fifty-six battalions at home, including the ten battalions of Guards and the six battalions in the Rhineland. The C.I.G.S. noted at this stage that: 'if the Expeditionary Force is removed from England to prosecute a war which is unpopular with any appreciable portion of the industrial community, the residue of regular infantry units left in England will be totally inadequate to provide the necessary backing to the police in maintaining internal order.'[27] The Crisis in Manchuria in 1931 prompted the Chiefs to challenge the Rule, stating that it made the achievement of government policy impossible. Britain's ability to defend its own territory, never mind its colonies in the Far East, was in doubt in the face of Japanese imperialism – and since the Washington Naval Treaty, the Japanese could no longer be counted as friends. Nor would the Chiefs be able to find resources for a continental expedition should it be required to carry out its Locarno commitments. On 22 March 1932 the Committee of Imperial Defence accepted the Chiefs' views and the Cabinet agreed the next day, so that the Rule was dead.[28]

As well as shortages of men and equipment, there also remained the issue within the Army of the want of professionalism. Before 1914 the Army, in spite of the reforms it had made after the Crimean and South African Wars, maintained the ethos among the Officers of an amateur force.[29] The Great War, through its scale and complexity, forced the Army to adapt, innovate, expand and transform, so that by 1918 it had perfected the tactics of infantry-artillery cooperation and learned to use petrol-engined lorries, tanks, radio, other armoured vehicles, gas and aircraft. However, after the war the old attitudes came back. Officers in smart regiments were not to be seen studying; and there was a belief that, since imperial defence was going to be the Army's mission for the foreseeable future, Officers should not spend too much time thinking about military doctrine – or indeed thinking at all.[30] It was a commonplace in many Regiments at this time that the majority of Officers thought and talked of nothing but the social scene, hunting, racing and polo. The German champion of armoured warfare, Heinz Guderian, had no

---

*   1st and 2nd Battalions of the Royal Irish Regiment, Royal Dublin Fusiliers, Royal Munster Fusiliers, the Leinster Regiment, the Connaught Rangers; the 2nd Battalions of the Royal Irish Fusiliers and Royal Inniskilling Fusiliers – who also shared a depot; the 3rd and 4th Battalions of the Royal Fusiliers, the Worcestershire Regiment, the Middlesex Regiment, the 60th Rifles and the Rifle Brigade. The cavalry amalgamations were the 1st and 2nd Life Guards, 3rd and 6th Dragoon Guards, 4th and 7th Dragoon Guards, 5th and 6th Dragoons, 16th and 5th Lancers (the 5th had been degraded in seniority because of a misdemeanour during the 1798 Irish Rebellion), 13th and 18th Hussars, 14th and 20th Hussars; 15th and 19th Hussars; 17th and 21st Lancers.

opposite number in Britain, for neither Basil Liddell Hart nor J.F.C. Fuller, its chief proponents here, were serving Officers.[31]

Problems with Officer recruiting, education, retention and promotion exacerbated the problem. The simple fact of post-war life was that the Army was not attracting many intelligent Officer candidates. The Generals of the Great War had a reputation, often exaggerated and in very many cases completely undeserved, for stupidity and callousness. After the war the stereotype lingered and grew, aided by some of the memoirs and novels already mentioned in the late 1920s and early 1930s – resented as these often were by veterans who angrily failed to recognise the picture they painted.

There had, however, been considerable discussion about the future of Officer training and of the two fee-paying colleges at Sandhurst and Woolwich.* Suggestions from Leslie Hore-Belisha[32] and committees under Lord Willingdon in 1937[33] and Lord Strathcona in 1938,[34] had all looked at ways to bring in more Officers as well as to widen the social base from which most Officers were drawn; but on the eve of the Second World War, around 90% of the Army's Officers were still from the public schools and 30% from ten public schools with Army Classes.† Most of the cadets at Sandhurst and Woolwich in the 1920s and 1930s came from military families, for other men would not accept the low pay and conditions of service of a young Officer. The sense of belonging to a tight military caste was palpable.

The teaching at the Royal Military College, Sandhurst, was at this time largely confined to military subjects rather than any broader education: the curriculum included the study of military administration; military law; sanitation and military hygiene; tactics, topography and field sketching, field engineering and trench warfare; French, German, or Hindustani; drill; equitation; physical training, bayonet training and sports; and musketry.[35] Hugh Stockwell, later the Force Commander at Suez, recalled similar memories to those of David Niven and John Masters: 'Life was a continual rush, changing from one set of clothes for another for parades (the puttees were a curse to get on properly), for Physical Training, or for the halls of study where we tackled map reading, tactical mountain warfare or Field Service Regulations. There was very little academic work then.'[36]

The management and riding of horses, and of polo and hunting, was also of great importance.[37] Sports and games were enthusiastically followed: there were soccer, cricket, rugby football, swimming, boxing, fencing and athletics. The few clever men who entered the service had to struggle not to have the brightness beaten out of them. There was no training in leadership. The object of training seemed to be to prevent rebellion, originality, or departure from the accepted norm. Life in the field army did nothing to correct this. Peacetime service was dull, especially for the veterans of the Great War. Field manoeuvres were often a joke, with undermanned units using flags to represent tanks.

The then Lieutenant, later Colonel, Jack Willes wrote that:

> The Battalion [1 R.W.F.] was very under strength and on exercises sections were represented by red flags placed on bushes. Because I am red/green colour blind I had to have my orderly

---

*   The Royal Military College Sandhurst trained Officers for the infantry, Royal Tank Corps and the cavalry; the Royal Military Academy Woolwich trained Officers for the Royal Artillery, Royal Engineers, Royal Signals, Royal Army Ordnance Corps and Royal Army Service Corps.

†   Eton, Harrow, Marlborough, Wellington, Rugby, Winchester, Hurstpierrepoint, Tonbridge and Felsted.

beside me to tell me which flag was displayed. I remember when we were in the experimental brigade we had scout platoons for which the vehicles provided were taxis, complete with a taxi driver … some of the taxi drivers were quite bolshie and refused to park tactically … Even on brigade and higher formation exercises a tremendous amount of time was spent on marching, which stood us in good stead when we went to France in 1940.[38]

The ambitions of most young Officers were limited to getting into a decent regiment and, in due course, commanding it. In due course, because promotion was by regimental vacancy, not time, and hard to come by. During the 1920s and early 1930s, spending ten years as a subaltern was not unusual. This was because of the system of promotion by regimental vacancy during the inter-war years.[39] Only when a senior Officer retired or died would a vacancy be created, and those eligible could make a step up the ladder. Matters were improved by Hore-Belisha's reforms based on the report of the Willingdon Committee, which replaced promotion by seniority with promotion by time. By 1938, an Officer could expect promotion to Lieutenant after three years, Captain after eight years, and Major – a rank which was guaranteed – by seventeen years at the latest. Importantly, too, Hore-Belisha demolished the log-jam at the top of the Army by reducing retirement ages to 47 for a Major, 50 for a Lieutenant Colonel, and so on. On 1 August 1938, 2,000 Officers were promoted in a single day.[40] In the Royal Welch Fusiliers, this resulted in the following promotions:[41]

To Colonel	To Major	To Captain
Bt Lt Col T.D. Daly MC	Bt Lt Col H.A. Freeman-Attwood OBE MC	Lieutenant H. de B. Prichard
	Bt Major S.O. Jones MC	Lieutenant J.A.M. Rice-Evans
	Captain T.S. Griffiths	Lieutenant E.H. Cadogan
	Bt Major D.S. Watson DSO	Lieutenant R.J.F. Snead-Cox
	Captain W.P. Kenyon MC	Lieutenant N.C. Stockwell
	Bt Major H.C. Watkins MC	Lieutenant R.A.F. Hurt
	Captain D.I. Owen	Lieutenant O.T.M. Raymont
	Bt Major M.B. Dowse	Lieutenant W.S.A. Clough-Taylor
	Captain B.E. Horton	Lieutenant J.R. Johnson
	Captain R.G. Davies-Jenkins	Lieutenant W.L.R. Benyon
	Captain R. de B. Hardie	Lieutenant L.H. Yates
	Captain W.H. Bamfield	Lieutenant & QM Jones DCM MM
	Captain Ll. Gwydyr-Jones	
	Captain R.L.K. Allen	

Beyond Lieutenant Colonel, promotion was by selection board; to which Hore-Belisha added the responsibility for appointments as well. This system should have been impartial, but there remained plenty of scope for nepotism.[42] Boards looked for the consistent qualities of honesty, trustworthiness, loyalty, sobriety, zeal and energy, and cheerfulness; and evidence that as age and experience grew, so too did industry, initiative, tact, honour and the capacity to command.[43]

Bringing together the results of receiving a staff college education, and the board system with its required qualities, one commentator noted that 'By the late 1930s, it had become impossible for an Officer to reach a senior post without having the psc [passed staff college] qualification.'[44] This process might have occurred even sooner but for the fact that over 200 of the 628 staff college graduates on the *Army List* in 1914 died in the Great War, and the limited size of the post-war entry to the Colleges at Camberley and Quetta meant that by 1928, the total had only risen to 671. On the eve of the Great War, two out of four members of the Army Council, six out of eight Command or District Commanders, and ten out of twenty of divisional commanders were staff college graduates – good odds for those who were not psc. This percentage remained roughly constant during the War.[45]

However, by the middle of the 1930s the average age of senior commanders was seven years older than in 1913,[46] and those younger men who had been waiting for promotion were losing their will to push things forward.[47] One effect of all issues was to produce Officers who lacked the qualities required for modern warfare.[48] In 1942, the then C.I.G.S., Alan Brooke, wrote in his diary, that 'Half our Corps and Division Commanders are totally unfit for their appointments, and yet if I were to sack them, I could find no better! They lack character, imagination, drive, and power of leadership.'[49]

The British regimental system also prevented the development of any coherent battlefield tactical doctrine. Under this system, regiments with linked battalions rotated between Britain and overseas. But because they rotated, their organisation had to be identical, even when one might be under-strength. The Regimental System also built the idea of family, but Regiments were against any sort of standardisation. Every Regiment therefore did things its own way. This had not been the case during the Great War when things were far more coherent.[50] Now the Regimental System closed Officers' minds and obstructed reform.[51]

Not all British Officers were stupid or resistant to change; some of the best commanders of the Second World War, men like Montgomery, Wavell, Slim, Alexander, Dill and Pile, studied hard in their own time.[52] The limited debate on doctrine was focused on mechanisation. In this field, in spite of every obstacle, progress was made throughout the 1920s and by the mid-1930s Britain was a leader in tank design, the techniques of mechanised warfare, and the grouping and training of mechanised formations.[53] However the spread of opinion on armoured warfare was very broad within the Army. At one end of the spectrum was a small group which believed that future warfare would be all about tanks. These included J.F.C. Fuller* and Percy Hobart.† Another group supported the revision of tactical doctrine but saw the need for all-arms cooperation rather than the total dominance of the Tank Corps. These included Alan Brooke and Montgomery. A third group were content to work within their own parts of the service in order to solve the tactical problems of the Great War. They were suspicious of mechanisation until the late 1920s. Another group, which included many cavalry Officers and considerable numbers

---

*   Major General John Frederick Charles Fuller CB CBE DSO (1878–1966) had been Chief of Staff of the Tank Corps in 1918 and was an early theorist of modern armoured warfare. He was also a practising Satanist.
†   Major General Sir Percy Cleghorn Stanley Hobart KBE CB DSO MC (1885–1957), also known as 'Hobo', commanded the 79th Armoured Division during the Second World War. He was responsible for many of the specialised armoured vehicles, 'Funnies' that took part in the invasion of Normandy and the campaign in North-West Europe.

in the infantry, did not see a need for change at all. Many were not against some aspects of mechanisation, but saw tanks only as useful for infantry support when needed. The final faction opposed mechanisation totally and saw no need to give up their horses.[54]

The interwar history of the Royal Tank Corps illustrates the debate led by J.F.C. Fuller and others within the climate of tight budgets and intellectual rigidity. From August 1918 onwards, the British Army had won its victories using a combination of tank-infantry, armoured car-cavalry-artillery, and infantry-artillery tactics, supported by aircraft, balloons for observation, machine guns and gas. Now, there appeared to be little use for tanks in imperial policing, and they were expensive. The Tank Corps was reduced from twenty battalions to four, and survived by switching to armoured cars, which were more useful outside Europe. Without the prospect of a major war, limited motorisation seemed most attractive. The maintenance of the Ten Year Rule until 1932 also caused the Committee of Imperial Defence to state that limitations on spending 'would not in any way hamper the development of ideas but would check mass production until the situation demanded it.[55]

In spite of the obstacles, the Army was able to continue research and development. By the mid-1920s, the best tank in Britain – perhaps in the world – was the *Vickers* Medium, which had a revolving turret and was capable of road speeds of up to 30 m.p.h (50 k.p.h.). The Army had a variety of armoured cars and light armoured fighting vehicles known as 'tankettes'. In 1924, Brigadier George Lindsay proposed forming all these into a 'Mechanical Force': Although unsuccessful at first, and although the Secretary of State for War, Sir Laming Worthington-Evans, approved the idea in 1925, its implementation had to wait until Field Marshal Sir George Milne[*] took over as C.I.G.S. in February 1926.[56] Milne and his successors faced a lack of money and a want of any clear mission outside imperial policing. Nor could they simply ignore reactionaries in the army and there was considerable doubt as to the practicality of the some theories given the state of technical capability at the time.[57] The most important work of innovation took place between 1926 and 1932. In 1926, Milne directed the formation of the Experimental Mechanized Force along the lines that Lindsay had suggested.[58]

The Army's first major exercises after the end of the war took place in 1925 with six infantry and one cavalry divisions. The lessons drawn from these were that too few senior Officers had experience of the command at this level and those that did thought in terms of trench warfare.[59] Over the next three years the Army carried out field trials, training was however constrained by outbreaks of foot-and-mouth disease in 1924 and in 1926. In the first year every available type of vehicle took part, and the force practiced many of the tactical techniques that the Germans would later call *Blitzkrieg,* or 'lightning war'. Later the force benefited from the introduction of battlefield radio, which convinced some that the problems of controlling rapidly-moving tracked and wheeled formations had been solved. But other more conservative Officers decided that the Force had provided all the lessons it was likely to do and it was disbanded in late 1928.[60]

Plans were then put in place to establish a mixed light armoured force on Salisbury Plain in 1929, followed by a new tank brigade in 1930 or 1931. Exercises with such a brigade under Brigadier Charles Broad[†] took place in 1931, and these emphasised the need for radio; in the final exercises,

[*]   Field Marshal Sir George Francis Milne, 1st Baron Milne GCB GCMG DSO (1866–1948) was C.I.G.S. from 1926 to 1933. He served in the Second Boer War and during the Great War commanded the British forces on the Macedonian front.
[†]   Later Lieutenant General Sir Charles Noel Frank Broad KCB DSO (1882–1976).

Broad was able to control the entire brigade through a sequence of movements in thick fog from the turret of his tank.[61] The Kirke Committee, which Milne created in 1931 to study the lessons of the Great War, was in favour of armoured units, but only within the context of a combined-arms grouping.[62] Many other problems of armoured warfare, like infantry-tank and artillery-tank cooperation, or the integration of vehicles with varying capabilities, had not been solved. Had the British continued to develop their ideas, however, they could have developed a force by 1940 that would have matched the Germans. However Milne shelved the Committee's recommendations in 1933. When the government told the Army to prepare for war in March 1939, the War Office reported that only sixty of the required 1,646 heavy 'infantry' tanks – those designed to equip armoured brigades and to support the infantry divisions – were in service. When Britain went to war, 1,000 of its 1,300 tanks were light tanks, suitable only for imperial policing and security.[63]

Experiments in 1934 with a 'Mobile Division' – the Army Tank Brigade and a motorised infantry brigade – gave poor results. The Imperial General Staff came to view this Division as an extension of the cavalry; its role was to be limited to reconnaissance, screening, and flank protection, rather than breakthrough or exploitation.[64] In 1935, the Army turned firmly away from the armoured division as a concept and instead divided the roles of armoured forces. The Army Tank Brigade would provide infantry-support units and would be equipped with heavy, so-called Infantry (I) tanks – when money became available. The Army's mobile units would consist of the cavalry regiments, equipped with lorries, armoured cars and light or medium ('Cruiser') tanks, which would eventually form Mobile Divisions.[65] In the meantime, the Army would convert the horse transport in its standard infantry battalions and the artillery to lorries – with the result that in 1939, the British Army was the only Army in the world that did not still rely on horses for its logistic support.[66] However, even after the Army had made good its shortages of equipment in 1939, it continued to use its forces in a way that gave an advantage to the Germans in the campaigns of 1940 in Norway, France and Belgium, with disastrous results.

The summer of 1939 was a period of chaos in the British Army. Its aim was to create a force of twenty-eight infantry, seven anti-aircraft and four armoured divisions; but only six infantry divisions already in existence went to France in September.* These were poorly-trained and short of equipment, especially tanks, medium and heavy artillery and anti-aircraft guns. In May 1939, to find the 500,000 men needed for its target force, Britain introduced conscription into the Regular Army (but not the Reserves). Even with more manpower, the British Expeditionary Force (B.E.F.) had to improvise its communications, logistics and its command and control structures after mobilisation; nor was there a nominated commander until Lord Gort was appointed after the declaration of war.[67] In the meantime, the Germans occupied the remainder of Czechoslovakia and took control of its armaments industry; Britain, France and Poland signed a mutual assistance pact; and Germany and Italy concluded the *Stahlpakt*, or Pact of Steel. After the surprise agreement of the Molotov-Ribbentrop Pact between Germany and the Soviet Union, on 23 August 1939, the Germans invaded Poland. On 3 September, Britain and France declared war on Germany.

It is very easy to blame the policy of all governments for the waning in British military power and indeed the figures quoted in this chapter show the severity of the cuts in funding and their

---

*   1st, 2nd, 3rd, 4th, 5th and 48th. They were followed by the 42nd, 44th and 50th. There were also two armoured brigades and an anti-aircraft division as well as a large number of units commanded at Army and corps level and not included in the totals of divisions.

effects, made worse by the inability to recruit and keep up with high levels of military commitments. These factors combined to stop the British Army from introducing the numbers and types of modern systems needed to train for and fight a European war. However the Army also had itself to blame, because of its resistance to change, its inability to set out clear strategic or tactical doctrine and its eagerness to return to pre-war organisations rather than build on the flexible, combined-arms structures of 1918. There was too, a lack of professionalism in military training and education. All these factors therefore combined to create an Army that was unable to fight and win the Great War again, let alone what was to come.

Notes

1   Geoffrey P. Megargee, *The Army Before Last: British Military Policy 1919–1939 and its Relevance to the US Army Today* (RAND Paper, Santa Monica USA, 2000), p. 2.
2   *Encyclopaedia Britannica*, Supplement Vol III, 1926; Niall Ferguson, *Empire: How Britain made the Modern World* (London, 2003); Megargee, p. 2.
3   Megargee, p. 2.
4   Tom Wintringham, *New Ways of War* (London, 1940).
5   F.O. Miksche, *Blitzkrieg* (London, 1941) but based on earlier material from the Spanish Civil War.
6   Richard Simpkin, *Deep Battle: The Brainchild of Marshal Tukhachevsky* (London, 1987).
7   G.R. Searle, *A New England? Peace and War 1886–1918* (Oxford, 2005) pp. 742–744; Megargee, p. 2.
8   Brian Bond, *British Military Policy Between the Two World Wars* (Oxford, 1980) pp. 2–5.
9   See, for example, Anthony Clayton, *The British Empire as a Superpower, 1919–1930* (University of Georgia Press, 1986), p. 1; Bond, *Military Policy*, pp. 10–12.
10   J.P. Harris, 'The British General Staff and the Coming of War, 1933–1939' in *The British General Staff: Reform and Innovation 1890–1939* ed. David French and Brian Holden Reid (London, 2002), pp. 175–178.
11   Megargee, p. 2.
12   Clayton, p. 19; Megargee, p. 6–7.
13   Corelli Barnett, *Britain and Her Army*, 1509–1970 (London, 1971) pp. 411, 412.
14   www.measuringworth.com, accessed 14 February 2018 and using the real price comparator.
15   The figures are from Peter Silverman, 'The Ten Year Rule,' in *R.U.S.I. Journal* CXVI (March, 1971), p. 42. There is evidence that the Cabinet had originally only meant the Rule to apply for one year but, although the Rule did not come up for formal review again until 1924, its assumptions remained in place.
16   Keith Jeffery, *The British Army and the Crisis of Empire 1918–1922* (M.U.P., 1984), pp. 12, 159; Clayton, *Superpower*, pp. 2, 17; Bond, *Military Policy*, pp. 40–41; Megargee, p. 7.
17   Higham, p. 6.
18   Jeffery, pp. 35–42.
19   Bond, p. 21.
20   Bond, pp. 10–11, 29, 102; Clayton, pp. 7, 26–27; Megargee, p. 5.
21   Bond, pp. 24–25; see also Silverman, 'Ten Year Rule.'
22   Keith Jeffery, *The Military Correspondence of Field Marshal Sir Henry Wilson 1918–1922* (Army Records Society, 1985), pp. 120–122. See also Megargee, pp. 3, 8.
23   Jeffery, p. 22; Bond, p. 26; Megargee, p. 6.
24   Higham, p. 234
25   Megargee, p. 7.
26   Silverman, 'Ten Year Rule', p. 44.
27   Bond, pp. 91–92.
28   Bond, pp. 94–96; Megargee, p. 7.
29   See Timothy Travers, *The Killing Ground. The British Army, the Western Front and the Emergence of Modern Warfare 1900–1918* (London, 1987) Part 1, Megargee, p. 11–12, and Brian Bond, *The Victorian Army and the Staff College* (London, 1972).
30   Corelli Barnett, p. 411.

31   Megargee, p. 12.
32   The National Archives, War Office Papers, T.N.A. WO 32/4461 dated 6 September 1937.
33   T.N.A. WO 32/4461, Second Report.
34   T.N.A. WO 32/4544, August 1938.
35   Royal Military College Cadet Register, 1921. See also *Provisional Regulations Respecting Admission to the Royal Military College Sandhurst and for first Appointments there from to the Regular Army* (WO 43/ RMC 414 attached to Army Orders, 1 August 1917).
36   Liddell Hart Archive, Stockwell Papers, KCL/Stockwell/1/2. See also John Masters, *Bugles and a Tiger* (London, 1956), p. 41; and David Niven, *The Moon's a Balloon* (London, 1971), p. 55.
37   Brigadier Sir John Smyth Bt VC MC MP, *Sandhurst. The History of the Royal Military Academy, Woolwich, the Royal Military College, Sandhurst, and the Royal Military Academy Sandhurst 1741–1961* (London, 1961), pp. 154–155.
38   Interview with Col J.E.T. Willes by Lt Col L. Egan (R.W.F. Museum).
39   See, for example, David Niven *The Moon's a Balloon*, p. 72; Montgomery *Memoirs*, p. 21; Montgomery, *Memoirs*, p. 40; and Jeremy Crang, *The British Army and the People's War*, p. 45.
40   Jeremy Crang, *The British Army and the People's War*, pp. 45–46.
41   *London Gazette*, 5 August 1938.
42   David French, 'An Extensive Use of Weedkiller: Patterns of Promotion in the Senior Ranks of the British Army, 1919–1939' in David French and Brian Holden Reid (ed), *The British General Staff. Reform and Innovation 1890–1939*, pp. 159–162.
43   David French, 'An Extensive Use of Weedkiller', pp. 164–165.
44   David French, 'An Extensive Use of Weedkiller', p. 168.
45   David French, 'An Extensive Use of Weedkiller', p. 168.
46   Megargee, p. 13.
47   Barnett, *Britain and Her Army,* p. 411.
48   Megargee, p. 12.
49   *Field Marshal Lord Alanbrooke, War Diaries 1939–1945* (ed. Alex Danchev and Daniel Todman), (London, 2001) p. 243.
50   This was very well developed in the German Army in both World Wars. See Timothy Lupfer, *The Dynamics of Doctrine: The Changes in German Tactical Doctrine during the First World War* (Combat Studies Institute, U.S. Army Command and General Staff College, 1981).
51   See the discussion in Megargee, p. 14.
52   Jay Luvaas, *The Education of an Army. British Military Thought, 1815–1940* (University of Chicago Press, 1964), p. 331; Megargee, p. 15.
53   J.P. Harris, *Men, Ideas and Tanks. British Military Thought and Armoured Forces, 1905–1939* (M.U.P, 1995), p. 202. See also Megargee, p. 15.
54   Megargee, pp. 15–16.
55   General Sir William Jackson and Field Marshal Lord Bramall, *The Chiefs. The Story of the United Kingdom Chiefs of Staff* (London, 1992), p. 134. see also Megargee, pp. 15–16, 17.
56   Harris, pp. 208–210; Shelford Bidwell and Dominick Graham, *Fire-power. British Army Weapons and Theories of War 1904–1945* (London, 1982), (an analysis of articles in the *Journal of the Royal Artillery*), p. 168.
57   Megargee, p. 18.
58   Harris, pp. 211–213.
59   Higham, p. 96
60   Megargee, p. 20.
61   Harris, pp. 220–221, 225.
62   Bidwell and Graham, pp. 197–200.
63   Clayton, p. 274; Bond, p. 328; Megargee, p. 11.
64   Harris, p. 261.
65   Megargee, p. 21.
66   Bidwell & Graham, p. 191; Bond, pp. 170–172.
67   Harris, p. 188; Bond, chapter 11; Clayton, pp. 258–259, 274.

Chapter 2

Infantry Battalion Deployment, Organisation, Equipment and Service 1918–1940

i. Infantry Battalion Deployment

Once the post-war demobilization process had been completed, as described in Chapter 1, and once the Geddes Committee recommendations had been implemented, regular infantry battalions were deployed as follows:[1]

    United Kingdom – 67 (56 after 1927; 64 after 1929)
    India – 45 (plus 82 Indian Army)
    Egypt – 6
    Palestine – 1 (9 after 1936)
    Hong Kong – 2 (plus 2 Indian Army)
    North China – 17 (after 1927)
    West Indies – 1
    Rhineland – 8 (until 1929)
    Aden – 1
    Iraq – 2 (until 1931)
    Ceylon – ½
    Singapore – ½ (plus 2 Indian Army)
    Gibraltar – 1
    Malta – 2
    Southern Africa – 4½
    Mauritius – ½

In addition there were bodies of colonial troops commanded by British Officers. These included the Royal West African Frontier Force, the King's African Rifles, the West India Regiment, the Bermuda Regiment, the Iraq Levies, the Iraq Army, the Transjordan Frontier Force, the Hong Kong Volunteers, the Straits Volunteers, and the Somaliland Scouts. The Dominions – South Africa, Australia, New Zealand, Canada, and Newfoundland – maintained their own forces not under the authority of the British War Office or General Staff.

ii. Organisation

Between the wars there were numerous changes to the infantry battalion establishment; some took account of economic realities and others the introduction of new weapons. The figures given reflect the establishments authorised by the War Office, but the realities on the ground were often very different. This was particularly so in the case of Home Service battalions which were starved of manpower in order to keep Foreign Service battalions up to strength. In April 1924, for example, 1 R.W.F. in India was at a strength of twenty-nine Officers and 869 men – only fourteen men short of its establishment; while 2 R.W.F. in Pembroke Dock was at a strength of twenty-five Officers and 515 men, three Officers and 234 men below the establishment. In January 1937, 2 R.W.F. was in Shanghai with thirty Officers and 880 men – twenty-seven men over establishment; while 1 R.W.F in Woking numbered twenty-nine Officers and 611 men, 152 below the establishment.[2]

In 1920 the War Office issued 'The Small Wars Establishment' for infantry battalions. Henceforth a battalion would comprise Headquarters (nine Officers & 129 O.R.s) and four rifle companies (six Officers & 209 O.R.s each). Each company had a Company Headquarters (two Officers & thirty-one O.R.s) and four platoons (each of one Officer and forty-three O.R.s). A platoon had two rifle and two L.M.G. sections, the latter equipped with a *Lewis* gun. The total strength was thirty-three Officers and 965 O.R.s. There were also five attached personnel, one of whom was the chaplain. The transport was entirely horse-drawn and comprised ten riding horses, thirty-seven draught horses and seven pack mules. The vehicles included limbered wagons, kitchens, water carts, and an Officers' mess cart.[3]

The first significant change occurred two years later and was brought about by the War Office decision to disband the Machine Gun Corps as a cost-cutting measure in 1922. This made available their arsenal of *Vickers* machine guns for distribution to infantry battalions. A Headquarters Wing was established which comprised all those elements not included in the rifle companies. It was divided into four groups under Wing H.Q. which had a C.S.M., C.Q.M.S., clerks, storemen and orderlies. No 1 Group was composed of a light mortar section with two light mortars; signallers, scouts, and stretcher bearers, the latter coming from the Band; and anti-aircraft gunners equipped with *Lewis* guns. No 2 Group was then armed with eight *Vickers* machine guns. No 3 Group, which contained personnel employed primarily on administrative duties, was under the Quartermaster and was available to fight when necessary. Finally, No 4 Group was responsible for the transport. The organisation of the four rifle companies was unchanged.[4]

The 1928 (War Establishment) reorganisation was brought about by the creation of a Machine Gun Company, and the reduction of the rifle companies from four to three. Within H.Q. Wing, No 1 Group now comprised the battalion H.Q. staff, including signallers, the intelligence section, stretcher bearers and clerks. No 2 Group became the Anti-Tank Group with four anti-tank guns. No 3 Group was responsible for administration under the Quartermaster and Transport Officer. The total strength of H.Q. Wing was eight Officers and 195 O.R.s. The peace establishment contained a No 4 Group comprising drummers, buglers and bandsmen. The M.G. Company had four platoons, each commanded by a subaltern and equipped with four *Vickers* machine guns. In practice, in peacetime, there were only three platoons. Platoon strength was one Officer, two senior N.C.O.s, and thirty-seven O.R.s. The three rifle companies each had four platoons of four sections. Platoons had a strength of one Officer, one senior

N.C.O., and thirty-three O.R.s. Each rifle company, including company H.Q., had six Officers, one Warrant Officer, five senior N.C.O.s, and 151 O.R.s. The total strength of the battalion was thirty-two Officers, six Warrant Officers, thirty-four senior N.C.O.s, and 755 rank and file, giving a total of 827 all ranks. There were also 112 horses/mules and twenty-one bicycles.[5]

In 1936 there was an Army-wide reorganisation. In the infantry battalion, H.Q. Wing was renamed H.Q. Company and comprised four platoons: signals, L.M.G.s for anti-aircraft and ground defence, mortars, and administration and transport. The M.G. company was disbanded and the fourth rifle company restored, but each platoon was reduced to three sections. Each section had a *Bren* L.M.G. which replaced the *Lewis* gun. The 2-inch mortar and the *Boys* anti-tank rifle were introduced at this time. Machine Gun battalions were created, as divisional troops units, in which the four rifle companies were converted to three machine gun companies of three platoons, each of two sections equipped with two *Vickers* machine guns; and later a 4.2-inch mortar company. The battalion thus had a total of thirty-six machine guns. At the same time horses in all types of infantry battalion were replaced by mechanical transport, numbering some sixty vehicles.[6]

The final reorganisation of the infantry was undertaken in 1939 just prior to the outbreak of war. The infantry battalion had a battalion H.Q. (four Officers and forty-two O.R.s), an expanded H.Q. company with six platoons: signals, anti-aircraft (four A.A. L.M.G.s), mortars (two 3-inch mortars), carriers (with ten tracked vehicles), pioneers, and administration. The strength of the company was five Officers and 213 O.R.s. A rifle company had three Officers and 124 O.R.s. Only one platoon in the company was commanded by a subaltern, the other two by Platoon Sergeant Majors, a new rank of W.O. III introduced in 1938 to make up for the shortage of Officers. In platoon H.Q., in addition to its commander, was the platoon sergeant, a runner, and two men on the 2-inch mortar. Sections had a corporal and seven men, two of whom manned the *Bren* L.M.G.[7] Anti-tank guns were not issued directly to the infantry battalions until after the outbreak of war. During the campaign in France, each infantry brigade included an Anti-Tank Company of three platoons, each platoon equipped with three 25-mm guns provided by the French, or three 2 pdr Ordnance guns, and one such platoon could be attached to each battalion.

Under this last organisation, the numbering of platoons was as follows:

H.Q. Company	A Company	B Company	C Company	D Company
1 – Signals	7	10	13	16
2 – Anti-aircraft	8 Rifle Platoons	11 Rifle Platoons	14 Rifle Platoons	17 Rifle Platoons
3 – Mortars	9	12	15	18
4 – Carriers				
5 – Pioneers				
6 – Admin				

iii. Ranks

The rank structure of a pre-Second World War infantry battalion differed only slightly from its modern equivalent. Companies were, by the mid 1920s, usually commanded by majors rather than captains. Specially meritorious service both at regimental duty and on the staff could be recognised by the grant of brevet promotion to the next higher rank. A brevet commission (discontinued in the mid-1960s) was only by courtesy. Officially, both titles were used: 'Major and Brevet Lieutenant Colonel so-and-so'. Originally the term designated a promotion given on occasions such as a coronation, or the conclusion of a war, but after the Crimean War, it was limited to cases of distinguished service in the field and on the principle of seniority, and brevet commissions were confined to ranks between captain and lieutenant-colonel. The Brevet conferred rank in the army, but not in the regiment. When an Officer served with his regiment, only regimental rank counted; if the regiment was with a larger formation then brevet rank could be used to determine command of temporary units formed for special purposes. Thus it was possible for a regimental Major to hold a brevet Lieutenant-Colonelcy with seniority over the commission of his own commanding Officer. Appointment to a brevet also counted towards the requirement to have served for a sufficient time in a lower rank to be eligible for promotion to a more senior one. [8]

The rank of Colour-Sergeant was limited to Company Quartermaster Sergeants; other Sergeants with specific responsibilities in H.Q. Wing being known as Staff Sergeants. The rank of Lance Sergeant still existed. This N.C.O. was usually a corporal acting in the rank of sergeant. The rank appeared first in the Royal Marines, then in the Army, during the 19th Century and could be removed by the soldier's commanding Officer, unlike that of a full sergeant, who could only be demoted by court martial. The rank was abolished in 1946, except in the regiments of Guards, which abolished full corporal instead.

Throughout the period, boys were enlisted routinely, usually as band boys or drummers but also occasionally in other trades, such as runners and signallers, more usually in the T.A. Boys' service began at the school leaving age of 14, and ended when a boy reached the age of 17, at which point he was re-enlisted into adult service. Following public disquiet at the deaths of boys in the Great War – boys who had often lied about their age and enlisted as adults – the minimum age for active service overseas was set at 19. However with the return of peace, boys accompanied their battalions overseas and there is no evidence to suggest that they were left out of battle in Ireland, Waziristan or North China.

In 1938, to make good a shortage of Officers to command at platoon level, the rank of WO III was introduced.[9] In the infantry, they were known as Platoon Sergeant Majors, and wore a large crown badge on the lower sleeve of the tunic; W.O. IIs wore a crown within a wreath. Eleven W.O. IIIs were allocated to each infantry battalion – the scale was different for M.G. battalions – and were distributed three to H.Q. Company, one each in No 2 (Anti-Aircraft), No 3 (Mortar), and No 5 (Pioneer) Platoons; and eight to the rifle companies, two of the three platoons per company being commanded by a W.O. III and one by an Officer.

Promotions to the rank were suspended by Army Council Instruction 804 of 1940, however those holding the rank would retain it until they were promoted or discharged from the service. The rank was finally abolished by A.C.I. 991 of 1947.

iv. Regimental and Army Numbers

Prior to 1920, each regiment issued its own service numbers to non-commissioned ranks, which were unique only within that regiment; thus a number could exist simultaneously in many regiments; if a man transferred between regiments or corps then he would be issued with a new number. No numbers were allocated to Officers before 1920.

A recognisably modern system, but still regimentally based, was brought in by Army Order 338 in August 1920. Numbers for non-commissioned ranks were a maximum of seven figures, although during the Second World War, eight figure numbers were used. Numbers were issued to all members of the Regular Army, Territorial Army, Special Reserve/Militia and the Army Reserve. Regiments and corps were allocated blocks of numbers, that given to the Royal Welch Fusiliers being 4178001 to 4256000. If a man changed regiments, he would retain his number. Officers were given six-figure numbers, allocated regardless of regiment or corps, by seniority.

v. Weapons

The Short Magazine Lee Enfield rifle (S.M.L.E.), a bolt-operated rifle firing a .303-inch round, which had been the personal weapon of the infantry throughout the war, continued to be so up to and during the Second World War. In 1926 it was re-designated the No 1 Rifle, the fact of which most soldiers were blissfully unaware. In 1931 the No 4 Rifle appeared. It was still the S.M.L.E., but slightly modified to aid mass-production and with a heavier barrel to improve the accuracy of the shooting. It was issued with a spike bayonet.[10]

The .303-inch *Lewis* Mark 3 light machine gun was introduced in May 1918. It was a pan-magazine-fed, gas operated automatic weapon 50.5 inches (128 cm) long weighing 28 lbs (13 kg). It had an effective range of 880 yards (800 metres).

The .303-inch *Vickers* medium machine gun was a water-cooled, belt-fed gun weighing 56 lbs (23 kg) all-up. It had a three-man crew and an effective range of 2,187 yards (2,000 metres). In various marks, it was in service from the Great War until the early 1960s.

The *Bren* .303-inch light machine gun was a magazine-fed, gas-operated gun designed in Czechoslovakia. It weighed 22 lbs (10.35 kg) and a barrel length of 43.9 inches (115 cm). Its maximum effective range was 600 yards (550 metres). It remained in service, re-barrelled to 7.62 mm, until 1992.

The *Hotchkiss* .303-inch Mk I machine gun was a French-designed gun generally used by the cavalry and Tank Corps. It was, however, fitted to the *Carden-Lloyd* carrier in service with the infantry. It could be belt or magazine fed and had a maximum range of 3,500 yards (3,211 metres).

The Ordnance Mk I 2-inch mortar had been issued in 1918, but withdrawn from service in 1919. The Mk II was issued in 1938 with H.E., smoke and illuminating rounds. It weighed 10.5 lbs (8.5 kg) and with its first-line scale of bombs required a crew of two. It had an effective range of 500 yards (460 metres). It remained in service until the late 1980s.

The Ordnance Mk II 3-inch mortar superseded the *Stokes* Mk I trench mortar in the early 1930s. It comprised a base-plate, bipod, barrel and sight, the whole weighing 112 lbs (50.8 kg). Its range was limited to 1,600 yards (1,463 metres), however improvements in the ammunition and components increased this to 2,800 yards (2,560 metres) by 1942. It had a crew of three and was an indirect-fire weapon, directed by a mortar fire control party. It remained in service until the late 1960s.

The *Mills* grenade was declared obsolete in 1918 but in 1936 the No 36 grenade was issued. This was a cast-iron, pineapple cast bomb with a central fuse and striker held by a close lever and secured by a pin. It weighed 1 lb 11 ozs (765 g), could be thrown to about 45 yards (41.2 metres) and had a danger area of around 100 yards (91 metres). It remained in service until the late 1970s.

The standard pistol of the British Army from 1887 to 1963 was the *Webley* .455" revolver, with a six-round chamber. From 1918 to 1945, the Mk IV was in general use. This weighed 2.4 lb (1.1 kg) and was effective to a maximum of 50 yards (45 metres).

The *Boys* 5.5-inch anti-tank rifle was in service from 1937 to 1943. It was effective against light armoured vehicles, achieving a penetration 23.2 mm (just under one inch) at 100 yards (90 metres). It was a bolt-action weapon fed by a 5-round magazine and was long and heavy: 5 feet 2 inches long (1.57 metres) and 35 lbs (16 kg) in weight.

The Ordnance 2 pdr anti-tank gun appeared in 1936. Its calibre was 40mm (1.57-inch) and had a range of 1,000 yards (914 metres) and was generally effective against all but the frontal armour of main battle tanks. The *Hotchkiss* 25 mm SA 34 anti-tank gun was introduced in small numbers in 1940 to make good shortages of the 2 pdr.[11]

vi. Personal Equipment

The adoption of new weapons, the re-organisation of the infantry into M.G. and rifle battalions, and the development of mechanization, all necessitated a review of the web equipment that had been introduced into service in 1908 and had been in use ever since. Trials were undertaken with a view to lightening, as far as possible, the weight carried by soldiers when on foot and when in action, based on the following principles: first, that basic individual equipment would be common to all arms; secondly, additional items of equipment, which differed for various individuals, should be carried in separate pouches or satchels which could be attached to the basic webbing.

The basic individual equipment, which was introduced in 1937, consisted of a web belt, braces, and haversack. These were of separate construction and detachable, and formed the framework on which to attach additional items. For the infantry these included ammunition pouches for the Lee-Enfield rifle and grenades; pistol holster; binocular case; gas mask haversack; first aid haversack. A large pack for use as a suitcase to hold personal articles and a sausage-shaped kitbag were also issued. These were normally carried in transport.[12] In peacetime, the brass fittings on the web equipment were polished and the webbing itself dressed with green *Blanco;* or white in the case of bands, drums, pioneers and military policemen.

vii. Vehicles

The *Carden-Lloyd* carrier was in service in infantry battalions in experimental formations during the late 1920s and early 1930s. It was a very small vehicle protected against small-arms fire and splinters. It carried only one weapon, a *Hotchkiss* gun, and this could be fired from the vehicle.

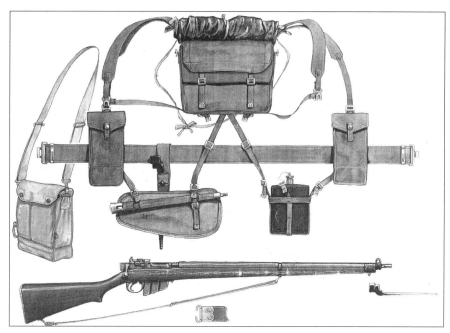

The 1937-pattern web equipment.
(*Journal of The Queen's Royal Surrey Regiment Association*, May 1991)

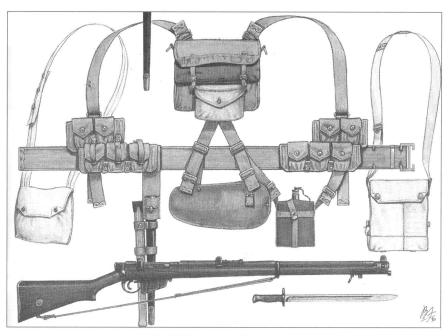

The 1908-pattern web equipment.
(*Journal of The Queen's Royal Surrey Regiment Association*, November 1990)

The troops were carried in a trailer. Its average speed cross-country was around 6 m.p.h. (10 k.p.h.) and on roads, 15 m.p.h. (24 k.p.h.) A relatively complicated vehicle, it required a high standard of training for efficient upkeep, repair and handling.[13] Only three vehicles per battalion were issued. The *Universal* Carrier, also known as the Bren Gun Carrier, was a light-armoured tracked vehicle built by Vickers-Armstrong and other companies. The first carriers – the *Bren* Carrier and the Scout Carrier with specific roles – entered service before the war, but a single improved design that could replace these, the *Universal*, was introduced in 1940. *Universal* Carriers were usually used for transporting personnel and equipment, mostly support weapons, or as machine gun platforms. With some 113,000 built throughout its life until the 1960s, it was the most-produced armoured fighting vehicle in history. It weighed 3 tons 16 cwt (3.75 tonnes), was powered by a V8 petrol engine and could achieve a speed of 30 m.p.h. (48 k.p.h.) and a range of 150 miles (240 km). It had a crew of three.

In addition, battalions were issued with the *Crossley* 25/30 tender in Ireland from 1919 to 1922; and after 1938 with a mix of 15-cwt and 3-ton petrol-engined lorries for troop and supply lift.

Other vehicles were used by experimental battalions. These are detailed in the Chapter 7, dealing with 1 R.W.F. in the experimental role.

viii. Communications

Until the introduction of radio, the Signal Platoon would pass messages by dispatch rider, runner, heliograph, telegraph using Morse buzzers, or flags.[14] The standard radio set introduced at the beginning of the Second World War was the Wireless Set No. 18. This was a portable man-pack set in service from 1940 for short range communications in forward area between battalion headquarters and the companies; there were no radios below company level. A single 18-set weighing 32 lbs (14.5 kg) with accessories (headphones, microphone, battery, spare battery and antenna) was carried on the back by one man and used by a second, the operator. Communication could be by radiotelephony (R/T), i.e. voice, or 'continuous wave' (C.W.), i.e. Morse code. In 1938, a new phonetic alphabet was introduced:[15]

1938	Ace	Beer	Charlie	Don	Edward	Freddie	George	Harry	Ink	Johnnie	King	London	Monkey
	Nuts	Orange	Pip	Queen	Robert	Sugar	Toc	Uncle	Vic	William	XRay	Yorker	Zebra
1918	Ack	Beer	Charlie	Don	Edward	Freddie	Gee	Harry	Ink	Johnnie	King	London	Emma
	Nuts	Orange	Pip	Queen	Robert	Esses	Toc	Uncle	Vic	William	XRay	Yorker	Zebra

ix. Barracks and Non-Commissioned Ranks' Quartering

From 1919 to the early 1930s, the world that a new recruit joined was little different from that which his predecessors had entered in 1914. He was issued with the same uniforms, weapons and equipment. In the larger garrisons he was accommodated in late-Victorian brick built barracks, but elsewhere he lived in temporary wooden-hutted camps built during the previous war and which were to survive until after the next one.[16] By 1927 the space allocated per man was 600 cubic feet (roughly 8 feet 3 inches x 9 feet x 8 feet), the equivalent of 17 cubic metres,[17] and it was reported that the installation of electric light should be almost completed by 1936.[18] The accommodation, although improving, nevertheless acted as a deterrent to recruiting. Prior to the Great War even army barracks were a marked improvement on the slum dwellings from which most of the soldiers came. The same could not be said afterwards when families increasingly lived in the comparative comfort of a new 'council' house on a modern housing estate, with which, in terms of privacy and amenities, a barrack room, even a modern one, came a poor second.[19] By 1939, it was planned that each soldier would have a partitioned bed-space fitted with a wardrobe; barrack rooms would be centrally heated, and blocks would be provided with modern sanitation and baths with hot and cold running water. The old dining rooms would be refitted as restaurants, and all cutlery, glasses, mugs and plates would be kept on the premises. Inevitably, some of these improvements were delayed by the war.

In India and Egypt, every soldier could afford servants to do the menial barrack jobs they had to in Britain. Native sweepers cleaned rooms and latrines; a barber 'nappy' shaved soldiers in bed before reveille; washer-men, or 'dhobi-wallahs' did their washing; and every section had a boy who cleaned boots, buttons and brasses.[20]

In 1921, the Army Council handed the management of canteen facilities to the Navy, Army and Air Forces' Institute (N.A.A.F.I.) but in the same year, the Treasury attempted to save money by reducing the quantity and variety of rations issued. However matters improved and menus gradually became better and more varied. By 1927, for example, 2 Buffs reported that the men's breakfast consisted of tea, bacon and beans, bread, margarine and marmalade, with eggs on Sundays.

Marriage was relatively rare among the Officers and men of the inter-war Army. All ranks had to obtain their Commanding Officer's permission to marry and this effectively ensured that the regiment's view of matters could be enforced. After 1920, soldiers who married after the age of 26, with permission, were also granted a marriage allowance. After 1938, married soldiers were granted either free quarters or marriage allowance, along with extra allowances for their children. After 1939, any marriage by a soldier aged over 20 was similarly recognised. Wives, when they joined a regiment, took on the same status as their husbands and families were closely supervised by regimental Officers. In foreign stations, they were subject to military law and married soldiers were held accountable for the behaviour of their wives and children.

Married quarters for non-commissioned ranks varied widely. In Calcutta in 1931, a married quarter consisted of a single room flat, which was about the size of an army hut, divided into rooms by hessian screens. The family slept on basic army beds which inevitably they shared with the insect life. In most garrisons in Britain, Victorian red-brick terraces were the standard quarters, from which wives who misbehaved could be immediately evicted. By 1939, efforts were in hand to ensure that every quarter had hot and cold running water, gas and electricity. The best married quarters were new flats in London, a new block built in 1936 in St John's Wood and housing sixty-eight families. These consisted of varying numbers of rooms depending on the size of families. Here, the equipment was up-to-date and included gas cookers, fitted wardrobes (holding rifle racks in addition), bathrooms, balconies, 'pram' garages and rubbish chutes. The rents were 7/- (35p) a week.[21]

x. Pay and Terms of Service

Officers

There were no 'short-service' commissions in the inter-war Army. On being commissioned from Sandhurst or Woolwich, Second Lieutenants were appointed to probationary commissions for their first three years. During this time, infantry Officers would attend a course at the School of Musketry, Hythe and then spent several months either at the Regimental Depot or in their battalions, doing drill, learning the interior economy of the unit and if they were lucky, being taught something of tactics by their seniors. At the end of three years, an Officer's commission might be terminated if the C.O., Senior Major and Adjutant did not agree that that the subaltern was efficient. If he passed this test, a subaltern then had to pass examinations for promotion to captain and to major – based on the tactical employment of a company and battalion respectively. Finally, majors who aspired to the rank of lieutenant colonel had to pass an examination to test their fitness to command, based on the employment of a mixed force of brigade strength. This examination included a written paper and a practical test.[22]

Rates of pay in 1919 were as follows:[23]

> Lieutenant Colonel, £2/7/6d (£2.37½p) per day plus 10/- (50p) command pay if a C.O.
> Major, £1/11/6d, (£1.57½p) rising to 37/- (£1.85p) after five years
> Captain, £1/3/6d (£1.17½p)
> Lieutenant, 16/- (80p) to 19/- (95p)
> Second Lieutenant, 13/- (65p) to 16/- (80p)
> An additional £74 per annum marriage allowance was paid to those over 30 who married with the C.O.'s permission.

By 1925 post-war deflation meant that the cost of living had fallen so it was decided to cut by a corresponding amount the pay of all Officers by 5½%.[24] Rates were again reduced from 1 October 1931, by 7%. Matters did not begin to improve until 1938 but even then rates were still below what they had been in 1919:[25]

> Lieutenant Colonel, £2/3/- (£2. 15p) per day plus 10/- (50p) command pay if a C.O.
> Major, £1/8/-, (£1.40p) rising to £1/13/6d (£1.67½p) after five years
> Captain, 19/6d (97½p) to 23/6d (£1.17½p)
> Lieutenant, 13/- (65p)
> Second Lieutenant, 11/- (55p)

For a lieutenant, therefore, his pay amounted for much of this period to about £18 per month, from which £10 would be spent on mess bills, along with extra pay for his servant and groom.[26] Jack Willes, who overspent his pay by a considerable margin, recalled that 1 R.W.F.'s mess had a large number of living-in members during the 1930s because marriage was forbidden until the age of 26 and entitlement to marriage allowance did not begin until 30:

> I had an allowance of £200 a year from my father and with that I could run a car, an MG *Midget*, with petrol at 9d (3.75p) a gallon (4.55 litres). I also had a horse, and a groom who

cost about 5/- (25p) a month. My mess bill, which included drinks, and food for the horse, was about £21 a month. I would go up to London twice a week, and during the season attended debutantes' balls.

The Officers' Mess remained very much a gentlemen's club. Behaviour likely to cause dissension, such as the discussion of politics or religion, practical joking and gambling, were all forbidden, as was talking 'shop'. Officers were required to preserve the same decorum in the Mess as they would in any gentleman's house. Officers wore mess dress on all but two or three evenings every week, usually Monday, Tuesday, Thursday and Friday. On Wednesday, Saturday and Sunday, dinner jackets were worn. Dinner was a parade and no Officer could leave until all had finished unless prior permission had been obtained, for example, to go to the cinema, in which case a suit could be worn at an early supper. Every Thursday was a band night and once a month there was a guest night. On these occasions, all silver, pictures and movable objects were cleared from the ante-room and everyone joined in hectic games like 'high-cockalorum' until the room and the participants were reduced to a complete shambles. Second Lieutenants were expected to keep quiet. As Jack Willes remembered: 'As a newly-joined subaltern – we were known as warts – you were not expected to express an opinion unless it was asked for, and one was kept very much down in the early years.'[27]

After 1918, the War Office granted a marriage allowance to Officers over the age of 30. In practice however, subalterns and captains could rarely afford to marry unless they had private means, but most regiments frowned on marriage for junior Officers. Divorce among Officers which involved another Officer's wife would require the resignation or retirement of the guilty party by the Army Council. Cases not involving another Officer's wife would incur the displeasure of the Army Council. In 1936, the Army Council warned all Officers that if they became involved in divorce proceedings, it would be noted in their records.

N.C.Os and Soldiers

Soldiers' lives were more regulated than the Officers. The standard enlistment was for twelve years, seven with the Colours and five with the reserve, later reduced to three.[28] Except for those few soldiers who reached Warrant rank, it was not possible for men to have a full career in the Army.

If accommodation was a deterrent to recruiting so also was pay. At the outbreak of war in 1914 a private soldier had been paid one shilling (1/-, or 5p) a day. This was increased by one (old) penny when in a war zone, and on 29 September 1917 a further three (old) pence were added. With troops refusing to return to France after the Armistice because of their anger over demobilisation plans, Winston Churchill was appointed Secretary for War in January 1919. He immediately doubled the pay of the Armed Forces, and on 1 July new pay scales were introduced. A representative example of the daily and annual rates after two years service is as follows:[29]

RSM – 14/- (70p), or £255 p.a.
Sergeant – 7/- (35p), or £128 p.a.
Corporal – 5/- (25p), or £91 p.a.
Private – 3/6d (17½p), or £64 p.a.

On joining, a private soldier was paid 2/9d (14p) a day, or £51 p.a. until he had completed training. Compulsory deductions were made for barrack damages and some items of replacement clothing. As one soldier who enlisted in 1920 wrote: 'We lads did not get much pay. Friday was pay-day and, after we had bought our bits and pieces such as soap, toothpaste and boot polish from the N.A.A.F.I. Canteen, by Sunday we were broke.'[30]

In 1923 the Army Council stated that whilst they generally approved of the 1919 pay code they considered that the level of pay of the lower ranks of both Officers and men was unnecessarily high and suggested the daily rates for the above should be: RSM, 10/- (50p); Sergeant, 5/- (25p); Corporal 3/- (15p); and Private, 1/6d (7½p). These rates, however, were not adopted. By 1925 post-war deflation meant that the cost of living had fallen so it was decided to cut by a corresponding amount the pay of those enlisting after 25 October 1925, thus introducing a two-tier system whereby men in the same regiment doing the same job might be on different rates of pay. Rates of pay of those already serving were unchanged. The new rates were considerably less, as the following figures show:[31]

> Sergeant – 6/- (30p), or £110 p.a.
> Corporal – 4/- (20p), or £73 p.a.
> Private – 2/- (10p), or £37 p.a.

But worse was to come. In July 1930 there were just over 2,000,000 unemployed, but in the wake of a European financial crisis it rose to nearly 2,800,000 in twelve months. The government collapsed after cutting unemployment benefit and in August a National Government was formed. Income tax was immediately increased and in September the National Economy Act was passed. This meant a cut in the pay of public employees, including those in the Armed Forces. The new rates for those who had enlisted before 26 October 1925 were:[32]

> RSM – 12/8d (64p), or £234 p.a.
> Sergeant – 6/6d (37½p), or £119 p.a.
> Corporal – 4/6d (22½p), or £82 p.a.
> Private – 2/6d (12½), or £46 p.a.

In mid-September naval ratings on ships of the Atlantic Fleet at Invergordon on the Cromarty Firth mutinied. No violence was used and no disrespect shown to Officers. The Commander-in-Chief Atlantic Fleet represented the men's grievances to the Admiralty which re-instated the pre-1925 pay for the ratings. It caused a panic on the London Stock Exchange and a run on the pound. A few sailors were gaoled and more discharged.

By the outbreak of war in 1939 new rates of pay had made a slight improvement. A private solder was still not much better off than an agricultural labourer, however. The new rates, after two years' service, were:[33]

> RSM – 14/- (70p), or £255 p.a.
> Sergeant – 7/- (35p), or £128 p.a.
> Corporal – 5/- (25p), or £91 p.a.
> Private – 3/6d (17½p), or £64 p.a.

Before 1939, marriage allowance was paid to all non-commissioned ranks on the married quarters roll. This varied from 7/- to 10/- (35p to 50p) per week according to a man's rate of pay and length of service. The Defence budget of 1938 introduced a flat rate, to be paid from the start of the financial year 1939, of 17/- (85p) for all married soldiers over the age of 26. Additionally, 5/6d (27½p) per week was granted for the first child, 3/6d (17½p) for the second, and lower rates for others.[34]

Marriage allowance continued to be paid until 1970 when, with the introduction of the Military Salary, pay was increased and single Officers and men were paid the same rates of pay as their married peers. Everyone then paid income tax and N.I.S., and was charged for their accommodation and in the case of single Officers and men, their food. At the same time the weekly pay parade at which soldiers were paid in cash was phased out; by 1976 pay was automatically paid monthly into bank accounts.

Before 1946 the promotion of N.C.O.s and Warrant Officers rested entirely with regiments, a serious weakness as it did nothing to equalise the quality between regiments nor provide opportunity for the most talented to gain accelerated promotion through transfer. Prospective N.C.Os usually had to complete a cadre course for promotion to lance-corporal and thereafter sit a promotion exam, the Army Certificate of Education (A.C.E.) 2nd Class from lance-corporal to corporal and A.C.E. 1st class from corporal to sergeant. The best candidates could expect promotion to lance-corporal in about three years, corporal in about six years and sergeant in about nine years. 30–32 was not uncommon as the average age of a W.O. II in the late 1930s.

In 1936, the Adjutant General identified petty, irksome discipline as a major cause of the Regular Army's difficulty in finding recruits. A number of measures were therefore put in hand to change established practices. All soldiers at home who were over 21 and who had completed recruit training were given a permanent pass to sleep out of barracks except when military duty required their presence. All soldiers were now allowed to wear plain clothes when off duty, and were no longer expected to polish barrack room utensils and mess tins.[35]

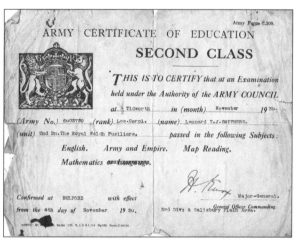

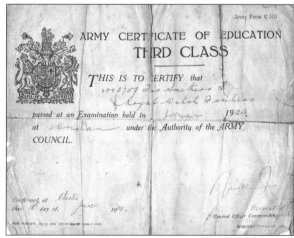

Certificates of Education awarded to R.W.F. soldiers between the World Wars.

xi. Troopships

Before and during the Second World War, troopships were the principal method of moving troops between Britain and the overseas garrisons, principally India. This remained the case until the advent of air trooping in the 1950s. The best-known troopships of the inter-war years in regular service were the British India Steam Navigation Company's *Dilwara*, *Dunera*, *Neuralia* and *Nevasa*; and the Bibby Line's *Devonshire*, *Dorsetshire*, *Lancashire* and *Somersetshire*. The peace-time Bibby Line trooper had an attractive livery of a white hull with a broad blue band and a yellow funnel: this caused them to be known as 'margarine boats' after the popular *Blue Band* margarine.

Troopships were generally around 9,000 tons gross, with a speed of fifteen knots. Each was designed to carry a complete infantry battalion and a number of drafts and individuals. On board, conditions for the Officers and families were comfortable, but for junior ranks, mess decks were of the broadside type, typical of Nelson's day. The troops slept in hammocks, and the younger soldiers had to accustom themselves to this, and to the ship's routine. The day at sea started with the call 'Rouse up, there! Lash up and stow!' Hammocks had then to be lashed up with blankets inside them, and stowed in racks above the mess tables. Each man was supplied with a sea kit bag for everyday use, and this too was kept in the hammock rack. Conditions were cramped enough in calm conditions, but in a storm, such as might be encountered in the Bay of Biscay, the ship would roll like a pig and the lower decks would be a maelstrom of stench and vomit.

Life on a troopship was tedious and, for the soldiers, not particularly pleasurable. Whereas Officers and families were provided with comfortable cabins, the men were treated as third class passengers and ate, slept, and were confined in bad weather to their own decks, two or three below the main deck. Decks were divided into messes of twenty men where meals were eaten at collapsible tables. At night hammocks were slung. The routine varied rarely and began at 06.00 hrs with reveille. This was followed by breakfast at 07.00 hrs, guard mounting at 09.00 hrs and 'boat stations' at 10.00 hrs. It was followed by the daily ship's inspection. The men's dinner was at 12.30 hrs and tea at 17.00 hrs. Cocoa and biscuits were served at 21.00 hrs and lights out was at 22.15 hrs. The hammocks were usually so close together that the battalion orderly Officer had to crawl under them as he went from one side of the ship to the other when visiting the sentries. It could be an unpleasant task in bad weather.

Whilst the ship's captain exercised overall authority, the day-to-day discipline and administration of the soldiers was in the hands of O.C. Troops, often an ageing Lieutenant Colonel, assisted by a small staff. The voyage to India in the 1930s took up to three weeks and the daily routine on board rarely varied. The most important part of the day was Boat Stations when everyone, including families, fell alongside their allotted life boats and were inspected by the Captain or First Officer to ensure that lifeboats were correctly adjusted and that the drill for 'abandon ship'; was understood. This was followed by Ship's Inspection which closely resembled a C.O.'s weekly inspection in barracks. Much of the time soldiers were left to their own devices to while away the long hours spent on board. Housey-Housey, better known as Bingo, and furtive Crown-and-Anchor schools flourished. Physical exercise was limited to P.T. parades, boxing and jogging round the boat deck. Food was generally agreed to be good. There were occasional evening concerts performed by the embarked troops, and Church parades every Sunday.[36]

xii. The Reserves

The Territorial Army is dealt with in a separate section. For the Regular Army, the reserves comprised three major bodies: the Army Reserve; the Special Reserve, or pre-war Militia, until 1924; and the Supplementary Reserve.

By 1939, the Army Reserve numbered, on paper, 131,000 men, all of whom had completed their period of Colour service and remained liable for call-up by Royal Proclamation if needed. However, only 3,700 of these could be considered as fully trained at any one time, having left the Colours within a year. The remainder might have been on the reserve for up to thirteen years and would require considerable re-training on modern weapons and tactics.[37] Their recall, training, equipment and onward movement to regular units were the responsibility of regimental depots and home-based Regular battalions under the Cardwell system, introduced between 1868 and 1874.

The Militia was transformed into the Special Reserve as part of the Haldane reforms of the post-1906 Liberal government. In 1908, all militia infantry battalions were re-designated as 'reserve' and a number were amalgamated or disbanded. Altogether, 101 infantry battalions, thirty-three artillery regiments and two engineer regiments of special reservists were formed.[38]

Special Reserve units remained in the United Kingdom throughout the Great War, but their Officers and men did not, since the object of the special reserve was to supply drafts of replacements for the overseas units of the regiment. The original militiamen soon disappeared, and the battalions became purely training units.

The Special Reserve reverted to its militia designation in 1921, and was then converted into the Supplementary Reserve in 1924, though the units were effectively placed in suspended animation until disbanded in 1953 (see *Regimental Records Volume VI*).

The Supplementary Reserve consisted of 42,600 men by 1939. The majority of these were tradesmen, such as mechanics, drivers and engineers, whose civilian occupations, in theory at least, fitted them for service in certain technical corps of the Army immediately upon mobilisation; however only about half had ever done any military training.

xiii. Conscription and Mobilisation, 1939

Mobilisation, according to the Army's own doctrine between the wars, was the completion of the force to its war establishment, involving the call-up of the Army Reserve and Militia, including the Supplementary Reserve.[39]

On 27 April 1939, after a lapse of twenty years, Parliament re-introduced a limited form of compulsory military service with the Military Training Act to assist in mobilizing a sufficient force for a continental war. This required some 200,000 men between the ages of 20 and 21 to register for service in June. These men were known as Militia, and were allowed to state their preferred choice of service and were drafted accordingly. The first batch of 34,000 men arrived for training in the Army in July.

Conscription was extended on 6 September 1939, shortly after the declaration of war on the 3rd, by the National Service (Armed Forces) Act, which made all physically fit males between the ages of 18 and 41 liable for call-up. In 1941, a further Act extended the upper age limit to 51, and made women also liable for service – although in practice, very few men over 41 and none over 45 were ever called up. These measures brought 727,000 registrations by the end of 1939 and 4,100,000 by the end of 1940, bringing the strength of the Armed Forces from 381,000 in 1938 (of which 224,000 were in the Army) to 2.25 million by the end of 1940. By early 1945, one-third of the adult male work-force was in uniform and the Army – not counting Indian and other Dominion and Empire troops – had reached a strength of 3,000,000 in 47 divisions.[40]

Notes

1   *R.U.S.I. Journal*, No LXVII (1922), p. 380.
2   Information compiled by Lt Col P.A. Crocker from the *Digests of Service.*
3   G. Blight, *History of the Royal Berkshire Regiment 1920–1947* (London, 1953), Appendix III.
4   *Infantry Training, Volume I, Training*, 1922 (Provisional).
5   *Field Service Manual*, 1930, Infantry Battalion.
6   *Infantry Training*, 1937, Training and War; W.J.P. Aggett, *The Bloody Eleventh: History of the Devonshire Regiment, Vol III*, 1914–1969 (Exeter, 1995), Appendix D.
7   *Field Service Pocket Book*, Pamphlet No 1, 1939, Glossary of Military Terms and Organization in the Field.
8   *R.U.S.I. Journal,* No LXXII (1927) p. 209.
9   Army Order No 197 of 1938, 17 September.
10   H.C.B. Rogers, *Weapons of the British Soldier*, (London, 1968).
11   George Forty, *British Army Handbook 1939–1945* (Sutton, 1998), p. 212.
12   *R.U.S.I. Journal*, No LXXXII (1937), p. 656; Mike Chappell, *British Infantry Equipments 1908–1980*, Men-at-Arms Series 108, pp. 14–21.
13   *R.U.S.I. Journal*, No LXXV (1930), p. 777.
14   Major James Hawkes, *Private to Major* (London, 1938) p. 154.
15   *Signal Training All Arms*, 1938.
16   J.M. Brereton, *The British Soldier: A Social History, 1661 to the Present Day*, (London, 1986) p. 141.
17   Army Quarterly, Vol 14 (1927), p. 131.
18   *R.U.S.I. Journal,* No LXXV (1930), p. 893.
19   Brereton, p. 157.
20   Frank Richards, *Old Soldier Sahib*, pp. 192–193.
21   *R.U.S.I. Journal,* No LXXXI (1936), p. 893.
22   David French, *Military Identities. The Regimental System, the British Army, and the British People c 1870–2000* (Oxford, 2005), pp. 154–157.
23   *R.U.S.I. Journal* No LXIV (1919), p. 757.
24   *R.U.S.I. Journal* No LXIX (1924), p. 380.
25   *R.U.S.I. Journal* No LXXXIII (1938), p. 878.
26   Anthony Clayton, *The British Officer* (London, 2006), p. 157.
27   Interview with Colonel J.E.T. Willes by Lt Col L.J. Egan (R.W.F. Museum).
28   Higham, p. 91.
29   *R.U.S.I. Journal* No LXIV (1919), p. 757.
30   A.C. Kennett, *Life is What You Make It* (Durham, 1992) p. 26.
31   Army Order 366 of 1925.
32   Royal Warrant for the Pay of the Army, 1931, Amendment No 22.
33   Royal Warrant for the Pay of the Army, 1940.
34   Brereton, p. 159.
35   A.G.3 to all G.O.C.s-in-C at home, 1 Sep 1937; Bond, p. 330.
36   *R.U.S.I. Journal* No LXXX (1935), p. 875; No LXXXI (1936) p. 200.
37   David French, *Raising Churchill's Army. The British Army and the War against Germany 1919–1945* (O.U.P., 2001, pp. 63–64.
38   *London Gazette*, 10 April 1908.
39   *Field Service Regulations, Volume I, Organization and Administration*, 1930 (War Office, 13 December 1939 edition), pp. 6–7.
40   George Forty, *British Army Handbook 1939–1945*, pp. 5–6.

Section II

The Regiment in the Inter-War Years, 1918–1939

Chapter 3

Postscript to the Great War

i. Background

Volumes III and IV of *Regimental Records* end on the day of the Armistice, 11 November 1918, with a short postscript dealing with the generalities of demobilisation. However the War did not end then – it was not over until the signing of the Treaty of Versailles in 1919; moreover the Army was still committed to operations during this period: on the North-West Frontier and Afghanistan, in Russia and the Trans-Caucasus, in Turkey, in Egypt, in Iraq, in Ireland and in Germany. This chapter completes the story of the

R.W.F. soldiers at Kinmel Camp, 1919.

Regiment in the Great War and in particular covers the activities of all those battalions which were afterwards disbanded and do not therefore receive coverage elsewhere in this Volume, from the armistice until they returned to the U.K., less those which served in Egypt; the significant moves and the post-armistice activities of battalions that served in Egypt where insurrection broke out in March 1919; the moves and disbandment of Home Service battalions; and the Volunteer battalions.

When the war began the Regiment had seven battalions: two Regular, the 1st and 2nd; the 3rd (Special Reserve); and four battalions of the Territorial Force (T.F.), the 4th (Denbighshire), 5th (Flintshire), 6th (Caernarvonshire & Anglesey) and 7th (Merioneth & Montgomeryshire). During the war another thirty-three battalions were formed which bore the Regiment's title,[1] excluding any amalgamations and re-designations, and the five battalions of

The 3rd (Special Reserve) Battalion, 1919.

the Volunteer Force (see below). This last point is important because the figure forty is at variance with the *Army List*, which gave forty-two, and *Regimental Records*, which has forty-four.[2] Only Brigadier James gives forty battalions.[3] In terms of the numbers of men who served in the Regiment, either exclusively, or as a result of transfer in from elsewhere, or before transferring out, an exact figure is very difficult to come by. However, the best available research, by Mr Richard Ward, gives a maximum figure of 70,019 men who served in the Regiment during the War years; of these, research by John Krijnen records that 10,967, or 15.5%, were killed, or died of wounds, sickness and other causes while serving. This broad figure masks huge variations in the casualty levels in different battalions, depending on where they served.

Immediately following the armistice the subject of demobilisation became a highly emotive subject until Churchill was appointed Secretary of State for War and applied common sense to the problem. When the Armistice took effect, Britain had 3,500,000 men under arms,[4] most of whom were serving overseas. By early January 1919, Officers and men overseas were demanding a prompt return to civilian life: from France, Sir Douglas Haig reported that the Army was on the verge of disintegration.[5]

The scheme for demobilisation devised during the war was announced by the War Office on 7 January 1919. It gave priority to those with four months service and immediate offers of work, which meant that for 3,000,000 men, some of whom had served for four years, there was no likelihood of an early return home. On 10 January Winston Churchill took over as Secretary of State for War in the coalition government of Lloyd George, who had won the General Election of December 1918. Churchill realised that the problem of demobilisation was exacerbated by the urgent need to provide several Armies of Occupation in addition to the troops needed in Palestine, Mesopotamia and India, as well as in the United Kingdom. Haig estimated that over 1,000,000 men would be required. A week later Churchill and his advisers agreed that those who had enlisted in 1914 and 1915 – about 2,200,000 men – would be demobilized as soon as transport could be arranged, but that those who had enlisted after 1 January 1916 would be retained as part of the Army of Occupation. Those retained would receive extra leave and a substantial increase in pay.[6]

After initial disagreement with Lloyd George, Churchill obtained his support and the proposals received Cabinet agreement on 28 January. Straightaway he briefed the press. On the previous day Churchill had secretly informed Lord Northcliffe who agreed that the papers of which he was the proprietor – *The Times, Evening News, Daily Mail* and *Daily Mirror* – would support them. The final details included the immediate demobilisation of all who had enlisted before 1916; no one over the age of forty to be retained; and conscription to remain for those required for the Armies of Occupation. By the end of January nearly 1,000,000 men had been sent home.[7]

When he presented the Army Estimates to the House of Commons on 3 March Churchill declared:

> There are two maxims which should always be acted upon in the hour of victory … The first is: "Do not be carried away by success into demanding or taking more than is right or prudent." The second is: "Do not disband your army until you have got your terms." The finest combination in the world is power and mercy. The worst combination in the world is weakness and strife… We plead earnestly for the maintenance in these times of trouble of a strong armed Power, to be used with sober and far-sighted moderation in the common

good. Believe me, it is far the cheapest, far the safest, and far the surest way to preserve for long and splendid years the position which our country has attained.[8]

ii. R.W.F. Battalion Moves

As this scheme took effect, all battalions overseas experienced a steady weekly reduction in strength as demobilisation gained momentum. No sooner had victory been achieved than training began, largely as it had been before the war, with the emphasis on drill, route marches and sport. There were also lectures on subjects such as demobilization, venereal disease and education; and also vocational classes. Fatigue parties for a variety of jobs were always required, as were men for camp duties. A popular innovation – at least with the 2nd Battalion – was the introduction of 'chip fryers,' at least it was until the fat caught fire and the canteen hut burnt to the ground.[9] The moves of the 1st and 2nd Battalions are dealt with in the appropriate chapters and they are not considered further here.

1/4th (Denbighshire) Battalion (T.F.) served in France and became a pioneer battalion on 1 September 1915, in the 47th (London) Division. On 11 November 1918 it was at Bizencourt, north-east of Tournai. It reached Raimbert on the 28th and remained in the area until moving to Le Havre on 11 May 1919. The cadre embarked for Britain on the 15th and proceeded to Wrexham. It was disbanded on 11 June.[10]

The 1/5th (Flintshire) Battalion (T.F.) served in 158 (Royal Welsh) Brigade of the 53rd (Welsh) Division at Gallipoli and in the Middle East. On 2/3 August 1918 it was amalgamated with the 1/6th Battalion to become the 5th/6th Battalion (see below).[11] On 2 August 1919 the cadre of the battalion arrived in Wrexham and was disembodied on the following day.

The 1/6th (Carnarvonshire and Anglesey) Battalion (T.F.) served in 158 (Royal Welsh) Brigade of the 53rd (Welsh) Division at Gallipoli and in the Middle East. On 2/3 August 1918 it was amalgamated with the 1/5th Battalion to become the 5th/6th Battalion (See below):[12] 'On Monday [4 August 1919] a cadre of the 1/6th Royal Welsh Fusiliers, who [sic] arrived in Dover on Sunday, reached Carnarvon … and were entertained by the Town Council to luncheon at the Sportsman Hotel, the Mayor (D.R. Parry) presiding.'[13] Amongst those present were Lieutenant Colonel J.G. Tuxford and Captain J. Cottrill. On 27 September a reception was held in Caernarfon for the 4,000 who had served overseas and had accepted the invitation. The salute was taken by David Lloyd George outside the Castle.[14]

During a speech in London in September 1914 Lloyd George had said:

> I should like to see a Welsh Army in the Field. I should like to see the race that faced the Normans for hundreds of years in a struggle for freedom, the race that helped to win Crécy, the race that fought for a generation under Glyndwr against the greatest captain in Europe – I should like to see that race give a good taste of their quality in this struggle in Europe; and they are going to do it.[15]

On 21 September a provisional committee was formed with the idea of raising a Welsh Army Corps (W.A.C.). The Welsh National Executive Committee (W.N.E.C.) was set up in Cardiff and at a representative meeting there on 29 September the W.A.C. was launched amid scenes of great enthusiasm. Formal authority for the raising of the W.A.C. by the W.N.E.C. was given by the Army Council on 10 October which gave sanction '… to raise the necessary troops in Wales and Monmouthshire and from Welshmen resident in London, Liverpool and Manchester to form a Welsh Army Corps of two divisions…'[16] Ten Royal Welch battalions – the 13th to 22nd, of which the 13th to 17th and the 19th served overseas – as well as battalions of the South Wales Borderers and the Welch Regiment were raised by the W.N.E.C. and were formed into the 38th (Welsh) Division. The 38th (Welsh) Division, with 113, 114 and 115 Brigades did not come into being until 29 April 1915, its original title having been the 43rd Division, with the 128, 129 and 130 Brigades. At about the same time the idea of forming a Welsh Army Corps was abandoned.[17]

8th (Service) Battalion was a Kitchener (K1) battalion formed at Wrexham in August 1914.[18] It served in 40 Brigade of the 13th Division at Gallipoli and in the Middle East. On the day the armistice with Turkey took effect, 31 October 1918, the battalion was in the area of Kirkuk and Kifri, north of Baghdad. On 26 November the battalion moved into a tented camp near Abu Hajah. Much time was spent repairing roads but on 5 December a battalion attack was carried out for the benefit of the Corps Commander who expressed great satisfaction with the battalion's performance. On 15 January it moved into Tabar Camp seven miles below Al-Amara. A gale and heavy rains forced the battalion to build a bund around the camp to avoid flooding. The strength of the battalion on 31 January was seventeen Officers and 614 Other Ranks. In March 1919 the division reduced to cadre, but on 7 April, 8 R.W.F. arrived in India.[19] Having been reduced to cadre it arrived in Wrexham on 16 August and was disbanded five days later;[20] a number of its men subsequently served with 6th Loyals on the North-West Frontier campaign.

9th (Service) Battalion was a Kitchener (K2) battalion formed at Wrexham in September 1914.[21] It served in 58 Brigade of the 19th Division in Britain, and in France from July 1915. On 11 November 1918 it was at Eth, west of Bavai in France. It moved into billets at Berteaucourt on 12 December. On most days training was undertaken in the morning and sport in the afternoon. On 22 January 1919 at a ceremonial parade a silk Union Flag was presented to the battalion by the Divisional Commander. On 23 February it moved to Villers L'Hopital where, by 31 March, it had been practically reduced to cadre.[22] On 25 May it arrived at Sandling, Kent and was disbanded on 2 June.

The Presentation of the Union Flag to 9 R.W.F. at at Berteaucourt-les-Dames, 12 January 1919. (R.W.F. Mus 2420)

11 R.W.F. in Constantinople, 1919.

10th (Service) Battalion was a Kitchener (K3) battalion formed at Wrexham in September 1914.[23] It served in France with 76 Brigade of the 25th Division, which was transferred to the 3rd Division in October 1915. The battalion was one of those selected for disbandment in early 1918 because of manpower shortages and on 15 February 1918 the battalion was amalgamated with 19 R.W.F. to form 8th Entrenching Battalion, a non-R.W.F. unit.[24]

11th (Service) Battalion was a Kitchener (K3) battalion formed at Wrexham in September 1914.[25] It served in 67 Brigade of the 22nd Division in Britain, France and Salonika. On 30 September 1918, when the armistice with Bulgaria took effect, the battalion was north-west of Lake Doiran in Macedonia. During November it moved by rail and on foot to Stavros where the usual training, recreation, sport and duties filled the days until, on 13 January it moved to Flynek Camp. On 27 February a detachment of two Officers and 138 Other Ranks entrained at Kilindir for Constantinople, leaving behind seven Officers and 143 Other Ranks. On 19 March the battalion, or what was left of it, arrived at Constantinople where it proceeded to Tash Kishla Barracks and took over regimental stores and equipment from the 2nd East Surreys. The strength of the battalion was sixteen Officers, plus two attached, and 317 Other Ranks. The time now was filled with company parades and guards. The battalion was still at Constantinople when the last entry was made in the war diary on 30 April.[26] It disbanded on 14 October 1919.[27]

13th (Service) Battalion, initially known as the 'North Wales Pals', began to form at Rhyl, North Wales on 2 October 1914. It was raised by the Denbigh and Flint Territorial Force Association and was transferred to the W.N.E.C. on 10 October.[28] It incorporated the University and Public Schools battalion in the counties of North Wales.[29] It served in 113 (Royal Welsh) Brigade of the 38th (Welsh) Division in France and Flanders. On 11 November 1918 it was Wattignies, north-east of Avesnes. The battalion moved to Sarbaras where, during a route march on 3 December, it formed up on the side of the road whilst King George V proceeded down the line. On the 29th it moved into billets at Franvillers, near Amiens. On 16 January 1919 all battalions in the division, less 2 R.W.F., were presented with a silk Union Flag by the Divisional Commander, Major General T.A. Cubitt, at Allonville. The Prince of Wales visited the battalion and chatted to the men on 6 February. The cadre reached Blangy-Tronville on 17 March[30] and Newmarket on 23 May. It was disbanded on 4 June.[31]

14th (Service) Battalion, initially known as the 'Caernarvon and Anglesey' Battalion, began to form at Llandudno on 2 November 1914 under the auspices of David Davies M.P., who raised and commanded it until relieved in France in 1916. He was a close friend of Lloyd George and was later created the 1st Lord Davies of Llandinam. It served in France and Flanders, in 113 (Royal Welsh) Brigade of the 38th (Welsh) Division. On 11 November 1918 it was at Dimont, north-east of Avesnes. By 23 November the battalion was at Sarbaras, where, during a route march on 3 December, it formed up on the side of the road whilst King George V proceeded down the line. On the 29th it moved into a hutted camp at Warloy, seven miles north-west of Albert. On 16 January 1919 all battalions in the division, less 2 R.W.F., were presented with a silk Union Flag by the Divisional Commander, Major General T.A. Cubitt, at Allonville. The Prince of Wales visited the battalion and chatted to the men on 6 February. Two days later the battalion was reorganised into three groups: for the Army of Occupation; for demobilisation; and for cadre. On the 28th the strength was down to twelve Officers and seventy Other Ranks. On 17 March the cadre joined the other cadres of the division at Blangy-Tronville.[32] The cadre arrived at Newmarket on 23 May and was disbanded on 4 June.[33]

15th (1st London Welsh) (Service) Battalion was formed by Welshmen in London on 16 September with headquarters at Gray's Inn, Holborn. It served in France and Flanders in 113 (Royal Welsh) Brigade of the 38th (Welsh) Division but was disbanded during the reorganisation of the Army in France on 6 February 1918.[34]

16th (Service) Battalion was formed at Llandudno by the W.N.E.C. in November 1914 from men surplus to the needs of the 13th Battalion. It joined what became in April 1915 113 (Royal Welsh) Brigade of the 38th (Welsh) Division. It served in France and Flanders. On 11 November 1918 the battalion was at Dimechaux, north-east of Avesnes. From the 23rd to the 30th it marched to Sarbaras where it occupied billets. During a route march on 3 December, it formed up on the side of the road whilst King George V proceeded down the line. On the 29th it moved into a hutted camp at Warloy, seven miles north-west of Albert. On 16 January 1919 all battalions in the division, less 2 R.W.F., were presented with a silk Union Flag by the Divisional Commander, Major General T.A. Cubitt, at Allonville. The Prince of Wales visited the battalion and chatted to the men on 6 February. The cadre reached Blangy-Tronville on 17 March[35] and Newmarket on 23 May. It was disbanded on 6 June 1919.[36]

17th (Service) Battalion was raised by the W.N.E.C. and started to form at Llandudno and Blaenau Ffestiniog in January 1915.[37] It subsidiary title was '2nd North Wales'. It served in France and Flanders in 115 Brigade of the 38th (Welsh) Division. On 11 November 1918 it was at Aulnoye Station. From 29 to 31 December the battalion moved to Blangy Tronville. On 16 January 1919 all battalions in the division, less 2 R.W.F., were presented with a silk Union Flag by the Divisional Commander, Major General T.A. Cubitt, at Allonville. The Prince of Wales visited the battalion and chatted to the men on 6 February.[38] The battalion was reduced to cadre in France and reached Newmarket on 25 May and was disbanded on 7 June 1919.[39]

19th (Service) Battalion was raised by the W.N.E.C. in February 1915 as a bantam battalion, i.e., men under the minimum height limit for the infantry of 5 feet 3 inches.[40] It joined 119 Brigade in the 40th Division. Almost all the men in the brigade, in four Welsh battalions, were bantams. The other brigades were mixed in height and the division was unusual in having six English, four Welsh and two Scottish battalions. By December 1915 the division was established in the Aldershot area. On 2 June 1916 the battalion disembarked at Le Havre. On 6 February 1918 it sent eight Officers and 150 Other Ranks to 2 R.W.F. and the remainder of the battalion left the division and joined VI Corps Reinforcement Camp. On 15 February 1918, having been among those battalions selected for disbandment to make good manpower shortages, 19 R.W.F. was taken, with 10 R.W.F., into the 8th Entrenching Battalion, a non-R.W.F. unit.[41]

24th (Denbighshire Yeomanry) Battalion (T.F.) was formed in Egypt on 1 March 1917 when the 1/1st Denbighshire Yeomanry (1/1st D.Y.) changed its role and became an infantry battalion in the Royal Welch Fusiliers.[42] It served in 231 Brigade of the 74th (Yeomanry) Division in the Middle East and in 94 Brigade of the 31st Division in France. On 11 November 1918 it was moving from Avelghem to Renaix. By the end of the month the battalion had reached Tatinghem, near St Omer. On 29 January 1919 it moved to the Staging Camp at Hondeghem where it relieved 26 R.W.F. of its duties. On 19 February the battalion paraded – strength twelve Officers and 115 Other Ranks – for the presentation of a silk Union Flag by Brigadier General L.P.J. Butler. On 4 March it moved to St Omer.[43] Having been reduced to cadre in France, it arrived in Catterick and was probably disbanded on the 28th.

25th (Montgomeryshire and Welsh Horse Yeomanry) Battalion (T.F.) was formed in March 1917 by the amalgamation of the 1/1st Montgomeryshire Yeomanry (1/1st M.Y.) and the 1/1st Welsh Horse Yeomanry (1/1st W.H.Y.) which had changed their role to become infantry. 25 R.W.F. joined 231 Brigade of the 74th (Yeomanry) Division and fought in Palestine and, in May 1918, moved to France. On 11 November it was at Perquise. Between the 15th and 20th the battalion moved to La Tombe, Tournai. On 7 December, The King visited the 74th Division and ten days later the battalion arrived at Grammont. On 16 June 1919 the cadre – Major W.S. Thomas and fifteen Other Ranks – left Grammont and embarked at Boulogne on the 21st.[44] On arrival in England it proceeded to Welshpool where, on the 29th, it was disbanded.

1st Garrison Battalion was formed on 18 July 1915 at Wrexham. It arrived in Gibraltar on 23 August. It left Gibraltar for Crowborough on 4 November 1919 and was disbanded on 14 February 1920.[45]

4th Garrison Battalion was formed at Bebbington on 19 May 1916. In June 1916 it went to France and became the 4th Garrison Guard Battalion. It was re-designated the 26th (Service) Battalion on 16 July 1918. See below.

iii. Battalions in Egypt after November 1918

The following battalions served in Egypt after the end of the war:

    5th/6th Battalion until July 1919
    1/7th Battalion until January 1920
    26th Battalion from May to December 1919
    2nd Garrison Battalion until September 1919
    6th Garrison Battalion until June 1919

The armistice with Turkey came into force on 31 October 1918. G.H.Q. Egyptian Expeditionary Force under General Allenby was at Bir Salem, some 250 miles (400 kilometres) from Cairo. By 15 November the 53rd (Welsh) Division was complete at Alexandria. Demobilisation began in December and by 7 March the 159th Brigade had been reduced to cadre strength. By 7 June the division was down to 75 Officers and 1,429 Other Ranks. Eight days later divisional cadres moved to Port Said en route for England, leaving behind in Egypt the 5th/6th and 1/7th Battalions, and the 4th/5th Welsh.[46]

The principles formulated by President Wilson of the United States of America in the closing stages of the war had considerable effect on the Egyptian educated classes. In November 1918 an Anglo-French declaration announced that the Allies were considering the enfranchisement of the peoples who had been oppressed under Turkish rule. Egyptians considered their right to manage their own affairs to be even stronger than that of Syria, Mesopotamia or of Arabia.

At the end of 1918 a Nationalist Committee was formed under the chairmanship of Saad Zaghlul.[*] His proposal to go straight to England with a programme for complete autonomy was rejected. By this time many Moderates had rallied to the Nationalists. On 20 February the 75th Division was selected for the Army of Occupation in Egypt. On 8 March Zaghlul and three of his most important followers were arrested and deported to Malta. The immediate effects revealed the gravity of the internal situation in Egypt which had probably been under-estimated. Anti-British demonstrations in Cairo required military intervention. There were disturbances at Tanta and in the Delta provinces where British soldiers and civilians were attacked. Railway lines were torn up, telegraph wires cut and by the middle of March, Cairo was isolated. H.Q. 75th Division and one brigade was at Alexandria and the other brigades at Heliopolis and Ismailia. At Dairut station a British inspector of prisons, two Officers and five Other Ranks in the train 'were butchered amid scenes of indescribable savagery; responsible Egyptian officials in the vicinity did nothing to restrain the fury of the mob… The Police, without their European Officers, were as useless and supine in the later outbreak as in the earlier; their attitude was that it was not their business to protect foreigners.'[47] Mobile columns were rapidly despatched to disturbed areas and before the end of March the situation was under control.

On 25 April H.Q. Egypt handed over command in Egypt to XX Corps which comprised the 10th (Irish), 54th (East Anglian) and 75th Divisions. The latter was given responsibility for the Eastern Delta up to the Suez Canal, renamed 75th Division Area on 1 June with its H.Q. at Ismailia. The area included Zigazig, Belbeis and Benha Districts, as well as Port Said, Ismailia and Suez areas. Many additional units, including elements of 1/7th R.W.F., were attached to the division for the necessary garrisons and protective work in this large district.[48]

Lord Allenby, the Commander-in-Chief, who had left the country for the Paris Peace Conference at the height of the disorder, was ordered to return. He adopted a policy of conciliation and the removal of the embargo on travel entailed the liberation of Zaghlul and his associates. The British Government decided to send a mission to Egypt under Lord Milner to enquire into the causes of the recent disorders and to report on the existing situation and the form of the constitution which, under the protectorate will be best calculated to promote its peace and prosperity. The mission reached Cairo on 7 December 1919. Special measures were taken for its security but students picketed the hotel, there were repeated assaults on British soldiers, and assassination attempts were made on Egyptian ministers. A visit to Tanta provoked riots in the city.

---

[*]   Saad Zaghlul (1859–1927), Egyptian revolutionary and politician. He served as Prime Minister of Egypt from January to November 1924.

5th/6th R.W.F. marching past General Allenby in Alexandria, 1919. (Mrs Dilys R. Glover, from the collection of Lt Col H. Maldwyn Davies). Allenby later wrote to the C.O. and told him that the battalion was the smartest in the entire parade.

5th/6th Battalion was formed on 2 August 1918 in Palestine by the amalgamation of the 1/5th and the 1/6th Battalions. On 2 November 1918 the battalion arrived at Hadra Camp, Alexandria, Egypt. On St David's Day a 'Special Welsh Eisteddfod' for Welsh troops was held at the American Mission, Alexandria. On 12 March the battalion was stood-to in response to the

A group of the 5th/6th Battalion in Egypt. (R.W.F. Mus)

alarm given under the Alexandria Defence Scheme, later reduced to one company on standby. On the 17th there was a small disturbance with some natives. Three days later twenty-seven Officers and 550 Other Ranks moved to Damanhour and came under command of Brigadier General F.H. Borthwick, G.O.C. Damanhour Force and former Commanding Officer of 5 R.W.F., leaving three Officers and ninety-one Other Ranks to guard Hadra Camp. On the 24th a platoon was despatched by tug to guard a bridge over the Nile at Dessuk until further notice. On the 29th A and C Companies lined the streets of Damanhour for Mudir's visit and D Company found a guard of honour. The next day C Company searched the village of Kafr El Dawr. On 3 April A and B Companies under Captain Kingsbury were required to man a picquet line from 06.00 hrs until 18.00 hrs whilst the cavalry searched villages north of a line Damanhour – Teh El Barud. Each man wore fighting order and carried 80 rounds of ammunition. On the 5th the battalion relieved the 1st Battalion Cape Corps on special duty guarding the railway line from Kafr El Dawr to Tewfikieh including stations and bridges. No 2 Sub-Section under Captain Y.R.D. Wigan (H.Q. at Abu Hommos) with B Company (two Officers and sixty-eight Other Ranks; H.Q. at Kafr El Dawar) and D Company (four Officers and 108 Other Ranks; H.Q. at Abu Hommos). No 1 Sub-Section under Captain J.B. Marston (H.Q. at Teh El Barud) with C Company (four Officers and seventy-four Other Ranks; H.Q. at Damanhour) and A Company (three Officers and ninety-two Other Ranks; H.Q. at Teh El Barod). On 16 April mounted troops were replaced with infantry for the protection of the railway line, with No 1 Sub-Section being the responsibility of the 1st Cape Corps and No 2 Sub-Section 5th/6th R.W.F. (H.Q. at Damanhour), with detachments located at Sahalli, Abu Hommos, Dessunes, Maawel El Quizaz and Kafr El Dawar. A redistribution of troops took place on 15 May: C and D Companies took over No 2 Sub-Section, with A and B Companies moved into camp at Damanhour. Two-man patrols were required to operate on foot along the line between stations from dusk until dawn and examine all culverts, pipes, track, and telegraph and telephone lines. At this point the war diary ends.[49] The cadres of both battalions, the 1/5th and the 1/6th, reached Wrexham and Caernarfon respectively at the beginning of August.

1/7th (Merioneth & Montgomery) Battalion (T.F.) was attending annual camp at Aberystwyth on 4 August 1914. It served in 158 (Royal Welsh) Brigade of the 53rd (Welsh) Division at Gallipoli and in the Middle East. On 31 October 1918, the day the armistice with Turkey came into force, it reached Alexandria, Egypt. The battalion settled into the routine experienced elsewhere at the end of the war and which comprised drill, physical training, sport, route marches, assault course and lectures, interspersed with duties and fatigues. On 2 January 1919 it

7 R.W.F. Football team, British Army champions in Egypt and Palestine, 1919.

moved to Mex and began working at the Ordnance Depot. Its stay was to be short-lived for on 10 February it arrived at Sidi Bishr where it was employed on road fatigues and picquets. On 15 March, as trouble began, the battalion became part of the Army of Occupation. Guards of up to platoon strength were sent to guard trains at Tanta, Nouzha and Hadra, and one of company size went to the Police Barracks at Bodoni. Other places that had to be guarded included Gabbary Station and oil tanks, 644 Company R.A.S.C., and Mex Wood Quay.

On 17 May orders were received for the battalion, less two companies, to go to Cyprus on the 19th at a strength of fifteen Officers and 450 Other Ranks. The move was postponed until the battalion was up to strength. This was achieved and the battalion embarked on the HT *Abbassieh* at Alexandria on 18 June. Departure was, however, delayed for a further three days because of boiler problems. It eventually arrived at Famagusta on the afternoon of the 23rd, where it relieved the 1st Royal Scots and assumed responsibility for all garrison duties, prisoner of war guards and Garrison Police. In the meantime, the two companies that remained in Egypt joined 234 Brigade, 75th Division, on 15 June,[50] and were soon responsible for guarding the R.E. Dump at Victoria and the Main Supply Dump at Sidi Bishr.

With signs that the internal trouble was dying down the two companies in Egypt moved to Sidi Bishr together with attached personnel of 5th/6th R.W.F. and 4th/5th Welsh on 9 July. On the 14th a detachment of seventy-four Other Ranks under the Detachment Commander attended the Naval and Military Celebrations Parade which was followed by a public holiday with sports, fetes, etc in the town.

For the rest of the year guards and picquets, P.T. and sport, including cricket with the Other Ranks defeating the Officers, who beat the sergeants. From July, Officers were regular members of Field General and Summary General Courts Martial, Summary Military Courts, Boards of Officers and Courts of Inquiry, presumably in connection with the insurrection.

Meanwhile in Cyprus, with the 1/7th Battalion still based in Famagusta, Lieutenant Colonel E.W. Brighton of the Bedfordshire Regiment assumed command. Sport seems to have been the main pastime when guards and duties permitted. Eventually, the battalion was relieved on 29 December by a company of 2nd Sherwood Foresters. On the return voyage the *Abbassieh* anchored off Beirut which was in quarantine. As a result the battalion was not allowed initially to disembark at Port Said. However, it did so on 2 January 1920 and immediately entrained for Kantara and marched to a Segregation Camp where it remained until the 5th.

Fusilier John Jones and friends, 26th Battalion, Egypt 1919.

On 19 January the Port Said detachment of the battalion was broken up. During the first fortnight in February the battalion was reduced to cadre at the Combined Base Depot at Kantara. On the 16th the cadre, which comprised Captain N.M. Corke MC (O.C.), Lieutenant F.D. Buchan (Adjutant), Lieutenant H. Delany (Q.M.), Lieutenant P.E. Lloyd, RQMS Jenkins and forty-five Other Ranks, moved to Port Said, and from there to Alexandria on the 21st where it embarked on HT *Czar* for home. The cadre arrived at Newtown on 2 March 1920 and was demobilised on the 12th.

26th (Service) Battalion came into existence in France on 16 July 1918 when the designation of the 4th Garrison Guard Battalion (see above) was changed. 26 R.W.F. was in 176 Brigade/59th (2nd North Midland) Division, the division of its predecessor. The battalion fought with the division in France until the end of the war and on 11 November 1918 it was at Delpré. On 16 November the battalion was billeted in Faches – Thumesnil, near Lille where it remained until 6 December doing education, recreation and a little military training. From 7 December it was accommodated in Hutment Camp at Barlin until, on 1 January, it moved into Borre Becque, one-and-a-half miles (2 kilometres) from Hondeghem, prior to taking over the Demobilisation Staging Camp. Work revolved around improving and running the camp which ceased to function as such

A group of the 2nd Garrison Battalion in Egypt.
(R.W.F. Mus)

on the 18th. On the 17th a silk Union Flag was presented to the battalion by the G.O.C. On the 28th the battalion had a ration strength of sixteen Officers and 421 Other Ranks and on the following day the camp was handed over to 24 R.W.F. On the 31st, 26 R.W.F. took over a demobilisation camp at Dunkirk where it remained until 20 March when it moved to Malo-les-Bains. On the 23rd the three battalions of 176 Brigade left Calais for Marseilles, en route for Egypt which was reached on the 28th.[51] In July H.Q. 176 Brigade was reduced to cadre and returned to England. 26 R.W.F. remained in Egypt until being reduced to cadre in December. The battalion arrived in England on 6 January 1920 and was disbanded shortly afterwards.[52]

2nd Garrison Battalion was formed at Garswood Park, near Wigan on 18 July 1915. It sailed from Devonport on 6 March 1916 for Egypt where it remained until disbanded on 17 September 1919.[53]

6th Garrison Battalion was formed at Aintree on 1 October 1916. In January 1917 it went to Egypt where it remained until reduced to cadre on 24 June 1919.[54]

iv. Home Service Battalions

3rd (Special Reserve) Battalion, which had existed since 1908, was at annual camp at Pembroke Dock on 4 August 1914 from whence it returned to Wrexham. Its role was to train recruits for battalions serving overseas, and also to act as a holding battalion on whose strength the long term sick and wounded could be held until they were considered fit enough to return to operational duties. On 12 May 1915 it moved to Litherland, Liverpool where it remained until moving to Limerick, Ireland which was reached on 6 November 1917. It continued in its role but in addition was meant to act as a deterrent to violence by dissident Irishmen following the attack on the Central Post Office in Dublin at Easter 1916. On 11 November 1918 the massed buglers of the battalion sounded the 'Cease Fire' in the centre of the square at Limerick. During the war it sent out drafts totalling over 20,000 Other Ranks. The battalion was absorbed by the 2nd Battalion on 6 August 1919 and was disembodied on the 23rd.[55]

When war broke out the Territorial Force of part-time soldiers had no overseas commitment. When Kitchener became Secretary of State for War he called upon T.F. units to volunteer to serve abroad. The many that did so were referred to as 'Imperial Service' (I.S.) units. On 31 August 1914 the County Associations responsible for the T.F. were authorised to form a reserve infantry battalion for every I.S. battalion – one in which 60% had volunteered for overseas service – and distinguished from it by the word 'Reserve' in brackets in its title, e.g. 4th (Reserve) Battalion The Royal Welsh Fusiliers.[56] Reserve battalions for the 4th, 5th, 6th and 7th Battalions were raised in September at their home stations at Wrexham, Flint, Caernarfon and Newtown respectively.[57]

In January 1915 the titles of the original battalions (known as 1st-Line battalions) were changed to 1/4th, 1/5th, etc, and the Reserve battalions – now known as 2nd-Line battalions – became the 2/4th, 2/5th, etc. 3rd-Line battalions were raised in March 1915 (3/4th and 3/5th), May (3/6th) and June (3/7th) at the pre-war stations of the 1st-Line. Their role was to supply reinforcements to the 1st- and 2nd-Line battalions. The second Welsh Division was formed in January 1915 and was concentrated at Northampton, its war station, by April. In mid-August it was named the 68th (2nd Welsh) Division with 203, 204 and 205 Brigades, and had a Home Service role.

2/4th (Denbighshire) Battalion (T.F.) was raised at Wrexham on 11 September 1914. It moved to Northampton in November and to Cambridge in the following month. It joined 203 (Royal

Welsh) Brigade in the 68th (2nd Welsh) Division in April at Northampton. In July and August the division moved to Bedford to replace its 1st-Line division – the 53rd – when the latter left Bedford for Gallipoli. In November the 68th Division joined First Army, Central Force, in the United Kingdom. By September 1916 it had moved into General Reserve, Home Forces and 203 Brigade. By May 1917 the 68th Division had been transferred to Northern Army, Home Forces with 203 Brigade at Halesworth. Following a further transfer to XXIII Corps the division moved into winter quarters in October with 203 Brigade at Yarmouth. Disbandment was authorised on 13 January 1918.

2/5th (Flintshire) Battalion (T.F.) was formed at Flint on 11 September 1914. In April 1915 it moved to Northampton and joined 203 (Royal Welsh) Brigade in the 68th (2nd Welsh) Division. Its moves followed the same pattern as the 2/4th Battalion. On 16 March 1918 the battalion was disbanded.

2/6th (Carnarvonshire and Anglesey) Battalion (T.F.) was formed on 11 September 1914 at Caernarfon. In April 1915 it moved to Northampton and joined 203 (Royal Welsh) Brigade in the 68th (2nd Welsh) Division. Its moves followed the same pattern as the 2/4th Battalion. The battalion was disbanded on 8 September 1917.

2/7th (Merioneth and Montgomery) Battalion (T.F.) was formed at Newtown in September 1914. In April 1915 it moved to Northampton and joined 203 (Royal Welsh) Brigade in the 68th (2nd Welsh) Division. In November 1916 the battalion moved to Wrentham and absorbed the 2/1st Brecknockshire Battalion T.F.[58] Otherwise its moves followed those of the 2/4th Battalion. The battalion was disbanded on 8 September 1917.

3/4th (Denbighshire) Battalion (T.F.) was formed at Wrexham on 25 March 1915.[59] On 8 April 1916 it became the 4th (Reserve) Battalion (T.F.)[60] (See below)

3/5th (Flintshire) Battalion (T.F.) was formed at Flint on 25 March 1915.[61] On 8 April 1916 it became the 5th (Reserve) Battalion (T.F.).[62] On 1 September 1916 it was absorbed by the 4th (Reserve) Battalion.[63] (See below).

3/6th (Carnarvonshire and Anglesey) Battalion (T.F.) was formed at Caernarfon on 29 May 1915.[64] On 8 April 1916 it became the 6th (Reserve) Battalion (T.F.).[65] On 1 September 1916 it was absorbed by the 4th (Reserve) Battalion (T.F.) (See below).[66]

3/7th (Merioneth and Montgomeryshire) Battalion (T.F.) was formed at Newtown on 5 June 1915.[67] On 8 April 1916 it became the 7th (Reserve) Battalion (T.F.).[68] On 1 September 1916 it was absorbed by the 4th (Service) Battalion (T.F.) (See below).[69]

4th (Reserve) Battalion (T.F.) came into being on 8 April 1916 with the re-designation of the 3/4th (Denbighshire) Battalion (See above). On 1 September 1916 it absorbed the 5th, 6th and 7th (Reserve) Battalions[70] at Oswestry in the Welsh Reserve Brigade T.F. In March 1918 it moved to Kinmel Park, near Rhyl. In July it moved to Herne Bay in Kent.[71] It possibly served briefly at Ipswich in January 1919 before returning to Herne Bay. It was disbanded on 23 September 1919.[72]

12th (Reserve) Battalion was formed at Wrexham in October 1914 as a Service battalion of K4. On 10 April 1915 it moved to Kinmel Park, near Rhyl and became a Second Reserve battalion.[73] On 1 September 1916 it became the 62nd Training Reserve Battalion, a non-R.W.F. battalion.[74]

18th (Reserve) Battalion (2nd London Welsh) was raised at Gray's Inn, London in January 1915 as a Service battalion. It was handed over to the W.N.E.C and moved to Bangor, North Wales in June and joined the 38th (Welsh) Division. In August it moved to Kinmel and became a Local Reserve battalion in 14 Reserve Brigade. On 1 September 1916 it amalgamated with the 20th (Reserve) Battalion to become the 63rd Training Reserve Battalion, a non-R.W.F. unit.[75]

20th (Reserve) Battalion was raised by the W.N.E.C. in North Wales in March 1915 from the Depot companies of the 13th to 17th (Service) Battalions, probably as a Second Reserve battalion.[76] By April 1916 it was in 14 Reserve Brigade at Kinmel Park. On 1 September 1916 it amalgamated with the 18th (Reserve) Battalion to become the 63rd Training Reserve Battalion, a non-R.W.F. unit.[77]

21st (Reserve) Battalion was raised by the W.N.E.C in North Wales in March 1915, probably as a Second Reserve battalion. By April 1916 it was in 14 Reserve Brigade at Kinmel Park. On 1 September 1916 it amalgamated with the 22nd (Reserve) Battalion to become the 64th Training Reserve Battalion, a non-R.W.F. unit.[78]

22nd (Reserve) Battalion was raised by the W.N.E.C. in North Wales in March 1915, probably as a Second Reserve battalion. By April 1916 it was in 14 Reserve Brigade at Kinmel Park. On 1 September 1916 it amalgamated with the 21st (Reserve) Battalion to become the 64th Training Reserve Battalion, a non-R.W.F. unit.[79]

23rd Battalion (T.F.) was formed on 1 January 1917 by the re-designation of the non-R.W.F. 47th Provisional Battalion, which had been formed in summer 1915 with Home Service personnel of T.F. battalions. It was at Mundesley in 224 Brigade with which it remained until disbanded. In June the Brigade moved to Bacton and in September to Hemsby, Norfolk where it was disbanded on 21 March 1919.[80]

3rd (Reserve) Garrison Battalion was formed at Wrexham on 18 July 1915. In November 1916 it was at Abergele, then Rhyl and Gobowen. In June 1917 it was at Oswestry until November when it moved to Cork, Ireland. In March 1918 it went to Crosshaven where it remained until disbanded on 16 May 1919.[81]

5th (Home Service) Garrison Battalion was formed at Wrexham on 22 August 1916. It moved to Barrow-in-Furness and in August 1917 became the 12th Battalion Royal Defence Corps, a non-R.W.F. unit.[82]

7th Garrison Battalion was formed on 1 January 1917,[83] possibly at Bebbington. It appears to have been disbanded in February.[84] According to *Regimental Records*, W. McG. Armstrong was appointed Commanding Officer.[85]

v. Summary

In summary, the forty battalions of the Regiment in the Great War were made up as follows:

    Regular: 1st and 2nd
    Special Reserve: 3rd
    Territorial Force: 1/4th, 1/5th, 1/6th, 1/7th, *2/4th, *2/5th, *2/6th, *2/7th, *3/4th, *3/5th,
        *3/6th, *3/7th, *23rd, 24th and 25th
    Service: 8th, 9th, 10th, 11th, *12th, 13th, 14th, 15th, 16th, 17th, *18th, 19th, *20th, *21st,
        *22nd and 26th (counts as one with 4th Garrison)
    Garrison: 1st, 2nd, *3rd, 4th (counts as one with 26th), *5th, 6th and *7th

*Battalions that served at home only.

Lloyd George with Royal Welsh Fusiliers, 1919.
(PA Images)

H.R.H. The Prince of Wales inspects R.W.F.
battalions in 38th (Welsh) Division, Allonville,
6 February 1919.

All battalions not mentioned above are deemed to have been re-designations or amalgamations. These include the 4th, 5th, 6th and 7th (Reserve) Battalions T.F. (re-designations), the 5th/6th Battalion T.F. (amalgamation), the 62nd, 63rd and 64th Training Reserve Battalions (non-R.W.F.), and the 8th entenching Battalion (non-R.W.F.).

vi. The Volunteer Force

Soon after the start of the war patriotic fervour led to the formation of units all over the country for local defence. They were entirely unofficial and were variously called the Volunteer Training Corps (V.T.C.), National Guard, Volunteer Defence Corps, etc. From a very early date, and certainly by December 1914, the Corps had its own magazine called *The Volunteer Training Corps Gazette*. In Wales, one of the earliest was the Cardiff Exchange Volunteer Corps which was formed at a meeting held on 7 August.[86] In November 1914 the organisation of V.T.C.s was recognised by the War Office, subject to certain stringent conditions, and control was vested in the Central Association of Volunteer Training Corps. There was no standard V.T.C. uniform but several styles of grey/green jacket or Norfolk jacket were permitted. Units were distinguished by means of button-hole badges and members were allowed to wear a red armlet bearing thereon the letters 'GR' in black. Military ranks were not permitted and Officers had titles like 'Platoon Commander', 'Sub-Commandant', etc. Training was carried out at weekends as all members did their normal civilian jobs during the week.

On 19 April 1916 the War Office authorised the raising of volunteer units under the Act of 1863 as amended by subsequent Volunteer Acts. The V.T.C. became 'The Volunteer Force,' and Central Association V.T.C. became the 'Central Association of Volunteer Regiments.' The grey/green uniform was officially recognised and the red armlet was only worn with civilian clothes. Volunteers on temporary service were subject to Military Law and liability for service in the

Regular or Territorial Forces was not affected by enrolment in the Volunteer Force. The establishment of a battalion (four companies) was 600 to 1,000, and for a company (four platoons) 150 to 250. A platoon numbered anywhere from forty to seventy men.[87]

In October 1916 the special rank badges were replaced by those in normal used by the field army. In December the special uniform was replaced by khaki. In May 1917 web equipment was issued and in July greatcoats. From May 1918 men granted exemption certificates by Military Tribunals, under the Military Service Acts, were liable to serve in the Volunteer Force as a condition of exemption from compulsory service in the Army. In response to an appeal by the Under Secretary of State for War on 27 May 1918, Volunteers served for periods of up to three months in Special Service Companies between June and October 1918 to relieve Regular troops required for active service in France. The terms of service permitted the enlistment of men over military age, men of military age referred by tribunals, and youths between 17 and 18 years of age. There was no medical and the only requirements were the ability to march five miles and to shoot with the aid of spectacles. Training involved fourteen drills per month for recruits and ten for others. Training was confined to drill, musketry, bombing, bayonet fighting and physical training. Liability for actual military service was to be called out in the event of an invasion being imminent.[88]

The final change in the constitution of the Volunteer Force came in July 1918 when Volunteer regiments (with the exception of London) became Volunteer battalions of line regiments and were authorised to wear their badges. The Royal Welsh Fusiliers thus gained five battalions:[89]

> 1st Battalion Anglesey Volunteer Regiment became 1st Volunteer Battalion The Royal Welsh Fusiliers
>
> 1st Bn Denbighshire Volunteer Regiment and 1st Battalion Flintshire Volunteer Regiment became 2nd Volunteer Battalion The Royal Welsh Fusiliers
>
> 1st Battalion Carnarvonshire Volunteer Regiment became 3rd Volunteer Battalion The Royal Welsh Fusiliers
>
> 1st Battalion Merionethshire Volunteer Regiment became 4th Volunteer Battalion The Royal Welsh Fusiliers
>
> 1st Battalion Montgomeryshire Volunteer Regiment became 5th Volunteer Battalion The Royal Welsh Fusiliers

An official Volunteer Force List appeared in October 1919, the year in which the units were disbanded. An extract of this is included in the Annex on Regimental Appointments.

Notes

1   T.N.A. WO 380/17 Register of Formations, Amalgamations and Disbandments 1914–1920.
2   *Regimental Records*, Volume III, pp. 29–31.
3   Brigadier E.A. James, *British Regiments, 1914–1918* (London, 1978).
4   Martin Gilbert, *World in Torment: Winston Churchill, Volume IV, 1917–1922* (London, 1975), p. 181.
5   Martin Gilbert, p. 181.
6   Martin Gilbert, p. 184.
7   Martin Gilbert, pp. 191–194.
8   Martin Gilbert, p. 194.
9   *Regimental Records, Volume IV*, pp. 268–269.
10 T.N.A. WO 95/1280 and WO 95/2721 (War Diaries).
11 T.N.A. WO 95/4323, WO 95/4626 and WO 95/4627 (War Diaries).

12 T.N.A. WO 95/4323, WO 95/4626 and WO 95/4627 (War Diaries).
13 *Carnarvon and Denbigh Herald*, Friday 8 August 1919.
14 *Carnarvon and Denbigh Herald*, Friday 12 September 1919.
15 Speech by Lloyd George at Queen's Hall, London on 19 September 1914.
16 Army Council Instruction No 103 of 1914.
17 Major A.F. Becke, *Order of Battle of Divisions, Part 3B* (Newport, 1989) p. 88.
18 Army Orders 324 and 382 of 1914.
19 According to WO 380/13. The last entry in the battalion war diary [WO 95/5162] was on 28 February.
20 T.N.A. WO 95/4303 (War Diary).
21 Army Order 382 of 1914.
22 T.N.A. WO 95/2092. (War Diary, last entry 31 March 1919).
23 Army Order 388 of 1914.
24 Lt Col F.N. Burton (ed.) *The War Diary of 10th (Service) Battalion Royal Welch Fusiliers* (Plymouth, 1926).
25 Army Order 388 of 1914.
26 T.N.A. WO 95/4858 (War Diary), which starts in December 1915 and WO 95/4922.
27 According to T.N.A. WO 380/17. It is not known where it occurred.
28 Brigadier E.A. James, *British Regiments 1914-18*, p. 67.
29 Welsh Army Corps, 1914–1919. Report of the Executive Committee (Cardiff, 1921).
30 T.N.A. WO 95/2555 (War Diary) which ends on 30 April 1919
31 T.N.A. WO 380/17.
32 T.N.A. WO 95/2555 (War Diary) which ends on 31 March 1919.
33 T.N.A. WO 380/17.
34 *Welsh Army Corps, 1914–1919. Report of the Executive Committee* (Cardiff, 1921).
35 T.N.A. WO 95/2556 (War Diary) which ends on 30 April 1919.
36 T.N.A. WO 380/17.
37 According to T.N.A. WO 380/17. However, in *British Regiments 1914–1918*, p. 67, the date is given as 2 February.
38 T.N.A. WO 95/2561 (War Diary) which ends on 30 April 1919.
39 T.N.A. WO/380/17.
40 T.N.A. WO 380/17.
41 *Order of Battle of Divisions*, Part 3B, pp. 102–106.
42 T.N.A. WO 95/4427 (1/1st DY war diary) which ends on 31 December 1916.
43 T.N.A. WO 95/4679 and WO 95/2366 (War Diary) which ends on 30 April 1919.
44 T.N.A. WO 95/4679 and WO 95/3154 (War Diary) until 21 June 1919.
45 T.N.A. WO 380/17 and *Regimental Records, Vol IV*, p. 403.
46 *Order of Battle of Divisions*, Part 3A, p. 123.
47 Earl Winterton, 'England and Egypt', *The Nineteenth Century and After*, CVII, October 1930, p. 764.
48 *Order of Battle of Divisions*, Part 3A, p. 130.
49 T.N.A. WO 95/4627 (War Diary).
50 'Stations of the Royal Welch Fusiliers, 1914–1946' [a card index held in Historical Branch, MoD London].
51 *Order of Battle of Divisions*, Part 2B, p. 23.
52 T.N.A. WO 95/409 and WO 95/3021 (War Diary).
53 T.N.A. WO 380/17 and *British Regiments 1914–1918*, p. 68.
54 T.N.A. WO 380/17 and *British Regiments 1914–1918*, p. 68.
55 *Regimental Records, Vol III*, pp. 24–29.
56 Army Order 399 of 1914.
57 *Order of Battle of Divisions*, Part 2B, p. 88.
58 *British Regiments, 1914–1918*, p. 68.
59 T.N.A. WO 380/17.
60 Army Council Instruction No 768 of 1916.
61 T.N.A. WO 380/17.

62   Army Council Instruction No 768 of 1916.
63   Army Council Instruction No 1528 of 1916.
64   T.N.A. WO 380/17.
65   Army Council Instruction No 768 of 1916.
66   Army Council Instruction No 1528 of 1916.
67   T.N.A. WO 380/17.
68   Army Council Instruction No 768 of 1916.
69   Army Council Instruction No 1528 of 1916.
70   Army Council Instruction No 1528 of 1916.
71   *British Regiments 1914–1918*, p. 67.
72   T.N.A. WO 380/17.
73   *British Regiments 1914–1918*, p. 67.
74   *British Regiments 1914–1918*, p. 67.
75   Army Council Instruction No 1528 of 1916.
76   Welsh Army Corps, 1914–19. Report of the Executive Committee (Cardiff, 1921).
77   Army Council Instruction No 1528 of 1916 and *British Regiments 1914–1918*, p. 68.
78   Army Council Instruction No 1528 of 1916 and *British Regiments 1914–1918*, p. 68.
79   Army Council Instruction No 1528 of 1916 and *British Regiments 1914–1918*, p. 68.
80   Army Council Instruction No 2364 of 1916, T.N.A. WO 380/17, and *British Regiments 1914–1918*, p. 68.
81   Army Council Instruction No 2364 of 1916, T.N.A. WO 380/17, and *British Regiments 1914–1918*, p. 68.
82   Army Council Instruction No 2364 of 1916, T.N.A. WO 380/17, and *British Regiments 1914–1918*, p. 68.
83   T.N.A. WO 380/17 and Army Council Instruction Nos 212, 276, 421, 818 and 225 of 1916.
84   *British Regiments 1914–1918*, p. 68.
85   *Regimental Records*, Vol IV, p. 403.
86   *The Volunteer Training Corps Gazette*, 12 December 1914.
87   Army Council Instruction No 1024 of 1916 (19 May), Volunteer Force Order No. 1, Regulations for the Volunteer Force.
88   *Radnor Society Transactions*.
89   Army Order No 208 of 1918 (July) and appendix.

Chapter 4

The 1st Battalion at the Close of the Great War, 1918–1919[1]

On 4 November, 1918, the day on which the Armistice between Italy and Austria-Hungary was to be signed, the 1st Battalion was on the right bank **November 1918** of the Tagliamento River, near Postoncicco. Shortly after 14.00 hrs a message was received from 22 Brigade Headquarters that no armistice had been signed and that the advance across the river would continue. The crossing began at 07.30 hrs on the 5th and encountered no opposition. A patrol under Lieutenant J.C.L. Edwards entered Turrida and found 200 Austrians, without their arms, who promptly surrendered. At 10.00 hrs, the Brigade Major informed the Commanding Officer that the armistice would come into force at 15.00 hrs and that all territory occupied at that time would be held. The battalion moved forward and by 12.30 hrs had occupied its objectives, with Battalion Headquarters based at San Lorenzo. On the following morning 20 Brigade was withdrawn to the west side of the Tagliamento and 22 Brigade was left to hold the entire front of the 7th Division, with 1 R.W.F. holding from Meretto (exclusive) to San Lorenzo. On the 6th, the brigade crossed to the west of the river and the battalion moved into billets at Provesano. Major Ll. A.A. Alston returned from hospital and assumed command of the battalion vice Captain E.G. Hawes. Between 8 and the 13 November 1 R.W.F. marched to Treviso, via Rorai Piccolo, Orsago, Vazzola and Breda di Piave, and entrained for Montecchio Maggiore, north-west of Padua, which it reached the next day and where it remained at least until the end of January 1919, and probably until leaving Italy. On 27 November the battalion marched to the aerodrome at Castelgomberto where Victor Emmanuel, the King of Italy, reviewed troops from XIV (British) Corps. Whilst at Montecchio much of the time was spent by the soldiers on education and sport, whilst some of the more fortunate ones, mainly miners, were repatriated to England for demobilisation. On 11 December, **December 1918** the Divisional Commander presented medal ribbons to Officers and soldiers who had been decorated for their bravery in the recent operations on the Tagliamento River. Thereafter the battalion was reduced to cadre strength. A proper celebration of Christmas was possible for the first time since 1913.

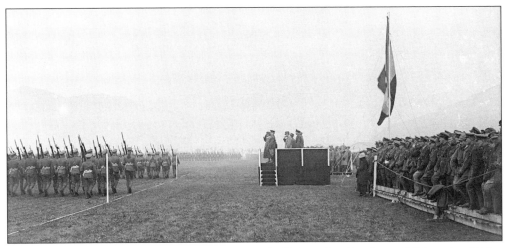

The 1st Battalion marches past King Victor Emmanuel of Italy at Castelgomberto, 27 November 1918.
(IWM Q26788)

On 23 February 1919 the cadre of the battalion, under Brevet Lieutenant
Colonel W.G. Holmes DSO* and comprising Captain T. Bluck MC,† Captain
G. Bromley, Lieutenant and Quartermaster A.J. Down and forty-four N.C.Os and Fusiliers,
left Italy and disembarked at Southampton on the 28th. On the following day, at 13.00 hrs, it
arrived at Wrexham station where it was met by the Mayor and Corporation, who laid on a civic
luncheon for the entire party.

February 1919

On 1 April 1919, Captain J.C. Wynne-Edwards joined as Adjutant and on 4
April, T/Major E.L. Mills MC joined and took over command. Orders had been
received that the battalion was to re-form and a steady stream of Officers arrived at Wrexham;
167 men joined during May, 363 during June and July. As conscription had been extended, it is
possible that many of these men were conscripts, however the Digest of Service makes no distinction. On 24 April the battalion moved to Park Hall Camp at Oswestry. On 10 May, Lieutenant
B.E.C. Boucher, who had only rejoined three days earlier, was killed in a car accident near
Shrewsbury. He had been commissioned in March 1917 and joined the 1st Battalion in France
in July. He accompanied the battalion to Italy and for his actions at the capture of the island of
Grave di Papadopoli in the Piave River in late October 1918 he was Mentioned in Despatches
and awarded the Italian *Croce di Guerra*. He was buried at Cheddleton in Staffordshire five days
later aged only 21.

April 1919

The embryonic battalion was inspected on 29 May by the Inspector
General of Infantry. On 10 June Lieutenant Colonel J.B. Cockburn DSO‡

May – July 1919

*   Later Lieutenant General Sir William Holmes KBE CB DSO (1892–1969). He was G.O.C.-in-C
     Ninth Army during the Second World War, retired in 1945 and emigrated to the U.S.A.
†   Captain Bluck was the only member of the Regiment during the war to win an MC and two Bars,
     the first as the RSM.
‡   Lieutenant Colonel Sir John Bridges Cockburn Bt (of the Ilk) DSO *Ld'H* (1870–1949). Awarded
     the Silver Medal of the Royal Humane Society for an act of conspicuous gallantry, in jumping into

The Officers of the re-formed 1st Battalion,
Oswestry, 1919. (R.W.F. Mus 4161)

The Paris Victory Parade, 14 July 1919.

assumed command of the battalion. On the
30th, the battalion took part in a ceremonial parade at Oswestry Park in celebration
of the signing of the 'Terms of Peace'. On
1 July Captain (Brevet Lieutenant Colonel)
W.G. Holmes was appointed Adjutant. This
pointed up one of the problems faced by
many able Officers after the war. Although
aged only twenty-six he had commanded the
1st Battalion from September 1916 to the
end of the war, winning a DSO and bar, and
earning four Mentions in Despatches and

The London Victory Parade, 19 July 1919.

the Italian Silver Medal whilst doing so. He was now faced with doing a captain's job for three
years. Although he was only a substantive Captain in the Regiment, he had been promoted to
the rank of Brevet Lieutenant Colonel in the Army in January 1919. This highlighted another
problem which was not to be resolved until shortly before the Second World War – the slowness
of promotion described in Chapter 1.

The battalion was represented at the Allied Victory Parade in Paris on 14 July by Lieutenant
W.P. Kenyon MC, Lieutenant H.B. French, 9115 CSM Hall DCM, 10886 Sergeant A.
Workman DCM MM, 9672 and Sergeant C. Rush DCM. The Colours were also taken. The
same party, plus 9694 Sergeant A. Evans (Orderly Room Clerk) was present at the Victory
Parade in London five days later.

On 21 July the Commanding Officer brought to the attention of the General Officer
Commanding at Oswestry an act of heroism by 56920 Private D.W. Davies. Whilst on ration
fatigue the horses attached to a R.A.S.C. G.S. wagon took fright and bolted out of control,
the driver having been thrown off the box. Davies ran after the wagon and climbed on. Then,
he ran along the pole until he was able to retrieve the reins which were trailing on the ground.

the Cameroon River, which is infested with crocodiles, when in high flood, in an attempt to save a
bluejacket of HMS *Cumberland* who had fallen overboard. Retired 1923 and succeeded his brother as
11th Baronet in 1947.

Although in great danger of falling off and suffering serious injury he managed to climb back on the box and after about five minutes brought the horses under control.

Because of a police strike the battalion was sent to Liverpool where it remained, billeted in the Rotunda Theatre, from 3 to 13 August when C Company moved to St George's Hall, and A, B and D Companies returned to Park Hall Camp. C Company joined them on the 19th. The next day the battalion was warned for a move to India, prob- **September – October 1919** ably on 15 September. In the event it was the advance party of five Officers and twenty Other Ranks under the command of Captain the Honourable G.R.B. Bingham that embarked at Liverpool on the SS *Teucer* on that date. On 29 September the battalion was ordered to 'stand-to' for duty in connection with a national railway strike if required, however the strike was settled on 7 October and the battalion stood-down.

The Officers, and the Band, Drums, Colours and Colour Party attended a Memorial Service at Wrexham Parish Church on 18 October for those of the Regiment who had given their lives in the War. The King was represented by the Colonel of the Regiment, Lieutenant General Sir Francis Lloyd. On the 22nd the battalion was inspected by Brigadier General C.T. Shipley CB who also presented British War Medals and Victory Medals. Three days later it entrained at Gobowen for Liverpool where it embarked on the HT *Northumberland*, which sailed at midnight. The strength of the battalion, including the advance party, was twenty-two Officers and 830 Other Ranks.

The first port of call was Port Said where everyone was entertained by the Egyptian conjurors who came aboard, and by the young boys who dived for pennies thrown by the troops. In the Red Sea the first anniversary of the Armistice was commemorated by a two minutes' silence, and at Aden Captain J.B. Venables DSO was put ashore for an appendix operation.

Note

1   Taken from T.N.A. WO 95/5400 (1 R.W.F. War Diary) for 1918 and 1 R.W.F. Digest of Service thereafter.

Chapter 5

The 1st Battalion in India, and on Operations on the North-West Frontier, 1919–1930

i. Lucknow, 1919–1921

On arrival at Bombay on 16 November, the battalion entrained for Kirkee where it camped until the 23rd. Two days later it reached its destination, **November 1919** Lucknow, where it was to be stationed at Outram Barracks for the next two years. A telegram awaited the battalion when it arrived at Bombay. It said simply 'Coming Bombay Tom'. Tom – otherwise Mahomed Ismail – had been the faithful *charwallah* – Contractor* – of the 2nd Battalion in India before the war, and he was to remain with the 1st Battalion until they left in 1930.[1] It was said that the attempts by N.A.A.F.I. to operate in India had been thwarted by the combined efforts of the regimental contractors.[2]

When 1 R.W.F. arrived in India, Lucknow was not under the command of one of the four great geographical commands (Northern, Southern, Eastern and Western) into which India was divided. Instead it came directly under Indian Army H.Q., commanded in 1919 by General Sir Charles Monro,[†] who was succeeded in 1920 by General Lord Rawlinson.[‡] The 8th (Lucknow) Division was commanded by Major General Sir Walter Scott,[§] who had assumed command only two months before the battalion arrived. In November 1920, the division became United

---

[*]   Battalions in India engaged a sutler to provide canteen and other services to the troops. The sutler paid a sum of money to the PRI or Regimental charity and recovered his outlay through profits on sales, but at controlled prices. He would also be engaged, and paid, to provide meals at times for the whole unit. Many sutlers ran the business as a family affair and would remain engaged with the same regiments for generations.

[†]   General Sir Charles Carmichael Monro, Bt GCB GCSI GCMG (1860–1929) was commissioned into The Queen's. He oversaw the successful evacuation from Gallipoli and, after commanding First Army in France, was Commander-in-Chief, India 1916–1920. He later served as Governor of Gibraltar from 1923 to 1929.

[‡]   General Lord (Henry Seymour) Rawlinson, Baron (1919) GCB GCSI GCVO KCMG (1864 –1925), is best known for his roles in the Battles of the Somme (1916) and Amiens (1918). He was C-in-C India 1920–1925.

[§]   Major-General Sir Walter Maxwell-Scott (1875–1954) Bt CB DSO was the Great-Great-Grandson of Sir Walter Scott.

Provinces District. 1 R.W.F. was assigned to the Lucknow Infantry Brigade, later 19 Indian Infantry Brigade, under Brigadier General J. H. de C. O'Grady,* who arrived in January 1920.

In spite of the ever-present problems of internal security duties in the cities, and service on the North-West Frontier, the soldier's lot was far better in India than at home. His pay went much further, he was a *sahib*, and could afford bearers and servants to look after him and his kit. In country places, elderly men would dismount from their donkeys, close their sun-umbrellas and remain respectfully halted when he passed by.[3] New barracks had been built in many stations and most had electricity, proper ablutions and sanitary facilities. Work generally stopped at midday, followed by sport in the afternoon, and Thursdays were always free time. All families accompanied the battalion and were given well-appointed quarters, again with servants. There were few civilised amenities, however, and for the single men, no European female society. Inter-communal riots could arise without warning and unless

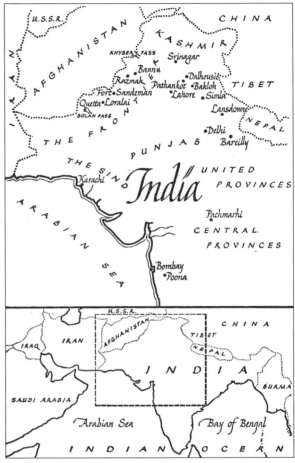

Map 5.1 Northern India, showing the locations of the major garrisons.

quickly stopped could lead to widespread death and destruction. Muslims and Hindus would fly at each others' throats with little provocation in what would rapidly become an orgy of arson, rape and murder if not stopped by the rapid intervention of British troops.

Less than a month after its arrival, the battalion was inspected for two days by the Brigade Commander.[4] This was followed by the celebrations of the Peace which were spread over three days and included a brigade sports day, a concert and a boxing tournament.

January 1920

On 1 January 1920, the Proclamation Parade was held throughout all the garrison towns in India. This was the anniversary of the day in 1877 when Queen Victoria had been declared Empress of India. Ceremony, pomp and circumstance were to be seen at their

---

*   Brigadier General James Henry de Courcy O'Grady CIE had served in the 52nd Sikhs and commanded in East Africa under Smuts during the Great War.

The Colours, 1st Battalion, Lucknow 1919. (R.W.F. Mus AB 3592)

very best. First the proclamation was read by the senior Officer; this was followed by a march-past of troops, both British and Indian – the cavalry in brigade order and the infantry in battalions – as the bands played the regimental marches. This in turn was followed by a *feu de joie*, a ceremonial firing of blank rifle shots which began with a thundering salute by the gunners of the Royal Artillery. Then the infantry rifles were aimed at the sky, the firers' heads statue still and eyes looking straight to their front. On the command 'fire' the right marker, the rifleman on the extreme right of the front rank fired one round, then, in rapid succession each man along the whole of the front rank fired one round immediately after the man on his right had fired. This produced a great rippling of rifle shots along the whole of the front rank; then, without pause, it was taken up by the rear rank, starting with the left marker. 'The effect was startling. First one saw little puffs of smoke sprouting from the muzzles of the rifles the length of

'Crump' Norman, by David Jones.
(R.W.F. Mus 2998b)

the ranks, and then came the sounds, single shots like a prolonged burst of machine-gun fire.'[5]   **March–April 1920**

The Annual General Inspection was made on 10 March by the Brigade Commander. On 7 April, Lieutenant Colonel J.B. Cockburn returned to the United Kingdom on medical grounds because of an eye wound and was replaced by Lieutenant Colonel C.C. Norman.[*] Lieutenant Colonel Cockburn had served with the Regiment for twenty-six years. Meanwhile D Company with detachments from A, B, and C Companies left Lucknow for the hill station of Ranikhet. In March each year, the diurnal winds heralded the approach of the hot weather which lasted until October. During this time, troops would spend some time away from the heat of the plains in hutted camps at places like Ranikhet. Here, away from the furnace of the plains, the cool air made sleep possible and much sport could be played. There were pony races, tennis, golf, shooting at leopard or panther, and tournaments against other regiments. For those left behind, work during much of the day was impossible and men were confined to their barracks. At night, men often slept, or tried to sleep, on the roofs of their bungalows.[6] On 16 June, B Company, the Band and details of A, D and C companies changed over with those at Ranikhet, returning in early August. While at Ranikhet, an incident occurred of which the exact circumstances are not known. However two soldiers, Privates W. Morris and W. Mason, were found guilty of mutiny and insubordination by a General Court Martial and were given death sentences, but these were later reduced to five years penal servitude.[7]   **July 1920**

Another disciplinary incident occurred in July, when the 1st Connaught Rangers, disturbed by Black and Tan activities in Ireland, mutinied. At Jullundur, Regimental Officers regained control but at Solon, where there was an attempt to storm the armoury, three battalions including 1 R.W.F., had to be deployed to overawe the Rangers. Two mutineers were shot dead. Fourteen were subsequently sentenced to death by court martial, but only one, Private James Daly, was actually executed. Six others received life sentences.[8]

On the sports field the battalion won the Murree Association Football Cup. Officers' polo was restarted for the first time since the war. On 13 August the battalion received a bronze replica of a gold medal presented by the King of Italy in commemoration of the Great War. Seven such medals and diplomas were sent to the Army Council in London.   **August 1920** After consultation with the Earl of Cavan, who had commanded British Forces in Italy from March to November 1918, seven regiments, 1 R.W.F. among them, were selected to receive medals as representatives of the British forces engaged in Italy

Another change of command occurred when on 10 September Lieutenant Colonel C.S. Owen[†] replaced   **September–December 1920** Lieutenant Colonel C.C. Norman, who went to command the 2nd Battalion. On 18 October, the battalion was inspected by the G.O.C and on 13 November, by the C.G.S. India. On the 20th, the battalion provided a Guard of Honour for the Viceroy, which the C-in-C Eastern Command stated was 'the best I have seen since the war. The turn-out was excellent.'[9]

The battalion took part in the Proclamation Parade on 1 January 1921 and immediately afterwards moved to Kakori for training,   **January–May 1921** returning on 22 January. St David's Day was celebrated as usual on 1 March. On 3, 4 and 5

---

*   See his biographical entry when in command of 2 R.W.F.

†   Later Brigadier C.S. Owen CMG DSO (1879–1959). He had a reputation as a tough soldier.

March, a number of Officers and men entered the Lucknow Garrison Assault-at-Arms, an athletic sports tournament, achieving the following places:[10]

1 mile, Second Lieutenant M.B. Dowse, 2nd
440 yards, Corporal Guston, 1st
Obstacle race, Corporal Jones, 1st and Pte Brown, 2nd
Sack race, Private Walsh, 2nd and Corporal Guston, 3rd
Alarm Competition, Battalion team, 2nd
Tug-o' War, Battalion team, 2nd
Relay race, Battalion team, 2nd.

Elements of C Company left for Ranikhet on 21 March. On the 26th, Headquarter Company was formed. On 2 April, the whole battalion was on parade for the proclamation of Lord Reading as Viceroy. On the 5th, C Company with elements of the other companies left for Ranikhet. The Digest of Service also notes the departure after two years' service of a draft of men, who appear to be among the last drafts of post-war conscripts. In exchange, a draft of 126 men joined the battalion from home. The draft members challenged the rest of the battalion to a boxing competition which took place over two days, 18 and 19 May. The draft emerged victorious in every weight.

In early June, A Company and detachments of the other companies exchanged with those at Ranikhet, returning on 8 August. On **June–September 1921** the 20th, a warning order for service in Waziristan was received; an advance party of two Officers, twenty men and one Indian 'follower' departed for Waziristan on 10 September.[11] The battalion remained at Lucknow until, following the receipt of orders, the main body left Lucknow by train on 2 December 1921 for India's North-West Frontier, to join the Waziristan Field Force. Shortly after 13.00 hrs the train, bearing 600 members of the battalion, their chargers, dogs, and baggage steamed out of Lucknow Station and began its leisurely and comfortable two-and-a-half-days progress via Bareilly, Amritsar, and Lahore, to the Indus at Mari Indus.

The prospect of active service was much welcomed:

> Although we loved Lucknow it was not a good place for us because there were too many distractions, both for the Officers and men. Going up to the frontier was the best possible thing, individually and collectively. You would have thought the Army existed only for fun … and we did have a very good camp, Kokori, ten miles outside Lucknow. Being in barracks you only thought about the afternoon, when you were going to play polo or cricket, and the men only thought about football and brothels.[12]

Troop trains in India were a distinctive khaki colour, consisting of about ten coaches hooked up to a steam engine, combining greatest capacity with as much air and coolness as possible. Each coach held sixty-six men, six to a compartment, seated on two benches or lying on folding shelves; their arms and equipment were stowed on racks above. The coaches were fitted with electric light and fans, with drinking water in special tanks which kept out the heat. Officers and all families could be in either ambulance coaches or in railway first or second class coaches, which also had baths; blocks of ice were provided to keep drinks and baby food cool. Every train had a kitchen car; meals were served at halts and fresh rations taken on board. There was also a canteen, from which drinks, fruit and some food could be bought at any time, operated by the battalion's Contractor. Finally there were baggage and horse wagons. A British battalion usually required two troop trains.[13]

On the platform at Amritsar the battalion was greeted by Lieutenant Colonel W.H. Stanway* and Captain E.J. Glazebrook.† At Mari Indus they detrained and were ferried across on river steamers to Kalabagh rest camp. The next three days were spent moving the battalion by narrow gauge railway over the Piesu Pass to Tank, so it was not until 8 December that the march proper began. It took two days to reach Jandola, the last standing camp on their journey, and the end of the road for the motor transport which had carried the baggage. From now on it would be carried on the backs of 400 'oonts', the camels to which the battalion was introduced for the first time.

STAFF LIST, 1 R.W.F. LUCKNOW, 1919–1923

Lieutenant Colonel
J.B. Cockburn DSO (10 June 1919)
C.C. Norman CMG CBE DSO (7 Apr 1920)
C.S. Owen CMG DSO (23 Sep 1920)
Major
J.D. Venables DSO (to Nov 1921)
Bt Lt Col C.C. Norman CMG CBE DSO
Bt Lt Col E.J. de Pentheny O'Kelly DSO
Bt Lt Col C.S. Owen CMG DSO
E.O. Skaife OBE (Sep 1921)
Captain
Ll. A.A. Alston DSO MC
Bt Lt Col W.G. Holmes DSO (Adjt)
J. Cuthbert MC (to Feb 1921)
Hon G.R.B. Bingham
Quartermaster
Lt G.M. Schofield
RQMS C.J. Shea
Attached
Capt W.W. Burke
(Educational Officer)
E.H.P. White *I.A.*
A.R. Johnson *I.A.*

Lieutenant
H.D.T. Morris
E.C. Tunnicliffe
B.E. Horton
G.B. Wright (to Nov 1920)
F.O. Mahon (to Mar 1921)
B.L.N Dickenson[1]
A.N. Griffiths
E.W. Gillbe MM (to May 1921)
B.E.C. Boucher
H.B. French
W.P. Kenyon MC
A.M.G. Evans (Capt May 1921)
G.E. Cardwell MC (Sep 1921)
S.O. Jones MC (Sep 1921)
H.A. Freeman MC
H.E.B. Goldsmith
H.D'O. Lyle
2nd Lieutenants
B.E. Horton
G.B. Wright
E. Hall
C. Duffy MC
D.R. Evans
M.B. Dowse (Lt Dec 1920)
O.L. Richards (to Aug 1921)
B.H.R. Hopkins (Lt Dec 1920)
R.G. Davies-Jenkins (Lt Aug 1921)

W.O. I
A. Smith
W.O. II
J. Hall DCM
W. Gorham
H. Beardmore
T. Hannon MC DCM
Staff Sergeants
ORC A. Evans 94
Sergeants
- Gunston
A. Workman DCM
MM
C. Rush DCM
- Page
A. Dufty
Lance-Sergeants
J. Bean

---

*   Lieutenant Colonel W.H. Stanway DSO MC had begun the war as a Company Sergeant Major in the 2nd Battalion and ended it as C.O. 6 Cheshires (*Y Ddraig Goch*, May 1922, p. 7).

†   Edward John Glazebrook had served as RSM of the 8th Battalion at Gallipoli where he was awarded the DCM. He was commissioned and remained with the battalion in Egypt and Mesopotamia. He was mentioned in despatches and subsequently awarded the MBE and MSM.

ii. Operations in Waziristan, 1921–1923

1 R.W.F. marches in to Kotkhai in Waziristan. (R.W.F. Mus 8152)

The arrival of the battalion at Kotkai on 10 December was greeted by the pipes and drums of the 110th Pioneers. On the following night, at Sararogha, they sustained their first casualty at the hands of the Mahsuds who twice sniped their camp, at 07.30 and 09.30 hrs. The next morning it was discovered that Company Sergeant Major C. Rush DCM of A Company had been killed in the second burst.* The final move from Sararogha to Ladha Camp had to be carried out in two detachments on the 12th and 13th so as to make possible the relief of The Queen's Regiment whom the battalion was replacing. The journey from Tank to Ladha, some 53 miles (84 kilometres), had taken six days, but from Sararogha the climb had became more pronounced and the going increasingly rough. On each day could be seen the permanent picquets on the hilltops, and the road protection troops who came out to guard the convoy on its passage up country. On arrival at Ladha the battalion joined 9 Indian Infantry Brigade which comprised 2/6th Gurkha Rifles, 1/69th Punjabis, and 2/39th Garwhal Rifles, under the command of Colonel Commandant C.J.L. Atkinson CMG CIE DSO.

December 1921

India's North-West Frontier was the most remarkable frontier of the whole imperial era, showing most clearly concepts of client-states and security in an area of extreme geographical difficulty and particularly unruly people. The area was also a major strategic frontier, peopled by Pathan tribesmen. They were characterised by an extreme independence and ferocity of temperament. Recourse to the gun was normal and death when inflicted could be unbelievably cruel. The difficulties of administering the Pathan hill peoples were thought to be insuperable and a large area was officially described as 'non-administered', where Britain's main concern was that there should be no trouble despite the 140,000 rifles estimated to be in the hands of the local

*   Charles Rush was born in 1887 and enlisted into the 3rd Battalion (S.R.) in 1904. He transferred to the Regular Army in 1905 and served with 1 R.W.F. throughout the Great War, winning the DCM in 1916 and also being mentioned in despatches.

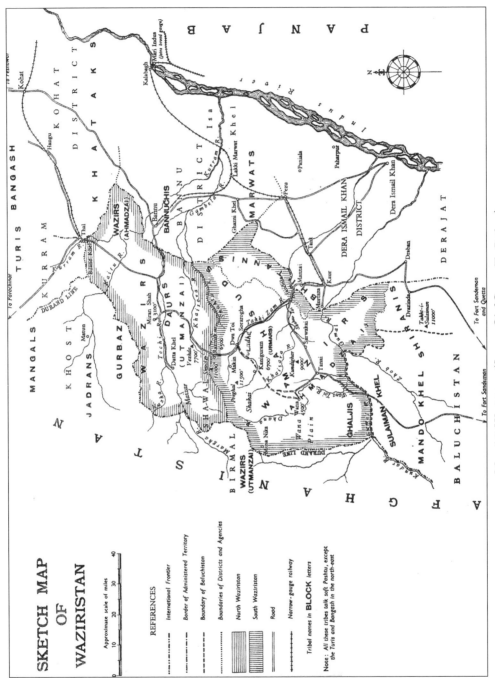

Map 5.2 Waziristan. (Source: Olaf Caroe, *The Pathans*)

inhabitants. Various local 'Scouts' and 'Militias' were stationed in fortified camps, with regular British and Indian troops mainly concentrated as reserves in certain strategic areas.[14]

In spite of the peace treaty that followed the Third Afghan War in 1919, unrest continued on the Frontier with attacks by Waziris and Mahsuds against the British forces. During 1921 operations were designed to wear down the remaining hostile sections with the result that by the autumn only the Jalal Khel and the Abdur Rahman Khel sections of the Mahsuds remained openly hostile in South Waziristan. During November and December it was decided to raise a new locally recruited force of 'Khassadars' for road protection duties between Sararogha and Ladha.

Ladha Camp was situated just under a mile north-west of Ladha village, at an altitude of some 5,000 feet (1,700 metres), in wild, desolate mountain country. The barbed-wire perimeter fence extended for 4,000 yards (1,800 metres). Only tented accommodation was provided, with twenty men in each 160-pounder tent. The terrain was arid, with much thorn scrub and juniper on the sides of the steep ridges. Tops of ridges were generally 'turtle-backed' and clear of scrub thus affording some fields of fire. At the time there were no roads; the sole means of communication being along tracks which were cleared along the river beds by the laborious process of picking and laying aside boulders and leaving a smooth surface of wet gravel. Ordinarily two or three ankle deep streams would meander down these beds, converge, meet, and separate again. They were, however, liable to sudden, heavy spates which were dangerous and which brought movement to a standstill and destroyed the painstakingly constructed tracks*. The climate was generally pleasant and quite warm in summer but in winter it could be very cold with heavy falls of snow.

The battalion's first-line transport was chiefly pack mules for the Machine Gun Platoon. All other transport was provided by camel companies of the Indian Army Service Corps. Field hospitals had a few ponies which proved useful for the sort of polo played in Waziristan – that is, on rough, confined pitches. Evacuation of the sick and wounded was by stretcher slung on each side of a camel – a ghastly experience for the occupant.

On arrival at Ladha the battalion was placed under the instruction of the 2/6th Gurkhas. Operational duties consisted **January 1921–April 1922** mainly of route protection for the daily convoys, the garrisoning and resupply of permanent picquets, and the 24-hour picqueting of the camp itself. Night duties were frequent. Danger was ever-present and slackness of any sort would only encourage enemy sniping and the risk of casualties. The Mahsuds never wasted ammunition and would rarely fire unless they were certain of their target. They were a most patient enemy and would wait for days or weeks until someone became slack or careless. Despite the physical and mental strain on all ranks morale remained high throughout the tour of duty in Waziristan.

From each of the four battalions in the brigade there was always the best part of a company out of camp manning the permanent picquets, which looked down some 4-500 feet on to the nullah bed below which took the place of a road. These picquets, consisting of an Officer or Non-Commissioned Officer and sixteen men, lived in rough stone *sangars*, surrounded by barbed wire and roofed with canvas or matting stretched on poles. Picquets remained in place

---

*   Spates were liable to occur in the months of January/February and July/August. When they occur there is great danger to convoys or any human beings or animals caught in a defile in a river bed. The spate comes as a wall of water and allows no time to escape.

The view from Razmak towards Tauda China. (R.W.F. Mus 6067)

Khirgi Camp, Waziristan. (R.W.F. Mus 6067)

for 8–10 days and were resupplied with rations and water every 4–5 days. The picquets were insufficient on their own to protect the long convoys of slow-moving camels from Mahsud snipers lurking in dead ground. Whenever the road was open, usually on four or five days a week, road protection troops were deployed from Ladha to link up with other troops from the next post down the line. Sometimes Khassadars were used, and when they were, one battalion was at five minutes notice to deploy in support of them. The Ladha brigade was responsible for a six mile (9 kilometre) stretch of road which required five companies supported by *Vickers* machine guns. The two companies which manned the first sector were required to leave camp an hour before the departure of the 'down' convoy. Moving in single file down the steep-sided *nullah*, picquets or patrols were deployed at every place of danger. All movement had to be covered, and the company did not move on until the picquet signalled that it was in position. The process was repeated until the end of the sector was reached. Picquets remained in position until a large red flag indicated the passage of the last camel in the 'up' convoy. In reverse order the picquets were hastily withdrawn, every move again being covered by the rifles and *Lewis* guns of their comrades. Sector after sector was thus evacuated until, about thirty minutes after the last camel had entered the security of Ladha Camp, the *nullah* bed was clear of men. [15] This lengthy system was the result of many years of hard experience on the frontier, for the Wazirs were formidable opponents who knew every inch of the ground and were murderously patient, punishing any lapse with a sudden, unexpected, attack. This was the pattern of life throughout 1921 and into 1922, as Captain P.C. Kenyon recalled:

> We went up a very inexperienced Battalion. We trained and did some very good schemes from Lucknow. Each camp is self-contained and surrounded by barbed wire, and you are responsible for a certain amount each side of the frontier. You defend yourself inside your camp and, when the natives misbehave, you go out and burn down their houses... Waziristan was very good training for a British battalion, far away from the fleshpots of places like Lucknow. Every day the Bn guarded the road which is in the valley. Picquets on the hilltops, some permanently occupied, and others only by day.[16]

St David's Day 1922 was celebrated in traditional manner on 1 March but not without concern that the leeks would arrive on time from India. Various entertainments groups were formed to provide some sort of off-duty diversion. These included a camera club, male voice choir, a theatrical group and a concert party.[17] On the 3rd a highly successful concert was performed in camp at the end of which a terrific storm arose, completely demolishing the Brigade Theatre and nearly destroying the camp itself as the result of sparks blown onto the tents, some of whose occupants had a narrow escape from being burnt alive. On the 6th the battalion football team achieved a notable success beating 2/3rd Gurkhas 6-1 in the final of the Climo Cup which was open to all units in Waziristan.

On 10 May the battalion sustained another casualty when Sergeant D. Hanscombe was mortally wounded by a Mahsud sniper whilst superintending **May 1922** a wood-cutting party at Prospect Picquet. The Commander in Waziristan, Major General Sir Torquhil Matheson* visited Ladha Camp from 22 to 24 May and carried out an inspection of

---

* General Sir Torquhil George Matheson, 5th Baronet, KCB CMG (1871–1963).

the battalion. In spite of heavy operational demands and training requirements there was still time for sport and recreation. The annual boxing tournament was held in June for the Owen Cup, presented by Lieutenant Colonel C.S. Owen, and ninety soldiers out of 650 competed. In the following month 119 participated in the novices boxing competition. The Male Voice Choir gave their second concert at Ladha, supplemented with humorous songs and balalaika solos by Lieutenant Colonel W.G. Holmes and Captain the Honourable G.R.B. Bingham respectively. The concert was given in the open with the result that the soldiers in one of the permanent picquets over a mile away took up the beautiful strain of *Mae Hen Wlad fy Nhadau*. On 4 July it was learnt that the Goat had died at the battalion's depot at Dalhousie. General Sir Claud Jacob,* Chief of the General Staff of India, visited the battalion on the 16th.

The threat of danger was ever-present with the enemy regularly sniping at the permanent picquets and Ladha Camp itself, and the battalion was about **July 1922** to receive a salutary reminder of this fact. On 29 July, two platoons of D Company under the command of Lieutenant R.G. Davies-Jenkins were the covering troops for the relief of Prospect Picquet. The covering party reached the picquet without incident and then pushed forward to occupy a small feature beyond it called Windy Snip, which was closely covered with thick scrub and small trees. Whilst the leading platoon under Lance Sergeant Davies was advancing to the top of Windy Snip, very heavy fire was opened on the leading sections by Mahsuds from a range of only 5 to 10 yards. Privates Lloyd and Bowen were killed instantly, and four others seriously wounded one of whom, Private Tevendale, died two hours later in Prospect Picquet. Fire was immediately returned by the platoon and from Prospect Picquet with the result that the enemy hastily made off into the thick scrub. The ambush was carried out by a gang of about forty men from the Abdul Rahman Khel section of the Mahsuds. They were divided into six groups. The first, numbering about ten, were carefully camouflaged behind a large rock that looked like a breastwork, with the second in position above and behind them. Two groups covered approaches from the flanks, whilst the remaining two groups, which could also engage Prospect Picquet if required, were held in reserve.[18] *The Times* newspaper reported later on the aftermath: 'As a reprisal for the attack on the Welsh Fusiliers on 29 Jul, when two Fusiliers were killed, one died from wounds, and three were wounded by the Abdur Rahman Khel Mahsuds near Ladha, aeroplanes have bombed Baddar Toi, near Kanigoram'.[19]

The rest of the year passed without major incident except that the tour in Waziristan, which was expected to end in the autumn, was **December 1922** extended to April 1923. On 6 December, an earthquake occurred but caused no casualties, and on the 13th, General Sir William Birdwood,† General Officer Commanding Northern Command, visited the battalion in Ladha Camp.

During the spring, it had been decided to relocate the main garrison of Waziristan at Razmak instead of Ladha, because the former, being on a plateau 6,000 feet (1,900 metres) above sea level, had a healthier climate. Since it was situated on the boundary between the tribal areas of the Mahsuds and the Waziris, it was well-placed to deal rapidly with anything started by either tribe, and also to carry out punitive shelling of the Mahsud settlements at Makin with

*   Later Field Marshal Sir Claud William Jacob GCB GCSI KCMG (1863–1948).
†   Later Field Marshal Baron (William Riddell) Birdwood, Baron (1938) GCB GCSI GCMG GCVO CIE DSO (1865–1951). He was the first commander of the A.N.Z.A.C. Corps in Gallipoli and on the Western Front. He was C.-in-C. India 1925–1930.

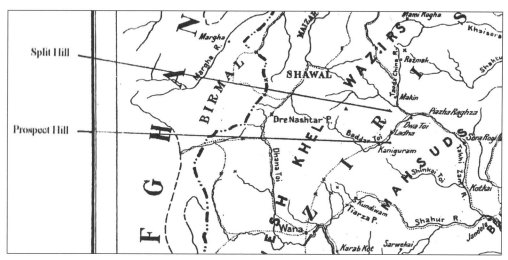

Map 5.3 Prospect Picquet and Split Hill Picquet.

Split Hill Picquet, 1924.
(R.W.F. Mus 2123)

A *Vickers* section of 1 R.W.F. in
Waziristan, 1921.

heavy artillery. The general situation remained good until the autumn when the decision was taken to occupy Razmak by 14 January 1923, **January 1923** and surplus stores at Ladha were successfully back-loaded. The Mahsud situation now began to deteriorate because of rumours that the government intended to abandon Razmak, rumours which gained additional credence by the evacuation of stores from Ladha in a direction other than to Razmak. Mahsud attacks increased, culminating on 12 December with the murder of Lieutenant Dickson of the Royal Engineers whilst working on the new Tochi to Razmak road.

The Officers, 1 R.W.F., at Tauda China on the North-West Frontier, 1923. (R.W.F. Mus 6067)

Tribesmen on the North-West Frontier, 1923. (R.W.F. Mus)

In the meantime, preparations had been progressing for the advance from Tochi to Razmak of the Razmak Force, comprising 5, 7 and 8 Indian Infantry Brigades under Major General A. le G. Jacob,* General Officer Commanding Kohat District. Operations began in December 1922 and the Razmak Plateau was eventually occupied in a blinding snowstorm on 23 January 1923. It was now decided to undertake punitive operations against Makin for the renewed hostilities of the Mahsuds during the latter part of the year and the many outrages they had perpetrated, particularly the murder of Lieutenant Dickson. Major General Matheson was made responsible for the operations and in addition to 9, 10 and 21 Brigades, 7 Brigade from the Razmak Force was placed under his command. Operations were required to be completed and forces withdrawn to Jandola by 25 February without fail. This very tight schedule was further complicated by the fact that it was necessary to replace the stocks of equipment, ammunition and engineer materials that had been back-loaded from Ladha earlier.

Makin was not so much a tribal village as an area dotted about with a number of villages of sub-sections of the Mahsuds, not all of whom were hostile. The area was in a large basin of walled terraces of cultivated land. On the west were very high precipitous mountains through which flowed the Dara Algad by way of a very steep gorge. Four miles (6 kilomtres) into the mountains lay Mandech: a large, inaccessible and hostile village of the Abdullai Mahsuds.[20]

On 1 February 1923, 9 Brigade evacuated Ladha as snow began to fall, and by late afternoon the battalion had reached Piazha Raghza where it remained until the 3rd. That night the troops camped on the right bank of the Dara Toi below Marobi. The next day, 7 Brigade moved south from Razmak to Tauda China, about two miles (three kilometres) south-east of Makin, where it was joined by 9 Brigade which had advanced north from Marobi. The force so formed was known as the Makin Column. The enemy, who were surprised by the advancing troops, withdrew to the hills to the north-east.[21]

On 5 February the battalion was detailed to establish and garrison a permanent picquet on Split Hill, assisted by men from the 23rd Sikh Pioneers. By 09.45 hrs, B and C Companies were in position on the northern and southern spurs. A Company, having discovered the site of the permanent picquet occupied during the 1919–1920 campaign, the company commander, Captain A.M.G. Evans, ordered 4 Platoon (Lieutenant H. D'O Lyle) to advance beyond Split Hill to watch the forward slope to the North. Its move was covered by 2 Platoon. As 4 Platoon was about to occupy its final position the enemy opened a heavy and accurate fire on 2 Platoon from the area which 4 Platoon was approaching. Fire was immediately returned and the enemy withdrew, but not before two men from 2 Platoon had been wounded. 4 Platoon established itself on the position and was reinforced by 3 Platoon. Intermittent sniping continued, mainly at 4 Platoon, but the Pioneers also suffered casualties. Whilst this was going on a group of the enemy, taking advantage of the thick bushes, crept up to within ten yards of 4 Platoon and opened a heavy burst of fire killing Private West and wounding two others. The platoon replied with hand and rifle grenades, and with the help of two sections of 3 Platoon under Lieutenant B.H.R. Hopkins which moved round the left flank and threw bombs, the enemy was repulsed with loss. At noon, Captain Evans ordered the two sections of 3 Platoon and 4 Platoon to withdraw to the rear and this was successfully accomplished without further casualties, although a couple of rifles were hit by enemy fire.

February 1923

---

*   Major General Arthur Le Grand Jacob CB CMG CIE CBE DSO ADC (Gen) (1867–1942).

There now followed a short lull in the firing, but after thirty minutes sniping began again with increasing intensity from the area of Red Tower, and Lieutenant Hopkins was wounded. Ammunition was beginning to run short. Company Quartermaster Sergeant G. Grindley, acting Company Sergeant Major of A Company, and Private Williams were severely wounded whilst returning to Company Headquarters, and Private A. Jones, the Company Runner, was hit in the arm and leg when he crawled out to attempt their rescue. Captain Evans ordered his Support Platoon (1 Platoon) to move forward to reinforce the other platoons. Once it was in position, Privates Murphy and W.H. Owens attempted to reach Grindley and Williams, but after Murphy had been mortally wounded Owen was forced to crawl back to cover.

Several more attempts were made to reach the wounded but to no avail as the enemy was bringing heavy fire to bear at this point. At the request of Captain Evans, a platoon of C Company occupied a spur running towards Kote village, and made a further attempt to rescue the casualties which had to be abandoned after Drummer Sherriff and Private Heath were both killed. Because the exact position of the enemy could not be identified the artillery were ordered to engage Red Tower and Kote village.

In spite of the battle raging around them the picquet had been completed and garrisoned. The battalion, however, would not withdraw whilst the wounded still lay in the open, but the accurate fire of the snipers precluded any further attempts in daylight. It was decided therefore to relieve A Company with Support Company under Captain Ll. A.A. Alston. By 17.30 hrs the relief was complete, but not without sustaining another casualty as Support Company entered the picquet. The battalion then withdrew under cover of artillery fire to Tauda China without further loss. During the night, helped by a good moon, the remaining bodies, except that of Company Quartermaster Sergeant Grindley, were recovered. In all the battalion had lost six killed and eight wounded*. Grindley's body was found later by the 2/39th Royal Garhwal Rifles.[22]

On the following day, 6 February, the battalion was in force reserve at Tauda China where they buried their fallen comrades. During 7 and 8 February a heavy snowstorm raged. Nearly a foot of snow fell and operations could not take place. Consequent extensive floods prevented the passage of motor transport and camel convoys for several days. A joint operation involving both 7 and 9 Brigades was carried out on 10 February for the destruction of the villages of Tora Tizha and Dinaur on the south side of the Makin basin. An account by an Engineer Officer describes what was done:

> A house is prepared for burning by making a few holes, some two feet across, in the roof …
> breaking open all doors and windows, so that there may be a good draught, and then filling
> the room with all the dry fodder and brushwood available. This is piled up under the main
> beams and kerosene oil is poured over it … Towers were blown up as soon as they were

---

*   The names of those killed were as follows:
4179610 Company Quartermaster Sergeant G. Grindley MM
2731111 Private B. Murphy
4180437 Private West
4181586 Drummer Sherriff
4114088 Private F. Jones
5094434 Private H. Heath

ready, but the burning was not so simple, owing to the dense clouds of smoke given off ...
Some damage was also done to the retaining walls of fields and fruit trees.[23]

The battalion provided cover for the burning of Tora Tizha, B and D Companies being assisted greatly by two R.A.F. aircraft as they occupied their positions. During the withdrawal a soldier was hit by a sniper, and four sepoys leading the machine gun mules of the battalion were seriously wounded when engaged at close range. A number of rifles and some ammunition were lost, and seven mules killed. On the 12th the battalion was ordered to seize and hold Split Hill for the artillery and escort three pack batteries onto the position. Throughout the morning these batteries, together with the 6-inch howitzers from camp completely wrecked objectives in the Dara Algad. The destruction of the Makin area was now complete. Of the six British Other Ranks killed and seventeen wounded during the operations of the Makin Column, all those killed and eight of the wounded were members of the battalion.

On 21 February the Abdullai petitioned for peace. As a result, Major General Matheson saw their representatives at a *jirga*[*] held at Tauda China on the following day, at which the guard of honour was provided by the Royal Welch. The terms were accepted and on the 23rd, 7 Infantry Brigade returned to the Razmak Force, and the Makin Column as such ceased to exist. It had carried out a difficult task with success in the face of the opposition of the strongest Mahsud clan. The terrain favoured the enemy and the weather was the worst possible.[24]

Notification was received on 25 February of the immediate award of Military Medals to four members of the battalion for their gallantry at Split Hill. The citations were as follows:[25]

4181397 Fusilier Jackson, P. (Burnley), and
4179475 Fusilier Williams, R.J. (Gelli Lydan, Blaenau Festiniog)
During the heavy fighting which took place on the 5th February, 1923, in connection with the construction of Split Hill Picquet, three attempts were made to bring in wounded who were lying out exposed to fire from the enemy. All three attempts were without success. Later, Fusiliers Jackson and Williams, regardless of heavy and accurate fire, directed at the particular spot, took advantage of a burst of gun fire, rushed out and each succeeded in bringing in a wounded man.

4179528 Fusilier Jones, A. (Formby)
During the fighting which took place on the 5th February, 1923, in connection with the construction of Split Hill Picquet, this soldier showed considerable courage in bringing up ammunition under fire. Later, when the C.S. Major had been hit and another man had been wounded in the endeavour to recover him, Fusilier Jones rushed out under an accurate fire and started to drag the C.S. Major in, but was then wounded in the arm and leg and forced to go back to cover.

4180533 Fusilier Owens, W.H. (Cwmaman, Aberdare)
During the fighting which took place on the 5th February, 1923, in connection with the construction of Split Hill Picquet, the C.S. Major was shot and lay in the open exposed

*   Tribal gathering.

to heavy and accurate fire from the enemy. Fusilier Owens displayed great courage in an attempt at rescue.

The battalion remained at Tauda China until 27 March 1923 carrying out minor operations such as picqueting, reconnaissance, road protec- **March 1923** tion, and the provision of working parties on the motor road being constructed to Razmak. St David's Day was celebrated with leeks from India, beer and other extras. At a large dinner in the Officers' Mess a mess tin had to do duty as a loving-cup. In spite of the much improved political situation Private Freegrove, temporarily employed on the Garrison Police, was killed by a sniper on 11 March. The weather during this period was appalling, and when the camp was not covered in snow, heavy rain turned it into a quagmire. On the 23rd a large Guard of Honour of 150 men was provided for a *jirga* attended by the Force Commander, the staff, and the Resident.

It was now necessary to deal with the situation at Wana without delay. Hostile gatherings during February had been dispersed by air attack, but there was plenty of evidence of the continuance of Afghan intrigues in this area where the garrison was exceptionally isolated. It was therefore decided that the South Waziristan Scouts should evacuate Wana and that strongly held Scouts posts should be established instead along the new road from Jandola to Sarwekai. The evacuation of the Scouts from Wana along the fifty-one miles (83 kilometres) of road to Jandola required the full support of a column of all arms. 9 Brigade was selected for this purpose[26].

The Brigade evacuated Tauda China on 27 March and proceeded by way of Piazha Raghza, Sararogha, and Kotkai to Wana Camp.[27] The column, accompanied by 700 South Waziristan Scouts left Wana Camp on 2 April, and after halting at Sarwekai to build up a reserve of supplies, reached Rogha Kot on the 12th. On the 13th the Scouts evacuated Wana without interference, and by the 17th the column was back in Wana Camp **April 1923** having left Scouts' posts established at Sarwekai, Haidari Kach, and Chagmalai.[28]

On 18 April, Major General Matheson paid his farewell visit to the battalion in Wana Column Camp. The following letter[29] was handed to the Commanding Officer:

> Now that you are about to leave the Force I wish to say good bye to you and to all ranks of the battalion under your command and to thank you for your good work while in Waziristan. You have spent 1 year and three months in the Force all of which with the exception of the recent operations you spent as part of the striking force at Ladha. You also took part in the operations against Makin in February and March of this year and in April 1923 you formed part of the column which marched from Jandola to Wana to withdraw the S.W. Scouts there and establish them at Sarwekai. In the Makin operations you showed the fine spirit that animates your Battalion and carried out every task set you with dash and courage regardless of losses, thereby winning the admiration of your comrades and the wholesome respect of the enemy. The fine spirit I refer to was never better shown than on 5th February 1923 at Split Hill when Officers and men deliberately courted death to help wounded comrades. I congratulate you particularly because a year ago your Regiment consisted mostly of very young soldiers who have now developed into a fine and well disciplined body of men. I regret to see that you had 37 casualties while in the Force of which more than half occurred in a gallant combat in the recent Makin operations. I also wish to congratulate you on your smartness and discipline in Camp. I regret that your departure from the Force should have

to take place in the present heat, but as you know it was unavoidable owing to the operations and I trust that you will have as comfortable a journey as possible. I hope you will enjoy your well earned rest in a peace station and I know that you will always in the future maintain and add to the fine records of your Regiment both in peace and war."

T.G. Matheson
MAJOR-GENERAL COMMANDING WAZIRISTAN FORCE
Dera Ismail Khan
17th April 1923

On 19 April, following a farewell speech by the Brigade Commander, Colonel Commandant R.P.C. O'Kelly,[*] the battalion marched out of Wana Column Camp for the last time. When they reached Khirgi later the same morning they were greeted by the bands of the 117th Mahrattas and the 37th Dogras. Four trains were provided for their journey to Multan which was reached on 23 and 25 April by B Company, half of A Company and H.Q. Wing, four hours late, where they were met by the Commander and Brigade Major of the Ferozepore Brigade Area and the band of the 46th Punjabis. The rest of the battalion arrived the following day.[30]

Staff List, 1 R.W.F. Waziristan, 1920–1923

Commanding Officer	Lt Col C.S. Owen CMG DSO
Second-in-Command	Maj E.O. Skaife OBE
Adjutant	Capt (Bt Lt Col) W.G. Holmes DSO
	Lt M.B. Dowse (Mar 23)
A/Adjt	Lt B.H.R. Hopkins
RSM	WO I G.R. Whyley
ORS	Sgt C. Evans 31[2]
ORC	Sgt H.F. Bradstreet

A Company	**B Company**	**C Company**	**D Company**
Capt A.M.G. Evans	Lt D.R. Evans	Capt H.F.	Lt H.B. Harrison MC
CSM C. Rush DCM	CSM A. Lungley	Garnons-Williams	CSM E.J. Smith
(kia 11/12 Dec 21)	Sgt E. Lewis 96	CSM C. Jones 14 DCM MM	CSM W. Gorham
A/CSM G. Grindley	Sgt E. Davies 17	Sgt J. Bacon	CQMS S. Farr
(dow 1922)		Sgt A.R. Worthington	Sgt S. Whitley
CQMS W.J. Swan			Sgt W. Howells
Sgt L. Jones 94 MM			
Sgt J. Soane			
Sgt A. Dufty			
Sgt E.T. Morse			

Headquarter Company

Quartermaster	**Band**	**Admin**	**Support Group**
Lt G.M. Schofield	Sgt M. Roberts	Capt S.J. Parker DCM MM	Capt Ll. A.A. Alston
RQMS R.W.	**Drums**	CSM H.F. Beardmore	DSO MC

---

[*]   Colonel Commandant R.P.C. O'Kelly CMG DSO. The rank of Brigadier-General had been abolished and was replaced by the rank of Colonel Commandant.

Chambers	Sgt Dmr J.P. Hall	CQMS G. Grindley	**Attached**
	Pioneers		Capt J.C. Rowley
			A.E.C.
	Sgt J.J. Hall		AQMS McMillan
			R.A.O.C.
Depot, Multan	**Unplaced**		
Capt the Hon G.R.B.	Bt Lt Col E.J. de	Lt E.C. Tunnicliffe	Sgt Gunston
Bingham	Pentheny O'Kelly DSO	Lt B.E. Horton	Sgt Hudson
Capt H.F. Garnons-	Capt E. Wodehouse	Lt B.L.N.	Sgt Jones 38
Williams (Jan 22)	Lt H. D'O Lyle (Capt	Trotman-Dickenson	Sgt W.H. Jones
Lt H.A. Freeman MC	Jan 23)	Lt A.N. Griffiths	Sgt Workman DCM
(Sep 22) (Capt Jan 23)	Lt H.D.T. Morris (Capt	Lt G.E. Cardwell MC	MM
C.S.M. – Hannon	Jan 23)	Lt B.E.C. Boucher	Sgt – Page
	Lt W.P. Kenyon MC	Lt S.O. Jones MC	LSgt J. Bean
	Lt T.S. Griffiths	Lt C. Duffy MC	LSgt I.G. Smalldon
	Lt R.G. Davies-Jenkins	Lt H.B. French	
	Lt H.E.B. Goldsmith	2Lt E. Hall	
	Lt G.B. Wright		

iii. Multan, 1923–1925

Multan came within Lahore District, part of Northern Command, and here the battalion joined the Ferozepore Brigade, with 10/2nd and 10/16th Punjabis, under Colonel Commandant R.J.F. Hayter CB CMG DSO. 1 R.W.F. occupied Edwards Barracks, with one company detached in the fort about one mile (1,600 metres) away. As one veteran recalled, 'The Orderly Officer would bicycle there during the night (sometimes in bright moonlight) wearing white mess kit, with overalls and Wellington boots, and sword in a metal scabbard.'[31] Multan itself was a typical Indian town with cantonment and bazaar. The barracks were thick-walled stone or brick, single-storey bungalows with verandas. There was electricity, but the ablutions were in separate build-ings some distance from the accommodation. The Officers lived in small bungalows, divided in the middle to make two rooms. These bungalows were stone, and usually thatched. There was no actual ceiling, but a ceiling cloth which was suspended where the ceiling should have been; cats could often be seen walking across the cloth, hunting the mice and rats that lived in the thatch.[32]

On 26 April, Major General A.E.C. Wardrop,* Commander Lahore District, inspected the battalion and welcomed the Officers and men to their new Station. The married families had already moved in October and November 1922.[33] On the following day Major E.O. Skaife presented British War and Victory Medals to all those who had not received them owing to their service in Waziristan.

Between 28 April and 5 May the battalion was reorganised onto the new Establishment (see Chapter 3), of four rifle companies and H.Q. Wing. No

May 1923

sooner had this been completed than A Company was ordered to stand-to a platoon as there was trouble in Multan between Hindus and Muslims; in the event the platoon was not required and preparations began for the move of the Hill Detachment to Dagshai for the hot weather. H.Q. Wing, B Company and details from the other companies left for the hills on the 7th, not

---

*   Later General Sir Alexander Ernest Wardrop GCB CMG (1872–1961).

No 14 Platoon, D Company, 1 R.W.F. wearing blue patrols in the Indian winter.

Lewis Gun section of No 14 Platoon, D Company, 1 R.W.F., wearing khaki drill.

1 R.W.F. at Multan, 1926. (R.W.F. Mus 4157)

a moment too soon as Captain S.J. Parker and three Fusiliers were taken to hospital suffering from heat stroke at Ferozepore. Indeed the heat was particularly bad that summer, reaching 120°F (50°C) and there were also frequent sand storms. So bad was it that Orderly Room Sergeant C. Evans, who had served with the battalion throughout the Great War, died of heat stroke on 8 July; Fusilier J. Barton of A Company died of malaria on 1 July[34]

During the hot weather, Officers and men wore khaki drill shirts with the sleeves rolled above the elbow, shorts, socks and hosetops, puttees and boots; the solar topee was worn during the day. At night, sleeves were rolled down and slacks replaced shorts, as a precaution against mosquitoes, and a side hat or peaked cap replaced the topee. For parades, a drill jacket was issued. In cold weather, especially in the hills, service dress could be worn. Soldiers had to appear in uniform at all times, whether on or off duty.

A number of N.C.Os and Privates received Force Commander's Certificates from the G.O.C. Waziristan Field Force:[35]

H.Q. Coy	A Coy	B Coy	C Coy	D Coy
RSM G.R. Whyley	CQMS W.J. Swann	CSM A. Lungley	CSM C. Jones 14	CQMS S. Farr
Sgt (ORC) H.F.	Sgt L. Jones 94	Sgt E. Lewis	Sgt J. Bacon	Sgt W. Howells
Bradstreet	Sgt J. Soane	Sgt E. Davies 17	Pte C. Williams 29	Sgt S. Whitley
	Cpl A. Harris	Pte R. Fay	Pte W. Condon	Cpl G. Davies 49
	LCpl R. Collier	Pte B. Jones 96		LCpl G. Cassidy
	Pte H. Wright			Pte A. Williams 84
	Pte J. Wheeler			Pte F. Green
	Pte W. Dellow			
	Pte S. Dallman			
	Pte E. Jones 05			

On 1 June, H.Q. Company ceased to exist as the battalion reorganised onto the new Establishment. In its place, H.Q. Wing was established with four groups (see Chapter 3).[36] In August, news was received that Privates in Fusilier Regiments would henceforth be called 'Fusilier' (see the chapter on Regimental Events). Instructions were also received on the wearing of miniature medals and collar badges in Mess or Evening Dress (see the Annex on Dress).

The Hill party changed over in the first week of August. As the weather began to cool, sport picked up. In September, the battalion football team entered the Durand Tournament, beating Shuztuz F.C. by 8 goals to nil, but

August 1923

losing to the 1st Cheshires by 3 goals to nil. A novice boxing competition was held on 17 and 18 October. Fusilier Bromley of C Company won the Bantamweight series; Fusilier Morris of C Company won the Featherweight series; Fusilier Langford of A Company won the Lightweights; Fusilier Johnson won the Middleweights and Fusilier Wilkins won the Welterweights. A battalion team subsequently entered the Mussoorie Station tournament, coming second to the 1st Royal Fusiliers overall.

A station rifle meeting was held on the last three days of October on Multan ranges, followed by platoon training and the various rounds of the Cockburn Cup, for hockey, a concert on 10 November and the Armistice commemoration on 11 November. On 22 November, the W.Os and Sergeants' Mess contested the Alma Cup, which was won by CQMS S. Farr; the Officers and Sergeants fired for the Annual Rifle Cup. The Sergeants won.

Entrenchng tools were withdrawn in October as 'becoming obso- lete'.[37] A series of inspections also took place. Major General Wardrop November 1923 inspected the battalion in review order on 30 November and then observed a field day on 1 December; Sir William Birdwood then inspected the battalion on 4 December. The report on the Annual Inspection was received some time later and in this, the District Commander concluded by writing 'A fine Battalion with great spirit and sporting instincts that makes the best of an isolated station'. This was endorsed by Sir William Birdwood, with the words 'I concur. A fine Battalion'.[38]

Christmas was celebrated in traditional style, and telegrams were sent to the King and the Prince of Wales. An All-Ranks Dance was January 1924 held on Boxing Day.[39] The Proclamation Parade was held as usual on 1 January 1924. Four days later the battalion marched eighteen miles (28 kilometres) to camp at Muzaffargarh, arriving back in Multan on 25 January where a draft of twenty-three men had arrived from the 2nd Battalion.[40] During February, a full programme of sports and games was pursued, with boxing, athletics, hockey, and cross country. The Boxing team won the Lahore District Boxing Competition on 22 February, going on to become Northern Command champions in March. This was followed with shooting, boxing in the Northern Command League, and individual training. The Brigade Commander carried out his annual inspection on 14 March, followed by a tactical exercise the next day, with which he expressed himself as being extremely pleased.

On 31 March, the first party of families left Multan for the hill station of Dalhousie, followed by the second party next day. The first April 1924 Hill Party from the battalion, comprising A and D Companies, the Band, Sick, Boys, and Goat left for Dalhousie on 14 April, slightly earlier than in 1923, with a total strength of 365 all ranks. On 23 April, Lieutenant Colonel C.S. Owen went on home leave. These furlough periods could last for up to eight months, including travelling time. Accordingly, Brevet Lieutenant Colonel P.R. Butler assumed command. A few days later, Major General Wardrop again carried out an inspection.[41]

The heat at Multan was again severe, passing the previous year's records, with many days over 100°F. Indeed Multan was famous for its oppressive heat and the chance to spend a month in the cool of the hills was heartily welcomed by all. For those at Multan, all work ceased at noon, although sport was played in the early evenings, and many men slept at night on the roofs of barrack blocks or bungalows. 'When the rains came, men sleeping on the roof of the barrack blocks would leap up naked and dance in the rain.'[42]

A Messing Meeting in late March decided that every man would subscribe 1½ Annas per day to buy fresh fruit and green vegetables for the mid-day meal during the hot weather in Multan because of the insufficiency of the Government allowance of 3½ Annas per day. On 15 May, spine pads were taken into wear. These were intended to protect the bone marrow in periods of extreme heat but in practice they were much disliked as being uncomfortable, and did no good at all. On 19 May, pith helmets were ordered to be worn for further protection against the sun. These were to be worn from 07.30 to 18.30 hrs daily.

On 28 April, following the decision by the War Office, the Government of India approved the wearing of the Flash in Service June 1924 Dress by non-commissioned ranks on ceremonial parades and when walking out.[43] On 4 June, news was received that the Battle Honours for the Great War had been issued in Army Orders for April. Five days later, on 9 June, news came in to Multan that the Boxing team had won the

All India Boxing Tournament at Mussoorie, with a score of 89½ points. 2 Brigade R.FA. were the runners-up with 77 points and 1st Royal Fusiliers in third place with 74.[44] The team was:

Featherweight, Fusilier Lodwicke, Fusilier Davies
Flyweight, Fusilier Westwell, Bandsman Galbraith, Fusilier Russell, Fusilier Ross
Bantamweight, Fusilier Pearce, Fusilier Sheppard, Fusilier Joyce, Fusilier Davies 47, Fusilier Evans
Lightweight, Lance-Corporal Rowlands, Fusilier Langford
Welterweight, Lance-Corporal Griffiths, Lance-Corporal Borrie, Fusilier Jenkins
Middleweight, Corporal Speed, Lance-Corporal Edwards 72
Light Heavyweight, Fusilier Jones
Heavyweight, Fusilier Strong
Individual cups were won by Sergeant E. Morse (Trainer's Cup), Lance-Corporal Edwards 72, Fusilier Westwell and Fusilier Strong.

From 19 to 20 June, the battalion proceeded by night march to Bandar Ghat, four miles (six kilometres) from Multan for a short camp and swimming, in order to escape the worst of the heat.

1st Royal Welch Fusiliers Winning Team. Mussoorie All India Boxing Tournament, 1924.
Back Row from left: Fus Sheppard, Fus Speed, Bdsm Galbraith, Fus Russell, Fus Joyce, Fus Evans
2nd Row: Fus Lodwicke, LCpl Griffiths, Fus Jones 27, Fus Langford, Fus Jenkins, Fus Davies,
LCpl Rowlands, Fus Davies 47
Seated: Fus Strong, Fus Ross, Fus Edwards 72, Lt H.B. Harrison, Sgt E. Morse, Fus Westwell,
Fus Nedderman
Seated in front: Fus Pearce, LCpl Borrie

On 24 June, the *London Gazette* of 27 February was received, in which were announced awards of Mentions in Despatches for distinguished service in Waziristan The awards were made to Major E.O. Skaife, Captain H.D.'O Lyle, 4178899 RSM G.R. Whyley, 4179129 Sergeant H.F. Broadstreet and 179938 Sgt J. Soane.

On 2 July, news was received that three American aircraft under Lieutenant Lowell Smith, which were making a round-the-world flight, **July 1924** were expected at Multan the following morning. The three battalions in the station decided to hold a combined dinner in 1 R.W.F. Officers' Mess to entertain the crews. The following morning a telegram was received from Ambala confirming the arrival time at 10.00 hrs and the three battalions formed a cordon around the airfield to watch the arrival. At noon, a train of I.A.S.C. bullock carts arrived with tins of aviation fuel and jars of distilled water, but no aircraft. At 13.00 hrs, still nothing. At 13.45, the heat was becoming dangerous and Lieutenant Colonel Butler dismissed most of the men, only for the three aircraft – *Boston, Chicago,* and *New Orleans* – to arrive fifteen minutes later. After three hours spent preparing the aircraft for the next leg to Karachi, a very late lunch was taken followed by a sleep in a bungalow in the cantonments. Thirty-four Officers and guests then sat down to dinner at 21.00 hrs, the party dispersing at midnight, and the Americans making an early start next morning. Their safe arrival in Karachi at 13.00 hrs was telegraphed.[45]

On 4 July, Fusilier Worthington of C Company died of pneumonia at Lobar; Fusilier Jordan of D Company died on 8 August from the same cause, followed on 19 August by Fusilier Holcombe of H.Q. Wing.[46] On 12 July, the first Hill Party returned from Dalhousie, and the second left Multan. Lieutenant Colonel C.S. Owen re-assumed command of the battalion on 24 July after three months away.

In mid-October, the Hill Party returned and standards were immediately tightened in the Officers' Mess, which had clearly **October–December 1924** fallen into slack ways during the hot weather. In future, Mess Dress at dinner was to be 'overalls and Wellington Boots' and not 'slacks and Oxford shoes'.[47] A large draft of one Sergeant and 123 men joined arrived from the 2nd Battalion at the beginning of November. Christmas 1924 was again celebrated at Multan, with a Christmas tree party for the children on Christmas Eve, the Officers and Sergeants serving the men's dinners on Christmas Day, and a concert on Boxing Day given by the Red Dragon Concert Party, an import from the 2nd Battalion.

1 January 1925 was Proclamation Day. All troops in the Garrison marched past in column of companies under Lieutenant Colonel C.S. **January 1925** Owen, with 1 R.W.F. under the command of Brevet Lieutenant Colonel P.R. Butler. The parade was witnessed by a great number of Indians from the local bazaars and the City. On the 3rd, Major General Wardrop attended a battalion Field Day at Muzaffargarh after the battalion had marched eighteen miles, and also the finals of the Inter Company Boxing Competition in the evening. Colonel Commandant Hayter visited another Field Day in February, in spite of a violent dust storm during the afternoon.[48]

The Annual Inspection took place after St David's Day, on 3 March. The inspection took the form of a ceremonial parade followed by a **March 1925** march past, and the inspection of barrack rooms and documents. On 8 March, the boxing team again won the District Championships and on 14 March, the athletics team won the Brigade Competition. The boxing team followed up its success on 15 March by beating the 2nd Seaforth Highlanders to win the Northern Command Championships. The *Civil and Military Gazette* reported that:

The 1st Bn The Royal Welch Fusiliers, are fortunate in possessing several boxers of a high standard. Quite recently they won the Team Competition in the Northern Command Boxing Championships at Rawalpindi, and it is noteworthy that only two of their representatives were beaten... Those who won their weights were Lt [J.H.] Lipscomb and Fusiliers Griffiths, Edwards, Jones and Ross. Griffiths is a Welterweight possessing much skill and ability. His final ... against Pte Duncan of the Seaforth Highlanders called for great endurance... Fus Edwards too, who is a Middleweight, hits powerfully and forces the pace and he won ... by knocking out Sgt Booth of the Sherwood Foresters. It shows commendable enterprise that this Battalion should also enter a team for the Ferozepore Brigade Boxing Tournament which was held concurrently with the Northern Command Championships, and at Ferozepore they also won the Team Competition... To win two championships at the same time in different centres requires a large number of boxers who can be fully relied upon. From the boxing point of view, it seems a little unfortunate that Multan, their Station, entails much travelling to obtain much experience against boxers outside their own Unit.

On 21 March, the Regimental Colour was trooped at Multan under the command of Lieutenant Colonel Owen. All Multan Cantonment was invited to the Parade and the attendance was large. *The Pioneer* of 26 March 1925 reported the event:

TROOPING THE COLOUR – KEEPING THE ARMY'S SOUL AT MULTAN CEREMONY If the age of chivalry has departed, it can still leave behind it, down to this very day, manifestations which help keep humanity on good terms with itself. The further we get from the days of pomp and panoply, of plumes and polish, the more necessary it is to recall now and then: and in the Army the dreary destiny of "mechanisation" would work havoc with its soul were it not that from time to time there is a harking back to the cherished things of yesterday... Yet every time an honoured custom is discouraged or forbidden, a badge removed, a bugle call abolished, something that is very precious suffers. A uniformity secured at the cost of esprit-de-corps is not worth having.

... the more beastly war becomes the greater the need is for symbolism. And of the symbolism which is still left to the British Army, surely there is nothing more stirring or of grander appeal than "Trooping the Colour".

But there comes an added poignancy... when the ceremony is performed by a khaki clad line battalion from England, under an aching Sun, with a little of background save Maidan, Mud Walls, and Metallic Sky, and under foot a dust such as no watering will allay. Certainly Multan – where this beautiful Ceremony was gone through on the 21st March 1925 by the Royal Welch Fusiliers – does little enough to remedy these drawbacks, but ... their successful overcoming, and the hard fact of the Cantonment's historic place in the British Army Annals, can turn disadvantages into advantages, and can make rich capital out of deprivation, and to those who watched the Parade on Saturday its success, both as pageant and Ceremony was complete, its symbolism unmistakeable. Not only were the various movements formed with a precision and steadiness worthy of the best days of the old Army, but the inner meaning of it all came home to one with quite peculiar force... Perfect precision ... joined symbolism that reflects all that is best in a soldier's calling – it takes not only steady troops to do it, but troops which have been steady for a couple of hundred years. At Multan there was little doubt about the precision and less about the symbolism.

It is by regard for symbolism that the Regiment keeps its soul.

The following were on parade:

Lieutenant Colonel C.S. Owen CMG DSO commanded the Parade
Captain F.S. Lanigan-O'Keefe MBE commanded the Escort to the Colour
Lieutenant D.R. Evans was Subaltern
Second Lieutenant P.L. Bowers carried the Colour
Sergeant G. Johnson, Fusilier Nicholson, and Fusilier Christian comprised the Colour Party
Lieutenant & Adjutant M.B. Dowse
Major C.H. Edwards
Captain Ll. A.A. Alston DSO MC
Captain S.O. Jones MC
Captain H.D.T. Morris
Lieutenant G.E. Cardwell MC
Lieutenant B.E. Horton
Lieutenant B.H.R. Hopkins
Lieutenant B.L.N. Trotman-Dickenson

The boxing team was unable to repeat its triumph of 1924 and on 23 March came second to the 2nd Seaforth Highlanders in the All India Boxing Championships; however on 27 May they won the team competition by nine points. On 21 April, the families left for Dalhousie, the Hill Station allotted to the battalion for the hot weather, followed on 28 April by B and D Companies, H.Q. Wing, and the sick. With their departure, hot weather routine was taken into force. On 6 May, cholera precautions were implemented because of an epidemic in the Multan Ice Factory.[49]

Up in Dalhousie, the Assembly Rooms were hired for dances and whist drives to take place most evenings, whilst at Multan: 'The weather at this period was about as trying as it could be. For days on end the maximum temperature would register up to 120° [F] and the minimum seldom went below 85°[F]. Battalion bathing parades took place on the left bank of the Chenab River, near Bhandar Ghat, in order to provide some relief. However, 2731256 Fusilier Lunt was drowned. These bathing expeditions took place every two weeks, and were described later by Major P.R. Butler:

The march out would generally take place towards evening, the companies proceeding across country in their own time, dressed in "clean fatigue" (which generally meant the minimum of clothing), and with only a small picquet carrying arms. (No doubt there are those in the Battalion who still could talk of the exploit of a certain Company Commander, who marched his men off the parade-ground as if making for the river, but when behind his barrack-rooms embarked them in a score of waiting "tongas," all paid for by voluntary contributions!)

… If it was not exactly cool, along those sandy river-stretches, it was at all events not stifling. There was the water, and a breeze. There was the freedom of great spaces. One was quit, for a brief interval, of mosquitoes, mud-walls and the teeming Indian population.

After darkness had fallen and dinners (prepared by the company cooks, who had come out with the rations) had been eaten, the whole Battalion would gather round the torches for a "sing-song". Welsh music and Welsh songs are beautiful at any time; but for supremacy commend me to "Land of my Fathers", sung by 500 Royal Welchmen on the banks of a Punjab river, on a starlit Indian night![50]

After a night bivouac, early morning swim and breakfast, the battalion would return early to barracks to resume normal routine.

On 15 July it was announced that the Clasp 'Waziristan 1921-24' for the India General Service Medal 1908 would be issued to all Officers and men who had served in Waziristan between 21 December 1921 and 31 March 1924.

July 1925

Major General Wardrop inspected the battalion on 27 July and especially complimented the smart turn-out of the mules. B and D Companies returned from Dalhousie on 1 August and the next day, A and C Companies left.

On 10 September Lieutenant Colonel H.V. Venables Kyrke* assumed command vice Lieutenant Colonel C.S. Owen, who had completed four years in command. Colonel Owen was placed on the half-pay list with effect 10 September 1925, having completed his service. He finally left Multan on 9 November. As the Digest of Service reported: 'Colonel Owen had endeared himself to everyone by his personality, efficiency, justice, fairness and hard-working qualities. He had ... through his own personal efforts ... raised the Battalion to the high state of efficiency in which he left it.' Kyrke was described by the then Lieutenant M.H. ap Rhys Pryce:

September 1925

> An extremely pleasant, hard-working man, with a delightful wife. He was short, slim and wiry. He did not interfere with his subordinates. He was active and once took me pigsticking. His horse somersaulted and ran off. I went after it, caught it, and brought it back. He thanked me and said "you should have kept on after the pig." At the age of 19 he had been at the Relief of Ladysmith and the subsequent forced march to Mafeking. He played a vigorous game of polo and rode in point-to-points.[51]

The battalion was reorganised in accordance with new Peace Establishment for India in early September, and on 1 October, cold weather routine came into force even though the maximum daytime temperature was recorded as 101°F (38°C), going down only to 76°F (25°C) at night.[52] On 22 October, Colonel Commandant Hayter inspected the battalion and watched a tactical exercise.

A draft of 112 men arrived from the 2nd Battalion on 29 October and on 30 October, the Hill Detachment rejoined from Dalhousie. The detachment, under Captain S.O. Jones MC, had carried out manoeuvres in mountain warfare, with detachments from 2nd Royal Scots Fusiliers. The exercises had been directed by the G.O.C., and Gurkhas from Bakloh and Dharmsala had acted as enemy. The operations were carried out in full marching order; weather conditions were bad, and all ranks bivouacked for three nights. Colonel Commandant D.I. Shuttleworth, Commanding the Jullundur Brigade

October 1925

---

*   Lieutenant Colonel Henry Vernon Venables Kyrke DSO (1881–1933) had been commissioned in 1898 and served in South Africa 1899–1902 – where he commanded the R.W.F. mounted infantry and became the only R.W.F. Officer to qualify for the clasp "Relief of Mafeking" on the Queen's Medal. He served with the W.A.F.F. and the Egyptian Army before and during the Great War. He was twice mentioned in despatches.

Area, wrote to the C.O., saying: 'I would like you please to thank all Officers and men, Royal Welch Fusiliers, for the way they worked both in the advance and in the withdrawal. It is evident that your Battalion is a quick-moving, well-trained unit.'[53] On 4 December, the incoming Commander-in-Chief, Field Marshal Sir William Birdwood, inspected the battalion, accompanied by the G.O.C. His Excellency spoke to many N.C.Os and men, and after the parade had a personal interview with each Officer. The battalion's tour of duty in Multan was now coming to an end and the G.O.C. bade them farewell on the following day. General Wardrop expressed his regret at the departure of the battalion from Lahore District. He said that the battalion had, at work and play, upheld the best traditions of the Regiment, and mentioned its boxing success. He was very sorry that the battalion was not going to a bigger station, which it fully deserved.

On 6 December, the families and heavy baggage left Multan for the new station, Nasirabad, and on the 11th, the battalion, with a strength **December 1925** of 820 all ranks, left Multan and proceeded to Pipri, near Karachi, for the Sind-Rajputana District manoeuvres, arriving at Pipri on 13 December. 'A bivouac camp was pitched in a howling desert and the battalion took part in manoeuvres which involved marching miles out and back over the rocky desert for three days.'[54] Five days later the battalion left Pipri and on 19 December, arrived at Nasirabad, although the Cook Sergeant had to be taken off the Troop Special [train] at Hyderabad suffering from smallpox. Fortunately it did not spread.

The Digest of Service observed that:

> It was with no regret that the Bn left Multan, sharing as it does with Jacobabad the very doubtful honour of being the hottest Station in India it was never very pleasant. There was little to amuse the men, and no one in the Station to compete with except at hockey and very occasionally cricket.

Staff List, 1 R.W.F. Multan, 1923–1925

Lieutenant Colonel
C.S. Owen CMG DSO
H.V. Venables Kyrke DSO (Jul 25)
Major
C.H. Edwards
Bt Lt Col P.R. Butler DSO (A/C.O. April–July 24)
Captain
F.S. Lanigan O'Keeffe MBE (Jan 25)
H. D'O. Lyle
Ll. A.A. Alston DSO MC
S.O. Jones MC
H.F. Garnons-Williams
H.D.T. Morris
S.J. Parker MC DCM
Quartermaster
Lt G.M. Schofield MBE
RQMS R.W. Chambers
Attached
SSgt J.A. McMillan *R.A.O.C.*

Lieutenant
H.B. Harrison MC
C.A. Anglesea-Sandels MBE MC
R.G. Davies-Jenkins
T.S. Griffiths
G.E. Cardwell MC
J.A. Pringle MC
B.E. Horton
B.H.R. Hopkins
R.E. Lampen
M.B. Dowse (Adjt)
D.R. Evans
B.L.N. Trotman-Dickenson
2nd Lieutenant
J.H. Lipscombe
H.A. Freeman MC
M.W. Whittaker
P.L. Bowers
Sergeants
V. Fraser

W.O. I
RSM G.R. Whyley
BM S.V. Hays
W.O. II
CSM C. Fell
CSM C. Jones DCM MM
CSM A. Lungley
CSM W.J. Swan
CSM S. Farr
CQMS
W. Howells
P. Ireland
B.C. Pratt
T. Ledington DCM
O.J. Stanley
Staff Sergeants
ORC L. Roberts
ORS H.F. Bradstreet
Pnr Sgt J. Hall DCM
Sgt Dmr J.P. Hall

WO II W. Stack *A.E.C.*
Lance-Sergeants
R.A. Richardson
G.H. Jones 20
G. Davies 49
W. Woods
A. Harris
P. Fox
J. Lewis 41
L. Roberts 35 (ORC)
R.R. Jones 48

E. Tinsley
P. Hewer
E.T. Morse
V.S. Smart
I. Hughes
E. Lewis
A. Jefferies
C. Morrissey
S. Whitley
W. Robinson
J. Bean
E. Davies 17
J. Soane
E. Davies 78
L. Jones 94
R.O. Jones 31
C. Rogers

Band Sgt W. Tubby
Sergeants
I.G. Smalldon
A.J. Fisher
S. Sherriff
R. Hayward
G. Johnson
W. Edwards
T.E. Roberts 75
J. Dodd
R. Thomas 78

iv. Nasirabad, 1925–1928

Nasirabad, 1926. (R.W.F. Mus)

Nasirabad lies 400 miles (600 kilometres) south of Multan, to the east of Jodhpur. At 1,800 feet above sea level (500 metres), the climate was better than Multan. It was an old and out-of-the-way station, very much on its own. It was a typical small cantonment with bazaar, cinema and railway station and the barracks were about a mile from the town. The men lived in substantial, brick-built, high-ceilinged bungalows which were roomy and airy; each one housed a platoon. There were no company dining rooms and at meal times, men took their plates and mugs to the cookhouse and then carried their meals back to the barrack room, making sure that no hawk or kite swooped down and stole the food! The Officers' and Sergeants' Messes were also in bunga-lows and each comprised a dining room, ante-room and kitchen.[55]

Here, 1 R.W.F. joined the Nasirabad Brigade Area under Colonel Commandant G.S.C. Crauford,* with the 10/6th Rajputs and the 5/14th Punjabis. Nasirabad in turn was part of Sind-Rajputana District, commanded by Major General H.F. Cooke,† and ultimately under the authority of Western Command which at the time of the battalion's arrival was commanded by Lieutenant General Sir Warren Hastings Anderson,‡ and from October 1927 by General Sir Charles Harington.§ One company was detached at Ahmadabad, nearly 300 miles (470 kilometres) south-west, close to the coast. It was placed there because of the possibility of civil unrest and had to march through the bazaar at least once each month to overawe the local populace.[56]

After Christmas, the first major event of 1926 was the departure of the Guard for the visit of H.E. the Viceroy, Earl Reading, to H.H. the Gaekwar of Baroda, on 19 January. The battalion was detailed to find a Guard of Honour, and an Officer's Guard over the Markapura Palace in which the Viceroy stayed. The Guard of Honour consisted of one Officer, four Sergeants, five Corporals and fifty-five Fusiliers. The following went to Baroda:

January 1926

> Captain E. Wodehouse, Commanding Guard of Honour
> Lieutenant & Adjutant B.H.R. Hopkins
> Lieutenant M.B. Dowse, Subaltern of Guard of Honour
> Lieutenant B.L.N. Trotman-Dickenson, Commanding the Officer's Guard
> Lieutenant D.R. Evans, Officer in Waiting on Guard
> Lieutenant M.H. ap Rhys Pryce, Ensign for the King's Colour
> RSM G.R. Whyley
> A/CSM S. Farr
> Sergeant G. Johnson (B Company), and Sergeant R. Thomas 78, Colour Party
> 250 Other Ranks.

H.E. the Viceroy complimented the battalion on the smartness of the Guard of Honour. Colonel Worgan, the Military Secretary, and the A.D.C. said they had not seen such a smart guard and such smart sentries in India. The heat was terrific but at no time was there any slacking off in keenness. Those not on guard were taken on a tour of Baroda City in lorries and watched the State sports tournament. The Guard returned on 27 January 1926.[57]

On 2 February the battalion was inspected by the G.O.C.-in-C. Western Command, who reported that the battalion 'drilled well – its interior economy is good – the turnout was good and it seems well commanded'.[58]

The Warrant Officers' and Sergeants' Mess Ball on St David's Day was attended by all Officers and their wives from Nasirabad, the Agent to the Governor General of Sind-Rajputana, and the Commissioner for Ajmer-Merwara. The

March 1926

---

*   Later Hon Brigadier General Sir Standish George Gage Crauford, 5th Bt (of Kilbirnie) CB CMG CIE DSO, late *Gordon Hldrs* (1872–1935).
†   Major General Herbert Fothergill Cooke CB CSI CBE DSO (1871–1936).
‡   Lieutenant General Sir (Warren) Hastings Anderson KCB (1872–1930).
§   General Sir Charles Harington GCB GBE DSO DCL (1872 –1940), commanded British forces in Turkey during the Chanak crisis. He became Governor of Gibraltar in 1933.

The Royal Welch Fusiliers.
Winners of All India Boxing Championship
1926.

The 1st Battalion boxing team, All-India Champions 1926. (R.W.F. Mus)

event was somewhat overshadowed by news of the death, on 26 February, of Lieutenant General Sir Francis Lloyd, Colonel of the Regiment, after a long and painful illness.

On 12 March the battalion side was defeated in the final of the Western Command Football Championships by the 1st Cameronians after extra time. On the previous day, the final had ended in a draw, but bad light precluded extra time being played. On 20 March, however, the boxing team, led by Lieutenant M.H. Ap Rhys Pryce and trained by Sergeant E.T. Morse, continued its progress by winning the All India Army Championships at Rawalpindi, with 2nd R.U.R. as runners-up, and 2nd Hampshires 3rd. In the individual competitions, Fusilier Edwards 72 (Light Heavy) won the Scots Belt, and Fusilier Griffiths 58 (Middle) won the Locks Elliot Belt.

On 22 March, the battalion received its Annual Inspection from the Commander Nasirabad Brigade Area, after which the Commander wrote 'to convey to your Bn his appreciation of its general efficiency which has reached a high standard in the field, on parade and in interior economy'.[59] The strength of the battalion on 30 June was reported as follows: W.O. I – two; W.O. II – 6; Staff Sergeants and Sergeants – thirty-three; drummers – sixteen; junior N.C.Os and Fusiliers – 828, a total of 885, not including Officers, against an establishment of twenty-eight Officers and 881 men.[60]Little activity other than interior economy was undertaken throughout the hot weather, however the Digest of Service did note that 'Owing to the fact that 160 ranks were treated for dog-bite during 1926, the number of dogs per Company and H.Q. Wing is reduced to 8'. Many men went on leave during this time, usually to the leave depot at Kasauli in the lower Himalayas. Four Fusiliers once hired a bullock wagon, loaded it with camp gear, food, shotguns, rifles and beer, and went off for a four-week trek around the country.[61] The Officers could ride and play polo, usually early in the morning, and in the cold weather there was excellent duck shooting nearby. Polo, hunting, and riding generally, were very much required of an Officer. Indeed on 24 March 1924, the A.A. & Q.M.G. of Lahore District had issued an order to the effect that 'The G.O.C. is not prepared to recommend as a candidate for the Staff College any Officer who cannot give proof of his capacity to ride hard and securely over an ordinary country.'[62] The then Second Lieutenant J.G. Vyvyan recalled that:

> The first thing the Adjutant ["Hoppy" Hopkins] said to me was "Well Vyvyan, you play polo?" We all had to subscribe to the Polo Club whether we played polo, wanted a pony, or not. Anyway the Polo Club supplied me with a pony, and three times a week one used to play; the other days one used to train one's pony. One never played tennis or golf; that was "not done, my dear".[63]

In December, the M.C.C., which was touring India, played two matches at Ajmer. Nearly 400 members of the battalion were present **December 1926** on each of the four day games. Afterwards, RSM Whyley received a letter from Mr A.E.R. Gilligan, Captain of the M.C.C. team saying that: 'I can tell you that we all very much appreciated the great interest shown by yourself, the Sergeants' Mess, and the Rank and File, and helped us tremendously to achieve a good victory'.[64] At Christmas there was an All Ranks Dance, a concert by A Company's concert party, and a well-received Illusionist Show by Fusilier Tipper. The children's Christmas tree party had to be postponed until 11 January because of a delay in the arrival of mail, which included the presents.

The proclamation parade was held as usual on 1 January 1927 and on the 14th, the battalion was inspected by the G.O.C Sind-Rajputana **January 1927** District. On 28 January, two Guards were provided for the unveiling of the 6th Rajputana Rifles War Memorial at Nasirabad. On 31 January, the battalion's reported strength had declined slightly: the figures were given as follows: W.O. I – two; W.O. II – six; Staff Sergeants and Sergeants – thirty-three; Drummers – sixteen; Junior N.C.Os and Fusiliers – 809, a total of 866, without Officers.[65]

On 26 February 1927, Nasirabad Brigade Area ceased to exist; 1 R.W.F. was placed under H.Q. Central Provinces District, with its Headquarters at Mhow. A series of inspections followed. The Annual Administrative Inspection was conducted by Colonel Commandant Crauford on 5 March; another inspection by Major General W.M. St G. Kirke,* Deputy C.G.S. India was held on 28 March, and a tactical exercise carried out the next day.

Summer scale routine began on 24 April with the dreaded spine pads taken into use a month later. A most successful Military Tattoo **April–August 1927** was held at Mount Abu under Major J.G. Bruxner-Randall, as a result of which 600 Rupees (£60) were handed over to the Regimental History Fund. On 6 August, the battalion completed its re-equipment with the new model of the *Lee-Enfield* rifle (See Chapter 3). On 6 August, new rules concerning education for promotion issued. C.O. decided that no N.C.O. would in future be considered for promotion to CQMS unless he was in possession of a 1st Class Certificate of Education. Lance-Corporals and Fusiliers who did not obtain a 3rd Class Certificate within

*   Later General Sir Walter Mervyn St George Kirke GCB CMG DSO (1877 –1949. He was Commander in Chief British Home Forces during the Second World War.

their first three years of service, and 2nd Class within their first four years, were henceforth to attend school for two hours every afternoon except Thursdays and Sundays.

Following a directive from the C.O., the first silver canes for the best guard turn-out were presented to 4071518 Fusilier G. Jones (A Company), and 4179010 Fusilier H. Edwards (B Company). The Goat having died, application was made for a replacement from the Royal Herd; however the Lord Chamberlain's response was that goats sent to India did not fare well, and that the battalion should obtain a goat from Kashmir for the duration of its service abroad.[66]

The battalion's short stay in Nasirabad was already drawing to a close and on 16 October, the Advance Party left for the new **October–November 1927** station, Quetta, under Captain H.C. Watkins and Captain and Quartermaster G.M. Schofield. On the 31st, the battalion was inspected by Lieutenant General Sir Harold Walker, G.O.C-in-C., Southern Command.[*] A and B Companies, and the *Vickers* guns then went off to Bithur Camp for Field Firing; D Company replaced A and B on 23 November, returning on the 30th. Earlier in the year, the C.O. had directed the establishment of a savings scheme for soldiers known as the Thrift Fund. On 28 August a letter was received from Field Marshal Sir William Birdwood, C.-in-C. India, conveying 'his appreciation of your efforts to organise a Thrift Association in the unit under your command. He especially notes that your scheme has only been recently introduced and trusts that it may progress till every man of the unit is a subscriber. He hears on all sides that the success of this scheme is extremely beneficial and much appreciated by the men themselves when they go to civil life'. By 7 December, the fund had 465 depositors and amounted to 73,465 Rupees.[†]

Christmas was again celebrated in Nasirabad; on Christmas Eve, eight men were discharged at the end of their term of service and took **December 1922** advantage of a scheme being offered by the Government of Australia to emigrate there. At the end of the year, battalion strength had increased through drafts received to the following: W.O. I – two; W.O. II – seven; Staff Sergeants and Sergeants – thirty-three; Drummers – sixteen; Junior N.C.O.s and Fusiliers – 866, a total of 924, not including Officers.[67] In addition, the battalion had a platoon of Indian soldiers attached, under a *jemadar* (lieutenant), with three *havildars* (Sergeants), two *naiks* (Corporals) and thirty-four sepoys.

After Christmas and the Proclamation Parade, the Annual Inspection for 1928 took place on 13 January and was conducted by Major General **January 1928** H.E. Hendon.[‡] This took the form of a tactical scheme in the morning, and all Officers were interviewed in the afternoon. A week later, on 20 January, the battalion left Nasirabad in two trains for Quetta, crossing the desert to Hyderabad where the troops transferred into two different trains for the onward journey to Quetta, where they arrived on 23 January 1928.

---

[*]   Lieutenant General Sir Harold Bridgwood Walker KCB KCMG DSO (1862 –1934) had commanded 1st Australian Division during the Great War.

[†]   About £7,400 – approximately £300,000 at 2018 values.

[‡]   No biographical details found.

Staff List, 1 R.W.F. Nasirabad, 1925–1928

Lieutenant Colonel
H.V. Venables Kyrke DSO
Major
C.H. Edwards
J.G. Bruxner-Randall (Oct 26)
G.E.R. De Miremont DSO MC
(May 26)
Bt Lt Col P.R. Butler DSO
Captain
H.C. Watkins MC (Mar 27)
F.S. Lanigan-O'Keeffe MBE
(Maj Aug 27)
E. Wodehouse
S.O. Jones MC
W.P. Kenyon MC (Apr 26)
J.A. Pringle MC (Nov 27)
H.B. Harrison MC
Quartermaster
Capt G.M. Schofield MBE
Attached
WO II D. Mahoney *A.E.C.*
AQMS G. Lloyd (Jan 27)
SSgt Jenkins *R.A.O.C.*
(to Jan 27)
S.C. Fosdike *I.A.R.O.*
(Aug 1927)
2Lt F.T.A. McCammon *I.A.*
(Oct 27)
2Lt A.R.Green *I.A.* (Oct 27)
2Lt F.J. Whittington *I.A.*
(Oct 27)

Lieutenant
B.H.R. Hopkins (Adjt from Jul 25)
C.A. Anglesea-Sandels MBE MC (to
Dec 25)
M.B. Dowse
B.L.N. Trotman-Dickenson
T.S. Griffiths (to Aug 25)
D.R. Evans
M.H. ap Rhys Pryce
H.A. Freeman MC
M.W. Whittaker
G.E. Cardwell MC
(to Sep 27)
M.B. Dowse (to Apr 26)
R.G. Davies-Jenkins
2nd Lieutenant
J.G. Vyvyan
J.H. Lipscombe (Lt Apr 26)
P.L. Bowers
E.M. Davies-Jenkins
T.W.L. Grey-Edwards
(to Dec 1927)
S. Goodchild
T.D. Butler (May 26)
H.A.S. Clarke
RFA David (Mar 27)

W.O. I
RSM G.R. Whyley
BM H.P.G. Perdue ARCM
W.O. II
J.M. Kensett
W.J. Swann (to Jul 26)
CQMS
J.J. Hall DCM
S. Sherriff
T. Ledington DCM
V. Smart (Oct 26)
Staff Sergeants
Band Sgt W. Tubby
ORS H.F. Bradstreet
Pnr Sgt A.C. Richards DCM
Sergeants
G. Johnson
R. Thomas 78
H.E.Spalding DCM
- Jefferies
W. Edwards 26
- Hughes
J. O'Brien
E. Davies 49
P. Sullivan
E. Davies 17
Morrissey
Hill 39
Lance-Sergeants
- Taylor
Davies 26
C. Kelly

v. Quetta, 1928–1930

Quetta, in Baluchistan, on the North-West Frontier of India, was to be the battalion's final station of its twelve years' service in India. Quetta, unlike the battalion's previous stations, was a major garrison containing two infantry brigades and some divisional troops units, as well as No 3 Wing of the R.A.F. in India. Here, 1 R.W.F. joined 4 (Quetta) Infantry Brigade, along with the 2/10th Gurkhas and the 4/15th Punjabis, and occupied White Barracks on the north-east side of the cantonments. The brigade was commanded by Colonel Commandant E.C. Alexander,[*] who was succeeded in May 1928 by Brigadier H.C. Duncan[†] – the rank of Brigadier having been reintroduced on 1 April 1928. In 1929, Duncan was succeeded by

[*]   Brigadier E.C. Alexander CIE DSO. No further biographical details found.
[†]   Brigadier Herbert Cecil Duncan OBE (1895 –1942) commanded 45 Indian Infantry Brigade during the Battle of Malaya. During the retreat from the Muar River on 19 January Duncan was badly concussed during an air attack on his headquarters. The following day, during an attempt to breakout of a Japanese encirclement in concert with Australian forces, he was killed whilst mounting a counter-attack against a Japanese attack on the brigade's rear.

Brigadier E.C. Gepp.[*] 4 Brigade was in turn subordinated to the 2nd Indian Division under Major General J.W. O'Dowda,[†] which, like Nasirabad, was within Western Command. Given the proximity of Quetta to the frontier, there was much more emphasis on collective training for war here, rather than internal security, than in Multan or Nasirabad. The battalion was joined by a platoon of Jats who replaced the platoon which had been under command in Nasirabad. The Jats looked after the M.G. Platoon's mules. This platoon remained with the battalion for the rest of its service in India, commanded by an N.C.O. known as 'Old Bill' because of his resemblance to Bruce Bairnsfather's character. 'One day he shut his moustache in the bolt of his rifle, much to the amusement of all.'[68]

It was cold and wet on arrival in Quetta and on the following day there was snow on the ground, for the climate here was pleasant and dry, although up to 100°F (38°C) in summer and below freezing in winter. White Barracks consisted of the usual thick-walled single-storey accommodation for the soldiers but there was electricity. Training facilities and ranges were excellent. Being a large station, Quetta had an active social life for all ranks. The Officers hunted with the Quetta hounds, played polo three times a week, and shot hill grouse and

The 1st Battalion's calendar for 1928.

duck. One could motor to Chaman on the Afghan border and, in the right season, train loads of peaches and grapes came from Khandahar. The soldiers had the Sandes Soldiers Home, a club run by English ladies, but there were also 'inspected brothels in the town.'[69] Health was generally good, although on 27 January, just after the battalion arrived, 4179472 Fusilier E. Cullen (A Company) died of carbon monoxide poisoning.

Members of the Jat Platoon, attached to 1 R.W.F., whose task was to care for the transport animals. (R.W.F. Mus)

*   Later Major General Sir Ernest Cyril Gepp KBE CB DSO (1879–1964).
†   Later Lieutenant General Sir James Williamson O'Dowda KCB CSI CMG, late *Queen's Own* (1877–1961).

The Brigade Commander carried out a ceremonial inspection on 8 February. On 14 March, Sir Charles Harington attended the W.Os' and Sergeants' Mess St David's Day Ball. On 12 April, B and C Companies marched to camp at Kach Road, returning on 2 May; A and D Companies then went to camp until the 24th. Four days later, **February–March 1928** the whole brigade turned out for a ceremonial parade followed on 30 May by a brigade night operations exercise.[70] The next day, A Company won the Regimental Cup at the Baluchistan District Assault-at-Arms Competition. The brigade night operations exercise was followed by a divisional scheme on the same subject on 13 June, between 20.00 and 07.30 hrs.

On 27 June, a Torchlight Tattoo was held. The Band, in period dress, and the Welsh Choir gave very effective performances in **June–July 1928** a Battle of Waterloo musical piece. On the 29th, the Polo Team won the Cadet College Polo Tournament and in July, followed this up by winning the Quetta Handicap Tournament and in August they won the Zero Polo Team tournament at the Quetta Horse Show.

Another divisional night operations exercise was held on 2 July; the battalion covered 20 miles (32 kilometres) between 15.30 hrs on the 2nd and 04.00 hrs on the 3rd. On 20 July, the R.A.F. gave a demonstration of machine gunning and bombing and on the 25th, the battalion took part in a mountain warfare scheme. The G.O.C. inspected the battalion in marching order on 10 August. On the 14th, at about 05.30 hrs, the Goat was killed by some wild animal, possibly

The King's Birthday Parade, Quetta, 1928.

The Goat of the 1st Battalion which died in India in 1928.

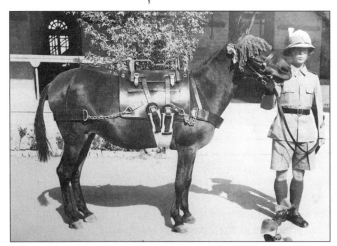

A pack mule prepared for the
Quetta Horse Show. (R.W.F. Mus)

A pair of mules prepared for the
Quetta Horse Show. (R.W.F. Mus)

A Company Officers and Sergeants,
1 R.W.F., c. 1928, showing the
tropical mess dress then worn
by both messes. (Norman Weale
Collection)

a wolf or hyena. On 20 August, a battalion field firing scheme was carried out, supported by 18 pdrs and 3.75 mm pack howitzers. The rest of August was given over to a full and varied programme of training and recreation: rifle classification was completed; all companies carried out field firing; battalion route marches were held once a week and company schemes were run in preparation for manoeuvres. There were also ceremonial parades once a week. All junior Officers were required to attend T.E.W.Ts, military law lectures and an examination by the Assistant Judge Advocate General. Much cricket was played and several dances held at which Regimental dance band and C Company's band played. An open-air concert was laid on in aid of the Regimental History Fund, at which the best talent in Quetta gave their services free. Finally, in the Quetta Horse Show, the battalion came first in the *Vickers* gun Mules, and 3rd in *Lewis* gun Mules. Several individual prizes were won by Officers.[71]

D Company 1 R.W.F. lining up for dinner in Camp at Gwal during manoeuvres in 1928.

A Company 1 R.W.F. on the march, manoeuvres, 1928.

September 1928

The busy programme continued during September. On the 1st, there was a battalion route march and tent pitching practice; a rifle meeting on the 6th; and field manoeuvres which began on the 12th when the battalion marched to the 12th milestone on the Pishin Road. The next day, another thirteen miles (21 kilometres) were covered, marching to Yaru, and on the 14th, a further twelve miles (19 kilometres) to Spring Camp. The marching was 'very good throughout.' There were two cases of fever but no one fell out. The Drums accompanied the battalion and played steadily.[72] At camp, from 15 to 26 September, training was conducted in 'civilised' – that is, European, warfare. There were battalion and brigade schemes and small column exercises and the battalion had the chance to work in co-operation with, and in operations against, cavalry, tanks and aircraft. On 27 September, the battalion marched ten miles (16 kilometres) to Shal Mills and another seven miles (11 kilometres) the next day to Manzanai, under 'service' conditions. This took from 08.00 to 15.00 hrs, as all picquets were opposed by an enemy force which had to be cleared.

From 29 September, the battalion began training in frontier warfare, first building a secure perimeter and settling in. From 1 to 7 October, training was carried out in mountain warfare. The Digest of Service reported that:

The Bn gained a very high reputation especially with regard to rapidity. On 4 Oct the GOC-in-C, Sir C Harington, and Gen O'Dowda watched a demonstration by the brigade of village burning. Bn provided covering troops and its withdrawal at speed gained high praise. Considerable experience was gained in picqueting and perimeter camp routine. A swimming pool was discovered ¼ mile up the nullah and was used daily by the Bn.

On 8 October the brigade marched back to Shal Mills, where on the following day an inter-brigade exercise against 5 Infantry Brigade, **October 1928** with 1 R.W.F. acting as 4 Brigade's Advance Guard, began. The battalion marched into camp at Pishin at 15.00 hrs. On 12 October, divisional manoeuvres began. At 07.15 hrs, the battalion moved from the 31st milestone as part of the main body. About 11.00 hrs, two companies deployed and drove the enemy from small hills on the left flank, rejoining the main body at about 13.00 hrs at the 24th milestone. At 17.00 hrs, the battalion reached the 18th milestone, where a two-hour halt was called. At dusk (about 19.00 hrs), orders were received to take over the outpost line from 5 Brigade. Two companies were in position by 19.30 hrs, and the remainder by 21.30 hrs, having passed the whole of 5 Brigade in the dark. After hot tea, bully beef and biscuits, two companies went on reconnaissance at midnight. They reached Kutchlagh (at the 14th milestone) with Brigade Headquarters, and were joined at 07.15 hrs on 13 September by the remainder of the battalion which had left at 06.00 hrs and covered five miles (eight kilometres) along the railway track in 1¼ hours. At 08.30 hrs the battalion took over the left of the divisional front with its left on the Quetta road. At 11.00 hrs, the whole division began to advance. After some opposition it reached the forming-up point for the final assault on Baleli Ridge at 14.30 hrs. This took place at 15.00 hrs and at 15.30 hrs the 'no parade' was blown, signalling the end of the exercise. After a halt for tea from the Contractor at the 8th milestone, the battalion moved off at 16.30 hrs and was met by the Band at the 6th milestone. After marching past the G.O.C.-in-C. at Sheikh Manda, and with only one ten-minute halt, the battalion reached White Barracks at 19.15 hrs.[73]

From 5 to 10 November, the Western Command Rifle Meeting was held. Thereafter, the leave season for non-commissioned ranks began **November 1928** and a large part of A Company went on furlough. Meanwhile, a very successful section leaders' cadre, which had been begun during the brigade and divisional manoeuvres, continued until 22 December, being visited on 11 December by the G.O.C. who watched bayonet fighting, P.T. and drill. The programme had included two days field firing, night firing, night operations, and three days of examinations. 'All passed successfully and the standard was good'.[74]

Christmas was celebrated in Quetta. At the end of the year, battalion strength had declined a little, probably due to furlough, and was reported as follows: W.O. I – two; W.O. II – five; Staff Sergeants and Sergeants – thirty-three; Drummers – fifteen; Junior N.C.Os and Fusiliers – 764, a total, excluding Officers, of 819.[75]

1929 opened with bitter blizzards from 27 to 31 January; the battalion concentrated on individual training, during which the Brigade Commander's Annual Inspection took place on 11 February. Soccer, hockey and rugby were played on every available occasion, and boxing also re-commenced. On 1 March, St David's **January–March 1929** Day was celebrated: hounds met at the Officers' Mess. On 15 March the G.O.C. ran a short exercise to test his brigadiers, during which the battalion covered twenty miles (32 kilometres).

D Company's mess set for Christmas dinner, 1928. (R.W.F. Mus)

On 4 April, Brigadier Gepp, the new Brigade Commander, was welcomed with a Ceremonial Parade. The following day, an unofficial start was made to forming the new M.G. Company out of D Coy, under Captain E. Wodehouse (See Chapter 3); the official date for the adoption of the new establishment was 1 July. On 6 April, a new distribution of areas and infantry units within the District to Brigades for administration and training came into effect. 4 (Quetta) Infantry Brigade now comprised 1 R.W.F., 4/15th Punjabis, 5/5th Royal Mahratta L.I. all barracked in Quetta; and 1/7th Gurkha and 2/19th Hyderabadis in Chaman. 5 (Quetta) Infantry Brigade comprised the 1st East Lancashires, 1/10th Gurkhas, 2/10th Gurkhas and the Hazara Pioneers, all in Quetta; and 2/4th Bombay Grenadiers at Pishin and Hindubagh.

4 April 1929

On 8 April, A and C Companies marched to Spring Camp at the 7th milestone on the Hanna Road. Here, the companies carried out section, platoon and company training in all phases of war, in open and mountain warfare. To get sub-units up to strength was a problem because of the '140-odd Garrison employed'.[76] On the 28th, A and C Companies changed with B and D Companies, who returned to barracks on 18 May. The Corps of Drums, which attended this camp, was trained in intelligence duties. D Company, No 2 Group of H.Q. Wing, and an attached Indian platoon trained together as the M.G. Company.

Meanwhile, on 15 April, a lecture was given by the C.G.S. India on 'Mechanisation in India' to all Officers and Warrant Officers in Quetta. Summer dress – K.D. in place of serge – came into wear on 23 April. On 4 June, the battalion put on a demonstration of laying out a night forming-up line for a dawn attack to the rest of 4 Infantry Brigade. This was followed on 14 June by an artillery demonstration attended by all Officers, Warrant Officers and N.C.Os.

Following the death of the goat in the previous year, a male and a female goat arrived from Ladha, 'but owing to some mistake the male goat's horns are so twisted it is impossible for him to appear on parade. Hopes of breeding are entertained'.[77] On 17 June, the battalion team beat the East Lancashires to win the District Boxing Tournament. In the nine weights of the individual novices and opens, the battalion had sixteen winners and runners up.

June 1929

On 3 and 10 July, there were brigade night exercises and on the 12th, several Officers attended an artillery shoot cooperating with aircraft. This was followed by a 'very instructive' day on 22 July when twenty-eight Officers and N.C.Os were given aircraft flights to study the appearance of the ground from the air. On 31st, a divisional night operations exercise took place. 5 Brigade attacked at 19.00hrs, 1 R.W.F. having carried out a reconnaissance before dark. The exercise was felt to be: 'Very realistic. Hostile artillery fire (smoke puffs), own barrage (smoke candles), guns, traffic, prisoners, casualties, etc. Bn moved out of barracks at 03.00 on 1 Aug. On forming-up line at 0500. Zero 05.30. Went straight through and "Cease Fire" blew 06.10. Marched straight back.'[78]

July 1929

A battalion night operations exercise was held on 6 August against a skeleton enemy force from 4/15th Punjabis. The exercise was set by the brigade commander: 'A successful night march across country followed by an attack at dawn. Bn waited on forming-up line from 04.00 to 05.40. Very cold.'[79] On 20th, an artillery and mountain warfare scheme was conducted under the G.O.C. The battalion's M.Gs and the guns of 9th Mountain Battery fired live ammunition.

August 1929

On 28 August the battalion trooped its Regimental Colour, which was the last major event of Lieutenant Colonel Kyrke's five years in command. Kyrke addressed the battalion for the last time on the 31st and on 1 September, Lieutenant Colonel E.O. Skaife assumed command.

The build-up to brigade and divisional training now began once more. On 7 September the battalion conducted a route march to the 8th milestone on the Quetta-Urak Road. On the 9th, a mountain warfare scheme was conducted around Spin Karez in the Hanna Valley, from 06.40 to 13.30 hrs. On the 11th, an attack scheme was conducted towards Sheikh Manda. On the 13th, Battalion H.Q. and M.G. Company took part in another artillery and M.G. attack scheme firing live ammunition.

September 1929

From 16 to 18 September, the battalion practised the occupation of, and withdrawal from, a camp in mountain warfare. The battalion moved off at 08.00 hrs, 480 strong, and with a train of carts and camels two miles (3 kilometres) long. During the withdrawal, ball ammunition was fired by the *Vickers* guns and the rearguard.

The battalion now had a short respite until 3 October, when it marched to Baleli Camp for manoeuvres. On the 4th, a twenty-four hour brigade exercise was conducted followed on 9 October by a three-day exercise to test the efficiency of a brigade column with full transport and artillery train against a mobile enemy with cavalry, mechanised artillery, armoured cars, and lorried infantry. Both sides used aircraft. The battalion struck tents at 05.45 hrs and marched at 07.30. With a section of mountain artillery, it acted as flank guard to the brigade's transport, which extended for 21,000 yards (twelve miles, or 19 kilometres). When, that night, the battalion halted it was in a defensive position on the left flank. It was a cold night and because of a mistake unloading the Divisional Train the troops had to sleep in their greatcoats. On 10 October there was an advance, followed, at 13.30 hrs, by a brigade frontal attack, and another general advance of ten miles (sixteen

October 1929

kilometres) with periodic skirmishes against cavalry. Contact with the enemy was lost and that night the brigade went into camp at Khanai Railway Station. On 11 October, the advance continued across country because of the presence of hostile aircraft. When the exercise ended, the battalion marched to Zarghun where the brigade camped for the night. The next day they marched to Balozai.[80]

Three days later, on 14 October, there was another brigade exercise, this time for twenty-four hours, and on the 16th, the battalion marched to Gwal where, for the first time since 8 October, the Officers and men slept under canvas. The next day the battalion took part in a divisional entrenching exercise for twenty-four hours. By 20 October, however, because of mandatory duties, the battalion was reduced to 226 fighting men, of whom ninety were in D (M.G.) Company. Even so, the battalion took part in the divisional exercise from 22 to 24 October. The Digest of Service reported that 'Many lessons were learnt on this exercise and the Bn had a strenuous 3 days. The initiative and rapidity of action of members of the baggage guard when the Div Train was attacked was a source of much congratulation for the Bn'.[81]

On 25 October the battalion marched twenty-one miles to Kuchlagh (33 kilometres). The Drums played throughout and the Band met the battalion five miles (eight kilometres) from camp. The next day, the battalion marched the fifteen miles (24 kilometres) back to Quetta. Throughout the period of training, the battalion had forty-three casualties, including two Officers, 'but most were old malaria cases'.[82]

Back in barracks, the Annual Inspection for the year by Brigadier Gepp was advanced to 5 November. From the 18th to the 23rd, the battalion won twelve individual prizes in the Western Command **November 1929**
Rifle Meeting. At the end of the year, according to the Digest of Service, battalion strength was as follows: W.O. I – two; W.O. II – six; Staff Sergeants and Sergeants – thirty-four; Drummers – sixteen; Junior N.C.Os and Fusiliers – 923, a total of 981, excluding Officers. However according to the return in W.O. 73/130, the total only six weeks before had been twenty-six Officers and 862 men – a significant discrepancy.

The Proclamation Parade, 1 January 1930. (Norman Weale Collection)

After Christmas, 1930 began with a series of route marches during January and February, during which the columns were attacked by **January–March 1930** aircraft with simulated bombs and machine-guns. In February, the first sanction was given to the use of company badges, which would continue in use until the end of the life of the Regiment. These are described in the chapter on Regimental Matters.[83] This scheme was later adopted throughout the Regiment and added to Regimental Standing Orders.[84]

On St David's Day, a Goat, which had been obtained locally in Sind, made its first public appearance. On 5 March, the boxing team defeated the Northumberland Fusiliers in the final of the Burt Institute Team Competition at Lahore.

On 1 April, B and C Companies marched off once more to Kutchlagh Camp where they carried out tactical training, changing with A Company on 7 May. There were clearly some disciplinary problems among the Officers. On 12 May, a General Court Martial was convened, at which Second Lieutenant J.H. Woods was dismissed the service for drunkenness. A second entry in the Digest of Service states that Major F.S. Lanigan O'Keeffe was 'removed from the Army with effect from 8 February 1930'.

On 16 May a new Regimental Goat, born on Dinas Bodwaen, Caernarvonshire on 1 March 1929, arrived at Quetta, displacing the **April 1930** locally recruited animal; this poor goat did not last long, however – it died of gastritis on 24 August. On the 21st, A and D Companies gave an excellent Gymkhana Meeting at Camp. The events included wrestling on mules, an obstacle race, *Vickers* gun race, and musical chairs on mules. The Band played. The two companies returned to Quetta on 26 May 1930, after carrying out a combined exercise.

On 28 May the whole battalion left barracks for an exercise, using pack mule transport only, spending the night at Urak and marching **May 1930** to Sra Khulla the following day. Here, a perimeter wall was built and picqueting practised. The battalion returned to Quetta on the 30th via the Kach Road, where the battalion marched past the G.O.C.

A week later, on 6 June, the battalion left barracks at 04.00 hrs to carry out an attack towards Baleli which ended by 09.30. On the 12th, **June 1930** the alarm was sounded at 02.30 hrs, and at 03.15 hrs, the battalion marched to the railway station and entrained, with its mules and carts, in less than an hour (fifty-seven minutes exactly). It then detrained and marched back to barracks.[85]

During June, there was much emphasis on sports and games. On the 13th, the Polo team defeated the Scinde Horse 7-1 in the final of the Quetta Cadet Polo Tournament. The team consisted of Major E. Wodehouse, Captain H.A. Freeman, Lieutenant M.F.P. Lloyd, and Lieutenant R.F.A. David. Cricket matches were played nearly every Thursday and Sunday, and games within the battalion were played almost every afternoon. Boxing and athletics training was carried out daily 'with great zeal by all ranks'.[86] On 10 July, the boxing team beat the 1st Devons 6-2 to win the Inter-Unit Shield in the District Boxing Tournament. Twenty out of twenty-seven finalists in the Open and Novices tournaments were members of 1 R.W.F.

At the beginning of July, brigade and divisional training once more began. On the 2nd, a divisional night operations exercise was held. **July 1930** The Digest of Service reported that: 'The Brigade Commander was very pleased with the way in which the men worked. Owing to careful attention to orders on the part of all ranks the operations went according to plan. March discipline was very good and the men were very quiet'.

On 5 August, orders were received for the battalion to be at six hours notice to move for I.S. duties at Sukkur. However from 16 to 19 **August 1930**

1 R.W.F. in Camp during the 1930 manoeuvres. (R.W.F. Mus)

August, about 300 men – almost the whole available strength of the battalion – took part in the Quetta Tattoo. The battalion contributed a 'Modern Guard' with the Goat, Pioneers, Band and Drums. B Company supplied a company of British troops for the attack on a village in a set-piece demonstration. A choir of 150 sang *Ar Hyd y Nos* and *Mae Hen Wlad Fy Nhadau* 'with great effect'. [87] The Quetta Horse Show was again held on 26 August. Battalion successes included winning the *Vickers* gun mules, the anti-tank carts, and the 'Handy Hunters' won by Major E. Wodehouse; the *Lewis* gun mules came second.

Field Firing exercises began on 23 August and ran through until 13 September, with each company spending five days on the range, and on 7 and 8 September, the brigade M.G. Concentration was held at Baleli. Western Command conducted a Staff Exercise involving battalion H.Q. and D (M.G.) Company for three days from 14–17 September.

Autumn training began on 24 September, but with Major Bruxner-Randall in command, as Lieutenant Colonel Skaife was in hospital with a broken leg. That day, the battalion, 548 strong, marched seventeen-and-a-half miles (28 kilometres). The following day, the battalion marched another fourteen-and-a-half miles (23 kilometres) to Saranan. On the 26th, nineteen miles (30 kilometres) to Killa Abdulla were covered in 'splendid going over hard flat desert … char-wallahs met us at 47 M.S. v welcome.'[88] The battalion made another eight miles (13 kilometres) to Camp Pani; and on 28 September, covered sixteen miles (25 kilometres) to Ting Kats via the Pasha Pass, at 1,500 feet (450 metres). During this series of marches, the battalion covered seventy-five miles (120 kilometres) and, with the exception of one man who sprained an ankle two miles out of Quetta, no one fell out. For the first time in India, the battalion experienced 2nd Line Motor Transport – but not for troop lift.[89]

September 1930

Battalion training until 4 October included attack, outposts, advance guard action, rearguards and defence.[90] Brigade training, from 6 to 12 October, included night advance and dawn attack schemes. During the second brigade exercise a new arrangement for feeding the battalion was tried out by the C.O. Instead of carrying haversack rations which became dry and unsavoury by the time they were eaten,

October 1930

A section of A Company at Kuchlak, 1930. (R.W.F. Mus 4157)

Drumhead service in the field, Baluchistan, 1930. (Norman Weale Collection)

1 R.W.F. on manœuvres, Quetta. (R.W.F. Mus 4157)

1 R.W.F. leaving Quetta, 28 November 1930. (R.W.F. Mus 4157)

rations (bully beef, bread and butter) were carried on two pack-mules per company. It proved an unqualified success and was much appreciated by the men.

There was a short break for recreation from 13 to 16 October, during which three boxing competitions were held. A few soldiers accompanied Officers when shooting *chikor* (partridges) and one fishing party brought back a complete mule load of fish. There was much bathing in a pool built by the Hazara Pioneers.

Another series of punishing marches began on 17 October, when the battalion marched twenty-two miles (35 kilometres) to Killa Abdulla and seven miles (11 kilometres) to Badwan on the 18th: 'Dust simply unbelievable all afternoon till about 6.00 p.m… men all dug themselves in and/or built sangars. Officers all bathed in a lorry two at a time. Great scheme.'[91] Eight miles (12 kilometres) were covered the next day as far as Shingari North. These marches were immediately followed by a brigade exercise from 20 to 22 October, after which the battalion marched seventeen-and-a-half miles (28 kilometres) and bivouacked. On 24 October, the battalion marched back to barracks in Quetta at the close of the autumn training period.[92]

On 10 November, the Annual Administrative Inspection was carried out by the brigade commander. Two weeks later,

November–December 1930

on 28 November, the battalion's farewell parade took place. The inspection was carried out by General Sir Charles Harington, G.O.C.-in-C. Western Command, accompanied by Major General O'Dowda. The battalion left Quetta on 8 December in two trains. The bands of the 1st Devons, 4/15th Punjabis, and 1/10th Gurkhas played the battalion on the march to the station. On 11 December 1930, 1 R.W.F. sailed from Karachi on the HT *Neuralia*. The battalion's strength on departure from India was reported as: fourteen Officers, eight Warrant Officers and 767 N.C.Os and Fusiliers.

Staff List, 1 R.W.F. Quetta, 1928–1930

Lieutenant Colonel
H.V. Venables Kyrke DSO
E.O. Skaife OBE (4 Sep 29)
Major
E.O. Skaife OBE (Aug 29)
C.H. Edwards (to Jun 29)
E. Wodehouse
J.G. Bruxner-Randall
F.S. Lanigan O'Keeffe MBE
   (to Feb 30)
Captain
H.A. Freeman MC (Adjt)
P.C. Kenyon MC
M.B. Dowse
B.H.R. Hopkins
J.A. Pringle MC (to Jul 30)
A.M.G. Evans (to Mar 29)
S.O. Jones MC (Mar 29)
G.F. Watson DSO (Oct 1929)
H.D.T. Morris
E.A. Morris MM (to Dec 30)
T.S. Griffiths (Dec 29)
Quartermaster
Capt G.M. Schofield MBE
(to Oct 29)
Lt G.R. Whyley (Feb 30)

Lieutenant
M.F.P. Lloyd (Dec 29, Adjt Sep 30)
R.F.A. David
J.G. Vyvyan
M.H. ap Rhys Pryce
(Adjt Jul 28–Sep 30)
R.J.F. Snead-Cox
D.R. Evans
P.L. Bowers
E.M. Davies-Jenkins
B.L.N. Trotman-Dickenson
T.D. Butler (Feb – Mar 30)
(to Apr 28)
M.W. Whittaker
G.R. Monkhouse
S. Goodchild (to Mar 29)
2nd Lieutenant
J.H. Woods (to May 30)
N.C. Stockwell (Mar 29)
J.H.T. Morris (to Nov 30)
E.H. Cadogan
S.C.H. Tighe (to Oct 29)
R.F.A. David (Lt Feb 30)
H.A.S. Clarke

W.O. I
RSM G.R. Whyley
RSM R.W. Chambers (Feb 30)
BM H.P.G. Perdue
W.O. II
E. Davies
J.M. Kensett
CQMS
Urquhart
Wilson
Fisher
Sergeants
S. Sherriff
Galbraith
Adams
Cheetham
Balfe
Johnson
Lance-Sergeants
Holmes
Attached
2Lt R.G. Hopkins *I.A.* (Apr 28)
2Lt D.D.H. Evans *I.A.*
   (Apr 28)
A.W. Percy *I.A.R.O.*
(May 28, Lt Jan 30)
2Lt C.F.D. Elliott *I.A.R.O.*
(Mar 29–Mar 30)
2 Lt Shiv Dev Verma *I.A.*
(Mar 29–Mar 30)
Lt J.B. McMurtrie *I.A.R.O.*
   (Capt Jan 30)
2Lt V.A. Wood *I.A.* (Mar 30)
2Lt C.E.S. Bentley *I.A.*[3]
Lt S.C. Fosdike *I.A.* (to Aug 30)

Table notes

1   Changed his name by deed poll to Trotman-Dickenson in May 1921.
2   Died of heat stroke on 8 July 1923 having been with the battalion throughout the Great War.
3   Died of typhoid fever, 8 August 1930 [1 R.W.F. Digest of Service].

Notes

1   R.W.F. Mus 4284/1; Interview by Lt Col L.J. Egan with Brig M.H. ap Rhys Pryce.
2   Interview by Lt Col L.J. Egan with Brig M.H. ap Rhys Pryce.
3   Brigadier G. Blight, *History of the Royal Berkshire Regiment 1920–1947* (London, 1953), p. 43.
4   T.N.A. WO 73/111–115 and 120–141, 1 R.W.F. Digest of Service.
5   Blight, p. 171.
6   Blight, pp. 46, 65.

7   Lawrence James, *Mutiny in the British and Commonwealth Forces 1797–1956* (London, 1987) p. 206 and T.N.A. WO 90/8, G.C.M.s abroad, 1917–1943.
8   A. Babington, *The Devil to Pay: the mutiny of the Connaught Rangers, India, July 1920* (Barnsley, 1991).
9   Letter from Sir Havelock Hudson to C.O. 1 R.W.F., 20 November 1920, in 1 R.W.F. Digest of Service.
10   1 R.W.F. Digest of Service.
11   1 R.W.F. Digest of Service.
12   Interview by Lt Col L.J. Egan with Maj P.C. Kenyon.
13   Captain R.M. Hall MC, 'Troop Trains in India', *R.U.S.I. Journal,* No LXXX (1935), p. 813; Interview by Lt Col L.J. Egan with Brig M.H. ap Rhys Pryce.
14   See, for example, Olaf Caroe, *The Pathans* (O.U.P., 1958) pp. 390–423.
15   *Y Ddraig Goch,* Series I, May 1922, pp. 4–5.
16   Interview by Lt Col L.J. Egan with Maj P.C. Kenyon.
17   J.C. Rowley 'Education on Active Service (Waziristan, 1921–1923)', *Journal of the Army Educational Corps,* Vol II No 1, March 1925, pp. 12–15.
18   *Y Ddraig Goch,* October 1922, p. 42, and 1 R.W.F. War Diary.
19   *The Times,* Monday 18 Aug 1922.
20   *Official History of Operations on the N.W. Frontier of India, 1920–1935* (New Delhi, 1945), pp. 9–28.
21   1 R.W.F. War Diary.
22   The account of the action at Split Hill is taken from 1 R.W.F. War Diary.
23   Major M. Everett DSO *RE, The Destruction of Makin – February 1923.* (A lecture given at the Staff College, Quetta).
24   *Official History*, pp. 26–27.
25   The citations appeared in the *London Gazette*, 13–18 September 1923.
26   *Official History*, pp. 27–28.
27   1 R.W.F. War Diary. The Official History says Jandoola.
28   1 R.W.F. War Diary and *Official History*, p. 28.
29   Attached to 1 R.W.F. War Diary.
30   *Y Ddaig Goch,* May 1924, p. 223.
31   Interview by Lt Col L.J. Egan with Brig M.H. ap Rhys Pryce.
32   Interview by Lt Col L.J. Egan with Brig M.H. ap Rhys Pryce.
33   *Y Ddaig Goch,* May 1923, p. 122.
34   *Y Ddaig Goch,* May 1924, p. 224.
35   1 R.W.F. Digest of Service.
36   1 R.W.F. Digest of Service.
37   1 R.W.F. Digest of Service.
38   1 R.W.F. Digest of Service.
39   *Y Ddaig Goch,* May 1924, pp. 227–228.
40   1 R.W.F. Digest of Service.
41   1 R.W.F. Digest of Service.
42   Interview by Lt Col L.J. Egan with Brig M.H. ap Rhys Pryce.
43   1 R.W.F. Digest of Service.
44   *Y Ddraig Goch, January 1925*, p. 292.
45   *Y Ddraig Goch, January 1925*, pp. 298–299.
46   1 R.W.F. Digest of Service.
47   1 R.W.F. Digest of Service.
48   1 R.W.F. Digest of Service.
49   1 R.W.F. Digest of Service.
50   P.R. Butler 'By Desert Waters' – A Memory of Multan,' *Y Ddraig Goch*, Series II, December 1933, pp. 195–196.
51   Interview by Lt Col L.J. Egan with Brig M.H. ap Rhys Pryce.
52   1 R.W.F. Digest of Service.
53   1 R.W.F. Digest of Service.
54   Interview by Lt Col L.J. Egan with Brig M.H. ap Rhys Pryce.

55   Interview by Lt Col L.J. Egan with Brig M.H. ap Rhys Pryce.
56   Interview by Lt Col L.J. Egan with Maj P.C. Kenyon.
57   1 R.W.F. Digest of Service.
58   1 R.W.F. Digest of Service.
59   1 R.W.F. Digest of Service.
60   1 R.W.F. Digest of Service; T.N.A. WO 73/123.
61   Interview by Lt Col L.J. Egan with Brig M.H. ap Rhys Pryce.
62   Order by Colonel E.C. Alexander, 24 March 1924.
63   Interview by Lt Col L.J. Egan with Lt Col J.G. Vyvyan.
64   1 R.W.F. Digest of Service.
65   1 R.W.F. Digest of Service.
66   1 R.W.F. Digest of Service.
67   1 R.W.F. Digest of Service.
68   Interview by Lt Col L.J. Egan with Brig M.H. ap Rhys Pryce.
69   Interview by Lt Col L.J. Egan with Brig M.H. ap Rhys Pryce.
70   1 R.W.F. Digest of Service.
71   1 R.W.F. Digest of Service.
72   1 R.W.F. Digest of Service.
73   1 R.W.F. Digest of Service.
74   1 R.W.F. Digest of Service.
75   1 R.W.F. Digest of Service.
76   1 R.W.F. Digest of Service.
77   1 R.W.F. Digest of Service.
78   1 R.W.F. Digest of Service.
79   1 R.W.F. Digest of Service.
80   1 R.W.F. Digest of Service.
81   1 R.W.F. Digest of Service.
82   1 R.W.F. Digest of Service.
83   1 R.W.F. Digest of Service.
84   *Regimental Standing Orders*, p. 71, 'The Parade Ground'.
85   1 R.W.F. Digest of Service.
86   1 R.W.F. Digest of Service.
87   1 R.W.F. Digest of Service.
88   M.H. Ap Rhys Pryce, *1930 Diary of Manoeuvres Sept 24th to Oct 23rd near Quetta, 1st Bn R.W. Fus* (R.W.F. Mus).
89   1 R.W.F. Digest of Service.
90   *1930 Diary of Manoeuvres.*
91   *1930 Diary of Manoeuvres.*
92   1 R.W.F. Digest of Service.

Chapter 6

The 1st Battalion in Sudan and on Internal Security Operations in Cyprus, 1930–1932

i. Sudan

Sudan is a huge country of approximately one million square miles (2.58 million square kilometres), roughly a quarter the size of Europe. Its greatest length north-south was 1,300 miles (2,080 kilometres) and east-west about 950 miles (1,520 kilometres). It was bordered to the north by Egypt, to the east by the Red Sea, Eritrea and Abyssinia, to the south by Kenya, Uganda and the Belgian Congo, and to the west by French Equatorial Africa and Libya. In 1930 it had a population of about 5,500,000 and was administered by a Governor General, and each of its fourteen provinces by a governor. There were few roads but thousands of miles of dry weather tracks.

Before the revolt of the Mahdi from 1881 to 1885, during which General Gordon was besieged and killed at Khartoum, it was known as Egyptian Sudan. Since its re-conquest by the Anglo-Egyptian expedition of 1896–1898 it had been under the joint sovereignty of Great Britain and Egypt. The limits of the condominium differed slightly from those of the Egyptian Sudan of the pre-Mahdi period. Sudan naturally fell into northern and southern Sudan, divided by the line of the Rivers Sobat – Bahr Al Arab. The northern zone of the country was a continuation of the Sahara Desert and here vegetation faded away and rainfall diminished as one got closer to the howling deserts of Libya. Almost all the people were Arabic speaking Muslims. By contrast, the southern zone was fertile, well-watered and in places densely forested. It lay wholly within the tropics and was very hot, even in winter, but as it is dry the climate is healthy. It belonged ethnologically to equatorial Africa of Uganda and Tanganyika and the native people were pagan black Africans. At Khartoum, the capital, the minimum temperature was 40°F (4.4 °C), the maximum 113°F (45 °C) and the mean annual 80°F (26.6 °C). January was the coldest month and June the hottest. Violent sandstorms were common from June to August, known as *haboob* – a wall of sand – which could travel at about 20–30 m.p.h. (35–50 k.p.h.) and lasted about three hours. Khartoum could expect about twenty-four of these each year. When the storm passed – as suddenly as it had come – it left sand in everyone's food, bed, and even in the most hermetically sealed safes.

For the size of country the garrison was tiny, consisting of only two British battalions (less one company detached in Cyprus); the Sudan Defence Force; and 47 (Bomber) Squadron R.A.F., all under the command of Brigadier S.S. Butler,* Commanding British Troops Sudan. The role of British troops was to guarantee the security of Khartoum and the road to Port Sudan. The Sudan Defence Force consisted of irregular mounted infantry, camelry and infantry, organised on a company basis and loosely grouped in various parts of the country; a large proportion of its Officers were British.[1] The Sudanese people appeared content with their British tutelage, and were obviously progressing towards a time when they would manage their own affairs.

Port Sudan, on the Red Sea, was always sticky and hot. In January the climate was tolerable for those already inured to tropical conditions. In Khartoum, the barracks were on the south bank of the Blue Nile. They were spacious, with wide verandas and some of the buildings were two-storied. Sand was everywhere, for the desert came up to the door. Outside the perimeter of wire and mud walls there were cactus plants, an odd palm tree, a string of camels, and little more.[2] Khartoum itself, at the junction of the Blue and White Niles, was a quiet pleasant city, but with little to offer the visitor. A tree-lined boulevard ran beside the Blue Nile, until it reached the White Nile, over which it was borne by a resilient bridge to Omdurman – a wholly native town, of considerable size. Along the boulevard were the Governor's Palace, official buildings and the residences of the principal officials. There were, elsewhere, three Cathedrals: Anglican, Catholic and Coptic; a college; and a colonnaded street of small shops. Life in Khartoum differed from that in India. As far as troops were concerned Khartoum was the Sudan, and the Sudan was Khartoum. There was no hill station and no different training area. There were three civil communities: government officials who were white and almost entirely British; merchants and traders were largely of Greek or Levantine origin; and the jet-black Sudanese. The official classes went on home leave much more often than the Indian Civil Service had done.[3] The early interest of the troops soon faded. The 'akker' (piaster) went less far than the 'chip' (rupee) had done in India, although one of the few advantages of serving in the Sudan was the payment of 6d (2½p) a day Colonial Allowance. Beer, only available bottled, was extremely expensive. There was little to see.

1 R.W.F. arrived in Port Sudan on 19 December and between then and the 23rd, moved to Khartoum by rail, a journey of some 400 miles (640 kilometres). The battalion was almost at full manning, with twenty-four Officers as against an establishment of twenty-eight; and the full established strength of 853 N.C.Os and Fusiliers.[4] C Company, initially under Major E. Wodehouse and later Captain H.A. Freeman,† remained on board HT *Neuralia* and sailed for Cyprus on Christmas Day. On arrival in Khartoum, the battalion was deployed with Battalion Headquarters, H.Q. Wing and D (M.G.) Company in Khartoum alongside the 1st Royal Warwicks, who were replaced by the 2nd Middlesex in April 1931; B Company went to Atbara and A Company to Gebeit,[5] where the conditions came as a pleasant surprise. The hutted camp was on a bushy plain surrounded by rugged hills with a railway line running through the middle. The facilities included a cinema, squash court, tennis court and swimming pool. Gebeit was situated about 220 miles (350 kilometres) W.N.W. of

December 1930

---

*   Later Major General Stephen Seymour Butler (1880-1964), *Northumberland Fusiliers* CB CMG DSO.

†   Later Major General Harold Augustus Freeman-Attwood DSO OBE MC *Ld'H* LoM (US) (1897–1967). He commanded the 46th Division from 1943 to August 1943, latterly in North Africa, but was dismissed the Service in that year by sentence of a General Court Martial on a charge of unlawful communication of information – in this case, in letters to his wife.

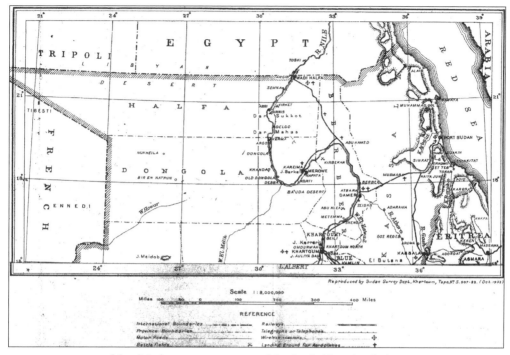

Map 6.1 A contemporary map of the Anglo-Egyptian Sudan.

The Sudan Club in Khartoum. (N.C. Stockwell)

Atbara on the road to Port Sudan from which it was about 75 miles (120 kilometres) distant. Atbara was in the desert about 200 miles (320 kilometres) north-west of Khartoum near the confluence of the Nile and Atbara Rivers. Although small, Atbara was an extremely important railway junction where the Cairo and Port Sudan lines met. It had a small British expat community of about a hundred. The barracks, pleasantly situated on the banks of the Nile, were better than expected and had sports fields, tennis courts and a basket ball court. The nearby Atbara Sports Club boasted a swimming pool. The Company had its own transport comprising a *Ford* truck, six *Morris* Commercials, three donkeys, two horses and a charger. There was also a rest camp at Port Sudan where men could go in parties of ten each week for a break.

Although training whilst in Sudan was restricted to section training **February 1931** because of the excessive heat, it was still possible to play sport and numerous competitions were staged, including cricket, football, hockey and swimming. In February, all companies competed at rugby football for the 'Rabbit Inter-Platoon Shield', which was won by No 13 Platoon of D Company. A Horse Show and Gymkhana were also held. The High Commissioner in Egypt, H.E. Sir Percy Lorraine, arrived for a visit on 4 February; the battalion mounted a ceremonial guard at Government House and the Band and Drums played in the gardens and at the formal dinner for His Excellency.

In March, St David's Day was celebrated in all locations. The **March 1931** Governor-General generously placed his steam launch, the *Elphin,* at the battalion's disposal. Eighty men enjoyed a cruise down the Nile. Brigadier Butler also lent his yacht, allowing another eighty men to enjoy a similar trip. Another 120 were given a conducted tour of the Battle of Omdurman by the Governor of Khartoum, Mr Sarsfield Hall. On the 9th, D Company under Captain M.B. Dowse found a Guard of Honour for H.R.H. the Princess Alice, Duchess of Athlone.[6]

In April, the temperature reached 111°F (45 °C) in the shade, **April 1931** prompting the remark that 'The climate certainly compared very favourably with an Indian hot weather.'[7] Four Officers returned from a big game-shooting expedition on the borders of Abyssinia. In spite of the heat, however, all companies were kept busy with training, especially shooting with the rifle, *Lewis* gun and M.M.G. There were also sports matches against the Sudan Defence Force. On 16 May, a joint celebration of the anniversary of the Battle of Albuhera in 1811 was held with the Middlesex. May closed tragically, with the death of Fusilier R. Walters, an excellent boxer and featherweight champion in Quetta, who was in a tent struck by lightning near Gebeit on 29 May; he was killed instantly.[8]

In June, D Company relieved A Company at Gebeit, where it would **June 1931** be able to complete its M.G. classification; A Company moved to Atbara and B Company to Khartoum. As the *Regimental Journal* noted, 'Both Gebeit and Atbara are very small worlds and, in spite of the efforts of even the most zealous organisers of distractions, are bound to become terribly monotonous if stayed in for more than six months – and it is possible to tire of Khartoum after a bit, particularly in the summer.'[9] Members of all companies attended R.A.F. courses in Army co-operation, and did a great deal of flying. It was also learned that the battalion would return to Britain earlier than expected, in April 1932, not November.

A flood at Gebeit in August caused some damage to the barracks; the **August–October 1931** railway was also torn up and houses wrecked by a spate of water three feet (one metre) deep. Troops were called out to assist in salvage and rescue work.[10] Between 10 and 13 September, another change of stations took place when D Company moved to Atbara, B

The camp at Gebeit in the Sudan. (R.W.F. Mus 3060)

Company to Gebeit and A Company to Khartoum, thus ensuring that each company had seen every station.[11] Plagues of locusts however did considerable damage – in particular, stripping the sports pitches at Khartoum of grass. A rabies scare then caused the death of some thousands of dogs, although a few pets in the barracks survived. Much sport was played in spite of the summer heat and the work of locusts, with soccer, hockey and boxing being especially popular. Rugby commenced in October, with the battalion team beating all opposition. A boxing tournament was organised by the 2nd Middlesex, the battalion team winning six of the seven cups.[12] The winning boxers were:

Flyweight, Lance Corporal Leahy
Bantamweight, Lance Corporal Durman
Lightweight, Lance Corporal Head
Welterweight, Lance Corporal Johns
Middleweight, Lance Corporal Griffiths
Boys' Contest, Boy Knox

At the end of October, the 2nd Middlesex departed after a tour of only one year, to be replaced by the 2nd Royal Ulster Rifles. On 25 November, a draft of one Officer and fifty-nine men under Lieutenant J.G. Vyvyan was sent from Sudan to reinforce C Company in Cyprus.[13] The remainder of the battalion carried out field training with R.A.F. aircraft and armoured cars. Christmas was celebrated so far as was possible in all locations.

Rifle section and Lewis gun team training in the Sudan, c. 1930. (R.W.F. Mus 3269)

With the return of hot weather, bathing in the Nile opened and was found most welcome – there being no swimming pools or baths in Khartoum for troops. In sport, the Ulster Rifles proved much tougher opponents than the Middlesex, beating the battalion at athletics and hockey. A St David's Day service was held in All Saints' Anglican Cathedral in Khartoum on 28 February, led by the Bishop, Llewellyn Gwynne.

January–March 1932

The battalion, less C Company, concentrated at Port Sudan and sailed for home on the HT *Dorsetshire* on 6 April. En route, the ship called at Gibraltar where on the 16th, the 1st and 2nd Battalions met. This meeting is covered in the chapter on Regimental Events. 237 men were transferred to the 2nd Battalion, which was to proceed to Hong Kong. The battalion, with thirty Officers and 461 N.C.Os and Fusiliers (including the detached C Company), 302 short of its established strength,[14] then continued its journey, arriving at Southampton on 21 April after eighteen years of foreign service. From there it moved to Bhurtpore Barracks, Tidworth.[15]

April 1932

ii. Cyprus

C Company, 125 strong, arrived in Cyprus in early January 1931 and moved to Polymedia Camp, Limassol.[16] Here it relieved a company of the 1st Cameronians and formed the major part of the garrison of the island, along with detachments of R.A.S.C. and R.A.M.C. There were in addition around 800 Cyprus Military Police distributed over the six districts of the island, with the biggest contingent in Nicosia. The chief Officers were British and the men about 60% Greeks and 40% Turks.

Cyprus had been ceded to Britain as a Protectorate by Turkey under the 1878 Treaty of Berlin. It had become a Crown Colony in 1922. The island, which has a Mediterranean climate, is 140 miles long (225 kilometres) at its greatest extent, and about sixty miles (96 kilometres) wide. Its population was divided between a majority of Greeks and a minority of Turks who lived chiefly in the north of the island.[17] The Greek majority had long sought union with Greece, or *Enosis*, and ironically Cyprus had been offered to the Greek government as an inducement to enter the Great War on the side of the Allies in 1914. The Greeks had refused, only to join the war later but without winning the prize of Cyprus.

In February the company took part in the Limassol knock-out soccer tournament, winning its semi-final match by 4 goals to 1 in front of a crowd of 4,000; and the final by 8 goals to 1 in front of 8,000 people. Thereafter the company's focus moved to preparations for the King's Birthday Parade in Nicosia; and in taking part in athletics events against local clubs. On 31 May the company took part in a boxing tournament against a Greek team and a team from HMS *Ormonde;* the Royal Welch won three of the four fights against the Greeks, and six of the seven against the Navy. The Birthday Parade took place on 3 June with seventy-five Officers and men from the company on parade, forming the right wing of the line along with the Cyprus Military Police and a party of seamen from the *Ormonde.* The salute was taken by the Governor, Sir Ronald Storrs,* after which a Royal Salute of twenty-one guns and a *feu-de-joie* were fired.

February–June 1931

---

*   Sir Ronald Henry Amherst Storrs KCMG CBE (1881–1955) served as Oriental Secretary in Cairo, Military Governor of Jerusalem, Governor of Cyprus, and Governor of Northern Rhodesia.

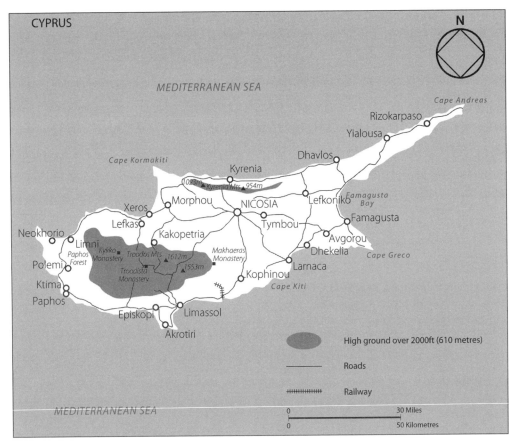

Map 6.2 Cyprus.

As soon as the parade was concluded, the company embussed in lorries and drove fifty miles (80 kilometres) to Troodos Camp, 6,000 feet (1,800 metres) up in the mountains.[18] Here, as soon as dinner had been eaten, a Guard of Honour was found for the Governor and the Anglican Bishop of Jerusalem, Dr Llewellyn Gwynne, at the consecration and opening of the new Troodos church. About a week later, the Governor having gone on leave, the Acting Governor inspected the company. Mr Henniker Eaton addressed the men, saying that: 'it is an honour to have as garrison on the island a Company drawn from a Regiment with such a glorious history as the Royal Welch Fusiliers. I was told the other day by a distinguished foreigner that in the long time he had spent on the island he had never known a company conduct itself in every way so splendidly as this one.'[19]

The routine of life in Cyprus changed dramatically in October.[20] At Midnight on 21/22 October, Captain Freeman was telephoned by the Colonial Secretary's office and told that because of violent disturbances in Nicosia, the company was required there immediately. There being no transport at Troodos, the company was ordered to march eighteen miles (28 kilometres) to Everykhou, where a special train had been arranged. Freeman realised that this would take far too long – it would be noon the following day before

October 1931

he arrived in Nicosia. He therefore sent an N.C.O. to commandeer all available transport in the local area. He also telephoned the station master in Nicosia, who arranged for ten cars to drive up from Morphou. By these means, he was able to arrive in Nicosia with one platoon in such transport as was immediately available at 07.30 hrs the following morning, with the rest of the company following in the cars from Morphou. The night was bitterly cold and the men moved with greatcoats on, 100 rounds of ball ammunition each, *Lewis* guns loaded and three days' rations in the haversack.

Freeman found that the previous evening, a meeting of Greek leaders had taken place in Limassol, at which it was decided that the time for *Enosis* – union with Greece – was at hand. This news had been telegraphed to Nicosia where the church bells had been rung and people collected. A crowd of 5,000 then marched on Government House and demands were made for a meeting with the Governor. The Governor refused to meet Greek leaders with a mob at their backs and ordered them to disperse. Stones were then thrown, the police arrived and the Riot Act was read. The crowd responded by burning police cars, trying to break down the door of Government House and indeed, setting it alight. By now there were more than eighty policemen in the area, fifty of them armed. Once the house had been set alight, the Governor gave the order to open fire. Twenty rounds were fired and the rioters withdrew leaving one dead man and sixteen wounded.

By daybreak the police under their Commissioner, Colonel Gallagher, had established picquets around the town, H.Q. British Troops in Egypt had been asked for reinforcements and the Royal Navy radioed for the presence of ships. Freeman decided to contain the rioters within the old town walls and therefore reinforced the police picquets with three of his platoons, concentrating on the Colonial Secretary's lodge, where the Governor had taken refuge, and the Government offices. The fourth platoon was held in reserve. At

Men of C Company 1 R.W.F. in Cyprus, 1931.

10.00 hrs the Governor convened a conference, during which a cable arrived from Egypt asking Freeman if he agreed with the need for more troops. Freeman asked for another company and was told that they would arrive by air that evening in aircraft from Cairo, via Rafah in Palestine. It was decided not to impose Martial Law, since it would be impossible to enforce, but to impose instead the Defence Order in Council of 1928. This was akin to Martial Law in the powers it gave the authorities, but control remained with the civil government and courts. This required the permission of the Colonial Secretary in London, which was granted three hours later.

As Nicosia was quiet, Freeman agreed to a request from Larnaca for reinforcements, and sent two platoons under Captain R. de B. Hardie and Lieutenant M.W. Whittaker – the only other Officers. Their arrival coincided with the end of a large meeting and as a result, the crowd there dispersed quietly. Leaving one platoon in Larnaca, Hardie sent the second platoon on to Famagusta, where British women and children had been evacuated to a ship in the harbour.

At 17.00 hrs Freeman was warned of a large crowd collecting near one of the picquets on the main street through the middle of the town, heading for the entrance to the town over a raised causeway which crossed the medieval moat; this was known as New Entrance. Here, Freeman had five men, five policemen and a *Lewis* gun in reserve under Sergeant Clements. Orders were given for people to return home; some obeyed but others did not. As a curfew had been ordered for 18.00 hrs, Freeman decided he must clear the causeway, not least because stoning had increased and he was afraid that his small detachment might quickly be overwhelmed. The picquet advanced with bayonets fixed, driving the crowd back while knife-rests were brought in by the police. Pressure continued, however, and Freeman made the Mayor come out and tell the crowd that anyone attempting to cross the police barrier would be shot. To underline this, the *Lewis* gun was brought up to the middle of the causeway. After this, matters calmed somewhat.

At about 20.00 hrs, Freeman was told that a crowd was again collecting. Freeman spoke to them and within half an hour all was quiet. Things were not so quiet in Limassol, where the Police Commissioner's house had been burnt down. Hardie and his platoon in Larnaca were ordered to move to Limassol. After that, the rest of the night was quiet. Various messages came in, telling Freeman that by great good luck, the Mediterranean Fleet was off Crete and that two cruisers, HMS *London* and *Shropshire*, and two destroyers, HMS *Acasta* and *Achates*, were due to arrive at 09.00 hrs the next morning under the command of Rear-Admiral J.C.W. Henley,[*] which they duly did, landing parties of armed seamen in Limassol, Larnaca, Paphos and Famagusta; Hardie and his platoon moved to Paphos, just in time to stop a crowd attacking the Police Commissioner's house there.

At 10.00 hrs on 23 October, another conference was called by the Governor. The main point at issue was the funeral of the man killed in the rioting in Nicosia. At least 5,000 people were expected to attend. This was allowed to proceed, but warnings were given that anyone leaving the proscribed route would be shot. An hour later, aircraft carrying a company of the 1st King's (Liverpool) Regiment flew in, 126 strong, with orders that they were to come under Freeman's command. The King's had been in Cyprus shortly before and therefore knew the island and its problems. Shortly afterwards another conference was held at which the Royal Navy assumed responsibility for the ports.

Intelligence suggested that after the funeral, there would be attempts to attack the Secretary's Lodge and the Government offices. Two platoons of the King's were therefore deployed to cover these points, in the end, after a few tense moments on the Larnaca cross-roads, the funeral passed off with only stone-throwing. That evening, the Royal Welch, who had had no sleep for forty-eight hours, were relieved by the King's and rested. From noon on the 24th, it was arranged that Nicosia would be divided into two parts, the King's being responsible for the Northern half and the Royal Welch the South. It was also determined, after some discussion, that the Bishop of Kitium, who had stirred up the trouble in the first place, would be arrested at 03.00 hrs next morning, since he was planning to arrive in Paphos to cause more disturbances. At the same time it was also planned to arrest five ringleaders in Nicosia. This was successfully achieved and the prisoners transferred to HMS *London* at Larnaca before dawn. The Bishop's arrest was equally successful and he was transferred to HMS *Shropshire*.

---

*   Later Vice-Admiral Joseph Charles Walrond Henley CB DSO DL (1879–1968). His career ended in 1932 when he took the blame, undeservedly, for the Invergordon mutiny and he was placed on the retired list.

On the 24th, the R.A.F. made a demonstration over all the main towns. Later on, the Bishop demanded to see the Governor; the Governor sent him to see Freeman. The Bishop threatened violence if all prisoners were not released and was told in no uncertain terms that all means available would be used to restore order if this occurred. Most civilians assumed that the prisoners were being held in Nicosia Central Prison, and Freeman therefore feared an attack there, reinforcing the gaol with two sections of troops. No trouble occurred here, although there was again a disturbance at the New Entrance picquet.

At 05.00 hrs on the 25th another Orthodox clergyman, the Bishop of Kyrenia, was seen trying to enter Nicosia. Freeman ordered his detention but before this could be achieved, the bishop returned to Kyrenia. Here he pulled down the Union flag, collected a crowd and delivered a seditious address. It was decided to arrest the bishop that night. His house was guarded by 500 rebels, who were to be reinforced by another 300. This latter party bumped into a picquet, was fired on and fled – taking with them the guard on the bishop's house. A platoon of the King's immediately entered the house, arrested the bishop and took him to join the other detainees.

Hardie meanwhile had been round half the island. He was ordered to go and spend a night in Troodos, then move via Pedoulas to Morphou and Lefka. **November 1931** In these places, telephone wires had been cut and forest huts attacked. On his travels, Hardie made villagers repair the damage they had caused. At Zodia he was attacked by a crowd and obliged to open fire, killing one man and wounding two others. He was later joined by a platoon of the King's Regiment. The damage was indicative of the fact that, although the main towns were now quiet, trouble had spread to the country districts. Another infantry company was therefore requested from Egypt to relieve the Navy. This company arrived by sea on 5 November along with a section of armoured cars from the 12th Lancers. A stringent curfew was now imposed all over the island and this, combined with the arrest of the leaders, brought the rebellion to an end. On 25 November, a draft of reinforcements, consisting of fifty-nine men under Lieutenant J.G. Vyvyan, was received from the 1st Battalion in Sudan, bringing C Company to a strength of 175 men.

Early in December, one company of the King's Regiment, the Lancers and the aircraft returned to Egypt, followed by the second King's company at the end of the month. **December 1931– February 1932** Freeman was left with his company H.Q. and two platoons in Nicosia, one platoon divided between Famagusta and Larnaca, and one platoon at Polymedia. It was not until the end of February that he was able to draw in the detachments. Before they left, training was given to the police in the use of rifles and a special constabulary organised, manned only by British expatriates.

The company remained on alert until it sailed from Cyprus on 22 April 1932 on the HT *Neuralia*. It left with a very high reputa- **April 1932** tion. Captain Freeman was awarded the O.B.E. for his actions while in command.[21] Sergeant Clements was awarded the B.E.M. for his coolness and determination at the New Entrance picquet. The *Neuralia* called briefly at Gibraltar as described in the chapter on regimental events. Here C Company transferred eighty-nine of its men to the 2nd Battalion. The remainder then continued to England, arriving at Southampton on 7 May and moving directly to Tidworth by train to re-join the 1st Battalion.[22]

Staff List, 1 R.W.F. Sudan and Cyprus, 1930–1932

Lieutenant Colonel
E.O. Skaife OBE
Major
T.D. Daly MC
E. Wodehouse
J.G. Bruxner-Randall
Captain
H.A. Freeman OBE MC
P.C. Kenyon MC
H. de B. Hardie
M.B. Dowse
G.N.H. Taunton-Collins
T.S. Griffiths
H.D.T. Morris
B.L.N. Trotman-Dickenson
Quartermaster
Lt G.R. Whyley

Lieutenant
M.F.P. Lloyd (Adjt)
R.F.A. David
J.G. Vyvyan
M.H. ap Rhys Pryce
R.J.F. Snead-Cox
M.W. Whittaker
H.A.S. Clarke
J.H. Liscombe
2nd Lieutenant
W.L.R. Benyon
N.C. Stockwell
E.H. Cadogan

W.O. I
RSM R.W. Chambers
BM H.P.G. Perdue
W.O. II
M.J. Kensett
I.G. Smalldon
J. Soane
A. Lungley DCM (to Feb 1932)
Staff Sergeants
DMaj J.M. Bacon
Band Sgt W. Tubby
Sergeants
C. Clements BEM
Davies
Attached
AQMS F.G. Moore

Notes

1   *R.U.S.I. Journal*, Vol LXXIX (1934), p. 535.
2   Blight, pp. 102–103.
3   Blight, p. 104.
4   T.N.A. WO 73/134.
5   1 R.W.F. Digest of Service; *Y Ddraig Goch*, Series III, June 1931, p. 21.
6   *Y Ddraig Goch*, June 1931, pp 21, 22.
7   *Y Ddraig Goch*, June 1931, p. 23.
8   *Y Ddraig Goch*, September 1931, p. 44.
9   *Y Ddraig Goch*, September 1931, p. 44.
10 *Y Ddraig Goch*, December 1931, p. 72.
11 1 R.W.F. Digest of Service; *Y Ddraig Goch*, March 1932, p. 6.
12 *Y Ddraig Goch*, March 1932, p. 5.
13 1 R.W.F. Digest of Service.
14 T.N.A. WO73/136.
15 1 R.W.F. Digest of Service.
16 1 R.W.F. Digest of Service.
17 George Gill, *British Colonies and Dependencies*, p. 120.
18 1 R.W.F. Digest of Service.
19 *Y Ddraig Goch*, September 1931, p. 45.
20 The following section is drawn from Captain H.A. Freeman 'The Rebellion in Cyprus, 1931' in *Army Quarterly*, Vol XXV (January 1933) no 2, pp. 268–280; 'Greek Rebellion in Cyprus, 1931', a report by Freeman to H.Q. British Troops in Khartoum dated 23 November 1931; Sir Charles W. Gwynn, *Imperial Policing* (London, 1936), Chapter XII – Cyprus, 1931; *Y Ddraig Goch*, St David's Day 1964, pp. 57–58; *Y Ddraig Goch*, St David's Day 1967, p. 179.
21 *LG* 3 June 1932.
22 1 R.W.F. Digest of Service; *Y Ddraig Goch*, September 1932, p. 53.

Chapter 7

The 1st Battalion in the United Kingdom, 1932–1939

i. Tidworth, 1932–1935

The battalion was complete at Tidworth on 7 May 1932 and within three days of arrival, dispersed for six weeks' furlough; the whole battalion re-assembled on 20 June 1932,[1] when all Officers paraded as spectators for the King's Birthday Parade in Tidworth Garrison. Tidworth, a small village on the border between Wiltshire and Hampshire, is on the north-eastern side of Salisbury Plain, the huge training area of 42,000 acres (65 square miles, or 168 square kilometres) purchased by the War Office in 1897. With a large increase in the size of the army at home at the start of the Boer War it was decided to build a new camp at Tidworth to house eight battalions, plus units of Royal Engineers, Army Service Corps, and garrison troops. Each building was of a standard type with long barrack blocks for two companies divided into

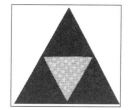

May 1932

The badge of the 3rd Infantry Division.

eight 12-man rooms. The rooms were connected by an external veranda, leading to full sets of stairs built between the veranda and two free-standing, square towers which contained N.C.O.s' rooms and company stores. Pairs of parallel barrack blocks were linked by covered ways to a separate dining room and between the two dining rooms was a central washhouse. The H-shaped unit thus formed held a half battalion. A second matching block formed a full battalion, with its own Officers' Mess and quarters, guardroom, Quartermaster's store, drill shed, Sergeants' Mess, canteen and stables. The eight barracks – Aliwal, Assaye, Bhurtpore, Candahar, Delhi, Jellalabad, Lucknow and Meanee – were named after battles in India and Afghanistan. Other buildings provided institutes, riding schools, married quarters, hospital, school, and garrison church which was built in 1914.[2] It was long rumoured that the barracks had originally been intended for Poona in India; oddly enough, the Poona garrison units to this day relate a story that *their* barracks were meant to have been built in a place in England, called Tidworth.

Here, the battalion occupied Bhurtpore Barracks and joined 7 Infantry Brigade, along with 1st K.O.Y.L.I. and 2nd Loyals, under the command of Brigadier C.C. Armitage* (in July,

---

*   Later General Sir Charles Clement Armitage KCB CMG DSO DL *Late R.A.* (1885–1973). M.G.O. India from 1938 until his retirement in 1942.

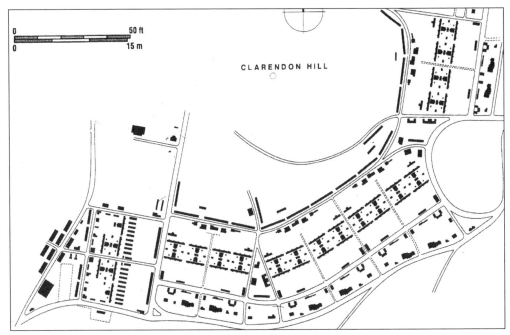

Map 7.1 Tidworth Garrison in 1930. (Source: English Heritage)

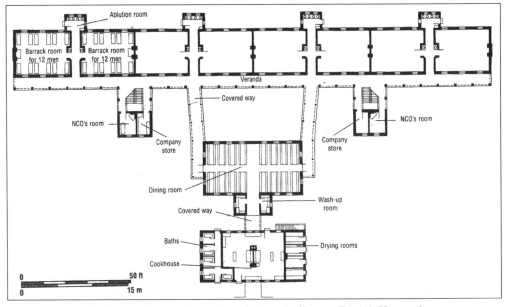

The layout of a barrack complex in Tidworth. (Source: English Heritage)

Major General G.M. Lindsay*) which was, as it had been in the 2nd Battalion's time, was an experimental mechanized formation assigned to the 3rd Infantry Division under the command of Major General H.H.S. Knox[†] until November 1932; then Lieutenant General W.W. Pitt-Taylor[‡] until October 1934; and then Major General R.G. Findlayson.[§] The division's other two brigades were 8 Infantry Brigade, from 1934 to 1936 commanded by Brigadier W.G. Holmes of the Royal Welch Fusiliers; and 9 Infantry Brigade.

As an experimental battalion, 1 R.W.F. was issued with a variety of vehicles. These were, first, the *Carden-Lloyd* Mark VI carrier, described in Chapter 3, which could act as a tractor for the lightweight *Oerlikon* 1 pdr anti-tank gun, or carry a *Vickers* M.M.G. and its crew. Secondly, a large *Burford-Kegresse* half-track, commonly used as an M.M.G. carrier. The tracks were made by the French firm Kegresse and were based on canvas and rubber, which was not robust, and was phased out in favour of metal tracks by 1929. Thirdly, a small 15/20-cwt half-track made by Crossley-Kegresse, which was used as a staff or command vehicle although there were some cargo variants. Fourthly, the *Morris Commercial* C.D. 6 x 4 reconnaissance car; last, the *Morris Commercial* D-Type 30-cwt cargo truck.[3]

As outlined in the previous chapter, the battalion transferred a large number of Officers and men to the 2nd Battalion in Gibraltar and as a result, was only 60% manned on its arrival in Tidworth, 302 short of its established strength. This situation slowly improved: a year

An *Oerlikon* 20mm gun of 1 R.W.F., 1931. (R.W.F. Mus)

later, the deficit was 229 and by January 1935, 178.[4] W.L.R. Benyon[¶] remembered that the battalion was not fully manned, however, 'I don't remember it ever being in the same state as the 2nd Battalion earlier... . I wouldn't say we had a full battalion, nothing like, but ... we were joined by this great batch of Officers who had come in when we were all abroad'.[5] N.R.G.

---

*   Major General George Mackintosh Lindsay CB CMG CBE DSO (1880–1956), was commissioned into the Rifle Brigade but transferred to the Royal Tank Corps. He was regarded as the most intellectually sophisticated of the RTC radicals between the wars but was shunted into obscurity and retired in 1939, only to be re-employed during the war first with the Civil Defence Corps and then the Red Cross.

†   Later General Sir Harry Hugh Sidney Knox KCB DSO (1873–1971), Adjutant-General to the Forces.

‡   Later General Sir Walter William Pitt-Taylor KCB CMG DSO (1878 –1950).

§   Later General Sir Robert Gordon-Finlayson KCB CMG DSO (1881–1956), Adjutant-General to the Forces.

¶   Later Colonel Wyndham Lethbridge Rex ('Winky') Benyon (1910–1997). He re-formed 2 R.W.F. in 1952 and commanded it in Britain, Germany and Malaya until 1954.

1 R.W.F. on parade at Tidworth in 1931, equipped as an experimental mechanised battalion. (R.W.F. Mus)

Carden-Lloyd Carriers of 1 R.W.F., Tidworth 1931. (R.W.F. Mus)

Bosanquet,[*] however, who was commissioned in August 1931 and joined 1 R.W.F. at Tidworth on its return from Sudan, recorded that: 'When I arrived I found myself with a platoon of four men and a sergeant'.[6] R.O.F. Prichard[†] was commissioned in January 1935 and joined 1 R.W.F. in Tidworth. He remembered that:

> I joined A Company and my Company Commander was Maurice Dowse[‡]… who ran an extremely good company. The second-in-command was Geoffrey Taunton-Collins… . My Platoon Sergeant was called Robins who looked after me very well until I learnt the ropes. The subalterns – in those days some had eighteen years' service – were Edward Cadogan,[§] Brian Doughty-Wylie[¶] and a Canadian called Bernatches, who had a good war, Commanded the "Vingt-deux" [Royal 22ème Régiment] and became a general… We

---

[*]   Later Lieutenant Colonel Neville Richard Gustavus Bosanquet (1911–2003). He commanded 2 R.W.F. in 1945 and 1 R.W.F. 1954–1957.

[†]   Later Colonel Robin Owen Forsyth Prichard OBE MC (1915–2002), C.O. 1 R.W.F. in Berlin and on operations in Cyprus, 1958–1960.

[‡]   Later Major General Sir Maurice Dowse KCVO CB CBE (1899–1986), Deputy Colonel of the Royal Welch Fusiliers 1952–1958. He organised the Coronation of H.M. Queen Elizabeth II in 1953.

[§]   Later Colonel Edward Henry Cadogan (1908–1993), son of Lieutenant Colonel H.O.S. Cadogan who was killed commanding 1 R.W.F. at Ypres in October 1914, father of Colonel H.M.E. Cadogan, C.O. 3 R.W.F. 1978–1980. He commanded 1 R.W.F. in Germany, 1948–1951.

[¶]   Later Lieutenant Colonel Brian Pierson Doughty-Wylie MC BA (1911–1982) son of the Hon Mrs Wilfred Thesiger but changed his name to Doughty-Wylie by deed poll 26 Sep 33. C.O. 2 R.W.F.

seemed to have a lot of elderly company commanders, unmarried, who had been in the 14-18 war and I can well remember the almost perennial President of the Mess Committee, Watty Watkins,* who was marvellous at it.[7]

Shortly after arrival, the battalion hosted the Oxford University O.T.C. for a week's training, while a number of N.C.Os went off to **July–August 1932** assist in training T.A. Battalions in 158 (Royal Welch) Infantry Brigade, especially in signalling with the heliograph, lamp and flags.[8] On 4 July, a representative party travelled to London to be received by His Majesty the King, Colonel-in-Chief. This occasion is covered in the Chapter dealing with Regimental Events. Thereafter all energies were devoted to preparations for the Southern Command Tattoo in the first week of August. The battalion provided the infantry for the modern battle scene, including a *Carden-Lloyd* M.G. section and an anti-tank section, as well as providing the band and drums. The Colonel of the Regiment also visited at this time, watched field training and inspected the battalion on parade. The Colonel expressed himself as being 'very satisfied with everything he saw on his visit.[9]

With the arrival of drafts from the Depot, battalion strength at the end of July stood at two W.Os I, five W.Os II, thirty Sergeants and Staff Sergeants, sixteen Drummers and 512 Junior N.C.Os and Fusiliers.[10] Battalion training as a mechanised force was carried out from 8 to 27 August, including river crossings on the Avon, in the hottest weather experienced in Britain for many years. Brigade training took place in September, with 7 Brigade and 9 Brigade on opposite sides. In spite of being in a mechanised formation, there was much in common with the regime in Quetta. W.L.R. Benyon recalled that:

> Training, ordinary regimental stuff, was interesting because there was much emphasis on marching in those days. Once a week there was a route march which lasted all day and I remember marching along all the roads round Tidworth. There was very little traffic and often the Band and Drums were in attendance. Even on brigade and higher formation exercises a tremendous amount of time was spent on marching, which stood us in good stead when we went to France in 1940... We were in the new mechanised brigade, so we had some enormous things that were twice as big as tanks, and we lumbered across country in them.[11]

The battalion was inspected on 10 October by the Brigade Commander, who was 'much impressed by the turnout, drill and steadiness on parade.'[12] Individual training and sport then became the main activities throughout the autumn and winter months. A novices' boxing competition was held in late October; in November, six boxers fought in a competition in Salisbury on behalf of the South African War Veterans Association; on 11 November, **October–November 1932** the Novices team beat the 11th Hussars by 15 points to 13 in the second round of the Salisbury Plain Area Novices Competition and in the semi-final on 24 November, beat 26 Field Brigade R.A. by 15 points to 14; and on 25 November Lance Sergeant Nedderman, Lance Sergeant Jones, Lance Corporal Taylor, Drummer Maloney, and Fusilier

---

Malaya 2 Apr – 27 Oct 55 until relieved of his command. He later served on the staff of Lieutenant General Sir Hugh Stockwell at Suez in 1956.

*   Later Lieutenant Colonel Harold Claude (Watty) Watkins OBE MC (1893–1974).

A Company of 1 R.W.F. on the march with its transport, Salisbury Plain 1932. (Minshull-Ford)

A halt on the march at a country pub, 1932. (Minshull-Ford)

The view from the ranks during a route march in 1932. (Minshull-Ford)

Gardner all boxed for the Salisbury Plain Area team against Royal Marines Portsmouth; all except Lance Sergeant Nedderman won their fights. In the S.P.A. final, the battalion team was beaten by 2nd Loyals by 17 points to 11. The following boxed in the competition:

Bantamweight, Fusilier Hoosnan
Featherweight, Lance Corporal Davies
Lightweights, Lance Corporal McCarthy, Fusilier Gilchrist, Fusilier Woodyat
Middleweight, Fusilier Page
Welterweights, Fusilier Nicholas, Fusilier Baker, Fusilier Roberts
Heavyweight, Second Lieutenant Barton

On 7 December, Second Lieutenant A.G. ff Powell, Lance Corporal Taylor and Fusilier Evans all boxed for S.P.A. against R.A.F. Salisbury **December 1932** Plain; Powell and Taylor both won their fights by a knock-out. The soccer team beat 4th/7th Dragoon Guards 12-4, 26th Field Brigade R.A. 4-1, 1st K.O.Y.L.I. 6-1, 5th Light Brigade R.A. 4-0 and drew 4-4 with the 11th Hussars in the Tidworth League. In the Army Cup, the team beat 3rd Division R.E. in the first round 4-2; 6th Medium Regiment R.A. 5-2 away and 2-1 at home in the second round. Rugby and hockey were also restarted with less favourable results. Cub hunting with the Tedworth and the Avon Vale Hounds also commenced, leading up to the start of the season. Twenty Officers hunted during the season.[13]

The battalion dispersed for leave over Christmas. In January, the battalion boxing team began its attempt on the inter-unit competition, taking revenge on 2nd Loyals in the first round by beating them 8 fights to 7; in the second round, on 31 January, the team defeated 1st Manchesters by 23 points to 21; and on 7 February, defeated 1st K.O.Y.L.I. by 11 **January 1933** fights to 4, or 26 points to 19, to win the Southern Command tournament. The team was composed of:

Bantamweight, Corporal J. Durman
Featherweights, Lance Sergeant Jones, Fusilier Cullen
Lightweights, Lance Corporal Taylor, Fusilier Carter, Fusilier Byrne
Middleweights, Fusilier Denner, Lance Sergeant Nedderman, Fusilier Lloyd
Welterweights, Lance Corporal Johns, Drummer Maloney, Fusilier Evans,
    Fusilier Gardner
Light Heavyweight, Lance Corporal Rowan
Heavyweight, 2nd Lieutenant A.G. ff Powell[14]

During January 1933, an inter-company small-bore shooting competition was held, won by D (M.G.) Company. The Officers took on the Wentworth Club at Squash, losing by 3 matches to 2; the team was composed of Major J.G. Bruxner-Randall, Captain G.N.H. Taunton-Collins, and Lieutenants R.F.A. David, R.C.M. Kelly and W.L.R. Benyon. R.O.F. Prichard recalled that:

We played a lot of games in those days including a tremendous amount of rugby and cricket. Of course we were also as a Regiment very horse minded, and many Officers hunted with the Avon Vale. There were one or two, especially Tony Raymont, who were keen on steeple-chasing and went around achieving a certain amount of success at Sandown Park and so on. There was an Army Company Rugby Competition in which my company got quite far before coming up against a company of 3rd Royal Tanks which had three internationals including Deane,* the English scrum-half.

On 28 February the battalion trooped its Regimental Colour on the barrack square in Tidworth in honour of St David, in the presence of the Colonel of the Regiment, General Sir Charles Dobell. Second Lieutenant A.J. Lewis was the Ensign and the escort to the Colour was under Sergeant S. Sherriff, with Lance Corporal H. Stone and Fusilier H. Stapley as sentries. C Company found the escort under Captain S.O. Jones, with P.L. Powers as Lieutenant. Each guard consisted of two Officers and fifty N.C.Os and Fusiliers. No 2 Guard was under Captain H.D.T. Morris, with Lieutenant E.M. Davies-Jenkins; No 3 Guard was under Captain H.F. Garnons-Williams, with Lieutenant N.C. Stockwell; and No 4 Guard was commanded by Captain H.C. Watkins, with Lieutenant E.H. Cadogan. Lieutenant Colonel Skaife commanded the parade, with Lieutenant M.F.P. Lloyd as Adjutant and RSM R.W. Chambers.[15]

> **February 1933**

The celebration of St David's Day continued with the usual dinners and sports; the W.Os' and Sergeants' Mess Ball was held on the 7th. The Red Dragon Cup was also competed for, for the first time since 1913, on 3 March. The race was run over a six mile (9 kilometre) cross-country course with a variety of fences and stone walls to be jumped, at Priddy Hill in the Mendip Hills, by permission of Mr H.A. Tiarks and other farmers. There was some snow on the ground but the weather had cleared by the time the twelve riders started: five were competing for the Red Dragon Cup, and seven for the Barnett-Barker Cup which was for government horses, rather than those in private ownership.† Eleven of the twelve competitors finished. The Red Dragon Cup was won by Captain H.C. Watkins on 'Airman'; the Barnet-Barker Cup by Major Ll. A.A. Alston on 'Cyllenius'. Lieutenant Colonel Skaife, on 'Mark Anthony', came down at the last fence but one and therefore did not finish.[16]

> **March 1933**

Training resumed with an Officers' Week from 12 to 17 March. Sport also continued, with the soccer team, coached and managed by Lieutenant G.R. Whyley and RSM Kensett, winning the S.P.A League Cup, the Tidworth Garrison League Cup and the Tidworth Garrison Challenge Cup. Rugby and shooting also continued.

On 16 May 1933, Lieutenant Colonel Skaife handed over command of the battalion to Lieutenant Colonel J.G. Bruxner-Randall. Skaife had learned classical Welsh, and Russian, while interned in the Netherlands following his wounding and capture in 1914. In 1933 he became a member of the *Gorsedd Ynys Prydain* and in later life was a prominent member of the Honourable Society of Cymmrodorion, the Druidic Order of the *Gorsedd*, the Welsh League of Youth (later the *Urdd*) and various *Eisteddfoddau*.[17] He was Colonel of the Regiment from

---

*   Geoffrey John ('Tinny') Deane (1909–1995) played for England against Ireland in 1931.

†   Brigadier Randle Barnett Barker DSO (1870–1918) was commissioned in 1891 and retired in 1906. He was recalled for service at the outbreak of the Great War and in January 1918 was promoted to the rank of Brigadier-General. He was killed in action commanding 99 Infantry Brigade on 24 March 1918, at the beginning of the great German offensive and is buried in Albert Communal Cemetery Extension; his grave is marked by a regimental headstone. He was a well-known equestrian, winning the Red Dragon Cup in 1904 and 1905, as well as numerous point-to-points. He presented two cups to the Officers' Mess. He has an impressive memorial window in St Mary's Priory Church, Abergavenny, placed there in 1922 by his widow and two sons.

Lieutenant E.H. Cadogan leads a convoy of vehicles on Salisbury Plain, watched by members of the battalion. (Cadogan family)

1948 to 1952 and knighted in January 1956, just before his death. His successor was rather more conventional. J.E.T. Willes,* who joined the battalion in February 1934, recalled that 'Bruxner-Randall was … very good and marvellous at training, and one felt that all the groundwork of one's tactical knowledge came from him. He was pretty strict on the way [training] went'.[18] R.O.F. Prichard recalled that:

> We trained quite hard. In the winter it was individual training, mainly weapon training, and in the spring we got on to platoon training. We used to train about two nights a week. In early spring we would go on a company march which was intended to get people fit for higher training, and lasted about a fortnight. The company second-in-command, Geoffrey Taunton-Collins, would carry out a recce during which he would visit people who owned estates in Wiltshire and arrange for the company to camp in their park overnight. We would march all day and cover about 20–25 miles [32–40 km] doing some tactical training on the way. Then in the evening we invariably played cricket against the local side if there was one. It was all very good fun and the company ended up by being pretty fit. This was

---

* Later Colonel John Edward Theodore ('Jack') Willes MBE (1913–2004), Colonel of the Regiment, 1965–1974.

followed by the musketry season when, for five or six weeks, we spent as much as four days per week on the range, either firing or supervising the firing point or butts. We were never a great shooting regiment but the C.O., Gerry Bruxner-Randall, demanded high standards, and I remember as subalterns being told that if we were not marksmen we would lose our Easter leave.

Battalion training with exercises watched by the Brigade Staff was followed by brigade then divisional exercises. I remember once doing a motorised exercise when we were all put into hired taxis and motor cars of all shapes and sizes and did an advance to contact across Salisbury Plain. When we met opposition we had to report back the relevant information. I suppose that we were trying out [the]concept of the reconnaissance regiment.

I also remember a small air movement exercise in which my platoon flew from Old Sarum to Andover, and for most of them it was the first time they had seen an aircraft. As we began the descent to Andover one of the soldiers stood up to get his kit down from the rack. He was shouted at by the other soldiers and told, "For God's sake don't do that, you'll turn it over".[19]

Members of the Anti-Aircraft Platoon, 1934. (Norman Weale)

Seven Officers entered events in the Southern Command Horse Show on 22 and 23 May, winning two seconds and one third place; Fusilier Lewis **May 1933** won third prize and the special prize for the best infantry draught horse with 'Yanto'. Battalion training took place during June in perfect weather, the final act of which involved a defensive position on Silk Hill, which was held against two cavalry regiments. A team was also sent to the Army Rifle Meeting at Bisley in July, winning only minor prizes but gaining in experience. The battalion again took part in the Tidworth Tattoo in August. In addition to performances by the Band and Drums, the battalion provided costumed archers and men-at-arms depicting the battle of Crécy. Inter-company and individual athletics competitions, the former for the Colonel Kyrke Cup, were held. CQMS W. Tubby was prominent, winning three track events and one field event, and coming second in two more. Hockey and cricket were also played.[20] The Regimental Band played for the Old Contemptibles' parade in Salisbury; at the Colonel of the Regiment's residence in Herefordshire; various engagements at Swindon, Bognor Regis, Marlborough School and Henley Royal Regatta; and then undertook a tour of towns in Devon.

The Southern Command Weapon Training Meeting was held on 29, 30 and 31 August. Thirty-six members of the battalion entered **July–August 1933** various events. In the Officers' rifle event, Second Lieutenant Lewis was placed sixth and Lieutenant Snead-Cox ninth. The Young Soldiers' team achieved third place in their event and the Anti-Aircraft Automatic team came second. The machine-gunners reached the knock-out semi-final and the Rifle and Light-Automatic team achieved fifth place.

Immediately afterwards, brigade manoeuvres began on 2 September in co-operation with 5th Royal Tanks, and progressed to divisional **September 1933** manoeuvres in the following week with 2 Cavalry Brigade acting as enemy. There were then two exercises involving troops from Aldershot Command: 3rd Division with 2 Cavalry Brigade, 5th Royal Tanks and 6 Medium Brigade R.A. opposed 2nd Infantry Division with 1 Cavalry Brigade, 2nd Royal Tanks and 1 Medium Brigade R.A.[21] At the end of September, Second Lieutenant D.M.C. Pritchard with two Warrant Officers and one Fusilier attended the funeral of the Reverend George Davies, who was believed to be the last known survivor of the Indian Mutiny, at Weston-Super-Mare. Davies had not served with The Royal Welch Fusiliers.

Hockey and Rugby then commenced. The hockey team entered the Army Cup and won its first two matches against the 11th Hussars 5-1 and 1st K.O.Y.L.I also 5-1. 1st K.O.Y.L.I. had their revenge by knocking the rugby team out in the first round of the Army Cup on 2 November, by 4 points to 3.* The Soccer team was also knocked out of the Army Cup in the second round, by 2-1 against 1st Survey Company R.E. A novices' boxing competition was held in October, principally to find replacements for several of the previous year's team. The new team then went on to the S.P.A. tournament, beating 5th R.T.C. by 18 points to 12. The match against 2nd Loyals was tied on points, but the battalion was judged victorious for having won the Welterweight first string fight.[22]

In late November, a large draft of eighty-five N.C.Os and Fusiliers was sent to the 2nd Battalion. The battalion dispersed for Christmas **January 1934** leave and reassembled in early January 1934. The annual Christmas Tree event for married families with children was not held until 16 January. Tea, games and presents from St Nicholas (Sergeant Davies) were much enjoyed.

Individual training and sport were the principal activities during the remaining winter months, with soccer, squash rackets, hockey, cross-country running and rugby being regularly played. A dozen Officers hunted regularly with the Avon Vale and Tedworth Hounds, although very cold weather put a stop to hunting from 2 December until Boxing Day. The novices boxing team continued their run of success by beating 26 Field Brigade R.A. by 20 points to 10, but then lost to 1st K.O.Y.L.I. by 16 points to 14. The team was composed as follows:

Bantamweight, Fusilier Whitcombe
Featherweight, Fusilier Cullen
Lightweights, Fusilier Chapman, Fusilier Davies, Fusilier Simmonds

---

*   From 1905 to 1948 points were awarded as followed: try – 3; converted try – 5; penalty goal – 3; drop-goal, except from a mark or a penalty – 4. Since a drop-goal is now worth only 3 points this explains how a score of 4–3 was possible.

Middleweight, Fusilier Turner
Welterweights, Fusilier Connor, Fusilier Higgins, Fusilier Tickle
Heavyweight, Fusilier Evans

Attention then turned to the Army Inter-Unit Championship. The team beat the 9th Lancers on 2 February by 27 points to 18 and 1st Hampshires on 5 February by 28 points to 16, although Second Lieutenant Powell received a broken nose in the latter contest, which stopped him fighting further. The team was knocked out of the competition in the Southern Command final by 2nd Loyals, by the narrow margin of 23 points to 21. The team was composed of:

Bantamweight, Fusilier Britton
Featherweights, Lance Sergeant Jones, Corporal J. Durman
Lightweights, Lance Corporal Taylor, Fusilier Cullen, Fusilier Davies
Middleweights, Fusilier Gardner, Lance Corporal Baker, Fusilier Page
Welterweights, Corporal Whatley, Lance Corporal Maloney, Fusilier Evans,
   Fusilier Malley
Light Heavyweight, Fusilier Denner
Heavyweight, Second Lieutenant A.G. ff Powell, Fusilier Devins[23]

Sergeant D.J. Jones beat Ron Brabyn, the Featherweight Amateur Champion of Wales, in Cardiff on 11 June to gain a place in the team representing Wales at the British Empire Games.

The battalion entered a team for the Roberts Trophy, a miniature range competition. Lieutenant Cadogan won the Bell Medal and the *Daily Mail* Certificate; Drum Major Williams won the *Daily Telegraph* Certificate, and CSM Sherriff won the *Daily Herald* Certificate.[24]

St David's Day was celebrated as usual with an all-ranks fancy dress dance, sports, dinners and the W.Os and Sergeants' Mess Ball; **March–April 1934** however for the first time since the 1911–1912 season in Ireland, the battalion was able to hold its own point-to-point races, at Steeple Ashton, by permission of Sir Alfred Slade. Races were held over two laps of the circuit, on a new course. The Red Dragon Cup was won for the second year by Captain Watkins, on 'Airman'.[25] Other races included an event for 2 Brigade R.H.A., an Open Nomination race, a farmers' race and the Government Chargers' race – the latter won by Major S.O. Jones on 'Marzipan'. On 11 April, a Regimental Race for past and present members was held at Windmill Hill, Tidworth, with fifteen entries but only four starters; Captain Watkins was again the victor.[26]

A fragment of the Crimean War Colours was restored to the battalion about this time, joining parts of the Regimental Colour held at the Depot. Full details are given in the Chapter on Regimental Events.

The battalion dispersed for leave over Easter and then at the end of March carried out section and platoon training, and weapon training, on Bulford Ranges.[27] The Battalion Rifle Meeting was held on 30 April and 1 May. RSM Kensett took the individual championship, Lance Corporal Fear won the Young Soldiers' competition, H.Q. Wing won the team competition and D (Support) Company won the tile shoot.

The Southern Command Horse Show was held on 11 and 12 May; **May 1934** Captain R. de B. Hardie won the class for Officers' Chargers on 'Marzipan', and Fusilier Lewis took 3rd place for pairs in the light draught horse event with 'Tim' and 'Yanto',

1 R.W.F. Drums in full dress, 1932–1934. (Norman Weale)

and carried off the special prize for the best individual horse with 'Tim'. Cricket, hockey and athletics were again pursued during the summer months, with mixed success. Further progress was made, however, at Bisley where Sergeant M. Roberts 14 was placed 6th in the Roupell Cup.[28] Progress was maintained in the Southern Command Weapon Training Meeting, where the Light Automatic Pairs team came third, the Young Soldiers came 6th, the Anti-Aircraft team came 5th, the Machine-Gunners 5th and the Rapid Fire team also 5th.[29]

On 1 June, the battalion took part in the 3rd Division's parade for the King's Birthday.[30] A large draft of 185 N.C.Os and Fusiliers was **June–July 1934** ordered to be prepared to join the 2nd Battalion, from an overall battalion strength of 620 all ranks. Battalion training commenced on 25 June and continued until 5 July, after which a demonstration was given to Officers of the Indian Army. Seven Officers, one W.O. II and seven N.C.Os assisted the T.A. Battalions at their camp at Porthcawl from 29 July to 13 August. The battalion also provided a large contingent for the Tidworth Tattoo in early August, after which it dispersed for two weeks' leave.[31]

On return from leave, brigade and divisional manoeuvres **August–September 1934** began on 31 August when the battalion marched to bivouacs on Marlborough Common. There would be little of experimental mechanised warfare in these manoeuvres, which had more in common with the autumn training in India. Sixteen miles were covered the next day, to a rendezvous with 2nd Loyals at Tockenham Wick. On 3 September, the brigade, less 1st K.O.Y.L.I., which was acting as enemy forces, marched to Chippenham for an exercise in night river crossing. This was followed by operations against irregular forces until 10 September, when divisional training commenced. The battalion was depleted in this period by the despatch of the draft of 185 men to 2 R.W.F., now in Hong Kong; however it was able to take its part in 7 Brigade's task of defending a factory complex, working with a screen of cavalry. At dusk on 13 September, the Brigade Commander, Major General Lindsay, realised that he was facing an advance by two full brigades, so emptied all available transport including buses, moved one-and-a-half battalions twenty-five miles (40 kilometres) around the enemy's flank covered by the cavalry, and attacked. A cavalry regiment was surprised asleep, an entire brigade surprised and divisional H.Q. missed by two minutes. Two engineer field companies and a medium artillery battery were captured. The attacking force withdrew in some confusion, to the chagrin, no doubt, of the G.O.C.[32]

This was in fact the last of the old-style manoeuvres involving 1 R.W.F., for on 17 September the brigade, now under Brigadier W. Platt,[*] returned to the Experimental Mobile Force which, as well as 7 Infantry Brigade, included 1 Army Tank Brigade, an armoured car regiment (12th Lancers) mechanised artillery (2 Brigade R.H.A.) and mechanised service support troops. Much of the infantry transport consisted of *Royal Blue* coaches, which proved very welcome as dormitories, as when the formation deployed into bivouacs near Gloucester, the rain came down in torrents. A night move to Hungerford was completed on the 21st, followed by the occupation of a somewhat immobile defensive position and a withdrawal on the night of the 20th which caused a major traffic jam between Hungerford and Newbury – a thing unknown at that time. 'Cease Fire' was sounded early on the 21st and a weary battalion at least enjoyed a rum issue with breakfast, followed by the luxury of motoring home, rather than marching.[33]

On 11 October, the Brigade Commander carried out his annual administrative inspection. On 15 October an all-ranks dance was held

October 1934

as a farewell to a further draft which was to depart the following morning for the 2nd Battalion in Gibraltar. In November, Captain and Brevet Major W.H. Albutt retired after thirty-seven years' service, most of which had been spent with the battalion. Major Albutt had served throughout the Great War and had been commissioned from the ranks, receiving the DCM and the OBE for his achievements. The battalion was joined by its first Canadian Exchange Officer, Captain P.J.F. Mignault, following the alliance with the Royal 22nd Regiment of Canada (see the Chapter on Regimental Events). Lieutenant R.J.F. Snead-Cox went to Canada, completing the exchange.[34]

Attention then turned once more to individual training and sport. Rugby, soccer and hockey were all played with more enthusiasm than concrete results. The Novices Boxing team beat the 9th Lancers and the 4th/7th Dragoon Guards in the opening rounds of the S.P.A. competition. Receiving a bye into the final, the team was beaten by 2nd Loyals in the Southern Command final by 18 points to 15. However Lieutenant Powell entered for, and won, the Officers' Heavyweight Individual Championship.[35]

The battalion took part in trials of the *Morris* truck and utility tractor on Salisbury Plain. This was a period of sustained heat and drought, the Digest of Service quoting Salisbury Plain

---

[*]   Later General Sir William Platt GBE KCB DSO (1885–1975). He was G.O.C.-in-C. East African Command in 1942 and as such, planned and directed the invasion of Madagascar in which 2 R.W.F. took part.

Area Orders in saying that the consumption of water in barracks had surpassed last year's total by 100,000 gallons (454,600 litres).

The battalion dispersed for leave over Christmas and the New Year on 11 December, although fifty men remained in barracks where **December 1934** a programme of entertainments with a first-rate Christmas dinner were laid on. Every man received a free ration of beer and cigarettes. Eighteen of these men had volunteered for research work at the Anti-Gas Experimental Station, Porton Down.[36]

The battalion reassembled on 12 January 1935, drafts from the Depot bringing its strength back up to 584 all ranks, less Officers, **January 1935** against an establishment of 763. Shortly afterwards, it received a visit from the Chinese Military Mission, whose fifteen members were 'vastly interested in our mechanized transport.'[37] A team from D (Support) Company won the Army Rifle Association's *Vickers* M.G. Cup, with a margin of more than 100 points over their nearest rivals. The team was composed as follows:

Captain: Lieutenant W.L.R. Benyon
Assistant: Sergeant R. Gendall

No 1 Detachment	No 2 Detachment	No 3 Detachment
Lance Corporal Henshaw	Lance Corporal E. Davies	Lance Corporal E. Davies
Lance Corporal Tickle	Lance Corporal Frith	Lance Corporal H. Stapley
Lance Corporal McCarthy	Fusilier W. Turner	Fusilier H. Scott
Lance Corporal I. Roberts	Fusilier Hoffman	Fusilier E. Davies

New Battalion Standing Orders to supplement Regimental Standing Orders, were issued on the authority of the Commanding Officer. St **March 1935** David's Day was celebrated as usual, with the Colonel of the Regiment attending. Other guests included Brigadier C.C. Norman and Colonel Hewitt, both former Commanding Officers; and Officers from brigade units and from the Regimental Depot. The Tedworth Hounds met by invitation that morning at the Officers' Mess. The point-to-point races were again held at Steeple Ashton, with the Red Dragon Cup won by Captain H.B. Harrison on 'Wild Duck'.

Soccer and rugby were also played and, with the coming of warmer weather, cricket and athletics. Corporal Whelan of H.Q. Wing beat **June 1935** CQMS W. Tubby to win the Victor Ludorum in the battalion athletics meeting at Tidworth Oval on 3 June. The battalion contributed as usual to the Tidworth Tattoo in late May and then moved on to its own collective training period before dispersing for two weeks leave in August. This was followed by the Southern Command Weapon Training Meeting, where the results fell short of previous years.

During brigade and divisional manoeuvres, which took place away from Salisbury Plain around Whitchurch and Winchester during **September 1935** late August and early September, in very poor weather, experiments were carried out in the use of the *Universal* carrier. Most of the manoeuvres seemed to consist of rearguard actions. Training culminated in Army manoeuvres, the first for many years. These began in a gale, while the battalion was under canvas at Fargo Camp near Larkhill and the storm blew away most of the camp, much of the men's kit and equipment, and soaked everyone to the skin. Thereafter, attention turned to the move from Tidworth, which was to be completed in the late autumn.

The Red Dragon Cup, 1935. From left, Bruxner-Randall, J.R. Johnson, B.E. Hopkins and S.O. Jones.
(R.W.F. Mus)

The Brigade Commander made his farewell visit on 4 December, **December 1935** followed by the G.O.C. 3rd Infantry Division on the 13th. On the 15th, the Advance Party under Captain H.D.T. Morris, with B Company, left Tidworth for Woking, followed on the 30th by the main body. The Brigade Commander wrote to the Commanding Officer, saying that:

> You have taken a considerable part in the many experiments for the future of the infantry, which have necessitated much work and thought by the Battalion. You have been most successful in the conduct of these experiments... You can move tomorrow, confident that, in the life and many activities of an Infantry Battalion, you have upheld your great reputation.[38]

Staff List, 1 R.W.F. Tidworth, 1932–1935

Lieutenant Colonel
Bt Col E.O. Skaife OBE
J.G. Bruxner-Randall (May 33)
Major
Ll. A.A. Alston (Oct 32) (HQ Wing)
T.D. Daly MC
E. Wodehouse (to Sep 32)
J.G. Bruxner-Randall

Lieutenant
M.F.P. Lloyd (Adjt to Dec 35)
R.F.A. David
J.G. Vyvyan
P.F. Pritchard (to Nov 35)
J.H. Liscombe
M.H. ap Rhys Pryce
R.J.F. Snead-Cox
M.W. Whittaker

W.O. II
J.M. Kensett
R. Thomas (Nov 34)
I.G. Smalldon
E. Davies 78
B. Clancy
J. Soane (to Dec 33)
W. Howells (to Dec 33)
J.M. Bacon (Jun 35)

D.M. Barchard
P.C. Kenyon MC
W.H. Albutt MBE DCM (to Nov 34)
D.H.W. Kirkby (Mar 35)
Captain
W.H. Bamfield (to Jun 35)
H.A. Freeman OBE MC
H.B. Harrison MC
R. de B. Hardie
P.J.F. Mignault *R.22eR.* (Nov 34)
M.B. Dowse
G.N.H. Taunton-Collins
S.O. Jones MC
T.S. Griffiths (Jun 35)
H.D.T. Morris (Mar 34)
H.C. Watkins MC
H.F. Garnons-Williams (to Jan 34)
A.M.G. Evans (Maj Jan 34)
Quartermaster
Lt G.R. Whyley MBE
Lt A.G. Bent MM (Jan 35)
RQMS H.F. Bradstreet
Attached
Sgt G. Walker *R.A.S.C.*
Sgt Coggins *A.E.C.*
Sgt A.C. Wright *Rhodesia*
Sgt R.A. Cummings *R.A.O.C.* (Nov 34)
WO I
RSM R.W. Chambers
RSM J.M. Kensett (Sep1933)
BM W.J. Watkins
Lance-Sergeants
F. Norman
W. Nedderman
D.J. Jones 92
J. Austin (to Dec 33)
C. Brooker (Dec 33)
P. Graham
J. Durman
J. Puschart
Freeman
Turvey
H. Jenkins (Sgt Dec 33)
W. Scammels (Dec 33)
F. Whitley (Dec 33)
W. Lodder (Dec 33)

E.M. Davies-Jenkins
H.A.S. Clarke (Adjt Dec 35)
C.H.V. Pritchard
P.L. Bowers
H. de B. Prichard
G.E. Braithwaite
N.R.G. Bosanquet
R. Snead-Cox
E.H. Cadogan
J.P.E. Bernatchez *R22eR* (Dec 35)
G.R.W.P. Lipsett (to Mar 33)
M.B. Courtney (Jun 35)
N.C. Stockwell
T.D. Butler (to Dec 33)
M.F.P. Lloyd-Harries (to Nov 34)
2nd Lieutenant
R.C.R. Price
W.L.R. Benyon (Lt Jan 34)
G.E.C. Barton
L.H. Yates
O.T.M. Raymont (to Jun 35)
H.A.S. Clarke
R.C.M. Kelly
D.M.C. Prichard
B.P. Doughty-Wylie
A.G. ff Powell
A.J. Lewis
J.E. Vaughan
J.W. Riley
F.C. Minshull-Ford
J.E.T. Willes (Dec 34)
R.O.F. Pritchard (July 35)
G.T.B.F. Dickson (Dec 35)
A. Forbes (Mar – Aug 33)
Sergeants
G. Davies 49 MM
Williams 64
Roberts 52
Wilkinson
W. Hawkins
Adams
Helier
W. Brown 19 (CSM Jun 35)
Jones 92
E.T. Kidgell
W. Cooper
S. Grindley

C. Morrisey (to Jun 35)
S. Sherriff (Dec 33)
S. Metcalfe (Dec 33)
G. Morris (Dec 33)
W. Brown 19 Jun 35
N. Ridings
CQMS
V.S. Smart
G. Johnson
O.J. Stanley
W. Tubby (Nov 33)
Ll. Jones 94
R. Gendall (Dec 35)
R. Thomas 78 (CSM Nov 34)
Brown (Mar 35)
Staff Sergeants
O.R.S. I. Hughes
O.R.C. G. Godfrey (Dec 35)
DMaj J.M. Bacon
DMaj G. Williams (1933)
SIM A.T. Currie
Armr Sgt F.G. Moore
Pnr Sgt F. Holehouse
Cook Sgt Kretzschmer (Jun 35)
Band Sgt A. Galbraith
Sergeants
W. Tubby
E. Davies
Brown 53
C. Clemence BEM (to Dec 33)
A. Cheetham (CQMS Sep 34)
M. Roberts 14 (CQMS Nov 34)
– Robins
S. Sherriff (CSM Dec 33)
J. Bean
Salisbury
W. Cowan
L. Macey (CQMS Mar 34, CSM Nov 34)
Neil
V. Fraser
G. Timmins
O. Jones 99
J. Cutler (Dec 33)
J. Jones 22
W. Norman (Mar 34)
R. Gendall (CQMS Dec 35)

ii. Woking, 1936–1937

The battalion exchanged barracks in Woking with the 1st Royal Warwicks, where it joined 6 Infantry Brigade, under the command

January 1936

of Brigadier N.M.S. Irwin,[*] part of the 2nd Infantry Division, at first under Major General A.P. Wavell;[†] and from 1937 to 1939 under Major General H. Maitland Wilson.[‡] It was to remain with this brigade, in different stations and theatres of operations, for the next ten years. Also in 6 Brigade were the 1st Durham L.I. and the 1st Duke of Cornwall's L.I., the latter at Blackdown. The battalion arrived in Woking with twenty-nine Officers and 611 N.C.Os and Fusiliers, 152 short of its established strength but complete in Officers.[39]

The barracks were actually a former women's prison; as W.L.R. Benyon recalled, the Sergeants' Mess bar was in the old condemned cells. He also recalled that:

> Woking was a super place to be, lovely cricket ground and it was really rather fun, we were just far enough away from Aldershot not to get everlastingly bothered, but close enough to be in the swim for the nice things that went on. I would say we were a thoroughly nice and happy battalion, a jolly good cricket team with people like Edward Cadogan, and Rodney David and others, all of whom had been of good school standard and we used to play matches against schools 2nd XIs.[40]

R.O.F. Prichard similarly recalled that:

> There was an excellent cricket ground and a lot of minor training areas on the doorstep. Old-fashioned things, like Church Parades, were made voluntary, so that if you happened to be in barracks you were expected to go, but if you were playing, golf or cricket, or you had gone home for the weekend you were excused… Before this we all used to march to church preceded by the Band and Drums.[41]

---

[*]   Later Lieutenant General Noel Mackintosh Stuart Irwin CB DSO MC (1892–1972). He played a prominent role in the British Army after the Dunkirk evacuation, and in the Burma Campaign. He was also instrumental in reforms to the training and equipment of British soldiers after the defeat in France in 1940.

[†]   Later Field Marshal Earl (Archibald Percival) Wavell, 1st Earl (1947) GCB GCSI GCIE CMG MC PC (1883 –1950) was later C.-in-C. Middle East, C.-in-C. India from July 1941 until June 1943 and Viceroy of India until his retirement in February 1947.

[‡]   Later Field Marshal Lord (Henry Maitland) Wilson, ('Jumbo') 1st Baron (1946) GCB GBE DSO (1881 –1964), was later G.O.C-in-C. British Troops in Egypt, Military Governor of Cyrenaica, Commander of the Commonwealth expeditionary force to Greece in April 1941 and G.O.C. British Forces in Palestine and Trans-Jordan in May 1941. He became G.O.C-in-C. Ninth Army in Syria and Palestine in October 1941, General Officer Commanding Persia and Iraq Command in August 1942 and G.O.C.-in-C. Middle East Command in February 1943. In the closing stages of the War he was Supreme Allied Commander in the Mediterranean, from January 1944, and then Chief of the British Joint Staff Mission in Washington D.C. from January 1945. He was one of the most consistently successful British Generals of the Second World War.

Here in Woking, the revised Establishment was adopted, as described in Chapter 3. The battalion was reorganised into four rifle companies, each of four platoons of three sections; each section had a rifle team and a light-automatic team equipped with the new *Bren* gun.[42] H.Q. Wing was renamed H.Q. Company and comprised four platoons: Signals, L.M.Gs for anti-aircraft and ground defence, Mortars, and Administration (Including transport). However at short notice, D Company was re-formed in January into a Machine-Gun Company.[43] As early as December 1935, a warning order was received to the effect that the battalion would be re-organised again as a machine-gun battalion during 1936.[44]

The badge of the 2nd Infantry Division.

R.O.F. Prichard recalled how, during the winter months, the Officers of 1 R.W.F. organised their hunting on a more or less permanent basis with the South Berks and the Vine Hunts. At least ten Officers hunted regularly, and others occasionally, and W.L.R. Benyon recalled that 'the policy was that those who hunted did so, and those who did not, did the work for those who did… If you did not own a horse you were not expected to drink a glass of port after dinner.'[45]

> We took a cottage at Mortimer near Reading, kept by an old farmer called Marks who was very keen on hunting. Our grooms stayed in the cottage during the season and Marks supervised them and our horses. We used to hunt a couple of days a week, usually with the South Berks or the Vine. You could hunt on practically nothing by getting a "fifteen bobber", an army charger, from a company commander who wasn't interested in hunting. You paid fifteen bob (15/- or 75p) a month and the Army provided the feed.[46]

On the night of 20 January 1936, King George V, Colonel-in-Chief, died and was succeeded by his eldest son as Edward VIII. A representative detachment of the battalion under Captain H.D.T. Morris with twenty N.C.Os and Fusiliers marched in the King's funeral procession from Westminster to Paddington Station on 28 January.[47]

The Boxing team entered the Army Cup for 1936 but were beaten in the first round by 2nd K.R.R.C. by 10 bouts to 5. The winners were Lance-Sergeant Jones (Featherweight, knockout), Lance-Sergeant Durman (Featherweight, points), Corporal Nedderman (Light Heavyweight, points), Corporal McCarthy (Lightweight, points) and Fusilier Higgins (Welterweight, knockout).[48] Soccer, rugby, hockey and cross-country running were also played extensiely.

St David's Day was celebrated as usual. The Red Dragon and **March 1936** Barnett-Parker races were held in the Garth Country on 13 March. The two races were held simultaneously over a five mile course with a variety of fences, starting at the George and Dragon Inn, Swallowfield Park. Major E. Wodehouse won the Red Dragon race on 'Benedict', and Lieutenant R.F.A. David won the Barnett-Barker race on 'Cherry Lad'.

Individual, section and platoon training were completed during the spring. In May, the battalion provided several teams for the Aldershot Tattoo including the physical training display, the Regimental Band and the Corps of Drums. A large detachment was also provided for administrative duties. While at Aldershot, much use was made of the facilities for swimming; and a great deal of machine-gun training was also carried out.

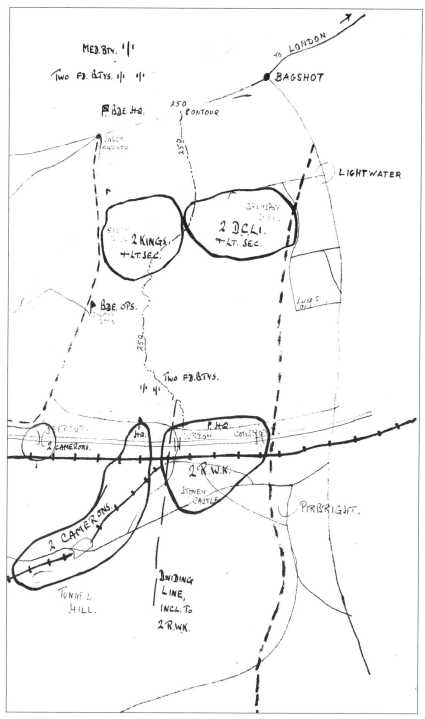

Divisional manoeuvres in the 1930s. (Minshull-Ford albums)

With the coming of warmer weather, athletics and cricket were pursued with more enthusiasm than success. A parade was held in honour of the King's Birthday on 23 June.[49]

The battalion moved to West Chiltington Camp, Sussex for battalion, brigade and higher formation training on 27 July,[50] returning on 19 August. The weather during the period was cold and wet. The culmination was Exercise *Golden Fleece*, a five day manoeuvre which involved marching eighty miles and ended with a phase of mechanized training,[51] devised by the G.O.C., Major General A.P. Wavell. R.O.F. Pritchard remembered that:

July–August 1936

> The exercise was designed to test the stamina of the troops taking part and to find out how long troops could continue to operate without sleep. In brief, our task was the capture the Golden Fleece, but after a long approach march each night it was found that the fleece had been moved, necessitating another long march during the next day and the following night. this process went on for a considerable period and it was the only time during peacetime that I have seen whole columns of men marching asleep, each man hanging on to the bayonet scabbard of the man in front. Two brother Officers, in another company, had to position their somewhat elderly company commander between them as left on his own he repeatedly simply walked into a ditch or hedge at the side of the road.[52]

Congratulating the battalion on its work during the exercise, the Brigade Commander wrote that:

> The long hours during which they were under Arms by day and night constituted a severe test on their physical fitness. The fact that they finished the last Exercise in such good

Divisional manoeuvres, 1936; 1 R.W.F. cyclists as enemy forces. (R.W.F. Mus 4161)

spirits and were ready to press on shows that all ranks are imbued with a good spirit and are physically fit.[53]

On 7 October, the Brigade Commander carried out his annual inspection. A draft of forty men was sent to the 2nd Battalion in Hong Kong and a draft of twenty-four recruits was received from the Depot, maintaining the battalion's strength at 630, without Officers.[54]

With effect from 1 November, the battalion was converted to the Machine-Gun role. The conversion began with the training of N.C.Os

November 1936

on the *Vickers* gun,[55] and progressed to the training of soldiers. D Company, having been M.G. Company, lost around 65% of its personnel to other companies both to provide a nucleus of expertise and to provide the required drivers, since the battalion's establishment of vehicles increased considerably.[56] As R.O.F. Prichard remembered, this meant that:

> … we were completely mechanised and everybody had to learn to drive. They became rather good at it. We trained very hard because we had all the new equipment, and we needed to train drivers and technicians, as well as mastering the new tactics that went with being a machine gun battalion. On the M.T. course at Aldershot we used to go on night driving exercises, round Hyde Park Corner and back! On Saturday mornings there was a recovery exercise. Each team had a u/s vehicle and when it was repaired the team were free to start their weekend.
>
> We had the *Vickers* gun and … the *Lewis* Gun, with its thirty-two stoppages, and the .303 rifle. The *Lewis* Gun was replaced by the *Bren* which had practically no stoppages compared with the *Lewis* Gun.
>
> The C.O., Gerry Bruxner-Randall, got on very well with Wavell and, as a result, we did rather more imaginative training than was usually done by battalions at that time…[57]

The expected Coronation of King Edward VIII never took place during 1936 and after the Abdication Crisis, George VI was proclaimed King on 11 December (see the Chapter on Regimental Events and the Annex on Colonels-in-Chief). Benyon, by now Adjutant, recalled how on 14 December:

> … We were sent to London to line the streets for the Heralds to drive through and proclaim the new King from the steps of St Paul's Cathedral. We were in Ludgate Hill just opposite the Old Bailey and we had the Goat with us, and whilst we were there a policeman approached me and said "I wonder, sir, if you could move that animal back behind, because the Chief Commissioner of Police is coming down in a minute or two to inspect the lines and I don't think his horse will like the Goat"! So I got rather pompous and said "What! Move His Majesty's Goat for a policeman? Total nonsense!" Anyway, nothing happened. Eventually a more senior Officer appeared and asked very nicely for the Goat to be moved. Meanwhile I had had second thoughts and realised that a Sovereign's Escort of the Household Cavalry was going to come up the hill any minute and if they were all going to stand on their hind legs at the sight of a goat, I might not be very popular. So, rather reluctantly, I had the Goat moved into the crowd. However, when the Chief of Police appeared his horse knew and refused to pass, so they had to make a detour down a back alley![58]

Immediately afterwards, the battalion dispersed for leave over Christmas and the New Year.[59]

In the New Year 1937, hunting was again prominent. At about this time, Lieutenant G.E. Braithwaite, who was then Adjutant of the 4th Battalion at Wrexham, built the Regimental point-to-point course at Marchwiel. This was generally agreed to be a terrific course with excellent fences: the Regimental Pioneers had been sent off to Cheltenham to do a course in fence-buildng:

> **January 1937**

> It was something that no other infantry battalion had ever done before … The first point-to-point at Wrexham was a marvellous meeting with a tremendous attendance. The last meeting before the War [1938 or 1939] there were thirty-two going in the nomination races which was really unbelievable.[60]

The boxing team prepared for the inter-unit competitions by competing in civilian tournaments around London. In the Aldershot Command Novices' tournament, the team beat the 4th Queen's Own Hussars in the semi-final by 13 bouts to 2, including nine knockouts. In the final, the team beat 1st D.L.I. by 22 points to 16. The team was:

> Featherweight, Fusilier Morgan, Fusilier Condick
> Lightweights, Fusilier Roberts, Fusilier Ross, Fusilier Wood
> Middleweight, Fusilier Weaver, Fusilier Parry, Fusilier Jones 19
> Welterweights, Drummer Hughes, Fusilier Murtagh, Fusilier Davies, Fusilier Knight
> Light Heavyweight, Fusilier Jones 62

A Company began training to convert to being an anti-tank gun company, with instructors being sent to the Armoured School at Bovington.[61] CSM W. Tubby and Sergeant S. Scammells achieved a distinction during the first course. Sergeant Whelan also achieved the same on the third course. All junior N.C.Os were put through a fire-control course by Major H.A. Freeman and Lieutenant H.A.S. Clarke. Six drummers were also trained as motor-cycle despatch riders along with most of the Signal Platoon.

St David's Day 1937 was observed as a holiday, with the usual celebrations. The W.Os' and Sergeants' Mess Ball was held in the N.R.A. Pavillion at Bisley. The battalion boys* were taken to London during the holiday. The Regimental Point-to-Point races were held on 13 March, with four races on the card. The Past and Present was won by Mr L.T. Lillington on 'Killadar; the Open Nomination, a field of twenty-six, was won by Mr P. Moseley on 'Carnaroy'. The Red Dragon Cup was won by Lieutenant B.P. Doughty-Wylie on 'Black Boy'. Finally, the Farmers' race was won by Mr W.F. Williamson on 'Dark Pointer'.[62]

> **March 1937**

On 17 April, a farewell parade was held on the barrack square for Lieutenant Colonel Bruxner-Randall. He was succeeded by Lieutenant Colonel Ll. A. A. Alston DSO MC.

---

*   Boys' service had been a feature of the British Army since the English Civil Wars. By the beginning of the Great War, boys service could start at 13 (reflecting the school leaving age). In some cases these boys were regimental orphans. In infantry battalions, boys were trained as drummers or bandsmen, and sometimes as apprentices to the Sergeant Tailor or Shoemaker. They could not be sent on active service but in peacetime finished their boys' service before mustering for man's service.

The 1st Battalion Coronation party. (R.W.F. Mus)

Front Row: Cpl. Beach, Sgt. Mills, Sgt. Randall, Sgt. Tubby, Lt. Benyon, Maj. H.R. Freeman, R.S.M. J. Kenset, C.Q.M.S. Roberts, Sgt. Austin, Sgt. Adams, Cpl. Moran.
Colour Party: 5. 6. 7. Second Row from left: Sgt. Simmons, Lt. Willes, Sgt. Priest.

The 1st Battalion Band dressed and ready for the Coronation. (R.W.F. Mus)

In April and May the battalion supplied a large detail for duties connected with the Coronation, as described in the Chapter on Regimental Matters. Demonstrations of anti-tank gunnery were given by A Company to Empire troops visiting for the Coronation; similar demonstrations were also given to the R.M.C. Sandhurst and the Staff College.[63] The Regimental Band and the Corps of Drums took part in the Aldershot Tattoo on 23 May. From 9 to 22 June, the battalion moved to Warminster for the Machine Gun Concentration Camp. Immediately afterwards, a large team was despatched to take part in the Aldershot Command Small Arms Meeting. In the competitions, the battalion secured fifth place overall in the Command and also won the Aggregate Cup and the R. & F. Rifle Match. Among the individual competitiors, Fusilier Davidson came 2nd in the Young Soldiers' Match.[64] At Bisley, CSM S. Sherriff won second place in Queen Mary's Prize with a score of 173, only one point behind the winner. He was awarded the A.R.A. silver medal and a cash prize of £15.00 (more than £800 in terms of purchasing power at 2018 rates).[65]

June 1937

A Guard of Honour of 100 N.C.Os and Fusiliers drawn from A and B Companies, with the Regimental Band, Corps of Drums, Pioneers and Goat, were on parade at Caernarfon on the occasion of the visit by The King and Queen on 15 July. The battalion had last undertaken a similar duty for the Investiture of The Prince of Wales in 1911. The Band and Pioneers travelled by train with the remainder moving in their five two-seater *Austins,* twenty-seven 15-cwt trucks and eight motor-cycles and one water truck (since no expense other than that allowed for normal training could be incurred) – and the Goat went by special truck via the Depot, where it spent the night under cover. The road march took three full days. The first day ended after 130 miles (209 kilometres) at Lee Castle, near Kidderminster. The second day ended near Bridgnorth for tactical training. The third day's march ended in Wrexham, with liberty to walk out that evening. The final day's march covered the journey to Caernarfon, via Llangollen, Capel Curig and Llanberis Pass. Astonishingly, all the vehicles made the round trip without mechanical failure.[66]

July 1937

His Majesty King George VI inspects the Guard of the 1st Battalion at Caernarfon, 15 July 1937. The Guard Commander is Major H.A. Freeman OBE MC, the Lieutenant is Second Lieutenant the Hon R.S. Best and the Ensign is Second Lieutenant H.G. Brougham. (R.W.F. Mus)

The whole detachment marched from Coed Helen across the swing bridge into Caernarfon. From the Water Gate of the Castle, the streets were lined by the Regiment's Territorial battalions and the detachment continued on across Castle Square, past the War Memorial, and on to the railway station – the whole way through dense crowds. The Royal train drew up on time at 15.30 hrs and after the usual presentations, the Guard greeted The King and Queen with a Royal Salute. The King then inspected the Guard and left for his visit. The troops then fell out for tea and were on parade again for Their Majesties' departure at 18.00 hrs. The King afterwards 'expressed his satisfaction at the turnout of the Guard and their steadiness on parade.' in a letter to the Colonel of the Regiment.[67] The parade state was:

Officer Commanding: Bt Major H.A. Freeman OBE MC
Second Lieutenant the Hon R.S. Best
Second Lieutenant H.G. Brougham, ensign for the King's Colour
RSM J.M. Kensett
Band Master W.J. Watkins
Pioneer Sergeant A. E. Evans
Drum Major G. Lavender

August–October 1937

After two weeks leave, the battalion moved to Branches Park Camp near Newmarket on 16 August for battalion, brigade and higher formation training in the East Anglian Manoeuvre Area,* returning on 11 September. From 16 to 21 September, Major T.D. Daly, Captain H.A. Freeman and Lieutenant J.E.T. Willes attended a War Office study and training period. Training did not prevent the annual families' outing which this year took place in September at Brighton, whither a large party of excited children with their parents was moved by motor-coach.

The Colonel of the Regiment, Lieutenant General Sir Charles Dobell, visited and inspected the battalion on 1 October. A Company then moved to Lydd ranges in Kent to fire the provisional anti-tank gun courses for the first time.[68]

On 25 October, the battalion moved once more, this time to Blackdown.[69]

Staff List, 1 R.W.F. Woking, 1935–1937

Lieutenant Colonel	Lieutenant	W.O. II
J.G. Bruxner-Randall	J.G. Vyvyan	I.G. Smalldon
Ll. A. A. Alston CMG DSO MC (18 May 37)	M.H. ap Rhys Pryce	E. Davies 78
	R.J.F. Snead-Cox (Nov 36)	J. Brown (to Jul 36)
Major	E.M. Davies-Jenkins (to May 37)	W. Brown 19
Bt Lt Col T.D. Daly MC	H.A.S. Clarke (Adjt, then Signals Offr) (to Mar 37)	F. Wilkinson (Jul 37)
J.G. Bruxner-Randall		J.M. Bacon
Ll. A.A. Alston CMG DSO MC	N.C. Stockwell	R. Thomas
D.M. Barchard	J.H. Liscombe	A.T. Currie

* Not to be confused with Stanford Training Area in Norfolk, requisitioned in 1940. The East Anglian Manoeuvre Area was simply an area of agricultural land around Newmarket which had been cleared for training.

P.C. Kenyon MC
D.H.W. Kirkby
Captain
Bt Maj H.A. Freeman OBE MC
(Dec 36)
H.B. Harrison MC (to Dec 36)
A.D.M. Lewis MBE
R. de B. Hardie (to Dec 36)
G.N.H. Taunton-Collins (to Jan 37)
W.H. Bamfield (Jul 37)
Bt Maj M.B. Dowse (to Mar 36)
Bt Maj H.C. Watkins MC
S.O. Jones MC
T.S. Griffiths
H.D.T. Morris (Maj Feb 37)
Quartermaster
Lt A.G. Bent MM
RQMS H.F. Bradstreet (to Jul 37)
RQMS S. Sherriff (Aug 37)
Attached
AQMS F.G. Moore
Sgt G. Walker *R.A.S.C.*
Sgt R. Cummings *R.A.O.C.*
WO I
RSM J.M. Kensett
BM WJ. Watkins

R.F.A. David (Adjt ?36) (to Jun 37)
C.H.V. Pritchard
P.L. Bowers
H. de B. Prichard
N.R.G. Bosanquet
C.E. Hill
E.H. Cadogan (to Feb 37)
J.P.E. Bernatchez *R. 22e R.*
W.L.R. Benyon (Adjt Dec 36)
2nd Lieutenant
R.C.R. Price
G.E.C. Barton
L.H. Yates
H.A.S. Clarke
R.C.M. Kelly
D.M.C. Prichard
B.P. Doughty-Wylie
A.G. ff Powell
R.O.F. Prichard
A.J. Lewis
J.E. Vaughan (Lt Sep 36)
F.C. Minshull-Ford
J.E.T. Willes (Lt Feb 37)
G.T.B.F. Dickson (Lt Sep 37)
Hon R.S. Best (Feb 37)
R.L. Boyle (Mar – Dec 36)
H.G. Brougham (Mar – Jun 36)
J.E.C. Hood (Sep 36–Mar 37)
F.B.E. Cotton (Feb 37)
M.G. Harrison (Feb 37)
E.D.K. Menzies (Sep 37)
Lance-Sergeants
W. Nedderman[2]
R.A. Cummings
C. Brooker
P. Graham
J. Durman
J. Puschart
- Freeman
- Turvey
F. Whitley
W. Lodder
F. Norman
J. Jones 22
- Balfe
J. Purcell
A. Chesters (to Dec 36)
R. Preest
E. Power
G. Whatley
- Clark (Sgt Jan 37)
G. Fender (Jan 37)
- Anders (Jul 37)

S. Metcalfe
G. Morris
Griffiths
N. Ridings
W. Hawkins
W. Tubby (Jul 36)
CQMS
V.S. Smart
G. Johnson
W. Tubby (CSM Jul 36)
Ll. Jones 94
A.T. Currie (CSM Jul 36)
- Watkins (Jan 37)
O.J. Stanley
M. Roberts 14
A. Cheetham
R. Gendall
M. Roberts 14
J. Harrison (Dec 36)
W. Leicester (Dec 36)
Staff Sergeants
ORS I. Hughes
ORC G. Godfrey
Band Sgt A. Galbraith
MT Sgt Curran
SIM J. Cutler
DMaj W.P. Williams[1]
DMaj G. Lavender (Jul
37)
Pnr Sgt F. Holehouse (to
Dec 36)
Pnr Sgt A.E. Evans
Cook Sgt Kretzchmer
Sergeants
E. Davies
S. Scammell
G. Timmins
A.R. James
J. Bean
H. Jenkins
W. Cowan
- Neil
- Brown 53
- Timmins
O. Jones 99
J. Cutler (Dec 33)
J. Jones 22
W. Norman
S. Grindley
E.T. Kidgell
W. Cooper (to Jan 37)
G. Davies MM
- Williams 64

- Marvin (Dec 37)
- Davies 79 (Dec 37)
P. Dwyer

- Roberts 52
T. Adams
- Helier
W. Leicester (CQMS Dec 36)
- Spencer
- Lowe
J. Dwyer (Dec 36)
G. Mills
E.T. Langford
W. Jones 92 (Jan 37)
F. Whelan
R. Austin

Notes

1   Died from injuries sustained in a traffic accident, April 1937.
2   Died from injuries sustained in a traffic accident, September 1937.

iii. Blackdown, and Preparations for War

At Blackdown, the battalion exchanged Dettingen Barracks with the Duke of Cornwall's L.I. with a strength, on arrival, of two W.Os I, four W.Os II, thirty Staff Sergeants and Sergeants, forty-four Lance Corporals and Corporals, sixteen Drummers and 507 Fusiliers, a total of 602 all ranks, without Officers.[70] The barracks in Blackdown were hutted and those huts which housed the Officers' Mess had been condemned after the Great War. R.O.F. Prichard remembered that

> One night, whilst changing for dinner, I put my foot through the floor of my room. While we were there a new mess was built and the King came to open it. Shortly before he arrived two ceilings collapsed so the rooms were locked and he was not shown around that particular building.[71]

It was here that, as the uneasy years of peace which separated the two Great Wars dragged out towards their inevitable climax, a new note of urgency became discernible in the pattern of Service training even though peacetime activities – tattoos, hunting, sports and games and so on – continued. To most people, perhaps, the Defence White Paper of 1937, with its doubling of the Territorial Army and its staggering additions to the Service Estimates, struck the first real warning note of the dangers that lay so close ahead. As its sombre warning became evident, a new determination by the nation to accept the inevitable challenge swept through the countryside.[72]

The years 1938 and 1939 were to be strenuous ones for the battalion, calling for a maximum effort on the part of every man to equip himself for the coming battle. One after another the German crises followed each other in Europe; the occupation of the Rhineland, the march into Austria, the annexation of the Sudetenland, the rape of Czechoslovakia, the seizure of Memel, and the final storm over Danzig. Each one told the same story, the steady growth of German military might and the insatiable lust for power which backed its growth. It was through that period of bewilderment, of alternate hopes of peace and threats of war, that the 1st Battalion carried through its final stages of peace-time training. Steadily, the battalion began to prepare itself for war, its eyes fixed firmly on the need for professional skill, endurance, and discipline. Though the work was unspectacular, though it called for a large degree of patient endeavour on the part of every Officer and man in times of particular difficulty, it was carried through with determination.[73]

Shortly after arrival, in November, the battalion Novices' Boxing team won the Aldershot Command Cup, beating 2nd Cheshires by 21 points to 17. The team was:

Featherweights, Lance Corporal Smith, Lance Corporal Monaghan
Lightweights, Lance Corporal Davies, Lance Corporal Thomas, Fusilier Roberts
Middleweight, Fusilier Cradle, Fusilier Gizzie, Fusilier Bishton
Welterweights, Fusilier Nolan, Fusilier Rees, Fusilier Jenkins, Fusilier Otton
Light Heavyweight, Fusilier Massey

Subsequently, the team was knocked out of the Army Cup in the semi-finals by the Welch Regiment.

In December 1937, B Company won the A.R.A. Machine Gun Fire Control Cup.[74] The G.O.C. 2nd Division, Major General H.M. Wilson, presented the cup on 6 February 198.

January–February 1938

The battalion dispersed for leave over Christmas and re-assembled for individual, section and platoon training during the early months of the year. On 12 February 1938, Lieutenant N.C. Stockwell, Second Lieutenant M.G. Harrison and a draft of 101 men left to join the 2nd Battalion, reducing the battalion to 517 all ranks, without Officers. A further draft of seventy-two men under Second Lieutenant E.D.K. Menzies left at the beginning of March. In exchange, the battalion received a draft of nineteen recruits from the Depot, and 194 men from the 2nd Battalion on 17 March, the net result was that the battalion's strength rose to 652 all ranks, less Officers.[75]

March 1938

St David's Day was celebrated as usual. In the Regimental Point-to-Point meeting at Marchwiel, the Red Dragon Cup was won by Lieutenant E.C. Parker-Jarvis on 'Henwyn', and the Barnett-Barker Cup by Lieutenant J.E.T. Willes on 'Clickety-Click'. The soccer team entered the Army Cup for 1938 and on 23 March beat the R.A.O.C. Depot Hilsea by 1-0 in the semi-final, having previously beaten 1st Welsh Guards 2-1, and 2nd Bedfords and Hertfords 1-0. In the final against R.A. Shoeburyness on 18 April, however, the team lost 0-3. The team was:

Sergeant J. Durman
Lance-Sergeant E. Power
Corporal H. Cutler
Lance-Corporals P. Glynn, H. Hooley and R. Jones
Bandsman L. Ridley
Fusiliers J. Davis, E. Wheeler, W. Hyde and A. Morgan 65.[76]

The King, as Colonel-in-Chief, sent a message of congratulation to the team on having reached the final; by a happy chance, the 7th Battalion had also reached the final of the T.A. Championship, which they won.[77] The King had learned of the matter from the Colonel of the

Royal Welch Fusiliers.

HISTORIC FOOTBALL MATCH,

1st. BATT. ROYAL WELCH FUSILIERS

(Finalists in the Regular Army Football Championship),

versus

7th BATT. ROYAL WELCH FUSILIERS

(Winners of the Territorial Army Football Championship).

AT NEWTOWN   ::   THURSDAY, MAY 5th, 1938.

OFFICIAL PROGRAMME, 1d.

The Royal Welch Fusiliers has always been noted as a regiment which takes great interest in all forms of sport.

Hardly a year goes by without some teams of the Regiment, both at home and abroad, achieving distinction in football, hockey, or boxing, etc.

This year, the football teams of the 1st Batt. and of the 7th Batt. reached the finals of the Regular Army Football Championship and the Territorial Army Football Championship respectively.

Such a feat has probably never happened before. It has seemed fitting, to arrange this match between the two Battalions, partly to commemorate this unusual event and partly to demonstrate the unfailing interest which the Regular Battalions always take in the Territorial Battalions.

Davies & Sons (Newtown), Ltd., Printers.

The programme for the football match between the 1st and 7th Battalions.

Regiment. Immediately afterwards, the battalion moved to Imber on Salisbury Plain to take part in the Command Machine-Gun Concentration.

A Company again won the A.R.A. Machine Gun Fire Control Cup; the team was led by Lance Sergeant R. Hayward. The battalion team won the Command Stretcher Bearer Competition. The Connaught Shield was presented by Lieutenant General Sir John Dill, the G.O.C.-in-C.* The team was:

Lance-Sergeant F.T. Smith

Lance-Corporals G.L. Bradbury, W. Lloyd, F. Hays, F.J. Downer, W. Burton, J. Nicolle and D. Knox

Bandsmen J.E. Barrett, L.W. Lowman, F.A. Clutton, N.F. Hanmer, A. Brown and G. Burden.[78]

The Battalion Rifle Meeting was held on 3 and 4 May. On 5 May, the soccer teams of the 1st and 7th Battalions, respectively finalists and winners of the Regular and Territorial Competitions, played an historic match at Blackdown.

On 20 May the battalion marched out to Tattoo Camp at Bourley Road, Aldershot, to begin preparations for the year's tattoo. The King's birthday was celebrated at Bourley Road on 9 June. The Tattoo seen by The King and Queen on 18 June. The battalion took part in three of the programmed events: physical training; an historical pageant; and the massed bands display.[79] Sergeant J.C. Bennett remembered that the battalion:

… was training for two items, the first a massive Indian club demonstration where the clubs were lit at the end with lights of different colours from batteries inside each club. This was done in complete darkness, except for the clubs, and about 300 men were involved. It was a fine sight. The second contribution was to be a performance of the story of the British Army climbing the Heights of Abraham … The Royal Berkshire Regiment was dressed in blue to represent the French. The two regiments were great rivals and there were some very funny things happening in that attack that weren't rehearsed.[80]

In August, a large number of promotions took place among the Officers as a result of the reforms to the promotion system (see Chapter 1).

September 1938

In September 1938, the Munich Agreement had seemed to put off the threat of war. The Colonel of the Regiment sent a telegram to The King on 30 September on behalf of the Regiment, asking him 'to accept their humble rejoicing that the KING is now relieved from the anxiety of War.'[81] However the subsequent German annexation of Czechoslovakia, the Molotov-Ribbentrop Pact, and German threats to Poland brought a sense of inevitability. Even so, many peacetime events continued as normal.

---

*   Later Field Marshal Sir John Greer Dill GCB CMG DSO (1881–1944) was C.I.G.S. from May 1940 to December 1941 and subsequently Chief of the British Joint Staff Mission in Washington D.C. He was then Senior British Representative on the Combined Chiefs of Staff and played a significant role during the Second World War in the formation of the 'special relationship' between Great Britain and the United States.

In November, A Company won the Machine Gun Fire Control Cup for the year, with a team led by Lance Sergeant Hayward.[82] Training also took place on the *Boys* anti-tank rifle. A Company, as anti-tank company, was responsible for conducting the training and running a firing period at Lydd ranges.

December 1938

At the end of the year, a large draft of one Officer and 200 men who were due for discharge at the end of their Colour service was received from the 2nd Battalion. Throughout the year, battalion strength had been maintained at just over 500, with drafts of recruits coming in from the Depot each month, but large drafts being sent during the trooping season to the 2nd Battalion abroad; C Company, for example, was reduced to only forty-eight Fusiliers.[83] At the end of December, battalion strength stood at two W.Os I, six W.Os II, five W.Os III, twenty-nine Sergeants and Staff Sergeants, fifty three Lance Sergeants and Corporals, eighteen Drummers and 558 Lance Corporals and Fusiliers, a total of 694, without Officers. This total rose further after Christmas, to 709.

The battalion dispersed for leave over Christmas and the New Year on 17 December 1938. From 15 January 1939, 1 R.W.F. reorganised once more as a standard infantry battalion, having been warned of the change in March of the previous year. This resulted from the reduction in the numbers of M.G. battalions to four, which were to become divisional troops units.

Hunting was seriously curtailed after Christmas by hard frosts and a serious outbreak of foot-and-mouth disease, so that the Officers were reduced to attending meets of the Aldershot Drag Hounds. The Novices' Boxing team began the new season by beating 2nd Cheshires in the opening round of the Command Cup on 18 January.

March–April 1939

St David's Day was celebrated as usual on 1 March, the last in peacetime. It was followed by the celebrations of the Regiment's 250th anniversary, described in the Chapter on Regimental Events. Shortly afterwards, on 12 April, The King and Queen Elizabeth visited Blackdown and watched a number of demonstrations laid on for them which included the various new weapons recently introduced (see Chapter 3). At the end of the visit:

> The King conveyed his appreciation of all [that] their Majesties saw and said how greatly their Majesties enjoyed the opportunity of spending a day among the troops and of seeing something of the conditions under which they train and live.[84]

The King, having been for many years a serving Royal Naval Officer, cannot have been too surprised at what he saw. 6 Infantry Brigade was not tasked with any of these demonstrations, however, and the battalion confined itself to forming up along the road to give The King and Queen a cheer as they passed through Blackdown.[85] One Fusilier did, however, meet The King. This was Band Boy Thomas 'Sonny' Frost, fourteen years old, and just 4 feet 8 inches tall and 84 lbs in weight. The King apparently stopped with a smile when he saw the young bandsman. 'My word', he said, 'You are a little man.' Frost was so surprised that he just managed to blurt out 'Sir!' in his best parade-ground manner and The King moved on. However Army publicity sensed an opportunity and within days, his photograph was in newspapers up and down the country. Because of his age, Frost did not go abroad with the battalion in September 1939 but had to wait until 1944 when he went to Normandy with the 6th Battalion. He was, by a nice irony, on parade with the 1st Battalion Band at the Victory Parade London in 1945 and had the quiet satisfaction of seeing the King once more on the balcony of Buckingham Palace.[86]

Partial conscription began in April 1939, as described in Chapter 2 and once the conscripts, or 'Militiamen', had completed their basic training at the Depot in Wrexham, drafts were received by the battalion.

The Aldershot Tattoo was held as usual in May with the battalion taking part in the massed bands. In the Aldershot Show, the battalion won the Farnborough Cup for the greatest aggregate of points gained in various classes. Individual successes included 1st and 2nd places in the Officers' chargers: Lieutenant Colonel Alston's 'Dragoon' and Major Evans' 'Silver Lad' respectively; and third place in the teams of Officers' chargers.[87]

The new Battledress and 1937-pattern web equipment entered service about this time, replacing the old Service Dress and 1908-pattern web equipment.

On 19 July, Lieutenant Colonel Alston completed his tour of command, the tenure of infantry battalion C.O.s having been reduced under the Hore-Belisha reforms from five years to two. He was succeeded by Lieutenant Colonel H.F. Garnons-Williams.[*]

With war approaching, R.O.F. Prichard noted that:

> It soon became clear that we were going to have to mobilise for war. Air Raid Patrol exercises were held and the Mobilisation Scheme got out and dusted down. It had some pretty curious directions in it. Eventually the day of mobilisation arrived and two reporters came down from London. The RSM, Joe Kensett, promptly put them in the Guard Room. My task as Carrier Officer was to go to the R.M.C. Sandhurst and erect a barbed wire entanglement around a water tower. When our Brigadier came to visit me he asked "What the hell are you doing here?" I said that "I am obeying instructions", to which he replied "Well, for goodness sake go back to barracks and look after your carriers". Before we actually moved [abroad] we had to pack up everything at Blackdown. I was ordered, together with a small escort, to take the mess silver, the Colours, and two Goats by train to Wrexham.[†] When we got to Farnborough station I found a number of other subalterns doing the same. I think the Notts & Derbys had a rather tired looking ram, and the Warwicks a springbok which sprang all over the place. So we shut all the animals with their respective soldier, Ram Corporal, Goat Major, etc, and wished them the best of luck. When we arrived at Crewe we found the soldiers stripped to the waist. The animals had not responded well to rail travel and in throwing themselves around had inflicted damage on their carers rather than the van in which they were being transported. It was with a sense of relief that we reached Wrexham and handed everything over to the Depot.[88]

As German intentions towards Poland became clearer, political tension heightened and various precautionary measures were put into
place. It was well known that the 2nd Division, of which the battalion was a unit, would be one of the first formations to leave the country for the field of battle, and it was this knowledge that

July–August 1939

---

[*]   Lieutenant Colonel Henry Fenton Garnons-Williams ('Garbage Bill') was commissioned on 5 August 1914. He served with the 1st and 3rd Battalions during the Great War and afterwards in Poland. Before taking command he had served in Palestine during the Arab Revolt, where he was mentioned in despatches.

[†]   The Goat died on 2 February 1944, aged 12 years [Regimental Newsletter, Second Series, No 2, February 1944].

set the standard during the last few weeks of peace. All leave was cancelled, and those away were recalled. Those on leave included four Officers from the 2nd Battalion who were ordered to report to the Depot. Three of these, Lieutenants A.J. Lewis, R.L. Boyle and Second Lieutenant J.E.C. Hood, subsequently joined the 1st Battalion. Office telephones were manned continuously and the Orderly Officer was detailed to sleep in the Adjutant's office. The Mobilisation Scheme was brought up to date and guards detailed off for vulnerable points. Vehicles were camouflaged and lights masked. Air Defence and anti-gas proofing were all made ready. By 1 September, every man had tested his gas mask in the gas chamber and all weapons had been re-zeroed. The B.B.C. news announced that all remaining reservists were to report to their Depots and that from 1 September, the evacuation of children to rural areas would begin. The spirit of the battalion was reported as 'very tense but cheerful.'[89]

At 16.00 hrs on 1 September, orders were received from H.Q. 6 Infantry Brigade to mobilise, the announcement of which was greeted **September 1939** with cheers from the troops. The battalion's strength on mobilisation was reported as twenty-six Officers and 792 N.C.Os and Fusiliers, one Officer and twenty-two men above the establishment.[90] The battalion mobilisation orders issued on 3 September, the day war was declared, gave instructions for the home detail; ordered that all vehicles should be fully loaded 'as for war', ready for weighing, by 10.45 hrs on the 4th; and issued a reminder on the orders for air raids – 'Every person in the Dettingen Sub-Area must be able ... to get to their AIR STATION within three minutes of the air raid WARNING RED.'[91]

On 8 September, The King visited Blackdown, driving along a road lined with cheering troops. When he arrived at that part of the route being lined by 1 R.W.F., he stopped the car, got out, and walked along the length of the battalion. Speaking to the C.O., he said that he thought the men looked fit and that their bearing was excellent and he wished all ranks the best of fortune.[92]

On 11 September, Brigadier Irwin, Commander 6 Infantry Brigade, inspected the battalion on parade. The Brigadier went round each company, asking the men questions and examining their fitness and state of training. At the end of the inspection he expressed himself as being 'most particularly satisfied' with what he had found. He described the battalion as a '[unreadable]-looking lot of devils' and said he expected to see it 'fight like Hell.'[93] The G.O.C. also addressed the battalion and in a fighting speech said he was proud to have the regiment in his division. On the following day, the Colonel of the Regiment visited. He went round the barracks and talked to as many Officers and men as possible, wishing everyone good luck and saying that he hoped to join them soon in the theatre of war.

The order to move to France came within a few days. On 14 September the Advance Party moved to Avonmouth under Captain E.C. Parker-Jervis. The road party of sixty-four vehicles under Lieutenant J.E.T. Willes, two other Officers and ninety-six N.C.Os and Fusiliers left Blackdown for Avonmouth on 19 September,[94] crossing to Brest, and four days later the main body embarked at Southampton in the HT *Manxman*, reaching Cherbourg at 06.00 hrs on the 24th.[95]

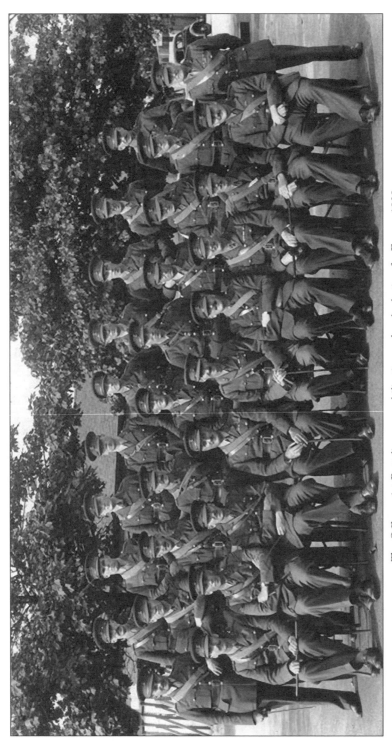

The Officers, 1st Battalion, on mobilisation and embarkation for France, 1939.

Back Row: Lt C. Griffiths, Lt A.R.B. Sugden*, 2Lt M.B. Kemp†, 2Lt J.L. King*, Lt J.C. Hood‡, Lt H.C. Brougham†, 2Lt W.J. Griffiths, 2Lt the Hon R.S. Best, Capt H.A.S. Clarke
Middle Row: Lt W.M. Shillington*, Lt A.R. ff Powell, Lt J.E.T Willes‡, Capt A.D.M. Lewis MBE, Capt A.J. Lewis‡, 2Lt F.M. Edwards†, Capt E.C. Parker-Jervis‡, Lt R.F.A. David*, Lt R.O.F. Prichard†, Lt & QM A.G. Bent MM
Front Row: Capt L.H. Yates, Maj R.L.K. Allen, Maj D.I. Owen†, Maj H.D.T. Morris, Lt Col H.F. Garnons-Williams‡, Capt & Adjt W.L.R. Benyon, Maj H.B. Harrison MC‡, Capt O.H. Raymont‡, Capt J.R. Johnson*

* wounded; ‡ killed; † captured

Staff List, 1 R.W.F. Blackdown, 1937–1939

Lieutenant Colonel
Ll. A. A. Alston CMG DSO MC
H.F. Garnons-Williams (19 Jul 39)
Major
J.G. Bruxner-Randall
H.D.T. Morris
D.I. Owen (Mar 39)
R.L.K. Allen (Jan 39)
P.C. Kenyon MC
D.H.W. Kirkby
Captain
Bt Maj H.A. Freeman OBE MC (Maj Aug 38)
Lance Sergeants
T. Purcell
R. Preest
E. Power
G. Whatley
P. Fender
W. Anders
- Marvin
- Davies 79
P. Dwyer
E. Power
F.T. Smith 05
- Muzzelle
- Davies 68
- Smith 44
- Greetham
- Merchant
J.C. Bennett
- Jones 09
- Ludlowv

Lieutenant
J.G. Vyvyan
M.H. ap Rhys Pryce
R.J.F. Snead-Cox (Capt Aug 38)
F.C. Minshull-Ford
R.O.F. Prichard
L.H. Yates
B.P. Doughty-Wylie
J.H. Liscombe (to Jan 39)
G.T.B.F. Dickson
A.G. ff Powell
P.L. Bowers
H. de B. Prichard (Capt Aug 38)
Sergeants
- Helier (Jan 39)
- Spencer
- Lowe
J. Dwyer
E.T. Langford
W. Jones 92
F. Whelan
- Clark (to Jan 39)
J. Lewis
M.C. Jones 86
- Freeman
- Dandy
Roberts 35 (to Mar 38)
- Baxendale
- Henshaw
- Curran (Jan 39)
A. Wright (Jan 39)
H. Jackson
A. Carr
F. Flanagan (CQMS Mar 39)
C. Brooker (CQMS Mar 39)

W.O. II
W. Tubby
G. Mills
W. Brown 19
F. Wilkinson (to Apr 38)
R. Thomas
A.T. Currie
G. Morris
J. Price
R. Thomas
W. Hawkins
A.R. James (Mar 38)
W.O. III
ORS I. Hughes
ORC G. Godfrey
Pnr Sgt A.E. Evans
MT Sgt Jones 57
DMaj G. Lavender
Band Sgt J. Durman
Cook Sgt C. Kretchmar
Sergeants
E. Davies
S. Scammell (to Sep 39)
G. Timmins
A.R. James (W.O. II Mar 38)
C. Scott
W. Cowan
O. Jones 99
J. Jones 22
W. Norman
S. Grindley
E.T. Kidgell
G. Davies MM
J. Williams 19
R. Davies 52
T. Adams

The following were listed in Mobilisation orders as posted to the home details with effect from 4 September 1939, although remaining on the strength of D Company for pay and rations:[96]

Maj A.M.G. Evans
CSM J. Price
PSM (W.O. III) R. Rayner
CQMS C. Brooker
CQMS J. Flanagan
Sgt C. Kretzchmer
Sgt J. Chelcy
Sgt R. Davies 52
Sgt J. Williams 19

Maj H.D.T. Morris
Cpl G. Wilson
Cpl T. Lee
Cpl S. Jones 75
Cpl W. Sandberg
LCpl M. Cousins
LCpl C. Ross
LCpl J.W. Gregory
LCpl R. Lang

Maj W.P. Kenyon MC
Fus G. Floyd
Fus E. Williams 54
Fus M. Trow
Fus J. Williams 76
Fus R. Wright
Fus C. Evans 19
Fus T. Phillips
Fus T. Mansfield

Sgt C. Scott	LCpl D. Thomas 52	Fus L. Howe
LSgt H. Jackson	LCpl A. Walker	Fus R. Costen
		Fus D. Simcoe
		Fus W. Stokes
		Fus W. Jones 94

The following joined the battalion on mobilisation:

Capt O.H. Raymont	2Lt C. Griffiths
Capt H.A.S. Clarke	2Lt J.L. King
Lt J.C. Hood	2Lt W.J. Griffiths
Lt A.R.B. Sugden	2Lt F.M. Edwards
Lt M.W. Shillington	2Lt M.B. Kemp
Lt H.C. Brougham	

In addition, the following Officers were ordered to other units and not to move to France with the battalion:

Maj R.L.K. Allen	Staff College
Capt J.A.M Rice-Evans	Other Ranks Training Unit (O.R.T.U.)
Capt W.S.A. Clough-Taylor	5 Infantry Brigade
Capt L.H. Yates	CC Details
Capt N.R.G. Bosanquet	Staff Captain, HQ 158 Infantry Brigade (T.A.)
Lt H.G. Brougham	Officer Cadet Training Unit (O.C.T.U.)
Lt R.L. Boyle	O.R.T.U.
2Lt J.B. Garnett	Royal Artillery (Civil Defence and Anti-Aircraft)
2Lt W.L. Rowlands (Spec Reserve)	T.A. via Depot
2Lt W.R. Crawshay (Spec Reserve)	T.A. via Depot

Notes

1   *Y Ddraig Goch,* September 1932, p. 52.
2   James Douet, *British Barracks, 1600–1914* (English Heritage, 1997).
3   Research undertaken by Mr Chris Hughes.
4   T.N.A. WO 73/178.
5   Interview with Colonel W.L.R. Benyon by Lieutenant Colonel L.J. Egan (R.W.F. Mus).
6   Interview with Lieutenant Colonel N.R.G. Bosanquet by Lieutenant Colonel L.J. Egan (R.W.F. Mus).
7   Interview with Colonel R.O.F. Prichard by Lieutenant Colonel L.J. Egan (R.W.F. Mus).
8   1 R.W.F. Digest of Service.
9   *Y Ddraig Goch*, December 1932, p. 84; 1 R.W.F. Digest of Service.
10   1 R.W.F. Digest of Service.
11   Interview with Colonel W.L.R. Benyon by Lieutenant Colonel L.J. Egan (R.W.F. Mus).
12   *Y Ddraig Goch*, December 1932, p. 86; 1 R.W.F. Digest of Service.
13   *Y Ddraig Goch*, March 1933, p. 12.
14   *Y Ddraig Goch*, March 1933, pp. 5–8.
15   *Y Ddraig Goch*, June 1933, pp. 58–61.
16   *Y Ddraig Goch*, June 1933, pp. 61–63.
17   See his obituary in *Y Ddraig Goch*, Winter 1956 1933, pp. 12–14.
18   Interview with Colonel J.E.T. Willes by Lieutenant Colonel L.J. Egan (R.W.F. Mus).
19   Interview with Colonel R.O.F. Prichard by Lieutenant Colonel L.J. Egan (R.W.F. Mus).
20   *Y Ddraig Goch*, September 1933, pp. 110–114.

21 *Y Ddraig Goch*, December 1933, pp. 168–170; 1 R.W.F. Digest of Service.
22 *Y Ddraig Goch*, December 1933, pp. 173–174.
23 *Y Ddraig Goch*, March 1934, pp. 10–11.
24 *Y Ddraig Goch*, March 1934, p. 11.
25 *Y Ddraig Goch*, June 1934, p. 5.
26 *Y Ddraig Goch*, June 1934, pp. 5–8.
27 1 R.W.F. Digest of Service.
28 *Y Ddraig Goch*, September 1934, pp. 4–13.
29 *Y Ddraig Goch*, December 1934, pp. 13–14.
30 1 R.W.F. Digest of Service.
31 1 R.W.F. Digest of Service.
32 *Y Ddraig Goch*, December 1934, pp. 10–12.
33 *Y Ddraig Goch*, December 1934, pp. 10–12 ; 1 R.W.F. Digest of Service.
34 1 R.W.F. Digest of Service.
35 *Y Ddraig Goch*, June 1935, p. 11.
36 1 R.W.F. Digest of Service.
37 *Y Ddraig Goch*, March 1935, p. 5.
38 1 R.W.F. Digest of Service.
39 T.N.A. WO 73/139.
40 Interview with Colonel W.L.R. Benyon by Lieutenant Colonel L.J. Egan (R.W.F. Mus).
41 Interview with Colonel R.O.F. Prichard by Lieutenant Colonel L.J. Egan (R.W.F. Mus).
42 *Y Ddraig Goch*, April 1936, p. 23.
43 *Y Ddraig Goch*, July 1936, p. 20.
44 WO 20/Infy/2472/A (SD 2).
45 Interview with Colonel W.L.R. Benyon by Lieutenant Colonel L.J. Egan (R.W.F. Mus).
46 Interview with Colonel R.O.F. Prichard by Lieutenant Colonel L.J. Egan (R.W.F. Mus).
47 1 R.W.F. Digest of Service.
48 *Y Ddraig Goch*, April 1936, pp. 13–14.
49 1 R.W.F. Digest of Service.
50 1 R.W.F. Digest of Service.
51 *Y Ddraig Goch*, December 1936, p. 11.
52 Notes by R.O.F. Pritchard, 1979 in R.W.F. Mus/Archives.
53 1 R.W.F. Digest of Service.
54 1 R.W.F. Digest of Service.
55 *Y Ddraig Goch*, December 1936, p. 9.
56 *Y Ddraig Goch*, December 1936, p. 13.
57 Interview with Colonel R.O.F. Prichard by Lieutenant Colonel L.J. Egan (R.W.F. Mus).
58 Interview with Colonel W.L.R. Benyon by Lieutenant Colonel L.J. Egan (R.W.F. Mus).
59 1 R.W.F. Digest of Service.
60 Interviews with Colonel W.L.R. Benyon and R.O.F. Prichard by Lieutenant Colonel L.J. Egan (R.W.F. Mus).
61 *Y Ddraig Goch*, January 1937, pp. 28–29.
62 *Y Ddraig Goch*, April 1937, p. 21.
63 *Y Ddraig Goch*, July 1937, p. 6.
64 1 R.W.F. Digest of Service; *Y Ddraig Goch*, December 1937, pp. 8–10.
65 www.measuringworth.com, acessed 24 September 2015.
66 *Y Ddraig Goch*, December 1937, pp. 14–15.
67 1 R.W.F. Digest of Service; *Y Ddraig Goch*, December 1937, pp. 5–6.
68 *Y Ddraig Goch*, January 1938, pp. 18–19.
69 1 R.W.F. Digest of Service.
70 1 R.W.F. Digest of Service.
71 Interview with Colonel R.O.F. Prichard by Lieutenant Colonel L.J. Egan (R.W.F. Mus).
72 *The Red Dragon*, p. 11.
73 *The Red Dragon*, p. 11.

74   1 R.W.F. Digest of Service.
75   1 R.W.F. Digest of Service.
76   *Y Ddraig Goch*, Spring 1938, p. 16.
77   1 R.W.F. Digest of Service.
78   *Y Ddraig Goch*, Spring 1938, p. 20.
79   *Y Ddraig Goch*, Summer 1938, p. 12.
80   Captain J.C. Bennett, *The Memoirs of a Very Fortunate Man* (Royston, nd), pp. 29–30.
81   1 R.W.F. Digest of Service.
82   *Y Ddraig Goch*, Winter 1938–39, p. 10.
83   *Y Ddraig Goch*, Winter 1938–39, p. 13.
84   1 R.W.F. Digest of Service.
85   *Y Ddraig Goch*, Spring 1939, p. 3.
86   Interview by George Rogers with Thomas Frost in *Weekly News*, Thursday 8 October 1992, p. 14.
87   *Y Ddraig Goch*, Spring 1940, p. 34.
88   Interview with Colonel R.O.F. Prichard by Lieutenant Colonel L.J. Egan (R.W.F. Mus).
89   Handwritten notes in R.W.F. Mus/Archives, writer unknown.
90   T.N.A. WO 73/142.
91   1 R.W.F. Mobilisation Orders dated 3 September 1939.
92   Handwritten notes in R.W.F. Mus/Archives, writer unknown.
93   Handwritten notes in R.W.F. Mus/Archives, writer unknown.
94   T.N.A. WO 167/843, 1 R.W.F. War Diary 18 September 1939–30 June 1940.
95   Lieutenant-Commander P.K. Kemp and John Graves, *The Red Dragon, The Story of the Royal Welch Fusiliers 1919–1945* (Aldershot, 1960) p. 12; 1 R.W.F. War Diary 18 September 1939–30 June 1940.
96   1 R.W.F. Mobilisation Orders dated 3 September 1939.

Chapter 8

The 2nd Battalion at the end of the Great War and on Operations in Ireland, 1918–1922

---

i. The End of the Great War, 1918–1919[1]

On 11 November 1918, 2 R.W.F. was at Aulnoye, 27 miles (43 kilometres) east of Cambrai, in 113 Infantry Brigade, part of the 38th **November 1918** (Welsh) Division, under the command of Lieutenant Colonel G.E.R. de Miremont.[*] Since arriving in France on 11 August 1914, the battalion had lost sixty-five Officers and 1,139 Other Ranks killed.[2] On the following day it was decided to re-form the Officers' Mess and working parties set about converting the huge waiting-room at the railway station into a mess.

On 3 December, The King passed through Aulnoye, accompanied by The Prince of Wales and the Duke of York, and inspected the battalion in 'loose fatigue order'. The next day, a party consisting of Lieutenant C.J. Roberts, Second Lieutenant A.L. Jones, Serjeant[†] Signaller G. Bracken, Serjeants E. Troman and F. Thorley, and Lance Corporal R. Williams, left for Wrexham to collect the battalion's Colours. The first Christmas celebrated in peacetime for five years included a Church parade in the morning followed by a first class lunch with plenty of beer under company arrangements. There **December 1918** was a concert in the evening. On 29 December the battalion left Aulnoye and marched on a very wet and stormy day to Hecq, where the inhabitants were most hospitable. Junior Officers were detailed in pairs to carry the cased Colours and found that the task outweighed the honour. On the following day, in better weather, 2 R.W.F. marched to Inchy where it was billeted in houses formerly occupied by the German High Command. Battalion H.Q. was in what had been General Hindenburg's quarters until late October. On the 31st it embussed at 07.30 hrs and reached its destination, a new camp near Blangy Tronville, in mid-afternoon.

During January 1919 the battalion was either training or working on camp improvements. On the 9th, A and B Companies under Captain **January 1919** G.E.B. Barkworth left camp at 03.30 hrs to round up Australian deserters who had been living rough and terrorizing the neighbourhood. Two were captured in pyjamas sleeping in a dug-out on an island west of Sailly Laurette and brought back to camp under escort. By the end of the month,

---

[*]   Major Guy Egon René de Miremont DSO MC▪ (1888–1929).
[†]   As explained in Chapter 15, the spelling of Serjeant differed between the two Regular battalions.

one Officer and 365 Other Ranks, including 202 miners, had been demobilised. Amongst them was Private Frank Richards DCM MM,[3] a signaller and one of the few remaining 'old originals', not in a battalion staff job, to serve throughout the war. On 7 February The Prince of Wales, later King Edward VIII, inspected the camp and lunched with the Officers. He was interested to meet the American Medical Officer. After lunch he insisted on 'having a look at the men' and talked to many of those wearing medal ribbons. On the 17th, the Regimental Band, fifty-three strong under Bandmaster W.O. I Clancy, arrived from Wrexham. It was accompanied by a Windsor Goat presented by the King. When the 2nd Battalion had embarked for France in 1914, the old Goat had been sent to the 3rd Battalion at Wrexham, where it had died during the course of the war.

Demobilisation continued with a further three Officers and 202 Other Ranks leaving during the month. For St David's Day, all ranks were issued with leeks. A joint dinner was held in the Officers' Mess with the 17th Battalion and guests included the G.O.C., Major General T.A. Cubitt,[*] and the Brigade Commander,

A group of the 2nd Battalion at Blangy-Tronville, 1918. (R.W.F. Mus 4161)

Brigadier H.D. De Pree.[†] The senior Regimental Officers present were Colonels J.B. Cockburn and C.C. Norman. The menu would have compared favourably with many pre-war dinners. On the 15th, the G.O.C. paid his farewell visit to the battalion. He expressed his regret at parting from 'his bloody little Welshmen' and concluded by saying that he never wished for better troops to command. A week later, 17 R.W.F. and 10th South Wales Borderers moved into the camp and a joint Officers' Mess was formed. On the 26th, Band Boy H. Williams was killed and three others injured when a bomb exploded on a dump near the camp. Williams, who was only fifteen years old and one of the youngest killed in the Regiment during the war,[4] was buried with full military honours in Austral Cemetery, on the Amiens-Villers road, on the 28th. When his companions rejoined at Wrexham from hospital, they were wearing wound stripes! On the following day, de Miremont relinquished command of the battalion and left to join the 46th Royal Fusiliers as part of the North Russia Relief Force.

Between December 1918 and the end of April 1919 eight Officers and 628 Other Ranks were demobilised. These were time-expired Regular soldiers and soldiers enlisted for the duration of the war. Men not eligible for demobilisation – those who had been conscripted under

*   Later General Sir Thomas Astley Cubitt KCB CMG DSO (1871–1939), Governor of Bermuda.
†   Later Major General Hugo Douglas De Pree CB CMG DSO (1870–1943), Commandant of the Royal Military Academy, Woolwich.

the Military Service Acts, 1916 – were sent to the 26th Battalion for duty with the Army of Occupation in Germany. These amounted to eight Officers and sixty-six N.C.Os and Fusiliers.

On 24 May the cadre of the battalion, consisting of five Officers and five N.C.Os, left Blangy for Britain. It sailed from Le Havre, after many

problems with officials over the import of the Goat, on the 29th, on HMT *St George*, arrived at Blackdown Camp, via Southampton, on the following day. It reached Wrexham on 6 June where it was met by the Officer Commanding the Depot, Major E.R. Kearsley, and Colonel Cockburn. With them were the Band of 1 R.W.F., all members of the Regimental Depot, and the Mayor and Corporation of Wrexham. The Cadre then marched along beflagged streets lined with people to the Guildhall to receive the official welcome. In the evening the Corporation gave a dinner for all concerned at the Wynnstay Arms Hotel.

The Cadre of 2 R.W.F. in May 1919.
Rear: Armourer SJt S. Belfield, Sjt Childs, Cpl Davies, LCpl Wright. Front: Capt W.H. Fox MC, Lt D. Roberts-Morgan DCM MM, Sgt Driver Dyer MM MSMm RQMS J. Hughes DCM, Dvr Carrol, Capt & QM H. Yates MC.

The composition of the Cadre when it arrived in Wrexham was:[5]

  Captain W.H. Fox MC, Officer Commanding
  Captain E. Howells Evans MC, Adjutant
  Major H. Yates MC, Quartermaster
  Captain Llewellyn Evans MC
  Lieutenant D. Roberts Morgan DCM MC
  5517 Temporary RSM W.H. Albutt DCM
  10961 Bandmaster W.J. Clancy
  9046 Acting Regimental Quartermaster Serjeant J. Hughes DCM
  6191 Company Serjeant Major E.R. Green
  4690 Acting Serjeant Driver W.J. Dyer MM

The Cadre dispersed on 13 June.

ii. The Re-formation of the 2nd Battalion, 1919

A letter from the War Office dated 16 May ordered the re-formation of the 2nd Battalion in Ireland. The basis of the newly-formed battalion was to be the 3rd (Special Reserve) Battalion which had been stationed at Limerick since November 1917. The letter laid down which of the key members of the battalion were to be selected from amongst those at the Depot or from those with the 3rd Battalion. On 16 July, Lieutenant Colonel O. de L. Williams[*] assumed command

---

[*]   Later Brigadier Oliver de Lancey Williams CMG DSO (1875–1959).

of the battalion and immediately made his selection, listed in the staff table below. A party of five Officers and seventy N.C.Os and Fusiliers, including the Band, and thirty-five tons of battalion baggage that had been stored at the Depot throughout the war, arrived at New Barracks, Limerick on 7 August 1919. 2 R.W.F. quickly absorbed the men of the 3rd Battalion thus giving it a temporary strength of 167 Officers and 2,379 men, which in a short time, however, was reduced to about 700.

July–August 1919

Officers and NCOs Selected to Re-form 2 R.W.F., 1919

C.O.   Lt Col O. de L. Williams CMG DSO
          Lt Col C.C. Norman CMG CBE DSO *Ch L d'H* (30 Oct 1920)

Appointment	Selected from Depot Personnel	Selected from 3rd Bn Personnel
Second-in-Command	Maj F.J. Walwyn DSO	
Adjutant		Lt L. Coote
Quartermaster		Lt C.J. Shea
Lewis Gun Officer		Lt E.T.P. Thomas
Transport Officer	Lt W. Gittins	
Signalling Officer		Lt Llewellyn
Company Commanders		
1		Capt G.L. Compton-Smith DSO
2		
3		Capt J.H. Courage
4		J.C. Wynne Edwards
Regimental Serjeant Major	5517 T/RSM W.H. Albutt DCM	
Regimental Quartermaster Serjeant	9046 A/RQMS J. Hughes DCM	
Company Serjeant Majors		
1	10210 CSM H. Spalding DCM	
2	10146 CSM W.H. Heirene	
3	8795 CSM T. Ledington DCM	
4		CSM Bauer
Serjeant Major Instructor in Musketry	9679 A/CSM E. Austin	
Company Quartermaster Serjeants		
1		6221 T/CSM A. Richards
2		6516 CQMS W.J. Woolman
3		16787 CQMS J. Hughes
4		52233 CQMS Yorke
Orderly Room Serjeant	9347 J. Widenbar	
Orderly Room Clerk		10201 Cpl E. Evans
Serjeant Driver		9285 Sjt Dvr E.E. Johnson
Provost Serjeant		200833 Sjt Jones
Signalling Serjeant		66583 Sjt Watkin
Signalling Corporal		72468 Cpl Taylor
Lewis Gun Serjeant		16647 Cpl Dyer
Pioneer Serjeant		91181 Sjt O. Smithurst
Serjeant Cook		24820 Sjt C. Bowen
Transport Serjeant		203041 Sjt Evans

Appointment	Selected from Depot Personnel	Selected from 3rd Bn Personnel
Officers' Mess Serjeant		5806 Sjt M. Malley
Serjeant Shoemaker		97897 Sjt Cross
Serjeant Tailor		11767 Sjt F. Halliday
Band Serjeant	11029 Sjt R. Howell	
Quartermaster's Storemen		46184 Pte Callow
		96195 Pte Thomas
Company Storemen		268106 LCpl McCabe
		87234 LCpl Cook
		59693 Pte Thomas
		60442 Pte Hammond

iii. Ireland, 1919–1922

The British General Election of 1910 saw the start of the most important period in the relations between Great Britain and Ireland since the Act of Union was passed in 1800. The Liberal Government was dependent on the support of the Irish Nationalists which could only be secured by a genuine effort to pass a Home Rule bill. Unionists, mainly but not exclusively from the north, were bitterly opposed to such action, as was the House of Lords. A Home Rule bill, the terms of which satisfied no one, was introduced in the House of Commons in 1912, but it was repeatedly rejected by the Lords. As attitudes hardened, increasing quantities of weapons and ammunition were imported illegally into the country for possible future use by paramilitaries. Companies of Ulster Volunteers were raised in the north, and National Volunteers in the South. It was clear that the Ulster Unionists were prepared to resort to arms if the need arose. In March 1914, Officers of the Cavalry Brigade at the Curragh, near Dublin, informed the Commander-in-Chief that they would accept dismissal rather than undertake operations against Ulstermen to impose the Irish Home Rule bill, which passed its third reading on 25 May. However, when war was declared in August, the Government decided to proceed as usual to the Royal Assent, but to postpone the implementation of the Act until after the cessation of hostilities, with the promise of an Amending Bill in the interests of Ulster. John Redmond, an Irish M.P., promised that Britain could be assured of Irish support during the war.

Sinn Fein ('We ourselves'), a fanatically republican political party which had not ruled out the use of force to achieve Irish independence, had been founded in 1905. The Irish Republican Brotherhood (I.R.B.) had been behind abortive uprisings in Ireland since 1867. By 1916 the two agreed that the time for action had arrived. On Easter Monday, 24 April 1916, the Irish Republic was proclaimed and, *inter alia*, the Post Office and the Four Courts in Dublin seized. The rising was foredoomed to failure and on the 29th the rebels surrendered unconditionally. Fifteen of its leaders were tried by court-martial and shot. From the date of the executions *Sinn Fein* and the Republican party began to acquire an influence and a following which, in a short time, made them dominant factors in Irish political life. In 1917 *Sinn Fein* led a revival of Irish nationalist feeling and three *Sinn Fein* candidates were returned in by-elections, including Eamon de Valera,* who had commanded a company during the Easter rising in Dublin, been

---

*   Eamon De Valera (1882–1975). A militant republican, he founded the *Fianna Fáil* political party in 1926. He was Prime Minister of Ireland 1932–1948, 1951–1954 and 1957–1959; and President 1959–1973.

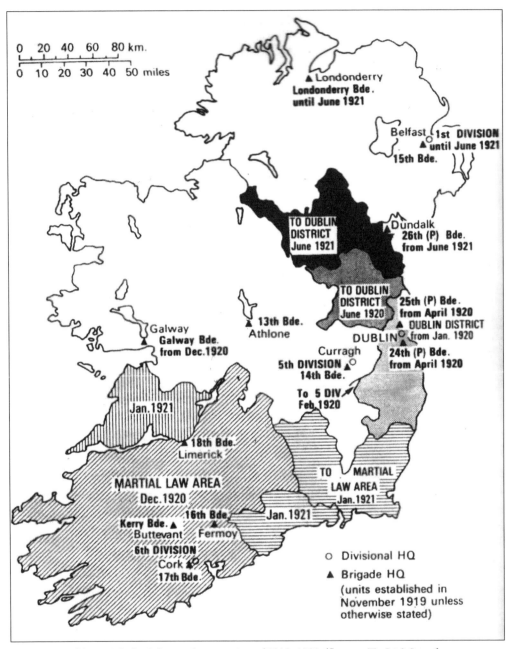

Map 8.1 Ireland during the campaign of 1919–1922. (Source: *The Irish Sword*)

sentenced to death, reprieved, and had just been released from prison. Not long afterwards he was elected President of *Sinn Fein*.

Although the rebellion of 1916 had not succeeded, it was seen as the start of the insurrection that was to continue until the truce in 1921. Trial by jury was suspended in April 1916. The wearing of unauthorised uniforms in public was banned, as was the carrying of firearms, illegal drilling, and the making of seditious speeches. After a period of calm many of these restrictions were openly flouted, and parades of up to 1,000 Volunteers were not uncommon. The Volunteers were, however, unarmed. By 1917, the homes of soldiers on leave were regularly raided for weapons. In late 1917 and early 1918 the War Office considerably increased troop levels in Ireland. In February 1917 the 65th (2nd Lowland) Division had replaced the 59th Division. In November, Irish battalions in Ireland were moved to England and replaced by twelve Reserve and Extra Reserve battalions. One of these was the 3rd (Special Reserve) Battalion The Royal Welsh Fusiliers which was based at Limerick in the south west. They were followed in 1918 by six Cyclist and eight Territorial Force battalions.

On 1 May 1918, Field Marshal Lord French became Lord Lieutenant of Ireland and the viceregal court was transformed into the headquarters of a military administration. Prominent members of *Sinn Fein* and the Republican Brotherhood were arrested, including de Valera. At the end of 1918, under the Defence of the Realm Regulations, certain areas were declared 'Special Military Areas' in which the military were empowered to prohibit the holding of meetings, assemblies (including fairs and markets) and processions, and to close premises used by the rebels for illegal purposes. At the General Election of 1918, out of 106 members for Irish constituencies, *Sinn Fein* returned 73, who immediately refused to take their seats in Parliament, formed themselves into the Assembly of Ireland, the *Dáil Eireann*, and on 21 January 1919 they elected de Valera as President of the Irish Republic with a number of departmental ministers answerable to the *Dáil*. On the same day, a declaration of independence was read and adopted. In May, de Valera was arrested and again imprisoned in England. In August, *Sinn Fein*, supported by the Catholic Church, launched a campaign against conscription and as a result many young men of military age joined *Sinn Fein*.

In June 1919 the *Dáil*, together with *Sinn Fein*, the Irish Volunteers and associated organisations, were declared illegal. During that month the first shooting by the Irish Republican Army (I.R.A.) – formerly the Irish Volunteers but reorganised on conventional military lines – of members of the Royal Irish Constabulary (R.I.C.) occurred. The campaign escalated and twelve months later military control was imposed on the worst affected areas, notably Cork, Limerick and Tipperary. In February, de Valera escaped from Lincoln Gaol and went to America to raise funds. Effectively, a state of war existed from 1919 to 1921, known to Republicans as the War of Independence. From 1919 the tactics of the I.R.A. amounted to the shooting of on- and off-duty policemen on the basis that the R.I.C., however Catholic and Irish its members might be, represented foreign oppression.

In August 1919 the British Army's Irish Command comprised three military districts: Northern (Belfast), Midland (Curragh) and Southern (Cork). On arrival at New Barracks, Limerick, on the 7th, 2 R.W.F. joined No. 12 Sub District in Southern Military District. The General Officer Commanding-in-Chief Irish Command was Lieutenant General Sir Frederick Shaw,* who

---

*   Lieutenant General Sir Frederick Charles Shaw KCB PC (1861–1942).

was succeeded in April 1920 by General Sir Nevil Macready.[*] The Command was reorganised in November when the Military Districts and Sub-Districts were replaced by Divisions and Brigades. The 5th Division with its headquarters at the Curragh had three infantry brigades; 6th Division at Cork, commanded by Major General Sir Peter Strickland,[†] had four brigades: 16 at Fermoy, 17 at Cork, 18 at Limerick, and Kerry Brigade at Buttevant. The reorganisation was completed in January 1920 with the formation of 1st Division in Belfast, and Dublin District with three brigades. The Command had a strength of 37,000, with thirty-four infantry battalions.

Until Martial Law was proclaimed in December 1920, the military operated in support of the civil power. What intelligence there was came from the R.I.C., but little was done to study the enemy's organisation, plans or equipment. Intelligence Branch at divisional headquarters at Cork consisted of one Officer, and the Intelligence Officer at brigade headquarters was a 2nd Lieutenant whose post was not established and who was frequently moved because of the exigencies of the service. Communication between formations, units and detachments was an ongoing problem. Mail using the Civil Postal Service was liable to intercept by rebel sympathisers. The Post Office Telegraph and Telephone system was used and although most of the operators were rebels they did not want to risk losing their jobs. Every un-coded telegram was public property and all telephone calls were listened to by operators. If the rebels had applied the tactic that led to the complete isolation of Fermoy for a week in July 1921 more assiduously, the implications would have been considerable. Despatch riders were used until the summer of 1920 when organised attacks led to their discontinuance. There were frequent attacks on armed mail cars and their use was only permitted when in convoy, and never for classified mail. By the summer of 1921, aircraft from No. 2 Squadron R.A.F. were providing a regular service between divisional and brigade headquarters, sometimes including battalion H.Qs. Even pigeons were used. Wireless had huge potential as it was virtually immune from enemy action, but in April 1920 there was only one wireless operator at Divisional H.Q. Prior to July 1921 equipment was difficult to obtain, and afterwards the provision of spares was inadequate.[6] It was not until after the start of the Second World War that wireless communications within infantry battalions became the norm.

The operational area of the 6th Division was the province of Munster in the south-west, which comprised the counties of Clare, Cork, Kerry, Limerick, Tipperary and Waterford, plus the counties of Kilkenny and Wexford which were in the province of Leinster. Without doubt the divisional area, with 28% of the population of the island, included the most violent counties. Half the total fatalities of the period occurred in the area, and 60% of all combatant deaths, including the forces of the Crown and the I.R.A.:

> In the South of Ireland … the war was waged far more vigorously and far more bitterly in some parts of the [divisional] area than in others. Cork and Kerry – especially the former – were the storm centres, whilst Wexford and Kilkenny were comparatively quiet… County Limerick, thanks largely to the very energetic force of constabulary in Limerick city – whose energies extended far outside the city itself – was fairly well in hand from the start,

---

*   General Sir Cecil Frederick Nevil Macready, 1st Baronet, GCMG KCB PC (Ire) (1862–1946), known as Make-Ready, also served for two years as Commissioner of the Metropolitan Police.
†   Lieutenant General Sir (Edward) Peter Strickland KCB KBE CMG DSO (1869–1951).

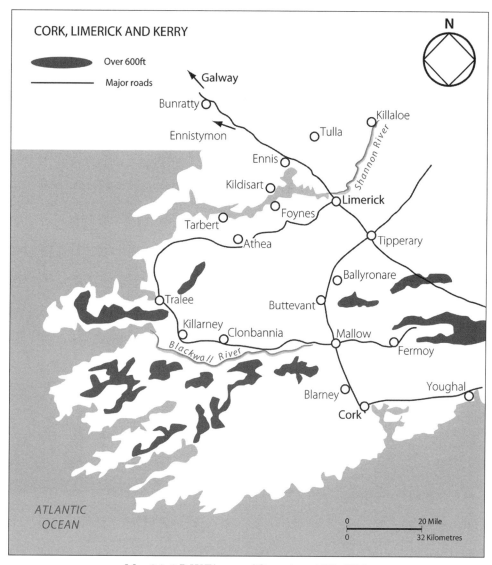

Map 8.2 2 R.W.F.'s area of Operations, 1919–1922.

and a large number of the outrages in south east Limerick were carried out by roving bands who came in from outside.[7]

Limerick was an attractive and ancient port city of about 40,000 people some 130 miles (210 kilometres) south-west of Dublin. It occupied both banks of the River Shannon, and an island on which stood a Norman fortress used as a barracks. The Shannon flowed through the rich lowlands beyond which rose the hills of Counties Clare and Tipperary. The port was the most important on the west coast. Industry was mainly agricultural and included flour-milling, bacon-curing and dairy products. The salmon fisheries on the Shannon were the most valuable in Ireland.

As a result of the reorganisation of Irish Command, 2 R.W.F. became part of 18 Brigade, commanded by Brigadier General A.R. Cameron, with 2nd Royal Scots, 2nd Yorkshires, 1st Oxford and Bucks L.I. and 1st Northamptons. On its arrival at Limerick the battalion found that 'the country was quiet and there were no demands for troops in aid of the Civil Power'.[8] In spite of this all Officers were issued with .38 Colt automatics which had to be carried at all times outside barracks. Detachments were deployed to Tralee, Killaloe, Ballyvonare, Kildysart, Tulla, Ennis and Ennistymon. By the end of the year demobilisation had reduced the battalion to fifty-four Officers and 583 Other Ranks. It was not a pleasant existence. Major B.L. Montgomery, who was Brigade Major in Cork, wrote that he went:

> ... straight into another war – the struggle against the Sinn Fein in Southern Ireland. In many ways this war was far worse than the Great War ... It had developed into a murder campaign in which, in the end, the soldiers became very skilful and more than held their own. But such a war is very bad for Officers and men; it tends to lower their standards of chivalry and decency...[9]

On 19 September a small party of soldiers from the K.S.L.I. was attacked by about forty rebels on its way to church at Fermoy.

2nd Battalion Drums on reformation at Limerick, 1919. (R.W.F. Mus 4147)

Band and Drums 2 R.W.F. in Caernarfon Castle September 1919. (R.W.F. Mus 4157)

Troops searching Irish civilians in Limerick, 1919. (*Irish Times*)

Although armed, the soldiers were not carrying ammunition, which was quite normal. This was the first serious attack on troops involving loss of life, as a soldier was killed.[10] In December, the Prime Minister, David Lloyd George, announced plans for the partition of Ireland, perhaps in recognition of the fact that throughout 1919 attacks on the R.I.C. had increased and isolated barracks had to be closed.

The year 1919 was considered a great success from the rebel point of view. They had set up their own Parliament, murdered many **December 1919** policemen, stolen a quantity of arms, intimidated the civil population into silence, and coerced juries into cooperation. Towards the end of the year, British battalions, including 2 R.W.F., began to appoint Intelligence Officers. Most were, however, 'new to the country, and it took them some time to get to know the people, their habits, their methods, and their haunts. These Intelligence Officers were fortunately young, keen and energetic and … they were men of action who definitely made their presence felt in their areas.'[11]

Rebel intelligence, on the other hand, was long-established and efficient. Many employees of the state, especially those working in the telephone or postal services, were well-placed to obtain information. Support for the rebels was very strong in many areas and in others, passive resistance to the authorities was the result of intimidation. One example of loyalty to the cause which occurred in the divisional area will suffice to illustrate the problems and how they might be turned to advantage. A girl of uncertain loyalty was employed as a maid by an Intelligence Officer. Ammunition left lying around at home disappeared and the maid appeared to be implicated. Carefully doctored rounds continued to disappear. When the girl applied for leave it was granted. She returned, in mourning, and admitted that her brother had been killed in an accident. He was a notorious rebel who had been killed when his pistol exploded during an attempt to murder a Resident Magistrate.

The use of troops as back-up for the police was a controversial issue, and it was not until early 1920, following the attempted assassination of the Lord Lieutenant, Lord French, that they began to be used as part of an overall offensive against the rebels. As the situation in Ireland began to deteriorate, 2 R.W.F. became increasingly involved in internal security operations as rebels continued to attack police barracks and patrols. Tasks included searches and arrests, the reinforcement of police barracks, and patrolling in Limerick city. On 3 January

An armoured column, 1920.

1920 a large number of police barracks throughout the area were subjected to surprise attacks by large parties of armed rebels who killed **January 1920** policemen, burnt barracks, and took arms and ammunition. A number of rebels were also killed. As a result, many vulnerable barracks were closed and the defences at others strengthened. The Government having decided that the rebel movement was military rather than political, plans were laid for the implementation of their decision. On the night of 31 January/1 February fifty-four men were arrested and deported next day to Wormwood Scrubs Prison. In March, the first 800 special constables of a force of 10,000 men of the Auxiliary Division known as 'Black and

Tans', arrived from England as police reinforcements to help put down the republican revolt.[12] British ex-servicemen dominated their ranks, but they paid little heed to policing. Their harsh tactics and behaviour only exacerbated the situation and led to even more extreme measures by the I.R.A. The division was to be responsible for some of the fiercest battles with the I.R.A's flying columns, as well as the most savage reprisals against civilians.[13]

On 26 April, at about 21.30 hrs, No. 24698 Private F.H. Quinn was walking unarmed down O'Connell Street in Limerick. Shots rang out **April 1920** and Quinn was shot in the head and seriously wounded. He died a few hours later. This was the first fatal casualty suffered by 2 R.W.F. in Ireland. The Commanding Officer, Lieutenant Colonel Williams, left the battalion on 9 May to command the South Wales Brigade. Major F.J. Walwyn assumed temporary command as Williams' replacement was with the 1st Battalion in India.

A dock and rail strike in May 1920 led to the embargo on supplies for troops and police and the battalion had to provide escorts for the **May/June 1920** vehicles carrying men and supplies. From June onwards duties became exceedingly heavy. Round the clock patrols were carried out in Limerick city, including regular searches for arms and seditious documents. It was decided to use some infantry battalions in small widely dispersed detachments, with support, when needed, being provided by battalions that remained concentrated in garrison towns such as Limerick. 2 R.W.F. was one of the latter. Two cyclist platoons were formed, one from B Company under Second Lieutenant the Hon F.J. Southwell, and the other from C Company under Lieutenant D.I. Owen. They did excellent work patrolling the surrounding countryside searching for rebels and arms, and restricting rebel movement.

By mid 1920 the difficulties of obtaining information led to an upsurge in attacks on Crown forces and forced a review of the Military Intelligence system. The intelligence staffs at divisional headquarters were increased and the Intelligence Officers' posts at brigade headquarters were upgraded to 'staff' appointments. At **July 1920** about this time, bloodhounds were introduced and proved to be effective. In June Brigadier General C.H.T. Lucas,* Commander 16 Brigade, together with two Colonels, was kidnapped in a fishing lodge just to the east of Fermoy. Lucas managed to escape on 30 July and made his way to the nearest police barracks. One of the first serious incidents involving troops and rebels in County Limerick occurred on 13 July when a mixed military-police patrol was ambushed by a large party of rebels. The engagement lasted for an hour and some of the Crown forces who were wounded had their arms and equipment taken. In a follow-up operation in a neighbouring village, and in spite of an I.R.A. ambush, a number of rebels were wounded and some captured, and weapons and ammunition recovered. On the 18th the so-called 'Battle of Cork', which resulted in the wounding by the rebels of soldiers and civilians, including two women, and the death of a number of rebels, led to the imposition of a 22.00 hrs curfew on Cork City. This was the first occasion on which the curfew was imposed in the divisional area although it was subsequently used as a punishment on towns and districts where outrages were committed. During the 'battle' some of the rebels took cover behind their womenfolk whilst firing at the troops.

Realising the potential for gaining information members of the security forces disguised as civilians were increasingly used to intercept and copy rebel communications. One such despatch

---

*   Later Major General Cuthbert Henry Tindall Lucas CB CMG DSO (1879–1958).

led to a number of arrests, including that of Terence MacSwiney, Lord Mayor of Cork and Commandant of an I.R.A. brigade. He subsequently embarked on a hunger strike in Brixton Prison which led to his death after eighty-three days. The rebels began to burn broken-down military vehicles temporarily abandoned whilst help was summoned. 'Q' lorries were designed (named after the 'Q' boats of the First World War) which mounted concealed weapons. One was sent to an area notorious for burning vehicles. When it broke down and the driver set off to call for assistance it was attacked by rebels. The picked crew opened fire on the astonished rebels, two of whom were killed and others wounded. After another successful operation in the Limerick area the rebels gave abandoned vehicles a wide berth. On 24 September an unsuccessful attempt was made to assassinate General Strickland in Cork.

For a number of reasons but chiefly because of attrition the rebels decided to change their tactics. From this emerged the 'Flying Columns' and 'Active Service Units'. The former were to be cyclist units with a strength of twenty-six first-rate, infantry-trained volunteers who would be permanently available at short notice for raids on stores, patrols, convoys, to demolish bridges, and to block roads with trees. Commanders were to have wide discretion to undertake operations on their own initiative. One of their first operations was the successful ambush of 1st Essex in October which resulted in the death of an Officer, with three soldiers killed and five wounded.

On 30 October, Lieutenant Colonel C.C. Norman arrived from India to take over command of the battalion.* His arrival coincided **October 1920** with an upsurge in rioting and violence across the country following the death of the hunger striker Terence MacSwiney. The ambushing and assassination of members of the Crown forces increased and, on 21 November, eleven unarmed British Officers were killed in their beds in Dublin by the I.R.A. on the suspicion that they were intelligence operatives. Later that day, Black and Tans fired into a football crowd, causing twelve deaths.

The safety of troops, both on and off duty, became a matter for concern. On 27 November, 'as the carriage of Brigadier General Cameron was leaving New Barracks at Limerick... a small group of **November– December 1920** men fired a volley of revolver shots at the vehicle. The driver, who was the only occupant of the car, was unhurt but two revolver bullets pierced the body of the vehicle.'[14] Officers had to be armed at all times, even when hunting. They were no longer allowed to sleep out of barracks, and married Officers were advised to send their wives back to England, which many did. A hotel for Officers for whom normal mess accommodation was not available was commandeered and placed under military guard. Non-Commissioned Officers and men were only permitted to walk-out in groups and town patrols were instituted for their protection. In order to combat rebel ambushes and outrages against them, some members of the security forces, but mainly the Black and Tans, resorted to unauthorised reprisals, such as the destruction of property owned by known rebels. The military authorities strongly opposed such action.

A major problem for the Crown Forces was the reliability of locally employed civilian staff as clerks, drivers, etc, and eventually staff for the more important posts were brought from England. Treachery by local employees led to the deaths of two Army Education Corps Officers

---

*   Later Brigadier Compton Cardew Norman CMG CBE DSO *Ch L d'H*, born 14 Dec 1877, commissioned 4 Jan 1899, commanded 1 R.W.F. for five months in 1920 before assuming command of 2 R.W.F. Retired 1934, died 15 Feb 1955. See E.L. Kirby *Officers of The Royal Welch Fusiliers 1689–1914*, p. 97, and David Langley *Duty Done*, p. 88, for full details.

and an R.E. Officer who were kidnapped in separate incidents and murdered. The bodies of the former have never been found. Operations such as this played an increasingly prominent part in I.R.A. activities. On 28 November a party of eighteen R.I.C. auxiliaries was ambushed by a Flying Column of the 3rd Cork Brigade and seventeen killed, the wounded being butchered with axes and bayonets. One of the most successful British operations of the year was a joint Military and Police raid on 20 December on a house in County Limerick. A whole rebel battalion was neutralised when five rebel leaders were killed and 138 others arrested, the latter receiving a total of 600 years imprisonment when tried by court martial. In the middle of December, Martial Law was imposed throughout the 6th Divisional area, but it was not as successful as anticipated as it appears to have been implemented half-heartedly. One result, however, was an increase in the number of Intelligence Officers at both divisional and brigade headquarters.

At the end of December, the battalion despatched a draft of 162 N.C.Os and Fusiliers to the Regimental Depot pending embarkation for 1 R.W.F. in India. This had the effect of reducing the military effectiveness of 2 R.W.F. to such an extent that 'with the exception of an occasional emergency town patrol, it was unable to carry out any duties other than the safeguarding of its barracks.'[15] The duties previously performed by the battalion in Limerick were handed over to the 2nd Royal Warwicks.

Official Punishments, or Reprisals, were introduced in 1921. For attacks on policemen, one of whom died, two houses were destroyed in Cork on 20 January. The punishments were 'if not always on the actual perpetrators, at any rate on sympathisers intimately connected with them.'[16] Between January and 6 June, when these Official Reprisals were forbidden by the Government, 191 houses had been destroyed in the divisional area. Another new measure was for 'hostages' to accompany road convoys. How effective it was as a deterrent on ambushes is uncertain, but hardly any subsequent convoy which included a hostage was attacked. In February a number of Loyalists were murdered and attacks on unarmed soldiers increased, presumably in response to the execution of rebel prisoners. On 5 March, Colonel Commandant Cumming, Commander of the Kerry Brigade in the 6th Division, was travelling in a convoy near Clonbanin in County Cork with forty soldiers as escort, when he was attacked by 100 rebels with a machine gun. Cumming was killed immediately on leaving his vehicle, and three more soldiers died during the engagement; six were wounded. It would appear that the rebels suffered no casualties.

January 1921

With the resumption of railway activity the battalion was required to provide train escorts to counter the new rebel policy of ambushing trains. In March 1921, evidence of the increasing boldness of the rebels became apparent with the systematic destruction of roads and bridges, and an increase in the frequency and scale of ambushes. Reprisals against individuals living in close proximity to the scene of an ambush were authorised and took the form of the destruction of property, fines and the seizure of goods. Large scale searches and the rounding-up of rebels were carried out by joint police and military forces. A large operation, by 150 troops, was launched at dawn on 19 March on a number of occupied rebel houses in County Cork which had been evacuated some hours before the attack. One party of troops was ambushed a few yards from the objective and another arrived on the scene late having lost its way. The Crown forces suffered ten killed and four wounded. Rebel casualties amounted to nineteen, six of whom were killed.

March 1921

During the first three months of 1921 some of the bloodiest **April 1921** encounters of the entire campaign occurred in counties Cork and Kerry, and although the losses to the security forces were considerable, they were outnumbered by those of the I.R.A. In one twelve-day period in April six individuals were targeted and murdered, or kidnapped first and then murdered by the I.R.A. Sir Arthur Vicars, an eminent antiquarian, was murdered in front of his wife at their home which was subsequently destroyed. As a reprisal for this outrage four shops were destroyed in a neighbouring village. An Officer was murdered whilst playing golf, and a Serjeant in a public house. On 16 April Major G.L. Compton-Smith of 2 R.W.F. was kidnapped by the I.R.A. near the village of Blarney, five miles north-west of Cork, and held as a hostage by them for the lives of four rebels under sentence of death at Victoria Barracks. He was shot on the 30th, the day after General Strickland had authorised the executions to take place. A full account of the incident is in the Annexes to this volume.

In May the battalion took over the Limerick City West Sub Area, **May 1921** with a detachment of the 1st Warwicks under command. The I.R.A. had formed flying columns of up to 200 volunteers in the city, which proved difficult for the security forces to pin down and engage, whilst tying up large numbers of troops. Because of the increased pressure training, other than individual and musketry, was impossible. In June, D Company under Major E.O. Skaife was employed for a week leading a flying column in the Tarbert-Athea-Foynes area. Sweeps were carried out in the countryside combined with cordon and search operations in the towns. Successes increased the pressure on the I.R.A.

An incident involving a family soon to be closely linked to the Regiment occurred at Ballyturin in County Galway. The Bagott family would often entertain Officers and their ladies who were stationed locally. Their daughter Molly was engaged to be married to Captain Bruxner-Randall of 2 R.W.F. On Sunday 21 May a party from the 17th Lancers drove over for tea and tennis. Shortly after they left, the groom rushed in and reported the sound of shots from the end of the drive. The party had been ambushed by ten men, and four of the party were dead. When Molly and her father went to investigate they were held up at gun point. Molly managed to slip away unnoticed. She met the groom who had used a different route. Between them they found a pony, put it into the trap and drove to Gort for help. Returning with twenty soldiers and police they had just started to search the grounds when a shot rang out and a policeman close to Molly was killed. There is no record of what followed. Amongst her wedding presents was a silver salver recording the gratitude of the Officers of the 17th Lancers for her bravery.[17]

A particularly unpleasant attack on 31 May was directed at the **June 1921** band of the 2nd Hampshires. Whilst marching to the range at Youghal, County Cork, a mine exploded in a wall killing seven and wounding twenty-one. By June 1921 the strength of the Army in Ireland had risen to fifty-one battalions; the 6th Division had twenty in its four brigades. The level of rebel activity during the next three months was maintained but chiefly in 17 and Kerry Brigade areas. Many successful operations, some large scale, were mounted in June involving hundreds of troops. A terror campaign against Loyalists resulted in kidnappings and house burnings by the rebels. The latter became more common when Official Reprisals were ended. At the end of June, the 6th Division began receiving considerable reinforcements with the arrival of seven infantry battalions and a brigade of four regiments of mounted rifles formed from surplus Officers and men of the

Royal Artillery.* Elaborate measures were taken to protect the new units as they moved by rail to their new destinations. Armoured trucks were attached to each train; air cover provided by the R.A.F.; and the line was patrolled by troops. The move passed off without incident, but on 8 July 2 R.W.F. found explosives on the line between Killaloe and Limerick.[18]

On the same day a truce was announced which was to start at noon on the 11th. All pending operations by the Security Forces were **July 1921** cancelled immediately. The I.R.A., however, continued murdering servicemen up to the very last minute. The terms of the truce required the I.R.A. to cease all attacks on the Crown forces; not to use arms; to cease military manoeuvres; to abstain from interference with public and private property; and to take no action likely to necessitate military involvement. By the end of August there had been 126 breaches in the divisional area alone.

The battalion was continually being called upon to provide guards, patrols and escorts. With the small number of men available for duties it was often the case that 'the soldier did a guard one night, a picquet the next, and the spent the following day in a Crossley [truck] visiting a detachment miles away from Limerick.'[19] On 10 July, 4179390 Private W.R. Williams was on duty riding a motorcycle in County Clare. Local residents on Bunratty **August 1921** Bridge gave no warning that a huge hole had been dug in it by the I.R.A. Williams fell through it. Neither his body, nor his machine, were ever found and he was presumed to have drowned. On 14 August, Private M. Moody was accidently killed by the discharge of an Officer's revolver being cleaned by a fellow servant. In spite of the pressures on the battalions caused by such a large roster of duties, nine Officers managed 105 days hunting between them during the 1921/22 season which opened on 21 September, and the Band went to Wales where they played in Cardiff for a visit by the Prince of Wales; the Bandmaster was presented with a suitably inscribed baton by the Lord Mayor of Cardiff.

The Anglo-Irish Treaty, which led to the formation of the Irish Free State, was signed in London on 6 December 1921. The Treaty was to **December 1921** come into force on 6 December 1922 and within one month Northern Ireland had to exercise its option of withdrawing from the Irish Free State. Support for the treaty amongst the Irish was far from unanimous with even the Irish President, Eamonn de Valera, opposing it. The *Dáil* voted to accept it but its opponents refused and this led to the Irish Civil War from June 1922 to May 1923, which claimed more lives than the War of Independence against Britain. Those in favour won, and the two main political parties in the Republic – *Fianna Fail* and *Fine Gail* – are the direct descendants of the opposing sides in the war. The majority of the Officers of the I.R.A. opposed the treaty.

In January 1922 the 6th Division began its withdrawal from Ireland. Units concentrated at Cork and Fermoy and then moved to **January–May 1922** the embarkation ports of Cork and Waterford. By April most of the division had left and the staff disbanded. On 18 May General Strickland departed having seen Victoria Barracks, Cork, the location of his own H.Q., taken over by the 1st Cork Brigade of the Irish Army. 2 R.W.F. was not amongst those leaving Ireland. On 21 March it moved from Limerick to Ponsonby Barracks, Curragh, County Kildare. In spite of the tension – an 'Officers' patrol' was mounted in the barracks at night – normal peacetime activities went on. Lieutenant M.H. ap Rhys Pryce

*   Units of this type had first been formed in the South African War of 1899–1902.

Troops with an armoured car in Dublin, 1921.

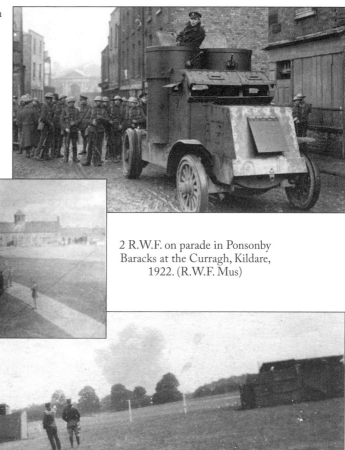

2 R.W.F. on parade in Ponsonby Baracks at the Curragh, Kildare, 1922. (R.W.F. Mus)

The smoke from the I.R.A. bombing of the Four Courts in Dublin seen from 2 R.W.F.'s camp. The short figure in breeches is the Quartermaster, Lieutenant L.J. Shea. (R.W.F. Mus 4155)

recorded in his diary: 'to races in the afternoon', 'nice ride on company charger and hectic guest night', 'Gallic [sic] hockey on lawn in afternoon'. In the Army Football Cup Final at Aldershot on 17 April the battalion team, which was presented to King George V before the match, lost to the 1st Wiltshires by three goals to one.

Another move occurred on 15 May when the battalion went under canvas in Phoenix Park, Dublin. Facilities for training were **August–September 1922** excellent but could not be fully utilised because the need for vigilance was still essential as a result of the lawlessness that existed, including sniping under cover of darkness. Disturbances were not as bad as they might have been because of the fighting that had broken out between supporters and opponents of the treaty. In Dublin there were occasional gun battles between the Free State troops and the rebels. On 31 August, Lieutenant Ap Rhys Pryce's 20th birthday,

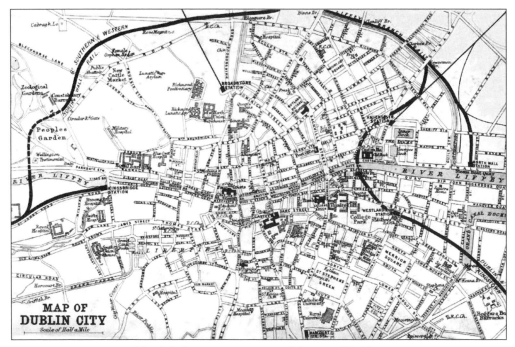

Map 8.3 A contemporary map of the city of Dublin.

he and a friend went to the Gaiety Theatre and during the performance there was a gun battle in the street outside. On the way home they were stopped by a Free State patrol and searched. Serjeant J. Chard, the Officers' Mess Serjeant, returned from town at midday with black powder marks on the collar of his tunic. A young man had detached himself from the lamp post against which he was leaning and fired a hand gun just in front of Serjeant Chard's face. On 16 September, 3903651 Corporal A. Roberts died of natural causes in Dublin. The Regimental Journal, *Y Ddraig Goch*, recorded the award by the Royal Life Saving Society of Diploma, Medal and Badge of the Order of Merit (the highest award possible) to Boy Meade; no records have been found of the details of this incident however.[20]

The weather, which started well, had gradually deteriorated into almost incessant wind or rain, or a combination of the two, and the nights were frequently cold. It was without regret that the battalion left Phoenix Park on 22 September and moved into the excellent premises of the recently evacuated Royal Hibernian Military School.*

Drafts to the 1st Battalion in India continued adversely to affect the battalion's operational capability with the result that it was 'hard put to find the men for the heavy garrison duties during October, the band and drums being finally called upon to complete the guard at Magazine Fort'.[21] On 1 December the battalion was re-organised into Headquarters Wing and four companies. H.Q. Wing comprised four groups: No 1 consisted of the Drums and Signals;

---

* The school was founded in 1769 to educate the orphaned children of members of the British armed forces in Ireland. By 1816 there were 600 children at the school. In 1922 the pupils were transferred to Shorncliffe and amalgamated with the Duke of York's Royal Military School.

2 R.W.F. machine gun section, Dublin, June 1922.
(R.W.F. Mus)

No 2, the Machine Gun Platoon with eight *Vickers* machine guns made available as a result of the disbandment of the Machine Gun Corps, and Light Mortar Section; No 3, the Quartermaster's Department and the regimentally employed;* and No 4, the Band and Regimental Transport.

The Colours of the 2nd Battalion at the last King's Birthday Parade in Dublin, June 1922: the Camp of the Fifteen Acres, Phoenix Park. King's Colour, 2Lt R.W.C. Martin, Sergeant J. Price on his right; CSM E. Austin; Regimental Colour 2Lt M.H. ap Rhys Pryce with Sergeant Davis on his left.
(R.W.F. Mus 2421)

On 5 December 1922 the Irish Free **December 1922** State was officially proclaimed. Ten days later the Royal Hibernian Military School was handed over to troops of the Irish Free State provisional government. The final evacuation of Ireland was carried out without any hostile activity. Early on the morning of the 15th the battalion Quarter Guard dismounted and was replaced by a guard of Free State soldiers. According to *The Times*:

> Four more battalions [1st Lancashire Fusiliers, 2nd Royal Welch Fusiliers, 2nd Loyals and 1st Northamptons] left Ireland. At 11 a.m. the outgoing troops marched past the Gough Memorial in the Phoenix Park, where General Sir Nevil Macready, Commander-in-Chief, took the salute. Great crowds thronged the streets as the four battalions marched through the city to the quays, and the troops were greeted with obvious great sympathy by thousands of onlookers. The Regimental Bands played lively airs as the men marched along the quays, and the Regimental Colours were saluted by many old soldiers as they were borne away from Ireland forever. Before the battalions left Phoenix Park General Macready said "goodbye" personally to all the Officers, and for the first time the King's Colours were saluted by a detachment of Free State troops as they were carried aloft from the park.

---

*   Regimentally employed soldiers included the Officers' batmen, cooks, and tradesmen such as the shoemaker and tailor.

As the troopships with the departing soldiers steamed down the Liffey from the North Wall today, all the ships in the harbour sounded their sirens and dipped their flags. When the troops arrived at the quayside, the military bands played, and when the National Anthem was struck up the King's health was drunk, amid cheers, in cups of tea.[22]

The battalion embarked at 14.00 hrs on 15 December and reached Holyhead at 18.15 hrs. It left Holyhead by train at 02.00 hrs the next morning, arriving at Pembroke Dock at 15.30 hrs, from where it then marched to Llanion Barracks.

2 R.W.F. leaves Phoenix Park Barracks, Dublin, in 1922.

Staff List, 2 R.W.F. Ireland 1919–1922

C.O.	Quartermaster	W.O. II
Lt Col C.C. Norman CMG DSO	Lt C.J. Shea	RQMS W.H. Kelly
Majors	**2nd Lieutenants**	ORS J. Hughes DCM
H.V.V. Kyrke DSO	Ll. Gwydyr-Jones	W.E. Heirene, C Coy
E.J. Pentheny O'Kelly DSO (to	The Hon F.J. Southwell	CSMI E. Austin
Jun 22)	A.D.M. Lewis	A. Simpson MC
Bt Lt Col W.B. Garnett DSO	R.W.C. Martin (Adjt Feb 23)	H. Spalding DCM, B Coy
Bt Lt Col J.R. Minshull-Ford	R.M. Farrant	W.H. Poole, D Coy
DSO MC		

Captains
G.E.R. de Miremont DSO MC
(Adjt)
J.H. Courage
T.D. Daly MC
Lieutenants
G.E.B. Barkworth (to Jun 22)
J. Edwards Evans
W.T.C. Moody
C.A. Anglesea-Sandels MBE MC
G.F. Watson DSO
W. Siddons DCM (to Jun 22)
H.C. Watkins MC
E.L. Morris (to Jun 22)
H.G. Williams
D. Roberts Morgan DCM MM
D.I. Owen
E.A. Morris MM
V.W. Ward DCM (to Jun 22)
G.E. Rees
R. de B. Hardie
J.A. Pringle MC

W.H. Bamfield
M.H. ap Rhys Pryce

W.O. I
RSM W.H. Albutt DCM
BM C.J. Clancey

A.H. Cumberland DCM MM,
A Coy
G. Ottaway
CQMSs
W.J. Woolman, A Coy
S.G. Davies MM, B Coy
E. Copping, D Coy
T. Ledington DCM, C Coy
Staff Sergeants
Sjt Shoemaker F. Witts
Master Tailor F. Holloway
Band Sjt R.W. Howell
Provost Sjt W.O.H. Smithurst
Sjt Driver A.P. Weeks

Notes

1   2 R.W.F. War Diary; J.C. Dunn, *The War the Infantry Knew* (London 1938).
2   David Langley, *Duty Done: 2 R.W.F. in the Great War* (Privately published, 2002).
3   Author of *Old Soldiers Never Die*, 1933, and *Old Soldier Sahib*, 1936.
4   War deaths included all those killed or died of wounds between 4 August 1914 and 30 September 1919; the Commonwealth War Graves registration continued until 1921 to take account of those who died of wounds.
5   2 R.W.F. Digest of Service 1 June 1919–31 March 1939 (R.W.F. Mus 294).
6   'The Irish Rebellion in the 6th Divisional Area. From after the 1916 Rebellion to December, 1921' in *The Irish Sword, The Journal of the Military History Society of Ireland*, Vol XXVII, Spring 2010, No 107, pp. 164–165.
7   *The Irish Sword*, p. 17.
8   2 R.W.F. Digest of Service.
9   *The Memoirs of Field Marshal the Viscount Montgomery of Alamein* (London, 1958), pp. 39–40.
10 *The Irish Sword*, p. 28.
11 *The Irish Sword*, p. 32.
12 They were called 'Black and Tans' after the markings of hunting hounds common in Ireland, because they were dressed in dark police tunics with khaki military breeches and puttees, with tam-o'shanters as their head-dress.
13 For more details see David Fitzpatrick, 'Militarism in Ireland, 1900–1922' in Thomas Bartlett and Keith Jeffery (ed), *A Military History of Ireland* (C.U.P., 1996), pp. 379–406.
14 *The Times*, Monday 29 November 1920.
15 2 R.W.F. Digest of Service.
16 *The Irish Sword*, p. 71.
17 Veronica Bamfield, *On the Strength: The Story of the British Army Wife* (London, 1974), pp. 206–208.
18 2 R.W.F. Digest of Service.
19 *Y Ddraig Goch*, Journal of the Royal Welch Fusiliers, Series I, May 1922, p. 8.
20 *Y Ddraig Goch*, October 1922, p. 51.
21 *Y Ddraig Goch*, January 1923, p. 88.
22 *The Times*, 16 December 1922.

Chapter 9

The 2nd Battalion in Great Britain and the Occupation of Germany, 1922–1929

i. Pembroke Dock, 1922–1926

Pembroke Dock had increased in importance since the Napoleonic Wars, when a Royal Dockyard had been established in the great natural harbour of Milford Haven. It had built over 250 ships for the Royal Navy and also five Royal Yachts, most recently the *Victoria and Albert* which had been launched in 1899. By the time of the Great War, it was, with its eleven slipways and its graving dock, one of the largest installations of its type in the country[1] and as such, the Admiralty and the War Office together represented the largest source of employment in the region; every home in Pembroke Dock contained a shipwright or skilled tradesman who had been a dockyard apprentice: the list of skills among the workforce included joiners, millwrights, blacksmiths, wheelwrights, painters, pattern-makers, and various metal smiths including armour plate specialists.[2] Thus the relationship between the town and the armed services was extremely close.[3]

The dockyard was protected by forts garrisoned by Regular and Territorial artillery brigades: 7 Siege Brigade R.G.A. with three regiments, and the Pembrokeshire Heavy Brigade R.A. (T.A.) which included the Royal Pembrokeshire Artillery Militia, reorganised in 1921 as P and Q Batteries Royal Garrison Artillery (T.A.). These in turn were protected from a seaborne enemy by one or two infantry battalions stationed within the garrison, which were not brigaded with other Regular units in the normal way and, although located within the Welsh Area, were under the direct command of the G.O.C.-in-C. Western Command.[4] In 1923 the only battalion in residence – indeed the only Regular infantry battalion stationed in Wales – was 2 R.W.F. which was based in Llanion Barracks, built in the 1850s just west of the southern end of the Cleddau Bridge, a much more recent construction. Although somewhat primitive – the heating was provided by coke stoves and electric lighting was some years in the future – the barracks were much appreciated, particularly by those who had been at war, in Europe or Ireland, for over eight years.

The soldiers of 2 R.W.F. were somewhat of a mixture, for while the majority were Welshmen from all over Wales, there was a leavening of this through drafts from London, Birmingham, and Liverpool. Before the War, one of the Regiment's nicknames had been 'the Brummagem Fusiliers'.[5] It was said that the Cockney drafts brought many of the brightest men, who frequently worked their way up to become Company Serjeant Majors, and the Birmingham draft also brought many high quality men into the Regiment. What the Welsh majority brought

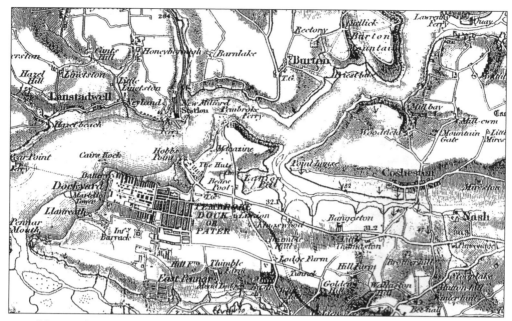

Map 9.1 A contemporary map of the area around Pembroke Dock. (Source: *Ordnance Survey*)

was a sense of national identity within the Regiment, shared by everyone whether Welsh or English, and a strong network of family traditions. The Regiment was permeated with fathers and sons, brothers and cousins, nephews and uncles, and untold connections by marriage. The Officers at this time were chiefly English Public School men, although there was always a contingent of North Wales landed gentry. Before the war these men had generally been able to combine military service with the pleasures of English country life, and after 1919 the pre-war, anti-intellectual, pattern generally reasserted itself. H.C. Stockwell, who joined the battalion in Pembroke Dock, recorded that he:

> … found little attention paid to the Welsh aspect of the Regiment and so far as I remember
> we were never encouraged either to learn Welsh, get to know Wales or study Celtic history:
> I think this was a pity. The exception was Eric Skaife,[6] who while a prisoner of war in the
> First World War, devoted himself to the study of Welsh and who when Colonel of the
> Regiment developed a strong personal Welsh background and living in Wales he became
> a Welsh bard.[7]

Lieutenant Colonel C.C. Norman, who had commanded the 15th Battalion, had been wounded three times during his service in West Africa and on the Western Front, would later command 158 (Royal Welch) Infantry Brigade and become Inspector General of the Royal West African Frontier Force, commanded the battalion. James Dunn had said of him that:

> … he showed a zeal for all-round efficiency and smartness that was bracing. He revived the
> practice of falling in to the drum, and surprised and shocked junior Officers by finding out

Officers 2nd Battalion Rhine 1928.

Rear: Lt C.J.L. Lewis, 2Lt H.de B. Prichard, Lt G.N.H. Taunton-Collins, Lt the Hon G.R. Clegg-Hill, 2Lt A.C. Heber-Percy.

Centre: 2Lt L.T. Lillingston, Lt G.R. Braithwaite, Lt M.B. Courtney, Capt F.I. Gerrard MC, Lt A.D.M. Lewis, Rev H.V. Griffiths MC C.F., 2Lt J.A.M. Rice-Evans, 2Lt M.F.P. Lloyd, Capt H.A. Davies MCE MC, Lt H.C. Stockwell.

Front: Capt D.H.W. Kirkby, Capt F.H. Shove, Capt T.C. Sharp, Capt & Adjt M.B. Dowse, Lt Col P.R. Butler DSO, Maj E.O. Skaife OBE, Lt & Q.M. W.H. Ablett DCM, Cap L.S. Lloyd, Capt H.D'O Lyle.

personally how much each knew of map reading. He could do smartly the things that every man in his command had to know.[8]

Among the Field Officers there were several men who had held high rank during the Great War, and now held brevet rank. They represented a fearsome array of battle experience: for example, Brevet Lieutenant Colonel John Minshull-Ford,* who had been wounded four times during the Great War, received the DSO and MC and had been six times mentioned in despatches, and had commanded a brigade; he would eventually command a division and be Colonel of the Royal Welch Fusiliers from 1938 to 1942. Then there was Brevet Lieutenant Colonel William Garnett, or 'Buckshee',† also a wartime brigade commander with pre-war service in South Africa, China and India; he too had won the DSO and had been mentioned in despatches four times, although J.C. Dunn had a poor opinion of him, and Siegfried Sassoon, who called him

---

*   Later Major General John Randle Minshull-Ford CB DSO MC, *b* 12 May 1881, commissioned 11 Aug 1900, retired 1938. Colonel of the Regiment 1938–1942. *d* 1 Apr 1948. See Kirby, p. 47 and *Who Was Who* Vol IV.

†   William Brooksbank Garnett DSO, *b* 31 Jul 1875, commissioned 5 May 1900, retired 1927, *d* 17 Aug 1946. His son, Lieutenant J.B. Garnett, was killed on 23 May 1940, aged 23, while commanding the Carrier Platoon of 1 R.W.F.

'Easby', judged him indulgent.[9] D.M. Barchard,* the Adjutant, had been taken prisoner at the battle of Langemarck in 1914, and had a deep and lasting loathing for the Germans. These were men whose background was in war, and whose business was fighting. They had little time for the niceties of the staff, and their influence on the post-war generation was profound. As well as Stockwell[†], the younger Officers included Ll. Gwydyr-Jones who had joined the battalion at Limerick in December 1920,[‡] and M.H. ap Rhys Pryce.[§] Stockwell described the influence of the senior Officers thus:

> Looking back on my first three years in the Army and my early days as a Regimental Officer, there is little doubt that with the experienced influence of the many senior Officers who had all survived the war in various theatres of conflict, we absorbed a great deal of knowledge: we learnt the responsibilities of an Officer, we learnt the basic tenets of leadership, we were knocked into shape and … those years – certainly for me – shaped my future life in my profession.[10]

2 R.W.F. was never more than 450 to 500 strong throughout its time in Pembroke Dock, and on arrival, only 300 strong – half its established strength. The battalion remained organised into four rifle companies and a Headquarters Wing.[11] Clothing and equipment was very much that in use during the late war, and was already looking obsolescent. As the home battalion of the Regiment under the Cardwell system,[12] 2 R.W.F. was responsible for training and finding drafts for the 1st Battalion of the Regiment, which was stationed at Lucknow in India, and the battalion Digest of Service is full of notifications of such drafts being sent off. This could be a dispiriting experience; the Regimental Journal *Y Ddraig Goch* described the situation thus:

> How pleased we all were some few weeks ago when a draft of seventy arrived from the Depot. The chests of Company Commanders swelled visibly… But now, alas, the hive seems strangely empty – another young brood has gone joyously forth … The chests of the Company Commanders have gone back to normal; and the Drill Serjeant now has a wintry smile; the Musketry Instructor has once more lapsed into silence. We always feel the same on the departure of a draft for India … [13]

The number and frequency of drafts depended on the rate of discharges in the overseas battalion, but if that battalion was in India or the Far East, drafts would only be sent out during the Trooping Season, outside the Monsoon. While with the home battalion, a recruit from

---

*   Later Brigadier David Maxwell Barchard, born 3 Nov 1891, commissioned 11 Oct 1911, retired to Kenya having commanded 21 (East African) Brigade in 1945, died 10 Mar 1954. See Kirby, p. 5.

†   Later General Sir Hugh Stockwell, GCB KBE DSO (1903–1986), Adjutant-General of the Army and DSACEUR.

‡   Later Brigadier Llewellyn Gwydyr-Jones DSO OBE. Known as Gwydyr, his name being anglicised and pronounced Gwider, to rhyme with 'wider'. See his obituary in *Y Ddraig Goch*, March 1987.

§   Later Brigadier Meyrick Home Ap Rhys Pryce, born 31 Aug 1902, commissioned 23 Dec 1921, was GSO1 of 53rd (Welsh) Division in Normandy in 1944, commanded 2 R.W.F. during the occupation of Japan in 1946, retired 23 Sep 1954, died 28 Mar 1996. See J.P. Riley *Regimental Records of The Royal Welch Fusiliers* Volume VI for more details.

the Depot would carry out section, platoon and company training to supplement what he had learned at the Depot, and therefore be able to take his place in a rifle company.

Inspections by senior Officers were frequent. On 3 March, just after the battalion had celebrated its first St David's Day at home, **January–April 1923** Lieutenant General Sir H. de Beauvoir de Lisle,[*] General Officer Commanding-in-Chief Western Command at Shrewsbury, inspected the battalion followed, on 4 April, by Major General Sir Archibald Montgomery-Massingberd,[†] General Officer Commanding Welsh Area. He was succeeded by Major General Sir Thomas Marden,[‡] who visited on 14/15 August. In contrast to Ireland, training could now be undertaken by all members of the battalion without the distraction of endless guards and picquets. Individual training in January and February was followed by section training. Then began intense musketry instruction in preparation for the Annual Range Course which was fired at Penally, just west of Tenby, from 12 April to 22 May. H.C. Stockwell recalled that:

> We went to Musketry Camp at Penally to the west of the Tenby golf course[§] – a hutted camp, but an exercise in itself marching there and setting up shop for our period in camp and this annual classification. On the march from Pembroke Dock we were accompanied by the field kitchen drawn by a pair of heavy draught horses, behind which the cooks marched brewing up a most delectable stew, hot and full of carrots and onions and potatoes and at the midday halt, the troops got down to it; not so the Officers as it was "infra dig" to eat with the troops and we sat aside eating stale and tasteless sandwiches while the air was full of the delicious smell of the hot stew from the field kitchen. This whole period we enjoyed, and took great pains to try and turn our Welshmen into decent shots. They weren't all that good – hours spent in the butts were boring and in those days we were glad of the bugle call "Cease firing" so that we might skid off into Tenby, the pub and the cinema. On our off days we struggled with golf on a lovely course full of sand-dunes and lumps and bumps, and now, of my golf balls.[14]

In June, authority was granted by the War Office for private soldiers in Fusilier Regiments to be known as 'Fusiliers',[15] a welcome addition to **June–July 1923** restoration of the spelling of 'Welch' in the Regiment's title that had been granted in 1920.[16] At Freshwater West on 5 July, 4180904 Fusilier A. Harwood got into difficulties whilst swimming. Captain M.L. Lloyd-Mostyn of A Company was awarded the medal of the Royal Humane Society for his gallant efforts in trying to save him. 'Had the current not been so furious we have no doubt that he would have been successful.'[17]

Sport played a prominent part in battalion life, and boxing was taken particularly seriously. The battalion Challenge Shield was won by D Company. Each evening there was an exhibition

---

[*]   General Sir Henry de Beauvoir De Lisle KCB KCMG DSO (1864–1955).

[†]   General Sir Archibald Armar Montgomery-Massingberd GCB GCVO KCMG DL (1871–1947) was Chief of the Imperial General Staff. He was later was the driving force behind the formation of a permanent Mobile Division, the fore-runner of the Armoured Division.

[‡]   Major General Sir Thomas Owen Marden KBE CB CMG (1866–1951) commanded the British occupying force in Turkey during the Chanak Crisis of 1921–1922. He had commanded 114 Infantry Brigade of the 38th (Welsh) Division on the Western Front during the Great War, including during the battle for Mametz Wood.

[§]   *Y Ddraig Goch* October 1923, p. 161, records this as being 12 April to 22 May.

by Serjeant Johnny Basham,* who coached
the battalion team which came fourth in
the Army Championships at Aldershot on
2/3 May, with Lieutenant R.W.C. Martin
winning the Officers' Heavyweights in the
team competition; Officers and men did
box in the same competitions, but at this
date there were still some Officers' only
matches. The hockey team won the Western
Command competition. The rugby team
entered the West of Llanelly League and
played two games a week. They were considered to be a great draw and could ensure a
good gate. Football was not so successful
but Corporal Twine was awarded the Gold
Badge of the Army Football Association,
and was selected to represent the Army
against the Royal Navy, Royal Air Force,
Rhine Army and the French and Belgian

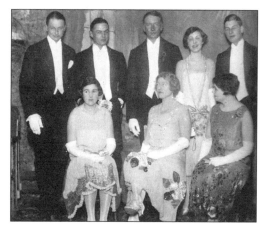

The *Red Dragons* concert party. The group includes
Lieutenant H.C. Stockwell, Lieutenant Moody,
Lieutenant F. Shove, Lieutenant Pringle, Mrs
Moody, Mrs Winnie Pringle and Mrs W.B. Garnett.
(Stockwell family)

Armies. Fusilier L. Voas was also capped against the French Army. The battalion team won
the Pembrokeshire Senior League, winning thirteen out of sixteen matches and losing only one.
H.C. Stockwell also recalled that:

> One of our activities was to lay out the new sports ground for the garrison – here we
> repaired for most of our working hours to load and fill *Decauville* trucks and run them on
> their rails to tip on the downward slope – the young Officers' team of truck pushers and
> tippers had no end of delight in racing the trucks through the mud and over the junction
> points to get them back to the loaders, who were drawn from the troops and were often
> trained miners at that, before they could load the next lot. No bulldozers then or machinery
> to do the job in a day or two – but we made a good job of the arena.[18]

The Officers enjoyed the hunting and were made particularly welcome by the Seymour Allen,
which met on Tuesdays and Fridays, while the Pembrokeshire Foxhounds met on Mondays and
Thursdays: there was, therefore, ample opportunity for all enthusiasts. A cup was given by the
battalion to be competed for in the Farmers' Race at Mr Seymour Allen's Point-to-Point, which
was to be run 'over a grass country with two or three fields of plough and good big grass faced
banks to jump.'[19] In May 1924, Second Lieutenant H.C. Stockwell won the Farmers' Race at
this event on a mare called 'Thoughtless', which was owned by a local farmer.[20]

The Band gave numerous charity concerts in Pembroke Dock
which were well reported on in the local press. The String Band

October–November 1923

---

*   John Michael (Johnny) Basham (1889–1947). He enlisted into the Regiment in 1911 and served
    throughout the Great War. He was British Welterweight Champion 1914–1920, and British and
    European Middleweight Champion in 1921. See his biography by Alan Roderick, *Johnny! The Story of
    the Happy Warrior* (Newport, 1990).

A meet of the South Pembrokeshire Hunt at the Officers' Mess, Llanion Barracks, Pembroke Dock on 1 March 1924.

was much in demand and performed at the Carmarthen Hunt Ball. The Band carried out a tour of North Wales in October/November to raise money for the publication of *Regimental Records*. Whilst there it was present at the unveiling of the memorial in Wrexham Parish Church to those Royal Welchmen who had lost their lives in Waziristan during the recent tour by the 1st Battalion.

The Goat presented by H.M. The King died at Pembroke Dock on 22 January 1924. In little over three weeks, on 17 February, a new Royal Goat arrived from the Royal Herd at Windsor. Its first parade was on 1 March, when the battalion trooped the Colour with, for the first time, all non-commissioned ranks wearing the Flash in Service Dress in accordance with Army Council Instruction No. 62. Hitherto, only Officers and Warrant Officers had been permitted to wear it in anything other than ceremonial dress. The new Goat apparently 'behaved with dignity and aplomb befitting a veteran.'[21] Second Lieutenant H.C. Stockwell was the Ensign for the Regimental Colour.

January–March 1924

The General Officer Commanding-in-Chief Western Command, Lieutenant General Sir John Du Cane,* inspected the battalion on 1 April. On 12 May, Lieutenant Colonel C.C. Norman, left the battalion and was succeeded by Lieutenant Colonel C.I. Stockwell.† Stockwell had commanded 164 Infantry Brigade in the 55th Division during the Great War and later in Ireland, was eight times mentioned in despatches, and had won the DSO and the *Croix de Guerre*. Frank Richards described him as 'cool as a cucumber', having 'plenty of guts', but being a 'first class bully.'[22]

April–May 1924

---

*   General Sir John (Philip) Du Cane GCB (1865–1947) was Master-General of the Ordnance.
†   Later Brigadier General CI Stockwell CB CMG DSO *CdeG* born 27 Sep 1879, commissioned 11 Feb 1899, retired 1932 but recalled to serve in WW2, died 4 Dec 1953. See Kirby, p. 122, Langley, p. 49, and *Who Was Who* Vol VII, p. 1048.

Siegfried Sassoon agreed with this assessment, and in *Memoirs of an Infantry Officer*, C.I. appears as the overbearing character Kinjack. Shortly after he had taken command, a series of inspections followed, begun by the recently appointed General Officer Commanding-in-Chief Western Command, Lieutenant General Sir Richard Butler[*] on 26 June who inspected the battalion in marching order. On the following day the Colonel of the Regiment, Lieutenant General Sir Francis Lloyd,[†] inspected it in review order. On 1 July 1924 and the three days following,[23] the General Officer Commanding 53rd (Welsh) Division (TA) and Welsh Area, Major General Sir Thomas Marden, again inspected the battalion. At the end of the inspection, he apparently told Stockwell that his battalion was 'not fit for war.' Given Stockwell's background and wartime experience, this, in H.C. Stockwell's words, 'caused C.I. to take off like a scalded cat – I doubt if his reply stood him in much good for his subsequent career.' H.C. Stockwell, who was the Commanding Officer's nephew, described some other aspects of that inspection:

> We Officers had been told to have our field glass graticuled at our own expense and arrangement, a tiresome exercise as it cost money and we had to send them away to be done. On the parade, the Officers were lined up and the General walked down the line asking each Officer "Have you had your field glasses graticuled?" and every now and then, after the Officer had replied "Yes", he took them and checked the answer. I know for a fact that Edward Morris[‡] on my right had not had his done and when asked he replied without the bat of an eye "Yes", gambling on the General checking his reply. He got away with it – he would, being an old soldier commissioned from the ranks during the Great War having won a Military Medal.[24]

Doubtless it was the result of the General's visit that the pace of field training and military activities was stepped up. This was divided between Penally and Freshwater: platoon training and range work at the former; and company training at the latter. On 8 July a party of fifty under Brevet Lieutenant Colonel J.R. Minshull-Ford left Pembroke Dock for Wembley to participate in the Empire Pageant at the British Empire Exhibition. The British Government wished to simulate trade across the Empire and based the exhibition around the new Wembley Stadium which would become an icon of British football. There were 27 million visitors to the exhibition. Numerous pavilions were erected across the site which represented the various countries of the Empire. The exhibition generated huge interest and there are numerous references to the Wembley Pageant during this period in the Regimental Journal. The exhibition was not a large financial success and so it was decided to run the exhibition on into 1925. The 2nd Battalion had two separate periods of duty at the exhibition. In this period at the exhibition, the party carried out a re-enactment of a Napoleonic era battle. In addition, five musicians from 2 R.W.F.'s Regimental Band were required to reinforce the musicians from the Army School of Music, Kneller Hall, Twickenham, London.

June–July 1924

---

[*]   Lieutenant General Sir Richard Harte Keatinge Butler KCB KCMG (1870–1935).

[†]   Lieutenant General Sir Francis Lloyd GCVO KCB DSO (1853–1926) was a Grenadier Guardsman and a Cardiff man. He raised the Welsh Guards in 1915, being at the time Major General Commanding the Brigade of Guards and General Officer Commanding London District.

[‡]   Edward Arnold Morris MM, born 13 Mar 1895, commissioned 28 Nov 1917, retired by 1932.

2 R.W.F. at the Royal Tournament, Wembley, 1924. (R.W.F. Mus 2642)

From 14 July 1925, a detachment of six Officers and 205 Other Ranks under Lieutenant Colonel Minshull-Ford and Captain Daly supported the exhibition for six weeks, returning in time for the Battalion annual autumn exercise in September. The whole of the Regimental Band also played a series of engagements at Wembley over a period of two weeks that summer.

D Company was sent out to a company training camp at Gupton Farm about one mile North-West of Castlemartin in West Pembrokeshire, near the entrance to Milford Haven, and just behind the sand-dunes on the edge of a superb sandy beach. Here the Officers and men were kept hard at work learning to attack and defend, and to master the practicalities of the tactical battle at the platoon and company level.

Sport continued to feature significantly in the summer and autumn of 1924. The football season was less successful than **January–April 1925** the previous one with the battalion team knocked out of the Army Cup by the eventual winners. Serjeant Twine played for England against Wales in an amateur international at Llandudno in March. During the season he also represented the Army in all their matches. Lieutenant R.W.C. Martin won the Quarter Mile at the Army Championships and went on to represent the Army in the Inter-Services Sports, and also to run in the Amateur Athletics Association meeting. Mr Seymour Allen's Point-to-Point was held at Flemington on 8 April 1925. This was the first time that the Officers' steeplechase for the Red Dragon cup had been run since 1913. The course was three-and-a-half miles (5.6 kilometres) long and there were sixteen starters, possibly a record. Seven finished, with Lieutenant W.H. Bamfield winning on 'Impediment' by twenty lengths.

On 14 June the Goat died after only a short period of service. **June–August 1925** His replacement, presented again by The King, arrived on 24 July. The new Goat had to master his duties more rapidly than usual: all companies marched off for five days' training in camp at Freshwater and then, in August, the battalion was ordered

Two pictures of 2 R.W.F. on Public Duties in London, 1925.

Major R.E. Hindson commands the St James's Palace Guard in August 1925; the Ensign is Lieutenant M.H. ap Rhys Pryce. (R.W.F. Mus)

to London to take over the guard duties on the Royal palaces and the Bank of England for six weeks, in order to provide a respite for the 3rd Battalion Coldstream Guards, which was to carry out brigade training.[25] These public duties were only rarely allocated to line or Colonial Regiments, and to take responsibility for the security of the Sovereign was a rare privilege. That it was granted to The Royal Welch Fusiliers was in recognition of the Regiment's outstanding war record, and of the fact that no less a person than His Majesty the King was Colonel-in-Chief of the Regiment. The imposing shape of Drill Serjeant W.G. Gingell MM of the Coldstream Guards soon appeared at Pembroke Dock and for three weeks, the battalion bashed the square in slow and quick time, and spent many hours at sword and rifle drill: Gingell established a good relationship with the battalion, and was allowed to stay on with 2 R.W.F. while the battalion remained in London. Here it was lodged with the 2nd Battalion Scots Guards in Chelsea Barracks where all ranks were generously entertained.

The battalion, dressed in drab khaki rather than the scarlet of the Guards – full dress had not been fully reintroduced after the war – began to undertake guards on Sunday 23 August 1925. In all, eleven King's Guards were undertaken at Buckingham Palace and St James, as well as duties at the Tower of London, Clarence House, the Magazine in Hyde Park and the Bank of England. A silver-mounted walking-out cane was presented to the smartest man on each guard. Whilst in London the battalion athletics meeting was held in Battersea Park. The battalion returned to Pembroke Dock on 25 September 1925.[26]

A concert party called the *Red Dragons* was formed under the direction of the Commanding Officer, based on Burnaby's popular and long running West End revue *The Co-optimists*,* and supported by a string band formed from the Regimental Band. Mrs Garnett was their Soprano, and other members included Mrs Moody and her husband W.T. Moody,† Gwydyr-Jones, and F.H. Shove‡ at the piano, H.C. Stockwell, and Winnie Pringle, a professional soubrette, or operatic soprano, from the London stage, who was married to J.A. Pringle, an Australian serving with the Regiment.§ The *Red Dragons* performed in Tenby and elsewhere: the Regimental Journal recorded one particular triumph:

> This concert party made its bow to the Battalion on the nights of April 3rd and 4th [1924] before crowded houses… the party gave a really first-class performance. The stage of the Canteen was entirely re-decorated in grey, with a huge Red Dragon in the centre-background …

The *South Wales News* enthusiastically described a performance during Tenby Hunt Week at the De Valence Gardens Pavilion.[27]

---

*   *The Co-optimists*, with Doris Bentley and Polly Ward, appeared at the Prince of Wales Theatre from 1923 to 1926, and at various other theatres thereafter until 1929. It was revived again in 1935. Several 78rpm records of the show were recorded, and these would certainly have helped the *Red Dragons*. For more details see Doris Bentley et al. *The Comic History of the Co-optimists* (Herbert Jenkins, 1926).

†   William Thomas Charles Moody, born 5 Feb 1897, commissioned 14 Jul 1915. Left the Regiment in 1929, later served in the R.A.O.C. until 1954.

‡   Frederick Harper Shove, born 30 Jul 1886, commissioned into the Royal Fusiliers 6 Jun 1917, transferred to R.W.F. 10 Feb 1923 as a Captain, retired 30 Jul 1931, but rejoined for war service with R.A.O.C. in 1940.

§   Jack Archibald Pringle MC, born 15 Jan 1897, commissioned 20 Jan 1916, left the Regiment about 1933 and died 19 Jun 1964 in Tasmania.

Five members of the battalion competed in the Army Individual Boxing Championships at Tidworth in February 1926. All put up a good show and Second Lieutenant M.B. Courtney reached the final of the Welterweights. Hunting continued as the favoured winter occupation of the Officers. Twenty-seven meets were attended and over five Officers on average attended each one, at a cost per day of about 16/- (80p). The Red Dragon Cup, again held during the Seymour Allen Point-to-Point, was won by Lieutenant Ll. Gwydyr-Jones ahead of another good field.

On 26 February 1926 the Colonel of the Regiment, Lieutenant General Sir Francis Lloyd, died at his home at Rolls Park, Chigwell, Essex. His funeral at the Guards Chapel in London on 4 March was attended by Colonel C.I. Stockwell, Major G.E.R. de Miremont and Major E.O. Skaife[*] from the 2nd Battalion. The new Colonel of the Regiment was Lieutenant General Sir Charles Dobell.[†] On St David's Day the battalion marched with its Colours to the garrison church in the dockyard, the King's Colour bearing for the first time the new battle honours from the Great War.

On 3 May 1926 the Trades Union Congress called the General Strike.[28] Even though they were government employees and of a highly conservative temper, the dockyard labour force came out solidly, along with the G.W.R. men from Neyland.[29] One platoon under Lieutenant P.F. Pritchard,[‡] was hurried off to Hereford by road in hired *Ford* trucks to guard an Ordnance Depot just outside the town, and a platoon of B Company under Lieutenant D. Roberts-Morgan[§] moved to secure the local ammunition depot at Pembrey.[30] The rest of the battalion was confined to barracks in case of trouble, except when a guard platoon was required at the Pembroke Dock Ordnance Depot. However it was quickly realised that there would be no trouble, and normal life resumed. This was scarcely surprising: the dockyard labour force was comprised of solid citizens, artisans, deacons of their chapels – not street ruffians. Besides, there was too much friendship between the town and the military for there to be any possible unpleasantness. The detached platoons rejoined, having had a dull time of it, when the strike was called off on the 13th. Thereafter the battalion returned to normal training, sporting, and social events, and in September went off to Freshwater for ten days in camp.

May 1926

In the aftermath of the General Strike, but primarily influenced by reductions in the size of the Royal Navy following the end of the Great War, came the closure of the Royal Dockyard. This had been announced almost a year before on Wednesday 2 September 1925, and it had a devastating effect on the local community. 4,000 skilled jobs were lost at a stroke as well as the effect on a host of other subsidiary businesses and institutions like the Coronation School in the dockyard. The Conservative M.P., Major Sir Charles Price, was a popular man but he was much blamed for closure with the result that at the next election he was turned out in favour of

---

[*] Later Brigadier Sir Eric Ommanney Skaife Kt CB OBE (1884–1956). Colonel of the Regiment 1948–1952).

[†] Lieutenant General Sir Charles Macpherson Dobell KCB CMG DSO (1869–1954). Colonel of the Regiment 1926–1938. Dobell preceded Allenby in command of British and Empire troops in the Middle East until he was dismissed following the failure of the Second Battle of Gaza. He was later Governor-General of Canada and was responsible for the establishment of the alliance with the Royal 22ème Régiment.

[‡] Later Lieutenant Colonel Philip Frederick Pritchard OBE MC. Commissioned 1924, transferred to I.A.S.C. by 1936. Known as 'the tall Mr Pritchard.'

[§] David Roberts-Morgan DCM MM, born 14 Mar 1886, commissioned from the ranks 5 April 1917, retired 14 Mar 1931, died 17 Sep 1939. See David Langley *Duty Done*, p. 21.

the Liberal candidate, Major Gwilym Lloyd George, son of the wartime Prime Minister, and member of the 15th (1st London Welsh) Battalion of the Regiment.[31] Arguably, the town has never really recovered from the blow, even with the arrival first of the Royal Air Force in 1939, and then the establishment of the oil refining industry in the 1970s. Many tradesmen moved to find work at the dockyards in Portsmouth, Plymouth and Chatham, establishing small colonies of Pembrokeshire folk in those towns.*

The battalion had already been warned for its next posting in Germany, since without the dockyard there was no further need of a garrison, and on 18 October the Advance Party left Pembroke Dock. Between 8 and 10 November the rest of the battalion left the deep depression of a jobless town with some

October–November 1926

relief, in three parties which arrived at Bingen in the Occupied Zone of Germany between the 10th and 12th. The Rear Party arrived on the 19th. There was a Regular battalion stationed in Pembroke Dock thereafter, until the activation of the Seaplane base during the Second World War. The strength of the battalion for the move was sixteen Officers and 694 Other Ranks, about 8% below establishment. They were accompanied by about a hundred wives and children. Travel was by rail from Pembroke Dock to Dover, ferry to Ostend, and then by train to Wiesbaden via Brussels, Metz and Saarbrücken.

Staff List, 2 R.W.F. Pembroke Dock, 1922–1926

Commanding Officer	Lt Col C.C. Norman CMG DSO
	Lt Col C.I. Stockwell CB CMG DSO (5 May 24)
Second-in-Command	Bt Lt Col W.B. Garnett DSO
	Bt Lt Col P.R. Butler DSO (1925)
Adjutant	Capt G.E.R. de Miremont DSO MC
	Lt D.M. Barchard (Feb 23)
	Lt R.W.C. Martin (Feb 26)
RSM	W.O. I W.H. Albutt DCM
	W.O. I W. Gorham MSM (Dec 24)
ORQMS	W.O. II J. Hughes DCM
ORS	LSjt S.L. Gysser

A Company	B Company	C Company	D Company
Capt M.L. Lloyd-Mostyn (Maj Jan 25) (to May 25)	Bt Lt Col J.R. Minshull-Ford DSO MC (to Jan 25)	Capt T.C. Sharp	Capt Ll. S. Lloyd
Lt G.E. Rees	Lt G.F. Watson DSO	Lt E.A. Morris MM	Lt R.M. Farrant (to Nov 23)
Lt A.D.M. Lewis	Lt Hon. F.J. Southwell (to Jun 23)	2Lt R.W.C. Martin	2Lt H.C. Stockwell (Mar 23)
CSM W.H. Dickinson DCM	2Lt M.H. ap Rhys Pryce (to Oct 25)	CSM G.T. Ottaway (to Dec 24)	CSM H. Spalding DCM
CQMS F. Witts	CSM S. G. Davies MM (to Jun 23)	CQMS H. Fox (to Feb 24)	CQMS E. Clopping
Sjt C. Cahill	CSM J. Wylie (to Dec 24)	CQMS M. Walshe	Sjt J.M. Kensett
Sjt N. Ridings	CQMS E. Eager	Sjt E. Cashmere	Sjt B.J. Kelly
Sjt E Moreton	Sjt W. Price	Sjt R.L. Davies	LSjt J. Brown
LSjt A. Carroll	Sjt H. Bath	LSjt W.J. Bowler	
LSjt J. Dale	LSjt J. Thatcher	LSjt T. Hutchings	
	LSjt W. Setterfield	LSjt W.H. Davies MM	
		LSjt T. Hutchings	

---

*   Among these were the family of Marie Lewis, archivist in the Pembrokeshire Record Office in Haverfordwest, who kindly supplied much background information for this chapter.

Headquarter Wing

Quartermaster
Lt C.J. Shea
RQMS W.H. Kelly
Sjt Master Tailor
J.W. Jordan
Sjt E. Shoemaker
Transport
Lt D. Roberts-Morgan DCM MM
Unposted
Lt C.A. Ryan (Mar–Apr 23)
Maj F.S. Lanican O'Keefe MBE (May–Nov 24)

Band
W.O. I (BM) W.J. Clancy
Sjt R.W. Howell
Drums
Sjt Dmr A.E. Gill
Pioneers
Sjt A.E. Evans
Provost
Sjt W.O.H. Smithurst
Training Staff
CSMI E. Austin
SIM S. Metcalfe
Attached
Lt A.C. Chamley *A.E.C.* (to Jan 23)

Admin
Capt F.H. Shove (to Apr 25)
Lt W.T.C. Moody
Lt H.C. Watkins MC (to Feb 25)
Lt D.I. Owen (to May 23, and from Jun 26)
Lt Ll. Gwydyr-Jones
Lt W.H. Bamfield
Lt D.H.W. Kirkby (May 25)
Lt H. Grismond Williams
Lt Ll. A. A. Alston (Dec 25)
Lt R. de B. Hardie (Feb–Jun 25)
Lt C.A. Anglesea-Sandels MBE MC
Lt G.F. Watson DSO (to Oct 24)
2Lt M.F.P. Lloyd (Mar 26)

CQMS W.J. Woolman
Sjt T. McCormick
Sjt J.W. Simkins
Sjt P. Chard

Unplaced
Maj C.H. Edwards
Maj J.G. Bruxner-Randall (Nov 25)
Capt T.D. Daly MC (to Jan 25)
Capt C.H. Wolff (Jun 26)

Capt R.E. Hindson (Dec 24)
2Lt M.B. Courtney (Sep 24) (Lt Aug 26)

2Lt G.N.H. Taunton Collins
2Lt G.E. Braithwaite (Sep 24) (Lt Aug 26)
2Lt Hon. G.R. Clegg-Hill (Sep 24) (Lt Aug 26)
2Lt C.J.L. Lewis (Oct 25)
2Lt P.F. Pritchard (Feb 25) (Lt Aug 26)
2Lt T.D. Butler (Mar 26)

W.O. II H.E. Callus DCM (Dec 24)
W.O. II W.H. Poole (Dec 24)
W.O. II C. Jones DCM MM (Dec 25)

CQMS P. Condon (Dec 25)
CQMS J.T. Wilde (Dec 24)
CQMS A. Bent MM (Dec

ii. Germany, 1926–1929

Under the terms of the Armistice, signed on 11 November 1918, the German Army was obliged to quit those parts of France, Belgium and Luxembourg that it occupied, together with the whole of Alsace-Lorraine. It was further required to evacuate all troops from German territory on the west bank of the Rhine, together with the three bridgeheads on the eastern bank of the river at Mainz, Coblenz and Cologne. French, American and British forces were to provide the army of occupation. To command the British contingent Haig chose General Sir Herbert Plumer on whose Second Army it was based. The Occupation Force originally comprised some 273,000 men, sixteen divisions of first-class troops. By March 1919 the original force had largely been demobilised and replaced by drafts of young soldiers and reduced to twelve divisions. After the signing and ratification of the Treaty of Versailles, the size of the force decreased rapidly.

The Treaty of Versailles, signed on 28 June 1919, made provision for the demilitarisation of the left bank of the Rhine. It also provided for the military occupation by Allied troops of this area, together with bridgeheads across the Rhine, for fifteen years from ratification of the treaty on 10 January 1920. The evacuation was to be implemented in three stages: that of Cologne in five years, that of Coblenz in ten, and that of Mainz in fifteen. These evacuations were, however, to be dependent on German compliance with the provisions of the treaty as a whole.

Following the ratification of the Treaty in January 1920, Britain's contribution to the army of occupation, through the Inter-Allied Military Commission, was titled the British Army of the Rhine (B.A.O.R). The British were responsible to the Inter-Allied Military Commission, and also for a short-term commitment to the Plebiscite Force in Upper Silesia in May 1921. The bulk

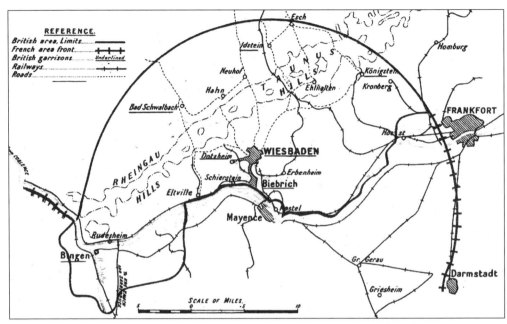

Map 9.2 A contemporary map of the Wiesbaden Bridgehead during the British occupation.
(Source: *Official History*)

of the occupation force was always French; the Americans and Belgians had also contributed in the early years. Between 1920 and 1925 the strength of B.A.O.R. steadily reduced from sixty to twenty thousand.[32] In January 1923, following the declaration that Germany was in voluntary default over the payment of reparations, France occupied the Ruhr, remaining there until July 1925.

When it first moved into the Rhineland, the British Army had taken responsibility for one of the bridgeheads astride the Rhine – the city of Cologne. Here an excellent relation-ship had developed between the Army and the German people, chiefly because the British were regarded as guarantors against French-inspired separatism as well as a bulwark against the popular upheavals of the early post-Armistice period, and periodic revolutions against the Weimar Republic. A sizeable British civilian population grew up, partly based on commerce, and partly on discharged soldiers who had married German women and preferred to stay on rather than face unemployment at home. By 1922, this population numbered about 2,500.[33] Between April 1924, when the Dawes Commission published its report on reparations, the London Conference of August 1924, and Locarno Pact of November 1925 – by which Britain, France, Belgium, Italy and Germany undertook to maintain their present frontiers, abstain from the use of force, and, in the case of Germany, recognise the demilitarisation of the Rhineland – a realisation dawned that the occupation would have to be ended. To comply with the treaty, the Rhineland was gradually demilitarised in tranches, from north to south. The British Army of the Rhine, which had been steadily reducing from the time that the Peace of Versailles had been signed, evacuated Cologne at the end of 1925, and moved south to the area of Wiesbaden. The last troops and families left Cologne on 30 January 1926.[34]

In Wiesbaden, the situation was markedly different from that in Cologne. Anglo-French relations were cordial – the discord which had followed the French occupation of the Ruhr between 1923 and 1925 and the strikes, riots, wholesale expulsion of German families, and collapse of the *Reichsmark* which followed – had been overcome after the fall of Poincaré.* Moreover, French troops had assisted the German authorities in putting down the separatist revolt in Wiesbaden in October 1923.[35] Because of this, the local German population here actively resented the occupation; perhaps also because the effects of U.S. and British contributions to German reconstruction, which more than offset the sums paid in war reparations, had not been felt in an area of French occupation. The area was far more rural than Cologne, and this, added to the transfer of some powers from the occupation forces back to local *Kreis* (county) officials, reduced contact at all levels. As time went on, however, reasonably cordial relations were established with few unpleasant incidents, although there were the inevitable battles in beer halls, and the infant Nazi Party, which had won its first twelve seats in the Weimar *Reichstag* in 1924, was responsible for some street affrays in 1929.[36]

In 1926, the population of Wiesbaden was about 102,000, and it was a popular centre for recreation and tourism as well as being the administrative capital of the state of Hesse-Nassau.[37] It boasted a *Kurpark*, a *Kurhaus*, or Civic Centre, in the neo-classical style; mineral baths; and many fine baroque buildings such as the theatre, and the *Neues Museum* which housed a fine collection of paintings including works by Corregio and Botticelli. Its historic connections with Britain and the British Army were underlined by the Waterloo memorial in the town centre.[38] For those, like most young Officers in the British Army, less

Khandahar Barracks, Wiesbaden, Germany.

inclined towards culture, the town boasted many restaurants, *bier kellern*, dance halls, hotels and night-clubs. It was, therefore, the natural centre for the social life of the men of the British Rhine Army and their families.

When 2 R.W.F. arrived in Bingen the General Officer Commanding-in-Chief was General Sir John Du Cane, who had been known to the battalion two years earlier when he was commanding Western Command. The strength of Rhine Army was now only about 7,800, some 1,400 below its establishment. General Headquarters was in the Hohenzollern Hotel in Wiesbaden, and its Army troops – a cavalry regiment (the 8th Hussars), field artillery brigade, field engineer company, signals regiment and administrative services – were also located in and around the town. There were two infantry brigades, both with their headquarters in Wiesbaden. 1st Rhine Brigade, under Colonel Commandant W.J. Maxwell-Scott,[†] comprised 1st Cameron

---

*   Raymond Poincaré (1860–1934), President of France 1913–1920; Prime Minister 1912–1913, 1922–1924 and 1926–1929.

†   Major General Sir Walter Joseph Constable-Maxwell-Scott Bt CB DSO (1875–1954).

Highlanders at St Andrews Barracks, Wiesbaden, 2nd Worcestershires, at Gheluvelt Barracks, Biebrich, and 2nd Royal Berkshires at Marne and Victoria Barracks in Bingen and Kandahar Barracks in Schierstein. 2nd Rhine Brigade, under Colonel Commandant H.K. Bethell,* had the 2nd Royal Fusiliers, 1st Oxford and Buckinghamshire Light Infantry, 2nd King's Shropshire Light Infantry and 1st Manchesters.

The Wiesbaden area, with the picturesque pine-clad Taunus Hills, depended on tourists as its major industry. The 'Rhine Army Amusements' staff set about providing facilities to satisfy the needs of the garrison and its families. A thousand-seat theatre was leased in Wiesbaden as a cinema and playhouse. A newspaper, the *Cologne Post and Wiesbaden Times* appeared twice weekly. There were football and hockey pitches, and cricket was played in the stadium, a large sports ground to the west of Wiesbaden. A derelict nine-hole golf course was taken over by agreement with the Germans, and improved. Thirty acres of level pasture land beyond Erbenheim were rented for polo and a pavilion erected, with the N.A.A.F.I. providing tea and refreshments. The locals were encouraged to build new tennis courts which were then requisitioned. Finally, an Officers' Club was organised in the basement of the Hohenzollern Hotel.

Sons and grandsons of Royal Welchmen, 2 R.W.F., 1926. (R.W.F. Mus 8355A)

Because of a re-location of battalions in 1st Rhine Brigade, 2 R.W.F., although relieving the 1st Cameron Highlanders, found itself taking over the barracks occupied by the 2nd Royal Berkshires, who were moved elsewhere. The battalion was split between Victoria and Marne Barracks in Bingen, and Kandahar Barracks in Schierstein, where the reserve of ammunition and explosives for the Army was stored. Two companies were based in Bingen and the two

---

*   Major-General Sir Hugh Keppel Bethell KBE CB CMG CVO DSO *C de G* (1882–1947), late of
     the 7th (Queen's Own) Hussars, had been the youngest divisional commander in the British Army's
     history up to the beginning of the Second World War.

others in Sicherstein. The reason for this dispersal was that, by agreement with the French, and in order to secure communications across the Rhine, the small Rhine port of Bingen and the district around it had been transferred to the British bridgehead.

All ranks of the Occupation Army received additional pay: for a Lieutenant this was a most welcome £1/8/- per week.[39] This naturally led to a spin-off for German businesses: it was estimated that the Rhine Army spent around £300,000 (at 1926 prices) annually on the local economy.[40] Given the nervousness after the hyper-inflation of 1923, and the effects of a weakening economy after the stock market collapse in U.S.A. with its consequent effects elsewhere, and by late 1929, 6,000,000 unemployed in Germany,[41] there is no wonder that the British had been welcomed in Cologne. W.S. Bainbridge had reported in 1923 that:

> In the British zone all seemed fairly normal … Walks of many hours … by day and by night, accompanied and unaccompanied, visiting shops, restaurants, cafes, beer gardens, movies and theatres, showed a fairly normal city. Show windows were full of luxuries as well as necessities. Theatres and movies were full, as were the cafes, beer gardens and restaurants. People were well dressed and there was no more evidence of poverty or lack of food as expressed in poor nutrition than in any of our large cities in America. The prices in marks are all enormous, but the wages are being changed frequently to conform to the rise and fall of the mark value and the related cost of living.[42]

The British garrison, just as in Cologne and indeed just as in the Rhine Army which was established after the Second World War, was largely self-sufficient. It ran its own schools, shops, and youth organisations such as the Scouts and Guides. It organised its own social and sporting affairs: dances, shows at the *Walhalla* theatre in Wiesbaden which was run as a cinema as well as for drama and variety. The 2 R.W.F. amateur dramatics troupe – the Red Dragons – all joined the Rhine Army Dramatic Society, taking part in productions of *War to the Death*, *Thanks*, and *A Man from Mars*. Sports were many and varied: horse shows, polo (at Erbenheim, south-east of Wiesbaden and next door to the suburb of Biebrich), cricket,* soccer, rugby, boxing, golf, tennis (at the *Hohenzollern* Hotel) and hockey were all actively pursued. The Army conducted its own military training, and was subject to its own military laws. For the Officers, life was therefore not much different from that in any other overseas station; social contact with the civilian population was discouraged, and German girls were much disapproved of. But the Officers of 2 R.W.F. enjoyed all these pursuits, as well as outings on the Rhine and evenings across the river in the *bier kellern* of Rudesheim. Things were, as ever, easier for N.C.Os and men who had much more freedom to meet German civilians in beer halls, cafés and at dance halls, and many learned to speak some German.[43]

All married families were housed, according to rank, in accommodation requisitioned from the local population in and around Bingen, a charming town of about 14,000 situated on the left bank of the Rhine and about one hour from Wiesbaden by train. They received generous rents from the British government. Lieutenant Colonel Stockwell was housed in the Villa Sachsen, an imposing and comfortable *schloss* to the east of the town. In Bingen alone of the outstations the people were really friendly from the beginning. Although fraternising with the local German

---

*   Cricket was played in the Stadium, a large ground attached to the barracks just west of Wiesbaden.

population was frowned upon, the way of life was pleasant enough with its well-ordered routine of military training, interspersed with recurring sporting and social events.

Operationally, the task of the Army of Occupation was first, to safeguard the defile of the Nahe River at Kreuznach, nine miles (14 kilometres) south of Bingen, which was the main line of communication for the much larger French Army which lay to the south and east around Frankfurt am Main, and the destruction of the Rhine bridge at Mainz. The ground in the bridgehead offered few advantages to a withdrawing force. The Rheingau and Taunus hills, which rise to about 1,600 feet (500 metres) mark the edge of a plateau running roughly from south west to north east, from which the country slopes down to the Rhine. Much of the country was then wooded, and traversed by marshy ravines, but was passable by infantry, cavalry and horse-drawn guns and transport. The deployment plan thus saw the brigades defending the approaches to Wiesbaden along the main roads, and covering the Mainz Bridge and Hindenburg road/rail bridge east of Bingen.[44]

Underlining the operational commitment was the detachment of C Company from April to June 1928, and B Company from January to March 1929, to form the Saar Railway Defence Force at Pétain Barracks, Saarbrücken, in the French zone of occupation.[45] Under the terms of the Treaty of Versailles, Germany ceded the territory of the Saar basin, with its extensive coal mines and other industries, to the League of Nations for a period of twenty-five years. The Territory of the Saar Basin, as it was known, was to be governed by a British and French Commission under a Mandate from the League; the underlying *raison d'être* being compensation for the destruction of French coal mining potential in Northern France between 1914 and 1918. At the end of the occupation period, in 1935, there was to be a plebiscite in which the inhabitants would vote either to join France, or return to Germany, or remain under the League

Lewis gun teams of 2 R.W.F. at Sonnenberg Camp, 1927. (Norman Weale collection)

Commission. A subsidiary issue was that of the Saarbrücken – Trier railway, which linked several industrial areas of Germany, and was to be used to take coal from the Saar to France. The railway administration was in the hands of a board of twelve directors, six French and six from the Saar Commission.[46] In 1926, the British and French governments agreed that after the withdrawal of troops from the Rhineland, planned for 1930, a small force would continue to be required to guard the railway for the remaining five years of the Agreement.[47] This force was set at 500 and was provided, initially, by the British and French occupation forces;[48] after 1929, however, the agreement lapsed and British troops did not re-enter the Saar until 1934 in preparation for the referendum.

The routine in B.A.O.R. followed a fairly set course. In 1927, the **January–March 1927** year started with individual training, followed in the spring by section, platoon and company training leading up to a battalion exercise in the spring at Budesheim. A shooting camp under canvas was held at the ranges at Sonnenberg and Rambach to which the battalion marched. In August and September the battalion participated in brigade and divisional manoeuvres for the first time since the end of the war at Fürfeld, about thirty miles (forty kilometres) south-west of Wiesbaden.[49]

In February 1927 the first draft of the year was sent to the 1st Battalion at Nasirabad in India. This regular drain on the battalion in order to maintain 1 R.W.F. at full strength ensured that 2 R.W.F. was sometimes as much as 25% below its establishment whilst with B.A.O.R. In April 1929 it was 188 men short.

In boxing the battalion were runners-up to the 2nd Manchesters in the Rhine Army Novices Championships. In March, Lieutenants R.W.C. Martin and G.E. Braithwaite played rugby for B.A.O.R. against the French Army. Fusiliers Morton (A Company), Morgan and Lewis (B Company) and Yorke (C Company) represented B.A.O.R. at football against the French. The battalion football team lost in the final of the Rhine Army Knock-out Challenge Cup to the 2nd Shropshire L.I. 1-0, but won the Rhine Army League. The athletics team came second to the 1st Oxford and Buckinghamshire L.I.

On 30 April Lieutenant General Sir William Thwaites* became **April–August 1927** the new, and last, Commander-in-Chief of Rhine Army. On 18 July, Lieutenant R.W.C. Martin, the capable and popular adjutant, was killed near Bingen when his motorbike skidded off the road, down an embankment and under a train. On 21 August, Lieutenant Colonel C.I. Stockwell relinquished command of the battalion and was succeeded temporarily by Major G.E.R. de Miremont.

On 12 October the battalion moved to Gheluvelt Barracks, **October–November 1927** Biebrich, exchanging with the 2nd Worcestershires. Biebrich was larger than Bingen with a population of just over 21,000, but not in such an attractive area. Its one great advantage, however, was that it was a suburb of greater Wiesbaden. The battalion was comfortably quartered in a one-time Officer Cadet School overlooking the Rhine.[50] In November the Commanding Officer approved the wearing of the Flash on blue patrol jackets by all Serjeants.

---

*   Later General Sir William Thwaites KCB KCMG (1868–1947). He commanded two divisions on the Western Front during the Great War and was Mentioned in Despatches six times, received eight foreign awards and a brevet – and yet gained no British award for gallantry.

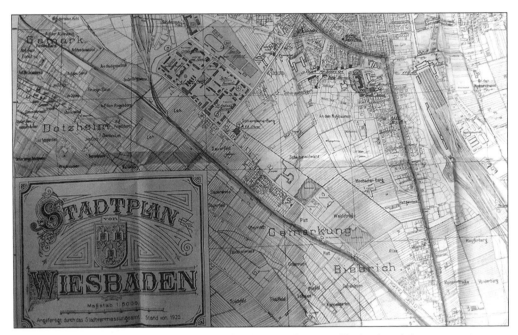

Map 9.3 A contemporary map of Wiesbaden showing the area of Biebrich and the main garrison locations.

On 6 February 1928 Lieutenant Colonel P.R. Butler assumed command of the battalion.[*] St David's Day 1928 was marked by a visit **February 1928** from the Colonel of the Regiment who inspected the battalion in review order. In his letter to the Commanding Officer the Colonel wrote of the visit as '… one of my most delightful experiences. Everybody made me so welcome and appeared so pleased to see me.' He alluded in the most complimentary terms to the turn-out and appearance of all ranks on parade and in barracks.

Ceremonial took up more time than in many stations and every opportunity was taken to hold reviews in the Exerzierplatz in Dotzheim. The Germans, deprived of military pomp of their own, attended in great numbers and would even flock to hear regimental bands on church parades. They came to admire the high standard of turn-out and military bearing of the British. The annual King's Birthday Parade was especially popular; massed bands and the Royal Welch Fusiliers' Goat were also great attractions. The newspaper *Frankfurter Zeitung*, referring to the changing of Guard by the Regiment, preceded by the goat and nine pioneers, said that it was 'the practice of this unit to relieve guard headed by its ration sheep for the day, followed by the nine butchers'.[51]

On 13 August 1928 the battalion marched the twenty miles (32 kilometres) to Tierpark Camp for the exercise season. Platoon, **August 1928**

---

[*]   Patrick Richard Butler DSO, transferred to R.W.F. from the Royal Irish Regiment in 1922 (on the creation of the Irish Free State). Commanded 2 R.W.F. until 1931, died in 1967. His obituary is in *Y Ddraig Goch*, Mar 1968.

company and battalion training were followed by brigade and inter-brigade manoeuvres, all of which involved marching long distances through the dusty German countryside. Stringent rules were issued which forbade the stealing of fruit.

At the unveiling in November of the memorial at La Ferté sous Jouarre to those who lost their lives in 1914 at Mons, the Marne and the Aisne, the battalion was represented by 4178909 RQMS J. Hughes DCM.

The King's Birthday Parade, B.A.O.R. 1928.

2 R.W.F. at Tierpark Camp, Germany, 1929. (R.W.F. Mus 2820)

In football the team again won the senior league, and also provided a number of players for the Rhine Army team. The boxers were again runners-up in the Open Championships, this time to 2nd Royal Fusiliers. The novices, however, won the Rhine Army final, beating 2nd Royal Berkshires by 7 bouts to 5. 3954720 Lance Corporal L. Davies, 4186705 Fusilier J. Evans and 4186022 Lance Corporal J. Jones all competed in the Army Individual Boxing Championships in London. The rugby team won the Rhine Army Challenge Trophy. Sporting instincts of another kind were strong among the Officers. In the Mess at Biebrich one night at dinner a discussion arose concerning the merits of the city of Koblenz, North of Wiesbaden on the Rhine. Argument then turned to the distance, either by the road that ran along the side of the Rhine, or by a road that ran over the *Hohewurzel* (an off-shoot of the Taunus Hills, north-west of Wiesbaden) through Bad Ems, which was just south east of Koblenz. The former, it was thought, was about sixty-four miles (102 kilometres), the latter some fifty-six (90 kilometres). Lieutenant Stockwell, who had been listening, piped up and said that he could walk to Koblenz from Biebrich in under twenty-four hours, and was taken up with a bet of £5* each from three of his brother Officers, on the proviso that he started the next day. Waking up next morning and feeling somewhat foolish he presented himself at the Orderly Room and asked for twenty-four hours leave starting from midday. Leave granted, he duly set off, and chose the road over the *Hohewurzel* and through Bad Ems:

> There is nothing very remarkable about walking fifty-six miles, but untrained and done on the spur of the moment, it had its chances. Luckily, I carried a pair of soft tennis shoes round my neck which were to prove invaluable. I called in at the Oxford and Buckinghamshire Light Infantry's Mess which lay on my way, where they thought I was mad, and had an excellent tea. Thus fortified, I set out on my way to walk through the night. I walked for two hours at a stretch and halted for twenty minutes. Luckily the German propensities for staying up drinking all night enabled me to find a 'hut' open in Bad Ems at about 4.00 am, where I quaffed a couple of pints of lager. Then having time on my side and my feet burning, and as it was raining, I lay down under a bench just clear of the town and fell into a deep sleep – to be woken two hours later by a motor bike roaring past my head. Then I put on my soft shoes and after a mile or so, which took some forty five minutes to rid myself of the stiffness, I warmed to my work and eventually sailed over the hard cobble stones, up to the Koblenzer Hof at 10.50am with an hour and ten minutes to spare, to demand a pint of lager, a bath and a telephone call back to Biebrich, to the somewhat startled Mess Serjeant. Eddie Chester-Master and "Moses" Shipley, both of the Royal Fusiliers, motored over to collect me – how kind they were.[52]

The possibility of the evacuation of the Second (10-year) and Third (15-year) occupation zones before the agreed times in January 1930 and January 1935 respectively, had been discussed by military and civilian leaders in early 1928. On 16 August a conference on the early evacuation of the Rhineland opened at The Hague. Further negotiations continued at Geneva in September 1928, but the new Labour government in Britain, elected on 31st May 1929, decided unilaterally to recall the Rhine Army by Christmas 1929.[53] A fortnight later the Foreign Ministers of the

---

* £270 at today's rates as a measure of income [www.measuringworth.com]

three occupying Powers informed Herr Stresemann, the German Foreign Minister, that the evacuation of the Rhineland would begin in September 1929 and the withdrawal of British and Belgian forces would be completed within three months.[54]

In view of the impending evacuation, little collective training was carried out during the battalion's last year in Germany. The winter of 1928/29 was abnormally severe. The hard weather began in mid-December and lasted until early March. The temperature was often 32°F below freezing and once reached 52°F below. The Rhine was completely frozen over and in some places over three inches thick.[55] During the worst period, the battalion was at Sonnenberg, firing its annual range courses, and accommodated in bell tents, sleeping six to a tent on duck boards. Before washing in the morning the ice had to be broken in a nearby stream. In order to avoid casualties from frostbite, sentries wore cap comforters under their normal caps and fur coats over regimental greatcoats. Sugar lumps were issued to them, braziers provided and watches reduced to one hour. At the start of April, platoon training was held at Tierpark Camp where the battalion, less A (Machine Gun) Company, again lived under canvas. As a result of the extreme cold the battalion returned to Biebrich before training could be completed.

December 1928–April 1929

The battalion's last year in Germany was its most successful in sporting terms. The Novice Boxers won the Rhine Army title by beating the 1st Prince of Wales's Volunteers 7-4. For the third successive year the battalion was runner-up in the Open Championships, losing again to 2nd Royal Fusiliers. The football team, for a record third year running, won the Senior Football League and the trophy became the property of the battalion. The Junior League was won by the 2nd XI. For the second year in succession the Rhine Army Rugby Challenge Trophy was won by the battalion. The committee decided that as the last holders it should become battalion property.

On 3 June, on the occasion of the King's Birthday, the battalion took part in a B.A.O.R. ceremonial parade on the Kurhaus Platz at Wiesbaden. Thereafter, the contrast between the victorious march to the Rhine in 1918 and the evacuation of B.A.O.R. could not have been starker. Evacuations of the garrison, which now stood at a total strength of only 5,300 all ranks, along with 342 wives and 915 children,[56] began on 14 September 1929 and continued by rail and barge over the next three months. In general, the military aspects went without a hitch. As the Rhineland was to be demilitarised, all military installations except barracks and railways had to be destroyed. This included the destruction of rifle ranges; the partial demolition and selling-off to civilians of the ammunition depot at Longerich and the ordnance depot at Nippes; the destruction of the Field Works School at Nippes, all telephone and electricity facilities, and all temporary accommodation.[57]

June–September 1929

2 R.W.F. was ordered to move on the 28th day of the evacuation, 12 October 1929,[58] to Assaye Barracks at Tidworth on Salisbury Plain. Crowds of well-wishers lined the platform at Wiesbaden station to wish the battalion God speed. General Thwaites himself was among them. At Trier, the train was met by the band and trumpets of a French cavalry regiment: the French bandmaster and trumpet major were invited to take wine with the Officers, and many toasts in Moselle wine were exchanged.[59] The battalion arrived safely at Tidworth during the evening of 13 October, complete with its families, numerous horses, ponies and dogs, and, of course, the Goat:

October 1929

By 14th November all women and children had been evacuated and every billet handed over. This considerably facilitated the completion of the evacuation; even the bulk of the three hundred cats and dogs had disappeared, also the goat of the R Welch Fusiliers, which was to be let off with 28 days' detention on arrival at Tidworth, the new station of the battalion, while the lesser animals had to undergo the usual 3-months' quarantine.[60]

2 R.W.F.'s Digest of Service recorded that

> At Trier the band and trumpets of a French Cavalry Regiment played stirring music during the halt, several French Officers of high rank being present as a special mark of comradeship and honour. The French Bandmaster and Trumpet Major were invited by Colonel Butler to take wine with the Officers, which they did; and toasts were exchanged in Moselle wine.
>
>   The Battalion arrived at Tidworth during the evening of 13th October and a successful detrainment was completed.
>
>   By special concession (which filled a column of the *London Gazette*) the goat was allowed to be sent to Quarantine at Tidworth. The numerous dogs accompanying the Battalion were sent to Quarantine elsewhere.

The final contingent of troops – from the G.H.Q. staff and the 2nd Royal Fusiliers – left Wiesbaden on 12 December and when General Thwaites and his troops arrived by train at Victoria Station in London, the reception, at the conclusion of what was after all an historical event, can only be described as low-key. Indeed the G.O.C.-in-C had to summon a taxi and have himself driven to his London house.

B Company leading 2 R.W.F. as it departed from Germany in 1929; the low strength of a home-service battalion is very evident. (R.W.F. Mus 3579 D)

Staff List, 2 R.W.F. Germany, 1926–1929

Lieutenant Colonel
C.I. Stockwell CB CMG DSO (to Aug 27)
P.R. Butler DSO (Feb 28)
Major
Bt Lt Col W.B. Garnett DSO (to Jul 27)
G.E.R. de Miremont DSO MC (to May 28) (a/C.O. 22 Aug 27–5 Feb 28)
R.E. Hindson (to Nov 27)
E.O. Skaife OBE (2ic May 28–Jul 29)
M.L. Lloyd-Mostyn (May–Jul 28)
Captain
D.M. Barchard (to Feb 27)
M.B. Dowse (Sep 27–Apr 29) (Adjt Jul 27–Apr 29)
H.D'O. Lyle (Jul 27)
Ll. S. Lloyd
W.P. Kenyon MC (May 28)
D.H.W. Kirkby (to Oct 28)
W.T.C. Moody (to Aug 29)
T.C. Sharp
C.H. Wolff (to Feb 27)
H.A. Davies (Apr 27)
Ll. A.A. Alston (to Dec 27)
F.H. Shove (Aug 29)
F.I. Gerrard MC (Mar 28)
Quartermaster
Lt W.H. Albutt DCM
Staff Serjeants
Band Sjt R.W. Howell (to Dec 27)
Band Sjt J. Evans (Dec 27)
Drum Major (Sjt Drummer) A. Gill (to Dec 27)
G. Moreland (Dec 27)
J. Edge (May 29)
Pioneer Sjt A.E. Evans
SIM S. Metcalfe (to May 29)
Pro Sjt W.O.H. Smithurst
ORS C. Burton (Dec 27)

Lieutenant
C.A. Anglesea-Sandels MBE MC
J.A. Pringle MC
H. Grismond Williams
E.A. Morris MM (Capt Sep 27)
D. Roberts Morgan DCM MM (to Dec 26)
G.N.H. Taunton Collins
G.E. Rees
W.H. Bamfield (to Mar 27)
A.M.M. Lewis MBE (Sep 28)
R.W.C. Martin, Adjutant (killed 18 Jul 27)
M.B. Courtney (to Mar 29)
G.E. Braithwaite
H.G. Williams (to Aug 27)
Ll. Gwydyr-Jones (to Sep 27)
D.I. Owen (to Apr 27)
H.C. Stockwell
Hon. G.R. Clegg-Hill (Adjt Apr 29)
P.F. Pritchard (to Feb 27)
2nd Lieutenant
H. de B. Prichard (Mar 27)
A.C. Heber-Percy (Sep 27)
C.H.V. Pritchard (Sep 27)
J.A.M. Rice-Evans (Mar 28)
L.T. Lillingston (Mar 28)
C.J.L. Lewis (Lt Sep 27) (to Nov 28)
M.F.P. Lloyd (Lt Feb 29)
T.D. Butler (to Nov 26)
W.M. Fox (May 28)
R.A.F. Hurt (Mar 29)

W.O. I
RSM W. Gorham MSM
BM W.J. Clancy
W.O. II
RQMS W.H. Kelly (to Dec 27)
RQMS J. Hughes DCM (Dec 27)
RQMS R. Howell (May 29)
ORQMS J. Hughes DCM
CSMI E. Austin
A. Bent MM (Dec 27)
E. Morse (Dec 27)
W.H. Dickinson DCM (to Dec 27)
H. Spalding DCM (to Dec 27)
N. Ridings (Dec 27)
H.E. Callus DCM (to Dec 27)
S. Metcalfe (May 29)
W.H. Poole (to Dec 27)
J. Kensitt (to Dec 27)
C. Jones DCM MM (to Dec 27)
A. Gill (May 29)
E. Box (May 29)
CQMS
M. Walshe (to Dec 27)
W. Woolman (to Dec 27)
E. Clopping (to dec 27)
P. Condon
A. Bent MM (to Dec 27)
J.T. Wilde (to Dec 27)
E. Box (Dec 27–May 29))
A. Otton (Dec 27)
W. Jones (Dec 27)
C. Morrissey (Dec 27)
S.G. Davies MM
F. Witts

Notes

1   James Anderson Findlay, *A Handbook of Pembroke Dock* (Haverfordwest, 1885); Hunt & Co's *Directory of South Wales* (circa 1920).
2   Findlay, p. 10.
3   Interview with Lord Parry of Neyland. Other information supplied by Mr Jamie Meyrick Owen.
4   Monthly *Army List*, 1926, pp. 49–50.
5   Research indicates that during the Great War, 40% of those killed while serving with the two Regular battalions gave Wales as their place of birth. See Peter Crocker, *Some Thoughts on the Royal Welch Fusiliers in the Great War* (R.W.F. Museum, 2001), citing *Soldiers Died in the Great War*.
6   Later Brigadier Sir Eric Ommanney Skaife Kt CB OBE (1884–1956), commissioned 1903. A fluent Russian speaker, he had been captured at Ypres in November 1914, and commanded 1 R.W.F. 1929 – 1933. He was the author of *A Short History of The Royal Welch Fusiliers*; and was Colonel of the Regiment from 1948 to 1952, died 2 Oct 1956. His biographical details can be found in J.P. Riley, *Regimental Records of The Royal Welch Fusiliers*, Volume VI, pp. 436–437, and in Peter Kirby, *Officers Of The Royal Welch Fusiliers 1689–1914*, p. 118. See also his obituary in *Y Ddraig Goch* Winter 1956 and *Who Was Who* Vol V.

7   Notes by General Sir Hugh Stockwell. See also his biography by Jonathon Riley, *The Life and Campaigns of General Hughie Stockwell* (Barnsley, 2006).

8   J.C. Dunn, *The War the Infantry Knew* (Abacus, 1994), p. 537.

9   J.C. Dunn, *The War the Infantry Knew*; Siegfried Sassoon *Memoirs of an Infantry Officer*; David Langley *Duty Done*, p. 80.

10   Notes by General Sir Hugh Stockwell.

11   Infantry Training Volume I (1926), p. 10, describes the organisation of a battalion in detail.

12   See, for example, Charles Messenger, *For Love of Regiment: A History of the British Infantry 1915–1994* (London, 1996).

13   *Y Ddraig Goch* January 1923, p. 88.

14   Notes by Sir Hugh Stockwell.

15   Army Order 222 of 1923.

16   Army Order 56 of 1920.

17   *Y Ddraig Goch*, October 1923, p. 194.

18   Notes by Sir Hugh Stockwell.

19   *Y Ddraig Goch* October 1923, p. 199.

20   *Y Ddraig Goch* May 1924, p. 234.

21   *Y Ddraig Goch*, May 1924, p. 234.

22   Frank Richards, *Old Soldiers Never Die* (London, 1933).

23   *Y Ddraig Goch* January 1925, p. 301.

24   Notes by General Sir Hugh Stockwell.

25   2 R.W.F. Digest of Service 1 April 1924–31 March 1925.

26   2 R.W.F. Digest of Service 1 April 1925–31 March 1926.

27   *South Wales News*, number unknown but possibly 15 January 1926.

28   Robert Graves and Alan Hodge *The Long Week-End. A Social History of Great Britain 1918–1939* (London, 1940), pp. 164–165.

29   Interview with Lord Parry of Neyland.

30   2 R.W.F. Digest of Service 1 April 1926–31 March 1927.

31   Interview with Lord Parry of Neyland.

32   F. Tuohy, *A Postscript to the Western Front* (London,1931).

33   David G. Williamson, *The British in Germany, 1918–1930* (Oxford, 1991), p. 212.

34   Williamson, p. 299, citing T.N.A./FO 371/11307 f.48. For a detailed description of the political developments see Sara Moore, *Peace Without Victory for the Allies 1918–1932* (Oxford, 1994).

35   Otto E. Fink, *Wiesbadener Bildchronik 1866–1945*. Supplied by the Library of the *Führunsakademie der Bundeswehr*, Hamburg.

36   J.E. Edmunds, *The Occupation of the Rhineland* (HMSO, 1944) [The Official History of the Military Occupation] p. 306; John Bradley, *The Illustrated History of the Third Reich* (London, 1978) p. 43.

37   *Pears' Cyclopaedia*, 51st Edition, p. 315; Albert Schaefer, *Wiesbaden* (Frankfurt, 1973), p. 193.

38   Monk Gibbon, *Western Germany* (London, 1955) pp. 97–99. Information also supplied by the Library of the *Führunsakademie der Bundeswehr*, Hamburg.

39   Explanatory Note by the Secretary of State for War (the Right Hon. Winston S. Churchill), 28 January, 1919, cited by Edmunds.

40   Edmunds, p. 305.

41   Bradley, pp. 42–45.

42   W.S. Bainbridge, *A Report on the present conditions in the Ruhr and Rhineland* (New York, 1923) p. 20. This account also gives a clear indication of the attitude common among Germans at that time, that the Treaty of Versailles was merely a truce, and that another war was on its way.

43   See, for example, the collection of photographs of Army life in Wiesbaden in the Thwaites' collection, Imperial War Museum 416.311, no 38145. Other accounts can be found in Williamson, Edmunds, and an account in *The Times*, 18 Sep 1929.

44   Edmunds, p. 288; Monk Gibbon, *Western Germany* (London, 1955) p. 125.

45   2 R.W.F. Digest of Service 1 April 1928–31 March 1929.

46   Agreement Between France and the Saar Territory Concerning the Operation of the Saar Railways, Article 6.

47   Dr Richard S. Grayson, *Austin Chamberlain and the Commitment to Europe: British Foreign Policy 1924–1929* (London, 1997), p. 96.
48   *House of Commons Debates*, Vol 204 c402W, 23 March 1927.
49   2 R.W.F. Digest of Service 1 April 1928–31 March 1929.
50   Tuohy, p. 245.
51   Edmunds, p. 304.
52   Riley, *Stockwell*, pp. 22–23.
53   Williamson, pp 327, 337.
54   Edmunds, pp. 312–313.
55   Edmunds, pp. 302–303.
56   Edmunds, p. 317.
57   Edmunds, p. 289.
58   Edmunds, p. 318.
59   2 R.W.F. Digest of Service 1 April 1929–31 March 1930.
60   Edmunds, p. 319.

Chapter 10

The 2nd Battalion as an Experimental Mechanised Battalion in Britain; and in the Garrisons of Gibraltar and Hong Kong, 1929–1937

i. Tidworth, 1929–1931

Tidworth, described in Chapter 7, was in Southern Command with its headquarters in Salisbury. Headquarters 3rd Division was based at Bulford, commanded by Major General Sir John Burnett-Stuart,[*] who had two future field marshals on his staff: Colonel A.P. Wavell and Lieutenant F.W. Festing. The division had three brigades: 7 Infantry Brigade at Tidworth; 8 Infantry Brigade at Devonport – commanded in 1934 by Brigadier W.G. Holmes of the Royal Welch Fusiliers; and 9 Infantry Brigade at Portsmouth. 2 Cavalry Brigade was also under its command. 2 R.W.F., in Bhurtpore Barracks, joined the 2nd Somerset L.I. – which was organised and equipped as a three-company machine-gun battalion, operating within the brigade – and 2nd King's Royal Rifle Corps in 7 Infantry Brigade under Brigadier C.C. Armitage.

The battalion was part of an experimental mechanised brigade which had been formed under the command of the 3rd Division, and based on 7 Infantry Brigade, on the orders of the C.I.G.S., Field Marshal Sir George Milne.[1] As a result most of the training was of an experimental nature and involved working with the 3rd and 5th Battalions of the Royal Tank Corps. Little marching was done by the soldiers, who found themselves being carried in private cars and charabancs – bearing such names as 'Silver Eagle' or 'Bournemouth Rambler' – because of the lack of military vehicles, until the issue of *Carden-Lloyd* carriers. For many this brought back memories of being carried in buses during the war. Mobility was the order of the day and exercises involved operations against mechanised and cavalry forces.

Every Saturday morning there was a Commanding Officer's or Company Commander's room inspection: 'There were floors to be scrubbed white on hands and knees, coal tubs to be burnished, ablution taps to be polished and windows cleaned.' Personal kit had to be laid out in a set order on the bed and bedding folded in the authorised way. Saturday afternoon was largely given over to sport. Every Sunday morning there was a Church parade when the Adjutant inspected the battalion before it marched to church preceded by the Band.[2] There was, therefore, no such thing as a 'week-end'. Officers and men had free time on Saturday evening, Sunday afternoon and Sunday evening only, except during periods of annual leave.

---

[*]   Later General Sir John Theodosius Burnett-Stuart GCB KBE CMG DSO DL (1875–1958).

Regimental Serjeant Major W. Gorham MSM left the battalion for civilian life after completing twenty-six years service in the Regiment in January 1930. He was replaced by W.O. I C. Jones DCM MM.

In July, a party of thirteen Officers and 100 N.C.Os and Fusiliers went to Porthcawl to assist the Territorial battalions at Annual Camp. The **July 1930** detachment included a mechanised machine gun platoon and a rifle platoon for demonstration purposes, commanded respectively by Lieutenant B.E. Horton and Second Lieutenant J.R. Johnson. The new *Carden-Lloyd* vehicles caused a certain amount of interest in Porthcawl, and a great deal during demonstrations for the T.A. and visiting Officers.

During September the battalion was engaged in five exercises, some of which were found particularly interesting. During the day **September 1930** the mobility of the cavalry made them very elusive, but by night the infantry came into their own, patrolling against enemy positions prior to launching night attacks. On one occasion, a night attack, followed by an advance, led to a stampede by the cavalry horses. On another the battalion covered 140 miles (225 kilometres) in twenty-seven hours. One exercise ended with a strong tank attack on C and D Companies 'which made one realize the feelings in war if discovered and hunted in the open by these "modern prehistoric monsters"'.[3] During this attack the Anti-tank Platoon was particularly commended by the Chief Tank Umpire for the excellent siting of its guns, represented by flags, as the guns themselves had not yet been issued (see Chapter 3).

The Band had a busy first year back in Britain. In July they visited Hastings, Margate, Southend, Brighton and Chester, before going on to perform at the Royal Welsh Agricultural Show in Caernarfon. In August the Band, Drums and Goat took part in the Southern Command Tattoo at Tidworth. The battalion's success in the boxing ring continued. They won the Southern Command Tournament by beating the 2nd Rifle Brigade in the final. One member of the battalion had a particularly successful year. Corporal J.D. Jones of Pontypridd won the featherweight title in the Southern Command, Army and Imperial Services championships. He represented the Army in Norway and Holland, and was narrowly beaten in the semi-final of the Amateur Championships of Great Britain. The football team, weaker than at any time since the war, did not have a particularly good season, but Lance Corporal Morton played a brilliant game for the Army against Aston Villa, and also played for Aston Villa and Everton Reserves.[4]

On 20 January 1931 Lieutenant Colonel C.C. Hewitt* assumed command of the battalion vice Lieutenant Colonel P.R. Butler who had been forced to relinquish command because of ill health. In February, 4185518 Fusilier W.P. Ross was knocked down and killed by a vehicle whilst repairing a broken down *Carden-Lloyd* carrier only a month before he would have completed his Colour service.[5]

The battalion was warned that its next posting, in October, was to be Gibraltar where it had last served between 1874 and 1880. Its place in Tidworth was to be taken by the 1st Battalion on its return from India and the Sudan. The retirement of Captain D. Roberts-Morgan at the same time marked the departure of one of the very few members of the battalion to have served with it throughout the war. He went out to France in 1914 as a Corporal and earned a

---

*   Later Brigadier Charles Caulfield Hewitt DSO MC (1883–1949). Originally an Inniskilling Fusilier he transferred in 1917.

reputation as a daring sniper. He was commissioned in the field for gallantry having won both the Distinguished Conduct Medal and the Military Medal.

A hugely successful St David's Day Ball for all ranks was held in the Garrison Theatre on 2 March, and four days later the Serjeants' Mess held **March 1931** their Ball at which there were 400 guests. The race for the Red Dragon Cup was on the card of the 2 Cavalry Brigade Meeting at Windmill Hill with twenty-one fences over a distance of 3¾ miles (6 kilometres). Mr R.A.F. Hurt won it on 'Orange Bill' by 20 lengths.[6] This was the closest available meeting to St David's Day, the battalion not having its own course available.

The Red Dragon Cup, Tidworth, 2 R.W.F., 1931. (R.W.F. Mus 4152)

Annual firing was conducted on the ranges at Perham Down. As in the previous year a party of Officers attended the Royal Welch Brigade camp at Tenby to help with the training of the Territorials. The King's Birthday Parade at **June–July 1931** Bulford on 6 June, the largest of its kind since the war, combined the pageantry of the drum horses, colours, bands and drums with the vehicles of a modern mechanized army including tanks and armoured cars. Because of the impending move to Gibraltar training was somewhat curtailed, but in spite of this, company camps were arranged in the local area, and the battalion participated in mechanised training in July.[7]

At the Southern Command Tattoo at Tidworth the battalion was represented by the Band, Drums, Pioneers and Goat, and also contributed a demonstration of physical training and horse work with 200 performers. Each performance was warmly applauded, especially on the last night when it was performed in heavy rain. One well-known Officer, not a Royal Welch Fusilier, wrote afterwards: 'May I say that for a first class exposition of how the British infantry carry through their job whatever the conditions, it was as good an example as one could wish to see. It did one good to be there. I take my hat off to the Battalion.'

During September the battalion went on embarkation leave prior to moving to Gibraltar. For many the return from leave meant a loss of pay, as outlined in Chapter 1. In 1930–1931 the Southern Command Team Boxing Championships were won by the battalion for the second year running. One of the best teams in recent years, it went on to the final of the Army Team Championships at Preston in April where it was beaten by the 2nd East Lancashires. Both teams were level on points but the East Lancashires took the title by winning eight bouts to seven. Corporal J.D. Jones extended his run of success at featherweight by winning the Army and Inter-Services Championships, and being runner-up in the Amateur Championships of Great Britain. Second Lieutenant T.A.G. Pritchard won the Army Heavyweight Championships for Officers. Lieutenant J.A.M. Rice-Evans was selected to play rugby for the Army during the 1930–1931 season.[8]

Before leaving Tidworth the Brigade Commander, Brigadier C.C. Armitage, addressed the battalion in the following terms:

> I do not think there is any regiment in the Army that has a finer tradition than The Royal Welch Fusiliers, the old 23rd Foot… Two years ago the Battalion arrived in Tidworth from the Rhine. They have been two strenuous years for you all … A Battalion that… arrives in a home station requires some time before it can adapt itself to the new conditions. I feel that you all have succeeded in overcoming these difficulties of home training. This has been accomplished by energy and hard work on the part of all ranks, and I congratulate you on it… .
>
> I will say now that nothing is finer than the discipline of your Battalion, its excellence at drill and ceremonial and the fine and soldierly bearing of all ranks. Whenever you march past I feel that your bearing stamps you as a hard fighting Regiment, where courage will never be lacking and which will never let you down in a tight place. These qualities are very marked in the boxing ring, which brings out that splendid offensive spirit… .
>
> I want to thank you all for what you have done in the 7th Infantry Brigade, for your splendid behaviour and example to other regiments in many forms of training and sport… I am proud and honoured to have had you under my command, that there is no regiment I would sooner go to war with, and that I shall always look upon you as one of the finest regiments in the Army.[9]

On 9 October, sixteen Officers and 546 Other Ranks assembled on the quay at Southampton under the command of Lieutenant Colonel C.C. Hewitt. A large gathering of friends was present to see them off, including: Generals Sir Charles Dobell and W.G. Braithwaite; Brigadiers R.A.W. Colleton and C.C. Norman; Colonels R.F. Williamson and R.I.B. Johnson; Lieutenant Colonel P.R. Butler; Major J.G. Bruxner-Randall; Lieutenant H.C. Stockwell; and most of the Officers from the Depot, as well as Mr W.J. Clancy and CQMS P. Condon. The battalion embarked on HT *Neuralia* for the four day voyage to Gibraltar.[10]

Staff List, 2 R.W.F. Tidworth, 1929–1931

Lieutenant Colonel
P.R. Butler DSO
C.C. Hewitt DSO MC (27 Dec 29)
Major
T.C. Sharp

Lieutenant
C.A. Anglesea-Sandels MBE MC
J.A. Pringle MC
G.N.H. Taunton Collins (Capt Jan 31)
C.H.V. Pritchard

W.O.I
RSM W. Gorham MSM
RSM C. Jones DCM MM (Mar 31)
BM W.J. Clancy

C.H. Edwards
J.G. Bruxner-Randall
Captain
H. Grismond Williams
Ll. Gwydyr-Jones
D. Roberts-Morgan DCM MM (Oct 30–Mar 31)
E.A. Morris MM
Ll. S. Lloyd
W.P. Kenyon MC
F.H. Shove
H.D'O. Lyle
H.A. Davies
W.B. Harrison (Jun 30)
F.I. Gerrard MC, Adjt Oct 30
Staff Serjeants
Band Sjt J. Evans (to Apr 30)
Band Sjt J. Flanagan (Apr 30)
Drum Major (Sjt Drummer) J. Edge
Pioneer Sjt A.E. Evans
Pro Sjt W.O.H. Smithurst
ORS C. Burton

Lieutenant
Hon F.J. Southwell (to May 30)
G.E. Braithwaite
H. de B. Prichard (to Nov 30)
B.E. Horton (May 30) (Capt Oct 30)
Hon. G.R. Clegg-Hill, Adjt to Sep 30
2nd Lieutenant
H. de B. Prichard
A.C. Heber-Percy (to Sep 30)
J.A.M. Rice-Evans
L.T. Lillingston (to Jun 30)
W.S.A. Clough-Taylor (Jun 30)
W.M. Fox
R.A.F. Hurt
J.R. Johnson (Mar 30)
W.L.R. Benyon (Mar 30–Jan 31)
Sir W.L. Williams Bt (Apr 30)
E.C. Parker-Jervis (Sep 30)
T.A.G. Pritchard (Feb 31)
H.P.A. Kempthorne (Sep 30)
Quartermaster
Lt W.H. Albutt DCM

W.O.II
RQMS R. Howell
ORQMS J. Hughes DCM
CSMI E. Austin
A. Bent MM
E. Morse
T. Dale (Mar 31)
N. Ridings
A. Gill (to Apr 30)
E. Box
S. Metcalfe
CQMS
J. Dodd (Apr 30)
W. Robinson (Apr 30)
A. Randall (Apr 31)
P. Condon
P. Chard (Apr 30)
G. Morris (Apr 30)
A. Otton (to Apr 30)
W. Jones (to Apr 30)
C. Morrissey (to Apr 30)
S.G. Davies MM (to Apr 30)
F. Witts (to Apr 30)

ii. Gibraltar, 1931–1934

Britain's great bastion in the western Mediterranean had belonged to it since it was captured in 1704 and then ceded by Spain under the terms of the Treaty of Utrecht in 1713. The whole territory is less than three miles in length from north to south and less than a mile at its widest point. The highest point of the Rock, O'Hara's Tower, is 1,408 feet. The climate is Mediterranean with long, hot summers and short, cool, usually wet

A view of Gibraltar, 1934.

winters. The proximity of the Atlantic Ocean ensures that the summers are not too hot nor the winters too cold. The most unpleasant climatic feature is the 'Levanter', a strong easterly wind with its warm, sticky presence which can be very wearing if it persists for more than a few days. The population, which is mainly of Italian extraction since the original Spanish population fled after the capture of the Rock in 1704, numbered less than 18,000 in 1930. It was a free port and a popular tourist centre even then. In 1895 the naval harbour and dockyard were completed, which made Gibraltar a significant asset for the Royal Navy.[11] For most servicemen and their

2 R.W.F., Guard Mounting, Gibraltar. (R.W.F. Mus)

families it was a good posting, with easy access to the Spanish beaches, and a local population who spoke English. The Governor, a General, was also the Commander-in-Chief.[12]

When the battalion arrived on 13 October 1931 the Governor was General Sir Alexander Godley.* The only other infantry battalion in the Command was the 2nd North Staffords which was replaced in 1932 by 2nd Duke of Cornwall's L.I. There were also two heavy artillery batteries, a fortress engineer company, a signal section, R.A.S.C. company and other minor services. The battalion relieved the 1st Lincolns in Buena Vista Barracks, located ¾ mile from the southern tip of the Rock, and about 1½ miles (3 kilometres) from the town. It had a good view of the entrance to the harbour and of the liners entering and leaving port. Not all the battalion was in the barracks and B Company had two platoons at North Front and two in Buena Vista. One of the advantages of being stationed abroad meant that for the first time since the end of the war, no drafts had to be sent to the 1st Battalion.

On 21 October the Governor carried out his first ceremonial inspection of the battalion. When His Excellency Don Leopoldo Ruiz Trillo Y Figueros, Governor of Andalusia, arrived to pay his respects to the Governor on 22 December the battalion provided a Guard of Honour. This was followed shortly afterwards by the filming by Gaumont Graphic Movietones of the daily Guard Mounting together with Band, Drums, Pioneers and Goat outside Government House.[13]

There is little doubt that sport suffered due to the lack of facilities in Gibraltar. Because of the shortage of military units on the Rock every opportunity was taken to compete against visiting Royal Naval ships, against which some satisfactory results were obtained. The boxers took on HMS *Devonshire* and after an excellent evening lost a close contest by 14 points to 13. In racing, the finest performance of the year was Lieutenant E.C. Parker-Jervis winning the Spanish Cup, the most coveted trophy of the year, on 'Bayard' in the Royal Calpé Hunt Point-to-Point meeting.[14]

---

*   General Sir Alexander John Godley GCB KCMG (1867–1957) is best known for his role as commander of the New Zealand Expeditionary Force during the Great War. He successfully commanded II Anzac Corps and then XXII Corps in France and Flanders. He is well described by Llewelyn Wyn Griffith in *Up to Mametz ... and Beyond* (ed Jonathon Riley) (Barnsley, 2010). He was also the godfather of Lieutenant Mervyn Richardson of 2 R.W.F., one of the diarists who described the 1914 Christmas Truce.

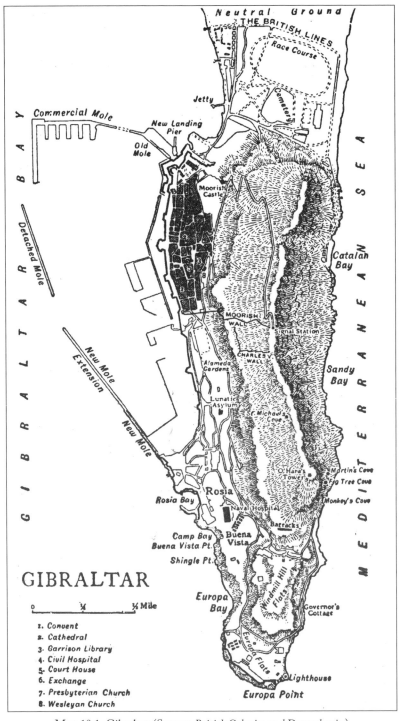

GIBRALTAR

1. Convent
2. Cathedral
3. Garrison Library
4. Civil Hospital
5. Court House
6. Exchange
7. Presbyterian Church
8. Wesleyan Church

Map 10.1 Gibraltar. (Source: *British Colonies and Dependencies*)

As well as a shortage of sports facilities, very limited training facilities meant that training was restricted to individual rather January–March 1932 than collective training. It consisted mainly of drill and ceremonial, physical training, education, and T.E.W.T.s (Tactical Exercises without Troops). The Annual Weapon Training courses were fired on the ranges at North Front.

St David's Day began well but the inter-company sports had to be cancelled because of bad weather. Dinner in the Officers' Mess was attended by the Governor and the Marquis Manzales, Master of the Royal Calpé Hunt. He was excused eating the leek 'as it was accepted that he had carried out this ceremony 43 years ago in the same mess.'[15] The Serjeants' Mess held their St David's Ball in the Garrison gymnasium on the 5th and this was followed, four days later, by an All Ranks Dance.

On 6 April the 1st Battalion, less C Company, arrived in Gibraltar on its way home. This historic meeting of the two battalions is April–May 1932 described in the chapter on Regimental Events. On 25 April the Governor carried out his Annual Administrative Inspection of the battalion. During May a party of sixty Warrant Officers, N.C.Os and Fusiliers went on a most successful three day trip to Tangier organised by the Commanding Officer.

The battalion participated in a Gibraltar Command ceremonial parade on the Race Course on 3 June to mark the birthday of H.M. The King. For June 1932 many it was the first experience of such a parade in the style normal before the war. Not only did it involve the firing of a *feu de joie* together with the Navy and the Duke of Cornwall's Light Infantry, but the battalion marched past in eight companies. All those on the saluting base, including the Spanish dignitaries, wore pre-war full ceremonial dress. A Guard of Honour consisting of two Officers and fifty Other Ranks with the Band, Ceremonial Pioneers, Colours and Goat was provided for the visit to the acting Governor on 17 September by Divisional Admiral Romeo Bemotti of the Royal Italian Navy.[16]

2 R.W.F. Polo Team 1932/33, from left, Ll. Gwydyr-Jones, B.E. Hopkins, J.R. Johnson, F.I. Gerrard. (R.W.F. Mus 2123)

The boxers continued to produce good results defeating teams from various ships including HMS *Nelson*, the flagship, and HMS *Malaya*, the Fleet champions. They ended the season by winning the Inter-Unit Boxing Championship of Gibraltar by beating the 2nd Duke of Cornwall's L.I. by 13 bouts to 2. The cricketers had a reasonably successful season, winning seven and tieing two of the sixteen matches. Both the ties were against the Royal Naval Detachment. Corporal W. Sollis and Bandsman Davies both scored centuries during the season. The latter topped the batting with 430 runs at an average of 31.6. Boy King was by far and away the best bowler with 47 wickets at 10.5 runs apiece.[17]

Early in 1933 the battalion participated in a combined exercise, on 14 February, to practice the defence of the Rock against a naval **January–July 1933** attack. On 20 March the Drums, Pioneers and Goat went on board HMS *Hood* to beat retreat. Afterwards the Captain sent the following message: 'The ceremony was both impressive and much appreciated by all who saw it, not only HMS Hood but HMS Renown and other ships too. We admired the way "Billy" surmounted all difficulties real and imaginary.'[18] On 2 July the Band, Drums and Pioneers gave a concert in the Bull Ring at Ronda in Spain, probably the first occasion on which a British military band had done such a thing. On 13 July, the battalion

participated in a ceremonial parade in honour of Their Excellencies, General Nunez Prado, the Captain General of Southern Andalucia, and General Gomez Morate, the Spanish Commander at Ceuta in Morocco. They were accompanied by their staffs and a number of other Officers from the Foreign Legion and the 15th Regiment from Algeciras in Morocco. The Order of Parade was printed in Spanish on the battalion printing press. After the parade twelve Spanish Officers were entertained to lunch in the Officers' Mess.[19]

Detachment on HMS *Hood* 20 March 1934. (LPH2131/4)

On the departure of the Governor, General Godley, on 9 October on the completion of his tour, the battalion provided the Guard of Honour and also helped with street lining. He had been a good friend of the battalion. The Guard was a composite one drawn from every company. It was commanded by Captain W.P. Kenyon, with Lieutenant E.C. Parker-Jervis and Second Lieutenant R.C.M. Kelly as subalterns. Afterwards the Commanding Officer received the following letter from the Governor: **October 1933**

> I take it to be a great honour that the last Guard of Honour mounted for me in my service should have been found by the Royal Welch Fusiliers, and that it should have been one which will serve me as a recollection for the rest of my life of how these things can, and should be done, by the crack Regiments of the British Army.[20]

On 24 October the same Guard of Honour was on duty for the arrival of the new Governor and Commander-in-Chief, General Sir Charles Harington.* Officers not on parade or on street-lining duties were in attendance at Government House to witness the ceremony of administering the Oaths of Office and the formal handing over of the Keys of the Fortress to the new Governor.[21] On the same day, Fusilier W.H. Fox died in the Military Hospital.[22]

A (Support) Company gave a demonstration of a machine gun barrage for the Governor on 19 December. Two targets, anchored in **December 1933** the sea about 200 yards apart and 1,000 yards from the shore, were engaged by all the battalion's sixteen machine guns.[23] The battalion boxing team defeated various ships from the Home Fleet. In the Garrison Individual Championships eleven out of twenty-two entries reached the final. For the second year running, 2nd Duke of Cornwall's L.I. were defeated by thirteen bouts to two in the Inter-Unit Championships. The Polo team won the Cup of Spain and were runners-up in the Inter-Regimental tournament. The Inter-Regimental Point to Point Race for the Godley Trophy was won by the battalion, as was the Subalterns' Cup. The football team won the League shield but was beaten in the semi-final of the Cup by the R.A. The cricketers became the Inter-Regimental Challenge Cup champions and went on to defeat a team drawn from the rest of the garrison. Out of eleven matches they only lost two.[24]

From 1st December 1933 to the end of March 1934, training consisted mainly of ceremonial drill, runs and education. The annual **January–April 1934** combined exercise for the defence of the Rock was held in February. A short ceremonial parade on the Alameda parade ground took place before the Colonel of the Regiment on St David's Day. At the Officers' Mess dinner in the evening one of the guests was Rear Admiral F.M. Austin, Rear Admiral Gibraltar, who as a Midshipman had been in charge of a pinnacle busy landing 2 R.W.F. for the advance to Tientsin in 1900.†

On the same day, in the United States, Major General Ben H. Fuller, Commandant of the U.S.M.C., was retiring from active duty. He had served in China in 1900 as had General Dobell. The proceedings were broadcast from Marine Headquarters in America and anyone with a short wave radio could hear them in Gibraltar:

> March 1st is St David's Day, dear in its memories to the Welsh people. In Wales, England and Gibraltar, the Officers of the Royal Welch Fusiliers know their friend, Major General Ben Hebard Fuller … a veteran of the Boxer Rebellion of 1900, retires today from active duty. The United States Marines and the Royal Welch Fusiliers rendered conspicuous service in that China campaign. Time has strengthened the friendship there cemented between the Royal Welch and the American Marine… The Royal Welch Fusiliers fought our forebears from 1775 to 1781. Tradition says they refused to permit their American battles to be written as battle honours on their Colours – they did not wish posterity to recall battles against the brothers… In 1917, when General Pershing landed at Liverpool,

---

*   General Sir Charles Harington Harington GCB GBE DSO DL (1872–1940), served for 46 years in the army, from the Second Anglo-Boer War, through the Great War, as Deputy Chief of the Imperial General Staff and then, between 1918 and 1920, he commanded the occupation forces in the Black Sea and Turkey during the Chanak Crisis.

†   Later Vice Admiral Sir Francis Murray Austin KBE CB (1881–1953).

later to command our armies in France, the Guard of Honour that received him was of the Royal Welch Fusiliers.[25]

The Commanding Officer was instrumental in re-introducing certain of the historic ceremonies associated with the Fortress of Gibraltar. With the approval of the Commander-in-Chief there was to be a weekly ceremonial guard mounting at Government House, with the Band and Drums in attendance. The Keys Ceremony was also to be performed once a week. The custom dates from the late eighteenth century after the Rock had been captured by the British and the governor of the day took steps to make it impregnable and to lessen the risk of capture by a coup de main attack. The Governor kept the keys of the three main gates on his sword belt and only handed them to the Key Sergeant who, escorted by an armed guard, was responsible for locking the gates at night and unlocking them in the morning. The duty was analogous to that carried out nightly at the Tower of London. To warn all non-residents that the gates were about to be shut the Drums of the regiment on duty accompanied the Key Sergeant on his round. For various reasons the custom fell into abeyance in 1927. The new procedure introduced by 2 R.W.F. in 1934 began half an hour before Retreat, when:

> … the Music of the Regiment on duty parades on the Alameda, directly below the old Signal Station… the bugles then sound the 'Long Dress', the Music then marches to Government House. Here the Key Sergeant, who has received the Keys from the Governor, joins the parade, escorted by an armed guard. The whole parade then moves as in times past, down Main Street to Casemates Square, where the Retreat is sounded. Meanwhile the Key Sergeant and his Escort march over to Landport Gate and this is duly locked. The Key Sergeant is then escorted back to Government House and the Keys are returned once more to the safe custody of His Excellency.[26]

In April the Commander-in-Chief carried out an annual inspection of the battalion; and in June the King's Birthday parade was held, as usual, on the Race Course. A Guard of Honour of two Officers and fifty men was provided for the visit of His Excellency General Urbano Palma, General Officer Commanding the 2nd Spanish Division at Seville, on 2 June. Another was found for the visit of the Emir of Transjordania on the 10 July.[27]

April–July 1934

A detachment of four Officers and seventy-nine Other Ranks from the United States Marine Corps, visiting Gibraltar on USS *Arkansas* and USS *Wyoming*, were entertained by the battalion on 24 July. Following a commemorative photograph lunch was provided in the Officers' and Serjeants' Messes and the Other Ranks' restaurant. There was much celebrating the repeal of the prohibition laws in America. In the afternoon there were opportunities for swimming, baseball and cricket. The following day six members of the Serjeants' Mess dined aboard the *Arkansas* and *Wyoming*.[28]

The boxers yet again defeated the 2nd Duke of Cornwall's L.I., this time by 11 bouts to 4. In the individual championships they won seven out of the eight titles they contested. The most memorable bout being the semi-final between Corporal Grindley of 2 R.W.F. and Corporal Rumble of 2nd D.C.L.I., which Rumble won on points after 'the finest fight for some period'. The Garrison Inter-Company Boxing Tournament was won by B Company which defeated A Company 2nd D.C.L.I. by nine bouts to two. At polo the battalion won the Inter-Regiment

Members of the U.S.M.C. join the 2nd
Battalion Sergeants' Mess in Gibraltar, 24
July 1934; formal and informal groups.
(R.W.F. Mus 5370)

Guard of Honour for the Emir
Abdullah of Transjordania, July 1934.
(R.W.F. Mus 3786)

Challenge Cup, the first infantry battalion to do so since 1910, and the Subalterns' Cup was won for the second successive year. Although the cricket team did not have a particularly successful season they played in a number of good matches. One such was against a Garrison Officers' team captained by the Governor. 2 R.W.F. made 223 all out but were well beaten by the Garrison Officers who passed the score for the loss of only two wickets. The battalion team was:

Major H.A. Davies
Captain the Hon. C.R. Clegg-Hill
Messrs H. de B. Prichard, J.R. Johnson and E.C. Parker-Jervis
RSM A. Bent
Lance Serjeant E. Sollis
Corporal H. Jackson
Lance Corporals T. King 17 and B. Talbot
Fusilier H. Jones 913.[29]

On 21 October 1934 the battalion handed over to the 2nd Gordon Highlanders. At 18.00 hrs it sailed from Gibraltar on HT *Somersetshire*. The voyage was good until the *Somersetshire* reached the China Sea when heavy seas were encountered and many suffered accordingly. The battalion landed twice for route marches on the way, at Colombo and Singapore. It eventually disembarked at Hong Kong on 22 November where it relieved the 1st South Wales Borderers.[30]

October–November 1934

Staff List, 2 R.W.F. Gibraltar, 1931–1934

Lieutenant Colonel	**Lieutenant**	**WOI**
C.C. Hewitt DSO MC	C.A. Anglesea-Sandels MBE MC	RSM C. Jones DCM MM
Major	J.A. Pringle MC	RSM A. Bent MM (Mar 33)
R.E. Hindson	H. de B. Prichard (Sep 31)	BM W.J. Clancy
T.C. Sharp	G.E. Rees	BM F. Burnett (Mar 33)
E.S.C. Grune (May 31)	C.J.L. Lewis	**WOII**
C.H. Edwards	C.H.V. Pritchard (to Oct 33)	RQMS R. Howell
J.G. Bruxner-Randall	J.A.M. Rice-Evans	RQMS C. Burton (Mar 33)
Captain	Hon. G.R. Clegg-Hill (to Sep 31	ORQMS J. Hughes DCM
H. Grismond Williams	and from Mar 32)	CSMI E. Austin
Ll Gwydyr-Jones	**2nd Lieutenant**	E. Morse
R. de B. Hardie (Oct 34)	H. de B. Prichard	J. Storer (Mar 33)
B.E. Horton	W.M. Fox	T. Dale
E.A. Morris MM	A.J. Lewis (to Apr 34) (Lt Aug 33)	N. Ridings (to Mar 33)
D.I. Owen (Nov 31)	W.S.A. Clough-Taylor (Lt Aug 32)	R. Hayward (May 32)
Ll. S. Lloyd (to Dec 31)	R.A.F. Hurt (Lt Jan 32)	E. Box
W.P. Kenyon MC (Mar 32)	J.R. Johnson (Lt Jan 33)	S. Metcalfe (to Mar 33)
F.H. Shove (to Jul 31)	Sir W.L. Williams Bt (to Jun 32)	E. Griffiths (Mar 33)
M.W. Whittaker (Dec 33)	E.C. Parker-Jervis (Jun 21) (Lt Aug	**CQMS**
R.K. Allen (Feb 34)	33)	J. Dodd
H.D'O. Lyle (to May 33)	H.P.A. Kempthorne (Lt Aug 33)	J. Edge (Mar 34)
E.R. Freeman (Nov 31)	T.A.G. Pritchard (Sep 31–Nov 34)	W. Robinson
A.D.M. Lewis (Apr 34)	(Lt Jan 34)	J. Price (Mar 33)

Bt Maj H.A. Davies MBE MC,
Adjt from Oct 33
W.B. Harrison (to Dec 31)
F.I. Gerrard MC, Adjt to Oct 33
M.H. ap Rhys Pryce (Mar 32)
G.F. Watson (to Oct 34)
Quartermaster
Lt W.H. Albutt DCM (to Feb
32)
Lt C. Jones DCM MM (Feb 32)

N.R.G. Bosanquet (Jun 32)
(Lt Aug 34)
L.H. Yates (Dec 32) (Lt Jan 33)
R.C.R. Price (Feb 33)
R.C.M. Kelly (Feb 33) (Lt Aug 34)
D.M.C. Prichard (Feb 33)
J.W. Riley (Nov 34)

P. Condon (to May 32)
P. Chard (to May 32)
G. Morris (to May 32)
C. Stanley (May 32)
T. Grinham (Mar 33)
E. Griffiths (May 32)
Staff Serjeants
Band Sjt J. Flanagan
SIM J. Costen
SIM A. LePoidevin (Mar 34)
Drum Major (Sjt Drummer)
J. Edge
Pioneer Sjt A.E. Evans
Pro Sjt W.O.H. Smithurst
ORS A. Randall (Mar 33)

iii. Hong Kong, 1934–1937

The Crown Colony of Hong Kong (Hiang-Kiang in Chinese, meaning 'sweet lagoons') is situ-ated on the South-East coast of China opposite the province of Kwang-tung (Canton) at the mouth of the Canton River. Very irregular in outline, the island is about eleven miles (18 kilo-metres) long and from two to five miles (3 to 8 kilometres) broad with a total area of thirty-two square miles (82 square kilometres). From the mainland it is separated by a narrow channel which, between Victoria, the island capital, and Kowloon Point, is about one mile (1.6 kilome-tres) wide. The island was occupied by Britain following the Opium Wars in 1841 and formerly ceded in the following year. The Kowloon peninsula was added in 1860, and the New Territories were leased from China in 1898 for ninety-nine years. The total area is 391 square miles (1,102 square kilometres), with a population in 1934 of almost 950,000, of which 97% was Chinese. Hong Kong was a free port – except for spirits, tobacco and petrol – and was the centre of a vast trade in many commodities. The terrain is mountainous, the highest point being Victoria Peak at 1,809 feet (551 metres). The New Territories contain peaks from 1,800 to 3,000 feet (550 to 914 metres). The hot season lasts from May to October with an average temperature in July of 87°F (30°C). When combined with humidity in excess of 90%, many Europeans found the climate unpleasant. During the winter months, from November to March, the climate is cooler and dryer, the average temperature in February being 63°F (17°C. The average rainfall is 85 inches (2,159 mm) of which 75% falls between May and September, when the south-west monsoon prevails.[31]

The General Officer Commanding British Troops in China, Major General O.C. Borrett,* was based in Hong Kong. His command included Hong Kong, Shanghai and Tientsin. He had under his command six infantry battalions, four of which were based in Hong Kong: 2 R.W.F., 1st Lincolns, 2nd East Lancashires, and the 1/8th Punjabis from India. The 1st Inniskilling

---

*   Later Lieutenant General Sir Oswald Cuthbert Borrett KCB CMG CBE DSO *Ld'H* was
    commissioned into the King's Own. He had commanded the 18th Division during the Great War.

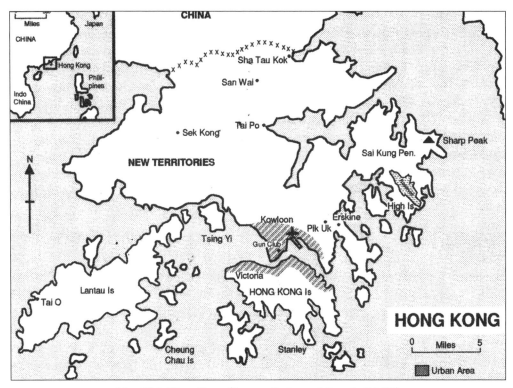

Map 10.2 Hong Kong. (Source: *Regimental Records, Vol. VII*)

Fusiliers were in Shanghai and the 2nd Worcesters in Tientsin. Their role was the protection of British commercial interests and, in the case of Hong Kong, internal security.

On arrival in Hong Kong the battalion had a strength of twenty-eight Officers, thirty Warrant Officers and Serjeants, and 796 Junior N.C.Os and Fusiliers. Accommodation was provided in four separate barracks on Hong Kong Island: Murray (B Company), Victoria (A (Support) Company), Wellington (C Company and Drums) and Mount Austin (D Company). Mount Austin on The Peak, a smart residential area, could only be reached by the Peak tramway.[32] The 2nd Battalion had last been stationed in Hong Kong in 1902.[33] Lieutenant Colonel R.E. Hindson assumed command of the battalion on 1 January 1935.*

The first three months of 1935 were taken up with training. The annual weapon training courses were fired at the Kowloon Ranges. **January–March 1935** From 8 February to 11 March the battalion carried out collective training at San Wai Camp in the New Territories, culminating in a battalion exercise. Detachments from the Royal Navy and Royal Marines were attached throughout. This was followed by a combined operations exercise, the Battalion Rifle Meeting and Hong Kong Area Rifle Meeting. In the Hong Kong Area Machine Gun Competition, numbers 3 and 4 Platoons succeeded in wresting the trophy from

---

*   Lieutenant Colonel Richard Eldred Hindson (1892–1966).

the 1st Lincolns.[34] The St David's Day ceremonial parade at San Wai Camp, where the battalion was under canvas, had to be cancelled because of the weather. The Serjeants' Mess Ball was held in the China Fleet Club and guests included the G.O.C. and Mrs Borrett.[35]

Boxing had begun early in 1935 as the Battalion Novices and Open Tournaments were held in February. The boxers were soon able, therefore, to start training for the Colony-wide competitions. The Novices began by winning the Inter-Unit Competition. In the Open Inter-Unit Competition the battalion were runners-up to the 2nd East Lancashires. Football teams competed in three leagues of mixed British and Chinese teams. The 1st XI was Lance Serjeant Grindley, Lance Corporal Ellis 78, and Fusiliers Keneghan, Rowlands, Wheeler, Keating, Hughes 465, Harrison, Dennis, Talbot and Roberts 35. Kenegan and Rowlands played for the Army. In rugby the Army Seven-a-Side Tournament found the two Royal Welch teams meeting in the semi-final. The 'A' team went on to win the competition. Two teams were entered for the Colony Seven-a-Side Tournament and the 'A' team were beaten 5 points to 8 in the final by the team from the Hong Kong Club. The competition drew large crowds of paying spectators and the proceeds were donated to charity. The following played rugby regularly for the Army XV:

Captain M.H. ap Rhys Pryce
Lieutenants J.A.M. Rice-Evans and R.C.R. Price
Lance Corporals Davies 52 and Bebb
Fusiliers Barry, Floyd, Morgan 09, Watts 29, Kelshaw, Anderson and Eagle.

Floyd also played for the Combined Services. A number of Officers hunted with the Fanling Hunt in the New Territories and the Polo players won the Royal Navy Cup. The annual Kowloon Marathon over 6½ miles (10 kilometres) of road was open to all Europeans in the Colony. The battalion did well with Fusilier Williams 47 coming 3rd, Fusilier Hall 4th, Fusilier Parry 67 5th and Lieutenant C.J.L. Lewis 7th.[36]

Between April and December 1935 the battalion provided eight Guards of Honour for a wide variety of visiting dignitaries to the colony, including: the Governor of Shan Tung Province and the Vice President of the United States of America, John N. Garner. The Annual Administrative Inspection by the G.O.C. was carried out on 24 April.[37] A review of troops by the Governor at Happy Valley Racecourse on 7 May on the occasion of King George V's Silver Jubilee was witnessed by hundreds of thousands of spectators. The Chinese celebrations lasted a week, the first day being devoted to magnificent processions, which included a 300 foot (100 metre) long Silver Dragon, decorated floats, tableaux of ancient Chinese legends, conjurors,

April 1935

The King's Silver Jubilee Parade, Hong Kong Racecourse, 1935.
(Thomas Williams)

jugglers, and so on. 'Even in the small villages in the New Territories, where, under the guidance of their village elders, thanksgiving celebrations and illuminations were arranged, while from Canton thousands and thousands of Chinese came in not only to see the processions, but to take part in them.'[38] Over a hundred thousand bulbs turned night into day in Victoria and Kowloon, and HMS *Hermes* and all the other naval ships in port were an amazing sight with their intricate illuminations.

On 5 October a Guard of Honour was provided on the occasion of Brigadier F.S. Thackeray[*] on his assuming the duties of **October–December 1935** Commander. Serjeant W. Setterfield died suddenly on 21 October aged 35 and was buried on the following day at Happy Valley with full military honours.[†] After Christmas, the battalion marched to Lo Wu in the New Territories for a camp, bivouacking en route on 28 December. Training consisted of field firing, platoon, company and battalion exercises carried out successfully in excellent weather. On 28 December Murray Barracks on Hong Kong Island was handed over to the 1st Royal Ulster Rifles and Shamshuipo Hutments (Hankow Barracks) on the mainland were taken over from the 1st Lincolns. This was the first time in four years that the battalion was all together in one barracks.[39]

On 20 January 1936, King George V, the Regiment's Colonel-in-Chief, died. On the 28th, representatives of the battalion **January–March 1936** attended a memorial service for His Late Majesty at St John's Cathedral. The immediate effect of the King's death was that the St David's Day celebrations on 29 February were very low key. The Regimental Colour was trooped with only the Regimental families as spectators. This was the first occasion since Pembroke Dock in 1924 that the Colour had been trooped. In the morning a party of one Officer and six Other Ranks laid a wreath on the Cenotaph. The Officers dined without guests and there were only two toasts, those of 'St David' and 'The King'. The Warrant Officers' and Serjeants' Mess Ball was postponed until after the period of court mourning.[40]

The Hong Kong Area Machine Gun Cup Competition was competed for at Lo Wu in February and won for the second year in succession by the battalion machine gunners. The battalion participated in a combined exercise from 21 to 23 March. Some elements were engaged in the defence of the Colony whilst the main body, under Major Ll. A.A. Alston, embarked on HMS *Medway* as part of the attacking force. A successful landing was made from destroyers under cover of darkness. The Annual Administrative Inspection by the G.O.C. took place at Shamshuipo on 17 April. The battalion **April–June 1936** participated in the Review by His Excellency the Governor at Happy Valley Racecourse on 23 June on the occasion of King Edward VIII's birthday. In order to get men away from Hong Kong the battalion established a holiday camp on Stonecutter's Island and each man was given an eight day holiday there. Holidays were taken by platoons and, provided the weather was fine, were popular.[41]

On 1 August the Commanding Officer, Lieutenant Colonel R.E. Hindson, retired on grounds of ill health. His successor, Lieutenant Colonel **August 1936** D.M. Barchard,[‡] joined the battalion on 2 November from 1 R.W.F. In the early hours of Sunday 17 August Hong Kong suffered a typhoon with winds reaching 130 m.p.h. (210 k.p.h.) and

---

[*]   Brigadier Frank Staniford Thackeray DSO MC ADC, late *HLI* (1880–1960).
[†]   In 1935/36 Fusiliers T. Lawton and Roberts 11 also died but no details are known.
[‡]   Later Brigadier David Maxwell Barchard (1891–1954).

accompanied by torrential rain. By 06.00 hrs the wind had abated somewhat and people felt safe enough to emerge from buildings and survey the damage. The stables had been razed to the ground and the church almost completely blown away. The sides of dining halls had been ripped away and wireless masts and cables lay in hopeless confusion. The damage done to life and property in the Colony was fortunately small compared to past storms. Those who lived afloat or in the ramshackle fishing villages suffered the most. Only one ship in harbour was seriously damaged, the remainder having left for the open sea when the typhoon warnings were received.[42]

At the beginning of November the battalion provided Guards of Honour for the arrival and departure of the Mayor of Canton and the **November 1936** President of the Kwantung Provincial Government. Afterwards the following extract from a letter was received by the G.O.C. from the Governor: 'I should be very grateful if your Excellency would convey my appreciation and thanks to all who supplied, commanded or took part in the Guards of Honour. Our guests before leaving expressed to me the greatest admiration of the military arrangements for their reception.'[43]

The end of the year was the time of the trooping season which meant farewells to old friends and the arrival of the new intake from the 1st Battalion. In 1936, over 250 N.C.Os and Fusiliers, almost a third of the battalion, left for England to join the Reserve. Fortunately not every year was a bad as this. The battalion marched to annual camp at San Wai for the third year running on 7 November. Training consisted of field firing and platoon, company and battalion exercises.

2 R.W.F. in camp, 1935. (R.W.F. Mus)

It was interesting and energetic and the test exercise set for the battalion involved covering vast distances on foot. It returned to barracks on 18 December after six weeks of virtually no rain.[44]

On 12 December representatives of the battalion **December 1936** were present at the Proclamation Parade in Statute Square, Hong Kong on the accession of His Majesty King George VI. Christmas festivities included a circus on the square on Christmas night produced entirely from talent within the battalion. Spectators included the families and also friends from the other Services all of whom thoroughly enjoyed the evening. After Christmas six weeks were spent on the Kowloon Ranges where the annual weapon training courses were fired.

The Novice boxers were beaten in the semi-final of the Hong Kong Area Championships by the 2nd East Lancashires. In polo, the team consisting of Captain

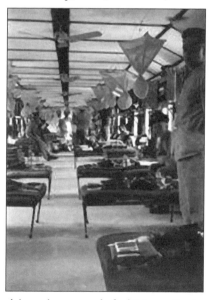

A barrack room ready for kit inspection in the 1930s. (Norman Weale)

A.D.M. Lewis, and Messrs Price, J.R. Johnson and Parker-Jervis were runners-up to the Royal Artillery for the K.O.Y.L.I. Cup, but won the Royal Navy Challenge Cup for the second year running. Eight members of the battalion played in the winning Army team for the Triangular Rugby Tournament. Lieutenant J.A.M. Rice-Evans, Fusiliers Morgan 09 and Floyd represented the Colony against a New Zealand Universities XV. Two battalion teams competed in the final of the Army Seven-a-Side Tournament and another reached the final of the Colony Tournament where they were beaten by the Hong Kong Club by 21 points to 13. At football, Fusilier Talbot represented the Colony against Shanghai. Corporal W. Wanklyn, and Fusiliers Talbot, Rowlands, Keating, Harrison, Roberts 35, and Coakley were capped by the Army.[45]

On 16/17 February 1937 the battalion performed well in a Command test exercise. In March they took part in a five day **February–April 1937** combined operations exercise. In the 'Services and Bisley' Rifle Meeting, battalion teams or individuals won the Platoon Match, Association M.G. Match, Light Automatic Match, Rifle and L.A. Match and the Falling Plate. They were runners-up in three other matches. The Annual Administrative Inspection by the G.O.C. took place on 20 April. On the same day 4191475 Fusilier B.M. Platt died of natural causes in the Military Hospital.[46]

The sporting instincts that had prompted the bet in Biebrich, ten years before, involving Lieutenant H.C. Stockwell's timed walk, came to the fore again in Hong Kong on St David's Day 1937. The *China Mail* reported under the headline 'Army Officer Wins a Wager. Walk round Territories And Half-Mile Race', recalling perhaps the great wager of Captain Robert Barclay,* that:

> Many years ago, it was quite a common occurrence for wagers to be made, as a result of which feats of sportsmanship were attempted for large stakes. I believe that the origin of an interesting bet which was decided yesterday, was a remark passed by Lt C.J.L. Lewis, of the Royal Welch Fusiliers, to the effect that he was one of the fittest Officers in the China Command. Lt [T.A.G.] Pri[t]chard,† the well-known cricketer and a brother Officer, hearing this, apparently issued a challenging comment with the result that the former offered to walk round the New Territories and then run the half mile in less than two minutes 40 seconds, all within the space of 24 hours. Lt Pri[t]chard took him up and a substantial wager was made. On Saturday afternoon at 2.30 p.m., accordingly, Lt. Lewis set off on his task and taking the Fanling route arrived on the Polo ground, Mong Kok, at 11.30 a.m. yesterday morning. After a bath and a short rest, he ran the half-mile on the Polo ground at about 2.00 p.m. and returned the very respectable time of two minutes 30 seconds to win the wager.[47]

---

*   He walked 1,000 miles in 1,000 hours, a mile in every hour, on a measured course on Putney Heath, for a prize of £1,000.

†   Later Lieutenant Colonel Trevor Alan Gordon ('Tag') Pritchard DSO OBE (1911–1986); Claud John Ledston ('Jackie') Lewis (1905–1987) served in the Regiment from 1925 to 1946. His war service included time with the 53rd (Welsh) Division in the U.K. and Northern Ireland and in India and Burma, where he was injured. He was the father of Lieutenant Colonel M.H. Lewis DL, C.O. 3 R.W.F. 1990–1992.

The battalion defeated the 1st Royal Ulster Rifles twice to win both the Inter-Unit Novices and Open Boxing Championships. In the Open Individual Championships 2 R.W.F. took three winners and four runners-up medals. A very successful football season ended in May. The First XI, often brilliant but inconsistent, came 5th in their league. The 2nd XI finished as runners-up in their league, and the 3rd XI won theirs, with Drummer Tatler equalling the Colony record by scoring eight goals in one match. The First XI were runners-up in the Colony Senior Shield Knock-out Competition. Both hockey XIs won their respective leagues and the battalion Ladies were developing into a strong team.

During April the Goat, which had been with the battalion since it joined at Pembroke Dock in 1925, had to be put down. It had seen service in England, Germany, Gibraltar and Hong Kong. In the words of the author of his obituary, 'Perhaps he may be our last Royal Goat. Let us remember him as a worthy and dignified bearer of this sad but proud title for his like will not be seen again.'[48] Fortunately this pessimistic view was soon forgotten when it was learnt that a new goat from the Royal Herd would be presented when the battalion returned to England. On 13 May the Coronation of King George VI and **May 1937** Queen Elizabeth was celebrated in Hong Kong with a military review at Happy Valley which began at 08.00 hrs. All ships in the harbour were dressed for the occasion with HMS *Eagle* standing out.[49] At midday a three mile long (4.5 kilometre) procession began which included representations from almost every big industry and firm. At night the sky was lit by searchlights and illuminations as the Chinese procession commanded everyone's attention.

Staff List, 2 R.W.F. Hong Kong, 1934–1937

Lieutenant Colonel
R.E. Hindson (to 1 Aug 36)
D.M. Barchard (2 Nov 36)
Major
Ll A.A. Alston DSO MC (2ic, Jul 35–Jan 37)
D.H.W. Kirkby (Jan 36)
T.C. Sharp
E.S.C. Grune (to Jan 37)
C.H. Edwards
J.G. Bruxner-Randall
Captain
H. Grismond Williams
R. de B. Hardie (to Nov 36)
Ll Gwydyr Jones
M.H. ap Rhys Pryce(to Jan 36)
H.B. Harrison MC (Jan 37) (Maj May 37)
B.E. Horton (to Jan 37)
E.A. Morris MM
D.I. Owen (to Oct 36)
W.P. Kenyon MC
M.W. Whittaker
R.K. Allen
E.R. Freeman
A.D.M. Lewis MBE (to Jan 36)
Bt Maj H.A. Davies MBE MC

Lieutenant
C.A. Anglesea-Sandels MBE MC
J.A. Pringle MC
H. de B. Prichard
G.E. Rees
C.J.L. Lewis
T.A.G. Pritchard, Adjt Jan 37
H.A.S. Clarke (Dec 36)
W.S.A. Clough-Taylor
R.A.F. Hurt
J.A.M. Rice-Evans
Hon. G.R. Clegg-Hill (Capt Sep 37)
R.C.M. Kelly
J.R. Johnson (to Aug 36)
H.P.A. Kempthorne
E.C. Parker-Jervis
N.R.G. Bosanquet
L.H. Yates
D.M.C. Pritchard
R.C.R. Price (to Jan 36)
A.J. Lewis
2nd Lieutenant
F.C. Minshull-Ford (Mar 36) (Lt Feb 37)
J.W. Riley (Lt Feb 37)
R.L. Boyle (Jan 37)
J.E.C. Hood (Nov 36)

W.O. I
RSM N. Ridings (Mar 35)
RSM S. Metcalfe (Mar 37)
BM F. Burnett
BM S. Hills ARCM (Jan 35)
W.O. II
RQMS C. Burton
CSMI E. Austin
E. Morse (to Mar 35)
J. Storer (to Mar 35)
G. Morris
T. Grinham
L. Macey (Mar 36)
J. Dale
R. Hayward (to Mar 35)
E. Box
E. Griffiths
CQMS
J. Dodd
A. Randall (to Mar 37)
J. Edge
J. Green
R. Price
A. Cheetham
T. Casson (Mar 36)
R. Wigham (Mar 37)

Adjt to Jan 37
Quartermaster
Lt C. Jones DCM MM

Staff Serjeants
Band Sjt J. Flanagan
SIM A. LePoidevin
SIM A. Ingram (Mar 37)
Drum Major C. Booker
Pnr Sgt W. Sollis
ORS V. Fraser
Cook Sgt C. Kretzschmar

Notes

1 Robin McNish, *Iron Division. The History of the 3rd Division, 1809–1989* (Privately published, 1989), pp. 70–71.
2 Notes made by WO I Reuben Jones MSM and held in the R.W.F. Museum. He was at the time a boy soldier having enlisted at 14 years of age.
3 *Y Ddraig Goch*, Series II, March 1931, p. 9.
4 2 R.W.F. Digest of Service; *Y Ddraig Goch,* June 1931, p. 25.
5 2 R.W.F. Digest of Service.
6 *Y Ddraig Goch,* June 1931, p. 30.
7 2 R.W.F. Digest of Service.
8 *Y Ddraig Goch,* June 1931, pp. 28–29.
9 2 R.W.F. Digest of Service.
10 2 R.W.F. Digest of Service.
11 George Gill, *British Colonies and Dependencies* (London, c. 1920), pp. 11–12.
12 Peter Dietz (ed), *Garrison: Ten British Military Towns* (London, 1986) pp. 177–200.
13 www.itnsource.com/en/partners/gaumont-graphic accessed 15 May 2015.
14 *Y Ddraig Goch*, March 1932, p. 9.
15 *Y Ddraig Goch*, June 1932, p. 35. As the last time a battalion of the Regiment had been in Gibraltar was in 1879.
16 *Y Ddraig Goch*, September 1932, p. 55.
17 *Y Ddraig Goch*, September 1932, pp. 59–60.
18 2 R.W.F. Digest of Service.
19 *Y Ddraig Goch*, September 1933, p. 120.
20 *Y Ddraig Goch*, December 1933, pp. 177–178.
21 *Y Ddraig Goch*, December 1933, p. 179.
22 2 R.W.F. Digest of Service.
23 *Y Ddraig Goch*, December 1933, p. 182.
24 *Y Ddraig Goch*, December 1933, pp. 173–192.
25 *Y Draig Goch*, Series III, June 1934, pp. 21–24.
26 *Y Ddraig Goch*, March 1934, pp. 48–50.
27 *Y Draig Goch*, September 1934, p. 18; 2 R.W.F. Digest of Service.
28 2 R.W.F. Digest of Service.
29 *Y Draig Goch*, September 1934, pp. 30–32.
30 2 R.W.F. Digest of Service.
31 George Gill, *British Colonies and Dependencies* (London, c.1920), pp. 114–115.
32 2 R.W.F. Digest of Service.
33 *Regimental Records,* Vol II, p. 299.
34 2 R.W.F. Digest of Service.
35 *Y Draig Goch*, July 1935, p. 51.
36 *Y Draig Goch*, July 1935, pp. 42–50.
37 2 R.W.F. Digest of Service.
38 *Y Draig Goch*, December 1935, p. 16.
39 2 R.W.F. Digest of Service.
40 2 R.W.F. Digest of Service.
41 2 R.W.F. Digest of Service.

42 *Y Draig Goch*, October 1936, p. 45.
43 2 R.W.F. Digest of Service.
44 2 R.W.F. Digest of Service.
45 *Y Draig Goch*, April 1937, pp. 34–45.
46 2 R.W.F. Digest of Service.
47 *China Mail*, Monday, 1 March 1937, p. 1. Information supplied by Lieutenant Colonel M.H.L. Lewis *R.W.F.*, C.J.L. Lewis's son
48 *Y Draig Goch*, July 1937, p. 29.
49 2 R.W.F. Digest of Service.

Chapter 11

The 2nd Battalion on Operations in China, in Sudan and in India, 1937–1940

i. The Sino-Japanese War

The Sino-Japanese War proper broke out in 1937 with the Japanese invasion of Tientsin (now Tianjin) and Peking (now Beijing), but this was only the latest phase of Japan's territorial designs on China. Manchuria had already been occupied in 1931 and the puppet state of Manzhuguo created in 1932. Nanking was invaded in December 1937 and most of north China was soon under Japanese control, in which state it would remain until the defeat of Japan in 1945.

In August 1937, strained relations between Japan and China had resulted in the concentration of 30,000 Chinese troops near Shanghai, where they were confronted by a force of 3,000 Japanese which had been landed by sea and supported by about twenty light cruisers and destroyers. Firing broke out on the 13th and as the Japanese brought reinforcements ashore their force soon reached about 8,000. The Chinese proved incapable of launching large scale attacks, quickly lost command of the air and were forced onto the defensive. By mid-October the Japanese had landed 150,000 men and although Chinese forces numbered half a million they were defeated by superior tactics, weapons and morale, and were forced to retreat to Nanking.[1]

The Shanghai International Settlement came into being after the defeat of the Qing dynasty of China by the British in the First Opium War of 1839–1842, and the subsequent Treaty of Nanking. Under the terms of the treaty, Shanghai and the treaty ports of Canton, Tientsin, Ningpo, Fuchow and Amoy were opened to foreign trade. The British, from their base in Hong Kong, quickly established a settlement along the banks of the Whangpo River. American and French involvement followed in Shanghai, with a settlement by the French in the South and the Americans to the north, carved out of the British settlement. In 1854, the three countries created the Shanghai Municipal Council to serve all their interests, but in 1862, the French concession dropped out of the collective arrangements. The following year the British and American settlements formally united to create the Shanghai International Settlement.

Unlike Hong Kong and Weiheiwei, which were sovereign British territories, the foreign concessions in Shanghai originally remained Chinese sovereign territory. However, during the Small Sword Society uprising of 1853–1855, the Qing government gave up sovereignty in the concessions to the foreign powers in exchange for their support in suppressing the rebellion. As more foreign powers entered into treaty relations with China, their nationals also became part of the administration of the settlement, but it remained a predominantly British affair. The threat to the concession by the outbreak of fighting between the Chinese and Japanese led to

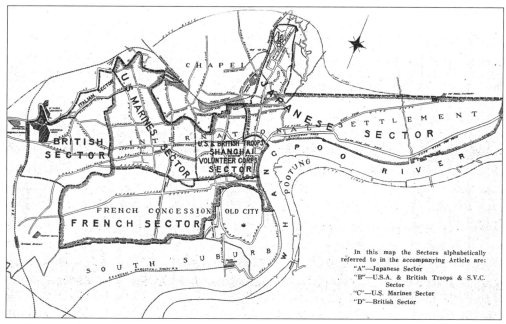

Map 11.1 Defence Sectors in Shanghai, a contemporary map. (Source: *The Army Quarterly*, 1938)

the deployment of British troops to protect national interests and citizens in both Shanghai and Tientsin.

ii. 2 R.W.F. in Shanghai

On 14 August 1937 the battalion embarked for Shanghai on the Blue Funnel cargo ship, SS *Maron*, normally a pilgrim ship. Its mission **August 1937** was to protect British lives and property endangered by the fighting between Chinese and Japanese troops in the area. The departure was delayed until 20.30 hrs because additional life-boats had to be made and taken on board. Arriving at the mouth of the Whangpoo at dawn on the 17th they found themselves amongst eleven Japanese warships.[2] In spite of the choppy sea the battalion transferred to HMS *Delight*, which had come post haste from Weihaiwei during the night, and continued up the Whangpo River to Shanghai. During the passage up the river, Japanese naval craft were engaging Chinese forces on both sides of the river and considerable aerial activity was observed. All along the deserted river banks destroyed buildings were visible everywhere. *Delight* drew alongside another British destroyer, whereupon everyone transferred to river craft which conveyed them to the jetty. By 13.00 hrs disembarkation was complete and the battalion en route in hired lorries to its billets at the Shanghai Race Club. The Officers were allocated accommodation in the Chairman's and Stewards' rooms and the men in the restaurants. As one veteran recalled, 'Despite travelling beneath an umbrella of shell fire from both of the warring sides, our arrival at the Shanghai Bund went off without incident.'[3]

Fusilier W. Fox and companion dressed
for lifeboat drill on the troopship heading
for Shanghai. (William Fox)

2 R.W.F. arrives by troopship
in North China. (F.C.
Minshull-Ford)

Troops going up the
Whangpoo to Shanghai
in the *Delight*. (F.C.
Minshull-Ford)

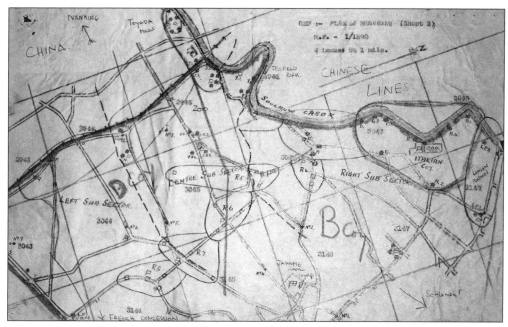

Map 11.2 A Plan of Shanghai from the album of Francis Minshull-Ford.

2 R.W.F. was placed under the command of H.Q. Shanghai Area which, until now, had only one British battalion, the 2nd Loyals. Additional British troops were on the way, the 1st Royal Ulster Rifles having left Hong Kong a day after 2 R.W.F., and 1st Middlesex was en route from Singapore. The Royal Ulster Rifles were later replaced by 1st Durham Light Infantry. The Commander was Major General A.P.D. Telfer-Smollett.* The International Settlement had been divided into sectors, occupied by regular troops from Britain, America – including the 4th and 6th Battalions U.S. Marines – France, and one unit of Russians. The Shanghai Volunteer Defence Corps (S.V.D.C.) was made up of British, Irish, French, Germans, Swedes, White Russians, Americans, and even Chinese and Japanese. Hard-pressed evacuation committees had been formed to get their nationals away to safety and ships full of refugees had been leaving port for Hong Kong, Taiwan, Saigon, Singapore, and even India and America.

The orders given to 2 R.W.F. were to take over on the following day in B Sector of the International Settlement, which the General described as the 'sticky sector'. Here, they were to relieve the 2nd (Russian) Battalion of the S.V.D.C.[4] Reconnaissance was carried out during the evening and at 14.00 hrs the following afternoon Battalion H.Q. and the companies set off for their sector.

The *Shanghai Evening Post* reported that:

---

*   Major-General Alexander Patrick Drummond Telfer-Smollett CB CBE DSO MC DL (1884–1954) was commissioned into the H.L.I.; he was David Niven's company commander and is described by him in *The Moon's a Balloon*. He was later Lieutenant Governor of Guernsey.

R.W.F. marching into Shanghai. (R.W.F. Mus 9184)

A coincidence which savours of the incredible has cropped up in Shanghai with the arrival of the Royal Welch Fusiliers from Hong Kong.

Way back in 1900 … detachments of the US Marines and the Royal Welch Regiment [*sic*] were among the International Relief Forces. Units of the two forces entered the walled city together on 14th August 1900, and until the quelling of the uprising were quartered close together. Thirty-seven years later almost to the day, groups of the same units met again and, as in 1900 they are in China to protect the lives and property of foreigners. At seven o'clock on the evening of 14th August 1937, the 2nd Battalion The Royal Welch Fusiliers left Hong Kong arriving here on the 17th, when they were rushed to the relief of the A Battalion SVC stationed in B Sector.

Defending that part of the Settlement Boundary directly next to theirs was the US Marines and … their successors exchanged the heartiest greetings.

There was one warrior of the Boxer Rebellion days … Brigadier General Richards, believed to have retired from the US Marines recently. The coincidence of dates … was instantly recognised by the war veteran who despatched a telegram from America to Colonel CFB Price [USMC], worded as follows:

"For Royal Welch and St David."

It was promptly handed over to Colonel Barchard.[5]

The battalion area was described as:

a very curious Sector, being a mass of streets, alleys and slums. Japanese posts 100 yards away on our right flank, facing us: our posts facing the Chinese on our front and left flanks, never further than 50 yards apart and mostly 10–15. We talk with both the Chinese and

Japanese sentries and go into the Chinese lines at North Station through an iron gate by one of our own block-houses.[6]

The area was in a disgusting condition as the Japanese had shot coolies from the Public Works Department trying to clear away the accumulated rubbish, filth and the dead bodies, both human and animal. The smell was appalling and flies were everywhere.

In the course of the next few days existing defences were enlarged and strengthened and additional emplacements constructed. Sandbags, barbed wire, rifle and machine gun posts brought home to everyone their close proximity to the battle area. Valentine Grevitt recalled that: 'It is highly unlikely our barricades would have deterred either the Chinese or the Japanese, particularly the latter, if they had been determined to sweep us aside.'[7] Because three sides of the sector were adjacent to Chinese and Japanese positions there was much bombing and shelling and several fires were started within the sector. Friendly relations, however, existed between the rival factions and the battalion, and the few Chinese people who had remained behind. Lieutenant D.M.C. Pritchard was talking to a Chinese sentry when a Chinese Officer approached and said, 'Weren't you in No 5 Company at Sandhurst, and isn't your name Pritchard?' They had been in the same company at the R.M.C.![8]

A view over the racecourse; the buses had been parked there for safety. (F.C. Minshull-Ford)

The Officers, 2 R.W.F. Shanghai. (F.C. Minshull-Ford)

Looking west from North Star.
(F.C. Minshull-Ford)

Stink Alley Post. (F.C.
Minshull-Ford)

On Monday 23 August, at noon, a bomb struck the Sincere Store in the heart of the Settlement near the junction of Nanking and Chekiang Roads. When the smoke cleared the scenes of carnage were horrific. The official estimate of casualties was 192 killed and nearly 600 injured. Shortly before, another bomb had landed on the U.S. Naval Storehouse but had failed to explode. On one occasion an incendiary fell close to the headquarters and the Japanese rang to say they would deal with snipers whilst the British soldiers fought the fire.[9]

On 27 August the battalion was relieved by the 2nd Loyals and returned to their billets. After five days they took over D Sector, the most westerly of the sectors, from the 1st Ulster Rifles. One half of the area was slums and the other a pleasant residential district with smart houses and gardens. People called at the posts at all hours of the day and night with gifts of coffee, tea, buns, cigarettes and beer. A detachment occupied the Toyada Mills which was vital for the successful defence of the Settlement. In spite of repeated bombing of the mills by the Japanese no casualties were suffered. On 5 September, 4189534 Fusilier G. Evans of B Company was killed in an accident. He had been a remarkably fine swimmer and had represented the battalion.[10] The battalion was relieved on the 7th and after a short rest it returned to the original sector, Sector B, which

September–October 1937

Situation Report from 2 R.W.F. to H.Q. British Forces Shanghai, October 1937. (Minshull-Ford albums)

it occupied until 7 November. There was daily Japanese bombing of neighbouring areas such as North Station, Chapei, Hongkew and Yangtszepoo, and long range artillery duels between ships in the river and the shore batteries. The Shanghai Waterworks at Yangtszepoo was also guarded by the battalion and although frequently shelled and bombed there were no casualties.

Early on 27 October, Chinese forces to the north and west of the sector carried out an orderly withdrawal during darkness which was not discovered by the Japanese until daybreak. During their withdrawal the Chinese set fire to a large number of houses and by nightfall a heavy pall of smoke stretched as far as the eye could see. As night progressed the fires assumed terrifying proportions and the threat to the sector was only averted by the efforts of the Shanghai Fire Brigade and the direction of the wind. Japanese mopping-up was completed with the exception of 400 Chinese soldiers, known as the 'Doomed Battalion'[11] who had occupied a very strongly constructed godown, or warehouse, situated on the south-west corner of the sector. In spite of repeated Japanese attacks on their position the Chinese continued to hold out.

About noon on the 29th, the Adjutant called the Officer Commanding C Company, Captain Ll. Gwydyr-Jones, to say that two Japanese pinnaces were making their way up the Soochow Creek, which was immediately to the rear of the Chinese position, with the intention of attacking the battalion in the godown from the south. They were to be stopped at all costs. The O.C. and his interpreter set off on bicycles to get the Chinese to block the creek with their boats. As soon as the word 'Japanese' was used the Chinese boatmen covered their heads and refused to move. Eventually they were prevailed upon to do what was required and a boom of junks and sampans was rapidly constructed. As the Japanese boats approached, Major H.B. Harrison, O.C. B Company, was clearly visible on one of the craft. Captain Gwydyr-Jones, using the Chinese boats as stepping stones, managed to get aboard the leading boat. The atmosphere was electric but he and Major Harrison managed to persuade the Japanese, already hemmed in by the Chinese boats, to stop. Gwydyr was 'not the sort of man who would stand by and

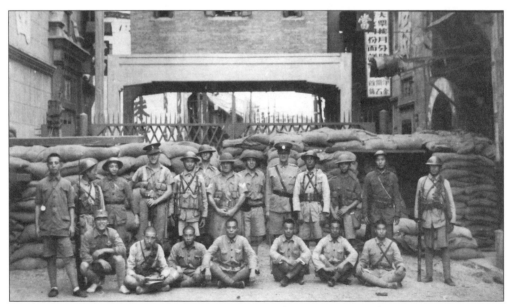

Liaison with the Chinese Army. (F.C. Minshull-Ford)

Captain F.C. Minshull-Ford on the Japanese front line. (F.C. Minshull-Ford)

The view from B Blockhouse. (F.C. Minshull-Ford)

A typical 2 R.W.F. post in Shanghai.

see men slaughtered when all the cards were stacked against them. Quite calmly he ordered his own machine gunner to extinguish the searchlights. For obvious reasons this was officially denied [later].'[12] Meanwhile the Commanding Officer and General Telfer-Smollett arrived on the scene just as two platoons from C Company, with loaded magazines, lined both banks. In the end, after long negotiations, the Japanese were forced to withdraw with considerable loss of face.[13]

Shortly before midnight on 30 October, Chinese troops began the evacuation of the godown, shepherded by C Company which was reinforced by two platoons from D Company. As the Chinese ran from the godown and crossed Thibet Road they were illuminated by searchlights and subjected to continuous Japanese machine gun fire. 'F' Blockhouse, which was in the direct line of fire, was vacated by C Company during the incident. Chinese casualties, which numbered about forty, were evacuated by C Company stretcher bearers, who first treated their wounds, to hospitals within the Settlement, but only about six or seven soldiers failed to make their escape. The remainder were disarmed and on the morning of the 31st, transferred to a concentration camp in the Settlement where they were guarded by the Russian battalion of the S.V.D.C. It was decided to reoccupy the Blockhouse and volunteers were called for. Practically the entire Company did so, but as only a small detachment was required it was decided that Lance Corporal Roberts 865, with Fusiliers Williams 66, Jones 62, Edwards 79 and Williams 88 should go. The reoccupation was achieved without casualties.

There were numerous reports of atrocities by both sides, but especially the Japanese:

> Stories of Chinese prisoners being used by the Japs for bayonet practice were commonplace … Photographers risked their lives to take photos of gruesome incidents happening within the battle area … Despite seeing the almost permanent fires raging in the fighting zone and hearing constant rifle, machine gun and shell fire one still tended to overlook the misery those fires and weapons inflicted on participants and inhabitants alike. It was as if we were in a cocoon completely protected from the dangers all around us. Perhaps in our ignorance we were sufficiently confident the Japanese would not attack us as long as we did not provoke them.[14]

Operations in the immediate vicinity of the sector now ceased and passed round to the western edge of the Settlement, towards Nanking, 170 miles (270 kilometres) north-east of Shanghai. The Chinese began to drift back to what was left of their homes and belongings. By 1 December the Sector garrison was reduced to one company, the

December 1937

The Potung district of the city on fire. (F.C. Minshull-Ford)

Artillery fire striking buildings in Shanghai. (F.C. Minshull-Ford)

The effect of artillery fire on the civilian population. (F.C. Minshull-Ford)

Chinese troops attacking Japanese positions in the Chapei district. (F.C. Minshull-Ford)

A Japanese armoured car coming up Range Road, firing on buildings to its left. (F.C. Minshull-Ford)

Fighting on the Chinese front line. (F.C. Minshull-Ford)

Chinese soldiers throw 'potato-masher' grenades from the Pantheon Theatre. (F.C. Minshull-Ford)

Japanese troops advancing through the city. (F.C. Minshull-Ford)

remainder of the battalion remaining in billets at one hour's notice, with one company at fifteen minutes' notice. On the 3rd a 'Victory March' by the Japanese was made through the International Settlement from West to East and a potentially serious situation was caused by a small bomb being thrown at the marching troops.[15]

The Sector garrison was further reduced to two platoons. A series of incidents caused by the alleged dropping of bombs on Japanese boats passing along the Creek continued to make negotiations difficult, and this resulted in further policing of this and other areas within the sector by the Shanghai Municipal Police who, since August, had cooperated closely with the battalion in the defence of the sector.

At Christmas C Company were on duty whilst the rest of the battalion stood down. An anonymous bard summed up their feelings as follows:

'Twas Christmas Day in the Sector,
And Ha! What a Shanghai Frost,
Three Captains called head and one tails, Sir,
And C Company lost the toss.

The lorry it comes pretty often,
And carries our food so to speak,
I'll bet you a hundred to one, Sir,
That it's carrying 'Bubble and Squeak".

It's not much use complaining,
We were on Active Service you see,
But at night when they come with the dinner,
There's another complaint, that's tea.

We've now got a coat called a Jerkin,
To keep out the cold and the frost,
If you don't stand six feet in your boots, Sir,
They just mark you absent or lost.

The Salvation Army has helped us,
By giving us bottled U.B.,
That's just a mistake on my part, Sir,
I mean with their cake and their Tea.

Well now my story is ended,
And I told you all that I can,
For I am now on the troopship Dunera,
And I'm off to a place called Sudan.[16]

Whilst the battalion was in Shanghai, the Rear Party in Hong Kong experienced another typhoon, this time a particularly serious one. It was first detected over the Pacific on 28 August. It struck the Colony at about 03.00 hrs on 2 September with gusts of up to 164 m.p.h. (260 k.p.h.) being recorded. Over six inches of rain fell in ten hours with 2.15 inches (63.5 mm) falling between 04.30 and 05.30 hrs. There was great loss of life in Taipo Market, but it was at sea that the worst effects were felt. The harbour was fuller than usual because of ships bringing refugees fleeing the conflict in China. Many of the smaller ships were carried from their moorings and thrown up on the sides of the harbour, others collided with larger ships. Most of the latter survived the storm but three whose moorings were interfered with by drifting vessels, including the luxury liner *Asama Maru*, were driven on to the shore. 90% of the yachts in their 'safe' haven at Causeway Bay suffered considerable damage. The barracks did not suffer too badly but the stables were blown away early on, fortunately after the ponies had been moved to the safety of an empty barrack room. Lance Corporal Falconer and Fusiliers Smith and Preece rowed out in a small dinghy to the assistance of two Chinese sailors seen clinging to the rigging of a sunken vessel in the bay. They were brought back through rough water in a state of collapse. Five of their colleagues were lost. It was estimated that about 2,000 lives were lost in the Colony and adjacent waters.[17]

Early in January 1938, information was received that the battalion was likely to return to Hong Kong at the beginning of February *en route* to the Sudan. In spite of the tense situation which the battalion had faced for much of the time whilst in Shanghai sport had continued to play a prominent part in battalion life. The Regimental Journal, *Y Ddraig Goch*, recorded that 'We can look back upon this season's rugger in Shanghai with complete satisfaction in regard to quality, variety, opportunity and results.'[18] The latter was borne out by the three XVs raised and the winning of thirteen out of the eighteen matches played. Football, hockey and polo were also played. As a token of their regard for the

January 1938

Cover of an unknown publication showing the alliance of the U.S.M.C. and R.W.F., Shanghai 1937.

The feu-de-joie being fired at the King's Birthday Parade in Shanghai, 1937. (R.W.F. Mus 9184)

battalion in the defence of Shanghai, the St David's Society, the representative body of the Welsh community in Shanghai, requested the honour of being allowed to present a Goat to the battalion. The presentation took place in the presence of a great number of people during the interval of the rugby match between the battalion and the Shanghai R.F.C., which the battalion won.[19]

Before departure the Commanding Officer received the following letter from General Officer Commanding British Troops, Shanghai:

> You have had a difficult task to perform in Shanghai during these last few months. You … did provide protection at a very critical period at the beginning of hostilities and during the hostilities under very trying circumstances. The fact that you succeeded in avoiding casualties in B Sector within a few yards of warlike operations reflects to your credit. You have, by your restraint and sound common sense, at all times maintained British prestige in Shanghai under the most difficult circumstances. I have a very vivid picture of your arrival in Shanghai … and it was an inspiring sight to see … your Regiment arriving opposite … and a spectacle which I shall never forget.
>
> Your departure from Shanghai will be regretted by the community at large, including the international garrisons, with whom you have co-operated. You will leave behind a reputation worthy of the traditions of your famous Regiment, which will long be remembered in Shanghai.[20]

Staff List, 2 R.W.F. Shanghai, 1937–1938

Lieutenant Colonel
D.M. Barchard
Major
D.H.W. Kirkby
T.C. Sharp
C.H. Edwards
H.B. Harrison MC
J.G. Bruxner-Randall
Captain
E.R. Freeman
H. Grismond Williams
Ll Gwydyr-Jones
E.A. Morris MM
W.P. Kenyon MC
M.W. Whittaker
Hon. G.R. Clegg-Hill
J.A.M. Rice-Evans
B.E. Horton
R.K. Allen
Quartermaster
Lt C. Jones DCM MM

Lieutenant
C.J.L. Lewis
T.A.G. Pritchard, Adjt
H.A.S. Clarke
W.S.A. Clough-Taylor
R.C.M. Kelly
N.R.G. Bosanquet
L.H. Yates
D.M.C. Pritchard
A.J. Lewis
F.C. Minshull-Ford
J.W. Riley
N.C. Stockwell
2nd Lieutenant
M.G. Harrison
R.L. Boyle
J.E.C. Hood
E.D.K. Menzies (Mar 38)

W.O. I
RSM S. Metcalfe
BM S. Hills ARCM
W.O. II
RQMS C. Burton
J. Harrison
R. Price
T. Grinham
L. Macey
CQMS
H. Armstrong
K. Kidgell
J. Green
C. Brooker
R. Wigham
Staff Serjeants
Band Sjt J. Flanagan
SIM A. Ingram
Drum Major J. Connor
Pnr Sgt W. Sollis
ORS V. Fraser
Cook Sgt C. Kretzschmar

iii. The Move to the Sudan

On 1 February the battalion paraded on the Racecourse in brilliant sunshine prior to leaving. It marched through the International
Settlement and Hongkew, along streets lined with thousands of people, led by the bands of the 4th and 6th Battalions U.S. Marines and supported by the band of the 2nd Loyals in the centre of the battalion. On reaching the quay it embarked on HT *Dunera*. She had been launched in 1937 and was only the second ship ever to have been designed as a troop transport. The first had been her sister ship, the *Dilwara*, which had been launched a year earlier.[21] She sailed the following morning for Hong Kong which was reached on the 5th. Five days later the battalion re-embarked and sailed on the 11th for the Sudan via Singapore and Colombo.[22]

St David's Day was celebrated on board ship on 28 February before reaching Port Sudan. Drummers went around early distributing leeks which had been smuggled on board at Hong Kong. The Officers and Serjeants waited on the men at lunch and afterwards the Officers were guests of the Warrant Officers' and Serjeants' Mess in the Second Class Smoke Room. Their ball that evening was held on the First and Second Class Sports Deck. It was preceded by a dinner to which were invited all Naval Petty Officers, R.A.F. Flight Serjeants and all the second class passengers. Because of an outbreak of measles, married Serjeants and their wives were prevented from attending. The leek eating ceremony was conducted with due dignity except that the toast to St David had to be drunk from a mess tin as all the mess silver was in the hold.[23]

iv. Sudan, 1938–1939

A description and map of the Sudan can be found in the Chapter dealing with 1 R.W.F.'s tour of duty there. In 1938, the Governor General was Lieutenant Colonel Sir George Stewart Symes.* The General Officer Commanding Troops in the Sudan was Major General H.E. Franklyn,† who was also Commandant of the Sudan Defence Force. His deputy was Brigadier R.G.W.B. Stone.‡

The move by rail of the battalion from Port Sudan to Khartoum began on 2 March 1938 and was completed by the 6th. On arrival it relieved the 1st Black Watch and then deployed with Battalion Headquarters, C Company, and A (Support) Company less
two platoons, at North Barracks, Khartoum, where an excellent new two-storey Officers' Mess had recently been built overlooking the Blue Nile. It was built as the direct result of pressure from Lieutenant Colonel E.O. Skaife when commanding 1 R.W.F. in Sudan from 1930 to 1932. D Company with 3 Platoon (M.G.) of A Company went to Atbara and B Company with 1 Platoon (M.G.) of A Company to Gebeit. The only other British battalion

---

*   Lieutenant Colonel Sir George Stewart Symes GCB GCMG DSO (1882–1962) was Governor of the Palestine North District from 1920 to 1925, Chief Secretary to the Government of Palestine from 1925 to 1928, Resident of Aden from 1928 to 1931, Governor of Tanganyika from 1931 to 1934 and Governor-General of the Anglo-Egyptian Sudan from 1934 to 1940.

†   Later General Sir Harold Edmund Franklyn KCB DSO MC (1885–1963). He commanded 5th Division in 1940 in the B.E.F. and then VIII Corps. He was C.-in-C. Home Forces from 1943.

‡   Later Lieutenant General Robert Graham William Hawkins Stone CB DSO MC (1890–1974).

in the Sudan was the 2nd Durham Light Infantry which was also based in Khartoum, in South Barracks. It was in turn replaced by the 1st East Surreys.[24]

B Company set off for Gebeit with some trepidation. Members of the 1st Battalion who had been there in 1932 had given unflattering reports of the conditions. It came as a pleasant surprise, therefore, to find things much better than expected. The hutted camp was on a bushy plain surrounded by rugged hills with a railway line running through the middle. The facilities included a cinema, squash court, tennis court and swimming pool. Gebeit was situated about 220 miles (350 kilometres) west-north-west of Atbara on the road to Port Sudan from which it was about 75 miles (120 kilometres) distant.

Atbara, the home of D Company, was in the desert about 200 miles (320 kilometres) north-west of Khartoum near the confluence of the Nile and Atbara Rivers. Although small, Atbara was an extremely important railway junction where the Cairo and Port Sudan lines met. It had a small British expat community of about a hundred. The barracks, pleasantly situated on the banks of the Nile, was better than

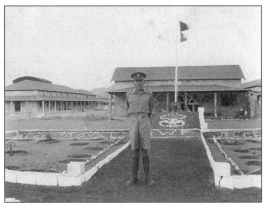

Battalion Headquarters in the Sudan.
(M.J.C. Stockwell)

A group of Fusiliers in the canteen at Khartoum, 1938.
(J. Underwood)

expected and had sports fields, tennis courts and a basket ball court. The nearby Atbara Sports Club boasted a swimming pool. The Company had its own transport comprising a *Ford* truck, six *Morris* Commercials, three donkeys, two horses and a charger.

Although training whilst in Sudan was restricted to section training because of the excessive heat, it was still possible to play sport and numerous competitions were staged, including cricket, football, hockey and swimming. The Sudan also provided an opportunity for Officers to participate in polo and pig sticking, the latter for the first time for many.

Nine Officers attended the Mulid El Nebi Festival at the Palace, Khartoum on 11 May. In May a rest camp was established at Port **May–June 1938** Sudan for those at Gebeit and parties of ten went each week for a break. On 5 June Captain M.W. Whittaker died of malaria at New Kideppo River, Equatoria Province. On the 12th the battalion attended a Memorial Service at Khartoum Cathedral. The King's Birthday Parade was held on 9 June on the Parade Ground at Khartoum North Barracks. At Gebeit, B Company was required to lay on the annual sports for the local natives, attended by the Governor General and the Commanding Officer. Some of the locals were fine athletes. The most spectacular events were a realistic mock battle with sticks, stones and shields, and a camel race.

Guard Picquet, Sudan 1938. (Thomas Williams)

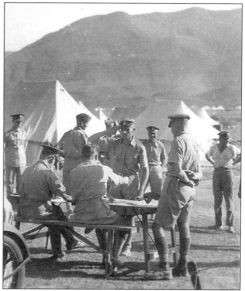

Pay parade, Sudan 1938. (Thomas Williams)

On 18 June instructions were received for the battalion to re-organise in accordance with the new 1938 establishment, as described in Chapter 3, however Support Company (A) was required to maintain trained personnel to man sixteen machine guns and thus continued with four platoons until leaving Sudan when it re-organised into three platoons. Also in 1938, in accordance with Army Council Instruction No. 398, the new rank of Warrant Officer Class III was introduced. The first to be promoted to the new rank were 4184195 CQMS H. Armstrong, 3906215 Serjeant J. Cutler, 4185263 Serjeant W. Beard and 4183041 Serjeant R. Rayner.[25]

On 21 June the battalion was warned for a move to Bareilly in India. Between the 28th and the 30th, companies exchanged locations. B Company took over from C in Khartoum, C took over from D at Atbara, and D replaced B at Gebeit.

On 29 September, 4189704 Fusilier A. Aubrey rescued a child who had fallen into the Nile. In the words of the Sudan Order:

> The Brigadier Commanding British Troops in the Sudan wishes to place on record the following act of gallantry performed by Fusilier A Aubrey … two children of El Daw Ahmed, Warder of the Khartoum Central Prison, were gathering wood on the Blue Nile River Bank when one, a small boy, fell in. Hearing the screams of the other child, Fusilier Aubrey dived into the river fully clothed and brought the child safely to the bank. Fusilier Aubrey's action involved considerable personal danger to himself owing to the river being in flood and the child's life was undoubtedly saved by his prompt action.[26]

The Annual Administrative Inspection was carried out by the G.O.C. on 29 October. On 24 November the battalion left Khartoum in two special trains for the slow and tedious journey to Port Sudan where two days later it embarked for India on the HT *Somersetshire*. It was relieved in the Sudan by the 1st Cheshires. Before leaving Khartoum all Officers present attended the Ramadan Bairam Levée which was held by the Governor General at the Palace. The ship was shared with the 2nd

November–December 1938

Queen's Own Cameron Highlanders en route from England to India. On 5 December the battalion disembarked at Bombay and entrained for Lucknow, its new destination, which it reached on 7 December, and moved into Outram Barracks.[27]

v. India

For a description and map of India see the Chapter dealing with the 1st Battalion's service from 1919 to 1930. In 1938, the Viceroy and Governor General of India was the Marquess of Linlithgow[*] and the Commander-in-Chief, General Sir Robert Cassels.[†] India was divided into four Commands: Northern, Western, Eastern and Southern. 2 R.W.F. was posted to 6 (Lucknow) Infantry Brigade which was commanded by Brigadier R.C. Money.[‡] The brigade was in Lucknow District, under the command of Major General F.L. Nicholson,[§] part of Eastern Command with its headquarters at Bareilly, where General Sir Harry Baird[¶] was the General Officer Commanding-in-Chief. In addition to the battalion, 6 Brigade comprised the 20th Lancers, 2nd Royal Berkshires, 3/2nd and 1/8th Punjabis. 2 R.W.F. had served with the latter recently in Hong Kong and with the Berkshires in B.A.O.R. ten years earlier.

India was the main overseas posting for the infantry and tours lasted for sixteen years and thus 2 R.W.F. did not expect to return home until 1954. Because of increased civil unrest caused by rising nationalism, aid to the civil power occupied more and more of a battalion's time. The quality of life for the single soldier had improved somewhat throughout the inter-war period. Electricity had reached the military cantonments, as had the cinema. Venereal disease was a major problem because, since garrison brothels had been banned in the 1890s, soldiers resorted to girls from the native quarter with all the attendant risks, although many towns had inspected brothels. The only alternative for many was to drink. Local leave could not be afforded on a man's pay and paid home leave could be taken only once in six years.

The battalion took part in the Proclamation Parade which was held on the Brigade Parade Ground, Lucknow on 2 January 1939. Between 3 January and 1 February collective training was carried out at Jhansi Camp. Twenty of the twenty-nine days were spent on exercise, including inter-battalion, brigade and inter-brigade ____January 1939____ exercises. This was quite an achievement as the battalion had had only nine days for training between its arrival in India and departure for Jhansi Camp. The last opportunity for collective training had been in Hong Kong in April 1937. As a result most commanders, particularly the most junior, were lacking in experience in leadership of troops in the field. No sooner had the battalion returned to Lucknow than it was put at six hours notice to move to Cawnpore to assist

---

[*]   Victor Alexander John Hope, 2nd Marquess of Linlithgow KG KT GCSI GCIE OBE TD PC (1887–1952).
[†]   General Sir Robert Archibald Cassels, GCB GCSI DSO (1876–1959) was the father of Field Marshal James Cassels, (1907–1996) Chief of the Imperial General Staff.
[‡]   Later Major General Robert Cotton Money CB MC (1888–1985), he commanded 15th (Scottish) Division during the early part of the Second World War.
[§]   Major-General Francis Lothian Nicholson CB DSO MC (1884–1953).
[¶]   General Sir Harry Beauchamp Douglas Baird KCB CMG CIE DSO (1877–1963).

2 R.W.F. pitching camp at Bamshawh. (R.W.F. Mus 3004)

in quelling communal disturbances. In the event their assistance was not required. The Brigade Commander carried out his Annual Administrative Inspection on 3 March.[28]

At the outbreak of war on 3 September the battalion was just concentrating again at Lucknow after avoiding the hot weather in the **September 1939** hill station of Landi-Kotal. On 11 September, Lieutenant Colonel E. Wodehouse* assumed command of the battalion. The battalion had just taken over Internal Security duties and was not, therefore, included in the order of battle of 6 (Lucknow) Infantry Brigade, the only formation in the area likely to see active service. All members of the battalion who were on leave in Britain were immediately posted to the 1st Battalion. A draft from the 8th Battalion soon brought 2 R.W.F. up to strength again.

Lucknow was little affected by the war although there was some excitement when orders were received to enclose a barrack block with barbed wire to form a prisoner of war cage. The excitement soon subsided when only eight Germans and two Italians and their families were confined in it, and they were soon moved elsewhere. The only other incident of note was a flag march to Gorakpur. For two days German radio described it as 'a brutal and tyrannical punitive expedition'. It was the battalion's first experience of an airlift when a number of Officers and men were transported from Lucknow to Gorakpur in antiquated Handley Page *Clive* aircraft.[29]

*   Later Brigadier Edmond Wodehouse CBE (1895–1960).

The Goat Major of the 2nd Battalion,
Christmas Day 1939. (R.W.F. Mus)

The Colours, King's Birthday parade, 1939.
(R.W.F. Mus)

vi. The Return to Britain

In early 1940 it became known that the battalion was likely to return home; the silver was packed for transport to Wrexham and the mess

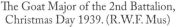

May 1940

fittings sold. After the fall of France in May 1940, 2 R.W.F. was chosen for combined operations training. This undoubtedly helped to preserve its identity as a Regular battalion throughout the war, and had a profound bearing on its performance when it saw action. The steady training, high morale, and comradeship was responsible, in part, for the surprisingly light casualties suffered by the battalion over the next five years. On 14 May, with two companies already back in the hill station 300 miles away at Ranikhet, the battalion was given five days' notice to move.[30] As it left Lucknow it was played out by the band of the 2nd Berkshires with whom a very special relationship had developed. It was a moving farewell for the battalion as the families were remaining behind in India with no idea of when they would be reunited. The Commanding Officer's wife, Persis Wodehouse, was a tower of strength comforting the wives and children and making arrangements for families to remain in contact. People were allowed to choose where to live and many chose Ranikhet, the popular hill station which they knew and which had a families' hospital. It was over two years before the families returned home. They eventually sailed from Bombay in November 1943 in the SS *Franconia*, a luxury liner converted for trooping. The voyage took five weeks and went via Durban, Capetown and Freetown, escorted at best by armed merchantmen.[31]

The battalion embarked on the SS *Aska* at Bombay on 6 June and joined a slow convoy for Durban. Cape Town was reached on the 23rd **June–July 1940** and many South Africans turned up to invite members of the battalion to spend the day at their homes. After calling at Takoradi for water and at Freetown for coal, the *Aska* sailed alone for a few days to a rendezvous in the Atlantic with a fast convoy for home. On 16 July she docked at Liverpool with the green hills of Denbighshire plainly visible.[32]

Staff List, 2 R.W.F. Sudan and India, 1938–1940

Lieutenant Colonel
D.M. Barchard (to Jul 39)
E. Wodehouse (17 Jul 39)
Major
D.H.W. Kirkby
T.C. Sharp (to Jan 39)
C.H. Edwards
H.B. Harrison MC (to Oct 38)
H.F. Garnons-Williams (to Oct 38)
T.S. Griffiths (Mar 39) (to Feb 40)
H. D'O. Lye (Feb 40)
J.G. Bruxner-Randall
W.H. Bamfield (Nov 38)
R.G. Davies-Jenkins (Mar 39)
Captain
J.G. Vyvyan (Nov 38)
J.H. Liscombe (Nov 38–Feb 40)
H. Grismond Williams
Ll Gwydyr-Jones (Maj Aug 38) (to Nov 38)
E.A. Morris MM
W.P. Kenyon MC (Maj Aug 38) (to Feb 39)
M.W. Whittaker (died 5 Jun 38)
Hon. G.R. Clegg-Hill (to Oct 38)
J.A.M. Rice-Evans
B.E. Horton (Maj Aug 38) (to Dec 39)
R.K. Allen
E.R. Freeman (Maj Feb 39) (to Feb 40)
H. de B. Prichard (Nov 38–Aug 39)
H. Clement-Davies (Feb 40)
Quartermaster
Capt C. Jones DCM MM

Lieutenant
T.A.G. Pritchard, Adjt to Nov 39 (Capt Jan 39) (to Dec 39)
H.A.S. Clarke (Capt Jun 38) (to Oct 38)
W.S.A. Clough-Taylor (to May 38)
R.C.M. Kelly (to Nov 38)
N.R.G. Bosanquet (to Nov 38)
L.H. Yates (Capt Aug 38) (to Nov 38)
H.J.E. Jones (Feb 40)
P.A.E. Jones (Feb 40)
J.W. Gregory (Nov 39)
D.M.C. Pritchard (to Dec 39)
A.J. Lewis (Capt Aug 39) (to Sep 39)
B.P. Doughty-Wylie (Mar 39)
J.E. Vaughan (Mar 39)
H.E. Pollicott (Jan 40)
F.C. Minshull-Ford (to Oct 38)
J.W. Riley (to Feb 40)
N.C. Stockwell (Capt Aug 38) (to Nov 38)
2nd Lieutenant
F.B.E. Cotton (Jun 38) (Lt Jan 40)
M.G. Harrison (Lt Jan 40)
R.L. Boyle (Lt Jan 39) (to Sep 39)
J.E.C. Hood (Lt Aug 39) (to Sep 39)
E.D.K. Menzies (Mar 38) (to Sep 39)
D.J.O. Thomas (Feb 39–Feb 40)
G.F.T.B. Dickson (Sep 38) (Lt and Adjt Nov 39)
I.W. Pitcairn-Campbell (Mar 39)
M.B. Howard-Williams (Apr 40)
S.R. Pearson (Feb 40)
P.C. Lucking (Feb 40)
J.A.B. Dickson (Sep 39)
R.C.H. Barber (Sep 39)
G. Demetriadi (Feb 40)
N.L.A. Vosper (Feb 40)

W.O. I
RSM S. Metcalfe
BM S. Hills ARCM
W.O. II
RQMS C. Burton
J. Harrison
R. Price
T. Grinham
L. Macey
J. Green
W.O. III
H. Armstrong
J. Cutler
W. Beard
R. Rayner
CQMS
W. Cowan
J. Flanagan
H. Kidgell
J. Green
C. Brooker
R. Wigham
Staff Serjeants
Band Sjt F. Payne
SIM A. Ingram
Drum Major J. Connor
Pnr Sgt W. Sollis
ORS G. Williams
Cook Sgt C. Kretzschmar
Attached
P.M. Chetwynd-Palmer *I.A.* (Sep 39–Jan 40)
J.R. Tilly *I.A.* (Sep 39–Jan 40)
H.O. Lincoln *I.A.* (Sep 39–Jan 40)

Notes

1   *Army Quarterly* 37/150 (1938).
2   *Memoirs of Valentine Frederick Loos Grevitt, Royal Welch Fusiliers, Shanghai 14th Aug 1937–Jan 1938* in R.W.F./Mus. No page numbering.
3   Grevitt, *Memoirs.*
4   2 R.W.F. Digest of Service.
5   *Shanghai Evening Post,* 19 October 1937.
6   *Y Ddraig Goch,* October 1937, p. 29.
7   Grevitt, *Memoirs.*
8   *Y Ddraig Goch,* October 1937, p. 29.
9   2 R.W.F. Digest of Service.
10 2 R.W.F. Digest of Service.
11 Grevitt, *Memoirs.*
12 Grevitt, *Memoirs.*
13 2 R.W.F. Digest of Service.
14 Grevitt, *Memoirs.*
15 2 R.W.F. Digest of Service.
16 *Y Draig Goch,* Spring 1938.
17 *Time* Magazine, Monday 10 September 1937. See also 'The Typhoon of September 1st to 2nd' in *The Hong Kong Naturalist,* March 1938.
18 *Y Draig Goch,* Spring 1938, p. 42.
19 2 R.W.F. Digest of Service.
20 *Y Ddraig Goch,* Spring 1938, p. 38.
21 H.C.B. Rogers, *Troopships and their History* (London, 1963) p. 179.
22 2 R.W.F. Digest of Service.
23 2 R.W.F. Digest of Service.
24 2 R.W.F. Digest of Service.
25 2 R.W.F. Digest of Service.
26 Sudan Order No. 241.
27 2 R.W.F. Digest of Service.
28 2 R.W.F. Digest of Service.
29 2 R.W.F. Digest of Service.
30 T.N.A. WO 166/4625, 2 R.W.F. War Diary 4 June 1940–31 July 1941.
31 Veronica Bamfield, *Cornucopia* (London, 2006) pp. 222–223.
32 T.N.A. WO 166/4625, 2 R.W.F. War Diary 4 June 1940–31 July 1941.

Chapter 12

The Territorial Battalions, 1919–1938

---

i. The Formation of the Territorial Army

At the close of the Great War, the Territorial Force was placed in suspended animation on 25 February 1919. It had already been decided by the Army Council, however, that it would be re-constituted as part of the permanent military forces of the Crown.[1] The Volunteer Force was allowed to continue until the Peace was signed at Versailles in 1919 although no general training was to take place. Its strength was recorded as 8,952 Officers and 238,453 men on 1 January 1919. It was disbanded on 1 September 1919.[2] Its Officers and men eventually received a letter of thanks from the King – 'a lukewarm printed message of thanks signed in an unintelligible hand' according to one recipient – and the right to retain uniforms and for Officers to retain honorary ranks.[3]

The task of resurrecting the Territorials before their wartime experience was lost fell to Winston Churchill, the newly appointed Secretary of State for War. Churchill had to solve the problem of finding some form of obligation acceptable to the Territorials yet flexible enough for the War Office to deploy them overseas. It was not until January 1920 that the Cabinet finally agreed the terms to be offered. The force was to be recruited on a four-year term of engagement with provision for re-engagement for one to four years up to the age of 40 (50 for N.C.Os). All those under 35 years of age would be liable to serve overseas but only after regular reservists had been called out by proclamation of imminent danger or great emergency, and after Parliament had legislated to authorise the actual despatch of Territorials abroad. Churchill promised that Territorial formations would retain their integrity in wartime. In what became known as 'the pledge' he effectively prevented the drafting of Territorials where they were most needed, in limited wars. An annual bounty of £5 was to be paid to those completing fifty drills, attending fifteen days' annual camp and firing an annual musketry course. Recruits would receive up to £4.[4] The legislation that gave effect to these proposals was the Territorial Army and Militia Act of 1921,[5] which turned the Territorial Force into the Territorial Army, and also returned the name 'Militia' to the Special Reserve. Recruiting had already opened, on 1 February 1920, five days after the Cabinet made its decision. The new organisation was to comprise fourteen infantry divisions and fourteen mounted brigades, but units were only to be recruited to 60% of their establishment.[6] These divisions would include 168 battalions of infantry.[7]

Churchill's decision to reorganise the Yeomanry because of their declining value in modern warfare led to the transfer of the Denbighshire Yeomanry, which had become the 24th Battalion

The Royal Welch Fusiliers in 1917, to the Royal Artillery. The Montgomeryshire Yeomanry, which had amalgamated with the Welsh Horse Yeomanry at the same time to become the 25th Battalion, was merged with the 7th Battalion The Royal Welch Fusiliers in 1920. The Welsh Horse Yeomanry which had been raised in 1914 was disbanded.

ii. 53rd (Welsh) Division

All Territorial units in Wales came under the command of Headquarters 53rd (Welsh) Division in Shrewsbury, the G.O.C. of which was also Commander Welsh Area which included Shropshire, Cheshire, Herefordshire and Monmouthshire and which was one of the three Areas which comprised Western Command; the others being West and East Lancashire. The division consisted of three infantry brigades, 158 (North Wales) in Wrexham, 159 (Welsh Border) at Shrewsbury and 160 (South Wales) at Cardiff. There were also three field brigades of Royal Artillery, one in Monmouthshire and Radnorshire, and two in Glamorgan; and the usual support arms and services including engineers, transport, ordnance and medical units. The Divisional Headquarters was very lightly manned, for apart from the G.O.C. and his aide-de-camp, there were only two staff Officers, a G.S.O. II (Major or Captain) and a Staff Captain, and a small number of N.C.Os. All other staff were either Territorials doing their jobs part-time, or civilians.[8]

The G.O.C.s of the Division during the period 1919–1940 were as follows:

Major General C.J. Deverell CB	July 1919–March 1922
Major General Sir A.A. Montgomery KCMG CB	March 1922–June 1923
Major General T.O. Marden CB CMG	June 1923–June 1927
Major General T.A. Cubitt CB CMG DSO	June 1927–October 1928
Major General C.B. Deeds CB CMG DSO	October 1928–June 1930
Major General C.J.C. Grant CB DSO	June 1930–December 1932
Major General J.K. Dick-Cunyngham CB CMG DSO	December 1932–June 1935
Major General G. Thorpe CB CMG DSO	June 1935–June 1939
Major General B.T. Wilson DSO	June 1939–July 1941

iii. 158 (North Wales) Infantry Brigade, later 158 (Royal Welch) Infantry Brigade

All R.W.F. battalions in North Wales were placed under the command of Headquarters 158 (North Wales) Infantry Brigade based at Hightown Barracks, Wrexham. In 1924, 158 Brigade became 158 (Royal Welch) Infantry Brigade.[9] The Brigade Headquarters was as thinly manned as the Divisional Headquarters, with only one Regular Officer, the Brigade Major, and that post not always manned but filled by a Territorial. During the period, the Commanders were as follows:

Colonel W.R.N. Maddocks CB CMG DSO	1919–1923
Colonel A.C. Girdwood CMG DSO	1923–1926
Colonel C.C. Norman CMG DSO Late *R.W.F.*	1926–1929

Colonel W.H. Freestun CMG DSO	1929–1932
Colonel B.E. Murray DSO	1932–1935
Colonel H.W.D. McCarthy-O'Leary DSO MC	1935–1938
Brigadier E.O. Skaife OBE Late *R.W.F.*	1938–1939
Brigadier J.P. Duke DSO MC	1939–1940

iv. The Royal Welch Fusiliers in North Wales

The Regiment retained its four battalions which had served with such distinction during the war, the 4th in France, and the 5th, 6th and 7th in Gallipoli, Egypt and Palestine. Their new titles were:

4th (Denbighshire) Battalion The Royal Welch Fusiliers (T.F.)
5th (Flintshire) Battalion The Royal Welch Fusiliers (T.F.)
6th (Carnarvonshire and Anglesey) Battalion The Royal Welch Fusiliers (T.F.)
7th (Montgomeryshire) Battalion The Royal Welch Fusiliers (T.F.)

In 1921, T.F. became T.A., as outlined above. In 1937, Army Order 168 amended the titles of the 6th and 7th Battalions to:

6th (Caernarvonshire & Anglesey) Battalion, The Royal Welch Fusiliers (T.A.)
7th (Merioneth & Montgomeryshire) Battalion, The Royal Welch Fusiliers (T.A.)

Battalions were organised on the same basis as regular units, but with a smaller establishment and a small number of regular staff: the Adjutant, Quartermaster, Regimental Sergeant Major and one Permanent Staff Instructor, a sergeant or W.O. II, per company. With four battalions to man, these P.S.Is sometimes came from the Welsh Guards, which had no T.A. unit in its order of battle.

Throughout the period, battalions opened and closed outstations at various times; these are summarised in the table below:

Battalion/Company	Main Location	Detachments
4 R.W.F.		
Bn H.Q. & H.Q. Company/Wing	Poyser Street, Wrexham	
A (M.G., or S, Coy 1930–1938)	Poyser Street, Wrexham	
B	Broughton	Brymbo, Summerhill, Llay Main Colliery
C	Ruabon	Chirk, Acrefair
D	Denbigh	Rhos, Corwen, Rhosllanerchrugog, Ruthin
5 R.W.F.		
Bn H.Q. & H.Q. Company/Wing	Mold	Rossett, Hawarden, Flint, Caergwrle
A	Mold	Northrop, Buckley, Caergwrle
B	Rhyl	Prestatyn, Abergele, St Asaph

Battalion/Company	Main Location	Detachments
C	Flint	Holywell
D (M.G., or S, Coy 1930–1938)	Hawarden	Connah's Quay, Shotton
6 R.W.F.		
Bn H.Q. & H.Q. Company/Wing	The Barracks, Caernarfon	Conwy
A	The Barracks, Caernarfon	Bangor, Llanberis, Penygroes, Bethesda
B	Porthmadog	Pwllheli, Criccieth
C	Conwy	Trefriw, Penmaenmawr, Dolgarrog, Menai Bridge
D (M.G., or S, Coy 1930–1938)	Holyhead	Beaumaris
7 R.W.F.		
Bn H.Q. & H.Q. Company/Wing	Newtown, Monts.	Llanidloes
A	Llanidloes	
B	Towyn, Mer.	Aberdovey, Dolgellau, Llanwddyn, Llansantffraid-y-Mechain
C	Welshpool	Llanfyllin, Llanfair Caereinion
D (M.G., or S, Coy 1930–1938)	Machynlleth	Montgomery, Llangurig (unofficial)

v. Territorial Service, 1919–1938

The T.A. suffered from severe problems for much of the inter-war period. The lack of a clear role was the first, with no commitment to foreign service and no resources available for home defence. The austerity drives of 1926 to 1936 meant that old equipment was not replaced while pay and allowances remained static. In 1922 the annual bounty reduced to £3 and £2/10/-;[10] in 1926 it was abolished,[11] and replaced by 'proficiency pay', worth only half as much and issued at a flat rate to all N.C.Os and soldiers who fulfilled the old bounty conditions;[12] moreover the cost of attending drills had to be carried by individuals. In 1922, T.A. brigades lost their brigade majors.[13] In 1926, annual camp was cancelled on economy grounds for many units and in 1932,[14] for all units. Proficiency pay was again reduced in 1927, to 30/-, and only saved at all after a hard fight. Overall T.A. strength declined, as a result, from over 140,000 in 1926 to 130,000 in 1929.[15]

Because of the relatively thin population of North Wales, few companies, other than those in Wrexham, were confined to a single location. Most had at least two, and some as many as four, outstations in order to provide easy access to Territorial soldiers in an age when car ownership was unusual, and public transport good but slow. In order to man a battalion fully, T.A. centres or Drill Halls had to be within walking or cycling distance of home for the men. Parades usually took place on one evening each week, supplemented in the summer months by additional range practices. One weekend per month (Saturday midday to Sunday evening) was also usually devoted to training. As well as Camp (see below) additional short Easter Camps or courses for specialists, Officers and N.C.Os were frequent in order that Officers and men could mark up the required number of days for their bounty. The annual commemoration of the Armistice on 11 November, and Remembrance Sunday, were always major events for T.A. battalions, which were on parade at war memorials throughout their areas.

Firing on a gallery range at Altcar, 1932. (R.W.F. Mus 8686e)

Nonconformism remained a problem for T.A. units trying to find recruits, as it had been before and in the early months of the Great War. Ministers of Religion were generally against military service, as were the left-wing Labour politicians who represented them. They were particularly opposed to parades and training on Sundays, however as most men worked at least five-and-a-half days, Sunday was the only day for T.A. activities.[16] Even with war looming, Buckley Council, for example, faced considerable opposition in granting permission for the 60th Anti-Tank Regiment to practice gun drill on their common on a Sunday.[17]

On the other hand, Wales was for the greater part dry on Sundays – that is, no alcohol was served – with no pubs open at all. A T.A. Drill Hall was one of the few places where men could get a drink on a Sunday, after training, and in spite of the hellfire rhetoric of their preachers, many men joined for this reason. The social life of T.A. battalions generally was very active, with company dances, parties and dinners being common especially during the winter months, in what were then more remote small towns and villages across North and Mid Wales. As well as the annual Sergeants' Mess Ball and the Officers' Mess Dinner for St David's Day, all companies would hold an annual dinner and prize-giving, followed by dancing. Even on a week-day drill night, there were social attractions to T.A. service:

> When "Drills" have finished for the evening, there is a dash for the door. No, not the exit for home … we enter the recreation room. It is like "The Movies"; the scene changes very suddenly and the sight that now meets the eye is strangely different. the room is taste-fully decorated, the colour scheme most soothing to the eye; plush curtains hang from the windows and doors; a quartet are doing their best to carry out the hints of Davis, the Snooker Champion, on "How to play Snooker" … at another corner of the room several band and drummer boys are gathered round the wireless listening to the B.B.C. jokes. Others are playing draughts and dominoes … the room boasts a fine library and the atmos-phere is one of ease and comfort. The room is open every evening from 6 p.m. to 10 p.m. Who wouldn't be in the Territorial Army?[18]

Sport was always a popular draw in terms of recruiting; shooting – full bore and small bore – and football were most popular in the R.W.F. battalions. A national T.A. Football Challenge

Cup was presented by Mr Harold Sumner OBE JP in 1922. R.W.F. units reached the final a number of times between then and 1938, as follows:[19]

Season	Match Details	Score
1922–1923	4 R.W.F. beat 4 R. Sussex	2-1
1923–1924	6 Hamps R. beat 7 R.W.F.	2-1
1930–1931	4 R.W.F. beat London Scottish	3-2
1931–1932	Bucks Battalion beat 5 R.W.F.	4-3
1934–1935	Devon & Cornwall Hy Bde R.A. beat 7 R.W.F.	1-0
1936–1937	7 R.W.F. beat Bucks Battalion	2-0
1937–1938	7 R.W.F. beat Bucks Battalion	7-3

The 1st and 7th Battalion football teams, 5 May 1938. (R.W.F. Mus 8686e)

The Prince of Wales donated a shield to be competed for at platoon level across the 53rd (Welsh) Division, usually at Camp. The various competitions included platoon and section formations/tactics, field signals, *Lewis* gun handling, guard and sentry duties, and platoon drill. The Regiment's T.A. battalions achieved the following successes:

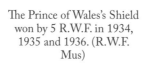

The Prince of Wales's Shield won by 5 R.W.F. in 1934, 1935 and 1936. (R.W.F. Mus)

	4 R.W.F.	5 R.W.F.	6.R.W.F.	7 R.W.F.
1932			1st in drill	
1933			1st in drill	
1934		Shield Winners		
1935		Shield Winners		
1936		Shield Winners		
1937			1st in L.M.G.	1st in Signals
1938	Shield Winners	1st in drill		

In 1922, Army Order 338 changed the regulations related to the Colours of Territorial battalions; from now on, in recognition of their service during the Great War and their full integration into the military forces of the Crown, they would be permitted to carry all the Battle Honours of their parent Regiment, not just those won by the Volunteers or Territorials. Previous to this, the four R.W.F. battalions had all carried the sole Battle Honour *South Africa 1899–1902* on their Colours, which had all been presented at Windsor on 19 June 1909.

In 1921, the coal miners came out in a national strike. It was feared that this might develop into a General Strike and the Regular Reserve was called up on 8 April; however the strike was resolved and the reserves stood down. During the General Strike of 1926, the Government called for volunteers for an armed military force; those from North Wales assembled outside Colwyn Bay at Rhuddlan Camp.[20] In addition the Royal Defence Corps in North Wales assembled at Kinmel Camp.[21]

In 1930, T.A. battalions were reorganised into three rifle companies and an M.G. Company, in the same way as Regular battalions. The M.G. Platoon in H.Q. Wing was abolished. This reduced the overall establishment of a battalion from 656 all ranks to 604.[22] In 1939, the establishment was amended again, in line with the Regular Battalion Establishment, to H.Q. Company with six platoons and four rifle companies.

In 1931 a new Efficiency Decoration for Officers and Medal for Other Ranks was introduced, designed to replace a number of British, Dominion and Colonial decorations and medals. Officers had to complete twenty years continuous service to qualify, but war counted double, and they received the post-nominals 'TD'. For non-commissioned ranks, twelve years continuous service was required; clasps were awarded after eighteen and twenty-four years. War service again counted double.[23]

In March 1936, War Minister Duff Cooper, faced with German rearmament, increased spending for the first time. Proficiency pay was increased to £3 along with a weapon training allowance of 10/- and an allowance for extra drills, restoring the overall payment to £5; travel allowances were also paid and a marriage separation allowance introduced for those over 23, rather than 26.[24] In the following year, extra clothing, including shirts, socks, ground-sheets and canvas overalls, was issued; battalions also received an issue of trucks. Finally, the *Territorial Magazine* was launched, a well-illustrated journal with useful and practical articles as well as reviews of the international situation, historical material and book reviews. These measures at least arrested an overall decline in numbers.[25] On 1 October 1938, the overall strength of the T.A. had risen to 186,689, with 53rd (Welsh) Division at 93.6% of its establishment of 9,500.[26] The Military Correspondent of *The Times* had noted the year before, that:

Units are in a much healthier condition than the shrinkage of their numbers might suggest. The type of Officer and man is better than it has been for some time past; training has definitely improved; and the closer association that has been brought about between Regulars and Territorials has produced good results… The biggest problem is employers who do not support their employees attending training and camps.[27]

1937 was the last year that the T.A. relied chiefly on horse transport. From Camp that year, hired civilian transport was used pending the issue of military vehicles; many units held special parades to mark the change, and the annual competitions for transport and Officers' chargers at Camp were marked by a particular poignancy.[28]

In 1938, many infantry units were converted to other duties, especially anti-aircraft artillery, searchlight and anti-tank artillery. Among these was the 5th Battalion The Royal Welch Fusiliers, which became 60th (R.W.F.) Anti-Tank Regiment R.A.* Under Leslie Hore-Belisha, the question of a role for the T.A. was at last addressed with four Territorial divisions being earmarked for service on the continent within six months of the outbreak of a war, while five others were assigned to air defence. T.A. infantry brigades, including 158 (Royal Welch) Infantry Brigade, were reduced from four battalions to three.[29]

The first test of the T.A. was the Czechoslovak Crisis of 1938, during which full mobilisation of the T.A. anti-aircraft divisions took place. In spite of bad weather, telegrams, telephone calls and the use of key men brought thirty searchlight battalions and twenty-four artillery regiments to full manning between 14.30 hrs on 23 September and dawn on 24 September.[30]

vi. Annual Camps

Camp was the highlight of the training year and usually lasted for two weeks. It was one of the few times when scattered units could be brought together and work as formed bodies, all other training being carried out on a company or even platoon basis, except for Officers' and N.C.Os' study days. It was thus a strenuous time for the regular staff, for the organisation began months before and the clearing up went on for weeks afterwards. Every man was expected to attend unless he could produce a valid reason, such as the refusal of his employer to release him, in which case he would discharge his Camp liability on a course or attachment. Failure to provide a valid excuse would result in a charge of absence, usually followed by discharge.

It was customary to locate a Camp where amenities were good and where a married man's family might also come in order to be close by; seaside towns like Aberystwyth, Porthcawl and Portmadog were therefore much favoured. Porthcawl was a particular favourite, being a large town with plenty of amusements, good bathing, and local training areas. On two occasions during the period, Camp was in the Isle of Man which from the point of view of interest and amenities was a great success, however from the military point of view it was less happy. The ranges and training areas were a long way from the campsite and the roads were few, and bad.[31]

---

*   The other infantry battalions converted to this role were 4 King's Own, 5 Surreys, 4 D.W.R. and 6 Hampshires; five Yeomanry regiments were also converted, as were a number of Regular and Territorial field regiments R.A.

The 53rd Divisional Camp in 1922. (R.W.F. Mus 8686d)

A kit inspection at Annual Camp some time in the 1920s. (R.W.F. Mus 8686d)

158 (Royal Welch) Brigade on parade at Annual Camp, Porthcawl, 1930. (R.W.F. Mus 4157)

Brigade orders group at Camp in the Isle of Man. (R.W.F. Mus 8686d)

Camp was twice cancelled between the wars. The first time was in 1926 during the General Strike, when it was thought possible that the T.A. might be called in to support the civil authorities. However this did not happen, partly because the legal grounds for such a move were dubious, and partly because many Territorials, especially from mining areas like Wrexham, were involved in the dispute. The second was in 1932 when after the financial crash of 1931, large-scale economies were necessary. At the same time, issues of new equipment such as light-automatics, wireless sets, mortars, 15-cwt trucks and Carriers were severely curtailed.[32]

There were three types of Camp during the inter-war years: first, Divisional Camps included supporting arms. These were never a success as the training areas were always too small for the 15,000 or so troops taking part. They did not produce enough interest for the soldiers, either in training or recreation. Finally they were disliked by local people as they were usually held during the tourist season. During the 53rd (Welsh) Division's Camp at Aberystwyth in 1922, for example, *The Times* reported that thousands of soldiers who had received their pay were in the town on the night of Friday 4 August. Two men were arrested by the police, which occasioned a riot by 500 men outside the main Police Station.[33] Secondly there were the more usual Brigade Camps, with three or four battalions – perhaps 3,000 men – in one location. Finally there were Battalion Camps, with a single unit in one location.[34]

Lieutenant, later Brigadier, H.S.K. Mainwaring recalled Camp at Ramsey in the Isle of Man in 1938:

> Territorial Camps were not the luxury affairs they have become in recent years. Just rows of bell-tents; sixteen per company, which meant eight or ten men in each with the Sergeants sharing one tent and the C.S.M. and C.Q.M.S. in another, with the Company Office at the end of the line. Each man had three blankets and a palliasse which was filled with straw on arrival, and a cape ground sheet which had to keep his bedding and himself dry when it was raining, an impossible task for one small piece of equipment and so one or the other inevitably got wet. The rifles were stacked in a 'spider' round the tent-pole, all else had to be on the ground. There was no hot water, baths or showers and no drying facilities. Shaving and washing had to be done in the open from a row of taps in a long pipe above a long line of narrow trestle tables. There was no Army Catering Corps or modern cooking appliances. All cooking was done in the open in Soyer stoves or in dixies over trench fires fed with logs. The standard of meals in each company depended upon the ability of each to recruit men able and willing to cook and get up at about 4 a.m. to light the fires and get the breakfast on the go in the open by 7 a.m.[35]

T.A. Camps were usually supported by the Regular battalions when at home. In 1929, Lord Silsoe recorded that it had become 'an understood thing' in the Regiment that not only would every young Territorial Officer attend a course or be attached to a Regular battalion, or to the Depot; but also that junior regular Officers, Warrant Officers and N.C.Os would help out at Camp:

> One year [between 1928 and 1931] … we had eight regular Officers attached to the brigade. Of these, two were outstanding – Major Eric Skaife and Major Bruxner-Randall. The latter got himself appointed year after year as Brigade Major [the permanent post having been abolished – see above] and Eric Skaife went round for a similar period to each of the battalions, mainly training Officers and N.C.O.s and even commanding platoons

on training. Liaison on a similar scale was arranged between the sergeants' messes – each battalion had a minimum of an RSM and three sergeants or higher attached as instructors. After a short period we had a regular as adjutant.[36]

The Order Book of 6 R.W.F. from 1926 to 1938, for example, gives a list of around a dozen Officers and N.C.Os attached to the battalion for Camp.[37] Camps from 1921 to 1938 were held as follows:

Year	Location	Remarks	Brigade Commander
1920	Rhyl		Colonel W.R.N. Maddocks
1921	Rhyl	6 R.W.F. at Blackpool	CB CMG DSO
1922	Lovesgrove Camp, Aberystwyth	53rd Division Camp	
1923	Porthcawl	Tented.	
1924	Llandudno		Colonel A.C. Girdwood
1925	Ramsey, I.O.M.	53rd Division Camp	CMG DSO
1926	No Brigade or Divisional Camp; 6 R.W.F. at Dyffryn	General Strike	
1927	Pwllheli	Tented. 6 R.W.F. at Dyffryn	Colonel C.C. Norman CMG
1928	Porthcawl	Tented. 6 R.W.F. at Pwllheli	DSO
1929	Porthcawl	Tented.	
1930	Porthcawl	Tented.	Colonel W.H. Freestun CMG
1931	Tenby	Tented.	DSO
1932	No Camp	Austerity measure	
1933	Lovesgrove Camp, Aberystwyth		Colonel B.E. Murray DSO
1934	Porthcawl	Tented.	
1935	Tenby	6 R.W.F. to Porthcawl in June; remainder in July/August	Colonel H.W.D. McCarthy-O'Leary DSO MC
1936	Douglas, I.O.M. Kinmel Camp, Denbighshire	4 and 5 R.W.F. 6 and 7 R.W.F.	
1937	Hereford	158 and 159 Brigades; 160 at Abergavenny	
1938	Ramsey, I.O.M.		Brigadier E.O. Skaife OBE

vii. The 4th (Denbighshire) Battalion, 1920–1938

The 4th Battalion, with its headquarters and H.Q. Wing at Wrexham, was under the command of Lieutenant Colonel C.H.R. Crawshay DSO. Its four companies were at Wrexham (A Company), Brymbo (B Company), Ruabon (C Company) and Denbigh (D Company). By the time that the battalion went to Camp in July 1920, it had recruited to its full established strength, the first T.A. battalion in Wales to do so and the second-strongest battalion in the entire T.A. after 4th K.S.L.I.[38] The battalion opened and closed a number of outstations in all company areas during the period, as shown in the Staff List.

158 Brigade, less 6 R.W.F., went to Camp for the first time post-war at Rhyl from 23 July to 6 August 1921. The strength of the 4th Battalion was sixteen Officers and 590 Other Ranks. Inspections were carried out by G.O.C. Western Command, Lieutenant General Sir Beauvoir

de Lisle KCB KCMG DSO MC, and Major General Deverell, the divisional commander.

In 1922, although recruited well up to establishment, the 4th Battalion was forced to close drill halls at Ruabon, Llangollen and Summerhill for economic reasons. Annual Camp was at Aberystwyth from 29 July to 12 August. Prior to going to camp Church Parades were held at Acrefair by C Company and at Broughton by B Company. The battalion deployed to camp at Aberystwyth with 614 all ranks. After a six hour train journey it arrived at Aberystwyth at 23.00 hrs and then marched the two miles (3 kilometres) to Lovesgrove where an excellent camp was found under canvas. In the first few days the Commanding Officer, Lieutenant Colonel Crawshay, was taken ill and returned home. His place was taken by Major G.C.W. Westbrooke MC, the Senior Major. The first week was devoted to drill and platoon and company training. On 3 August the Colonel of the Regiment, General Sir Francis Lloyd GCVO KCB DSO, arrived. He was entertained to dinner in the Officers' Mess and the next morning

The Colours, 4 R.W.F., Victory Parade London, 19 July 1919. (R.W.F. Mus 5262); King's Colour, Captain J.M. Davies MC; Regimental Colour, Captain C. Williams; escorts are CSM A.G. Otten DCM (Brymbo), Sergeant S. Davies DCM MM (Wrexham).

he inspected the battalion which was drawn up in line. After the inspection close column was formed and the battalion marched past in column, returning in quarter column. The Colonel complimented the battalion on its war record, its fine appearance and steadiness on parade, and its success in being one of the first Territorial battalions to reach full strength after re-forming. On Bank Holiday Monday the battalion route march through Aberystwyth was watched by thousands of visitors. The last week was devoted to battalion training and preparation for the visit by the divisional commander on 10 August Major General Sir A.A. Montgomery KCMG CB. On the following day the performance was repeated for the G.O.C. Western Command.

The 4th Battalion scored a notable victory in beating 7 R.W.F. to win the Brigade Football Competition and went on to win the Divisional Cup. The team was:

Privates D.T. Roberts, R. Griffiths, E. Banks, E. Davies, E. Roberts, C. Pierce
Lance Corporals J. Green, T. Millington
Corporal A. Webb, J.R. Hughes
Sergeant H. Webb

The following members of the battalion also won their fights in the finals of the Brigade Boxing Competition:

Flyweight, Private A. Flanaghan
Bantamweight, Private F. Hays
Middleweight, Corporal – Hodnott[39]

The 4th Battalion St David's Dinner was held at the Wynnstay Hotel, Wrexham on 2 March 1923. Thirty Officers attended and amongst the guests were Lieutenant Colonel C.S. Owen CMG DSO, Major E.R. Kearsley DSO, Major H.V. Venables Kyrke DSO, Captain J.G. Bruxner-Randall and Lieutenant R. De B. Hardie.[40]

The football team had a highly successful season which ended with victory in the final of the T.A. Football Cup at Wrexham against 4th R. Sussex by two goals to one. The Royal Sussex opened the scoring after twenty minutes but ten minutes later Private C. Pierce equalised from the penalty spot. A minute later 4 R.W.F. had a second penalty for handling in the goal mouth but failed to take advantage of it. Shortly before half-time a good centre by Private R. Griffiths was put into the back of the net by Private E. Roberts. Thanks to valiant saves by the goalkeeper, Private D.T. Rowlands, the battalion retained its lead until the final whistle. The cup and medals were presented by Lieutenant General Sir Noel Birch KCB KCMG, Director General of the Territorial Army.[41] 4 R.W.F. had previously won the Territorial Cup in 1910/11 when they beat the Notts and Derbys in what was the first year of the competition.

July 1923 found the 4th Battalion involved in a number of unveiling ceremonies of war memorials. C Company was present at Acrefair on the 8th, and on the 15th at Rhosymedre where the memorial was a pulpit. B Company was at Gwersyllt on the 23rd and four days later at Minera where the Commanding Officer unveiled the monument and helped to dedicate a peel of bells.

The St David's Day Dinner for 1924 was held at the Wynnstay Hotel, Wrexham, on 4 March; twenty-six Officers attended.[42] Camp took place without Lieutenant Colonel Crawshay, who had to give up command on health grounds and who was dined out on 28 June. The battalion rifle meeting was held on 5 July at Erddig Range, Wrexham, in terrible weather. The programme was cut short but the following shoots were completed:

500 yards application, won by Fusilier B. Slawson
600–500 yards fire with movement, won by Fusilier T. Cummings
300 yards snap shoot, won by Corporal A. Nicholls
200 yards recruits' shoot, won by Fusilier F. Jones 05
500 yards Pool Bull, won by Corporal C. Griffiths
300 yards Pool Bull, won by Fusilier A. Cummings[43]

In December 1924, Bandmaster Kelly retired after twenty years with the battalion; Captain H. Delaney took his place. During the early months of 1925 a series of courses was held for Warrant Officers and Sergeants. In sports, Second Lieutenant H.W. Griffith and Captain H.A. Freeman were placed 2nd and 3rd in the Western Command Race at Ruabon Point-to-Point. Corporal G. Griffiths and Fusilier W.G. Williams represented the battalion in the Divisional Boxing finals on 26 February.[44]

Information for the period 1926 to 1930 is scarce, as there was no *Regimental Journal* in those years, however the Minutes of General Meetings of the Denbighshire T.A.A. contain some information on the battalion's doings during those years.[45] In September 1926 the battalion's strength was reported as nineteen Officers and 625 men, one Officer and eleven men short of the establishment. There was no Camp in 1926 due to the General Strike. The battalion received an excellent report in the Annual Administrative Inspection for 1926. Camp in 1927 was at Porthcawl and the battalion reported no absentees; it was reported as a popular and successful Camp. The battalion came 7th in *The Daily Telegraph* National Challenge Cup competition for attendance at Camp in 1927; 598 all ranks attended, 91.1% of the total strength.[46] Porthcawl was again the venue for Camp in 1928, but a change was made in 1929 when the brigade went to Pwllheli. In 1929, the sum of £165 was provided by the County T.A.A. for new Home Service scarlet tunics for the Regimental Band.[47] The Bandmaster's frock coat, trousers, cap and badge, sash and sword belt alone cost £11/16/-; each bandsman's tunic, trousers, cap and badge cost £3/5/6d. For comparison, the relative value of £1 in 1929 at 2017 rates is £259.[48]

As part of the infantry battalion establishment changes, A Company became the battalion's machine-gun company in 1930 and remained so until 1938. Camp in 1930 was held at Porthcawl from 27 July to 10 August; four Officers and eleven N.C.Os were attached from the 2nd Battalion to assist with training. The battalion won the cup for the best *Vickers* gun team in the Division.[49]

The early months of 1931 were spent in shooting and social events. All companies took part in the Lord Wakefield Challenge Cup for small-bore rifles. The Officers' St David's Day Dinner was held at the Wynnstay Arms Hotel, Wrexham on 28 February, after which all companies held dances; the celebrations proved too much for the Regimental Goat, which died two weeks later from a chill. Lord Mostyn donated a replacement.[50] Recruiting had not been brisk during the first quarter of the year but even so, numbers had held up well. By March 1931 the battalion was only twenty men short of its establishment, although not all were trained soldiers. The battalion again won the T.A. Football Cup, beating 6th Sherwood Foresters 10-0, 6th West Yorks 1-0, 7th King's 1-0 and the London Scottish 3-2. The team was:

> Fusiliers F. Jones, F. Smallwood, G. Smallwood, W. Hughes, C. Hughes, H. Edwards, T.
>   Reeves and N. Williams
> Corporals T. Millington, H.H. Jones
> Sergeant A. Webb[51]

Camp for 1931 was held at Tenby from 26 July to 9 August; eleven Officers and 546 men attended. Visitors included the G.O.C. and the Colonel of the Regiment. Platoon, company and specialist training occupied the first week, along with sports; the second week was devoted to battalion training and a brigade scheme. While at Camp, Lance Sergeant E. Reynolds was commended by the G.O.C. for his gallant action in bringing under control a pair of horses harnessed to a limbered wagon who had bolted. Reynolds's action prevented the horses from causing a serious accident on the crowded main road near Penally Camp.[52] After Camp, attention returned to shooting and soccer.

The *Regimental Journal* recorded, not surprisingly, 'a feeling of disappointment' following the decision to cancel T.A. Camps for 1932, announced in 1931. In that year the football team reached the final of the Wrexham and District Amateur Competition, but were beaten after a tie by a team from Rhos. H.Q. Wing beat 4/5th Seaforths to win the Lord Wakefield Challenge Cup for small-bore rifle shooting, in which 502 teams competed. On 31 July, over 300 men attended a Battalion Church Parade at Wrexham, the first time since 1914 that the outlying companies had attended this parade.[53]

The Officers' St David's Day Dinner was held at the Wynnstay Arms Hotel on 1 March 1933; forty members attended; the Drums and Pioneers were on parade before the dinner in the High Street in full dress, Retreat was beaten and the Officers' Mess call was sounded at 20.00 hrs. After dinner, most of those present adjourned to the Drill Hall, where the Sergeants' Mess Ball was in full swing.[54]

4th Battalion Officers at the Court Levee, 1933.
(R.W.F. Mus 4173)

At Camp, at Aberystwyth, in 1933, the Signallers won the Brigade competition; C Company won the Sports Cup; and No 9 Platoon was placed 4th in the Division in the Prince of Wales's Shield for drill. In the autumn, the Commanding Officer, Lieutenant Colonel (Bt Colonel) G.R. Griffith retired after twenty years with the battalion. He was succeeded by Lieutenant Colonel R. Fenwick-Palmer, late of the Life Guards and 61st Medium Regiment R.A. (T.A.).

The winter months of 1933/34 were as usual devoted to shooting, social events and recruiting. The Sergeants' Mess Ball was held on 1 March 1934 and was attended by 350 members and guests. In March 1934, H.Q. Wing reported that it had completed its established strength, although the other companies reported recruiting as slow.[55] A pre-Camp T.E.W.T. was held for all Officers at Horseshoe Pass, Llangollen, on 29 April, which was also attended by all Officers from the Regimental Depot. The battalion went to Camp at Porthcawl from 29 July to 13 August in very indifferent weather. Although training was not affected, a ceremonial parade planned for 11 August had to be cancelled. The Battalion Rifle Meeting was held at Llangollen on 25 August. Sergeant Turner won the Sergeants' Shield and Second Lieutenant H.A.N. Jones won the Officers' Cup.

The battalion lost a number of men in the Gresford Colliery disaster, which is detailed in Regimental Matters and in the Roll of Honour. B Company opened a new Drill Hall at Llay Main Colliery.[56]

On 23 January 1935 the *Regimental Journal* recorded the sort of event that made the T.A. such a draw for social reasons during the inter-war years:

Lieutenant Colonel P.H. Hansen VC DSO MC ... staged a most successful Cinematographic Show in the Drill Hall [Wrexham]. The Show was divided into three parts; (1) Great Events of 1935 ... (2) Military Sunday at Chester... (3) The Jamaica Tattoo... Col. Hansen, in addition to showing the films himself, produced a running commentary ... The Drill Hall was packed; Officers and their wives, representation from all Companies, the Depot, R.W.F., and the local Battery were present.[57]

The Band received a full set of new instruments in early 1935, the gift of the people of Denbighshire. The privilege of wearing blue patrol uniforms, at individual expense, was extended to all ranks. The Officers' St David's Day Dinner was held as usual at the Wynnstay Arms Hotel; fifty-three Officers and guests, including the Brigade Commander, were present; after dinner, most of those present went on to the Sergeants' Mess Ball which was in progress in the Drill Hall in Poyser Street. The new Drill Hall at Llay was opened by the Director-General of the T.A., Lieutenant General Sir Charles Bonham-Carter* on 27 May. A Guard of Honour of fifty men under Major T.W. Mottram was on parade with the Regimental Colour, the Band and Corps of Drums. After the Drill Hall was declared open, Jubilee Medals were presented, as recorded in the Annexes to this Volume.[58]

Camp for 1935 took place at Tenby in beautiful weather and the brigade was well received by the local people and visitors – 'a great contrast to the atmosphere at Porthcawl.'[59] Training was again assisted by the attached regular Officers and N.C.Os. After Camp, a T.E.W.T. near Chester on 19 and 20 October, 'based on an actual war episode which took place in Italy [in 1918], and was most interesting and instructive.'[60]

The Officers' St David's Day Dinner, which took place at the Wynnstay Arms Hotel on 28 February was much overshadowed by the death of the Colonel-in-Chief, H.M. King George V. The battalion was represented at the King's funeral by Major H. Allsebrook. Detachments attended memorial services for the late King, and the ceremonies around the Proclamation of King Edward VIII, in towns throughout the battalion's area.

4 R.W.F. returning from Camp, Wrexham General Station, 1936. (R.W.F. Mus 5088)

---

*   Later General Sir Charles Bonham-Carter GCB CMG DSO (1876–1955) was later Governor of Malta.

In March, the battalion was reported as 'still a little under strength.'[61] Pre-Camp training went on much as usual along with recruiting, so that by the time the battalion went to Camp at Douglas, I.O.M., strength was reported as twenty-six Officers and 582 men.[62] Here the battalion was in Camp with the 5th Battalion and two battalions of the Border Regiment, the 6th and 7th Battalions being at Kinmel Camp, Denbighshire. A full programme of training was run, in mixed weather. The battalion received a visit from the Governor, Sir Montagu Butler, on sports day, at which he presented the prizes. The Commander 126 (East Lancashire) Infantry Brigade, Colonel G. Darwell MC, wrote to the Commander 158 (Royal Welch) Brigade, saying that: 'I want to … tell you how impressed I was with the bearing and drill of the 4th and 5th Battalions when they marched past the Governor here. I have never seen a parade so well carried out by the T.A. before. Their turn-out was excellent.'[63]

After Camp, the Officers' and Sergeants' Shoot took place at Llangollen on 30 August; Captain G.E. Braithwaite won the Officers' competition and CSM R. Gendall won the Sergeants' competition. In the Divisional M.M.G. Competition, A Company gained third place. The Officers' St David's Day Dinner was held as usual at the Wynnstay Arms Hotel in Wrexham, on 1 March 1937. The attendance was a record high and afterwards, most of those present went on to the Sergeants' Mess Ball in the Drill Hall at Poyser Street.

Detachments from all companies took part in the Coronation Parade in London in May 1937, as recorded in the Chapter on Regimental Matters. Other detachments were on parade in towns across the battalion's area for Coronation celebrations and services. The battalion went to Camp in 1937 at Hereford, in beautiful weather but without the attractions of a Camp by the sea, with a strength of 582 all ranks, only six under its establishment; this included nearly 250 men who had less than eighteen months' service.[64] The paper strength of the battalion was 631; of those on the strength who did not attend camp, thirty-one were absent through sickness or no leave of absence from their work. The remaining eighteen were immediately discharged. As a result, the battalion comfortably won the Mayor of Hereford's Cup, a competition on the lines of the *Daily Telegraph Cup* for attendance at Camp. With the international situation becoming tenser, Camp was noticeably harder than in some previous years, with many afternoon demonstrations in place of sports, and the culmination being a battalion test exercise – including a night attack – followed immediately by a brigade exercise, the first for many years. It was also noted that food was much improved, with a fourth meal, supper, being added to the daily ration. In the various competitions, the battalion was placed third overall in the Prince of Wales's Shield, second in the signals test, and 9th in the M.M.G. competition.[65]

On 1 November 1937, Lieutenant Colonel R.G. Fenwick-Palmer handed over command of the battalion after four years to Lieutenant Colonel J.M. Davies MC. During the winter, several Officers were attached to the 1st Battalion during the divisional manoeuvres in East Anglia. D Company's *Lewis* gun team came first in the 53rd (Welsh) Division in the T.A.R.A. Competition for 1937/38, and fourteenth in the T.A.; the battalion team came first in the Division and fourth in the T.A. in the Imperial Tobacco Cup; A Company came second in the Divisional M.M.G. Competition.

The Officers' St David's Day Dinner, followed by the Sergeants' Mess Ball, were held as usual on 1 March. The latter was attended by 600 members and guests.[66] On 3 March 1938 the battalion reached a strength exceeding 100% of its establishment.[67] In the spring, pre-Camp training began, assisted by regular N.C.Os from the Depot. The battalion sent a team of fifteen to Bisley; seven company T.E.W.Ts, two battalion T.E.W.Ts and a signal exercise were held. The battalion went to Camp at Ramsey, I.O.M. from 31 July to 13 August 1938 with a strength of twenty-two Officers and 609 men. The battalion won the Prince of Wales's Shield, coming first in the signals, A.A. and stretcher-bearers' tests. Unusually, Camp included a full twenty-four hours in the field.[68]

STAFF LIST, 4th (Denbighshire) Battalion, 1920–1938

Battalion Headquarters (Wrexham)

Commanding Officer	Lt Col J.R. Minshull-Ford DSO MC	30 Mar 20
	Lt Col C.H.R. Crawshay DSO	3 May 21
	Lt Col G.C.W. Westbrooke MC	3 May 24
	Lt Col G.R. Griffith OBE TD	3 May 29
	Lt Col R.G. Fenwick-Palmer CBE	1 Nov 33
	Lt Col J.M. Davies MC	1 Nov 37
Senior Major	Maj G.C.W. Westbrooke MC	
	Maj A. Wynne	1934
	Maj (Bt Lt Col) J.M. Davies MC	1935; Bt Lt Col 34
	Maj H. Allsebrook	Nov 37
Adjutant	Capt M.L. Lloyd-Mostyn	24 Feb 20
	Capt Hon G.R.B. Bingham	1 Mar 23
	Capt H.A. Freeman MC	1 Sep 24
	Lt E.R. Freeman	1 Sep 27
	Capt H.B. Harrison MC	16 Dec 31
	Capt G.E. Braithwaite	16 Dec 35
R.M.O.	Lt A. MacDonald *R.A.M.C.*	1933; Capt 34
Chaplain	Rev N.S. Baden-Powell *C.F.*	
Quartermaster	Capt T. Mansfield	1 Jul 12
	Lt J.H. Randles	3 Jul 27
Regimental Sergeant Major	W.O. I H.E. Callus DCM	1921
	W.O. I R. Leonard	Jul 25
	W.O. I J.S. Mallett	Dec 1932
	W.O. I A. Lovell *W.G.*	Dec 35
	W.O. I R. Gendall	Dec 36
	W.O. I W.J. Hawkins	1938
O.R.Q.M.S.	W.O. II W. Preen	to Nov 33
	W.O. II P. Chard	1934

H.Q. Company/H.Q. Wing (Wrexham)

Officer Commanding	Maj (Bt Lt Col) J.M. Davies MC	1932; Bt Lt Col 34
	Capt G.E. Wood	1935; resigned 1938
	Maj M. Bennetts MC	1938
Signal Platoon	Lt G.W. Higginson	Jun 25
	Lt H.A.N. Jones	Jun 36
	Sgt Turner	1936
M.M.G. Platoon (disb 1930)	2Lt C.A. Hayes	Jun 25
Pioneers	Sgt W. Williams	1936
Bandmaster	W.O. I – Kelly	1904
	Capt H. Delaney	Dec 24
Corps of Drums	DMaj Lawlor	1936
Officers' Mess	Sgt T.S. Roberts	died 1937
W.Os' & Sgts' Mess	Sgt H. Webb	
	W.O. II – Parry	1936
Company Sergeant Major	W.O. II F. Newbold	to 1936
	W.O. II – Simpson	1936

	W.O. II P.W. Jones	1937–1938*
C.Q.M.S.	Sgt J. Kenny	
Instructor	Sgt A.J. Markey	1922
	Sgt Hanley	Feb 23
	Sgt W. Byles	Jun 25
	W.O. II A. Hughes	1936

A Company (Wrexham) (1, 2, 3 Platoons) (M.G., or S, Company 1930–1938)

Officer Commanding	Capt A.L. Phillips	
	Capt Ll. Davies	Jan 25
	Capt A. Wynne	Jul 25
	Capt T.W. Mottram MC	Jun 32
	Maj J.M. Davies MC	1933
	Capt M. Bennetts MC	1935; Maj 38
Second-in-Command	Capt Ll. Davies	Feb 23
	Capt M. Bennetts MC	Mar 33, from R of O.
	Capt F.D. Williams	1937; to B Coy 38
Platoon Commander	Lt Ll. Davies	
Platoon Commander	2Lt M.C.P. Dennis	Lt Jul 22
Platoon Commander	2Lt J. Turner	
Platoon Commander	2Lt G.W. Higginson	Jul 22
Platoon Commander	2Lt S. York	Jul 25
Platoon Commander	2Lt F.D. Williams	1934; Lt 36
Platoon Commander	2Lt W.J. Hulton	1935; Lt 37, to D Coy 38
Platoon Commander	2Lt W.B.N. Kington	1936
Platoon Commander	2Lt E.S. Dobb	1938
Platoon Sergeant	Sgt A. Meades	died 34
Platoon Sergeant	Sgt Nicholas	1936
Company Sergeant Major	W.O. II – Parry	1930
	W.O. II – Royce	1936
C.Q.M.S.	Sgt W.H. Jones	1930–1938†
Instructor	W.O. I H.E. Callus DCM	
	W.O. I R. Leonard	Feb 24
	Sgt G.A. Archibald	1930
	Sgt W. Oliver MM	1932
	Sgt W. Norman	1934
	Sgt G. Timmins	1937

B Company (Broughton, Summerhill, Brymbo and Llay Main Colliery) (4, 5, 6 Platoons)

Officer Commanding	Capt H.V. Davies MC	
	Capt G.E. Wood	Jun 32
	Capt T.W. Mottram MC TD	1935, Maj Nov 36
	Capt F.D. Williams	1938
Second-in-Command	Capt A. Wynne	to Jun 25
Platoon Commander	2Lt O.A. Davies	Lt Jun 22
Platoon Commander	2Lt O.E. Roberts	
Platoon Commander	2Lt J. Houghton	Lt Aug 22
Platoon Commander	2Lt G.E. Wood	Jul 25; Lt 27
Platoon Commander	2Lt H.A.N. Jones	1934
Platoon Commander	2Lt A.G. Owen	1933; Lt 36

*   Joined 4 R.W.F. in 1903.
†   Joined 4 R.W.F. in 1900.

Platoon Commander	2Lt H.K. Woods	1935
Platoon Commander	Lt H.K. Roberts	1936
Platoon Commander	2Lt J.V. Shepherd	1936
Platoon Commander	2Lt F. Owen	1933; Lt 36
Platoon Commander	2Lt F.E.D. Griffiths	1938
Platoon Sergeant	Sgt A.H. Webb	
Platoon Sergeant	Sgt H.W. Jones	1934
Platoon Sergeant	Sgt Wightman	1936
Platoon Sergeant	Sgt W.A. Jones	
Company Sergeant Major	W.O. II A.G. Otten DCM	
	W.O. II A.E. Hughes	to Nov 34
	W.O. II Williams	1935
C.Q.M.S.	Sgt A. Griffiths	1930
Instructor	Sgt W.J. Lewis	
	Sgt J.H. Randles	Feb 23
	Sgt G. Owens DCM	Jun 25
	W.O. II A. Lovell *W.G.*	Nov 33
	W.O. II R. Gendall	1935
	W.O. II C.A. Hunt *W.G.*	1937

C Company (Ruabon, Chirk and Acrefair) (7, 8, 9 Platoons)

Officer Commanding	Capt (Bt Maj) R.W. Richards MC	
	Capt H.M.P Dennis	Oct 22
	Capt A.C. Lloyd Edwards	Jun 25
	Capt H. Allsebrook	from 7 Warwicks, Jun 32
	Capt A.E. Davies	1937
Second-in-Command	Capt H.M.P. Dennis	
	Lt A.E. Davies	1935; Capt 37
Platoon Commander	2Lt H. Rogers	Jun 25
Platoon Commander	2Lt D. Hulse	Jun 25
Platoon Commander	Lt A.E. Davies	1933
Platoon Commander	2Lt W. Lewis	1936
Platoon Commander	2Lt J.L. Parker	1936
Platoon Commander	2Lt T.A. Jones	1936
Platoon Commander	Lt A.G. Owen	1933; Lt May 36
Platoon Sergeant	Sgt Spencer	1932
Platoon Sergeant	Sgt Pennington	1932
Platoon Sergeant	Sgt B. Griffiths	1932–34
Platoon Sergeant	Sgt J.R. Griffiths	1935
Platoon Sergeant	Sgt Williams	1933
Platoon Sergeant	Sgt Wightman	1935
Platoon Sergeant	LSgt Humphries	1936
Platoon Sergeant	LSgt Heyward	1937
Platoon Sergeant	LSgt Bartley	1937
Company Sergeant Major	W.O. II G.T. Ottoway	
	W.O. II H. Spalding DCM	Oct 22
	W.O. II J.J. Mallett	Jan 23
	W.O. II A. Morris	1930
	W.O. II J.R. Griffiths	1938
C.Q.M.S.	Sgt T.H. Pritchard	1930
	Sgt Clutton	1938
Instructor	Sgt H.J. Kite	to Oct 22
	Sgt Spencer	1932
	Sgt A. Wright	1936

D Company (Denbigh, Rhos, Corwen, Rhosllanerchrugog and Ruthin) (10, 11, 12 Platoon)

Officer Commanding	Capt P.R. Foulkes-Roberts MC	
	Capt G.R. Griffith OBE	Jun 25
	Capt B.E.R. Williams	1932; resigned 1938
	Capt W.J. Hulton	1938
Second-in-Command	Capt P.W. Brundrit	died Nov 22
	Lt J. Hughes MC	Dec 22
	Lt W.J. Hulton	1935
Platoon Commander	Lt J. Hughes MC	
Platoon Commander	2Lt P.A.F. Roberts	to Jun 25
Platoon Commander	Lt J.A. Roberts	Jun 25
Platoon Commander	2Lt H.W. Griffith	Jun 25
Platoon Commander	2Lt J.W. Griffith	Jun 25
Platoon Commander	2Lt B.E.R. Williams	Jun 25
Platoon Commander	2Lt W. Lewis	Jun 32
Platoon Commander	Lt R.O. Roberts	1930
Platoon Commander	2Lt M.E. Beale	1933, Lt 36
Platoon Commander	2Lt H. Clement Davies	
Platoon Commander	2Lt D.E.G. Griffiths	1933; Lt 36; to R.A.F. 38
Platoon Commander	2Lt H.A.N. Jones	1936; from C Coy. Lt 36
Platoon Commander	2Lt J.A. Hughes	1936
Platoon Commander	2Lt R.W. Soden	1937
Platoon Sergeant	LSgt J. Richards	
Platoon Sergeant	Sgt D. Evans	1930
Platoon Sergeant	Sgt W.G. Jones	1933
Platoon Sergeant	Sgt W.F. Pritchard	1930
Platoon Sergeant	Sgt R.W. Jones	1938
Company Sergeant Major	W.O.II M. Wood	to Oct 22
	W.O. II P.W. Jones	1923–1937
	W.O. II W.F. Pritchard	1937
C.Q.M.S.	Sgt W.F. Pritchard	
	Sgt J. Richards	1937
Instructor	Sgt A.J. Markey	
	Sgt C. Hanley	Jan 23
	Sgt J.H. Randles	Jun 25
	Sgt J.H. Bacon	1932
	Sgt G. Davies	1935
	Sgt S.H. Platt *W.G.*	1937

Unplaced
Captain H.C. Davies

viii. The 5th (Flintshire) Battalion, 1920–1938

The 5th Battalion had its Headquarters and A Company at Mold, B Company at Rhyl, C Company at Flint and D Company at Hawarden. All companies opened and closed detachments at various times throughout the period, as shown in the Staff List.

The Battalion went to Camp in 1921 with 158 Brigade at Rhyl from 23 July to 6 August. The strength of the battalion was sixteen Officers and 580 men. Inspections were carried out by G.O.C. Western Command, Lieutenant General Sir Beauvoir de Lisle KCB KCMG DSO MC, and Major General Deverell.

On Thursday 13th July 1922, the anniversary of its departure for Gallipoli, the 5th Battalion's war memorial was unveiled at the Drill Hall at Rhyl. In the presence of the Lord Lieutenant for Flintshire the memorial, a bronze plate set in granite and bearing the words, 'To the Officers, Non-Commissioned Officers and Men of the 5th Flintshire Battalion Royal Welch Fusiliers who fell in Gallipoli, Egypt and Palestine during the Great War', was unveiled by Mrs B.E. Philips* of Mold and Mrs Tuck of Hawarden. The dedication was by His Grace the Archbishop of Wales.

5 R.W.F. Battalion Headquarters in Mold. (Mrs Dilys R. Glover, from the collection of Lt Col H. Maldwyn Davies)

In 1922, 5 R.W.F. B Company at Rhyl was particularly active. The first monthly supper of the season was held in October and was followed by a lecture on 'Mental tests in the American Army' by Captain J. Mostyn MC. Later in the month the winter entertainment programme began with an excellent boxing tournament, followed by whist drives and a shoot. D Company at Hawarden reported its strength at 213 after over 100 discharges.

In 1922, Camp was at Aberystwyth from 29 July to 12 August. The first week was devoted to drill and platoon and company training. The last week was devoted to battalion training and preparation for the visit by the divisional commander on 10 August Major General Sir A.A. Montgomery KCMG CB. On the following day the performance was repeated for the G.O.C. Western Command.

Lieutenant Colonel T. Freer Ash relinquished command of the 5th Battalion on 8 March 1923 and was succeeded by Lieutenant Colonel E.H.W. Williams. Major H.A. Jefferson handed over the duties of adjutant in April 1923 to Captain H.A. Davies MBE MC who had been awarded his MBE in the previous New Year honours list. He was invested on 1 March, the first time a leek had been worn at Buckingham Palace.[69] The St David's Dinner at the Drill Hall, Rhyl was also the occasion for bidding farewell to Colonel Freer Ash and Major Jefferson. Colonel H. Maldwyn Davies made a presentation from the Officers of the battalion to each.

Camp at Porthcawl was well attended in 1923 and was generally regarded as the best camp since the re-formation of the battalion. No 8 Platoon of B Company won the Prince of Wales's Cup at Camp as champion platoon in 158 Brigade. Each man was given a silver-topped cane by the Commanding Officer.[70] The Prince of Wales visited Rhyl after Camp; B Company found a Guard of Honour with the Regimental Band in pre-war full dress.

A Machine Gun Platoon was formed within H.Q. Wing at the beginning of 1924, the men attending a two-week course with the 2nd Battalion at Pembroke Dock.[71] In February, the battalion began the formation of an honorary members company, whose main focus of activity was to raise funds for sporting and social purposes. The early members included several senior managers from Llay Hall and Llay Main Collieries, in which many men from A Company in

*   The widow of Lieutenant Colonel B.E. Philips who was killed commanding 5 R.W.F. at Gallipoli on 10 August 1915.

particular were employed. In April 1924, the battalion reported its strength as eighteen Officers and 530 men, two Officers and 106 men below the establishment.[72] Much of the shortfall was in C Company where it was reported that the P.S.I., Sergeant Burgin, was under arrest awaiting trial and therefore there was no permanent presence at the Drill Hall.

The Honorary Colonel, Colonel J. Sheriff Roberts, who had served with the battalion from 1881 to 1905, died in post in March 1925; no Honorary Colonel was appointed to replace him.[73] The battalion found a Guard of Honour and Firing Party, with the Regimental Band, for the unveiling of the war memorial in Caergwrle on 11 April 1925. By June 1925 the shortfall in strength had been more than made up, with the battalion's strength reported at twenty Officers and 669 men.

Information on the period from 1926 to 1930 is thin, since the *Regimental Journal* was not published during these years. When it did resume publication, the battalion provided no notes until December 1931. The Minutes of the Flintshire T.A.A. do however record something of the battalion's doings in these years.[74] There was a very strict attitude towards attendance at Camp; in 1925, there were sixteen absentees, of whom three were prosecuted for absence without leave. There was only a local camp in 1926 because of the General Strike; Camp in 1927 was at Pwllheli and a Rifle Meeting was held at Llangollen. Camp in 1928 was attended by twenty-three Officers and 572 men out of a total on strength of 633. Camp in 1929 was at Porthcawl; all but sixteen of the battalion's 600 men attended.

D Company became the battalion's machine-gun company in 1930, as part of the establishment changes for the infantry, and remained in this role until 1938. The rifle meeting was again held at Llangollen and Camp was at Porthcawl once more.

During 1931 the Battalion Rifle Meeting was held at Sealand Range on 14 June. On 28 June, the eliminating rounds for the Prince of Wales's Shield, for platoon drill, were held at Hafod-y-Coed, with No 5 Platoon under Lieutenant C.E. Malley coming first in the brigade and 4th in the division. Annual Camp was held at Tenby in excellent weather; the battalion won the brigade cross-country running competition and the brigade football competition, and came 2nd in the inter-battalion signalling competition.[75]

The Officers' St David's Day Dinner for 1932 took place on 27 February at Rhyl; thirty-six Officers and their guests were present including the G.O.C. A new departure, the Sergeants' Mess Ball, was held at Halkyn on 12 March.[76] No Camp was held in 1932 for reasons of economy. In place of Camp, as many additional days of training as possible were laid on, including drill, signalling and machine-gunning. The battalion rifle meeting was held at Sealand on 3 July, with H.Q. Wing winning the Recruits' competition, B Company the Lewis gun competition and CSM G. Norry winning the champion shot trophy.[77]

During the winter of 1932/33, all companies held N.C.O. cadre courses; four Officers and sixteen men were attached to the Regimental Depot for periods of instruction.[78] The Officers' St David's Day Dinner was held at Rhyl on 25 February; the G.O.C.-in-C. Western Command, Sir Cyril Deverall, and the Archbishop of Wales were the principal guests. In June, Lieutenant Colonel E.H.W. Williams handed over command, having held the appointment for ten years, and was succeeded by Lieutenant Colonel H. Maldwyn Davies, who had been Second-in-Command throughout the entire period.[79]

The battalion went to Camp at Aberystwyth in 1933 with a strength of 506 all ranks, of whom 150 were recruits.[80] After Camp, attention turned to shooting and social events. The

Sergeants' Mess Ball was held on 24 February 1934 at Rhyl; 120 members and guests attended. The Colours were displayed and the leek eaten at dinner.[81]

In the run-up to Camp for 1934, the battalion won the Prince of Wales's Shield for military skills and was placed second in the Division M.G. competition. These successes came just before the death of the Honorary Colonel, Colonel E.H.W. Williams, who had for many years ardently wished the battalion to win the Shield. A series of church parades was also held in towns throughout Flintshire, with the Band and Corps of Drums in full dress. The Rifle Meeting was held at Sealand on 12 July in very fine weather. Eighteen Officers and 460 men attended Camp in 1934.[82] The battalion went to Camp at Porthcawl from 29 July to 13 August in very indifferent weather. Although training was not affected, a ceremonial parade planned for 11 August had to be cancelled.

The winter months of 1934/35 were as usual given over to the training of specialists, recruits and N.C.Os, and to the customary round of dances, dinners and parties. The Officers' St David's Day Dinner was held on 3 March, the Bishop of St Asaph was the principal guest. The Sergeants' Mess Ball was held at the Mold Drill Hall on 16 March. The Rifle Meeting took place at Sealand on 30 June: B Company won the inter-company shoot and the recruits' competition; C Company won the *Lewis* gun competition. The individual championship was a tie between Sergeant C.C. Claridge, Sergeant W. Colgate and Corporal G. Jones. Fusilier R. Williams of B Company was best recruit. Camp took place with the rest of the brigade at Tenby from 28 July to 12 August 1935; the battalion again won the Prince of Wales's Shield for military skills.

5th Battalion Officers at the Court Levée, March 1938, (R.W.F. Mus 5359B). Front row, from left: Major H. Maldwyn Davies OBE TD, Lieutenant General Sir Charles Dobell, Lieutenant Colonel E.H.W. Williams DSO, Captain D.I. Owen, Captain J. Mostyn MC. Back row, from left: unknown, Captain F.P. McManus, unknown, Captain E.O. Burton, Captain J.R.O. Charlton, unknown, Captain H. Sherriff Roberts.

The autumn and winter were devoted to individual training, recruiting and various social events. The *Regimental Journal* noted a higher-than-usual tempo of individual training courses and cadres, and that drills were 'being exceptionally well attended,'[83] helped by the introduction of training films provided by the Adjutant, Captain C.H.V. Pritchard. The battalion provided detachments for the various memorial services for the late King, most notably at Rhyl on 28 January 1936, where the parade was under the command of the Commanding Officer. The T.E.W.T. for all Officers on 1 March was marred by bad weather, and concluded with all present listening to the first broadcast of His Majesty King Edward VIII on the wireless.

In April, the foundation stone of a new Drill Hall was laid at Connah's Quay. The Rifle Meeting was held on 14 July at Sealand, in poor weather. In the various shooting matches, H.Q. Wing won the High Sheriff's Challenge Shield; B Company won the B.S.A. Guns Ltd Challenge Trophy and the *Lewis* Gun Challenge Trophy; and Fusilier B. Worrall of C

Company won the Young Soldiers' Championship.[84] A pre-Camp tactical instruction day was held at Pentre Halkyn on 23 July.

Camp was held, with the 4th Battalion, at Douglas, I.O.M. from 26 July to 9 August 1936; the rough sea caused more than a few cases of sickness on the ferry crossing from Liverpool and poor weather continued throughout camp. A full programme of training and sport was, however, completed and for the third year in succession, the battalion won the Prince of Wales's Shield; Sergeant J.D. Jones and the St Asaph Platoon won the field training event by forty-four points.[85]

The new Connah's Quay Drill Hall was opened on 5 December 1936 by the G.O.C.-in-C. Western Command, Lieutenant General Sir Henry Jackson. A guard of honour was found by D Company under Captain Clough-Taylor, with Lieutenant McCully as ensign for the Regimental Colour. A large number of guests attended. The opening ceremony was followed that evening by a dance.[86]

Recruiting began to pick up noticeably in early 1937, so much so that two nights each week were allocated for paid drills with a third voluntary evening also available. In the spring, a mortar platoon was formed in H.Q. Wing under Lieutenant J.R.O. Charlton.[87] Representatives from all companies went to London to take part in the Coronation in May 1937; other detachments were on parade at ceremonies and services around the battalion's area on Coronation Day.

The battalion went to Camp at Hereford with the 53rd (Welsh) Division; like the 4th Battalion, the Officers and men noted a higher tempo of training than in previous years. Recruiting and low-level training carried on during the winter months. The Officers' St David's Day Dinner was held at Rhyl on 5 March and the Sergeants' Mess Ball at Connah's Quay. The battalion received its issue of nine 15-cwt trucks in the Spring.

Camp for 1938 was at Ramsey, I.O.M. with the rest of the brigade; the battalion was at full strength. A Boys' Platoon was formed in H.Q. Wing during 1938.[88]

On 16 November 1938, the battalion was re-organised as an anti-tank artillery regiment and re-designated 60th (R.W.F.) Anti-Tank Regiment, R.A. Its story is continued in Chapter 14.

STAFF LIST, 5th (Flintshire) Battalion, 1920–1938

Battalion Headquarters (Mold)

Commanding Officer	Lt Col T.H. Parry DSO	16 Feb 20
	Lt Col R.C. Lloyd DSO MC TD	1 Sep 20
	Lt Col T. Freer Ash TD	8 Mar 21
	Lt Col E.H.W. Williams DSO	20 Jun 23*
	Lt Col (Bt Col) H. Maldwyn Davies TD	27 Apr 33
	Lt Col S.H. Burton TD	27 Apr 38
Senior Major	Maj H. Maldwyn Davies TD	
	Maj S.H. Burton TD	1931
	Maj H. Sheriff Roberts	1936
Adjutant	Maj H.A. Jefferson DSO	
	Capt H. Alban Davies MBE MC	Apr 23
	Capt D.I. Owen	12 Apr 27
	Capt D.R. Evans	1 Nov 31
	Lt C.H.V. Pritchard	1 Nov 36
I.O.	Lt G.H. Alletson	1933

*   Williams commanded the 5th Battalion for ten years, unusual even in the 1920s.

Quartermaster	Capt G. Claridge TD	
	Lt E.F. Hollobon MM	30 Apr 25, Capt 33
R.M.O.	Capt J.R. Griffiths *R.A.M.C.*	Mar 24
Chaplain	Rev T.S. Perrott *R.A.Ch.D.*	Oct 23
Regimental Sergeant Major	W.O. I G. White	
	W.O. I H.W. Bloxham	Jan 23
	W.O. I Clancey	Jun 25
	W.O. I E. Davies	1933
	W.O. I S. Sherriff	Nov 35
	W.O. I Currie	Nov 37
Bandmaster	W.O. I H. Walsh	to 1935
	W.O. I S. Pratt	Jul 35
R.Q.M.S.	W.O. II R.W. Chambers MSM	to Jun 23
O.R.Q.M.S.	Sgt C.C. Claridge	1935

H.Q. Company/H.Q. Wing (Mold and Rossett)

Officer Commanding	Maj E.O. Burton	1934
	Capt F.P. McManus TD	1935, Maj Jul 36
	Lt L.M. Theakstone (acting)	1936
	Lt L.G.S. Clough-Taylor	1935; Capt Jul 36
Second-in-Command	Lt L.M. Theakstone	1937
Signal Platoon (Caergwrle)	Sgt H.P. Harmes	Jun 23
	Lt L.G.S. Clough-Taylor	1931
	Lt L.M. Theakstone	1933
	Lt H.E. Bolton	1937
M.M.G. Platoon (Disb 1930)	Sgt F.J. Bowyer	Jan 24
Mortar Platoon (Hawarden)	Lt J.R.O. Charlton	1937
Admin Platoon	2Lt B.G. Jefferson	1932; Lt 35
	Sgt R. Roberts (Horse Transport)	
Regimental Band (Flint)	Sgt H. Bailey	1935
Corps of Drums (Mold)	DMaj W.F. Woods	1934
Instructor	Sgt Neil	1937

A Company (Mold, Northop, Buckley and Caergwrle) (1, 2, 3 Platoons)

Officer Commanding	Capt H. Newton Jones	resigned May 23
	Capt R.A. Davies-Cooke	Jan 24; resigned 34
	Capt R.S. Williams	1934; died 1936
Second-in-Command	Lt R.S. Williams	May 23
	Lt E. Williams	1936
Platoon Commander	Lt R.G. Evans	
Platoon Commander	2Lt R.S. Williams	
Platoon Commander	Lt C.E. Malley	1931
Platoon Commander	2Lt R.A. Davies-Cooke	1932
Platoon Commander	2Lt H.E. Bolton	1933–34
Platoon Commander	2Lt T.M. Nash	1937
Platoon Commander	2Lt E. Evans	1937
Platoon Sergeant	LSgt R.W.C. Jarvis	1934
Platoon Sergeant	LSgt H. Stanton	1934
Platoon Sergeant	Sgt H.T. Ellis	1934
Platoon Sergeant	Sgt Whitley	1936
Platoon Sergeant	Sgt Roberts	1936
Platoon Sergeant	LSgt J.H. Davies	1936
Company Sergeant Major	W.O. II J.T. Jones	
	W.O. II Clarke	Jan 24

C.Q.M.S.	Sgt Houghly	
Instructor	Sgt J. Evans *W.G.*	
	Sgt R.H. Sowrey	
	Sgt E. Jones DCM *Oxf Bucks*	died Mar 23
	Sgt H. Clarke	Jun 23
	Sgt S. Grindley	1931
	Sgt C. Clemence	1934
	Sgt W. Leicester	1934
	Sgt W. Jones 92	1935
	Sgt W. Cooper	1937

B Company (Rhyl, Prestatyn Abergele and St Asaph) (4, 5, 6 Platoons)

Officer Commanding	Capt F.P. McManus	
	Maj S.H. Burton TD	1933
Platoon Commander	Lt F.C. Gibson	
Platoon Commander	Lt G.T.O. Pritchard	
Platoon Commander	2Lt – Priddle	resigned 34
Platoon Commander	Lt A.E. Crockatt	1935
Platoon Commander	2Lt E. Williams	1934
Platoon Commander	2Lt T.H.M. Owens	1935; Lt 37
Platoon Commander	2Lt G. Hemelryk	1937
Platoon Commander	2Lt W.O. Hill	1938
Platoon Commander	2Lt M.A.J. Thomas	1938
Platoon Commander	2Lt J. Ellis Evans	1938
Platoon Sergeant	Sgt Williams	1934
Platoon Sergeant	Sgt J.D. Jones	1934
Platoon Sergeant	Sgt D.W. Jones	1934
Platoon Sergeant	Sgt Vaughan	1935
Platoon Sergeant	Sgt R.C. Jarvis	1935
Platoon Sergeant	Sgt G. Jones	1936
Platoon Sergeant	LSgt H.W. Ottley	1936
Company Sergeant Major	W.O. II F.W. Arnold MM	
	W.O. II D.W. Jones	1936
C.Q.M.S.	Sgt E. Simmonds	
Instructor	W.O. II H.W. Bloxham	
	Sgt A.P. Weeks	Jun 23
	W.O. II G.R. Morris	1930
	W.O. II J. Soane	Nov 33

C Company (Flint and Holywell) (7, 8, 9 Platoons)

Officer Commanding	Capt G.A. Parker	
	Capt E.O. Burton	1934; Maj 37
Platoon Commander	Lt R.O. Jones	
Platoon Commander	Lt T.D. Morgan	Jun 23
Platoon Commander	Lt R.O. Charlton	1931
Platoon Commander	Lt C.E. McCully	1930, Lt 32
Platoon Commander	2Lt H.S.K. Mainwaring	1935; Lt 37
Platoon Sergeant	Sgt D. Davies	to 31
Platoon Sergeant	Sgt E.L. Williams	1937
Platoon Sergeant	Sgt Jones	1938
Platoon Sergeant	LSgt Salisbury	1938
Company Sergeant Major	W.O. II – Bowler	1920
	W.O. II B. Clancy	1936
Instructor	W.O. I G. White	

	Sgt A. Boyle	
	W.O. II D.R. Roberts *W.G.*	1936
	W.O. II H. Claydon *W.G.*	1937

D Company (Hawarden, Connah's Quay and Shotton) (10, 11, 12 Platoons) (M.G., or S, Company 1930–1938)

Officer Commanding	Maj H.M. Davies	
	Capt S.H. Burton	May 23
	Capt E.O. Burton	1931
	Capt H. Sheriff Roberts	1934
	Capt L.G.S. Clough-Taylor	1936
Second-in-Command	Capt J. Mostyn MC	
Platoon Commander	Lt D.B. Robb	Capt Jan 23; retd May 23
Platoon Commander	Lt E.O. Burton	
Platoon Commander	Lt T.D. Morgan	to Jun 23
Platoon Sergeant	Sgt W. Carter	
Platoon Sergeant	LSgt E. Cooksey	1934
Platoon Sergeant	Sgt S. McAllister	1937
Platoon Sergeant	Sgt – Marland	1937
Platoon Sergeant	Sgt W. Colegate	1938
Company Sergeant Major	W.O. II D.G. Norry	1932
C.Q.M.S.	Sgt R. Norrey	1935
Instructor	W.O. II R.W. Chambers MSM	
	Sgt E. Williams	
	Sgt F.H. Quinn	Jun 23
	Sgt F. Wilkinson	1932
	Sgt – Ribton *W.G.*	1934
	Sgt – Lowe	1938

ix. The 6th (Caernarvonshire & Anglesey) Battalion, 1920–1938

The 6th Battalion was based at Caernarfon under Lieutenant Colonel F.J. Walwyn DSO. A Company was at Caernarfon with outstations at Bangor, Llanberis and Penygroes. B Company H.Q. was at Porthmadog with outstations at Pwllheli and Criccieth, C Company H.Q. was at Conwy with an outstation at Trefriw, and D Company H.Q. was at Holyhead with an outstation at Beaumaris.[89] All companies opened and closed detachments at various locations throughout the period, as noted in the Staff List.

Before the war the 6th Battalion had had a company on Anglesey, but on re-forming, Anglesey had been allotted to the Royal Army Service Corps. The platoon in Caernarfon was chiefly made up of employees of the Castle Company's brick works, where the platoon commander was also the works manager.[90] Being largely a rural area except for the slate mines around Blaenau Ffestiniog, the men were mainly from an agricultural background, as Lieutenant Kyffin Williams, later in command of the Nefyn Platoon, recalled in a somewhat sarcastic passage of his memoirs:

> The men were poachers, farm labourers, railwaymen and slaughterers from an abattoir; an ill-assorted lot who had joined specifically to enjoy a fortnight's holiday each summer when the battalion went to camp. The detachment consisted of about twelve Joneses, ten

Williamses, ten Robertses and a sprinkling of Owens, Parrys, Lloyds and Griffiths, most of whom were naturally referred to by nicknames. There was Will Chimp.... Huw Baboon ... General Franco ... Willie Christmas, Little Titch and hollow-legged Hughie ... A Finn called Ezra Johannes Eklund added a little continental flavouring.

Some of the men of the Nefyn contingent could speak only Welsh, which complicated their training. Will Jones was killed in Burma without ever having mastered any English.[91]

Recruiting was slow to start, but improved rapidly from July 1921 so that by the end of the month the strength of the battalion had reached twenty-one Officers and 651 Other Ranks. As no R.A.S.C. unit was raised, permission was obtained from the War office for the battalion to recruit on Anglesey.[92]

The first Annual Camp was held in 1921. For some reason, possibly because of a lack of suitable accommodation and training facilities for all battalions of the brigade to be together, the 6th Battalion went to Squires Gate, Blackpool on its own in August.[93] A total of twenty-one Officers and 650 Other Ranks attended. The weather was excellent and the inter-company drill and football competitions were won by D and A Company respectively. The G.O.C. 53rd (Welsh) Division carried out an inspection and expressed 'complete satisfaction'.

In September, the 6th Battalion War Memorial was unveiled at Christ Church, Caernarfon by Major General F.F. Mott CB who had commanded the 53rd (Welsh) Division during the late war. The memorial was of Kuhn brass and contained the 'names of some 300 Officers and men who gave up their lives in the War.'* Prior to the service the battalion was inspected by General Mott in the Castle. The impressive service was attended by detachments from the companies, with the Band, Drums and a Colour Party.

During the year electricity was installed in the Drill Hall at Caernarfon where the 6th Battalion held its annual Officers' Mess Ball in March, followed by one for the Warrant Officers and Sergeants' Mess.

In 1922, Annual Camp was at Aberystwyth from 29 July to 12 August. 6 R.W.F.'s strength was twenty Officers and 573 Other Ranks. The mornings were spent on military training and the afternoons devoted to sport. A Company won the football cup and the Parkia Drill Competition, and B Company the shooting trophy. In the B.S.A. Ltd Trophy Competition for shooting, fired under the conditions of the T.A. Rifle Association, B, C, and A Companies respectively secured the top three places.[94] The battalion rifle meeting was held at Penmon Range on 23/24 September. Accommodation was provided at Kingsbridge Camp, Beaumaris. The Lord Lieutenant of Caernarvonshire's Silver Challenge Cup for teams of eight all ranks was won by D Company, as was the Glasfryn Memorial Silver Challenge Cup for teams of eight Other Ranks. The Plas Coch Silver Challenge Cup for the best individual score in the Lord Lieutenant's Cup went to Sergeant R. Davies of C Company who also received the 'Battalion Jewel' and was styled 'Champion Shot of the Battalion' for the next twelve months. The Oakwood Silver Challenge Cup for Officers was won by Captain C.E. Vivian MC.

On Armistice Day 1922 the Caernarfon Town War Memorial was unveiled. A Company 6 R.W.F. provided a guard of honour under Captain H. Gordon Carter MC and a firing party under RSM H.A. Richards. The Commanding Officer of the 2nd Battalion, Lieutenant

---

*   *Y Ddraig Goch*, Vol I, May 1922, No 1, p. 19. The actual number of Other Ranks who died was 246.

Colonel C.C. Norman CMG DSO, and the 2nd Battalion Band attended, having travelled from Dublin. A special enclosure in front of the Memorial had been reserved for the relatives of the fallen. Wreaths were laid by the Mayor, and by Dame Margaret Lloyd George on behalf of her husband who was campaigning prior to the imminent General Election. 'It was a moving and pathetic sight to see the widows and orphans proudly wearing the medals of their fallen fathers and brothers… .'[95] After the parade the Band and Colonel Norman were entertained to dinner in the Royal Hotel. Colonel Norman, responding to a speech by the Mayor, said that, 'Many of the men whose names were inscribed on the Memorial were personally known to him and served with him in France in the 2nd, 13th and 17th Battalions which he had commanded … during the war.'[96]

The pressure of affairs forced the Commanding Officer to resign and he was succeeded by Lieutenant Colonel C.E. Vivian MC on 10 January 1923. In March 1923 the Adjutant, Captain J.N. More[*] was replaced by Captain (Brevet Lieutenant Colonel) C.C. Norman CMG DSO.[†] Norman stayed only six months, being replaced that autumn by Captain A.M.G. Evans.

The battalion provided Guards of Honour, with the Band of the 2nd Battalion, for the Prince of Wales's tour of North Wales in the autumn of 1923, at Caernarfon on 31 October, under Captain H. Gordon Carter MC, with Second Lieutenant F.D. Colebourne as Ensign for the King's Colour; at Bangor on 1 November, under Captain A.M. Trustram Eve, with Second Lieutenant S. Goodchild as Ensign; and at Conwy on 2 November under Major J. Douglas Porter OBE, with Lieutenant W.P. Lines as Ensign:

> The Guards of Honour on each occasion were … well turned out and very steady on parade. The Prince talked to several of the Men of the Guard on each occasion, especially to any man who was wearing a decoration.[97]

In 1923 D Company again won the B.S.A. Trophy for the battalion in shooting; D Company also won the High Sheriff's Shield and the Divisional inter-company recruits' shoot. CSM J.T. Jones and Lance Sergeants R.J. Thomas and J. Owen of C Company were selected for the Divisional team of ten men for Bisley in 1924; Jones made the Army 100; he and Owen both returned with prizes. The Battalion Rifle Meeting was held at Holyhead Rifle Range on 7, 8 and 9 June 1924 and was attended by twelve Officers and 130 men; the prizes were presented by Colonel A.C. Girdwood, Commanding 158 (Royal Welch) Infantry Brigade. At Camp, C Company took the Brigade Drill Cup for platoons.[98]

B Company had installed a wireless set at Company H.Q., which was a great draw for special programmes and events. In 1924, these included the opening of the British Empire Exhibition by His Majesty King George V: 'Though unable to witness the gigantic spectacle. All who were present agreed that they had been treated to "the next best thing".'[99]

The Rt. Hon. David Lloyd George unveiled the Pwllheli War Memorial on 12 June 1924, B Company found a Guard of Honour.

---

[*]   Author of *With Allenby's Crusaders*, nd [c.1923] and *Dugout Doggerels from Palestine*, nd [1922].

[†]   A brevet lieutenant colonel, he had commanded 15 R.W.F. in 1917/18 and although continuing to hold appointments as a Lieutenant Colonel until 1921, with the reduction in size of the post-war Army he reverted to his substantive rank. He was however restored to a Lieutenant Colonel's command in 1923.

The St David's Day Ball was held at the Barracks, Caernarfon, on 6 March 1925, and dinner was followed by dancing. More than 100 Officers and their guests attended. Information is scarce for the period 1926 to 1930, as the *Regimental Journal* was not published during those years although the Caernarvonshire & Anglesey Territorial Army Association minutes record at least some of the battalion's doings.[100]

The battalion went to Camp at Dyffryn, near Llanbedr, just south of Harlech, in 1926 for an unofficial Camp, there being no official Brigade Camp.[101] Dyffryn was again the venue for Camp in 1927, while the rest of the brigade went to Pwllheli, and it was 'One of the best places for training a brigade ... There were hundreds of acres of *morfa* [i.e. grassy sand-hills] and an excellent rifle range'. Camp was however a sad affair for the battalion as the Commanding Officer, Lieutenant Colonel Vivian, was clearly unwell when he arrived. Eventually the Brigade Commander and the Senior Major, Major Trustram Eve, persuaded him to go home; he died soon afterwards.[102]

R.W.F. at Camp in Porthcawl, 1929; Lieutenant Colonel Trustram Eve, RSM Howells, Captain and Adjutant F. Garnons-Williams. (R.W.F. Mus 2134)

Camp for 1928 was at Pwllheli, a single-battalion Camp close to home, for reasons of economy, while the rest of the brigade went to Porthcawl. In the same year, the battalion formed a corps of drums, in common with all other battalions in the brigade. The battalion received an excellent report in the Annual Administrative Inspection of 1929, and joined the brigade Camp at Porthcawl. A new Drill Hall was opened at Conwy on 4 May 1929 by the G.O.C.-in-C. Western Command. The Drill Hall had cost £4,024 and included a miniature range, was wired for telephone and electric light, and had central heating throughout. Soon afterwards, modernisation began at the Caernarfon and Penygroes Drill Halls. At the end of the year, the battalion reported its strength as ninety-one men below the establishment.[103]

The brigade Camp for 1930 was at Porthcawl for the third year in succession, a long and difficult journey from the remoter stations of the battalion's area. Some men needed fourteen hours to complete the journey.[104] A number of Officers and N.C.Os from the 2nd Battalion were attached to assist with training. In 1930, Lieutenant Colonel Trustram Eve was asked by a number of Officers if he would take them to a Levée at St James's Palace. As he recorded:

> I agreed only if they would wear "full regimentals". On 2 June, I took twelve Officers (the seven most senior and five subalterns, including the M.O.) to the Palace. There were Officers from other Regular battalions there, but they were all wearing khaki. We were presented by the Colonel of the Regiment, who brought back a message of congratulation from the King on our full dress.[105]

A weekend Camp was held at Easter 1931, followed by the battalion's Rifle Meeting at Whitsun; B Company carried off seven of the ten cups offered, and held a celebratory parade in Portmadoc on their return home.[106] Another new Drill Hall was opened at Menai Bridge on 26 September 1931, housing a platoon of C Company.

In the spring of 1932, about fifty N.C.Os and potential N.C.Os went through a two-month cadre in section and platoon drill and tactics. An Easter Camp attended by those junior N.C.Os and Fusiliers selected for promotion was a great success. From April onwards, all companies concentrated on completing the annual weapon training courses and in selecting teams for the annual Rifle Meeting: 'Such was the enthusiasm that many rushed home for a quick tea before catching a special bus to the ranges, often ten miles from their homes.'[107] At the Rifle Meeting, which took place at Holyhead on 18 and 19 June, CSM Sullivan took the battalion Gold Jewel for the third successive year, a feat previously unequalled. Later in the year, D (Machine Gun) Company won the Brigade M.G. Test.[108] In the summer, the Corps of Drums beat Retreat in Conwy on several occasions.[109]

The Goat died in 1932; a replacement was provided by Captain R.E. Griffith. Lord Penrhyn was appointed Honorary Colonel: 'a large number of men in the battalion are employed by him and all know what great interest he has always shown in our welfare.'[110] There was no Camp during 1932 in consequence of the economic situation, however all companies held training schemes at weekends during the summer in compensation. No 13 Platoon of D Company won the brigade M.M.G. Test during the summer.

The winter months of 1932/33 were devoted to full bore and miniature range shooting. The Battalion Rifle Meeting was held at Sealand on 24 and 25 June, attended by all Officers and 100 men; C Company was again champion company and Sergeant J. Owen of Portmadoc won the Gold Jewel. Fusilier R.J. Burnell of Holyhead won the recruits' Silver Medal. Camp at Aberystwyth was generally regarded as 'not so bad as it was painted' – it was a Divisional Camp – and a full programme of training and sport was completed. No 13 Platoon again came first in the brigade in the Prince of Wales's Shield for drill and third in the Division.[111]

After Camp, attention returned to shooting and to various dances, parties and company dinners. In the early spring of 1934, courses for specialists and N.C.Os were held. The Rifle Meeting was held at Holyhead on 23 and 24 June; CSM J.T. Jones won the Gold Jewel.[112] On 14 July, H.R.H. the Princess Royal visited Penrhyn Castle to inspect detachments of Girl Guides; the Regimental Band played at the parade.

The battalion went to Camp at Porthcawl from 29 July to 13 August 1934 in very indifferent weather. Although training was not affected, a ceremonial parade planned for 11 August had to be cancelled. On 3 October, a reunion dinner was held at the Holborn Restaurant in London for all Officers who had served in the battalion during the Great War.

Jubilee parades were held in all towns across the battalion's area. A Company and the Band were on parade in Caernarfon, B Company at Pwllheli, C Company at Conwy and D Company at Holyhead.[113] The battalion went to its own Camp at Porthcawl in 1935 from 9 to 22 June, in poor weather, while the rest of the brigade went to Tenby a month later. The Rifle Meeting was held during Camp.

Normal training continued throughout the winter months along with the usual round of social events. The Officers' St David's Day Dinner was cancelled as mark of respect to the late King George V and a guest night held instead; the Sergeants' Mess Ball did not take place and it too was replaced by a guest night. Camp for 1936 took place with 7 R.W.F. at Kinmel Camp.

During the winter months of 1936/37, the battalion received the first of its planned fleet of motor transport, along with spare parts and instruction manuals; all spurs were reported as being returned to the Quartermaster. On 31 December 1936, battalion strength was reported as twenty Officers and 486 N.C.Os and Fusiliers,[114] an increase of thirty men on the previous year. By 31 March, this had increased further to eighteen Officers and 498 Other Ranks.[115] Recruiting was greatly helped by the increases in bounty and allowances outlined in Chapter 13. All companies were on parade as usual for the Armistice Commemoration in November, and for the proclamation of His Majesty King George VI in December.

The Sergeants' Mess Dinner was held later than usual, on 3 April 1937. The battalion sent a contingent to London for the Coronation in May 1937, as described in Chapter 15; several Officers and men received Coronation Medals as outlined in the Annexes to this Volume. All companies provided detachments for Coronation parades and services in towns across the battalion's area, notably in Caernarfon, Conwy, Bangor, Porthmadoc and Pwllheli. By July, strength had again risen to twenty-four Officers and 500 men.[116]

On 15 July, the battalion provided a street-lining detachment, along with other detachments from the 4th and 5th Battalions, for the Royal Visit to Caernarfon. This event is covered in detail in Chapter 6. A temporary camp was established at Coed Helen, where the troops were assembled and fed: It was a day of real hard work. The crowd was a large one and as all were anxious to obtain a good view of Their Majesties, control was at times difficult. It says much for the tact with which the troops handled the situation that the crowd were kept in good humour and did not resent being pushed back.'[117] Kyffin Williams, as always with an eye for the absurd, recalled being on parade:

6th Battalion Officers at the Court Levée, 1937.
(R.W.F. Mus 5359B)

Khakied and putteed, we were joined by an impressive detachment of the Welsh Guards, resplendent in scarlet and bearskins, who were to act as the Royal Bodyguard. The 6th Battalion Royal Welch Fusiliers were merely detailed off for street-lining duties.

Up at the barracks in the morning, Edward Cadogan, the regular adjutant, instructed the young Officers in sword drill, and afterwards I unwisely had a glass of lager. We were shown our positions on the Royal route, and I found that I and my farm labourers had the doubtful honour of lining up outside the public lavatories, on top of which a statue of Lloyd George fiercely waved its fist, and directly under Queen Eleanor's Gate [of the Castle] where the Royal couple were to make their appearance. A misguided benefactor had presented the platoon with a barrel of beer and we smuggled it into the Gents. All through that hot summer afternoon "Permission to fall out, sir?" came the continual cry, and Fusilier after Fusilier dived for the sanctuary of the public lavatories and the refreshing ale.[118]

The title of the battalion was amended slightly under Army Order 168 of 1937, to 6th (Caernarvonshire & Anglesey) Battalion, The Royal Welch Fusiliers (T.A.).

Camp was held at Hereford with the rest of 158 (Royal Welch) Infantry Brigade. The higher tempo of training and demonstrations, especially of new equipment, were remarked upon, as in other battalions. B Company came first in the *Lewis* gun handling event. Her Majesty Queen Mary visited Hereford during Camp; the battalion provided a street-lining detachment.

Recruiting, shooting and social events were the focus for the winter months of 1937/38, along with the Commemoration of the Armistice in November. The Sergeants' Mess Ball was held at Conwy on 5 March 1938. On 28 April 1938, *The Cheshire Chronicle* reported that the battalion was only thirty men short of its full war establishment of thirty-one Officers and 600 men. The *Regimental Journal* gave the battalion's strength as fifty-three Officers and 553 men;[119] probably a misprint, as the actual strength in Officers was more likely to be twenty-three.

The Goat died in the spring of 1938; a replacement was captured on the Great Orme. Camp was held at Ramsey, I.O.M. with the rest of 158 Brigade. Tactical training on the rough hills was found testing and there was much emphasis given to training in anti-gas precautions. 'It was a strange camp that year' recalled Kyffin Williams. 'The War Office had become aware of Hitler; so we had orders to parade every afternoon. There was a near mutiny over this, for the annual camp had always been regarded as a sort of holiday. Indignation abounded and we had a sorry time enforcing the new regulations.'[120]

On 14 November 1938, Major General Sir John Brown, the Deputy Director-General of the T.A., addressed a large gathering at Penrhyn Castle, the seat of the Honorary Colonel, on the subject of recruiting. The next day, the General addressed another meeting on Anglesey and afterwards visited all the battalion's Drill Halls in Caernarvonshire.[121] On Christmas night the Goat broke out of his field and was found half drowned in a river, and unfortunately died during the night.

STAFF LIST, 6th (Caernarvonshire & Anglesey) Battalion, 1920–1939

Battalion Headquarters (Caernarfon)

Commanding Officer	Lt Col F. Mills DSO	16 Feb 20
	Lt Col F.J. Walwyn DSO	31 Dec 20
	Lt Col (Bt Col) C.E. Vivian MC	10 Jan 23
	Lt Col A.M. Trustram Eve MC	10 Jan 27

	Lt Col (Bt Col) M.L. Lloyd-Mostyn	10 Jan 31
	Lt Col J.M. Evans	10 Jan 37
Senior Major	Maj J. Comlyn	
	Maj J. Douglas Porter OBE	1923–1924
	Maj (Bt Lt Col) A.M. Trustram Eve MC	1926
	Maj J. Gilbert MC TD	1927–1936
	Maj I. Griffith	1936
	Maj R.R. Davies	1937
Adjutant	Capt J.N. More	
	Capt (Bt Lt Col) C.C. Norman CMG DSO	Mar 23
	Capt A.M.G. Evans	Sep 23
	Capt H.F. Garnons-Williams	12 Sep 27
	Capt D.H.W. Kirkby	6 Dec 30
	Capt P.L. Bowers	6 Dec 34
	Capt J.A.M. Rice-Evans	Jul 38
	Capt E.H. Cadogan	1 Nov 38
Quartermaster	Capt T. Deane	1915
	Lt R.E. Griffiths	1925
	Lt W.H. Kelly	29 Jan 26; Capt 30
	Lt R.W. Howell	20 Dec 35
Regimental Sergeant Major	W.O. I H.A. Richards	
	W.O. I W. A. Simpson MC	Nov 23
	W.O. I T. Evans	1925
	W.O. I H. Howell	1927
	W.O. I G. Johnson	1934
	W.O. I J. Brown	Jan 38
Bandmaster	W.O. II D. Evans	1929
	W.O. I H. Walsh	to 1935
	W.O. I – Pratt	Jul 35
R.Q.M.S.	W.O. II J. Hughes	1920
	W.O. II F. Twine	1933
	W.O. II V.S. Smart	1935
O.R.Q.M.S.	W.O. II H.J. Williams	

H.Q. Company/H.Q. Wing (Caernarfon, Pwllheli, Bethesda)

Officer Commanding	Capt W.P. Lines	1927
	Maj N. Gilbert MC TD	1930
	Capt E.L.O. Williams	1933
	Capt H.W.R. Williams	1935
	Maj I. Griffith	1936–1937, to D Coy
	Capt D.R. Llewellyn	1937
Second-in-Command	Capt J. Morris Jones	
	Capt H.G. Carter MC	1930
Signal Platoon	Capt N. Gilbert MC	
	2Lt R.C. Newton	1927
	2Lt D.R. Llewellyn	1932; Lt 32
	2Lt O.E.H. Hughes	1937
	Sgt S.H. Vickers	1927
	Sgt A. Vale	1929
	Sgt R. Roberts	1935
Instructor	Sgt R.J. Price	1931
	Sgt A.R. James	Dec 32
M.M.G. Platoon (Disb 30)	Lt S. Goodchild	Mar 24
	Lt S. Farthing	1926

	Sgt W. Doughty	1927
Admin Platoon	2Lt R.C. Newton	1926
	Lt H. Williams	1930
	2Lt W.L. Woods	1937
	Sgt R.J. Thomas	1929
Corps of Drums (Conwy)	DMaj W.H. Kelly	1921
	DMaj E. Jones	1929
	DMaj J. Hughes	1931
	DMaj W.J. Coton	1933
	DMaj J.G. Harper	1935
Regimental Band (Beaumaris)	Sgt J.W. Stone	1929
Pioneers (Conwy)	Sgt R.J. Thomas	1930, from D Coy
Cooks (Conwy)	Sgt R. Nicholson	1932, from B Coy
	Sgt G. Pritchard	1936
Officers' Mess	Sgt J. Morris	1926
	Sgt J. Owen	1933
Provost Sgt	Sgt J. Owen	to 33
	Sgt R.J. Thomas	1933
Company Sergeant Major	W.O. II P.C. Cush	1925
	W.O. II G. Owen	1929
	W.O. II B.J. Kelly	1933
	W.O. II G. Brereton	1934
C.Q.M.S.	Sgt W.J. Williams	1925
	Sgt J. Turnbull	1931
	Sgt A. Vale	1933
	CSgt O.C. Simms	1934
	CSgt D. Hughes	1938
Instructor	Sgt L. Jones	1926
Sergeants	Sgt D. Hughes	Sgt W. Harwood
	Sgt W. Doughty	Sgt E. Edwards
	Sgt E. Hannan	Sgt G. Evans
	Sgt R.E. Jones	Sgt A.R. Heighway
	Sgt E. Jones	Sgt R. Lewis
	Sgt R. Edwards	Sgt D. Williams
	Sgt H.J. Williams	Sgt W. Thomas
	Sgt R.G. Rees	Sgt R. Roberts

A Company (Caernarfon, Bangor, Llanberis, Bethesda and Penygroes) (1, 2, 3 Platoons)

Officer Commanding	Capt H.T. Finchett Maddock MC	
	Capt H. Gordon Carter MC	1923; Maj Feb 27
	Capt (Bt Maj) I. Griffith	1930: Maj Apr 36
	Capt R.C. Newton	1935; Maj 37
Second-in-Command	Capt H. Gordon Carter MC	1921
	Lt R. Roberts	1926
	Capt R.C. Newton	1931
	Lt G.P. Jones	1936
	Capt D.R. Llewellyn	1937
Platoon Commander	2Lt O.M. Williams	1926
Platoon Commander	Lt I. Griffith	1927
Platoon Commander	Lt D.R. Jones	1926
Platoon Commander	Lt G.R. Evans	1926
Platoon Commander	Lt F.D. Colebourn	1926
Platoon Commander	2Lt R.C. Newton	1925, Lt 27
Platoon Commander	2Lt E.G. Owen	1931; Lt 33

Platoon Commander	2Lt T.E. Owens	1931
Platoon Commander	2Lt G.P Jones	1932; Lt 35
Platoon Commander	Lt D.R. Llewellyn	1934
Platoon Commander	2Lt J.W. Fletcher Townley	1936
Platoon Commander	2Lt D.S. Davies	1936
Platoon Commander	2Lt D.A.E. Roberts	1937
Platoon Sergeant	Sgt O.J. Jones	1920
Platoon Sergeant	Sgt W.A. Roberts	1926
Platoon Sergeant	Sgt T.O. Smith	1926
Platoon Commander	Sgt D. Roberts	1926
Platoon Sergeant	Sgt H. Thomas	1926
Platoon Sergeant	Sgt W.H. Roberts	to 1937
Platoon Sergeant	Sgt B. Kelly	1927
Platoon Sergeant	Sgt R.O. Griffiths	1927
Platoon Sergeant	Sgt M. Jones	1929
Platoon Sergeant	Sgt R. Nicholson	1929
Platoon Sergeant	Sgt H. Thomas	1929
Platoon Sergeant	Sgt J.W. Evans	1930
Platoon Sergeant	Sgt J.T. Jones	1930
Platoon Sergeant	Sgt W.H. Roberts	1930
Platoon Sergeant	Sgt O.C. Simms	1933
Platoon Sergeant	Sgt F. Thomas	1935
Platoon Sergeant	Sgt R. Hughes	1935
Platoon Sergeant	Sgt A. Rogers	1936
Platoon Sergeant	Sgt T.J. Williams	1936
Platoon Sergeant	Sgt T. Parry	1937
Platoon Sergeant	Sgt D.H. Edwards	1938
Company Sergeant Major	W.O. II J. Billing	1920
	W.O. II D.G. Bracegirdle	1925
	W.O. II T. Evans 74	1926
	W.O. II P. Sullivan	1927
	W.O. II R.D. Griffiths	1931
	W.O. II J.W. Evans	1932
	W.O. II B. Kelly	1936–1938
C.Q.M.S.	Sgt I. Jones	1920
	Sgt J.L. Evans	1929–30
	Sgt E.R. Hughes	1930–33
	Sgt B. Kelly	1931
	Sgt A. Vale	1935
	CSgt E.J. Jones	1938
Instructor	Sgt R.H. Sowrey	1921
	Sgt S. Dibble MM	Feb 24
	Sgt E. Griffiths	1927
	Sgt A.R. James	1934
	Sgt D. Robbins	1936
	Sgt M. Jones	1938

B Company (Porthmadog, Pwllheli and Criccieth) (4, 5, 6 Platoons)

Officer Commanding	Capt A.M. Trustram Eve MC	1920
	Capt J.N. More	Nov 23
	Capt R.O. Jones	1927–29
	Capt F.D. Colebourn	1929
	Capt R. Vaughan Humphries	1931
	Maj R.E. Griffith	1934; died 1935

	Capt R. Vaughan Humphries	1935
Second-in-Command	Lt T.A. Shone	1922
	Capt P.R. Price	1927–29, from C Coy
	Capt A. Roberts	1935
	Capt R. Homfray	1937
Platoon Commander	Lt W.T. Williams	Jun 25
Platoon Commander	Lt R.E. Griffiths	1926
Platoon Commander	Lt F.E. Colbourn	1926
Platoon Commander	Lt E.R. Jones	1927
Platoon Commander	2Lt R. Homfray	1930
Platoon Commander	2Lt D.M.S. Parker	1932
Platoon Commander	2Lt D.E. Owens	1932
Platoon Commander	2Lt D.S. Davies	1932
Platoon Commander	2Lt C.L.E. Haigh	1932; Lt 32
Platoon Commander	2Lt I. Hughes	1936
Platoon Commander	2Lt S.T.A. Livingstone-Learmonth	1936
Platoon Commander	2Lt T.W. Whittaker	Jan 37
Platoon Commander	2Lt J.W. Williams	Jan 37
Platoon Commander	2Lt J.K. Williams	1937[*]
Platoon Commander	2Lt H.G. Jones-Roberts	1938
Platoon Sergeant	Sgt H. Griffiths	1926
Platoon Sergeant	Sgt C. Griffiths	1926
Platoon Sergeant	Sgt W.H. Jones	1926
Platoon Sergeant	Sgt M. Jones	1931
Platoon Sergeant	Sgt S. Williams	1931
Platoon Sergeant	Sgt H. MacMillan	1933
Platoon Sergeant	Sgt J. Owen	1933
Platoon Sergeant	Sgt R. Nicholson 81	1933
Platoon Sergeant	Sgt R. L. Jackson 51	1929; died 33
Platoon Sergeant	Sgt I. Jones	1935
Platoon Sergeant	Sgt O.J. Jones	1935
Platoon Sergeant	Sgt J.T. Jones	1936–1937
Platoon Sergeant	Sgt D. Green	1936
Platoon Sergeant	Sgt – Hildige	1936–1937
Platoon Sergeant	Sgt W.T. Williams	1937
Company Sergeant Major	W.O. II E.O. Jones	1920
	W.O. II J. Rowlands	1926
	W.O. II J. Wilde	1927
	W.O. II W. Jones	1929
	W.O. II P. Sullivan	1929
	W.O. II W. Howells	Dec 36, from PSI C Coy
C.Q.M.S.	Sgt H. Morris	1920
	Sgt A. Evans	1929
	Sgt V. Smart	to 1936
Instructor	Sgt T. Evans	1924
	Sgt W. Robinson	Nov 26
	Sgt C. Brooker	1931
	Sgt L. Lawrence *W.G.*	1933
	Sgt Nicholl *W.G.*	Dec 36

[*]   Later Sir John 'Kyffin' Williams KBE RA, (1918–2006); see his entry in the Annex on writers and artists.

C Company (Conwy, Penmaenmawr, Dolgarrog, Menai Bridge and Trefriw) (7, 8, 9 Platoons)

Officer Commanding	Capt J. Douglas Porter OBE	Maj Jul 22
	Capt W.P. Lines	Dec 24; to H.Q. Coy 1927
	Maj J.M. Evans	1931
	Capt R.C. Newton	1936
	Capt R.M. Turton	1937–1938
	Capt D.S. Davies	1938
Second-in-Command	Capt J.M. Evans	1927
	Capt R.M. Turton	1936
	Capt E.L.O. Williams	1937
Platoon Commander	2Lt J.M. Evans	1921, Lt 24
Platoon Commander	Lt W.P. Lines	1922
Platoon Commander	Lt C.J. Roberts	1922
Platoon Commander	Lt P.R. Price	Dec 23
Platoon Commander	Lt E.L. Llewellyn	1929
Platoon Commander	2Lt D.W. Darbyshire	1929; Lt 30; to R. of O. 1934
Platoon Commander	2Lt E.R. Jones	1929–30
Platoon Commander	Lt R.M. Turton	1931, from 5 Border
Platoon Commander	Lt H.W.R. Williams	1932
Platoon Commander	2Lt D.S. Davies	1932
Platoon Commander	2Lt J.M. Layton	1934, from H.A.C.
Platoon Commander	2Lt C. Vere-Whiting	Jan 37
Platoon Commander	2Lt R.H.D. Williams-Bulkeley	Jun 37
Platoon Commander	2Lt J.W. Bloor	Nov 38
Platoon Sergeant	Sgt H. Williams	1920
Platoon Sergeant	Sgt H.J. Barther	1921
Platoon Sergeant	Sgt W. Hughes	1926
Platoon Sergeant	Sgt J.E. Jones	1926
Platoon Sergeant	Sgt R. Davies	1926
Platoon Sergeant	Sgt R.I. Jones	1931
Platoon Sergeant	Sgt R. Goosey	1931
Platoon Sergeant	Sgt S. Williams	1933
Platoon Sergeant	Sgt Ll. Lloyd-Williams	1935
Platoon Sergeant	Sgt J. Williams	1935
Platoon Sergeant	Sgt A. Rogers	1937
Company Sergeant Major	W.O. II R. Williams	1920
	W.O. II R. Jones	1927
	W.O. II J.T. Jones	1929
	W.O. II P. Sullivan	1931
	W.O. II G. Brereton	1934
	W.O. II S. Williams	1937
C.Q.M.S.	Sgt L. Jones	1922
	Sgt R. Jones	1929
	Sgt H. Morris	1931
	CSgt R. Goosey	1934
Instructor	W.O. II J. Wylie	Feb 24
	W.O. II J. Wilde	1927
	W.O. II W. Howells	1933
	W.O. II J. Brown	1936
	W.O. II F. Wilkinson	1938

D Company (Holyhead and Beaumaris) (10, 11, 12 Platoons) (M.G. Company from 1930–1939)

Officer Commanding	Maj C.E. Vivian MC	
	Capt J.N. More	1922

	Capt A.M. Trustram Eve MC	Nov 23
	Capt J. Morris-Jones	1925
	Capt N. Gilbert MC	1926; Maj 31; res May 36
	Capt R.C. Newton	1933
	Capt E.L.O. Williams	1935
Second-in-Command	Lt D.M.S. Parker	1936; died 1938
Platoon Commander	2Lt R.C. Jones	1921
Platoon Commander	2Lt S. Goodchild	Jun 22
Platoon Commander	2Lt T.W. Grey-Edwards	Aug 23
Platoon Commander	2Lt E.L.O. Williams	1926
Platoon Commander	2Lt H.W.R. Williams	1927
Platoon Commander	2Lt E.L.C. Williams	1927
Platoon Commander	2Lt J.R. Jones	1929
Platoon Commander	2Lt C. Fanning Evans	1929
Platoon Commander	2Lt R.H.G. Sharp	1931–33
Platoon Commander	2Lt D.S. Davies	1931, from Supp Res
Platoon Commander	2Lt G.P. Jones	1932
Platoon Commander	Lt D.M.S. Parker	1935, from B Coy
Platoon Commander	2Lt E. Roberts	May 38
Platoon Sergeant	Sgt J. Jones	1920
Platoon Sergeant	Sgt N.D. Lambert	1920
Platoon Sergeant	Sgt G. Brereton	1926
Platoon Sergeant	Sgt R.J. Thomas	1926
Platoon Sergeant	Sgt F.W. Turner	1926
Platoon Sergeant	Sgt R.E. Jones	1926
Platoon Sergeant	Sgt W.J. Pratt	1929
Platoon Sergeant	LSgt J. Owen	Sgt 36, retired 1937
Platoon Sergeant	Sgt A.L. Williams	1932
Platoon Sergeant	Sgt N.T. Doughty	1933
Platoon Sergeant	Sgt A. Pratt	1933
Platoon Sergeant	Sgt E.J.J. Pierce	1933
Platoon Sergeant	Sgt R. Lloyd	1936
Platoon Sergeant	Sgt T.G. Jones	1936
Platoon Sergeant	Sgt J.E. Jones	1937
Platoon Sergeant	Sgt H.G. Evans	1938
Platoon Sergeant	Sgt W.L. Jones	1938
Company Sergeant Major	W.O. II J.T. Jones	1923
	W.O. II J.E. Jones	1938
C.Q.M.S.	Sgt W. Doughty	1926
	Sgt N.T. Doughty	1935
	Sgt R.J. Burnell	1938
Instructor	Sgt Mann	1921
	Sgt J.B. Kelly	Nov 23
	Sgt Evans	Nov 23
	Sgt L. Jones 94	1927
	Sgt W. Cowan	1929
	Sgt W. Lowe	Oct 32
	Sgt G. Williams	1936
	Sgt R. Preest	1937

Attached

Capt I. Wynne-Jones *R.A.M.C.*		1926
Lt A. Roberts *R.A.M.C.*		1930; Capt 32
Rev R.W. Hughes *C.F.*		1920–1927

Rev A.R. Morgan MC *C.F.*   1927–1930
Rev W.P. Webb *C.F.*   1930

Unplaced
2Lt I. Hughes   Jun 36

Instructors (on re-formation, companies not identified)
W.O. I H.A. Richards
W.O. II E.J. Smith DCM (to Jun 23)
Sgt A.H. Quinn
Sgt W. Dunne (to Jun 23)
Sgt G. Cuel (to Jun 23)
Sgt T. Evans MSM
W.O. II A. Simpson MC, vice Smith (to Mar 23)
Sgt D.C. Urquhart MM, vice Cuel
Sgt B.V. Wright, vice Dunne
Sgt A.E. Waller DCM (May 22)

x. The 7th (Merioneth & Montgomeryshire) Battalion, 1920– 1938

The 7th Battalion was re-formed under the command of Lieutenant Colonel R.O. Crewe-Read DSO. Its headquarters were at Newtown; A Company was at Llanidloes; B Company at Towyn (Merionethshire) with detachments at Aberdovey and Dolgellau; C Company at Welshpool with detachment at Llanfyllin and Llanfair Caereinion; and D

R.W.F. on parade in Llanidloes, c.1923. (R.W.F. Mus 8686d)

Company at Machynlleth with a platoon at Montgomery. All companies opened and closed detachments at various locations throughout the period, as shown in the Staff List.

The battalion went to Camp with 158 Brigade at Rhyl from 23 July to 6 August 1921. The strength of the battalion was fifteen Officers and 531 men. The brigade and divisional football cup was won by the 7th Battalion which beat the 4th by four goals to one. Inspections were carried out by G.O.C. Western Command, Lieutenant General Sir Beauvoir de Lisle KCB KCMG DSO MC, and Major General Deverell, the divisional commander.

The battalion annual shoot, always a popular event with 7 R.W.F. before the war, was held at Penarth Range on Whit Monday. Glorious weather helped to ensure a most successful day with the Battalion Cup – presented by Sir Edward Pryce-Jones Bt TD, Honorary Colonel since 1908 – was won by the Welshpool team under CSM Herbert Evans. The Silver Challenge Cup for the highest aggregate score went to Private E.W. Pugh of Welshpool. The Commanding Officer provided lunch for competitors and visitors in marquees specially erected for the occasion. On returning home the Welshpool Company (C) received a warm reception, the Regimental Band playing them through the streets to the Armoury. The same evening C Company hosted a dance to which 250 attended. Music was supplied by the Regimental String Band under Bandmaster Sidney Jones.

The battalion won the 53rd Division football competition at Shrewsbury, defeating 2nd Welsh Field Ambulance from Cardiff 11-4.

The Band and a Guard of Honour of 130 Other Ranks under the command of Captain G. Latham MC was provided by 7 R.W.F. on the occasion of the visit of Field Marshal Earl Haig to the *Eisteddfod* at Meifod. Lieutenant Colonel Crewe-Read acted as A.D.C. to the Field Marshal. The G.O.C. 53rd Division visited the battalion on 28 and 30 June.

In 1922, Camp was at Aberystwyth from 29 July to 12 August. The first week was devoted to drill and platoon and company training. The last week was given over to battalion training and preparation for the visit by the divisional commander on 10 August Major General Sir A.A. Montgomery KCMG CB. On the following day the performance was repeated for the G.O.C. Western Command.

When the balance of bounties came to be paid to members of 7 R.W.F. on their return from Camp, many soldiers re-engaged. As the battalion had a waiting list it could afford to select only those of the required quality. In October C Company provided a party under Lieutenant E.H. Farmer for the unveiling of the Llanfair Caereinion War Memorial. In November a dinner and smoking concert was held at Llanidloes for the presentation of the Battalion Efficiency Cup to A Company. An excellent dinner was provided by the Queen's Hotel. The Company, of whose members 141 out of 144 had attended annual camp, had won the football, cross-country – with six in the first nine to finish – and recruits' cups, and scored the highest in musketry efficiency.

The D Company 7 R.W.F. Drill Hall at Machynlleth was improved by the addition of a new storeroom and armoury, billiard room, N.C.Os' room, kitchen and 30-yard range. The County T.A. Association provided billiard tables for all drill halls.

Colonel Sir Watkin Williams Wynn Bt CB accepted the invitation to become Joint Honorary Colonel with Colonel Sir Edward Pryce-Jones.

According to the *Regimental Journal*, the 7th Battalion was the 'Best Battalion in the Welsh Division' in 1923. Among other awards, it won the County Shooting Shield:

> The presentation to the 7th Royal Welch Fusiliers of the Lord Lieutenant's Shield for shooting, which took place on 23 February [1923], proved to be a highly successful and interesting function for rallying interest in Montgomeryshire Territorial units. The torch light procession made by the Regiment through the town headed by the Regimental Band … to take the trophy from the railway station to the Drill Hall.[122]

The shield was presented to the Commanding Officer, Lieutenant Colonel Crewe-Read, by the Lord Lieutenant, Sir Watkin Williams Wynn. It was the first time that the shield, open to T.A. units throughout the county, was awarded. One of those present was Sergeant Drummer Evan Jones, survivor of Rorke's Drift.*

7 R.W.F. provided a guard of honour under Captain F.A.D. Evans MC on the occasion of the unveiling of the County War Memorial at Montgomery on 28 April 1923 by the Lord Lieutenant, Sir H.L. Watkin Williams Wynn. The Adjutant, Captain T. Picton of the Royal

---

*   Evan Jones (1859 – 1931) served in the R. Monmouthshire R.E., the 24th Foot, the S.W.B., the Northumberland Fusiliers and the R.W.F.

Sussex Regiment, was made MBE in the Birthday Honours list. He had served in the ranks of The Royal Welch Fusiliers before being commissioned.[123]

The Prince of Wales visited Welshpool on 25 July 1923 when the 7th Battalion provided the Band and a Guard of Honour of 130 men under Captain E.P. Price MC. The other Officers were Captain F.A.D. Evans MC and Lieutenant E.H. Farmer. Lieutenant A.E. Wilson DCM was the Ensign for the King's Colour.[124]

In June 1923, battalion strength was reported as twenty Officers and 610 N.C.Os and Fusiliers. 'This is considered satisfactory, as all men over the age of 40 years have been discharged.'[125] After Camp, courses of instruction in signalling, light-automatic (*Lewis* gun), *Vickers* M.M.G. and N.C.O. duties were held.

The battalion Rifle Meeting was held on Whit Monday 1924, the prizes being presented by the Honorary Colonel, Colonel Sir Edward Pryce-Jones Bt TD. C Company was the champion company and the prize for the best aggregate score was won by Fusilier M.A. Morgan. The battalion's annual Prize-Giving and Dinner took place at the Drill Hall in Newtown in September, which was also the battalion's farewell to Lieutenant Colonel Crewe-Read and Captain Picton. The Honorary Colonel presented a new Regimental Goat to commemorate the occasion.[126]

R.W.F. Signallers, winners of the 53rd Division championship 1923–1926. (R.W.F. Mus)

In the T.A. Rifle Competitions for the year 1924, the battalion was placed 5th in the Lord Lieutenant's Shield (68 entries), 6th in the B.S.A. Ltd Trophy (128 entries), 2nd in the Imperial Tobacco Challenge Cup (28 entries), and 17th in the M.G. Challenge Cup (76 entries). The battalion also won the Divisional Recruits' Competition, the Tredegar Aggregate Shooting Competition and the Inter-Battalion Competition; was placed 2nd in the Inter-Platoon Competition; and 5th in the Shropshire T.A. Association Miniature Range Competition.[127]

The St David's Day Ball in 1925 was held at the Drill Hall, Newtown, and it 'was again a brilliant assembly of uniforms and colours.'[128] A large number of Officers from the 2nd Battalion and the Depot attended, along with the Band of the 2nd Battalion; an all-ranks dance was also held, at Newtown, on 19 March.

Little information is available for the period 1926 to 1930, as no *Regimental Journal* was published. However the minutes of the County Territorial Army Association record battalion strength in 1926 as sixteen Officers and 562 men against an establishment of twenty Officers and 636 men. Local newspapers in Montgomery and Merioneth also published regular articles on the doings of their local T.A. companies. In 1929, the Regimental Band was put into full dress and an allowance of £100 per annum made for its upkeep.[129]

In 1930, A Company was able to secure the use of a 12-acre training area close to its T.A. Centre. The company paraded in Llanidloes with the Regimental Goat, Pioneers, Band and Drums on 21 June; 120 Officers and men were on parade. B Company opened a new Drill Hall in Llansantffraid. In May 1931, D Company held a field training day on Lord Londonderry's estate near Machynlleth; seventy Officers and men attended.[130] The M.G. Company won the Brigade Competition at Camp in 1931 by 120 points, and were runners-up in the Divisional Competition.

The 7 R.W.F. Officers' St David's Day Dinner in Newtown, 1927. (R.W.F. Mus 8686d)

7 R.W.F. in Camp, 1927. (R.W.F. Mus)

The winter months of 1931/32 were enlivened by courses and small-bore rifle competitions. The signallers won the Brigade Signalling Competition and were runners-up in the Divisional Competition. A T.E.W.T. on 17 January was attended by sixty Officers and N.C.Os but 'unfortunately funds do not permit for more than a few of these enjoyable meetings.'[131] The Sergeants' Mess held its first post-war St David's Day Ball at Welshpool on 3 March 1932. It was well attended and became a regular event. However the *Regimental Journal* recorded later in the year that: 'This last year has been, possibly, the most trying period for the Battalion. Everybody has felt very keenly the loss of our annual training in camp, but fortunately everything has been done to keep men together and to keep their interest up.'[132] In July, a sports meeting was held at Newtown, attended by 200 Officers and men. The Rifle Meeting took place on 1 August, also at Newtown, and was visited by the G.O.C. The Signal Platoon again won the Brigade Cup and came second in the Divisional competition. During the summer, eight Officers were attached for periods of instruction with the 1st Battalion. On 24 September, 200 former members of the battalion who had served during the Great War attended a dinner in Towyn. [133]

On the Friday afternoon next before Christmas, A Company in Llanidloes put on a Christmas Tree party for the children of the company's members, and those of the Regimental Band – which was also the Llanidloes Town Silver Band. About ninety sat down to tea, followed by games and presents. The Officers' Ball, having not been held in 1932, was held on 6 January 1933 at Welshpool, followed on the Sunday by a T.E.W.T. for Officers and N.C.Os.[134] The Sergeants' Mess St David's Day Ball was held a month later, on 24 February, in one of the worst snow-storms in living memory. Even so, sixty members and guests managed to attend; however the orchestra did not make it and the event was deemed a financial disaster. The Officers' St David's Day Dinner at Welshpool on 4 March was more successful.[135]

Camp at Aberystwyth in 1933 was generally regarded as the best the battalion had had since 1920. In the various competitions, the battalion came second in the brigade signals, second in the brigade M.G. and seventh in the division, and second in the brigade and sixth in the division in the Prince of Wales's Shield for drill.[136] After Camp, attention returned to shooting and training a large number of new recruits, especially in A Company.

The Officers' St David's Day Dinner for 1934 was held at the Bear Hotel, Newtown, on 3 March 1934 and the Sergeants' Mess Ball for 1934 took place at the Scala Theatre, Newtown, on 9 March. The Rifle Meeting took place at Penarth Range, Newtown, on Whit Monday; Corporal J.D. Williams of Towyn won the Individual Championship.[137] The battalion went to Camp at Porthcawl from 29 July to 13 August 1934 in very indifferent weather. Although training was not affected, a ceremonial parade planned for 11 August had to be cancelled. The Signal Platoon came first in the Divisional competition and the M.M.G. Company came third. The Llanwyddyn Platoon under Lieutenant A.H. Williams was placed third overall in the Prince of Wales's Shield for military skills.[138]

In 1935, the Officers' St David's Day Dinner was held in the Bear Hotel, Newtown, attended by thirty-five Officers and guests, the latter including the G.O.C., Major General A.J. Dick-Cunyngham.* The battalion football team reached the final of the T.A. Challenge Cup,† losing to the Devon and Cornwall Heavy Brigade, R.A. (T.A.) by 1-0 after extra time.[139] Jubilee

---

*   Major General James Keith Dick-Cunyngham CB CMG DSO (1877–1935) left the command soon after this for the 4th Infantry Division, but died soon thereafter at the early age of 58.

†   The 7 R.W.F. team was also the Llanidloes town team.

The Silver Jubilee celebrations in Newtown, 7 R.W.F., 1935. (R.W.F. Mus 8686d)

The 7 R.W.F. Guard of Honour for H.R.H. The Prince of Wales's visit to Dolgellau. (R.W.F. Mus 8686d)

parades were held across the battalion's area; those members of the battalion who received the Jubilee Medal are listed in the Annexes to this Volume.

The battalion took part in the Brigade Camp at Tenby in 1935 from 28 July to 12 August; the warm welcome accorded by the Mayor and Corporation, and the people generally, was much remarked upon. The first week was devoted to section and platoon training, the second week to company and battalion training. On 3 August the whole brigade (less 6 R.W.F.) was inspected by the Colonel of the Regiment, Lieutenant General Sir Charles Dobell. The Signal Platoon again won the brigade competition. During Camp, the annual reunion of veterans of Suvla Bay was held, among them three Officers and nine men from 7 R.W.F.[140]

During the winter of 1935/36, electric lighting and heating was installed in all the battalion's Drill Halls.[141] The soccer team again won the Divisional Cup, beating 53rd Divisional Signals in the final on 21 December 1935. In the T.A. Cup, the team beat 9th Manchesters 5-4 but lost the semi-final to 8th D.L.I. 2-1. Drills and other courses were curtailed by the building work, but training was fully under way again by early April 1936. The Rifle Meeting was held as usual on Whit Monday, with C Company winning the championship.

The battalion went to Camp with the 6th Battalion at Kinmel Camp, Denbighshire, from 26 July – 9 August 1936, in very bad weather. Section and platoon training occupied the first week, company and battalion training the second. 'Our numbers were a little more than usual, but employment kept a number of men away, though employers were very helpful in letting as many men off as possible.'[142]

The autumn and winter of 1936/37 were devoted to low-level training, recruiting and social events, including the Llanidloes children's Christmas party, and the Armistice Commemoration in November. The Officers' St David's Day Dinner was also the farewell to the Commanding Officer, Lieutenant Colonel C.S. Price-Davies, who left after eight years in command.

In the T.A. Football Challenge Cup for 1937 the battalion football team defeated the 53rd Divisional Signals 3-0, 5th Prince of Wales's Volunteers 4-2, 8th D.L.I. 5-3 in extra time and then the Buckinghamshire Battalion 2-0 in the final at the H.A.C. Ground, Armoury House, London. The team was:

> Fusiliers R.E. Price, E.V. Price, D.C. Jones, E.R. Gamble, W.E.R. Morris, J. Beedlecombe, R. Jones
> Lance Corporals H.B. Mills and J. Price.[143]

A contingent from the battalion took part in street lining duties at the Coronation in London in May 1937, as detailed in Chapter 15. Other detachments took part in Coronation parades and services in towns across the battalion's area, especially in Newtown, Welshpool, Llanidloes and Machynlleth, Dolgellau and Llanfyllin.

The battalion's title was amended by Army Order 168 of 1937, to 7th (Merionethshire & Montgomeryshire) Battalion, The Royal Welch Fusiliers (T.A.), reflecting the true geographic spread of the battalion across mid-Wales.

On 15 July the battalion mustered 300 all ranks to line the streets for the visit of Their Majesties King George VI and Queen Elizabeth to Aberystwyth, while the 4th, 5th and 6th Battalions were carrying out the same duty in Caernarfon. Some detachments from outlying districts paraded at their Drill Halls before 05.00 hrs and then entrained for Aberystwyth, where the battalion concentrated for breakfast at 08.30 hrs. The parade was concluded by noon

King George VI visits Aberystwyth, 1937.
(Ceredigion Council)

Queen Mary's visit to Hereford, 29 July 1937.
(R.W.F. Mus 8686e)

and after their dinners, the men were given liberty in Aberystwyth until entraining once more at 19.30 hrs for a very late return home after a long day.[144]

Camp was held at Hereford with the rest of the brigade in what was described as tropical heat. During Camp, the battalion provided a detachment for street-lining in Hereford during the visit of Her Majesty Queen Mary, the Queen Mother. During Camp, the Signal Platoon again won the Divisional Competition and the M.G. Company was placed second.

In the 1938 T.A. Football Challenge Cup, the battalion football team defeated 6th Welch 7-1 after a replay, 8th D.L.I. 2-1 and then the Buckinghamshire Battalion 7-3 in the final at the H.A.C. Ground, Armoury House, London on 23 April 1938. This was the second year running that the team had won the final against the Buckinghamshires:

> Fus H.L.W. Roberts scored the first goal for the Welch after four minutes play. It was not until the Welch Fusiliers had increased their lead by two more goals, obtained by Fus D.C. Jones and LCpl H.B. Mills, that the Bucks Battalion started to show their form. After the Bucks Battalion's first goal, Fus Roberts again scored for the Welch Fusiliers.[145]

After the match the D.G.T.A., General Sir Walter Kirke, presented the challenge cup and medals. The Royal Welch team was:

> Fusiliers R.E. Price, E.V. Price, D.C. Jones, H.L.W. Roberts, W.E.R. Morris, E.R. Gamble, J. Price, J. Beedlecombe, R. Jones
> Lance Corporals H.B. Mills and J. Price.

Recruiting proved more challenging for the 7th Battalion than for the other three T.A. battalions of the Regiment, given its low density of population. By mid 1938, A and C Companies reported being over their established strength, but B, D, and H.Q. were all below strength.[146] Increases in pay for drills, allowances, and bounties did, however, help. Camp was taken at

7 R.W.F. arrives at Ramsey, I.O.M., for Annual Camp. (R.W.F. Mus 8686d)

Ramsey, I.O.M., with the rest of 158 Brigade, from 31 July to 13 August. For many men, an early start was needed to get to the rendezvous outside Birkenhead by 11.00 hrs on Sunday 31 July and it was 19.00 hrs that evening before the brigade disembarked from the ferry SS *Benmychree** and marched into camp, watched by a large crowd. In addition to tactical exercises, including the use of gas, Camp included a Brigade *Eisteddfod* and a ceremonial parade in front of the Governor of Man.

STAFF LIST, 7th (Merioneth & Montgomeryshire) Battalion, 1920–1938

Battalion Headquarters (Newtown)

Commanding Officer	Lt Col T.H. Harker DSO *K.R.R.C.*	
	Lt Col R.O. Crewe-Read DSO *S.W.B.*	16 Feb 20
	Lt Col G.R.D. Harrison TD	28 Feb 25
	Lt Col C.S. Price Davies MC TD	28 Feb 29
	Lt Col W. Roberts MC	28 Feb 37
Senior Major	Maj G.R.D. Harrison TD	Sep 24
	Maj R.W.J. Arbuthnott-Brisco TD	Jun 25
	Maj E. Powell-Price MC TD	1930
	Maj (Bt Lt Col) W. Roberts MC	1934
Adjutant	Capt J.C. Wynne Edwards	17 Mar 20
	Capt T. Picton MBE MC	
	Connaught Rangers [later R. Sussex R.] 1923	1 Oct 21
	Capt G.F. Watson DSO	16 Oct 24

*   Later used as a transport ship for the assault on Pointe du Hoc by the U.S. Rangers on 6 June 1944.

	Lt R.G. Davies-Jenkins	14 Nov 28
	Lt J.H. Liscombe	14 Nov 32
	Capt R. de B. Hardie	14 Nov 36
R.M.O.	Maj E.W. Ashworth *R.A.M.C.*	to 1938
Chaplain	Rev S. Bailey *R.A.Ch.D.*	1930
Quartermaster	Capt T.W. Grist	22 Mar 20
	Capt R. Leonard	13 Nov 29
Regimental Sergeant Major	W.O. I W.P. Allen	
	W.O. I W. Martin	Oct 23
	W.O. I Dickenson DCM	Oct 22
	W.O. I W. Martin	May 23
	W.O. I N. Ridings	1931
	W.O. I E. Davies	Oct 34
	W.O. I W.J. Hawkins	1938
Bandmaster	W.O. I S.J. Jones	1921
R.Q.M.S.	W.O. II R. Riley	1937

H.Q. Company/H.Q. Wing (Newtown)

Officer Commanding	Maj R.W.J. Arbuthnott-Brisco TD	
	Capt A.E. Wilson DCM	Oct 24
Second-in-Command	Lt Ll. Llewellyn Rowlands	Oct 23
Signal Platoon	Lt D.R. Manuel	
	Capt V. Makey TD	1933; Maj 38; resigned 38
	Sgt W. Blayney	
M.M.G. Platoon	Lt H. Player	Oct 23
Mortar Platoon (1937)	Lt W.E. Lewis	
Admin Platoon	Lt A.E. Wilson DCM	
	Lt J.J. Turner	1938
	Sgt E.H. Jones	
	Sgt J.P. Owen	
	Sgt – Bowen	1938
Pioneers	Sgt – Walters	
Regimental Band (Llanidloes)	Sgt – Benbow	1937
Corps of Drums	DMaj J.R. Owen	1933
Company Sergeant Major	W.O. II S.J. O'Hare	1936
Instructor	Sgt A. Cox	1926
	Sgt H. Roberts	1936
	W.O. II E.T. Langford	1937

A Company (Llanidloes) (1, 2, 3 Platoons)

Officer Commanding	Capt G.L. Bennett Evans	Oct 23; retired Oct 36
	Capt R.B.S. Davies	1930; Maj 33
	Capt J.H. Williams	1938
Second-in-Command	Capt G. Latham MC	
	Capt E.D. Vaughan Jones	1929; R of O 35
	Capt L. Ll. Jones	1935
Platoon Commander	Lt T.R. Wilson-Jones MC	
Platoon Commander	Lt W.F. Cooke	
Platoon Commander	Lt F.G. Smith	
Platoon Commander	Lt C.B. Lloyd	Oct 23
Platoon Commander	2Lt R.S. Davies	Oct 23
Platoon Commander	Lt E.D. Vaughan Jones	1924
Platoon Commander	Lt R.G. Mills	1930
Platoon Commander	Lt J.H. Williams	1930

Platoon Commander	Lt R. Tonner	1933
Platoon Commander	Lt D.F. Jones	1935
Platoon Commander	2Lt B.G.B. Pugh	1938
Platoon Sergeant	Sgt W. Vaughan	
Platoon Sergeant	Sgt J. M. Rowlands	1933
Platoon Sergeant	Sgt A. Toy	1933
Platoon Sergeant	Sgt P. Price	1938
Platoon Sergeant	Sgt C.L. Rees	1938
Company Sergeant Major	W.O. II T.M. Evans	died Nov 33
	W.O. II – Mason	1933
	W.O. II R. Thomas	1936
C.Q.M.S.	Sgt D.W. Jones	
	Sgt J.M. Rowlands	1933
Instructor	Sgt A.C. Bent MM	1922
	Sgt W. Price	Mar 25
	W.O. II C. Morrisey	1930
	Sgt J. Mains *King's Own*	1931
	W.O. II R. Thomas	1935

B Company (Towyn, Dolgellau, Llanwyddan, Llansantffraid and Aberdovey) (4, 5, 6 Platoons)

Officer Commanding	Capt G.L. Bennett Evans	
	Capt F.A.D. Evans MC	Oct 23
	Capt E.P. Price MC	Jul 24
	Capt L. Baxter Jones	1931
Second-in-Command	Lt W. Roberts MC	Oct 23
	Capt L. Jones	1931
Platoon Commander	Lt A. Vaughan	
Platoon Commander	Lt V. Makey	
Platoon Commander	2Lt G.E. Roberts	1933
Platoon Commander	Lt R. Turner	1933
Platoon Commander	2Lt A.H. Williams	1934
Platoon Sergeant	Sgt – Needham	1935
Platoon Sergeant	Sgt – Boden	1935
Platoon Sergeant	Sgt – Warrilow	1936
Company Sergeant Major	W.O. II E. Tippett	
	W.O. II Wildblood	1931
C.Q.M.S.	Sgt Roberts	1930
W.O.II Instructor	Sgt J.M. Jones	
	Sgt E.W. Tanner	
	W.O. II A.H. Cumberland DCM MM	Oct 23
	Sgt – Morgan *W.G.*	1935

C Company (Welshpool, Llanfyllin and Llanfair) (7, 8, 9 Platoons)

Officer Commanding	Capt W. Williams-Wynn	
	Capt F.A.D. Evans MC	Jul 24
	Capt C.L. Bonshor	1937
Platoon Commander	Lt E.H. Farmer	retired May 24
Platoon Commander	2Lt R.E.C. Thomas	Lt Oct 23
Platoon Commander	2Lt C.L. Bonshor	1933; Lt 35
Platoon Commander	Lt A.F.V. McConnell	1934
Platoon Commander	2Lt J.J. Turner	1936
Platoon Commander	2Lt J.L. Holt	1936
Platoon Commander	2Lt C.L. Batty	1935; Lt 37
Platoon Sergeant	Sgt – Thompson	

Platoon Sergeant	Sgt R. Riley	
Platoon Sergeant	Sgt E. Jones	
Platoon Sergeant	Sgt E. White	1925
Platoon Sergeant	LSgt E.W. Pugh	1925
Platoon Sergeant	Sgt W. Sankey	1932
Platoon Sergeant	Sgt T.R. Davies	1937
Platoon Sergeant	Sgt W.R. Morris	1938
Platoon Sergeant	Sgt T. Powell	1938
Company Sergeant Major	W.O. II H. Evans	
	W.O. II R. Riley	1933
C.Q.M.S.	Sgt S. O'Hare	1934
Instructor	Sgt E.J.J. Pierce	
	Sgt F. Hughes DCM	1922
	Sgt A.A. Thompson	to Oct 23
	Sgt T. McCormick	Jun 23
	Sgt – Armstrong	1929
	Sgt – Helier	1931
	Sgt H. Roberts	1934
	Sgt G. Wills	1936; died 1938
	Sgt P.H. Owen *W.G.*	1938

D Company (Machynlleth and Montgomery) (10, 11, 12 Platoons) (M.G. Company 1932–1939)

Officer Commanding	Capt E.P. Price MC	
	Maj R.B. Davies	1934
	Maj A.O. Lloyd Owen-Owen	1938
Second-in-Command	Capt J. Glynn Jones MC	
	Capt A. O. Lloyd Owen-Owen	Jul 24
Platoon Commander	Lt H. Player	
Platoon Commander	2Lt A. O. Lloyd Owen-Owen	Lt Oct 23
Platoon Commander	2Lt E.O. Baxter-Jones	Oct 23
Platoon Commander	2Lt G.E. Roberts	1935; Lt 38
Platoon Sergeant	Sgt – Thomas	1931
Platoon Sergeant	Sgt E. Vaughan	1933
Company Sergeant Major	W.O. II I. Thomas	1936
C.Q.M.S.	Sgt – Edwards	
Instructor	Sgt G. Fleming	
	Sgt F. Cashmore	1923
	Sgt H. Cutler	1931
	Sgt – Croft *W.G.*	Nov 33
	Sgt J. Shepparrd *W.G.*	Nov 36

Unplaced

2Lt G.L. Allen		1924
Capt the Hon R.B.S. Beaumont MP		1930–38
Lt E. Nalder		to 1936
2Lt J.E.M. Dugdale		1938
2Lt K.A. Hoare		1938
2Lt J.E.P. Thomas		1938
2Lt E.D. Savage		1938
2Lt T.G. Cumberland		1938

xi. The Gresford Colliery Disaster, 22 September 1934

At 02.08 hrs on 22 September 1934 a huge explosion occurred in the Gresford Colliery near Wrexham. It was one of the worst mining disasters in British history. 266 men lost their lives, only eleven of whose bodies were recovered. Amongst them were twenty-seven serving and former members of the 4th Battalion of the Regiment. The King sent a message of condolence; the 1st Battalion did likewise, and raised a sum of money to assist the families of victims. A full list of the victims, with the King's message, is reproduced in the Annex dealing with the Roll of Honour from 1919 to 1939.[147]

xii. The Royal Defence Corps

The Royal Defence Corps was formed in March 1916 and disbanded in 1936.[148] It was initially formed by converting the Home Service Garrison battalions of line infantry regiments. Garrison battalions were composed of soldiers either too old or medically unfit for active front-line service; the Home Service status indicated they were unable to be transferred overseas. Eighteen battalions were converted in this way, including the 5th (Home Service) Garrison Battalion of The Royal Welsh Fusiliers which became 12th R.D.C. and was stationed at Kinmel

Defence Corps Officers, General Strike 1921, Kinmel Camp. (R.W.F. Mus 7624) 2nd row 1st left Maj G. Claridge MSM TD, 4th left 2nd row H. Jefferson, 2nd row 5th left Tom Parry, M.P. for Flintshire.

Camp. Although it ceased to be an R.W.F. unit at this point it retained a large number of R.W.F. Officers and men, who continued to wear the Regimental badges.

The role of the Corps was to provide troops for security and guard duties inside the United Kingdom; guarding important locations such as ports or bridges. It also provided independent companies for guarding prisoner-of-war camps. The Corps was never intended to be employed on overseas service.[149] It was mobilised for service during the Miners' General Strike of 1921 and the General Strike of 1926.

After its disbandment, the Corps was superseded by the National Defence Companies, described in the next chapter.

xiii. The Cadets

The title Cadet Force was introduced in 1908, providing an umbrella for the many companies of cadets that had formed as part of Volunteer battalions since the late 1850s. Some cadet companies were located in Territorial Force Drill Halls, others in schools. When in 1908 the Volunteers became the Territorial Army, administration of the Cadet Force was taken over by the Territorial Army Associations within counties. Cadets were allowed to enlist at the age of twelve and remain until they reached the age for enlistment into the Regular or Territorial Armies, or they left school in the case of those cadets in school contingents.[150] The Cadet Force expanded massively during the Great War, during which the War Office assumed responsibility for its administration and training.

In 1923, however, faced with austerity, the government withdrew financial support for the Cadet Force and control and administration reverted to the Territorial Army Associations. At about this time, the British National Cadet Association (B.N.C.A.) was formed in an attempt to ensure the survival of the Cadet Force and to win back government support. In 1932, The B.N.C.A. was permitted to run the Cadet Force under the guidance of the Territorial Army.

Ruthin College Cadet Corps in camp. (Philip Eyton-Jones)

A cadet unit affiliated to the Regiment existed in Caernarfon town before 1922, commanded by Captain T.W. Hughes, administered by the Caernarvonshire & Anglesey T.A.

A Cadet company existed at Ruthin School, from at least 1914, affiliated to the 4th Battalion.[151] The contingent went to Camp for one or two weeks each summer and was inspected each year by either the Adjutant of the Depot, or the Adjutant of the T.A. battalion to which it was affiliated. Some records of the Ruthin School contingent appear in the school journal, *The Ruthinian*. The corps had a PSI who was also the school's P.T. instructor. The journal records that financial and other support to the corps lapsed in 1930; the annual inspection of 20 October that year being the last one.[152] An entry in March 1931 records a rugby match against the Depot, which the school lost 9–3: 'A very crude Army side, but full of zeal and apologies … It is our modest opinion that methods would have been more orthodox if the Depot team had contained at least one of commissioned rank.'[153] Thereafter, all mention of the Cadet Corps ceases. A Scout troop was raised in September 1934.[154]

STAFF LIST, Ruthin School Cadet Corps

Officer Commanding	Captain J. Lloyd-Jones
Second-in-Command	Lieutenant W.H. Whittle
P.S.I.	Warrant Officer Class I – Mallet, to December 1929
	Sergeant – Roberts, January 1930–December 1932
Cadet Sergeants	F. Harland, 1930
	W.D. Owen, 1930
	J.V. Culey, 1931
	E. Hartley, 1931

Notes

1   Letter Viscount Milner to Winston Churchill dated 14 January 1919 in MOD Library S149, f 33.
2   MOD Library S149, f 36.
3   Ian F.W. Beckett, The Amateur Military Tradition 1558–1945 (M.U.P., 1991) p. 243.
4   Beckett, p. 245; MOD Library S149, f 51.
5   11/12 Geo V c 37.
6   *R.U.S.I. Journal*, Vol LXV (1920), p. 422.
7   Stanley Simm Baldwin, *Her Majesty's Territorials* (London, 1994), p. 125.
8   Brigadier C.N. Barclay, *The History of the 53rd (Welsh) Division in the Second World War* (London, 1956), pp. 9–10.
9   *R.U.S.I. Journal*, Vol LXX (1924), p. 382.
10 Army Order 131 of 1922.
11 *R.U.S.I. Journal*, Vol LXXII (1927), p. 728.
12 *R.U.S.I. Journal*, Vol LXXIII (1928), p. 311.
13 Army Order 131 of 1922.
14 Army Order 200 of 1932.
15 *R.U.S.I. Journal*, Vol LXXV (1930), p. 347.
16 Silsoe, p. 122.
17 *The Chronicle*, 22 April 1939, p. 12.
18 *Y Ddraig Goch*, April 1937, pp. 80–81.
19 *Territorial Magazine*, June 1938, p. 42.
20 Silsoe, Chapter 14.
21 See the pohotograph from the Regimental Archives included in the illustrations.
22 *R.U.S.I. Journal*, Vol LXXIX (1929), p. 196.
23 *R.U.S.I. Journal*, Vol LXXIV (1931), p. 197.
24 *R.U.S.I. Journal*, Vol LXXXI (1936), p. 444.

25 Peter Caddick Adams, 'The Territorial Army before The Second World War', *British Army Review* 1999, p. 33.
26 *R.U.S.I. Journal*, Vol LXXXIII (1938), p. 884.
27 *Army Quarterly*, Vol LXXXIXV (October 1935), p. 5.
28 Barclay, p. 16.
29 *R.U.S.I. Journal*, Vol LXXIII (1938), p. 885.
30 Baldwin, pp. 130–131.
31 Barclay, p. 12.
32 Barclay, pp. 12–15.
33 *The Times*, Monday 7 August 1922, p. 5g.
34 Silsoe, Chapter 14.
35 Hugh Mainwaring, *Three Score Years and Ten with Never a Dull Moment* (Printed Privately, 1976), pp. 18–19.
36 Silsoe, p. 129.
37 R.W.F. Mus 4387, 6 R.W.F. part 2 Orders 1926–1938.
38 *The Times*, Monday 26 July 1920, p. 11; Barclay, p. 10.
39 *Y Ddraig Goch*, Vol I, No 3, October 1922, p. 98.
40 *Y Ddraig Goch*, Vol I, No 4, May 1923, p. 147.
41 *Y Ddraig Goch*, Vol I, No 4, May 1923, p. 137.
42 *Y Ddraig Goch*, Vol I, No 7, May 1924, p. 245.
43 *Y Ddraig Goch*, Vol I, No 8, July 1924, p. 265.
44 *Y Ddraig Goch*, Vol I, No 10, June 1925, p. 334.
45 Denbighshire Record Office TA/D/6–7 Minutes of the Denbighshire T.A.A. General Meetings, 1922–1938.
46 *R.U.S.I. Journal*, Vol LXXIII (1928), p. 108.
47 Denbighshire Record Office TA/D/6–7 Minutes of the Denbighshire T.A.A. General Meetings, 1922–1938.
48 www.measuringworth.com, accessed 1 November 2015.
49 *Y Ddraig Goch*, Series II, Vol I, No 1, March 1931, p. 13.
50 *Y Ddraig Goch*, Series II, Vol I, No 2, June 1931, p. 32.
51 *Y Ddraig Goch*, Series II, Vol I, No 2, June 1931, p. 33.
52 *Y Ddraig Goch*, Series II, Vol I, No 3, September 1931, pp. 55–56.
53 *Y Ddraig Goch*, Series II, Vol I, No 3, September 1931, p. 67.
54 *Y Ddraig Goch*, Series III, Vol I, No 1, March 1933, p. 92.
55 *Y Ddraig Goch*, June 1934, pp. 72–73.
56 *Y Ddraig Goch*, December 1934, pp. 82–84.
57 *Y Ddraig Goch*, March 1935, p. 82.
58 *Y Ddraig Goch*, July 1935, pp. 88–91.
59 *Y Ddraig Goch*, December 1935, p. 60.
60 *Y Ddraig Goch*, January 1936, p. 66.
61 *Y Ddraig Goch*, April 1936, p. 74.
62 *Y Ddraig Goch*, October 1936, p. 64.
63 *Y Ddraig Goch*, October 1936, p. 65.
64 *Y Ddraig Goch*, October 1937, p. 62.
65 *Y Ddraig Goch*, October 1937, pp. 64–65.
66 *Y Ddraig Goch*, Spring 1938, p. 89.
67 *Territorial Magazine*, Summer 1938, p. 48.
68 *Y Ddraig Goch*, Autumn 1938, p. 77.
69 *Y Ddraig Goch*, Vol I, No 4, May 1923, p. 138.
70 *Y Ddraig Goch*, Vol I, No 6, February 1924, p. 208.
71 *Y Ddraig Goch*, Vol I, No 6, February 1924, p. 209.
72 Flint Record Office TA/F/6–8, Minutes of the Flintshire T.A.A. General Meetings 1913–1938.
73 *Y Ddraig Goch*, Vol I, No 10, June 1925, p. 335.
74 Flint Record Office TA/F/6–8, Minutes of the Flintshire T.A.A. General Meetings 1913–1938.

75   *Y Ddraig Goch*, Series II, Vol I, No 4, December 1931, p. 86.
76   *Y Ddraig Goch*, Series II, Vol II, No 1, March 1932, p. 14.
77   *Y Ddraig Goch*, Series II, Vol II, No 3, September 1932, p. 70.
78   *Y Ddraig Goch*, Series III, Vol I, No 1, March 1933, p. 37.
79   *Y Ddraig Goch*, Series III, Vol I, No 2, June 1933, pp. 91–92.
80   *Y Ddraig Goch*, Series III, Vol I, No 3, September 1932, p. 155.
81   *Y Ddraig Goch*, June 1934, pp. 76–77.
82   *Y Ddraig Goch*, September 1934, pp. 68–70.
83   *Y Ddraig Goch*, April 1936, p. 77.
84   *Y Ddraig Goch*, July 1936, p. 89.
85   *Y Ddraig Goch*, October 1936, p. 70
86   *Y Ddraig Goch*, January 1937, p. 87.
87   *Y Ddraig Goch*, July 1937, p. 91.
88   *Y Ddraig Goch*, Autumn 1938, p. 70.
89   Silsoe, Chapter 14.
90   Letter from Mr G. Roberts of Llanberis in R.W.F. Mus 4388.
91   Kyffin Williams, *Across the Straits* (London, 1973), pp. 114–115.
92   *Y Ddraig Goch*, Vol I, No 1, May 1922, p. 19.
93   *Blackpool Gazette and Herald*, 25 August 1921.
94   *Y Ddraig Goch*, Vol I, No 3, June 1923, p. 101.
95   *Y Ddraig Goch*, Vol I, No 3, January 1923, p. 102.
96   *Y Ddraig Goch*, Vol I, No 3, January 1923, p. 102.
97   *Y Ddraig Goch*, Vol I, No 6, February 1924, p. 209.
98   *Y Ddraig Goch*, Vol I, No 9, January 1925, p. 305.
99   *Y Ddraig Goch*, Vol I, No 8, July 1924, p. 267,
100 Caernarfon Record Office XD/115/1/10, February 1925–July 1932. Minutes of General Meetings of the Caerns T.A.A.
101 R.W.F. Mus 4387, 6 R.W.F. part 2 Orders 1926–1938.
102 Silsoe, Chapter 14.
103 Caernarfon Record Office XD/115/1/10, February 1925–July 1932. Minutes of General Meetings of the Caerns T.A.A.
104 *Y Ddraig Goch*, Series II, Vol I, No1, March 1931, p. 13.
105 Silsoe, p. 127.
106 *Y Ddraig Goch*, Series II, Vol I, No1, March 1931, p. 15.
107 *Y Ddraig Goch* June 1932, p. 44.
108 *Y Ddraig Goch*, Series II, Vol II, No 4, December 1932, p. 104.
109 *Y Ddraig Goch*, Series II, Vol II, No 2, June 1932, p. 46.
110 *Y Ddraig Goch*, Series II, Vol II, No 4, December 1932, p. 104.
111 *Y Ddraig Goch*, Series III, Vol I, No 3, September 1933, p. 156.
112 *Y Ddraig Goch*, September 1934, pp. 70–71.
113 *Y Ddraig Goch*, July 1935, p. 98.
114 *Y Ddraig Goch*, January 1937, p. 88.
115 *Y Ddraig Goch*, April 1937, p. 91.
116 *Y Ddraig Goch*, July 1937, p. 94.
117 *Y Ddraig Goch*, October 1937, p. 75.
118 *Across the Straits*, p. 116.
119 *Y Ddraig Goch*, Summer 1938, p. 71.
120 *Across the Straits*, p. 118.
121 *Y Ddraig Goch*, Winter 1938–39, p. 56.
122 *Y Ddraig Goch*, Series I, Vol I, No 4, May 1923, p. 143.
123 *Y Ddraig Goch*, Series I, Vol I, No 5, May 1923, p. 175.
124 *Y Ddraig Goch*, Series I, Vol I, No 6, October 1923, p. 175.
125 *Y Ddraig Goch*, Series I, Vol I, No 7, February 1924, p. 210.
126 *Y Ddraig Goch*, Series I, Vol I, No 10, June 1925, p. 335.

127 *Y Ddraig Goch*, Series I, Vol I, No 10, June 1925, p. 336; Merioneth County Record Office, ZM/6465/4, Minutes of the Territorial Army Association, 1908–1948.

128 *Y Ddraig Goch*, Series I, Vol I, No 10, June 1925, p. 336

129 Merioneth Records ZM/6465/4.

130 *Y Ddraig Goch*, Series II, Vol I, No 3, September 1931, p. 58.

131 *Y Ddraig Goch*, March 1932, p. 14.

132 *Y Ddraig Goch*, Series II, Vol I, No 4, December 1932, p. 106.

133 *Y Ddraig Goch*, Series II, Vol I, No 4, December 1932, p. 106.

134 *Y Ddraig Goch*, Series III, Vol I, No 1, March 1933, pp. 38–39.

135 *Y Ddraig Goch*, Series III, Vol I, No 2, June 1933, p. 95.

136 *Y Ddraig Goch*, Series III, Vol I, No 3, September 1933, p. 157.

137 *Y Ddraig Goch*, June 1934, pp. 78–79.

138 *Y Ddraig Goch*, December 1934, pp. 88–89.

139 *Y Ddraig Goch*, July 1935, p. 99.

140 *Y Ddraig Goch*, December 1935, p. 70.

141 *Y Ddraig Goch*, January 1936, p. 74.

142 *Y Ddraig Goch*, October 1936, p. 76.

143 *Y Ddraig Goch*, April 1937, p. 95.

144 *Y Ddraig Goch*, October 1937, p. 79.

145 *Territorial Magazine*, June 1938, p. 42.

146 *Y Ddraig Goch*, Summer 1938, p. 74.

147 *Y Ddraig Goch*, December 1934, p. 4.

148 *The Times*, 20 March 1916

149 T.N.A. WO 32/18622

150 *Evening Express, 25 August 1909 (Welsh Newspapers Online)*.

151 *Denbighshire Free Press,* 1 August 1914, p. 3 (Welsh Newspapers Online).

152 *The Ruthinian*, Vol 1 No 1, p. 10.

153 *The Ruthinian*, Vol 2 No 1, p. 8.

154 *The Ruthinian*, Vol 5 No 2, p. 11.

Chapter 13

The Territorial Battalions and Artillery Regiments, 1938–1940

---

i. The T.A. on the Eve of War

After the collapse of the Munich Agreement in March 1939, the Government doubled the size of the T.A. from its then-established strength of 212,000. Each T.A. unit was to create a double, or clone, of itself – but without sufficient weapons, vehicles or equipment. This was a tough task for most infantry battalions, which lost many of their best Officers and N.C.Os to create the cadres for the new battalions, referred to as Second-Line T.A. battalions. The process of duplication was carried out in much the same way for all units. In most infantry battalions of the 53rd (Welsh) Division, two complete companies and a proportion of specialists were sent across to the duplicate battalion; in each battalion, the two companies then split to form four new companies, which were filled up with volunteers and conscripts.[1]

In The Royal Welch Fusiliers, the 4th, 6th and 7th Battalions gave birth to the 8th, 9th and 10th Battalions; while 60th Anti-Tank Regiment formed 70th Anti-Tank Regiment. These new units were largely filled up by conscripts, or militiamen, as detailed in Chapter 1, but there were also many volunteers, since a man who volunteered for the T.A. could not be conscripted. The surge of manpower was enormous, with 400,000 attending annual camps in August 1939.[2] This surge allowed many elderly or unfit men to be combed out.

In 1939, the T.A. battalion establishment was amended again, in line with the Regular battalion establishment, to H.Q. Company with six platoons and four rifle companies. The M.G. Company was abolished.[3]

Camp for 1939 for 158 (Royal Welch) Brigade was held in early August at Porthcawl, shortly before the outbreak of war. The whole brigade also took part in the ceremony at Caernarfon Castle in July 1939 marking the 250th anniversary of the raising of The Royal Welch Fusiliers. In spite of the rhetoric of Lloyd George at that occasion, quoted elsewhere in this volume, there was widespread support for Chamberlain's policy towards Germany – few really wanted a re-run of the last war – and enormous relief at the outcome of the Munich conference. The *Daily Express* had this to say:

> The policy of this journal is to be sympathetic to those in trouble and at the same time to look after our own affairs … For us, in Britain, in the midst of these troubled times, it is the duty of all, every man and woman, to stand behind the Prime Minister, to support his deeds, to ratify his acts, to uphold his position.

But in the year following Munich, the mood changed, and a feeling of humiliated anger replaced that of relief. Rearmament gathered pace, conscription was introduced, and the signs of war were everywhere. There was much sadness too, however, for as Harold Macmillan put it, 'we survivors of the First War seemed to have failed in our duty and to have betrayed our fallen friends.'[4]

ii. The National Defence Companies

T.A. battalions also had affiliated National Defence Companies. After the end of the Great War, responsibility for home defence on land rested with the Territorial Army and also the Royal Defence Corps (see the previous chapter), which consisted of ex-Regular soldiers who were too old or unfit for General Service overseas. As a part of the response to the rise of Germany, Secretary of State for War Duff Cooper announced the disbandment of the Royal Defence Corps and the establishment of National Defence Companies that were to be a part of the Territorial Army, each with an established strength of four Officers and 107 men.[5] In a statement to the House of Commons on 21 July 1936, he said that the companies would be formed on a county or city basis, each being linked to their local Territorial battalion. Enlistment would start on 1 September of that year, and was open to 'ex-members of His Majesty's Forces, normally between the ages of 45 and 60 years'. Their role was stated to be 'to protect important points in Great Britain when war is threatening or has actually broken out, but members of the force will not be called up until these conditions arise, nor will they be called up on account of civil disturbance. Cooper stated that the national establishment would be 8,450 Officers and men, 'and I have every confidence that I shall have no difficulty in securing this number of men in a very short time'.[6] In North and mid Wales, these Companies were those of Denbighshire, affiliated to the 4th Battalion, under Major V.C. Roberts MC;[7] Flintshire, affiliated to the 60th (R.W.F.) Anti-Tank Regiment, under Captain R. Hyde-Linaker;[8] Caernarvonshire and Anglesey, affiliated to the 6th Battalion, under Captain T.A. Macmillan;[9] and Merioneth and Montgomeryshire, affiliated to the 7th Battalion, under Captain E.W. Edwards. These companies were under No 105 Group which also included the Shropshire Company under Major Paddock, and later Major W.G. Dugdale.[10]

The National Defence Companies were mobilised on 25 and 26 August 1939, in the week before war was actually declared.[11] In answer to a question in the House of Commons on 26 September, Leslie Hore-Belisha, who was now Secretary of State for War, said that he had 'in contemplation a change in the present method of manning vulnerable points.'[12] On 3 October, Sir Victor Warrender, the Financial Secretary to the War Office, announced that recruitment to the companies was 'not open at present'.[13] In November 1939, the National Defence Companies were formed into battalions attached to Regular Army Regiments and renamed 'Home Service Battalions'.[14] They would guard vulnerable points and Prisoner of War camps in the United Kingdom throughout the rest of the war. The four companies affiliated to the Regiment, along with the Shropshire and Herefordshire companies, were formed into the 11th (National Defence) Battalion. At this point they left the Territorial Army and their story is continued elsewhere in Part 2 of this volume.

iii. Mobilisation.

On 1 September, the General Mobilisation Order was issued to all units and formations by wireless, followed by telegrams confirming the order.[*] 158 Brigade's battalions received the orders at about 16.00 hrs and by 18.30 hrs, individual orders had been sent out to the Officers and men – around 1,200 in the case of each of the three battalions, since the 4th, 6th and 7th Battalions were still administering the newly-formed Second Line battalions. By 21.00 hrs that night, around 90% of the posted strength of each unit had reported, been clothed and equipped, and billeted in the Drill Hall.[15]

Unidentified TA Soldiers at Camp in 1939 wearing gas masks. (R.W.F. Mus)

iv. 158 (Royal Welch) Infantry Brigade

158 (Royal Welch) Infantry Brigade formed part of the 53rd (Welsh) Division, whose headquarters were in Shrewsbury. In 1938, Brigadier E.O. Skaife commanded it from the headquarters in Wrexham. The brigade staff consisted only of the Brigade Major, Major H.C. Stockwell, a chief clerk and a Quartermaster Sergeant. Much had to be delegated to the Adjutants and Quartermasters of the brigade's subordinate battalions. Even divisional H.Qs, like that of the 53rd (Welsh), consisted of only the G.O.C. and two staff Officers: in the case of 53rd (Welsh) Division, the G.S.O. 2 of the division in 1938 was Brevet Major G.W.R. Templer.[†] The brigade had no distinctive badge or sign, but flew a flag with the R.W.F. dragon and initials, surmounted by the brigade title.

The flag of 158 (Royal Welch) Infantry Brigade.

---

*   How this was achieved was laid down in *Regulations for the Territorial Army 1936*, pp. 23–25.
†   Later Field Marshal Sir Gerald Templer KG GCB GCMG KBE DSO (1898–1979). For details see his biography by John Clarke, *Templer – Tiger of Malaya* (London, 1985).

In general, the system of mobilisation and embodiment worked smoothly and well.[16] The immediate task was to take over Civil Defence duties. There were general arrangements for Civil Defence in the event of war: the whole of Britain was divided into Regions, each under a Commissioner, who boasted almost unlimited powers. The Welsh Region had its H.Q. in Cardiff and consisted of the whole of Wales – incredibly, not the same area as was covered by the Military District of Welsh Area and 53rd (Welsh) Division. Further to complicate matters, the military command was divided into four Zones, and the Welsh Area contained two of these, not contiguous with the divisional and brigade boundaries.[17] Thus from the start there was a misalignment of responsibility, accountability, and civil, military and financial authority: a recipe for chaos before ever the enemy took a hand in the matter.

Things were further complicated by the fact that, on embodiment, all troops whether from 38th or 53rd Divisions (which were inextricably interlinked and geographically mixed), or corps and army troops, were assigned to take over key point guards from the National Defence Companies; H.Q. 158 Brigade therefore took under command a number of divisional and corps troops units: All that said, the men were eager to do well, and by 12 September, Major Stockwell was able to report to H.Q. 53rd Division that his units were well settled.[18] However, although men had answered their call-up in large numbers, not all could be kept. In 4 R.W.F., for example, 1,200 men were called up but over the next two weeks, 136 were discharged to work in the mines and yet more released for work on the harvest. Other men had continually to be found for specialist duties, and still more were found to be unfit for active service. Units were shrinking rapidly. This hurried process was described as 'a complete muddle – a badly thought out plan and badly executed.'[19]

One considerable advantage of mobilisation for the Brigade H.Q. was that a number of Officers and N.C.Os were posted to the staff. Among these were Captain N.R.G. Bosanquet,* a Regular Officer, was attached as an additional staff captain.[20] The brigade suffered a blow on 13 September when Brigadier Skaife's *Humber* staff car ran into a bus and was completely smashed. Although Skaife returned briefly to duty on 6 October, he was too badly injured to remain in command and the next day he handed over to Brigadier J.P. Duke.† His loss was deeply felt by the brigade, as the Officers and men knew and trusted Skaife, and felt his commitment to them.

Had the brigade remained in North Wales, training and assisting with the harvest, Skaife would probably have been able to recover and continue in command. However on 26th, orders were received for a move to Northern Ireland.[21] The move was completed via Stranraer on 23 November. The move was conducted under conditions of strict security, but even so, Lord Haw-Haw‡ duly announced their arrival on the wireless. It was not anticipated that the

---

*   Later Lieutenant Colonel Neville Richard Gustavus Bosanquet, *b.* 10 October 1911, *comm.* 27 August 1931. Commanded 2 R.W.F. in 1945, and 1 R.W.F. 1954–1957, one of only two Officers to have commanded both Regular battalions of the Royal Welch Fusiliers – the other being Llewellyn Gwydyr-Jones. He died in 2003, having given the authors much valuable help.

†   Jesse Pevensey Duke (1890–1980). Commissioned into the Royal Warwickshire Regiment, served in Albania 1914, France and Flanders 1914–1918 (DSO, MC, Brevet Major), North Russia 1920. Retired in 1947.

‡   Lord Haw-Haw was the nickname given to wartime broadcaster William Joyce, remembered for his propaganda broadcasts on the medium wave station *Reichssender Hamburg* that opened with '*Germany calling, Germany calling*', spoken in an upper-class accent. Joyce was captured by British forces in northern Germany just as the war ended, tried, and eventually hanged for treason on 3 January 1946.

Germans would invade Ireland, although there was a possibility of seaborne raids, increased by the attitude of Eire, which maintained strict neutrality and which had, unbelievably, been given back control of the 'Treaty Ports.'* Air attacks on installations like the Harland and Wolff shipyard in Belfast, and Short's aircraft factories in Queen's Island and Castlereagh were also a possibility. There was also the threat of espionage and sabotage, since Germany maintained full diplomatic representation in Eire throughout the war, with consulates in some cases very close to the border.

The chief cause of nervousness, however, was the possibility of increased I.R.A. activity. This had already begun: from January 1939 onwards the I.R.A. had conducted a bombing campaign in mainland Britain and in Northern Ireland.[22] The internal security role further disrupted 158 Brigade's training for war, and also increased its dispersion. Kyffin Williams recalled that: 'The I.R.A. was invisible, yet active. We Officers had the humiliation of suffering escorts as we went around the town. All rifles were chained to the floor of the Armoury for fear of raids, and I had to impress on the guards of our company billet the importance of challenging in English, not in Welsh, which they invariably did.'[23]

Once established, the brigade was tasked to provide guards and security detachments, carry out route clearance operations, and to be prepared to assist the police in public order. However, Duke was determined that training for war was going to resume. A 'get fit campaign' was launched, as well as courses for specialists like pioneers and Carrier crews; weapon training and shooting; tactical training; and a series of T.E.W.Ts for the Officers. More drafts of reinforcements continued to arrive, with the majority being Londoners or Scots. By January 1940, there had been a marked change in the character of the brigade: 'The older T.A. N.C.O. is gradually fading from the picture, and the younger men are taking their places, a large proportion of the younger N.C.Os coming from the first Militia called up.'[24]

In December 1939, the divisional H.Q. and the balance of 160 Brigade also moved out to Northern Ireland. Reinforcement meant that internal security duties could be shared, and more transport became available. I.R.A. activity increased in February and March: on 11 February there was an attack on Ballykinler Camp, and on 16 March, the police station at Dungiven was raided; there were also disturbances in Belfast. As a result, the brigade was tasked with more frequent route clearance operations, providing mobile columns to support the police, and with more guarding commitments. By April 1940, the bulk of the division had concentrated in Northern Ireland.[25]

Then on 20 April, a sudden call was sent out for volunteers for irregular warfare units to go immediately on active service abroad – the Independent Companies had been born. Their story is continued elsewhere in this volume. The remainder of the brigade continued internal security duties in Northern Ireland; the story of the brigade after the evacuations from France and Norway is continued in Part 2 of this volume.

---

*   These were at Cobh (Queenstown), Berehaven in Bantry Bay, and Lough Swilly in Donegal. They had played a key role in the fight against German U-boats in the Great War, but very short-sightedly, had been evacuated by the British in 1938.

v. The 4th (Denbighshire) Battalion, 1939–1940

In January 1939, A Company ceased to be the M.G. Company and re-formed as a rifle company. The M.G. role was assumed by a new platoon in H.Q. Company. On 28 April 1939, *The Cheshire Chronicle* reported that the battalion was only just short of its full war establishment of thirty-one Officers and 600 men. At this point, the battalion split to provide the cadre for the 8th Battalion, and began additional recruiting efforts throughout its area.

When mobilisation was ordered on 1 September, the battalion concentrated with H.Q. at Wrexham, A Company at Rhos, B Company at Llay Main Colliery, C Company at Acrefair and D Company at Denbigh. Detachments of signallers, stretcher bearers and drivers were sent out to all companies. Within a few days, B, C and D Companies were all together at Llay Main, where the War Diary noted the considerable help and support that the colliery authorities gave in billeting the men. Here, Royal Engineer services and R.A.S.C. rationing took some time to provide proper support; nor was the battalion yet properly equipped, to the extent that it was still wearing the 1908 pattern uniform. However, morale was very high and crime of any sort completely absent.[26]

On 13 September, the cadre of 8 R.W.F. was formally separated from the battalion. On 16 and 19 September, two drafts of sixty and sixty-seven men were returned from the battalion to the coal-mines, as being in protected employment. On 20 September, A Company too arrived at Llay, followed on 26th by the Mortar and Pioneer Platoons and the Intelligence Section. On 4 October, the losses caused by the establishment of the 8th Battalion and the miners were made good by the arrival of a draft of 250 militiamen from Scotland.[27]

When orders were received for the move to Northern Ireland, the advance party left on 19 October, followed on the 20th by the transport. The main body departed by rail from Rossett on 22 October, arriving at 02.00 hrs on the 23rd. The troops embarked on the ferry *Princess Margaret* and disembarked at Larne at 05.30 hrs. Here, the battalion entrained for Belfast, where it arrived at 07.30 hrs and marched to billets.[28]

In Northern Ireland, serious training commenced, beginning with an intensive programme of P.T., sports and route marches to improve physical fitness. This was supplemented by individual cadres, courses, tactical training, T.E.W.Ts and shooting. However there was also much hospitality to be enjoyed from the local people.

On 27 November, the battalion was at last issued with Battledress and the 1937-pattern equipment although some items, such as ground-sheets, took more time to arrive. At the beginning of December, leave was started with drafts being sent to Wales and Scotland each week. On 15 December, the battalion was ordered to move to, and concentrate in, Victoria Barracks, Belfast. The advance party moved the next day, followed by the main body on 20 December.[29] Here, training for war continued, although a requirement to provide 'flying columns' for internal security duties, reminiscent of 2 R.W.F.'s tour of duty in 1920, had also to be met. Here in Belfast, the first Christmas of the war was celebrated in peace-time conditions, with the men's dinners served by the Officers and Sergeants and a holiday from work.

Normal training, guard duties and internal security duties continued after Christmas. On 6 February, special security measures had to be put in place in Belfast owing to the execution of two I.R.A. men in Birmingham. The situation continued to be tense until the 12th, with demonstrations in the city and a raid on Ballykinler Barracks. On 21 February, Lieutenant Colonel H. Allsebrook handed over command to Lieutenant Colonel M.K. Watson, who ate the leek when St David's Day was celebrated as usual on 1 March, with the men's dinners, the Sergeants' Mess Ball and the Officers' Dinner.[30]

A further large draft of 312 recruits arrived on 5 April and for the next three months, throughout the tense days of May while the B.E.F. struggled out of France and Belgium, intensive training, shooting, field firing, courses and security duties were the order of the day. 4 R.W.F. saw no active service at this time, however as described in Chapter 16, the battalion provided men for the formation of No 2 Independent Company, men they never saw again. The story of the battalion continues in Part 2 of this Volume.

STAFF LIST, 4th (Denbighshire) Battalion, 1939–1940

Battalion Headquarters

Commanding Officer	Lt Col J.M. Davies MC	
	Lt Col H. Allsebrook	1 Apr 39
	Lt Col M.K. Watson *Wilts*	21 Feb 40
Senior Major	Maj H. Allsebrook	to 1 Apr 39
	Maj R. De B. Hardie	19 Feb 40
Adjutant	Capt G.E. Braithwaite	
	Capt M.E. Beale	2 Feb 40
A/Adjutant	Capt M.E. Beale	
	2Lt A.S.D. Graesser[*]	2 Feb 40
I.O.	Lt W.C. Roberts	9 Mar 40
R.M.O.	Capt A. MacDonald *R.A.M.C.*	
Chaplain	Rev N.S. Baden-Powell *C.F.*[†]	
	Rev W.H. Reid *R.A.Ch.D.*	3 Sep 40
Quartermaster	Lt J.H. Randles	
Regimental Sergeant Major	W.O. I W.J. Hawkins	
O.R.Q.M.S.	W.O. II P. Chard	
Bandmaster	Capt H. Delaney	
Corps of Drums	DMaj – Lawlor	

H.Q. Company/H.Q. Wing (1-6 Platoons)

Officer Commanding	Maj M. Bennetts MC
Signal (No 1) Platoon	Lt H.A.N. Jones
	Sgt – Turner
Pioneer (No 5) Platoon	Sgt W. Williams
M.T.O.	Lt H.G. Jones-Roberts
Sgts' Mess	W.O. II – Parry
Company Sergeant Major	W.O. II P.W. Jones
C.Q.M.S.	CSgt J. Kenny

A Company (7, 8, 9 Platoons)

Officer Commanding	Not Identified
Second-in-Command	Lt W.B.N. Kington
Platoon Commander	2Lt E.S. Dobb
Company Sergeant Major	W.O. II – Royce
Instructor	Sgt G. Timmins

---

[*]   Later Major Sir Alistair Graesser DSO MC TD, Honorary Colonel of 3 R.W.F.
[†]   Baden-Powell was a civilian officiating chaplain, and not a member of the Royal Army Chaplains Department.

B Company (10, 11, 12 Platoons)

Officer Commanding	Capt F.D. Williams
Second-in-Command	Lt F.E.D. Griffiths
Platoon Commander	Lt F. Owen
Platoon Commander	Lt J.V. Shepherd
Platoon Commander	Lt H.K. Roberts
Company Sergeant Major	W.O. II – Williams
C.Q.M.S.	Sgt A. Griffiths
Instructor	W.O. II C.A. Hunt *W.G.*

C Company (13, 14, 15 Platoons)

Officer Commanding	Maj A.E. Davis
Second-in-Command	Lt T.A. Jones
Platoon Commander	Lt J.L. Parker
Platoon Commander	Lt W. Lewis
Company Sergeant Major	W.O. II J.R. Griffiths
C.Q.M.S.	Sgt Clutton
Instructor	Sgt A. Wright

D Company (16, 17, 18 Platoons)

Officer Commanding	Capt W.J. Hulton
Second-in-Command	Lt R.W. Soden
Platoon Commander	Lt J.A. Hughes
Platoon Commander	Lt D.E.G. Griffiths
Company Sergeant Major	W.O. II W.F. Pritchard
C.Q.M.S.	Sgt J. Richards
Instructor	Sgt S.H. Platt *W.G.*

Unplaced

Lt A.G. Owen	2Lt D.C. Harry	2Lt N.J.M. Anderson
Lt D.G. Craig	2Lt R.C.H. Fox	2Lt J.O. Burton
Lt D.S.F. Hunt	2Lt N.P. Cutcliffe	2Lt T.G. Demetriadi
2Lt W.E.D. Paul	2Lt E.M.S. Watkin	2Lt C.L. Wilding-Jones
2Lt H.G.M. Williams	2Lt L.A.C. Reade	2Lt A.G. Ruffhead
2 Lt A.E. David	2Lt G.R. Brasted	2Lt R. Humphries-Roberts
2Lt J.V.G. Hope	2Lt G.C.A. Adams	

vi. The 6th (Caernarvonshire & Anglesey) Battalion, 1939–1940

In January 1939, D Company ceased to be the M.G. Company and re-formed as a rifle company. The M.G. role was assumed by a new platoon in H.Q. Company. A new Goat was recruited in January; this turned out to be a fearsome beast, all but unmanageable, and was eventually unloaded onto the 9th Battalion when the 6th left for Northern Ireland.[31] The Officers' St David's Day Dinner, the last in peace-time, was held at the Oakley Arms Hotel on 25 February and the Sergeants' Mess Dinner at the Conwy Drill Hall on 25 March. Recruiting and low-level training was the focus for the first months of the year. B Company opened a new detachment at Criccieth and D Company a new detachment at Amlwch. The latter reached a strength of thirty-nine within two months.[32] Two further new detachments were opened at Beaumaris and Llandudno but these were passed to the 9th Battalion.

In April 1939, the battalion split to provide the cadre for the 9th Battalion, and began additional recruiting efforts throughout its area.[33] By April 1940, H.Q. and A Companies reported a combined strength of 300. D Company reported its strength as 222, including thirty-four men called Jones and thirty-three called Williams.

In August, the battalion took part in the 250th Anniversary celebrations at Caernarfon, which are described in Chapter 16; at the conclusion of the anniversary parade, new Colours were presented to the 6th Battalion, replacing those of 1909. These Colours are described in the Annexes.

The order to mobilise was received on 1 September, and immediately, war stores were drawn from R.A.O.C. depots. The battalion completed all documentation at noon on 3 September, at which time the Old and New Colours were sent to the Depot for safe-keeping. The Regimental silver was also removed from the messes and sent to the National Provincial Bank in Caernarfon, while the Drum Major's mace and sash were sent to the care of the County T.A. Association.[34] On the afternoon of 3 September, 9 R.W.F. was split from the battalion and moved to Coed Helen Camp, Caernarfon and the following day, 6 R.W.F. began its move to a concentration area at Old Colwyn where it was dispersed in billets, Battalion H.Q. taking up residence in the Tanycoed Cafe: the War Diary reported 'some trouble over Billets owing to numbers of old ladies, spinsters and medically certificated people.'[35]

Kyffin Williams recalled how:

> Two large buses drew up outside the Drill Hall on the harbourside, and groups of mothers, wives and sweethearts stood miserably in small whispering groups. Suddenly the word was passed around, "They're off to Egypt", and tears began to flow into the harbour. Handkerchiefs waved in the sun as we disappeared towards the unknown, but this turned out to be only Porthmadog, twelve miles away, and there in the Drill Hall the Company assembled under the command of Dick Homfray, a reassuring quarry manager from Blaenau Ffestiniog... We stayed for a peaceful and fruitful month in Old Colwyn. We learned to live with each other, and in a small way mastered such fearsome weapons as Bren guns, Boys anti-tank rifles and carriers... [36]

Over the next days the battalion settled into the routine of war service; the chief difficulty was in getting enough cookers to feed all the men on time. Training in accordance with instructions issued from Brigade H.Q. began on 7 September, along with a series of courses for young Officers and junior N.C.Os. Other N.C.Os went to Wrexham to form a training cadre, while parties of men were also detached to help bring in the harvest. A few men were also identified as being in reserved occupations and were accordingly discharged; this resulted in the loss of only nine men, however.

A draft of 209 men arrived from the I.T.C. on 4 October, all were Scotsmen, and appeared to be 'fine types of men.'[37] This raised the strength of the battalion to approximately 600. The training programme to date had, however, identified problems: a lack of well-trained weapons instructors; a large number of specialists and key N.C.Os being in medical categories D and C – meaning that they could not deploy on active service or go overseas; uncertainty on the future of the permanent staff instructors; the loss of the best N.C.Os as instructors at the I.T.C.; a want of M.T. drivers; and a shortage of some items of clothing and spare parts.

On 20 October the advance party of fifty-two N.C.Os and Fusiliers under Major R.C. Newton left for Liverpool, following the receipt of orders for the brigade to move to Northern Ireland. The main body of the battalion, 460 strong, with twenty tons of baggage, embarked at Liverpool on the SS *Duchess of Hamilton* on 23 October, the balance of the baggage being carried on the Mail Packet from Stranraer to Larne. The crossing was rough, and the 'troops very sick.'[38] The battalion arrived at Lurgan in three trains at 09.50 hrs, 11.10 hrs and 16.15 hrs and moved into requisitioned buildings: Battalion H.Q., A and D Companies in Brownlow House, B Company in Parochial buildings, C Company in an old school and a dance hall, and H.Q. Company, less the M.T. which was in a T.A. hutted camp, in the Ross factory.*

Once the battalion had settled in, Officers and N.C.Os were sent on training courses to resident Regular battalions of the East Lancashires and the Royal Sussex, along with driver training, to rectify some of the shortcomings identified earlier. On 30 October, a fitness campaign was inaugurated with regular and frequent P.T., route marches, sports and bayonet fighting classes.

A severe outbreak of 'flu interrupted training at the beginning of November but there was worse to come, as several men went down with typhoid fever.[39] In spite of this, brigade T.E.W.Ts, route marches and training in the preparation and occupation of defensive positions continued. A programme of leave was also initiated with each company being sent away for a week in advance of Christmas.

On 12 December the battalion at last received an issue of Battledress in place of the old Service Dress. On 14 December, all Medical Category C personnel were posted to the 50th Holding Battalion. On 20 December the battalion moved to Lisburn by route march, departing Lurgan at 09.00 hrs and marching past the Brigade Commander at Lisburn at 13.15 hrs. With the move to Lisburn came a change of both Commanding Officer and Adjutant, with Lieutenant Colonel A.M.G. Evans assuming command and Captain J.A.M. Rice-Evans taking over as Adjutant from Captain E.H. Cadogan, who was posted to 23 I.T.C.[40] Christmas Day was observed as a holiday, but training resumed on Boxing Day.

Individual training and fitness continued throughout the winter months. St David's Day was celebrated in traditional style on 1 March, after which all companies proceeded in turn to Dunmurray ranges for shooting. Further range work took place in late March at Ballykinler. The focus of training shifted to section and platoon level during April and on the 24th, the battalion provided a draft of twenty-four men under Second Lieutenant J.L. Anderson for No 2 Independent Company, men they never saw again and whose story continues in Chapter 16. Training continued throughout May as the B.E.F. struggled against the Germans in Belgium and France. The battalion saw no active service at this time. Its story continues in Part Two of this Volume.

STAFF LIST, 6th (Caernarvonshire & Anglesey) Battalion, 1939–1940

Battalion Headquarters (Caernarfon)

Commanding Officer	Lt Col J.M. Evans	
Senior Major	Maj R.B.S. Davies	
Adjutant	Capt J.A.M. Rice-Evans	1 Jul 38
Capt E.H. Cadogan	1 Nov 38	
I.O.	Lt D.A.E. Roberts	

---

*   According to the Lurgan Directory for 1939, this was a hem-stitching factory.

Quartermaster	Lt R.W. Howell MM
Regimental Sergeant Major	W.O. I J. Brown
R.Q.M.S.	W.O. II V.S. Smart
O.R.Q.M.S.	W.O. II H.J. Williams

H.Q. Company (1-6 Platoons)

Officer Commanding	Maj R.C. Newton
Signal (No 1) Platoon (Bethesda)	Lt O.E.H. Hughes
A.A. (No 2) Platoon (Conway)	
Mortar (No 3) Platoon (Menai Bridge)	
Carrier (No 4) Platoon (Penygroes)	
Pioneer (No 5) Platoon (Holy head)	
Admin (No 6) Platoon)	Lt W.L. Woods
M.T.	2Lt F.G. Jones-Roberts
Cook Sgt	Sgt G. Pritchard
Corps of Drums	DMaj J.G. Harper
Regimental Band (Llanberis)	W.O. I – Pratt
Company Sergeant Major	W.O. II Brereton
C.Q.M.S.	Sgt D. Hughes

A Company (7, 8, 9 Platoons) (Caernarfon)

Officer Commanding	Capt E.G. Owen	Jan 39
Second-in-Command	Capt D.R. Llewellyn	
Platoon Commander	Lt D.A.E. Roberts	
Platoon Commander	Lt J.W.F. Fletcher-Townley	
Platoon Commander	2Lt J.B. Williams	
Platoon Commander	2Lt – Carr	Mar 40
Platoon Sergeant	Sgt D.H. Edwards	
Platoon Sergeant	Sgt T. Parry	
Platoon Sergeant	Sgt T.J. Williams	
Company Sergeant Major	W.O. II B. Kelly	
C.Q.M.S.	Sgt E.J. Jones	
Instructor	Sgt M.C. Jones	to Mar 40
	Sgt S.G. Scammells	

B Company (10, 11, 12 Platoons) (Porthmadoc and Pwllheli)

Officer Commanding	Maj R. Vaughan Humphries	
Second-in-Command	Capt R. Homfray	
Platoon Commander	Lt J.W. Williams	
Platoon Commander	Lt J.W. Whittaker	
Platoon Sergeant	Sgt W.T. Williams	
Platoon Sergeant	Sgt D. Green	
Platoon Sergeant	Sgt O.J. Jones	
Company Sergeant Major	W.O. II W. Howells	Mar 40
C.Q.M.S.	Sgt E. Jones	
Instructor	Sgt A. Nicholl *W.G.*	

C Company (13, 14, 15 Platoons) (Conway and Dolgarrog)

Officer Commanding	Capt D.S. Davies	
Second-in-Command	Lt C. Vere-Whiting	
Platoon Commander	Lt J.W. Bloor	
Platoon Commander	Lt H.D. Williams-Bulkeley	
Platoon Commander	2Lt J.B. Williams	
Platoon Commander	2Lt A.J. Cox	Mar 40

Platoon Sergeant	Sgt Ll. Lloyd-Williams
Platoon Sergeant	Sgt J. Williams
Platoon Sergeant	Sgt A. Rogers
Company Sergeant Major	W.O. II S. Williams
C.Q.M.S.	CSgt R. Goosey
Instructor	W.O. II F. Wilkinson

D Company (16, 17, 18 Platoons) (Holyhead)

Officer Commanding	Capt E.L.O. Williams
Second-in-Command	Capt S.T.A. Livingstone-Learmonth
Platoon Commander	2Lt E. Roberts
Platoon Sergeant	Sgt W.L. Jones
Platoon Sergeant	Sgt H.G. Evans
Platoon Sergeant	Sgt J.E. Jones
Company Sergeant Major	W.O. II J.E. Jones
C.Q.M.S.	Sgt R.J. Burnell
Instructor	Sgt R. Preest

Attached

Rev C. Tudor *C.F.*

Unplaced

Capt G.P. Jones	Capt T.E. Owens	2Lt J.K. Williams
Lt H.G.J. Roberts	2Lt N. Jones	2Lt T. Phillips, to Mar 40
2Lt G.E. Gresty	2Lt K. Ll. Ellis	2Lt J.L. Anderson
2Lt W.R. Stones	2Lt E.G. Thomas	2Lt H.B. Gould
2Lt M.W. Cemlyn-Jones	2Lt J. Fitton	2Lt W.M. Jones
2Lt R.V.G. Williams	2Lt T.A. Pierce	2Lt W.A. Walford
2Lt J.T. Owen	2Lt A.J. Pritchard	2 Lt R.T. Williams

vii. The 7th (Merioneth & Montgomeryshire) Battalion

In January 1939, A Company ceased to be the M.G. Company and re-formed as a rifle company. The M.G. role was assumed by a new platoon in H.Q. Company. In April 1939, the battalion split to provide the cadre for the 10th Battalion, and began additional recruiting effort throughout its area.

The battalion received its orders to mobilise at 14.28 hrs on 1 September; embodiment began immediately with H.Q. Company concentrating at Newtown, A Company at Llanidloes, B Company at Llanfyllin, C Company at Welshpool and D Company at Machynlleth. Over the next days the companies were moved to the designated Civil Defence Area in Newtown (see sketch map), with air defence dispersal areas designated. On 8 September, a well-meaning R.A.S.C. message arrived to say that rations in kind were available to be drawn, at seven days' notice. The Quartermaster replied, declining the issue, and pointing out that while the R.A.S.C. was offering food, the R.A.O.C. had failed to issue cooking equipment.[41]

Training began at once, along with a myriad of fatigue duties required to make the temporary accommodation habitable. On 9 September, six permanent staff instructors and 391 men were posted to the 10th Battalion to make up its numbers. This necessitated a reorganisation of the battalion to complete H.Q. Company. Another sixty-four men under the age of 19 were sent to 10 R.W.F. on 12 October; the deficit was partly made up by the arrival of a draft of 199 militiamen – conscripts – on 5 October. Battledress was issued and worn for the inspection of the battalion by the G.O.C. on 17 October.[42]

On 21 October, orders having been received for the move of 158 Brigade to Northern Ireland, the advance party left for Portadown, followed on the 24th by the main body. The stay in Portadown was a short one, for on 14 December the advance party moved to

7 R.W.F. being inspected at Newtown after mobilisation, September 1939. (R.W.F. Mus)

Londonderry, followed on the 17th by the main body. Here, the battalion moved into Ebrington Barracks in the Protestant Waterside area of the city on the East bank of the River Foyle. Training began at once in the deployment of mobile columns to counter I.R.A. activity. The Senior Major, Major R.B.S. Davies recalled that:

> When 7 R.W.F. left for Ireland … it was duly announced by Lord Haw-Haw on German radio. We were the first British troops to arrive in Portadown, C. Armagh and received a great welcome. The wearing of the Flash created additional interest. The Royal Welch Fusiliers served at Carrickfergus nearly 250 years ago when they came over to support the cause of William of Orange … the welcome was an outstanding one, and during the whole of our stay the welcome lasted.[43]

On 22 December, the battalion's first non-T.A. Officers joined: Second Lieutenants B.K. Moir and E.H. Farmer, both Emergency Reserve Officers. Second Lieutenant D.C. Ellis reported on the 28th and that day, Captain A.H. Williams left to join the 1st Battalion in France; he would not return until 1944, after having been wounded in Belgium and later commanding the 1st Battalion in India and Burma, to take command of the 7th. On 11 January, Captain W.L.R. Benyon and Sergeant Stiff joined from 1 R.W.F., the former to take over the adjutancy a week later; and on 6 February the battalion received its first regular Commanding Officer since the end of the Great War, when Lieutenant Colonel G.F. Watson assumed command.* Major G.E. Braithwaite arrived in March as O.C. H.Q. Company. Second Lieutenant P.L.W. Stable, who had joined the battalion the week before, had to leave the battalion almost at once for the I.T.C. Wrexham, because of I.R.A. threats towards him 'on account of his father's position'.[44] His father was a High Court Judge.

---

*   Later Major General Gilbert France Watson CB DSO OBE (1895–1976). He served in France during the Great War where he was twice mentioned in despatches and made DSO. He commanded 183 Infantry Brigade in 1940 and then moved to the War Office in 1942, where on promotion to Major General he remained as Director of Manpower Planning until his retirement in 1946.

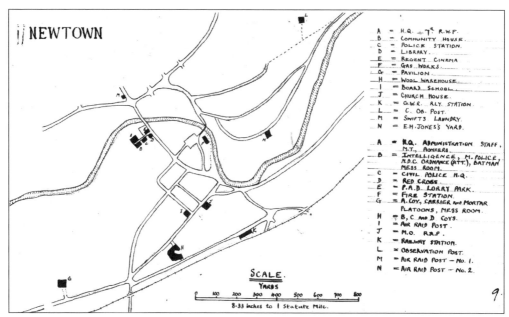

Map 13.1 7 R.W.F. Civil Defence Area in Newtown, on mobilisation, September 1939. (T.N.A. WO 166/4628, 7 R.W.F. War Diary 1 September 1939–31 December 1941)

The tempo of training increased from March onwards and at the end of the month the Brigade Commander carried out an administrative inspection. At 09.00 hrs on 3 April the battalion marched out of Ebrington Barracks and at 17.00 hrs that day, arrived at Glen Barracks, Newtownards. Here, the G.O.C. inspected the battalion on 9 April and on the 12th, a draft of 340 men arrived and was met at the railway station by the Corps of Drums. Between 25 April and 1 May, drafts under Second Lieutenant T.H. Davies and B.G.B. Pugh left to join No 2 Independent Company. These men never returned to 7 R.W.F. Their loss was more than made good by the arrival of a draft of ninety men on 16 May. Training continued as the situation deteriorated in Norway and in France and on 24 May, the battalion moved rapidly to Belfast to take up a defensive position at Harland and Wolff's docks and the Hamilton Road Yard, with A and C Companies detached to Sydenham airfield and B Company at the Power Station.[45] Here it was grouped with a troop of 175 Light Anti-Aircraft Battery R.A. The following night, five off-duty Fusiliers were held up by I.R.A. gunmen in a dance hall, fortunately without violence. The battalion remained in Belfast until 22 June when it was relieved by the 7th Glosters, and marched back to Newtownards, headed by the Corps of Drums. The story of the battalion following the fall of France is continued in Part 2 of this Volume.

STAFF LIST, 7th (Merioneth & Montgomeryshire) Battalion, 1939–1940

Battalion Headquarters

Commanding Officer	Lt Col W. Roberts MC	
	Lt Col G.F. Watson	6 Feb 40
Senior Major	Capt (T/Maj) E.G. Green-Emmott	
	Maj R.B.S. Davies TD	Feb 40

Adjutant	Capt R. de B. Hardie	
	Capt W.L.R. Benyon	17 Feb 40
I.O.	2Lt B.K. Moir	1 May 40
Chaplain	Rev S. Bailey *R.A. Ch. D.*	
Quartermaster	Capt R. Leonard	
Regimental Sergeant Major	W.O. I E. Davies	Oct 34

H.Q. Company (1–6 Platoons)

Officer Commanding	Maj G.E. Braithwaite	18 Mar 40
Bandmaster	W.O.I S.J. Jones	
Corps of Drums	DMaj J.R. Owen	
Signal Platoon (No 1)	Capt V. Makey	
Pioneer Platoon (No 5)	Sgt Walters	
Company Sergeant Major	W.O. II – Wilson	
C.Q.M.S.	Sgt Owen	
	Sgt Savage	Mar 39

A Company (7, 8, 9 Platoons)

Officer Commanding	Capt J.H. Williams	to 1 R.W.F. Dec 39
	Capt L. Ll. Jones	Dec 39
	Capt R.P. Turner	2 Feb 40
Second-in-Command	Capt L. Ll. Jones	
Platoon Commander	Lt D.F. Jones	
Platoon Commander	2Lt B.G.B. Pugh	
Platoon Sergeant	Sgt C.L. Rees	
Platoon Sergeant	Sgt P. Price	
Company Sergeant Major	W.O. II R. Thomas	
Instructor	Sgt – Brown	1939

B Company (10, 11, 12 Platoons)

| Officer Commanding | Capt W.J. Higson | 1 May 40 |
| Instructor | Sgt – Morgan *W.G.* | |

C Company (1, 14, 15 Platoons)

Officer Commanding	Capt C.L. Bonshor	
Second-in-Command	Lt C.L. Batty	
Platoon Commander	Lt J.L. Holt	
Platoon Commander	Lt J.J. Turner	
Platoon Sergeant	Sgt T. Powell	
Platoon Sergeant	Sgt W.R. Morris	
Platoon Sergeant	Sgt P. Price	
Instructor	Sgt P.H. Owen *W.G.*	

D Company (16, 17, 18 Platoons)

Officer Commanding	Capt A.O. Lloyd Owen-Owen	
Platoon Commander	2Lt G.E. Roberts	
Platoon Sergeant	Sgt W.L. Jones	
Company Sergeant Major	W.O. II I. Thomas	
Instructor	Sgt R. Shepheard *W.G.*	

Unplaced

Capt R.J.H. Cooke	Capt P.J. R. Davies	2Lt H.T.H. Moonfield, May 40
Capt W.J. Higson, to 1 May 40	Lt A.R. Hanmer	2Lt Hon D. Davies
2Lt G.W. Thomas	2Lt K.A. Hoare	2Lt J.E.M. Dugdale

2Lt J.E.P. Thomas	2Lt E.D. Savage	2Lt E.M. French, May 40
2Lt T.G. Cumberland	2Lt W.J. Simmons	2Lt R.W. Pannell
2Lt D.C. Ellis	2Lt E.H. Farmer, to Feb 40	2Lt G.E.R. Goring Thomas,
2Lt P.L. W Stable, to Feb 40	2Lt T.H. Davies, Feb 40*	Feb 40
2Lt D.E.H. James, Mar 40	2Lt D. Curtis, Apr 40	2Lt A. Roberts, Mar 40
2Lt L.F. Boston, Apr 40	2Lt E.L. Hardman, Apr 40	2Lt R.D.R. Evans, Apr 40
2Lt L.C. Thomas, May 40	2Lt E. Evans, May 40	

viii. 115 (Royal Welch) Infantry Brigade

When the doubling of the T.A. was announced, the 53rd (Welsh) Infantry Division's duplicate was the 38th (Welsh) Infantry Division, a division which had seen distinguished service on the Western Front in the Great War. The 38th Division again included 113, 114 and 115 (Royal Welch) Infantry Brigades. The Brigade was commanded by Brigadier C.S. Price-Davies, a former Commanding Officer of the 7th Battalion. It consisted of the three second-line battalions of the Regiment, the 8th, 9th and 10th Battalions and 115 Brigade Anti-Tank Company. 70th (R.W.F.) Anti-Tank Regiment was part of the 38th Division's support group. Like all second-line formations, 115 Brigade suffered from a lack of equipment and regular instructors, although there were many veterans of the Great War. In April 1940 the brigade moved from North Wales to south-west England, where it was widely dispersed guarding airfields, key points and sections of the coast. It was not until July 1940 when the brigade moved to Cheshire, that serious training could begin for the first time at company, battalion and brigade level, although equipment remained in short supply.

ix. The 8th (Denbighshire) Battalion, 1939–1940

The battalion was formed at Colwyn Bay as the second-line unit of the 4th Battalion. On mobilisation on 2 September 1939, the battalion concentrated with 4 R.W.F. and 'the men paraded in good spirits and were dismissed to their homes' after all documentation had been completed. Within a few days, the battalion was concentrated under canvas at Coed Helen Camp, Caernarfon.[46] However, there were no cooks, no weapons and little in the way of stores. Three cooks were borrowed from 4 R.W.F. but the men had to be dispersed into billets and fed there. The move to Coed Helen was, however, the first independent action of 8 R.W.F. and the efforts of the advance party under the Senior Major and Quartermaster were greatly appreciated, and the three attached cooks managed to have a hot dinner waiting for every man on arrival. Captain A. Macdonald joined as R.M.O – he was the only M.O. in the entire brigade, as the orders for the doubling of the T.A. had not taken account of the need for attached personnel.

Here at Coed Helen the battalion began to form; the G.O.C. visited very early on and was 'surprised at the raw state of the brigade'.[47] Why he was surprised is not clear. Shortly after arrival, the whole camp was re-pitched in an irregular pattern as an anti-air-raid precaution and some

---

*   kia with No 2 Independent Company in Norway.

rifles and *Bren* guns were received. A warning order was received for a possible move to Narberth in Pembrokeshire, however the recce party returned, reporting Narberth as an impossible place. Training in basic infantry skills therefore continued, with particular emphasis on weapon training and shooting with the few available weapons.

8th Battalion Officers on mobilisation, September 1939. (R.W.F. Mus 5137)

Although no wheeled transport was available, the first signs of an improvement in the situation were seen with the arrival of Carriers on 23 September; on 29th, new drums arrived from Boosey and Hawkes allowing the formation of a fife and drum corps. The battalion's first formal parade took place on 1 October when 8 R.W.F. marched past the Brigade Commander, led by its drums and pioneers under Sergeant Hughes and Corporal Roberts, en route for a new location at Llanberis. The march took three hours and in Llanberis the troops were dispersed in billets with H.Q. Company in the 6 R.W.F. Drill Hall, A Company in the Victoria Hotel ballroom, B Company at the Railway Station, C Company at Church House, and D Company in various council houses. The Officers' Mess was set up in the Victoria Hotel, the Sergeants' Mess in a café, and the cookhouse also in the Victoria Hotel.[48]

An informal group, 8 R.W.F., Oswestry April 1940. (Idris Morgan)

Training continued as before; on 6 October, volunteers were called for, for service 'in a tropical country'. A draft was selected and formed under Second Lieutenants G. Demetriadi and N.L.A. Vosper; after leave, the draft went to join the 2nd Battalion in India. In the meantime, a draft of twenty-two men from 4 R.W.F arrived, followed by sixty-one militiamen (conscripts). Another eighty arrived on 21 October along with eight men from 4 R.W.F. who were not fit to proceed overseas.

On 28 October the battalion received orders for a move to Leominster, on 10 November; however this was cancelled on 1 November. The battalion therefore adjusted its quartering arrangements, with the orderly room moving to better accommodation in the Mount Pleasant Hotel and the Officers' Mess moving to the Padarn Villa Hotel. Almost immediately, however, new orders were received for a move to Llandudno; a recce party went off straight way and soon reported that billeting arrangements were satisfactory.[49] Unsurprisingly this move was soon changed to Colwyn Bay. Arrangements were made with the N.D.C Company for guarding the only vital points in the area, Conway Bridge and Penrhos.

On 7 November, orders were received to form a mobile column of one company, held at three hours notice to move. This company was formed as a composite, with one platoon drawn from each rifle company and its transport was to be requisitioned buses from Messers Crosville in Caernarfon. Very bad weather now interrupted training, however, and the move to Colwyn Bay was delayed when the Divisional H.Q. staff condemned the proposed billeting arrangements, and directed the brigade staff to find better accommodation.

On 2 December the battalion posted forty-one young soldiers to duty with searchlight units in Cambridgeshire, however 100 men from an intake due on 9 January arrived early and were formed into a new company. Various senior Officers from the Divisional Headquarters visited during December and all were exposed to the battalion's shortages of equipment and poor accommodation. However on 15 December the advance party left for Colwyn Bay, followed two days later by the main body; the various road parties and the baggage were all complete at their destination at 14.22 hrs.[50] The Brigade Commander visited on 21 December to inspect all billets, 'which were approved but were very dirty and untidy. On the same day, Captain W. Siddons DCM assumed acting command of the battalion, which the War Diary noted as being the sixth change of command since the outbreak of war; however the diary did not record the previous incumbents.[51]

Christmas was celebrated as far as possible in traditional style and an all-ranks' dance was held in the evening. Training resumed on 26 December, although a concert was arranged in the evening. On 2 January, Major Sir Henry Tate took command of the battalion from Captain Siddons. The emphasis of training shifted in early January to cadre courses for specialists and employed men, junior Officers, and N.C.Os. The G.O.C. visited on 19 January and was 'more satisfied' with what he saw – not only with the state of training of the men, but also with the standard of administration and the cleanliness of billets.[52]

The weather, which had been wet and miserable since the autumn, turned much colder in late January, a situation not helped by the failure of the electric lights throughout the billeting area. To make matters worse, mumps broke out in the battalion at the beginning of February; the civilian fever hospitals being full, 38th Division had to open its own to care for the cases.

More weapons and equipment slowly trickled in during February; on 6th, the Mobile Column was called out. Although this was at eight hours' notice to move and it was called out at 08.50 hrs, the Column was on the move at 10.30 and at its destination in Rhyl by 11.00 hrs. On arrival, however, the War Diary reported that the exercise was poor and the requirement not clearly stated. 'The result was bad dispositions.'[53]

In mid-February the weather improved and route-marches recommenced; companies also took turns at working on the construction of a trench system in Eirias Park. A series of T.E.W.Ts was held for the Officers, a 30-yard range constructed and a boxing competition held.

St David's Day, the battalion's first, was celebrated, however training continued as there were by now sufficient rifles for companies to zero on the 30-yard range and then fire practices at Sealand. On 5 February, the battalion was warned for a move with the rest of the brigade to Dorset. The G.O.C. again visited on 15 March and appeared satisfied with all he saw; he also interviewed all N.C.Os as he went round the battalion.

On 25 March, Lieutenant Colonel R.G. Fenwick-Palmer took command of the battalion; Sir Henry Tate reverted to being Senior Major. A large draft of five Officers and 140 men joined from the I.T.C. and the 4th Battalion shortly before orders for the move were issued on 3 April. The baggage was packed and taken by rail to the new station at Burnham-on-Sea in Bridgewater Bay, Somerset. The battalion moved into billets in Burnham, Avonmouth and Shirehampton[54] which were fair, however the sanitation arrangements were very poor and a new kitchen and cookhouse had to be built. Here, the battalion took over responsibility for a section of the coast from 50th R.T.R. Detachments were sent to secure airfields and key points as far away as Wroughton, Hullavington, Monkton Farleigh, Ridge and Hudswell.

Shortly after arrival, the battalion boxing team won the 38th Divisional final at Cardiff, beating 15 Welch. A little later, on 10 May, the battalion also won the divisional cross-country competition.

On 22 April, Major W. Siddons was detailed as Officer Commanding No 9 Independent Company, which was formed from the division, along with a draft of Second Lieutenant D.T. Beddous and twenty-three volunteers from the battalion. A further draft of Second Lieutenant J.R.T. Waldron, Sergeant Pritchard, Corporal Walker and Fusilier Smith were also detailed a few days later. These men left for Ross-on-Wye on 27 April but never returned to the battalion, with the exception of Major Siddons, who was relieved of his command. Their story is continued in Chapter 16.

When the Germans invaded Belgium on 10 May, all leave was cancelled; all ranks were ordered to carry respirators at all times and the battalion was ordered to stand-to at dawn and dusk every day. A draft on forty-two men under Second Lieutenant G.A.F. Mostyn joined from the I.T.C. On 21 May, Second Lieutenant R.H.G. Sharp with a platoon from A Company left for Swanage to take over duties at the Air Ministry Research Station. Further detachments from B Company and the Signal Platoon were sent to Colerne and Lyneham airfields near Bath on 22 May. A further draft of 150 men from the 7th Holding Battalion arrived on 3 June. On 5 June, a warning order was received indicating that the brigade would move again, this time to Cheshire. The advance party moved on 24 June and the various detachments were relieved and pulled in over the following days. The main body began its move by a series of trains on 29 June and was complete in its new area on 7 July.[55] The battalion's story is continued in Part 2 of this Volume.

STAFF LIST, 8th (Denbighshire) Battalion, 1939–1940

Battalion Headquarters

Commanding Officer	Lt Col R.C. Lloyd MC TD	
	Capt (T/Lt Col) W. Siddons DCM (acting)	21 Dec 39
	Maj (T/Lt Col) Sir Henry Tate Bt	2 Jan 40
	Lt Col R.G. Fenwick-Palmer CBE	25 Mar 40
Senior Major	Maj Sir Henry Tate Bt	
Second-in-Command	Capt W. Siddons DCM	21 Dec 39
Senior Major	Maj Sir Henry Tate Bt	25 Mar 40
Adjutant	Capt S.V. Misa	
A/Adjt	2Lt D.T. Beddous	
Training Officer	Capt W. Siddons DCM	25 Mar 40
	Capt H.F. Cross MC	Oct 40
Quartermaster	Lt E. Davies	
Regimental Sergeant Major	W.O. I J. Bacon	
O.R.Q.M.S.	W.O. II – Casson	

H.Q. Company

Officer Commanding	Capt W. Lewis	
Signal Platoon (No 1)	2Lt R.T. Turner-Hughes	
A.A. Platoon (No 2)		
3-inch Mortar Platoon (No 3)	Lt H.C.P. Hamilton *R. Irish Fus*	Oct 39; Capt May 40
	2Lt R.W. Cookson	
Drum Major	Sgt – Hughes	

A Company

Officer Commanding	2Lt R.W. Soden	
Platoon Commander	2Lt N.L.A. Vosper	to Nov 39
Platoon Commander	2Lt R.H.G. Sharp	

B Company

Officer Commanding	Capt W.J. Higson	
	Capt H.F. Cross MC	Oct 39
Second-in-Command	2Lt A.A. Craddock	
Platoon Commander	2Lt T.G. Demetriadi	
Platoon Commander	2Lt A.H.H. Seldon	

C Company

Officer Commanding	Capt L.G.S. Clough-Taylor	
Platoon Commander	2Lt G. Demetriadi	to Nov 39

D Company

Officer Commanding	Lt J.L. Parker

Attached
Captain A. Macdonald *R.A.M.C.*

Unplaced

Major	Captain
T.W. Mottram MC TD	B.M.P. Dennis

Lieutenant
J.W. Riley, Mar 40

Second Lieutenants

W.M. Jones	**W.O.s**	
A.R. Tatton	– Wright	-
E.B. Watson-Smyth	Sgt	
W.D.A. Clare	– Price	
W.E.D. Watkins	– Pritchard	
A.J. Parish, Feb 40		
J.R.T. Waldron		
G.A.F. Mostyn, May 40		

x. The 9th (Caernarvonshire & Anglesey) Battalion, 1939–1940

The battalion was formed at Llandudno as the second-line unit of 6 R.W.F. It was planned that the six platoons of H.Q. Company would be distributed with the Signals and Mortars at Bethesda, A.A. Platoon and Carriers at Conway, Pioneers at Llanberis and the Admin Platoon distributed in all company locations. Battalion H.Q. was to be in Conway; A Company was to be at Llandudno, Llandudno Junction and Deganwy; B Company at Llanberis; C Company at Conway and Dolgarrog, and D Company at Bethesda.[56] On mobilisation, the battalion concentrated at Coed Helen Camp near Caernarfon and from there, when owing to inclement weather the camp became untenable, it moved to Penmaenmawr, near Conway.[57]

At Penmaenmawr the billeting was not entirely adequate and the training facilities were most unsatisfactory. With the arrival of a large draft of militiamen (conscripts) at the end of October, it became obvious that a move would have to be made; after a stern competition with the Ministry of Works for billets, the battalion marched to Llandudno at the beginning of December, replacing the 8th Battalion which moved to Llanberis. Here, the training facilities were better but like all the units in 115 Brigade, the battalion was lamentably short of Officers and N.C.O. instructors.

On 6 February 1940, Lieutenant Colonel R.R. Davies, who had not been really well for some time, was relieved in command by Lieutenant Colonel G.E. Malcolm MC of the Gordon Highlanders. Major B. Horton also joined as Senior Major and Captain N.R.G. Bosanquet joined as Adjutant from H.Q. 158 Brigade.

The battalion remained at Llandudno until early April 1940 when, with the rest of 115 Brigade, it moved to south-west England to guard vulnerable points. Battalion H.Q. was established at Andover airfield, with one company at the R.A.F. bomb dump at Chilmark, one company at Boscombe Down airfield, one company at Andover Airfield, and one company at the Chemical Experimental Station, Porton Down; from here, a platoon was detached to guard the new airfield then under construction at Middle Wallop. The Company at Porton Down had some interesting experiences while acting as guinea-pigs for gas experiments.

In April, a draft was sent to No 9 Independent Company and in early May, the battalion was ordered to concentrate at Popham Camp, near Basingstoke. Here it was told that it was to be sent to India. Considerable documentation and medical arrangements had to be hastily completed and all except those earmarked for Home Service only went on five days embarkation leave. The Officers were all instructed to buy tropical kit. However during the leave period, the evacuation of the B.E.F. from France was completed and the departure for India was postponed indefinitely – in fact it never took place. With the rest of 115 Brigade, therefore, the battalion moved to Winsford in Cheshire at the end of June and the beginning of July.[58] Its story continues in Part 2 of this Volume.

STAFF LIST, 9th (Caernarvonshire & Anglesey) Battalion, 1939–1940

Battalion Headquarters

Commanding Officer	Lt Col R.R. Davies	
	Lt Col G.E. Malcolm MC *Gordons*	Feb 40
Senior Major	Maj J.M. West	
	Maj B. Horton	Feb 40
	Maj J.M. West	Jun 40
Adjutant	Capt C. Vere-Whiting	
	Capt N.R.G. Bosanquet	Feb 40
Quartermaster	Lt J.T. Dale	
Regimental Sergeant Major	W.O. I W. Howells	

Captain	**Lieutenant**
T.A. Gloster	Sir R.H.D. Williams-Bulkeley Bt

Second Lieutenants

J.W. Bloor	R.T. Williams
H.B. Gould	J.B. Williams
T.E. Hughes	R.O. Watkin
P.L.W. Wintringham	W.A. Watford
P.G. Thomas	

xi. The 10th (Merioneth & Montgomeryshire) Battalion, 1939–1940

The battalion was formed at Newtown as the second-line unit of 7 R.W.F. On mobilisation, the battalion concentrated at Coed Helen Camp near Caernarfon, where individual training was begun at once, the general standard of training among the young soldiers being poor. A party of ninety-seven men under Major E.P. Price was sent to guard Penrhos airfield, returning on 19 September.[59]

On 2 October, the battalion moved into billets in Beaumaris, Anglesey. During the month, drafts of eighty-one men from

An informal group of 10 R.W.F. at Barmouth, 1939.

7 R.W.F., and 241 from the 7th Holding Battalion were received; four men were discharged as being medically unfit for service. At Beaumaris, A and D Companies moved into Red Hill on 18 October and individual training, with route marches and sports, continued. In November, training shifted to section and platoon level. In December, several cases of diphtheria occurred in B Company. On 9 December, the battalion was inspected by the Brigade Commander; twenty-two men were posted for duty with R.E. searchlight units. Their numbers were more than made up by the arrival of a draft of thirty-six trained soldiers from the I.T.Cs at Wrexham and Saighton. The strength of the battalion by companies at this point was:

H.Q. – 154
A – 138
C – 104
D – 64
(B Company acted as training company and was included in the H.Q. Company total)
Total – 460 all ranks.[60]

Christmas was celebrated in traditional style, as far as was possible. On 11 January 1940, Battalion Headquarters closed in Beaumaris and re-opened further along the North Wales coast at Rhos-on-Sea.[61] It was followed over the next week by the companies, with the exception of D Company which remained at Beaumaris. Further drafts totalling twenty-six, including eleven trained soldiers from 2 R.W.F., arrived during January. Training continued during February and March, and a number of Officers attended external courses. St David's Day, the battalion's first, was celebrated in traditional style.

On 1 April 1940 the advance party moved to Plymouth and Falmouth, along with the rest of 115 Brigade which was spread across a wide area of south-west England. The main body followed on 5 April. Battalion Headquarters opened at Millbay Barracks, Plymouth, with H.Q. Company in Zion Street Hall (later Ballard Institute, Millbay) B Company at Marshmills Camp and the rifle companies dispersed in Plymouth and Falmouth. Drafts of forty-nine men were received from the I.T.C. Wrexham on 11 and 16 April; however twenty-five men from low medical categories were posted for duty at PoW camps and on 27 April a draft of thirty volunteers under Second Lieutenant J.C.K. Purdey left to join No 9 Independent Company at Ross-on-Wye.[62] Most of these men, less ten who were sent back on 22 May as surplus to the establishment, never returned to the battalion and their story continues in Chapter 16.

In May, as the German invasion of Belgium and the evacuation of the B.E.F. unfolded, the battalion continued its duties. C Company under Captain A.R. Hanmer was sent as a mobile column to Corsham, Wiltshire. At the end of the month, a warning order was received to the effect that the battalion would move to Tidworth, less one company, where it would be accommodated under canvas. The advance party moved on 24 May to Windmill Hill Camp, Tidworth, followed by the main body on 28 May, less C Company which remained at Corsham. At the same time, Major C.L. Bonshor with 240 all ranks went to Burnham-on-Sea to provide a training cadre for all future drafts to 115 Brigade; on 30 May the first intake of 132 men arrived for training. Further drafts of 155 men arrived at the beginning of June.

On 4 June, the battalion was warned for a move with the rest of 115 Brigade to Cheshire. The advance party left for Tarporley on the 5th and the next day the main body, less C Company, moved to Oulton Park, Tarporley.[63] After de-training at Winsford Station, the battalion marched in full marching order to the camp, a distance of seven miles on a very hot day: testing perhaps, but not much when compared to what the 1st Battalion had endured in Belgium and France. The story of the battalion in Cheshire and elsewhere is continued in Part Two of this Volume.

STAFF LIST, 10th (Merioneth & Montgomeryshire) Battalion 1939–1940

Battalion Headquarters

Commanding Officer	Lt Col W.W. Kirkby DSO	
	Lt Col D.W.H. Kirkby	6 Feb 40
Senior Major	Maj C.L. Bonshor	
	A/Maj R.W. Thomas	Jan 40
	Maj E.R. Freeman	Feb 40
Adjutant	Lt H. Phibbs	
A/Adjt and I.O.	Lt J.L. Williams	Nov 39
Quartermaster	Lt W. Gorham MSM	
Regimental Sergeant Major	W.O. I N.T. Ridings	

H.Q. Company

Officer Commanding		
Signal Platoon (No 1)	Lt E.W. Timothy	
A.A. Platoon (No 2)	Capt W.E. Lewis	Jan 40
	Lt L.F.W. Barker	Feb 40

3-inch Mortar Platoon (No 3)

Carrier Platoon (No 4)	2Lt R.H.J. Daniel	Mar 40
Pioneer Platoon (No 5)	2Lt E.H. Holroyd	
Admin Platoon (No 6)	2Lt E.M. Kinsey	

A Company

Officer Commanding	Maj E. Powell TD	
Platoon Commander	2Lt W.H. Hicks	May 40

B (Training) Company

Officer Commanding	Capt W.E. Lewis	
	Capt C.R.L. Beatty	Jan 40
Second-in-Command	Lt S.I. Thomas	to Jan 40
	Lt L.W.F. Barker	
Weapon Training Officer	Lt G.E. Roberts	Feb 40, Capt May 40
Platoon Commander	2Lt A.R. Nash	
Platoon Commander	2Lt D. Anderson	

C Company

Officer Commanding	Maj E.P. Price MC TD	
	Capt A.R. Hanmer	Apr 40
Platoon Commander	Lt G.R. Llewelyn Jones	May 40
Platoon Commander	2Lt C.H. Oakley	Jun 40

D Company

Officer Commanding	Capt A.R. Hanmer	
	Maj C.L. Bonshor	Mar 40
Second-in-Command	Capt P.J.R. Davies	Mar 40
Platoon Commander	2Lt J.E.R. Williams	Mar 40
Platoon Commander	2Lt J.D.F. West	May 40
Platoon Commander	2Lt R.W. Thomas	

Attached

Maj A. Roberts *R.A.M.C.*

Unplaced

Captain	**Lieutenant**	
E. Powell TD	P.J.R. Davies	
	D. Fleming Jones	Capt 1 Mar 40
Second Lieutenants	A. Vaughan	to Sep 39
F.H. Shilton, Nov 39	E.D.V. Jones	to Jan 4
E.H. Holroyd	T.H. Davies	R.B. Evans (Capt Dec 39)
A.K. Rowe	H.P.M. Lewis	J.C.K. Purdey, to May 40
H. Lloyd-Jones	A. Roberts	
	A.R. Tatton	

W.O. II

E.T. Langford (to RSM 10 R.W.F., 1940)

xii. 60th (Royal Welch Fusiliers) Anti-Tank Regiment, R.A., 1938–1940

The Officers, 60th (R.W.F.) Anti-Tank Regiment R.A. conducting a T.E.W.T., 1939. (R.W.F. Mus)

Men of 60th (R.W.F.) Anti-Tank Regiment R.A. from 237 and 238 Batteries in Flint and Connah's Quay, on mobilisation, September 1939.

The Regiment was formed on 16 November 1938 by the conversion of the 5th Battalion. The *Regimental Journal* recorded that: 'The news last autumn that the 5th Battalion was to be converted from an infantry battalion into one of the new anti-tank units came as a sudden and disconcerting shock to all ranks and the phrase "We joined the Royal Welch – not the Army" was frequently to be heard.'[64] However the Regimental connection was maintained. Through the efforts of its Honorary Colonel, Sir Randle Mainwaring, the regiment continued to wear the R.W.F. collar badge, shoulder title – first in brass and later in cloth – and the Flash, with the R.A. cap badge and buttons. The Goat was also retained.[65] A dinner marking the change of title and role was given at Chester for the Officers by Major General J.R. Minshull-Ford, Colonel of the Regiment

H.Q. and H.Q. Battery were initially at Rhyl, but the H.Q. moved to Flint by August 1939 where a new Drill Hall was built.[66] A Company 5 R.W.F. at Mold became 237 Battery with outstations at Caergwrle and Buckley; B Company at Rhyl became 238 Battery with an outstation at Holywell; C Company at Flint became 239 Battery, with an outstation at Connah's Quay; and D Company at Hawarden became 240 Battery. The regiment remained part of 53rd (Welsh) Division (T.A.) under the Commander Royal Artillery (C.R.A.). The regiment was initially equipped with the 2 pdr anti-tank gun and was fully motorised, chiefly with 15-cwt trucks, although the new equipment took some months to arrive. The established peace-time strength was to be twenty-four Officers and 450 N.C.Os and men.

Many Officers and N.C.Os went on attachments to 21st Anti-Tank Regiment at Aldershot during the early part of the year; there were courses for junior N.C.O.s and gunners at all the regiment's Drill Halls. St David's Day was celebrated as usual. In April 1939, the regiment was reported as being at full war strength of thirty-three Officers and 571 men,[67] and was at this point split in order to form the second-line regiment, 70th (R.W.F.) Anti-Tank Regiment R.A. Recruiting began with a large public meeting and parade in Flint on 16 April[68]

The regiment went to Camp in 1939 at Trawsfynydd, and here fired the 2 pdr gun for the first time. On the declaration of war, which occurred while the regiment was still at Camp, the regiment concentrated at the Bolsover Colliery Company's holiday camp at Rhyl, which was commandeered for the purpose.[69] Mobilisation and concentration took place smoothly.[70] Here, all those unfit for service abroad were weeded out and their places taken by drafts of 150 regular reservists, all former gunners who had for the most part served in coastal batteries: '… none had been Anti-Tank Gunners; none wanted to become Anti-Tank Gunners; and all appeared to resent having to join what seemed to them to be a Territorial Infantry Battalion.'[71] Orders were received for a move to Lille Barracks, Aldershot in October, as H.S.K. Mainwaring, now the Second-in-Command, recalled: 'For the move the Regiment got its transport which consisted of civilian vehicles of all shapes and sizes, including a number of furniture vans. The road convoy moved off for a night drive while the men went by train.'[72] Here, training began in earnest and just before Christmas, orders were received for a move to France. The regiment's barracks were to be taken over by another unit, and the Officers and men were therefore temporarily dispersed into billets in Fleet: 'In order to get the regiment accommodated we had to erect mess-tents in private gardens … as things turned out our move to France was delayed and we spent nearly six weeks in those billets, including Christmas, which coincided with deep snow and severe frost of that winter.'[73]

While at Fleet the regiment was selected for conversion to a new type of unit, half anti-tank and half anti-aircraft, for service with the 1st Armoured Division. This meant the loss of two of the existing batteries, 238 and 240 – which were broken up and their numbers lost – and many of its original men, but the alternative was to have the regiment disbanded and used to reinforce 70th Regiment. The regiment was then re-designated 101st Light Anti-Aircraft and Anti-Tank Regiment R.A. Its story is continued below.

Three pictures of 60th
(R.W.F.) Anti-Tank
Regiment, 1939.
(R.W.F. Mus)

Winston Churchill
visits 60th (R.W.F.)
Anti-Tank Regiment,
being briefed by Major
J. Ellis Evans, 1939.
(R.W.F. Mus 6909F)

STAFF LIST, 60th (R.W.F.) Anti-Tank Regiment R.A., 1938–1940

Regimental Headquarters (Rhyl; to Flint by August 1939)

Commanding Officer	Lt Col S.H. Burton	
	Lt Col H. Sheriff Roberts	Jul 39
Senior Major	Maj H.S.K. Mainwaring	Sep 39
Adjutant	Capt C.H.V. Pritchard	
Quartermaster	Captain E.F. Hollobon MM	
Regimental Sergeant Major	W.O. I A.T. Currie	
Regimental Band	W.O. II S. Jones	

237 Battery (Flint)

Officer Commanding	Capt O. Leigh	
	Maj C.E. McCully	1940
Second-in-Command	Capt T. Owen	
Troop Commander	Lt C.D. Cleaver	
Troop Commander	Lt D. Wright	
Troop Commander	Lt R. Bowen Jones	
Troop Sergeant	Sgt R.G. Bird	
Troop Sergeant	Sgt T. Harmes	
Troop Sergeant	Sgt S. Cooper	
B.Q.M.S.	Sgt J.H. Prescott*	
Instructor	W.O. II B.F. Clancy	

238 Battery (Connah's Quay and Hawarden)

Officer Commanding	Maj H.S. Roberts

---

*   John Herbert Prescott was the father of Labour Deputy Prime Minister and Life Peer John Prescott.
He transferred into 60th A.T. Regiment from 5 R.W.F. in November 1938.

Troop Sergeant	Sgt B. Otley	
Troop Sergeant	Sgt J. Davies	
Instructor	W.O.II G. Norrey	

239 Battery (Mold and Buckley)

Officer Commanding	Maj G.E. Alletson	
	Maj J.R.O. Charlton	Feb 40
Troop Sergeant	Sgt H.T. Ellis	
Troop Sergeant	Sgt W. Cartwright	
Troop Sergeant	Sgt W. Jarvis	
Instructor	W.O. II D.R. Williams	

240 Battery (Rhyl and Holywell)

Officer Commanding	Capt H.S.K. Mainwaring	
	Capt J.R.O. Charlton	Oct 39
Troop Sergeant	Sgt D.W. Davies	
Troop Sergeant	Sgt H. Salisbury.	
Troop Sergeant	Sgt – Davies	
Instructor	Sgt F. Hughes	

Unplaced

Captain	Lieutenant	2nd Lieutenant
L.G.S. Clough-Taylor*	E.O. Burton	H.E. Bolton
J. Ellis Evans	V.H.O. Herbert	W.O. Hill
B.G. Jefferson	J. Hemelryk	M.J.A. Thomas
R. Steele-Mortimer		E. Williams
		R. Bowen Jones
		J.M.H. Owens
		Q.A. Thomas
		P.A. Walker

xiii. 70th (Royal Welch Fusiliers) Anti-Tank Regiment, R.A., 1939–1940

The regiment was formed in April 1939 as the second-line duplicate of 60th Anti-Tank Regiment. The regiment continued to wear the R.W.F. collar badge, shoulder title – first in brass and later in cloth – and the Flash, with the R.A. cap badge and buttons. The regiment, which consisted of Headquarters and four batteries – 277, 278, 279 and 280 – remained part of 60th Anti-Tank Regiment until after the order for mobilisation was received on 1 September 1939. H.Q. and H.Q. Battery were at Rhyl, 277 Battery at Mold, 278 Battery at Rhyl, 279 Battery at Flint and 280 Battery at Hawarden, all alongside their parent batteries of 60th Regiment. The regiment was initially equipped with the 2 pdr anti-tank gun.

On the day after mobilisation, the planned Camp at Porthcawl was cancelled. By 3 September, twenty-two Officers and 539 men had reported for duty at Rhyl; on the 5th, R.II.Q. closed at Rhyl and re-opened at Plas-yn-Dre, Holywell, with the batteries dispersed in the Assembly Rooms, various church halls, the Drill Hall and private houses; almost no accommodation

---

*   To 8 R.W.F. by December 1939.

stores were available.[74] On 16th, the regiment came under the command of H.Q. 38th (Welsh) Infantry Division.

Over the next month, drafts of militiamen (conscripts) arrived to join the regiment, along with consignments of stores, weapons and equipment. For a short time, 20 October to 4 November, the regiment was placed under the command of H.Q. 53rd (Welsh) Infantry Division. On 10 November the regiment moved to Pembroke Dock, where a number of under-age and low-category men were discharged or posted. Training and administration continued throughout November and December, along with familiarisation in the regiment's home defence duties around Milford Haven. These included the guards on various ammunition depots, airfields, bridges and static sites.[75]

On 22 April 1940, Lieutenant Colonel J.H. Colbourn assumed command, vice Lieutenant Colonel H.M. Davies. On 18 May the regiment was placed under the command of North Wales Area and moved to Trearddur Bay on Anglesey. Here it was to assist 11 R.W.F. in securing the Menai Bridge, the Port of Holyhead and possible landing sites on the island.[76] Key points included rail and road bridges, railway stations, the meteorological office and naval installations. Here the regiment remained until 5 July, when new equipment began to arrive and the regiment returned to the command of H.Q. 38th (Welsh) Division. Its story continues in Part Two of this Volume.

STAFF LIST, 70th (R.W.F.) Anti-Tank Regiment R.A., 1939–1940

Regimental Headquarters

Commanding Officer	Lt Col H. Maldwyn Davies OBE TD DL
	Lt Col J.H. Colbourn, 22 Apr 40
Second-in-Command	Maj G.H. Alletson
Adjutant	Capt J.J. Borthwick
Quartermaster	Lt C.A. Barnes

Unplaced

Captains	2nd Lieutenants
E. Williams	P.V.R. Pennant
B.G. Jefferson	H.F.P. Jones
T. Ockleston	D.E. Griffiths
	– Morgan-Davies
Lieutenants	F.P. McManus TD
T.D. Morgan	W.H.R. Roberts
J.H.M. Owens	I.G. Gruffydd
T.G. Edwards	R.W. Hampton
– Shearer	C.P. Roberts

xiv. 101st Light Anti-Aircraft and Anti-Tank Regiment R.A., 1940

The regiment was based on the R.H.Q. and two batteries of 60th Anti-Tank Regiment (R.W.F.) at Fleet: 237 Battery under Major C. E. McCully and 239 under Major J.R.O. Charlton were the two batteries selected and on 15 February 1940, R.H.Q. moved to Dawlish in Devon under Major L.H.H. Payne; and the two batteries to Puddletown in Dorset; the Signal Section was at Athelhampton and the Light Aid Detachment (L.A.D.) R.A.O.C. in Tolpuddle.[77] Here in Dorset, two anti-aircraft batteries joined them on 21 February to make up the new regiment. These came from two famous London regiments. The first was a battery of 11 (H.A.C. and City of London Yeomanry) A.A. Brigade R.A., formerly the Rough Riders (City of London Yeomanry); and the second a battery from 61st (Finsbury Rifles) A.A. Brigade R.A., formerly 11th Battalion (County of London) Regiment, or Finsbury Rifles. These became 43 and 44 Batteries respectively. As a result, the regimental title underwent its first change, to become 101st Light Anti-Aircraft and Anti-Tank Regiment, R.A. The regiment was assigned to the newly-formed 1st Armoured Division.

The Regiment now had batteries from three different sources, all equally proud of their old traditions and insisting on wearing their distinctive uniforms, badges and buttons – the Rough Riders in boots and breeches, the R.W.F. with their flashes and so on, as H.S.K. Mainwaring, the Second-in-Command, recalled.[78] After many criticisms from visiting senior Officers, an order was issued from Brigadier F.E. Morgan, commanding the Support Group of 1st Armoured Division, stating that the Royal Artillery uniform should be adopted throughout.[79] The unit was now essentially a gunner one, with gunner tasks, and it was necessary in the interests of efficiency that it should be readily recognisable as such. That this could be done without any lessening of pride in the Royal Welch antecedents was demonstrated in the years to come. In fact, St. David's Day 1940 was celebrated in the village hall of Puddletown with, if possible, even greater fervour than usual, the principal guest being General Sir Henry Jackson, a former G.O.C.-in-C., Western Command, who was living in retirement close by.

From then until May, the regiment concentrated on mastering its equipment, although this was in very short supply. Firing with the *Bofors* gun was carried out at St Agnes in Cornwall; and with the 2 pdr anti-tank gun at Lydd. *Bofors* guns had to be borrowed, for the regiment at this point held only *Bren* and *Lewis* guns.[80]

In May the regiment was mobilised at short notice for active service in France. Its story continues in a Chapter 17.

Notes

1   Barclay, p. 18.
2   Caddick Adams, p. 37.
3   WO 20/Gen/5689 (T.A.1) dated 10 October 1938.
4   Alistair Horne, *Harold Macmillan, Volume I: 1894–1956* (New York, 1989), p. 126.
5   Barclay, pp. 18–19.
6   *Hansard*, House of Commons Debates, 21 July 1936, vol 315 cc228–229.
7   R.W.F. Mus L/2655/325.
8   *The Cheshire Chronicle*, 18 February 1939.
9   R.W.F. Mus L/2655/325; Caernarfon Record Office XD/115/1/10.
10 R.W.F. Mus L/2655/325.
11 Frederick W. Perry, *The Commonwealth Armies: Manpower and Organisation in Two World Wars* (M.U.P., 1988), p. 50.
12 *Hansard*, House of Commons Debates, 26 September 1939, vol 351 c1183.
13 *Hansard*, House of Commons Debates, 3 October 1939, vol 351 cc1804.
14 Perry, p. 53.
15 See, for example, T.N.A. WO 166/4626, 4 R.W.F. War Diary September 1939–December 1941.
16 T.N.A. WO 166/1030–158 (Royal Welch) Infantry Brigade War Diary 1st September 1939–1st April 1941.
17 See the section on Commands and Districts in the *Monthly Army Lists 1938–1940* for details.

18 T.N.A. WO 166/1030–158 (Royal Welch) Infantry Brigade War Diary September 1939–April 1941.
19 T.N.A. WO 166/4626–4 R.W.F. War Diary September 1939–April 1941.
20 T.N.A. WO 166/1030–158 (Royal Welch) Infantry Brigade War Diary September 1939–April 1941.
21 T.N.A. WO 166/4626–4 R.W.F. War Diary September 1939–April 1941.
22 Robert Fisk, *In Time of War. Ireland, Ulster and the price of neutrality 1939-45* (London, 1983), pp. 73–75.
23 *Across the Straits*, p. 126.
24 T.N.A. WO 166/1030–158 (Royal Welch) Infantry Brigade War Diary September 1939–April 1941.
25 Barclay, pp. 30–31.
26 T.N.A. WO 166/4626, 4 R.W.F. War Diary, September 1939–December 1941.
27 T.N.A. WO 166/4626, 4 R.W.F. War Diary, September 1939–December 1941.
28 T.N.A. WO 166/4626, 4 R.W.F. War Diary, September 1939–December 1941.
29 T.N.A. WO 166/4626, 4 R.W.F. War Diary, September 1939–December 1941.
30 T.N.A. WO 166/4626, 4 R.W.F. War Diary, September 1939–December 1941.
31 *Y Ddraig Goch*, Spring 1939, p. 59; *Across the Straits*, p. 122.
32 *Y Ddraig Goch*, Spring 1940, p. 62.
33 See, for example, the *Holyhead and Anglesey Mail*, 21 April 1939; *Holyhead Chronicle*, 28 April 1939; *The County Herald*, 19 May 1939.
34 T.N.A. WO 166/4627, 6 R.W.F. War Diary, 1 September 1939–31 December 1941.
35 T.N.A. WO 166/4627, 6 R.W.F. War Diary, 1 September 1939–31 December 1941.
36 *Across the Straits*, pp 121, 123.
37 T.N.A. WO 166/4627, 6 R.W.F. War Diary, 1 September 1939–31 December 1941.
38 T.N.A. WO 166/4627, 6 R.W.F. War Diary, 1 September 1939–31 December 1941.
39 *Across the Straits*, p. 126.
40 T.N.A. WO 166/4627, 6 R.W.F. War Diary, 1 September 1939–31 December 1941.
41 T.N.A. WO 166/4628, 7 R.W.F. War Diary 1 September 1939–31 December 1941.
42 T.N.A. WO 166/4628, 7 R.W.F. War Diary 1 September 1939–31 December 1941.
43 Major R.B.S. Davies, *The Seventh – A Territorial Battalion 1908–1946* (Llanidloes, 1950), p. 26
44 T.N.A. WO 166/4628, 7 R.W.F. War Diary 1 September 1939–31 December 1941. No details found except that he had played cricket for Glamorgan since 1936.
45 T.N.A. WO 166/4628, 7 R.W.F. War Diary 1 September 1939–31 December 1941.
46 T.N.A. WO 166/4629, 8 R.W.F. War Diary 1 September 1939–June 1940.
47 T.N.A. WO 166/4629, 8 R.W.F. War Diary 1 September 1939–June 1940.
48 T.N.A. WO 166/4629, 8 R.W.F. War Diary 1 September 1939–June 1940.
49 T.N.A. WO 166/4629, 8 R.W.F. War Diary 1 September 1939–June 1940.
50 T.N.A. WO 166/4629, 8 R.W.F. War Diary 1 September 1939–June 1940.
51 T.N.A. WO 166/4629, 8 R.W.F. War Diary 1 September 1939–June 1940.
52 T.N.A. WO 166/4629, 8 R.W.F. War Diary 1 September 1939–June 1940.
53 T.N.A. WO 166/4629, 8 R.W.F. War Diary 1 September 1939–June 1940.
54 R.W.F. Mus 79/Mob/2778 T.A.1.
55 T.N.A. WO 166/4629, 8 R.W.F. War Diary 1 September 1939–June 1940.
56 T.N.A. WO 166/4627, 6 R.W.F. War Diary, 1 September 1939–31 December 1941.
57 There is no extant War Diary for 9 R.W.F. at this point; a letter from Lt Col Sir Richard Williams-Bulkeley, who served with the battalion, is the basis of this short resume (R.W.F. Mus L/2655/279).
58 R.W.F. Mus 79/Mob/2778 T.A.1.
59 T.N.A. WO 166/4631, 10 R.W.F. War Diary 3 September 1939–July 1940.
60 T.N.A. WO 166/4631, 10 R.W.F. War Diary 3 September 1939–July 1940.
61 R.W.F. Mus 79/Mob/2778 T.A.1.
62 T.N.A. WO 166/4631, 10 R.W.F. War Diary 3 September 1939–July 1940.
63 R.W.F. 79/Mob/2778 T.A.1.
64 *Y Ddraig Goch*, Spring 1939, p. 54.
65 WO T.A.2/B.M. 299 dated 21 April 1939.
66 *The Cheshire Chronicle*, 22 April 1939.
67 *The Cheshire Chronicle*, 28 April 1939.

68 *The Cheshire Chronicle*, 22 April 1939.
69 Mainwaring, p. 41.
70 *The Red Dragon*, p. 279.
71 Mainwaring, p. 41.
72 Mainwaring, p. 41.
73 Mainwaring, p. 42.
74 TNA W.O. 166/1642, 70 (R.W.F.) Anti-Tank Regiment War Diary 1 September 1939–31 December 1940.
75 TNA W.O. 166/1642, 70 (R.W.F.) Anti-Tank Regiment War Diary 1 September 1939–31 December 1940.
76 TNA W.O. 166/1642, 70 (R.W.F.) Anti-Tank Regiment War Diary 1 September 1939–31 December 1940.
77 T.N.A. WO 166/1702, 101st L.A.A. & Anti-Tank Regiment War Diary June – September 1940 (Addendum).
78 Mainwaring, p. 41.
79 *The Red Dragon*, p. 280; Mainwaring, p. 42.
80 T.N.A. WO 167/654, 101st L.A.A. & Anti-Tank Regiment War Diary February – May 1940.

Section III

The Regimental Institutions and the Training Organisation, 1918–1940

Chapter 14

The Regimental Depot, No 23 Infantry Training Centre and the Special Reserve

---

i. The Re-establishment of the Regimental Depot, 1919–1920

The Depot of the Regiment had been established at Hightown Barracks, Wrexham, on 10 August 1877. During the war years, the Depot had remained at Wrexham but the training functions had been carried out by the 3rd (Special Reserve) Battalion, first at Litherland Camp, near Liverpool, from May 1915 where the battalion had formed part of the Mersey Defence Force; and then from November 1917 at New Barracks, Limerick, Ireland. A letter from the War Office dated 16 May ordered the re-formation of the 2nd Battalion in Ireland. The letter laid down which of the key members of the battalion were to be selected from amongst those at the Depot or from those with the 3rd Battalion. A party of five Officers and seventy N.C.Os and Fusiliers, including the Band, and thirty-five tons of battalion baggage that had been stored at the Depot throughout the war, arrived at New Barracks, Limerick on 7 August 1919.

Like the T.A. battalions of the Regiment, the Depot was subordinated to the 53rd (Welsh) Divisional Area, which had its Headquarters at Shrewsbury, which in turn was under Western

Hightown Barracks, Wrexham, between the wars. (W.S.A. Clough-Taylor)

The main gate at the Depot, Hightown Barracks, Wrexham.   The Square at Hightown Barracks, Wrexham.

Command in Chester. With the re-formation of the two Regular battalions and the demo-bilisation of the 3rd Battalion in 1919, the Depot resumed its function of supplying drafts of trained recruits to the home-based battalion, from where, in accordance with the trooping seasons, further drafts were assembled and sent to the foreign-service battalion. The Depot was organised into a Headquarters, under command of a Major, a Headquarters Company or Wing; and two training companies each commanded by a Captain, with a Lieutenant, a Company Sergeant Major and C.Q.M.S., six Sergeants or Lance Sergeants, and ten Corporals or Lance Corporals. The usual routine was two squads of approximately platoon size undergoing training in each company with a third forming. Squads were named after the Regiment's Battle Honours, with Minden, Alma, Waterloo, Lucknow, Mons being particular favourites. N.R.G. Bosanquet remembered that:

> Soldiers joined and were put into a hut to await their squad. When there were enough, about twenty-four, they were given a name such as Alma or Albuhera Squad, and handed over to a Sergeant and two Corporals. Many were very thin and weak when they joined, but after the food and training they soon put on weight and became great chaps. Every now and then we were given a Cockney squad, and these Cockneys produced the sergeant majors and colour sergeants, of which the best known were Nobbler Albutt and Tommy Dale… A newly commissioned Officer usually went to the Depot before proceeding to his battalion. When I joined there were eleven young Officers at the Depot. We were put under two sergeants and did weapon training day after day.'[1]

Although the source of recruits for the Territorial Army was the 23rd Recruiting District of North and Mid Wales, recruits for the Regular battalions continued to be drawn, as they had been before the Great War, from all over Wales, the border counties of England, Birmingham and London. A survey of the average percentage of soldiers serving with territorial Regiments who were born in their regimental district between 1883 and 1900 placed the Royal Welch Fusiliers in the lowest percentage category, scoring only 18.9%.[2] Like Bosanquet, General Sir Hugh Stockwell recalled in a personal memoir of service with 2 R.W.F. in the 1920s that many of the best senior N.C.Os were Londoners.[3] There was at this point no method of selecting men for particular arms or services – where a man went depended partly on personal choice and partly on the identity of the recruiting sergeant who handled his enlistment.

The Depot routine at Wrexham was a settled one and it allowed for plenty of sport: many Officers hunted with the Wynnstay and the Vale of Clwyd, usually twice or three times each week depending on how many horses they could afford to keep. Colonel C.E. Hill remembered that:

> I was posted to the Depot in 1937. There was a very small staff there, and a few recruits ... We worked hard in the summer because we had to go round to all the [T.A.] camps. In the winter we worked hard when we were there, but we went hunting three days a week. When everybody went hunting the Q.M. was duty Officer. It worked really well.[4]

Major P.A. Kenyon likewise recalled that:

> I'll never forget putting my name in the book for leave. I was doing a lot of hunting and a certain amount of shooting, and it so happened that for the next twelve days I had invitations for either hunting or shooting. There was no problem about leave and ... I could have as much as I wanted.[5]

Kyffin Williams also remembered that 'I went on a course to our barracks at Wrexham and was surprised to find that the Officers were seldom out of hunting kit.'[6]

For the non-commissioned ranks, the Welsh Area included five Regimental Depots, those of the Cheshires, R.W.F., S.W.B., K.S.L.I. and the Welch. Every year, a programme of inter-depot sports was run which included novices boxing, shooting, athletics, soccer, hockey, rugby and cricket. There were also Command competitions, especially in boxing. The social programme of the messes was also active and varied.

The Depot also fulfilled the unofficial function of Regimental Museum. Items of historical interest presented to the Regiment, or brought back from abroad, were held either in the messes, or by the Quartermaster, or were displayed in the men's dining hall. The Depot also held all historical documents not sent on to the Public Record Office or the Adjutant General's Department.

There were various fixed points in the year. The Regimental Day was celebrated in the traditional style, with the recruits being served at dinner by the Officers and Sergeants, the leek eaten by the youngest Fusilier in each company, dinners or balls in the messes, and sports. It was also usual on St David's Day for the Wynnstay Hunt to meet at the Officers' Mess. The Depot was inspected each year by the G.O.C. 53rd (Welsh) Division, usually in July, and by the G.O.C.-in-C. Western Command. A highlight of the summer was always the Regimental Cricket Week, held at the Depot in the second week of August. The Regimental team would take on a number of local sides, usually the Vale of Clwyd Hunt, Sir Alfred McAlpine's XI, and South Wales Hunts among others. The annual Comrades' Reunion took place following Cricket Week. The Depot also provided assistance, and a good many entries in the equestrian events, at the Denbighshire and Flintshire Show, usually held at the Wrexham Racecourse in early August. The Depot staff and recruits were always on parade each year at the War Memorial in Wrexham on 11 November. At the end of the year, Christmas was celebrated with a carol service and the soldiers' dinners served by the Officers and Sergeants, and a children's Christmas Party for the married families.

ii. Infantry Basic Training between the Wars.

A platoon in training, 1925. (R.W.F. Mus)

From 1919 onwards, recruits were kept in training at the Depot for twelve weeks, after which further training was given in the Regular battalions. In 1922, this was increased to twenty weeks.[7] At the Depot, daily routine quickly taught recruits that from now on, the Regiment would determine how their time was spent, how they dressed, what they ate and how they kept their kit.[8] The training regime concentrated on three aspects: training the body physically through P.T., sports, and – most importantly – close order drill; secondly, developing a soldierly spirit, ethos and bearing through Regimental history, traditions, and ceremonies; and thirdly the technical aspects of training in the use of the rifle, bayonet, grenade and entrenching tool. Drill, as the means of teaching instant obedience, discipline, the sense of togetherness and the bearing of a soldier, was of paramount importance. In 1932, a recruit under training went through 420 hours of instruction, of which 104 hours were drill and only seventy-five hours were education.[9] According to *Infantry Training 1932*, 'The first and quickest method of teaching discipline is close order drill … close order drill compels the habit of obedience, and stimulates, by combined and orderly movements, the man's pride in himself and in his unit.'[10] So much for all that had been learned of low-level tactics in 1917 and 1918. When not on the barrack square, the ranges, the gymnasium floor or the sports pitch, recruits spent much time cleaning, repairing and polishing their kit, and laying it out formally for inspection every morning. There was, however, an increasing emphasis on education from 1928 onwards, in order to develop initiative and the ability to learn throughout a man's service.[11]

By 1937, with the prospect of war looming, the emphasis in training had shifted markedly, to the extent that it was officially accepted that the purpose of training was not just about obedience, but also about producing a soldier who was 'determined, inquisitive and self-dependent' and with the qualities of 'an expert hunter'.[12] With this change in approach, some of the more rigid aspects of discipline at infantry depots were relaxed. Time on the drill square described above declined to ninety-four hours, the balance being devoted to fieldcraft and tactics.[13] But although training could be hard, for most it was a positive experience, marking major changes in life: from a civilian to a soldier, from boyhood to manhood, from dependence on family to membership of a group and of a wider regimental family.

iii. The Depot, 1921–1939

On 9 August 1921 the Depot was the scene of the presentation of silk Union Flags to the wartime Service Battalions, described elsewhere under Regimental Matters and in the Annexes. In 1922, the Depot extended 'a hearty welcome' to members of various Irish Regiments which had been disbanded, who were transferred into the Royal Welch Fusiliers.[14]

In June 1922 the Depot was inspected by the G.O.C.-in-C. Western Command. After a full inspection and presentation of medals, the G.O.C. saw recruits in the second, fourth, eighth and twelfth weeks of training undergoing squad drill, musketry, guard mounting and the platoon in the attack respectively. The inspection also

The Depot staff on re-formation at Wrexham, 1920. (R.W.F. Mus); the Officer Commanding is Major E.R. Kearsley DSO, the Adjutant is Captain D.M. Barchard, the Quartermaster is Major H. Yates MC and the RSM is W.O. I A.M. Boreham MC.

looked at a new recreation ground, a W.Os' and N.C.Os' cadre course and the miniature range.[15]

On Alma Day 1922, a tablet was unveiled in the dining hall to those members of the Regiment who had won the Victoria Cross. Major General Sir Charles Dobell performed the ceremony in the absence of the Colonel of the Regiment. On 29 and 30 August 1923 the Depot was inspected by Major General T.O. Marden, G.O.C. 53rd (Welsh) Division and by Lieutenant General Sir Beauvoir de Lisle, G.O.C.-in-C. Western Command.

An outbreak of foot-and-mouth disease in 1924 curtailed both training and hunting; a very wet winter and early spring also caused the cancellation of many sports fixtures.[16] In July, a platoon under Lieutenant R. de B. Hardie joined 158 (Royal Welch) Brigade as demonstration platoon during Camp at Conway.[17] In November, the Depot took part in the unveiling and dedication of the Regiment's Great War Memorial, described elsewhere.

Information is unavailable on the activities of the Depot from 1926 to 1930, as no *Regimental Journal* was published, and the Depot did not submit a Digest of Service. In 1931, the Officer Commanding reported that recruiting was very strong and that 260 men had been sent to the home battalion, a total which included many Welsh soldiers: 'Their surroundings and prospects, and the atmosphere in which they live, compares more than favourably with the conditions existing in the good class homes from which the young soldier of to-day is recruited.'[18]

Around 1930, H.R.H. The Prince of Wales instituted a shooting competition for all infantry depots, consisting of three practices for a team of eight firers: ten rounds snap at 300 yards; ten rounds deliberate at 500 yards, and ten rounds rapid in the prone position at 300 yards, preceded by a run from the 400 yard firing point, the total time allowed being one minute.[19] The Regimental Depot began to compete in 1931, the team being trained by Sergeant S.M. Sheriff, scoring 628 points out of a possible 960; the winning team

The Colours of the 3rd (Special Reserve) Battalion outside the Depot Officer' Mess.

scored 709. In 1932 the team improved their score to 706; thereafter there is no further mention of the trophy in the *Regimental Joural*.

In 1935, full dress was resumed for the Quarter Guard, 4th Battalion drums and Goat Major on St David's Day.[20] On 6 May 1935, a ceremonial parade was held by the Depot, with the 4th Battalion and 244 Battery R.F.A., to celebrate the Silver Jubilee of Their Majesties King George V and Queen Mary. The Colours of the 3rd and 4th Battalions were on parade, with the Regimental Goat, Corps of Drums and Band of the 4th Battalion, all under the command of Colonel H.W.D. McCarthy-O'Leary, Commander 158 (Royal Welch) Infantry Brigade. A large crowd watched the parade, which included a *feu-de-joie* and a march past. In the afternoon, the Depot gave a physical training and gymnastics demonstration and in the evening an all-ranks dance was held in the gymnasium.[21]

On 27 May 1936 a Depot 'At Home' was held for the first time; this was henceforth intended to be an annual event, held as close as possible to Empire Day.* The Depot opened to the public at 14.30 hrs and there were a series of gymnastic displays, guard mounting, guided tours of the orderly room, barrack blocks, dining hall, sports ground, N.A.A.F.I. canteen, gymnasium, miniature range, fire engine shed, schools, gas chamber, hospital and the messes. There were also static displays of a howitzer, from 244 Medium Battery R.F.A.; vehicles and weapons from the 1st and 4th Battalions, and a complete equipment lay-out. Tea was provided, after which the Band and Drums of the 4th Battalion beat retreat. The day closed with an all-ranks dance.[22]

In September 1936, Class A Reservists were called up to the Depot for service in Palestine, as detailed elsewhere under Regimental Matters.

During 1938 the tempo of training increased to the extent that there were usually six squads in training at any one time, and the pressure on the accommodation – which was undergoing modernisation – meant that squads were sent to the at-home battalion, the 1st, after only six or eight weeks, there to complete their training with their instructors, who were therefore detached from their families – sometimes having only recently returned from five or six years' service

---

*   Empire Day was 24 May, and was an annual celebration from 1904 to 1958.

abroad. Even so, sport was played every afternoon and after years of very basic living conditions, things were improving:

> Four meals a day, and good ones at that, – hot tea and biscuits at 11 a.m., – hot shaving water at Reveille, – a Drill Shed for use when it is wet or cold, – a "Silence" Room where they can sit, read and write, and where even a coat hanger is supplied. No Barrack Damages, – no buying of Gym. Kit, – What a Life![23]

The modernisation included new kitchens and dining room, barrack blocks, washrooms and messes. The timing was not totally helpful, as at a time when expansion of recruiting and the consequences of conscription began to show, the Depot's living accommodation had been halved.

The Wynnstay Hounds met as usual at the Depot on St David's Day 1939 and the Sergeants Mess Ball was held on 3 March, the last of peacetime. Thereafter, the tempo, which had already begun to quicken, accelerated further:

> The old Depôt routine of "two squads and one forming" became a thing of the past; and Officers whose previous military experience at the Depôt had schooled them to expect at least 4 days hunting and two days shooting a week, became seriously alarmed. Then came news that certain reservists were to be called up; closely followed by the epoch-making announcement that by an Act of Parliament a modest quarter of a million militia or so were to be called to the Colours… Women and ex-sailors, if you please, suddenly appeared in the cookhouse … Then all our recruits abruptly left us and went down to Blackdown [i.e. to the 1st Battalion], and the first militia-man walked bravely through the gates.[24]

iv. No 23 Infantry Training Centre (I.T.C.), 1939–1940

This increase in activity was followed in September 1939 by the order for mobilisation:

> If you had told Bangor-on-Dee Rowing Club that it had got to expand into a naval base of the first magnitude, the reply would probably have come back, "Duw, man, … !" or words implying that the project was not feasible. But the Depôt became "this I.T.C." in one day.[25]

Matters were not helped by the poor state of preparedness of the R.A.O.C. and R.A.S.C. supply services: no cooking equipment was provided; and no food was issued for nearly three months, meaning that local purchase had to be employed. Ration cards were found to be invalid for the first month.[26] However the presence of many experienced reservists helped the Depot staff to solve problems and handle the increased numbers under training; so too did the quality of soldiers now coming in as a result of conscription – men of far greater intelligence and capability than the average peace-time Fusilier, it seemed:

> As for the militia – it would have been a pleasure to have written several pages about them, had time and space permitted. They tick over on a 60-hour week (about) and come up smiling and about three programmes ahead of schedule. You'd have to go a long way from

Sergeants' Mess, 23 I.T.C., 1939. (R.W.F. 4143)

Wrexham to find a "dud" militiaman. To think that one ever had doubts as to whether they would become real Royal Welchmen.[27]

The Regimental Depot ceased to exist as a training unit and became 23 I.T.C., still responsible for supplying trained recruits to the Regular, Territorial and Service battalions of the Regiment and as such continued in operation until September 1941.[28] It was also home to units of the Auxiliary Territorial Service (A.T.S.), the women of 15th (Montgomery) and 40th (Denbighshire) Companies.[29] The changed tempo was remarked on by Kyffin Williams, sent home from Northern Ireland:

> Floods of men poured in during our periodic intakes. Men from North and South Wales, from the hills of Montgomeryshire and Radnor, and also scousers from Liverpool and sharp boys from Birmingham, We formed them into squads under drill sergeants and at the end of twelve weeks gave lance-corporal stripes to the best.
>
> May came, and with it the fall of France. Our First Battalion was over there and soon news came back of men missing and killed. Gloom descended on the barracks, but Dunkirk was at hand and there was work to be done. A train-load of muddy warriors from innumerable British regiments arrived at Wrexham station. We formed them into threes and they straggled wearily up to the depot, shambled past the guard and collapsed on the Barrack square.[30]

STAFF LIST, Depot The Royal Welch Fusiliers and 23 I.T.C., 1919–1940

Depot Headquarters

Officer Commanding	Maj E.R. Kearsley DSO	27 May 19
	Maj H.V.V. Kyrke DSO	27 May 22
	Maj M.L. Lloyd-Mostyn	27 May 25
	Maj G.E.R. de Miremont DSO MC	27 May 28
	Maj Ll. A.A. Alston DSO MC	21 Oct 29
	Maj E. Wodehouse	21 Oct 32
	Maj A.M.G. Evans	21 Oct 35
	Maj H.C. Watkins MC	21 Oct 38
Adjutant	Capt D.M. Barchard	1919
	Lt J.G. Bruxner-Randall	Dec 22
	Lt D.I. Owen	29 Aug 23
	Capt M.B. Dowse	30 May 27
	Lt Ll. Gwydyr-Jones	30 May 28
	Lt G.E. Braithwaite	15 Oct 30
	Lt C.H.V. Pritchard	15 Oct 33
	Lt R.C. Rose Price	Mar 36
	Capt R.C.M. Kelly	1939
	Capt W.G. Daniel	5 Oct 40
Assistant Adjutant	Lt the Hon F.J. Southwell	1923
Quartermaster	Maj H. Yates MC	1921
	Capt A.M. Watson MBE	1925
	Capt W.H. Albutt MBE DCM	Feb 32
	Lt G.R. Whyley	12 Feb 30, Capt 37
Regimental Sergeant Major	W.O. I A.M. Boreham MC	2 May 19
	W.O. I W. Heirene	7 Jun 22
	W.O. I A.G. Bent MM	1930
	W.O. I A. Lungley	2 Feb 32
	W.O. I J.T. Dale	2 May 37
O.R.Q.M.S.	W.O. II H.G. Holderness	1933
	W.O. II – Hughes	1938
O.R.S.	Sgt H.G. Holderness	1922
	CSgt G. Evans, 1938	

Headquarter Company/Wing

Gas Officer	Capt W.H. Bamfield	1937
R.Q.M.S.	W.O. II F. Powell MC	1921
	W.O. II W. Gorham	1924
	W.O. II R. Howell	1933
	W.O. II – Davies	1937
	W.O. II R. Thomas	1939
Transport	Sgt W. Byles	1922
Bandmaster	W.O. I H.P.G. Purdue *(late Essex R.)*	1932
P.T.I.	W.O. II – James *A.P.T. Staff*	to 1923
	SSI J.M. Crane *Suffolk R.*	1923

Training Companies

Captains
J.G. Bruxner-Randall, 1921
C.G.H. Peppé, 1921
E. Wodehouse, 1924
W.P. Kenyon MC, 1930
H.C. Watkins, 1930
T.S. Griffiths, 1932
E.R. Freeman, 1933
B.E. Horton, 1935
G.E. Braithwaite, 1935
D.I. Owen, 1937
C.J.L. Lewis, 1938

Lieutenants
E.C. Tunnicliffe, 1921
R. de B. Hardie, 1921
W.P. Kenyon MC, 1923
T.D. Butler, 1930
H. de B. Prichard, 1930
Hon G.R. Clegg-Hill, 1932
J.G. Vyvyan, 1933
R.A.F. Hurt, 1933
E.C. Parker-Jervis, 1934
B.P. Doughty-Wylie, 1935
J.P.E. Bernatchez *R.22eR.*, 1935
C.E. Hill, 1937
R.F.A. David, to 1938

Company Sergeant Majors
W.O. II W.H. Poole, 1920
W.O. II C. Fell, 1922
W.O. II R. Burns, 1922
W.O. II J. Mallett, 1922
W.O. II G.R. Whyley, 1922
W/O. II – Bergen, 1923
W.O. II T. Hannon MC DCM, 1924
W.O. II I.G. Smalldon, 1933
W.O. II J. Storer, 1935
W.O. II J. Edge, 1937
W.O. II F. Tams, 1939
W.O. II A. James, 1939
W.O. II J. Soane, 1939

C.Q.M.S.
J. Reeves, 1921
J. Kirby, 1922
S. Lord, 1922
R. Leonard, 1922
P. Condon, 1924
P. Chard, 1931
R.O. Jones, 1933
C. Harrison, 1933
M Roberts 14, 1934
A. lePoiveden, 1937
J. Jones 22, 1937
D. Urquhart MM, 1937
O. Stanley, 1939
J. Dodd, 1939
A. Randall, 1939

W.O. III (P.S.M.)
W. Scammels, 1939
F. Fraser, 1939

Lance-Sergeants
W. McGuiness, 1939
D. Morgan, 1939
J. Jones, 1939
T. Williams, 1939
F. Smith, 1939
P. Price, 1939
W. Watson, 1939
T. Jones, 1939

Attached
CSMI S. Consitt *A.P.T.S.*, 1939
Sgt A. Ritson *A.E.C.*, 1939

Sergeants
W. Challoner, 1919
J.M. Kensett, 1921
F. Hughes DCM, 1921
J.T. Wilde, 1922
W. Barkley, 1922*
G.W. Jones MM, 1922
S. Thomas 58, 1922
H. Howells 88, 1922
J.D. O'Brien, 1922*
C. Hanley, 1922
P. Ireland, 1922
C. Barker, 1922*
G. Neene, 1922*
E. Griffiths 91, 1922
F.P. Newbold, 1924
E. Moreton MM, 1924
J. Thatcher, 1924
W.H. Setterfield, 1925
S.M. Sheriff, 1931
- Roberts, 1932
H.J. Jenkins, 1933
- Whalley, 1933
W. Lodder, 1933
R. Hayward, 1934
J. Austin, 1934
W. Parry, 1935
B. Brown, 1935
G. Davies, 1935
F. Whitley, 1935
T. Adams, 1935
- Mantle, 1936
- Philips, 1936
A. Chesters, 1937
W. Anders, 1937
G. Whatley, 1937
G. Evans 34, 1937
L. Grindley, 1938
- Curran, to 1938
F. Pepper, to 1938
E. Balfe, 1939
J. Williams, 1939
T. Vaughan, 1939
J. Whalley, 1939
S. Hares, 1939
G. Harris, 1939
A. Silk, 1939
J. Thatcher, 1939
S. Baxindale, 1939
W. Martin, 1939
J. Evans, 1939
G. Beech, 1939
G. Muzzelle, 1939
D. Brannan, 1939

*Believed to have joined from disbanded Irish Regiments in 1922.

v. The 3rd (Special Reserve) Battalion

In 1908, all militia infantry battalions were re-designated as 'reserve' and a number were amalgamated or disbanded.[31] The two Militia Battalions of the Royal Welch Fusiliers had been the 3rd (Denbigh & Flint) and the 4th (Caernarvon & Merioneth). In 1908 the 4th Battalion was disbanded. The 3rd Battalion then became the Special Reserve battalion of the Regiment.

The 3rd Battalion remained in the United Kingdom throughout the Great War, first at Wrexham, then from May 1915 at Litherland Camp near Liverpool, and then from November 1917 at Limerick in Ireland. Its Officers and men did not necessarily remain with the battalion throughout the war, since the object of the Special Reserve was to supply drafts of replacements for the overseas units of the Regiment. The original militiamen soon disappeared, and the battalions became purely training units.

The 3rd Battalion returned to Wrexham in cadre from Limerick after the re-formation of the 2nd Battalion in 1919 and in common with the rest of the Special Reserve, reverted to its militia designation in 1921; it was then converted into the Supplementary Reserve in 1923, but effectively placed in suspended animation. Its Colours remained with the Depot, which fulfilled many of its former functions, and were displayed in the Officers' Mess. These Colours were brought onto parade at Depot ceremonial events.

STAFF LIST, 3rd (Special Reserve) Battalion (Royal Denbigh and Flint Militia), 1919–1924

Commanding Officer	Lt Col A.R.P. Macartney-Filgate CBE	to Oct 23
Adjutant	Lieutenant L. Coote	
	Lieutenant D.M. Barchard	12 Ju 19
	Captain J.G. Bruxner-Randall	18 Aug 22
	No further appointment	from Oct 23
Quartermaster	Lieutenant C.J. Shea	1919–1923

Depot Strength, 1919–1939 (Combined with the 3rd Battalion until 1923)

Date	Station	Offrs	W.Os & Sgts	Dmrs	J.N.C.Os & Fus	Source
Jan 19	Limerick	25	52	3	216	WO 73/110
Jul 20	Wrexham	7	31	3	247	WO 73/113
Dec 20		7	35	10	158	WO 73/113
Jun 21		7	17	2	207[1]	WO 73/114
Dec 21		7	20	3	261	WO 73/115
Mar 22		7	22	7	262	WO 73/116
Dec 22		6	23	10	216	WO 73/117
Jun 23		5	11	3	202	WO 73/118
Oct 23		8	14	5	268	WO 73/119
Apr 24		7	13	2	227	WO 73/120
Apr 25		7	12	3	228	WO 73/122
Oct 26		7	13	3	243	WO 73/124
Apr 27		6	14	3	144	WO 73/125
Oct 27		7	13	3	214	WO 73/126
Apr 29		5	13	3	158	WO 73/129
Oct 29		7	13	3	167	WO 73/130
Oct 30		7	12	3	141	WO 73/132

Date	Station	Offrs	W.Os & Sgts	Dmrs	J.N.C.Os & Fus	Source
Jan 33		7	13	3	168	WO 73/136
Jan 34		7	13	3	166	WO 73/137
Jan 37		7	12	3	137[2]	WO 73/140
Jan 38		7	14	3	148[3]	WO 73/141
Jul 38		8	13	6	178[4]	WO 73/141
Oct 39	23 I.T.C.	33	48	16	914[5]	WO 73/142

Table notes

1   There were, in addition, 7 Officers and 335 O.R. mobilised reservists at the Depot.
2   59 recruits in last half year.
3   65 recruits in last half year.
4   123 recruits in last half year.
5   War Establishment.

Notes

1   Notes by Lieutenant Colonel N.R.G. Bosanquet in R.W.F. Mus/Archives.
2   David French, *Military Identities,* p. 60.
3   Notes by Sir Hugh Stockwell in R.W.F. Mus.
4   Notes by Colonel C.E. Hill in R.W.F. Mus/Archives.
5   Notes by Lieutenant Colonel P.A. Kenyon in R.W.F. Mus/Archives.
6   *Across the Straits,* p. 120.
7   *Y Ddraig Goch,* May 1923, p. 133.
8   Frank Richards, *Old Soldier Sahib* pp 30, 36.
9   David French, *Raising Churchill's Army. The British Army and the War against Germany, 1919–1945* (O.U.P., 2000), p. 56.
10   *Infantry Training, Vol I, Training* (W.O./G.S 1932), p. 11.
11   T.N.A. WO 32/2382, 26 November 1928.
12   *Training in Fieldcraft and Elementary Tactics, Military Training Pamphlet No 33* (W.O./G.S. 1937), p. 5.
13   French, p. 57.
14   *Y Ddraig Goch,* October 1922, p. 52.
15   *Y Ddraig Goch,* October 1922, p. 57.
16   *Y Ddraig Goch,* May 1924, p. 241.
17   *Y Ddraig Goch,* January 1925, p. 302.
18   *Y Ddraig Goch,* September 1931, p. 60.
19   *Y Ddraig Goch,* December 1931, pp. 82–83.
20   *Y Ddraig Goch,* July 1935, p. 62.
21   *Y Ddraig Goch,* July 1935, pp. 62–63.
22   *Y Ddraig Goch,* July 1936, pp. 70–72.
23   *Y Ddraig Goch,* Winter 1938–39, p. 49.
24   *Y Ddraig Goch,* Spring 1940, p. 55.
25   *Y Ddraig Goch,* Spring 1940, pp. 56–57.
26   *Y Ddraig Goch,* Spring 1940, p. 57.
27   *Y Ddraig Goch,* Spring 1940, p. 58.
28   *Newsletter,* Second Series, No 1, August 1943.
29   A.G. Card 28, War Establishments v/474/1 (Lower).
30   *Across the Straits,* p. 127.
31   *London Gazette,* 10 April 1908.

Chapter 15

Regimental Matters, 1919–1940

---

i. The Colonel-in-Chief

His Majesty King George V became Colonel-in-Chief of the Regiment on 21 December 1901, when he was still Prince of Wales. This was the first recorded formal use of the title.[1] His Majesty remained Colonel-in-Chief from his accession on 31 May 1910 until his death on 20 January 1936. On 21 August that year, the Regimental Committee decided to request that King Edward VIII should become Colonel-in-Chief in succession to his late father, however no action was taken on this request before the King's abdication in December. On 11 May 1937, following further representations by the Regimental Committee, His Majesty King George VI graciously consented to become Colonel-in-Chief.[2] Nothing had been known of The King's intentions until the publication of the Coronation Honours List. This contained the names of six Regiments of which The King was to become Colonel-in-Chief, leaving aside the Regiments of Guards.*

On 4 July 1932 a Representative Detachment of the 1st Battalion consisting of all Officers, Warrant Officers and Colour Sergeants; ten Sergeants and Lance Sergeants; ten Corporals and Lance-Corporals; twenty Fusiliers; the Regimental Band, Corps of Drums, Pioneers and the King's Goat left Tidworth for Chelsea Barracks where they were accommodated by the 1st Battalion Grenadier Guards. The Pioneers were carrying for the first time their new tools – mattocks, picks, axes and spades – replacing the axes previously carried by the whole platoon. On 5 July, His Majesty received the Detachment at Buckingham Palace, marking the return of the 1st Battalion from foreign and active service.[3] The detachment marched off at 10.00 hrs, through a large crowd, and formed up below the terrace in the private garden to the rear of the palace. At 11.00 hrs, The King came out, with Sir Charles Dobell, Colonel of the Regiment, and inspected the Detachment.

His Majesty then addressed the detachment:

> It gives me much pleasure to inspect this Detachment and to offer the First Battalion a warm welcome back to this country. I know how much you must all be looking forward to

---

* The others were 1st Tte Royal Dragoons, the King's Royal Rifle Corps, the Queen's Own Cameron Highlanders, the Royal Tank Corps, the Duke of Lancaster's Own Yeomanry and the Officers' Training Corps.

1st. Battalion Officers with H.M.King George V,
at Buckingham Palace 1932.

Top Row. Lt. R.J.F. Snead-Cox,2nd.Lt. N.R.G. Bosanquet, Lt. N.C. Stockwell, 2ndLt. G. Barton, 2nd. Lt. R.C.R.Price,
Lt. E.M. Davies-Jenkins, 2nd. Lt. Lipsett, 2nd. Lt. R.C.M. Kelly, 2nd. Lt. D.M.C. Pritchard, 2nd. Lt. L.H.
Yates 2nd. Lt. W.L.R. Benyon, Lt. E.H. Cadogan.
Centre Row. Capt. R. de B. Hardie, Lt. J.G. Vyvyan, Lt. R.F.A. David, Capt. G.N.H. Tounton-Collins, Lt & Q.M. G.R.
Wylie, Lt. J.H. Liscombe, Lt. H.A.S. Clarke, 2nd. Lt. A.J. Lewis, Lt. O.T.N. Raymont. Lt. M. Whittaker.
Front Row. Capt. M.B. Dowse, Capt. H.D.T. Morris, Major J.G. Bruxner Randall, General Sir Charles Dobell, H.M. King
George V, Col.-in-Chief, Lt-Col. E.O. Skaife, Major E. Wodehouse, Capt. T.S. Griffiths, Capt. H.A. Freeman.

After the King had inspected a representative detachment of 100 Rank and File of the 1st Battalion, on its return from
foreign service, the King was standing with the Commanding Officer on the steps leading from the Bow Room, before the
Officers were presented to him. All of a sudden he turned to the Commanding Officer and said "It is such a pleasure to
see you all wearing your Flashes. I had such trouble about it in the War. The War Office wanted to take the Flash off
the backs of the Royal Welch. Lord Kitchener was particularly difficult – they said it was too conspicuous. I said
the enemy will never see the Flash on the backs of the Royal Welch."

The 1st Battalion party at Buckingham Palace 1932. (R.W.F. Mus 0588)

a tour of home service, and to being with your families, relations, and friends. You began your foreign service in January, 1914, and of more than 800 Officers and men who left these shores for Malta, only four, whom I am glad to see here today, are still serving with the Battalion. The last eighteen years have added fresh lustre to the regiment both in peace and war.

During the South African campaign, King Edward conferred on me the honour of becoming your Colonel-in-Chief. Ever since that day I have always followed with unfailing interest your fortunes. As your Colonel-in-Chief I share your pride in your 117 Battle Honours, and I wish good luck and prosperity to my Royal Welch Fusiliers.

Lieutenant Colonel Skaife then replied:

> Your Majesty,
> The First Battalion of The Royal Welch Fusiliers value more deeply than words of mine can express the welcome home which Your Majesty has been graciously pleased to extend to them, firstly through the message received on their landing at Southampton and secondly through Your Majesty's command that this representative Detachment should be paraded here today.
>
> It will be the constant aim and endeavour of all ranks of the First Battalion both now and in the future to do their duty in such a way as to show their gratitude to their Colonel-in-Chief for the signal marks of favour which Your Majesty has been pleased to show them.

Lieutenant Colonel Skaife, CSM J.M. Kensett and Drum Major J.H.B. Bacon, who had all been with the battalion when it sailed from Southampton in January 1914, were then presented to the King. His Majesty then presented the MSM to Sergeant C. Clemence. The Detachment then gave three cheers, following which the Band played 'God Save the King'. The Detachment then marched back to Chelsea Barracks. Heavy rain fell, but the weather cleared by 13.00 hrs allowing a photograph to be taken of the whole Detachment, in addition to a photograph of the King with the Officers at Buckingham Palace.

ii. The Colonel of the Regiment

On 26 February 1926 the Colonel of the Regiment, Lieutenant General Sir Francis Lloyd GCVO KCB DSO died aged 73. He was succeeded by Lieutenant General Sir Charles Dobell KCB CMG DSO.[4] On 26 October 1938, General Dobell was succeeded by Major General J.R. Minshull-Ford CB DSO MC; General Dobell was the first Colonel since General Sir William Codrington, who assumed the appointment in November 1860, who had not died while serving as Colonel of the Regiment. The biographies of the Colonels can be found in the Annexes to this volume.

iii. The Spelling of 'Welch' in the Regiment's Title, 1920

Throughout its long history the Regiment has used 'Welsh' and 'Welch' indiscriminately and both also appeared in official documents, including the Army List. The 41st Foot which became nominally Welsh in 1831 favoured the spelling 'Welch'. Before the Great War a joint submission to the War Office to sanction the use of 'Welch' was rejected. Another attempt was made after the War and this time it was successful. Army Order No. 56 of 1920 stated that 'His Majesty The King has been graciously pleased to approve of the word "Welsh" in the title of the Royal Welsh Fusiliers and the Welsh Regiment being amended to read "Welch"'. It was made clear however in subsequent correspondence that this was:

> only in regard to the spelling in the Army List and Official Correspondence … large stocks of cap-badges, titles etc., are on hand and that as an immediate change with respect to

these articles would involve the loss of a large sum of public money, this change cannot take place until such stocks are used up… no public expense can be sanctioned in connection with Colours until new ones are required in the ordinary course.[5]

iv. The Spelling of Sergeant

In the 1st, 3rd and Territorial Battalions, Sergeant was spelled with a 'g' and this practice appears to have been followed in the Service and Home Guard battalions from 1940 to 1945. In the 2nd Battalion, however, Serjeant was spelled with a 'j'. The reason for this is not clear, unless it was a deliberate device to emphasize the difference between the two Regular battalions.

v. The Flash

Until 1900 the Flash was worn by Officers, Warrant Officers and Staff Sergeants, but on 2 June of that year, following an inspection of the 1st Battalion at Raglan Barracks, Devonport, by the Commander-in-Chief, Field Marshal Viscount Wolseley, Queen Victoria was 'graciously pleased to approve of all ranks of the Line Battalions … wearing on full dress a "Flash" somewhat similar to that now worn by the Officers of the Regiment.'*

On 6 May 1915 the Under-Secretary of State for War stated in Parliament that 'Recently it has been observed that some Officers of this regiment were irregularly wearing the "Flash" with service dress uniform, and instructions have been issued for this to be discontinued. The "Flash" is only authorised to be worn with the scarlet tunic.' Such was the feeling this caused that, only six days later the Under-Secretary, in answer to another question in the House, announced that 'this matter has been reconsidered, and authority to wear the flash with service dress will be given for the period of the War.'

The question of the Flash was finally settled in November 1923 by the personal intervention of King George V, Colonel-in-Chief. The King's Private Secretary wrote to the War Office to say that:

> The wearing of the Tunic … having been abolished, His Majesty considers that the distinction of the Flash should be worn on all Ceremonial and Church Parades and when walking out. It is most highly valued by the Regiment: and the King trusts that now, when similar privileges are being restored to Highland Regiments, this cherished distinction may be given back to the Royal Welch.

The Quartermaster-General replied that 'I do not anticipate there will be any difficulty in giving effect to His Majesty's wishes.' In January 1924, the Army Council issued an instruction approving the wearing of the Flash by all ranks, whether Regulars, Militia or Territorials,[6] and

---

*   This meant the Regular battalions of the Regiment, but it was also taken to include the Militia or Special Reserve battalions, which appeared on the Army List. It did not include the Volunteers or later the Territorial Force battalions – whom Robert Graves refers to in *Goodbye to All That*, for example, as 'the Flash-less Territorials'.

henceforward all ranks were permitted to wear the Flash in service dress on ceremonial occasions and when walking out.

When the Representative Detachment of the 1st Battalion was received at Buckingham Palace in 1932 (see above), The King remarked to Lieutenant Colonel E.O. Skaife,

> … It is such a pleasure to see you all in your Flashes here today. I had such trouble about it during the war. They wanted to take the Flash off the khaki uniform of the Royal Welch. Lord Kitchener was particularly difficult. They said it was too conspicuous. I told them that the enemy would never see the Flashes on the backs of the Royal Welch.

vi. Rank of Fusilier, 1923

Army Order No. 222 of 1923 stated, *inter alia*, that 'In future, private soldiers of Fusilier regiments will be described as "Fusilier".'

vii. The Senior Major

The use of the title of 'Senior Major' by the Second-in-Command of battalions refers to the period before the Great War when battalions only had one Major – companies being commanded by Captains. The title was first used in *Regimental Standing Orders* in 1912 but disappeared during the Great War. In October 1920 and January 1921, the Digests of Service for 1 and 2 R.W.F. respectively use the term; editions of *Regimental Standing Orders* in 1921 and 1935 use the title.

viii. Presentation and Laying-up of Union Flags of the Service Battalions

On 9 August 1919, on a beautiful day and in front of a large crowd at the Depot in Wrexham, the Colonel of the Regiment, Lieutenant General Sir Francis Lloyd, presented silk Union Flags to the 8th, 10th, 11th, 15th and 19th Service Battalions, and the 1st, 2nd and 6th Garrison Battalions to mark their significant contribution during the Great War. Details of the Union Flags are included in the Annexes to this Volume.

Some Flags had already been presented to Service battalions in France or Belgium in January 1919: on the 16th, the 14th, 16th and 17th Battalions' Flags had been presented at Allanville, France, and two days later the 13th received theirs at the same location. The 9th was given its Flag at Berteaucourt, France on the 22nd, and finally the 26th at Hondeghem, Belgium on the 17th.

The parade at Wrexham formed up as a three-sided square, with N.C.Os acting as Escorts to the Flags forming the base. On the approach of the Colonel of the Regiment the parade presented arms. Sir Francis Lloyd, accompanied by the Officer Commanding the Depot, Major E.R. Kearsley, advanced to meet the Archbishop of Wales, the Most Reverend Dr R.G. Edwards. The Flags were then marched forward and placed against the piled drums. The senior Officer of each battalion then uncased the Flag of his own battalion. The Archbishop then performed the ceremony of consecration. When this was complete the junior Officers acting as

The Presentation of Union flags to the Service Battalions at Hightown Barracks,
Wrexham, on 9 August 1919. (R.W.F. Mus)

Flag Bearers marched forward and halted facing the drums. The senior Officer of each battalion
in turn handed the Flag to the Colonel of the Regiment who presented to the kneeling flag
bearer. When all the Flags had been presented the Flag Bearers rose.

Sir Francis Lloyd then addressed the parade. He pointed to the significance of the Flags as
emblems of self-sacrifice and loyal devotion to a just and honourable cause, which was only won
by a high sense of duty and determination. He urged young soldiers to preserve untarnished the
reputation of the Regiment which had been gained before the War, and to which fresh lustre
had been added during the bitter struggle from 1914 to 1918.

The Flag Bearers were then turned to face the parade which then formed line. The Flags
being unfurled a Royal Salute was given. The Flag Bearers marched in slow time to their escorts
in the line while the Band played the National Anthem. The parade then marched past to the
Regimental quick-step, *The British Grenadiers*, the Colonel of the Regiment taking the salute.
The Flags of the 15th Service and 6th Garrison Battalions were marched off parade as they
were to be deposited at County Hall, London, and Liverpool respectively, reflecting where
these battalions had originally been raised. The remaining Flags, together with those of the 9th
and 26th Service Battalions, were then escorted to St Giles' Parish Church, where they were
laid on the altar and handed over to the Church for safe custody. The service was conducted
by the Archbishop, assisted by the Very Reverend Canon Davies. The Flags now hang in the
Regimental Chapel in the Church.

Some of the Union Flags were laid up elsewhere: those of the 13th and 17th Battalions in
Trinity Church, Llandudno on 6 June 1919; the 14th at Bangor Cathedral on 31 May 1919;
and the 16th at St Asaph Cathedral on 4 June 1919. Finally, the 15th Battalion (1st London
Welsh) was handed over to London County Council on 25 October 1921 for display in the old
County Hall, Spring Gardens. The fate of the Union Flag presented to the 24th (Denbighshire
Yeomanry) Battalion at Hondeghem on 19 February 1919 is unknown. The Flag of the 25th
(Montgomeryshire Yeomanry) Battalion was laid up in St Mary's, Welshpool on 20 September
1920, but there is no record of when it was presented.[7]

ix. Publication of *Regimental Records* Volumes I–IV, 1921–1929

No reference has been found to the decision to proceed with the publication of *Regimental Records* or when it was taken, but the first volume appeared in 1921. It covered the period from the founding of the Regiment in 1689 until 1815. The compilers of the first two volumes were A.D.L. Cary, Librarian of the Royal United Service Institution, and Captain Stouppe McCance (late R.A.S.C.). The lack of contemporary Regimental material is bemoaned by the Colonel of the Regiment in his Preface. In their Introduction the compilers state that they 'have been considerably handicapped in their task by the almost entire absence of letters, diaries, or journals of Officers who served with the regiment...' * They also acknowledged the advice received from, *inter alios*, members of the Regimental Records Committee, Brigadier General Sir Robert Colleton, and Major G.F. Barttelot. The structure for both volumes was in the form of a running narrative chronologically arranged, with a calendar of events. The first volume contained two appendices covering the Succession of Colonels and Regimental Mess Records, and there was also a short bibliography. The second volume, which appeared in 1923, dealt with the period 1816 to July 1914. Much more contemporary material was available including journals and diaries for the Burma War of 1885–1887, the Black Mountain Expedition of 1891, the Second Boer War 1899–1902, and Pekin 1900. Appendices include the Succession of Colonels, Costume and Equipment, Arms, Medals, Music, Sport, Colours, Commanding Officers, and the Flash. There was an even shorter bibliography of only ten items. In neither volume were there either footnotes or endnotes. Surprisingly, Volume II contained no reference to the Militia, Volunteers or the Territorial Force.

Volumes III and IV were written by Major C.H. Dudley Ward (late Welsh Guards), a well-known Great War historian who wrote histories of the Welsh Guards, 53rd (Welsh) Division, 74th (Yeomanry) Division, and also some novels. Volume III, published in 1928, covered the Great War in France and Flanders, including the expansion of the Regiment during the War. Volume IV, which appeared in 1929, dealt with other theatres from 1915 to 1918. The latter volume had sixteen detailed appendices, including Rolls of Honour of Officers and Other Ranks.

In July 1928 the Regimental Committee took exception to some passages that appeared in Volume III and instructed the publishers, Forster Groom & Co Ltd, London, to suspend circulation. In three instances deletions or alterations were made to the offending passages. In the original edition the penultimate paragraph on page 420 began thus: 'It is curious to find at this time, while the Higher Command was dithering with fear that the enemy might break through, a certain amount of fraternisation, etc, etc.' On page 436, the third paragraph mentions the problems of the 38th Division and ends with the words, 'the health standard of the division was low.' The next paragraph – almost certainly referring to 113 (Royal Welsh) Brigade with 13, 14 and 16 R.W.F. – has been deleted and replaced by a very short innocuous paragraph about the weather. The paragraph to which the Regimental Committee took offence reads as follows:

---

*   Subsequently, with the development of the Regimental Museum and its archives, much material from the American Revolutionary, French Revolutionary, Napoleonic and Crimean Wars has come to light.

Under the circumstances discipline suffered. At the beginning of May a company was found not wearing equipment in the front line; another company had no sentries at their posts, and no Officer on duty; in yet another company area everyone was found asleep at seven out of ten sentry posts.

The last two occurrences were in June 1918.[8]

In 1930 the Regiment owed the publishers £293. The Regimental Committee decided to take a bank loan using the property of the R.W.F. Philanthropic Fund, namely two fields at the Depot, as security if necessary.[9]

x. Regimental Standing Orders

Two editions were issued during the period. The first, in 1921, superseded the 1888 edition, which had been supplemented by sets of Standing Orders for the 1st and 2nd Battalions, in 1910 and 1912 respectively, since authority was given to Commanding Officers to vary *Regimental Standing Orders* according to circumstances. The second edition during this period was issued in 1935.

xi. The Regimental Journal, *Y Ddraig Goch*, 1922–1925 and 1931–1940

The first issue of the regimental journal, named *Y Ddraig Goch* ('The Red Dragon') was published in May 1922. In the Preface, the Colonel of the Regiment wrote:

> In a great Regiment such as ours, with great traditions of the past and an "esprit de corps" second to none, anything that binds us more closely together is a distinct asset. This publication is such, and is a long-felt need, it will be a means of conveying contemporary Regimental History to all Battalions... . I prophesy a great success.

The Editor in his Letter stated that, 'If this number proves a success both financially and in a literary sense, our aim is to edit a magazine quarterly.' The cost was one shilling (5p) for Officers and nine pence (3.75p) for Other Ranks. It ran to twenty-four pages and included notes from both Regular battalions – the 1st in Waziristan and the 2nd in Ireland – the Regimental Depot, and one Territorial battalion (the 6th). Much space was devoted to sport, including hunting, and the rest devoted to Comrades, staff lists, obituaries, and Sergeants' and Corporals' Messes. In fact, the Regular battalions devoted more space to sport than to their operational activities. There was only one freelance article about a Spanish poodle called 'Pickles' who was presented to H Company 2 R.W.F. in 1887 as its mascot. The author, Drummer Maynard, had charge of it.

The next issue in October was very much on the lines of its predecessor, with the 1st Battalion managing to devote seven of its eight pages to sport. So it continued, with about three issues a year, a total of ten issues in all, making up Volume I, until June 1925 after which no more issues appeared. The reason was not explained but, the editorial in May 1924 drew attention to the financial plight of the venture, with the printers demanding payment, and over £130 being owed from various sources.

In spite of unsuccessful pleas by the Regimental Committee for its revival, it was not until March 1931 that the next issue appeared, a very slim edition of only fifteen pages. It continued as Series II, with two Volumes each of four quarterly issues in March, June, September and December, until December 1932. Series III then began with Volume I, four quarterly issues in 1933. Thereafter there was no further Volume numbering, but four issues usually appeared each year, except in 1935 when there were three, 1939 when there were two, and 1940 when there was one. After the Spring 1940 edition the *Regimental Journal* was suspended for the remainder of the war. In most issues, sport always featured prominently, and company and platoon notes were usually obscure to any who did not understand the in-jokes and nicknames.

xii. The Regiment's Great War Memorial, unveiled 15 November 1924

The proposal to erect a Memorial to Officers and men of the Regiment who fell in the Great War was raised by a group of Officers in 1918. They formed a committee whose aim was to contact as many members and friends as possible in order to ascertain the form the Memorial should take and to invite subscriptions. A meeting was held in London in 1918 at which the Colonel of the Regiment presided. The original intention had been to erect a monument in each of the counties of North Wales but it soon became apparent that most communities were planning their own

monuments. At a meeting at the Depot in October 1919 it was decided to have a single Regimental Memorial at Wrexham, which was regarded as the home of the Regiment.

The Mayor and Corporation were very supportive and facilitated the selection of a suitable site.[10] The original planned location for the memorial was the High Street, but the Ministry of Transport advised against that location owing to the street being classified as an A road. The second planned location was Guildhall Square, off Chester Street, although that would have required the relocation of the statue of Queen Victoria, which had only been installed a few years before the war. The third planned location was the junction of the King's Mills Road, Bennions Lane and Salisbury Park Road.[11] Sir William Goscombe John must have investigated this

Lieutenant General Sir Francis Lloyd unveils the Regiment's War Memorial in Wrexham, 15 November 1924. (R.W.F. Mus)

location more closely, as the Town Clerk informed the Borough Council meeting in committee that the sculptor desired a better location for the erection of a memorial. The Council agreed to meet the Regimental representatives again to consider alternative locations. The site finally chosen, which was given by the Borough of Wrexham, was at the corner of Grosvenor Road and Regent Street. In 1959 the Memorial was moved to a new site off Chester Road (see *Regimental Records, Volume VI*).[12]

The unveiling and dedication of the War Memorial of The Royal Welch Fusiliers took place at Wrexham on Saturday 15 November 1924. The memorial perpetuates the sacrifices of the 10,934 Officers and men of the forty battalions of the Regiment (less the Volunteer Force) who gave their lives during the Great War; the figure includes those killed while serving with other units and those attached from outside.[13] It was unveiled by the Colonel of the Regiment, Lieutenant General Sir Francis Lloyd, and the dedication was conducted by the Archbishop of Wales, the Most Reverend Dr R.G. Edwards.

Before the ceremony the troops paraded at Hightown Barracks, and with the ex-Servicemen marched to the Guildhall, where they were joined by the Mayor of Wrexham, Councillor C.E. Hickman, the Corporation and officials. The procession then moved off in the following order:

> Band and Drums of 2 R.W.F. under Bandmaster W.J. Clancy.
> Major H.V. Venables Kyrke DSO, Officer Commanding Regimental Depot.
> Detachment 7 R.W.F. (TA).
> Detachment 6 R.W.F. (TA) under Captain A.M. Trustram Eve MC.[*]
> Guard of Honour found by Depot R.W.F., under Lieutenant W.P. Kenyon.
> The Colours of 2 R.W.F. with Lieutenant R.W.C. Martin in charge of the Regimental
>   Colour.
> A composite Firing Party, found by R.W.F. (TA) battalions.
> Detachment 5 R.W.F. (TA) under Captain J. Mostyn.
> Detachment 4 R.W.F. (TA) under Captain A. Wynne.
> R.W.F. Old Comrades.
> Mayors of Boroughs of North Wales.
> Mayor and Corporation Wrexham.

On arrival at the site they were joined by:

> Lord Kenyon, Lord-Lieutenant of Denbighshire
> Sir H. Williams-Wynn Bt, Lord-Lieutenant of Montgomeryshire
> Henry N. Gladstone, Lord-Lieutenant of Flintshire
> Viscount Southwell
> Rev. Mgr. Canon G. Nightingale, Vicar-General
> Rt. Rev. Dr R.G. Edwards, Archbishop of Wales

---

[*]   Later Brigadier Lord (Arthur Malcolm Trustram Eve) Silsoe, 1st Baron (1963), 1st Baronet (1943) GBE MC TD QC (1894–1976). An Officer of the Territorial Force, he served with 6 R.W.F. in Gallipoli, where he won an MC, and in Egypt and Palestine. He commanded 6 R.W.F. (T.A.) 1927–1931. As a Brigadier he commanded 158 (Royal Welch) Infantry Brigade (T.A.) in 1940 and 1941 in Northern Ireland. In 1942 he became Chairman of the War Damage Commission, responsible for paying compensation for private property damaged by enemy action.

Sir E. Pryce Jones Bt
Canon Lewis Pryce, Vicar of Wrexham
Rev. T. Owen Jones, representing the Evangelical Church Council

Immediately afterwards the Colonel of the Regiment arrived, attended by his Staff Officer, Captain J.G. Bruxner-Randall, and three A.D.Cs. He was received with a General Salute, after which he inspected the Guard of Honour. There followed a short service of hymns and prayers, at the conclusion of which the troops presented arms. General Lloyd then unveiled the memorial with the following words: 'In the name of the Ever-blessed, Glorious, and Undivided Trinity, and in memory of the gallant men of the Royal Welch who gave their lives for King and Country, I unveil this Memorial.'

The Union Flag which covered the Memorial then fell and everyone saluted. The Archbishop read the short dedicatory prayer, and the firing party fired three volleys. The Buglers sounded the 'Last Post' and then the 'Reveille'.

The Colonel of the Regiment in addressing those present said that that day their great historic Regiment celebrated perhaps the greatest epoch in the history of the world, and the greatest page in its own history. He closed his speech by formally handing over the Memorial to the Mayor and Corporation of Wrexham.

During the singing of the hymn, 'O valiant hearts, who to your glory came,' wreaths were laid at the foot of the statue, the first by Sir Francis Lloyd, followed by tributes from all sections of the Regiment, and finally private individuals. Whilst the Band of 2 R.W.F. played Chopin's '*March Funèbre*', wreath after wreath was laid around the base of the Memorial. The pronouncement of the Benediction by the Archbishop and the Vicar-General, the sounding the Reveille, and the singing of '*Hen Wlad Fy Nhadau*' and the National Anthem brought the ceremony to a close.

The Old Comrades' Reunion Dinner was held in the evening at Wrexham. Telegrams were sent to H.M. The King and to 1 R.W.F. in India.

The Memorial consists of a fine group in bronze by the distinguished Welsh sculptor, Sir William Goscombe John R.A. It represents two Fusiliers, one in the uniform of the Regiment at the time of Marlborough holding the Colours over the other, a Fusilier of the Great War who carries rifle, bayonet, shrapnel helmet and gas mask. The group stands on a pedestal which bears the inscription: 'To the immortal memory of the Royal Welch Fusiliers, 1914–1918. *Duw Cadw'r Brenin*' [God Save the King]. The monument is about twenty feet in height, the bronze group about ten.

xiii. Battalion Memorials

4th (Denbighshire) Battalion (T.F.) in the Great War
The Battalion war memorial, a plaque inscribed with the names of the fallen, was unveiled in Poyser Street Barracks, Wrexham, at a date unknown, but before 1926. It was later moved to Hightown Barracks.

5th (Flintshire) Battalion (T.F.) in the Great War
The unveiling of the battalion war memorial by the Lord-Lieutenant of Flintshire, Henry N. Gladstone, took place at the Drill Hall, Rhyl on Thursday 13 July 1922, the anniversary of the

battalion's departure for Gallipoli in 1915. The dedication was by the Rt. Rev. Dr R.G. Edwards, Archbishop of Wales. The Memorial consisted of a bronze plate on a granite background with the names of all men of the battalion who took part in the Great War.[14] This memorial was later removed to St Asaph Cathedral.

6th (Carnarvonshire & Anglesey) Battalion (T.F.) in the Great War
In September 1921, the battalion war memorial at Christ Church, Caernarfon was unveiled by Major General G.F. Mott, formerly General Officer Commanding 53rd (Welsh) Division. The memorial took the form of a tablet in Kuhn Brass, resting on a fumed oak background, and contained the names of some 300 Officers and men who gave their lives in the War. Underneath are the words: 'To the Glory of God and in Memory of the Officers, Non-Commissioned Officers and Men of the 1/6th Battalion Royal Welch Fusiliers who gave their lives for King and Country in the Great War.' The memorial which was subscribed for by relatives of the deceased, and by past and present Officers, was executed by Messrs. Mowbray, Margaret Street, London.[15]

53rd (Welsh) Division in the Middle East
A stone cross with memorial tablet was erected at Ram Allah in March 1918. After some post-war damage it was moved to the Mount of Olives outside Jeruslaem where it is cared for by the Commonwealth War Graves Commission.[16]

14th (Service) Battalion in the Great War
A stone seat was placed in Danzig Alley War Cemetery.[17]

15th (Service) Battalion (1st London Welsh) and 18th (Service) Battalion (2nd London Welsh) in the Great War
A bronze memorial tablet was unveiled on 30th June 1929 at Gray's Inn, London.[18]

16th (Service) Battalion in the Great War
A bronze plaque was placed in St Asaph Cathedral in June 1919.

17th (Service) Battalion in the Great War
A stained glass window was placed in Holy Trinity Church, Llandudno in 1934.[19]

24th Battalion (Denbighshire Yeomanry) (T.F.) in the Great War
A stone plaque was placed in St Asaph Cathedral at a date unknown.

Penmaenmawr
A Memorial listing the names of those men from Penmaenmawr, a mining town on the North Wales coast, was unveiled outside the Young Men's Institute on 31 May 1925. The majority of the names are R.W.F. and the memorial bears the Regimental badge.

1/5th R.W.F.
A memorial was placed in Higham Ferrers, Northampstonshire where the 53rd (Welsh) Division had concentrated before embarkation in December 1915, to commemorate the dead of Gallipoli.

R.W.F. Regular Officers in the Great War
A marble panel was placed on one of the columns in the Royal Memorial Chapel at Sandhurst on 5 November 1922, to commemorate those former Gentleman Cadets of the Royal Military College who died during the Great War.

The English Church in Ypres
A memorial brass plaque to the Regiment's fallen was placed in St George's Anglican Church in Ypres, in 1931.

1st Battalion in Waziristan, 1921–1923
In November 1923 a memorial tablet, on which were engraved the names of the eighteen members of 1 R.W.F. who lost their lives in Waziristan, was unveiled in Wrexham Parish Church. The ceremony was performed by Major General T.O. Marden, General Officer Commanding 53rd (Welsh) Division. The large congregation included the Mayor, Councillor H. Blew, and other members of Wrexham Town Council. The Band of the 2nd Battalion was in attendance, and a party of men from the Depot under Captain E. Wodehouse was on parade. Lieutenant W.P. Kenyon commanded the Guard of Honour and the Regimental Colour was carried by Lieutenant the Hon F.J. Southwell. On arrival, General Marden was accompanied by Major H.V. Venables Kyrke DSO, Officer Commanding Regimental Depot. The service in the Church was conducted by the Vicar, the Reverend Lewis Pryce, who gave a brief address. After the unveiling the buglers sounded the 'Last Post'. Following the Blessing, 'Reveille' was sounded, and the service concluded with the National Anthem.[20]

xiv. 158 (Royal Welch) Infantry Brigade (T.A.)

In 1924, 158 (North Wales) Infantry Brigade (T.A.) was re-designated as above. The 5th, 6th and 7th Battalions of The Royal Welch Fusiliers fought with the Brigade throughout the Great War in Gallipoli, Egypt and Palestine. With the addition of the 4th Battalion, the brigade was unchanged when it was re-formed in 1921, and remained so until 1938, when the 5th Battalion was re-roled as an anti-tank regiment R.A. Brigade Commanders during the period 1919–1940 included the following Royal Welch Fusiliers:

> Colonel C.C. Norman CMG DSO, 29 July 1927–29 August 1930
> Brigadier E.O. Skaife OBE, 18 October 1937–7 October 1939
> Brigadier A.M. Trustram Eve MC TD, October 1940–March 1941

xv. Queen Mary's Statuettes

In January 1936, Her Majesty Queen Mary presented two bronze statuettes to the Regiment, one of an Officer and one of a Fusilier, standing with arms reversed. The statuettes, 2 feet 11 inches high (0.9 metres) were the artists' models for the South African War memorial in St Giles's Church and were executed by T. Rudd of London, the memorial having been unveiled by King George V and Queen Mary on 8 May 1903. The statuettes were lodged at the Depot,[21] where they were fixed on stone shelves either side of the Officers' Mess entrance for many years. When the Depot closed they were sent to the Regimental Museum and then to the 1st Battalion, where at the time of writing they remain.

xvi. The Regimental Committee, 1927–1938

The Colonel of the Regiment, Lieutenant General Sir Charles Dobell, called a meeting at the Naval and Military Club, London on 18 January 1927, with Colonel C.I. Stockwell, Commanding Officer 2 R.W.F., and Major E.O. Skaife. The subject was the formation of a Regimental Committee. It was resolved that the formation of a Committee to deal with all matters affecting the Regiment as a whole was desirable. Under the chairmanship of the Colonel of the Regiment it was to comprise:

Commanding Officer of the Regular battalion on Home Establishment
Representative of the Regular battalion serving overseas
Chairman of the Old Comrades Association
'An Old Officer' of the Regiment to be appointed by the Committee for two years
Commanding Officer of one of the T.A. battalions

The Chairman nominated Major Skaife to represent the 1st Battalion, and Lieutenant Colonel J.B. Cockburn DSO as the 'Old Officer'. The Officer Commanding the Depot was to be the Secretary. The Committee was to meet annually at the Depot during Regimental Cricket Week. It was agreed that something needed to be done to revive the *Regimental Journal* which had ceased publication 1925. It was hoped that Major G.J.P. Geiger could be persuaded to take on the editorship, but at the next meeting (22 June 1927) those hopes were dashed. At the meeting on 21 July 1928, Volume III of *Regimental Records* was discussed in the light of the exception that had been taken to some passages. The publishers were informed by telegram to suspend circulation and the offending passages were re-written. The deleted passages may be seen above under Regimental Records.

On 16 August 1929 the proposal that all ranks should wear roses on Minden Day was rejected. It was decided that the Regimental Pioneers should carry the 'tools' on all occasions when aprons were worn. During the next two years the Pioneers came up for much consideration. In 1930 (18 July) it was agreed that in future they were to carry axes only, and on parade they were to lead the battalion ahead of the King's Goat. The former was changed in the following year (21 August) and the decision to carry three axes, two pickaxes, two shovels and a mattock substituted, and the latter decision – the position of the King's Goat on parade – was reversed in 1934. In 1932 (12/13 July) it was decided that Officers attending Levées would wear Full Dress, and the early marriage of young Officers was strongly discouraged. It was decided in 1934 (18 August) that future Regimental Dinners would be held at the Savoy during Ascot Week. This happened until 1936, but in 1937 the Dinner was cancelled. A strange decision was made in 1935 (26 July) that the cost of cleaning old stands of Colours deposited in churches should be borne by the battalion to which they had formally belonged. Strange, because normally Colours were netted and left to turn to dust. The Committee now began to meet biannually.

In 1936 the 250th Anniversary began to occupy the minds of the committee. A sub-committee under Lieutenant Colonel R.E. Hindson was formed and it was suggested that a permanent memorial might be established in the form of playing field for the youth of North Wales at Wrexham. Regrettably, it proved no longer possible, on financial grounds to develop the idea further. The 250th anniversary was, however, formally celebrated (see below). The full dress uniform of the late King was received by the Depot (21 August).

In 1937 (2 April) the Committee decided to investigate the cost of creating a Regimental Museum at the Depot; it also decided to hold a conference of serving and retired Officers at the Savoy before the Regimental Dinner to obtain suggestions regarding the 250th anniversary celebrations. At the second conference that year (13 August) it was directed that Regimental Sergeant Majors would be addressed as 'Mr' and not 'R.S.M.' It was also decided to ask H.M. King George VI if he would attend a Royal Review in the summer of 1939 to mark the 250th anniversary; this review might also include the presentation of Colours to T.A. battalions.

In 1938 (22 April), the matter of a flag, which had belonged to 9 R.W.F. during the Great War, was discussed. This had been found on a dead Royal Welchman between Bapaume and Hebuterne on 27 March 1918 during the great German offensive by Hauptmann Leo Ritter and had been returned by him to a deputation of Officers of the Regiment on 29 January.* Continuing the theme of flags, 158 (Royal Welch) Infantry brigade had asked to use the red dragon, 'R.W.F.' and 'HQ 158 (Royal Welch) Infantry Brigade' on its flag. The committee agreed to this. A plan for the 250th put forward by the home-based battalions and the Comrades was unanimously agreed.

On the outbreak of war, a Comforts Fund was established to benefit battalions in the field, and prisoners of war. Sir Edmund Bushby† was appointed Chairman.[22]

xvii. Alliances with British and Commonwealth Regiments, 1927

The informal but much-cherished alliance with the Royal Fusiliers, dating from the Peninsular War, continued, with Officers, Warrant Officers and Sergeants being received as honorary members in each others' messes.

In 1926 and 1927 the War Office gave its assent to a number of alliances between British and Commonwealth Regiments. Three such alliances with the Royal Welch Fusiliers were approved in 1927:

> 1st Battalion Australian Military Forces (Army Order No. 138 of 1927)
> 12th Infantry (Pretoria Regiment) Union of South Africa Citizen Force (Army Order No. 215 of 1927)
> The Royal 22ème Régiment, Permanent Active Militia of Canada (Army Order No. 265)

The title of the 1st Battalion Australian Military Forces soon changed to 1st Battalion (East Sydney Regiment). From 1930 to 1937 its title was 1st/19th Battalion (City of Sydney Regiment).

---

*   Now in the collections of the Regimental Museum.
†   Sir Edward Fleming Bushby Kt (1879–1943), a wealthy cotton merchant.

It then reverted to its 1927 title. The alliance with the Pretoria Regiment owed much to the initiative of the then Major E.O. Skaife. The alliance with the Royal 22ème Régiment, the 'Vandoos', came about because of the particular friendship that existed between Lieutenant General Sir Charles Dobell, then Colonel of the Royal Welch Fusiliers, who had been born in Québec and attended the R.M.C. Kingston, and General George Vannier, then Colonel of the Royal 22ème Régiment. From 1934 to 1937 the two Regiments exchanged Officers:[23]

R.W.F. Exchange Officer:
Lieutenant R.J.F. Snead-Cox, 1934–1937

R.22eR. Exchange Officers:
Captain P.J.F. Mignault, to the 1st Battalion 1934–1935
2nd Lieutenant J.A. Roberge, attached to the 1st Battalion, September – October 1935
Lieutenant J.P.E. Bernatchez,* to the 1st Battalion, 1935–1937

xviii. Presentation of the March 'The Royal Welch Fusiliers', by Lieutenant Commander JP Sousa *U.S.N.R.*, 5 June 1930

The warm feelings of comradeship, although not formally expressed as an alliance, that existed between the Regiment and the United States Marine Corps, resulting from shared experiences with 2 R.W.F. and the 4th Battalion U.S.M.C. in China in 1900, led to the composition of 'The Royal Welch Fusiliers March' by the noted composer Lieutenant Commander John Philip Sousa of the United States Naval Reserve. As well as serving together in Peking, the Regiment had provided a guard of honour for the arrival at Liverpool in June 1917 of General Pershing, the Commander of the American Expeditionary Force.

The Americans decided to send a delegation to England which, headed by the American Ambassador in London, would present the score to the Regiment. In the event, the delegation was headed by the American Chargé d'Affaires and included the 76 year-old Sousa and Brigadier General George Richards *U.S.M.C.*, a veteran of the Peking campaign. On 25 June, the delegation

Lieutenant Commander J.P. Sousa *U.S.N.R.* presenting his march, 'The Royal Welch Fusiliers' to the Regiment 30 June 1930. (R.W.F. Mus)

*   Later Major General Joseph Paul Emile Bernatchez CMM CBE DSO CD (1911–1983). He commanded the R. 22e R. 1941–1944 and was Commander 3 (Canadian) Infantry Brigade in Italy and N.W. Europe 1944–1945. Major General in 1951 and Colonel of the R. 22e R. in 1964.

arrived at Bhurtpore Barracks, Tidworth – the home of the 2nd Battalion – where it was met by the Colonel of the Regiment, Lieutenant General Sir Charles Dobell. There was a General Salute by the battalion drawn up under Brevet Lieutenant Colonel C.C. Hewitt, who was commanding in the absence of Lieutenant Colonel Butler. Sousa presented the score to General Dobell who in return gave Volumes III and IV of *Regimental Records* to General Richards. Colonel Hewitt then asked Commander Sousa to conduct the Band playing the March. After he had done so he remarked that, 'The boys played it fine.' The battalion then marched past to the new March and the Chargé d'Affaires took the salute. After the parade had ended and the visitors had had a chance to talk to Peking veterans, lunch was provided in the Officers' Mess.[24]

It is also of note that the 2nd Battalion when in Gibraltar in July 1934 entertained the U.S. Marine detachments on board two warships, the *Arkansas* and the *Wyoming*;[25] the 2nd Battalion also found itself serving alongside U.S. Marines when in Shanghai in 1937.

xix. Regimental Dinner for All Commanding Officers, 1930

On 29 July 1930 the 6th Battalion held a Guest Night in their Mess at which the Colonel of the Regiment and the Commanding Officers of the 1st, 2nd, 4th, 5th, 6th and 7th Battalions were present. Only the 3rd (S.R.) Battalion and the Depot C.Os were absent.[26] This was probably an unique occasion in the Regiment's history. The following C.Os were present:

Lieutenant Colonel E.O. Skaife MBE, 1st Bn
Lieutenant Colonel C.C. Hewitt, 2nd Bn
Lieutenant Colonel G.R. Griffths OBE TD, 4th Bn
Lieutenant Colonel E.H.W. Williams TD, 5th Bn
Lieutenant Colonel A.M. Trustram Eve MC TD, 6th Bn
Lieutenant Colonel C.S. Price TD, 7th Bn

xx. The Crimea Colours

In June 1934 it was reported that a fragment of the Regimental Colour carried in the Crimea had been restored to the 1st Battalion by retired Colour Sergeant N.T. Ridings, who had served with 2 R.W.F. from 1885 to 1906.[27] This fragment was one of the Rising Sun badges.[28] These Colours had been presented in 1849, carried throughout the Crimean War and the Indian Mutiny, and remained in service until 1880 when, very ragged, they were framed and placed on board the Royal Yacht, at the request of H.R.H. The Prince of Wales. When they were placed on board the Royal Yacht they had just come off parade and were 'crossed on the wheel of the Yacht' [and later] 'lashed to the bridge'. At the time of their retirement, however, this fragment had become accidentally detached and was retained by the then Drum Major Molloy, who afterwards passed it to Colour Sergeant Ridings. By the outbreak of the Great War, fragments of both Colours were preserved in the Depot Officers' Mess at Wrexham; the restored fragment joined the existing fragments.[29]

xxi. Adoption of Company Badges and Pioneers' Tools, 1930

In February 1930, the first sanction was given to the use of company badges in 1 R.W.F., a practice which would continue in use until the end of the life of the Regiment. These were as follows:

H.Q. Wing: a plain Red Dragon
A Company: the Rising Sun
B Company: the Prince of Wales's Plumes
C Company: the White Horse of Hannover
D (MG) Company: the Sphinx

When Support Company was later formed, it adopted the Minden Rose. It was further laid down that the badges to be used for marching past base were to be the Rising Sun at Point A; the Plumes at Point B; the Red Dragon at the saluting point in front of the inspecting Officer, the White Horse at Point D; and the Sphinx at Point E.[30] This scheme was later adopted throughout the Regiment and added to Regimental *Standing Orders*.[31]

At about the same time, new tools were adopted by the ceremonial pioneers, who had until this time carried axes on parade. When the representative detachment visited Buckingham Palace (see above), the Pioneers were carrying mattocks, axes, spades (or shovels) and picks.[32]

xxii. The Meeting of the 1st and 2nd Battalions at Gibraltar, 16 April 1932

The 1st Battalion, less C Company, disembarked briefly from the HT *Somersetshire* at Gibraltar on 16 April on its way home to England from the Sudan. The 2nd Battalion, and a considerable number of the civilian population, awaited their arrival at the Alameda Parade Ground. As

The meeting of the 1st and 2nd Battalions at Gibraltar, 1932. (R.W.F. Mus 549 B)

The Officers, 1st and 2nd Battalions, 16 April 1932, Gibraltar. (R.W.F. Mus 4157)

the 1st Battalion approached, the 2nd Battalion 'fell-in' in close column of companies, Officers taking post in Review Order. Headed by the Band, Drums and Goat the 1st Battalion marched on and halted facing the 2nd Battalion in the same formation. Lieutenant Colonel Hewitt gave a short speech of welcome, which was replied to on behalf of the 1st Battalion by Lieutenant Colonel E.O. Skaife. At 18.30 hrs Sir Alexander Godley arrived and addressed both battalions, saying that it was the first time in his whole career that he had ever had the opportunity to see a whole Regiment on parade. The battalions then fell-out and the Officers repaired to the Buena Vista Officers' Mess for dinner at 19.00 hrs. The *Somersetshire* was due to sail at 21.00 hrs, but as the Captain of the ship had been brought to the mess for dinner as well, her departure was somewhat delayed.[33] It was in fact the first time that the two battalions had met since Malta in 1914. On 2 May, C Company 1 R.W.F., returning separately because of their duties in Cyprus, paused briefly at Gibraltar en route to Britain on HT *Neuralia*.

xxiii. Keys of Corunna

Under the terms of the Will of the late Miss Hariette Lloyd Fletcher of Gwernhaylod, near Overton, who died on 10 May 1919, it was directed that the Keys of Corunna which were brought away after the evacuation in January 1809 by her father, Thomas Lloyd Fletcher, then a Captain in the 23rd Fusiliers, should, subject to the life interest of her sister, be given to the Regiment. In June 1934 the Keys were lodged at the Depot.[34]

xxiv. Reservists called up for service in Palestine, 1936

In 1936, thirty-seven Royal Welch Reservists were called up for the Palestine emergency where they served with the 2nd East Yorkshire Regiment.[35] They were as follows:

4187085 LCpl R.H. Harvey	4188479 LCpl T. Maloney	4188591 LCpl F.E. Dowding
754247 Fus D.J. Parry	4187627 Fus P.W. Butler	4187767 Fus R.H. Harvey
4187777 Fus W.C. Redler	4189015 Fus C. Stockley	4188063 Fus L. Jones
4188047 Fus W.J. Price	4188053 Fus R. Simmonds	4186928 Fus A.D. Handley
4188077 Fus E. Pearce	4188073 Fus J. Leonard	4188096 Fus A.W. Bedson
4188014 Fus T.M. Ryan	4188127 Fus F.A. Coote	4188318 Fus E. Smith
775992 Fus E.J. Carne	4188378 Fus E. Watts	4188391 Fus H. Jones
3650501 Fus J. Birchall	4188428 Fus J.R. Crompton	4188484 Fus G. Evans
4188522 Fus R.T. Davis	4188530 Fus L.G. Cook	4188526 Fus J. Priestly
4188531 Fus G.H. Johnson	4188581 Fus T.C. Gaughran	4188581 Fus M.S. Smith
4188592 Fus A.J. Moore	4074605 Fus T.N. Jones	4188596 Fus R.O. Hughes
3955136 Fus S. Evans	37712 Fus W.C. Morgan	4288428 Fus C. Bailey

xxv. The Coronation, 1937

Between 18 and 23 April, Lieutenants J.H. Liscombe, J.E. Vaughan and A.G. Bent MM, with eighty N.C.Os and Fusiliers drawn from B Company 1 R.W.F., moved to camp sites in Kensington Gardens and Hampton Court for administrative duties connected with the

Coronation of King George VI. The weather was extremely hot at this time and the work was hard, as the *Regimental Journal* reported: Everyone suffered from tired hands and excessive exposure to the sun's rays. In the first week thousands of tons of tentage and stores were unloaded and erected...'[36] Dismantling the camp took a great deal less time.

The administrative detail was followed on 1 May by Lieutenant R.J.F. Snead-Cox, Second Lieutenant H.G. Brougham with seventy men from D Company, also for administrative duties; Second Lieutenant R.O.F. Prichard and fifty men on 9 May for car park duties; Captain H.A. Freeman OBE MC and forty-one men for street lining duties on the same date – and in addition Lieutenant J.E.T. Willes with the Regimental Colour, escorted by Sergeants R. Preest and G. Timmins; Lieutenant and Adjutant W.L.R. Benyon with seven men also travelled to London to form a marching detachment in the procession. Those on parade wore Coronation blues with forage caps, the Officers and W.Os wearing Sam Browne belts.[37] Finally, Captains T.S. Griffiths and A.D.M. Lewis MBE, with two men, undertook accountancy duties from 8 May. The Coronation itself took place on 12 May:

> The great day arrived, rather dull, but not raining. Each man was issued with his pocket ration of two lumps of sugar, one packet of Horlick's milk tablets and a packet of Marching chocolate. Two halts were called to eat these... we were marshalled into position among the Infantry of the Line, seniority being from rear to front, each unit marching eight abreast and at two paces interval... in advance of Westminster Abbey we had to pass thousands of school children on the Embankment with their flags and cheers, and finally to halt just short of Piccadilly for fifty minutes. The Street Lining Troops of the 4th, 5th, 6th and 7th Battalions were also here.
>
> The final march began with the rain threatening, and not until we had reached Buckingham Palace did it really mean business, and so did the Gentlemen who had planned the route. It was then, and only then, that we commenced to march around London in the pouring rain and back to our muddy camps.[38]

All those not involved in London were given a holiday.[39] Fifteen Officers and men subsequently received Coronation Medals, as recorded in the Annex on Honours and Awards. Those taking part in the Coronation were as follows:

Procession
Lieutenant & Adjutant
W.L.R. Benyon
RSM J.M. Kensett
CQMS M. Roberts 14
Sgt R. Austin
Cpl G. Beech
LCpl E. Roberts
Fus T. Beck
Fus R. Maher

Colour Party
Lieutenant J.E.T. Willes
Sergeant R. Preece
Sergeant G. Timmins

Street Lining Troops
Captain and Bt Major H.A.
Freeman OBE MC
43 N.C.Os and Fusiliers

Car Park Duties
Lieutenant R.O.F. Prichard
50 N.C.O.s and Fusiliers

Finance Duties
Captain T.S. Griffiths
Captain A.D.M. Lewis MBE
2 N.C.Os

Administration, Kensington Gardens
Captain J.H. Liscombe
Lieutenant R.J.F. Snead-Cox
2nd Lieutenant H.G. Brougham
100 N.C.Os and Fusiliers

Administration, Hampton Court
Lieutenant J.E. Vaughan
Lieutenant & QM A.G. Bent MM
50 N.C.Os and Fusiliers

The four Territorial battalions each provided detachments of twenty-eight Officers and men for the Coronation. Details are incomplete but the following are known to have taken part:

	4th Battalion	5th Battalion	6th Battalion	7th Battalion
Procession	Lt Col R.G. Fenwick-Palmer	Lt Col H.M. Davies	Lt Col J.M. Evans	Lt Col W. Roberts MC
	DMaj Lawlor	CSM H. Norry	CSM J. Brown	RQMS J.D. Williams
	Cpl D.D. Jones	Sgt Wright	Sgt J. Lloyd Williams	LSgt E.T. Bond
	Fus T.O. Jones	Fus Lindrop	Fus E. McGuinness	Fus W.I. Roberts
Street Lining	Maj J.M. Davies MC	Capt & Adjt C.H.V. Pritchard	Maj R.C. Newton TD	Maj R.B.S. Davies
	Capt & Adjt G.E. Braithwaite	Cpl Windsor	Capt & Adjt P.L. Bowers	Capt & Adjt R. de B. Hardie
	Capt H.E. Davies	Cpl Underhill	Lt G.P. Jones	Lt R.J.H. Cooke
	2Lt J.L. Parker	Bdsm Owen	CSM W. Howells	CSM I. Thomas
	CSM P.W. Jones	Dmr Bevan	CSM J.T. Jones	CSM I. Roberts
	CQMS J. Kent		Sgt Ll. Williams	Sgt W.H. Hutchins
	Sgt Norman		Sgt R. Hughes	Sgt E. Needham
	Sgt Nicholas		Sgt I. Jones	Sgt W.H. Sankey
	Sgt Williams		Sgt J. Williams	SI H.T. Roberts
	Cpl F. Jones		Sgt A.L. Williams	LSgt J.D. Williams
	Cpl Lambert		Sgt R. Lloyd	Cpl E.E. Pugh
	LCpl W. Beech		Sgt R.J. Thomas	LCpl W.H. Pryce
	Fus T. Davies		LSgt D.H. Edwards	LCpl A. Evans
	Fus Langford		Cpl D.H. Jones	Dmr A.F.B. Cory
	Fus Williams		Cpl H.R. Simpson	Fus H.L. Hughes
	Fus A.W. Evans		Cpl W.T. Williams	Fus P.D. Vaughan
	Fus R.D. Snell		Cpl H.G. Evans	Fus J.L. Williams
	Fus B.J. Soden		LCpl W. Roberts	Fus R. Fleming
	5 un-named Fus from Denbigh		LCpl D.T. Edwards	Fus A.C. Davies
			Fus J. Ll. Carpenter	Fus E. Davies
			Fus E.G. Parry	Fus W. Hughes
			Fus S. Richardson	Fus H.L.W. Roberts
			Fus R.T. Hughes	Fus J. Cudworth
			Fus S. Humphreys	
			Fus H. Jones	
			Fus A. Parry	
			Fus F. MacGuiness	
			Fus E.R. Cox	
			Fus R. Greene	

Coronation services were held in towns within the recruiting areas of the Territorial battalions. In Denbigh, a detachment of three Officers and thirty men under Lieutenant D.E. Griffith led the 4th Battalion in the Mayor's procession to the castle for the Coronation Service; the Union and the Welsh national flag were broken out, the parade gave a Royal Salute followed by three cheers for His Majesty. In Caergwrle, eighty Officers and men of the 5th Battalion were on parade, including the band. In Conway, Captain R.M. Turton and sixty men from the 6th Battalion were on parade.

xxvi. Passenger Tender Engine 'Royal Welch Fusilier', May 1939

In May 1939 Captain J.C. Wynne-Edwards of Plas Nantglyn, Denbigh received a letter from the Chief Operating Manager of the London Midland and Scottish Railway Company (L.M.S.) in which he stated that, 'The request you made in your letter to Lord Stamp … for the engine named "Royal Welch Fusilier" to work on the "Irish Mail" has been passed to me. I am making arrangements for Class 6 (Royal Scot) passenger tender engine "The Royal Welch Fusilier" to be stationed at Holyhead in order that the engine may work on the "Irish Mail" express services between Holyhead and Euston, in accordance with your request.'[40]

The engine, No. 6118, was delivered to the L.M.S. in 1927. The first engine was named 'Royal Scot', hence the name of the class. It was decided to name the other forty-nine engines in the class after regiments as a way of commemorating the Great War memories of which were still fresh in people's minds. It seems that the Regiment would have been approached before consenting to the use of its name. There would have been a public naming ceremony almost certainly performed by the Colonel of the Regiment, accompanied by a Guard of Honour with a band. It is probable that No. 6118 was named in 1928.[41]

A photograph of the 'Royal Welch Fusilier' and its name plate are in the Regimental Museum.

xxvii. The Officers' Association

The Regimental Dinner between the wars. (R.W.F. Mus 6067)

The Association was founded in 1920. Membership was open to Officers who had served or were serving 'in any branch of the Regiment'. Its first annual dinner was held in 1921 and thereafter a dinner was held annually, either in Chester or in London. By 1934, there were 379 members.[42] Dinners known to have been held during the period were as follows:

16 December 1931	Grosvenor Hotel, Chester	
1932	Hotel Metropole, London	
7 October 1933	Grosvenor Hotel, Chester	86 present
27 October 1934	Restaurant Frascati, London	
26 October 1935	Hotel Victoria, Northumberland Avenue, London	
3 October 1936	Grosvenor Hotel, Chester	55 present
16 October 1937	Hotel Victoria	83 present
15 October 1938	Hotel Victoria	61 present

In addition, there was a 1st and 2nd Battalion Dinner Club which had been in existence since 1898.[43] This was originally open only to Regular Officers, however at some point the membership was widened to those who had served in the 1st or 2nd Battalions during the Great War. Dinners were held at the Savoy in Ascot Week from 1922 to 1924; the Naval and Military Club in 1934 and 1935; and the Savoy again in 1937 and 1938.

The 38th (Welsh) Division Dinner Club held an annual dinner, usually on 11 November, in London.

xxix. The Old Comrades' Association

The first meeting of the Old Comrades took place in October 1912. It was not until after the Great War, however, that the Old Comrades' Association was founded, in 1921, and 1925 before a trust deed officially laid out the purposes of the Association. These were, in essence, to foster contact between current and past members of the Regiment; to promote the well-being of the Regiment and foster *esprit de corps*; to provide financial assistance to those in need, as well as to widows or dependents. Membership was open to anyone, of any rank, who had served or was serving in a regular, militia, special reserve, territorial or service battalion, or any unit recognized by the Army Council as being part of the Regiment. It was renamed as the Comrades Association in 1945.

The following branches were maintained during the period:

THE RED DRAGON DINNER CLUB
38TH (WELSH) DIVISION.

Menu.
—
Huîtres Royale
—
Petite Marmite   Crème de Tomate
—
Filets de Sole Walewska
—
Carré d'Agneau à l'Anglaise
Petits Pois Etuvée
Pommes Noisettes
—
Faisan en Cocotte
Salade de Saison
—
Bombe Pralinée
Friandises
—
Canapé Baron
—
Café
—
Criterion Restaurant   November 11, 1922

The menu for the annual reunion dinner of the 38th (Welsh) Division at the Criterion in London, 11 November 1922.

An old soldier, 3607 Robert Hughes of Corwen, who served with 1 R.W.F. in India, the Sudan and South Africa; later 7 R.W.F. at Gallipoli. A very young soldier, believed to be Owen Jones, also of Corwen. (R.W.F. Mus)

The Old Comrades Reunion, 1930. (R.W.F. Mus 5032)

London and the South of England, Manchester, Liverpool and District, Birmingham & the Midlands, Shrewsbury, Lancashire, Yorkshire & the North, South Wales & West of England, North Wales, Cardiff, Swansea, Wrexham and Caernarfon & Anglesey.

A Reunion and Dinner had been held annually at Hightown Barracks, Wrexham, on the Saturday of the Regimental Cricket Week, usually the third week in August, since 1877; and on the following Sunday morning the Association formed up at the War Memorial, laid wreaths and marched to church, usually led by the 4th Battalion (T.A.) with its Band, Corps of Drums, Pioneers and the Regimental Goat.

There was in addition an annual London Welsh Reunion, the first of which on 15 March 1920 was reported in *The Times:*

> The reunion dinner of the 1st and 2nd London Welch (15th and 18th Battalions Royal Welch Fusiliers) took place on Saturday night at the Queen's Westminster Drill Hall, Buckingham Gate. The 500 Officers and men present were the guests of Major David Davies MP,* who presided. Among the company were Lieutenant General Sir Francis Lloyd, Lieutenant Colonel L. Price Davies VC, Judge Ivor Bowen KC (Treasurer of Gray's Inn), Mr Lewis Thomas KC, and Major J. Edmonds DSO MP.[44]

---

*   Later Lord David (Davies) of Llandinam. 1st Baron (1932) (1880–1940). He was Liberal M.P. for Montgomeryshire 1906–1929. He raised and commanded the 14th (Caernarvon and Anglesey) battalion of the Regiment at home and in France 1914–1916. He was then appointed Parliamentary Private Secretary to the Prime Minister, the Rt Hon David Lloyd George OM PC MP.

Thereafter this reunion was held annually throughout the period, coinciding with a parade at the Cenotaph, where the Colonel of the Regiment laid a wreath. Davies, it should be noted, held regular reunions for the 14th Battalion at his home, Plas Dinam, Llandinam, Montgomeryshire.

Other battalions held reunions at various times throughout the period. Most notable among these were the 9th Battalion, in Swansea, and the 17th Battalion, in Llandudno. The 6th and 13th Battalions also held less regular reunions.

xxix. The 250th Anniversary Celebrations, 2–6 August 1939

The climax of the celebrations took place during early August. On Wednesday 2nd – coincidently the anniversary of the battle of Blenheim – the Regiment was officially welcomed by the Mayor and Corporation of Wrexham at the Guildhall where an illuminated address was presented by the Mayor – a precursor of the granting of the Freedom of the Borough after the Second World War. The Regiment then marched past the Lord-Lieutenant of Denbighshire, Colonel Sir R.W.H.W. Williams-Wynn, the Mayor of Wrexham, and the Colonel of the Regiment, Major General J.R. Minshull-Ford. A tea party for 400 guests was held in the Barracks during which three trees – gifts of the Allied Regiments of Canada, Australia and South Africa – were planted. A silver Challenge Cup, a gift from the Regiment, was presented to the Mayor of Denbigh for annual competition by Junior Male Voice Choirs at the National Eisteddfod.

(Above) The 250th Anniversary parade in the Castle, Caernarfon, 1939. (Below) Lloyd George with the Goats of the 1st, 4th, 6th and 7th Battalions during the 250th Anniversary celebrations, 1939.

On Saturday the 5th, headed by the Band and Drums of the 1st Battalion, the Colonel of the Regiment and detachments or representatives of twenty Royal Welch Fusilier battalions – including many raised to serve in the Great War – marched through the square of Caernarfon where the Lord-Lieutenants of North Wales and the Mayor of Caernarvon took the salute. The order of march was as follows:

> Band and Drums, 1 R.W.F.
> Colonel of the Regiment
> 1 R.W.F.
> Company Colours representing 2 R.W.F., and escort
> Depot
> Representatives of Service Battalions: 8, 9, 10, 11, 13, 14, 15, 16, 17, 19, 24, 25 and 26 R.W.F.
> Commander 158 (Royal Welch) Infantry Brigade and staff
> Band and Drums, 4 R.W.F.
> 60th (5 R.W.F.) Anti-Tank Regiment R.A.
> Band and Drums, 6 R.W.F.
> 6 R.W.F.
> Band and Drums, 7 R.W.F.
> 7 R.W.F.

From the King's Gate of the Castle the Rt. Hon. David Lloyd George OM PC MP, Constable of Caernarvon Castle, crossed the lowered drawbridge to greet Brigadier E.O. Skaife OBE, commanding 158 (Royal Welch) Infantry Brigade, which was in Camp at Caernarfon. The Brigadier, speaking in Welsh, requested permission for the Regiment to hold its 250th Anniversary celebration within the Castle, to which the Constable, replying in the same tongue, graciously assented and handed over the massive key of the gate.

Inside, the grey castle walls were ablaze with banners, shields and flags. The Massed Bands of the 1st, 4th, 6th and 7th Battalions played as the troops entered by the various gates and took up their positions, with the Regimental Goats in line, in front, facing the dignitaries on the rampart beneath the Eagle Tower. After a speech by the Colonel of Regiment, the Colours of each battalion were marched into position in turn, while the Bands played a fanfare. Then a magnificently attired Herald recalled the great events in the history of the Regiment since 1689.

After a speech of congratulation by the senior Lord-Lieutenant, Mr Lloyd George, an almost legendary figure in his native land, addressed the gathering. Two sentences stand out from his speech:

> Should the menace to human liberties which now hangs in the firmament, like a dark thundercloud over our heads, burst into a raging storm, we shall all do our duty to save humanity from irretrievable disaster. It is a source of confidence to us that we know that this Regiment will once more face its responsibilities in a way which will be worthy of its glorious past and which will uphold that reputation for bravery which the Welsh people won in their age-long struggle for freedom.

The next day a Divine Service was held in the Castle, at which the Bishop of St Asaph, the Most Reverend Dr W.T. Havard, gave the address. At the end the Bishop consecrated the New Colours of the 6th Battalion, and the Regiment re-dedicated itself to the service of King and country. Four weeks later, Britain was at war with Germany.[45]

Notes

1   *London Gazette,* 20 December 1901.
2   *Y Ddraig Goch,* July 1937, p. 4.
3   Y Ddraig Goch, September 1932, pp. 54–55
4   Digest of Service.
5   20/Inf./1320 – A.G. 10 dated 27 January 1920 in 1 R.W.F. Digest of Service.
6   Army Council Instruction No. 62 of 1924; *Y Ddraig Goch,* May 1924, p. 234.
7   R.W.F. Chronology 1919–1939 by Lieutenant Colonel RJM Sinnett, Sixth Edition 2006; *Y Ddraig Goch,* May 1922, p. 15; Major E.L. Kirby, 'A Report of the Location of the Colours of the Royal Welch Fusiliers', March 1986 (unpublished).
8   A manuscript note in Dr J.C. Dunn's copy of the original edition of Volume III in the Regimental Museum and written in his handwriting (R.W.F. Mus 228).
9   Minutes of the Regimental Committee, 18 July 1930 (R.W.F. Mus 7999R).
10 *Y Ddraig Goch,* January 1923, pp. 106–107.
11 Research into the archives and records of Wrexham Council by Mr Jonathon Gammond, Wrexham Museum.
12 This is taken from *Regimental Records, Volume IV*, pp. 398–401, in which the full text of the address by the Colonel of the Regiment may be found.
13 Research by Dr John Kryjnen.
14 *Y Ddraig Goch,* October 1922, pp. 61–62.
15 *Y Ddraig Goch,* May 1922, p. 19.
16 Silsoe, p. 97.
17 *Y Ddraig Goch,* St David's Day 1967, pp. 84–85.
18 R.W.F. Mus 374.
19 *Y Ddraig Goch,* September 1934, p. 75.
20 *Y Ddraig Goch,* February 1924, pp. 204–205. The 1st Battalion could not be present as it was still serving in India.
21 *Y Ddraig Goch, April 1936,* p. 4.
22 Minutes of the Regimental Committee. Museum Acc No. 7999R.
23 Michael Glover and Jonathon Riley, *That Astonishing Infantry. The Royal Welch Fusiliers, 1689–2006* (Barnsley, 2008) Appendix 6, pp. 287–278.
24 *Y Ddraig Goch,* March 1931, p. 8.
25 *Y Ddraig Goch,* September 1934, p. 54.
26 2 R.W.F. Digest of Service.
27 1 R.W.F. Digest of Service.
28 *Y Ddraig Goch,* September 1933, p115; June 1934, p. 5.
29 Peter Kirby, 'The Crimean Colours – 1st Battalion The Royal Welch Fusiliers' in *Y Ddraig Goch,* December 1974, pp. 149–151.
30 1 R.W.F. Digest of Service.
31 *Regimental Standing Orders,* p. 71, 'The Parade Ground'.
32 1 R.W.F. Digest of Service, 1930.
33 *Y Ddraig Goch,* June 1932, p. 35.
34 *Y Ddraig Goch,* September 1934, p. 49.
35 *Y Ddraig Goch,* January 1937, p. 79.
36 *Y Ddraig Goch,* July 1937, pp. 7–8.
37 *Y Ddraig Goch,* July 1937, pp. 1, 9, 10.
38 *Y Ddraig Goch,* July 1937, p. 10.
39 1 R.W.F. Digest of Service.

40   Letter from T.W. Royle, Chief Operating Manager to Captain J.C. Wynne-Edwards, dated 16 May 1939.
41   Email to Lieutenant Colonel P.A. Crocker dated 24 May 2011 from Neil Burgess, Hon. Sec., London Midland and Scottish Society.
42   *Y Ddraig Goch*, March 1934, pp. 81–87.
43   *Y Ddraig Goch*, Summer 1959, p. 39.
44   *The Times*, Monday 15 Mar 1920, p. 13.
45   This is essentially the same as appeared in *The Red Dragon*, pp. 8–10.

Section IV

The Regiment on Expeditionary Operations, 1939–1940

Chapter 16

The 1st Battalion on Operations in France and Belgium September 1939–May 1940[*]

---

i. The Phoney War

1 R.W.F., under the command of Lieutenant Colonel H.F. Garnons-Williams, was brigaded with the 1st Royal Berkshires and the 2nd Durham Light Infantry in 6 Infantry Brigade, commanded by Brigadier N.M.S. Irwin,[†] forming part of 2nd Division, under Major General H.C. Lloyd.[‡]

---

[*] The account which follows has been compiled from various sources listed in the end-notes, among which the most significant are the battalion War Diary, which was in part reconstructed after the event; the Regiment's short war history, *The Red Dragon;* a series of interviews recorded during the compilation of *The Red Dragon*; Lieutenant J.L. King's account, *Farewell to Flanders,* which is a very detailed personal account heavily corrected by R.J.M. Sinnett; Captain W.S.A. Clough-Taylor's personal diary which was largely written after the event; and finally 'The Story of the 1st Battalion, Royal Welch Fusiliers Friday, May 10th – Monday, May 27th, 1940'. This latter was composed from the personal recollections of the surviving Officers of the battalion who were taken Prisoners of War. It was taken down at an early date, in the form of rough notes, which had to be concealed from the Prison Camp authorities. After a lapse of about three years, when conditions in the Camps became easier, it was transcribed and then subsequently typed out in England. Being based on the personal recollections of a limited number of Officers it is inevitable that a certain amount of the story has not been recorded. Three of the surviving Officers were platoon commanders who cannot be expected to know much about what went on outside their own relatively small orbit. Both the Officers from Battalion Headquarters who contributed were sometimes away on missions at the same time and something may have been lost to the narrative from this cause. In the final action at St-Venant, the battalion was widely deployed and from certain sub-units such as C Company, there was no one available to tell the tale of the last few hours. The account is accurate, however, to the extent that whatever has been written down has been vouched for by an Officer who was present at the time. As far as possible, I have verified the narrative from two or more sources.

[†] Later Lieutenant General Noel Mackintosh Stuart Irwin CB DSO MC (1892–1972). Five times mentioned in despatches during the Great War, he later commanded the 2nd Division when Lloyd became ill in May 1940; the land forces for the Dakar expedition in August 1940; and 38th (Welsh) Division at the end of 1940. In 1942 he took command of IV Indian Corps and then in command of the Eastern Army led the ill-fated Arakan expedition (see the 1st Battalion 1942–1943). He was removed by Sir George Giffard, G.O.C.-in-C. 11th Army Group, after this and was then eclipsed by Sir William Slim's rise.

[‡] Later Lieutenant General Sir Henry Charles ('Budget') Lloyd GCVO KCB DSO MC *CdeG* DL (1891–1973). In 1941, he took command of G.H.Q. Home Forces before moving on to be G.O.C-

With the 1st Division, under the command of Major General
H.R.L.G. Alexander,* they made up I Corps, under General Sir John
Dill. I and II Corps were the full complement, in these early days, of the British Expeditionary
Force, which by April 1940 had risen to ten divisions – half of them regular and half Territorial
– in three corps and a G.H.Q. reserve, plus three additional Territorial divisions employed on
labour duties.[1] Of these, it is of note that the 42nd Infantry Division was commanded by Major
General W.G. Holmes, late R.W.F.

The then Major General Bernard Montgomery[†] wrote of the B.E.F. that:

> It must be said to our shame that we sent our Army into that most modern war with
> weapons and equipment which were quite inadequate, and that we had only ourselves to
> blame for the disasters which overtook us in the field when the fighting began in 1940.[2]

The B.E.F. was under the command of Field Marshal Lord Gort,[‡] who with the Director
of Military Operations and Intelligence, Major General Henry Pownall,[§] and the Director-
General of the T.A., Major General Douglas Brownrigg,[¶] had vacated his post as C.I.G.S.
to take command of the expeditionary force. It had been expected either that Sir John Dill,
C.-in-C. Aldershot Command, or Sir Edmund Ironside,[**] Inspector-General of Overseas Forces,
would command the force. As Montgomery put things: 'These two candidates must have been
amazed when a third candidate got the job … the Army was certainly amazed. And it was even
more amazed when Ironside was made C.I.G.S… .'[3]

---

in-C. of Southern Command in 1942. His last appointment was as Major-General commanding the
Brigade of Guards and G.O.C. London District in 1944.

* Later Field Marshal Lord (Harold Rupert Leofric George) Alexander, 1st Earl Alexander of Tunis
KG GCB OM GCMG CSI DSO MC CD PC PC (Can) (1891–1969). He served in the Great
War and between the wars in Poland and Latvia against the Russians. He was C.-in-C. Allied Forces,
Mediterranean in the later stages of the Second World War and after the war was Governor-General
of Canada.

† Later Field Marshal Bernard Law Montgomery, 1st Viscount Montgomery of Alamein KG GCB
DSO PC (1887–1976), Commander 21st Army Group 1944–1945 and later Chief of the Imperial
General Staff.

‡ Field Marshal John Standish Surtees Prendergast Vereker, 6th Viscount Gort VC GCB CBE DSO
MVO MC (1886–1946) was later Governor of Malta and of Gibraltar, and High Commissioner
for Palestine. Personally fearless, he was out of his depth in 1940 although he must be given credit
for seeing clearly the imperative for the B.E.F. to break clean from the Germans and evacuate the
continent.

§ Later Lieutenant General Sir Henry Royds Pownall KCB KBE DSO (1887–1961). He was Chief of
Staff to the B.E.F. until the fall of France in May 1940. He was later Chief of Staff to Sir Archibald
Wavell until the fall of Singapore in 1942, and Chief of Staff to Lord Louis Mountbatten in 1943
and 1944.

¶ Later Lieutenant General Sir Wellesley Douglas Studholme Brownrigg KCB DSO (1886–1946).

** Later Field Marshal Lord (William Edmund) Ironside, 1st Baron of Archangel and Ironside
GCB CMG DSO (1880–1959). Ironside was a Major-General by the end of the Great War and
subsequently commanded the North Russia Relief Force, the military mission in Hungary, and
British Forces in Turkey and North Persia. He then served in India and in England and spent some
time on half-pay as Lieutenant of the Tower, before returning to active duty as a Lieutenant General
in 1933, first in India and then as Governor of Gibraltar. But for the war, he would have retired in
1939.

Firing the *Boys* anti-tank rifle on the beach near Etaples, 1939. (R.W.F. Mus)

The 2nd Division's transport, Carriers and Anti-Tank Company moved first, followed by 4 Brigade and the divisional M.G. battalion, then 5 and 6 Brigades.[4] Having disembarked at Cherbourg on 24 September 1939, 1 R.W.F. moved that night by train and arrived the following day at Noyen-sur-Sarthe, sixteen miles (25 kilometres) south-west of Le Mans. Here it detrained and marched six miles to Parcé-sur-Sarthe, near Noyon, where Battalion Headquarters, H.Q. and C Companies were housed. A, B and D Companies were billeted in outlying farms another two or three miles (3–4.5 kilometres) further on.[5] Over the next three days, Lieutenant P.D. Skillington and Lieutenant J.E.T. Willes arrived with twenty-seven of the battalion's vehicles, which had spent a night at Le Mans, quartered opposite the pits in the famous race-track.[6] Although B Echelon was still adrift, it appeared later. On the 29th, the battalion entrained once more and moved on to Achiet-le-Grand, thirteen miles (20 kilometres) south of Arras and there was faced with a night march of fourteen miles (21 kilometres) to Hendecourt-lès-Cagnicourt, nine miles (15 kilometres) south-east of Arras,[7] which it reached at 05.00 hrs on 1 October.

Here the battalion remained until orders for the expected move up to the Belgian frontier came on 6 October. The B.E.F. was to take over part of the line between the First and Fourth French Armies with the 2nd Division occupying the right of the British line, and with the French North African Division on its left.[8] 6 Brigade, on the right of the British line, was centred on Mouchin, not far from Lille, and on 6 October the battalion moved up to occupy, for the first time, a section of the Maginot Extension which was at a highly immature stage of construction. With Battalion Headquarters at Lannay and facing the still-neutral territory of Belgium, the battalion set to work strengthening the

October 1939

defensive positions.[9] On 9 October, most of the transport except for the C.O's *Humber*, five 15-cwt trucks, a water cart and four lorries was sent back to Flines-les-Raches, four miles (6 kilometres) to the south-west.[10] Here at Mouchin, the battalion remained until early May 1940, apart from occasional moves for training or guard duties.

Between the two wars French strategy had based itself upon fixed frontier defences, and the great Maginot Line had been built, at enormous expense, along the whole of the frontier with Germany. It extended from the Swiss border in the south, to Sedan in the north: a great concrete line of underground forts, with vast storage spaces, also underground, for ammunition and other stores. But from Sedan to the Channel coast there was little beyond the most rudimentary defences due to political sensitivities in regard to the neutral status of Belgium. This had, after all, been one of the chief *causae belli* of the Great War. Still clinging to the doctrine of fixed defences, the French Army had been, since the declaration of war, engaged in a belated attempt to extend the Maginot Line to the sea, though on nothing like the same scale. When 1 R.W.F. moved into the line, the defences consisted of little more than an anti-tank ditch and a few concrete blockhouses at intervals. J.L. King recalled that:

> The right boundary of the battalion's position was … laid out round a pill box … referred to as "P" pill box. For some unfathomable reason three of our political visitors, the Secretary of State for War, Leslie Hore-Belisha, the Prime Minister Neville Chamberlain and the First Lord of the Admiralty Winston Churchill, all felt it necessary to relieve themselves against the wall of this pill box.[11]

6 Infantry Brigade was to occupy its part of the line with 1st Royal Berkshires forward on the left of the line, 1 R.W.F. right forward and 2nd D.L.I. in depth. Each forward battalion had three blockhouses in its sector.[12] Here it set about constructing what became known as 'the Gort Line'.

French strategy and operational plans set the tone for the B.E.F. during the next few months. Throughout the autumn, all the battalion's energies were devoted to improving the defensive line by digging new trench systems behind a deep anti-tank ditch; wiring and mine-laying; installing additional anti-tank guns; constructing machine-gun pits and deep shelters.[13] The Gort Line as planned was to consist of three lines and a reserve position and to assist the work, twelve field companies of Royal Engineers drawn from T.A. divisions in Britain arrived to assist in the planning and implementation of the work, along with large consignments of defence stores: anti-tank mines, corrugated iron, metal pickets, barbed wire, sandbags and duckboards. 700 mechanical diggers and other machines were also brought into service and these were much in evidence in the battalion's area.[14]

Each of the brigade's three battalions occupied a forward line with three of its companies, and a reserve line with the remaining rifle company and H.Q. Company; in the case of 1 R.W.F., B Company was left forward, C centre, and A right, with D and H.Q. in the second line. H.Q. Company, when in the line, was to consist of two platoons, each platoon made up of half the Pioneer Platoon and a section of the Carrier Platoon. It was stated in the operation order that these positions would be held 'to the last man and the last round.'[15]

The battalion was kept hard at work, but when the winter set in with heavy rain, the whole area became a morass of thick mud, making all road movement difficult. Drainage became the major issue, with work on secondary defences and deep shelters much curtailed. Even so, much was accomplished: during the winter, the B.E.F. constructed forty miles of anti-tank ditches,

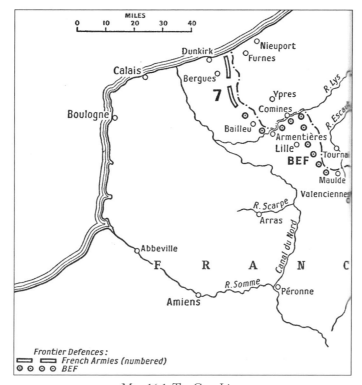

Map 16.1 The Gort Line.

400 concrete emplacements and hundreds of miles of trenches and switch positions.[16] J.L. King recalled that:

> The battalion took up a defensive position at Mouchin … Trenches were dug and revetted, duckboards were laid and where possible drains were made. My platoon was in a very low and wet area, which entailed building positions upwards, the water table being at about four feet below ground level. This involved the use of sandbags. Fortunately there were six reservists in the platoon who had served in Shanghai during the Japanese invasion of China; the strong points built around the British Sector of that city had been made of sand bags, and the Reservists were experts at laying them.[17]

The sense of urgency lessened as the first rush to construct defences eased, for there was something of a peace-time atmosphere to life: Battalion Part One Orders were published at least weekly, and there were opportunities for recreation, church parades, visits to the battlefields of the Great War and military training. Billets were occupied by those not in the line, just as in the last war, and there was plenty of food, wine and cigarettes: life was good, and cheap.[18] J.L. King remembered that 'the attractions of Arras [were] the Maison Blanche and the hotel opposite the Railway Station, which served lobster and a large variety of omelettes.'[19] A community centre was established at Mouchin, where men could go in turn in the evening to listen to B.B.C. programmes on the wireless. Mail deliveries were frequent, with letters taking about a week to get home, and vice-versa.[20] A rest camp was opened at Flines, and concerts were arranged in the divisional area, to which parties of men from the battalion were taken. One of the most remembered was that of the well-known performer George Formby with his new song 'Imagine me in the Maginot Line':

> Now imagine me in the Maginot Line
> Sitting on a mine in the Maginot Line
> Now it's turned out nice again
> The Army life is fine
> At night, myself to sleep I sing
> To my old tin hat I cling
> I have to use it now for everything
> Down on the Maginot Line[21]

It was during this period, on 10 November, that Lieutenant Colonel Garnons-Williams was killed in an aircraft crash near Aix, while over-flying the line on a reconnaissance;[22] the pilot of the aircraft, strangely, was unhurt. Garnons-Williams was buried at Douai the following day. His death was a sad loss to the Regiment, for he had been greatly respected by all ranks in the battalion and his death made the commemoration of the Armistice on Sunday 12 November all the more poignant. His place as Commanding Officer was taken by Lieutenant Colonel H. B. Harrison.*[23]

November 1939

The persistent rain of the early winter gave way in December to hard frost, which still further restricted work on the defences, especially in mixing and laying concrete for the deeper shelters. In place of the deep mud came rock-hard frozen surfaces, making the use of the roads almost impossible for vehicles. At one period of the great frost the battalion had to rely on an Indian mule company to bring up all rations and supplies: for the old hands, it was just like Quetta, only colder. Visits became more frequent: H.R.H. the Duke of Gloucester on 12 November, the Secretary of State for War, Leslie Hore-Belisha, on 18 November. J.L. King remembered one of these:

December 1939

> I was tapped on the shoulder and heard a Fusilier say "Sir!" I looked up and on the top of the side of the ditch I saw a pair of very shiny brown boots and then breeches and finally the red-capped figure of Major-General Alexander, whom I knew was acting Corps Commander. Very embarrassed I called the section to Attention, clambered out of the ditch, which was draining well and full of mud, found my cap and saluted. Unlike previous visitors, the General asked me to explain the platoon layout. He jumped on to the fire step and looked around him. Not only to the front but also directly behind him; we had built up the back of the trench so that when firing positions were taken up, our heads would not be silhouetted against the background. This the General had obviously appreciated. He inspected the field of fire from both section positions which covered the front of the blockhouse and asked about the Bren Gun fixed line positions. This he discussed with the section commanders. He only spoke to me, the section commanders and some Fusiliers.

---

*   Lieutenant Colonel Herbert Berkeley ('Harry') Harrison (1896–1940) had served in the Royal Dublin Fusiliers during the Great War and transferred to the R.W.F. in 1922.

The Colonel, Major Raymont and the Brigadier stood silently behind him. He was very interested in our use of sandbags. After he had inspected both section positions and the blockhouse, he stood talking with the remainder of the party. As he was about to leave, he walked over to us and said, loud enough for all to hear, "King, this is one of the best made platoon positions I have seen – well done!" I called my platoon to attention and saluted as he left. A satisfied air remained over the platoon. A little praise goes a long way. We had spent a long miserable wet and then freezing winter building our position and this was the first time that anyone of the rank of General had given us any words of encouragement.[24]

There were also visits from the press:

One member of the Press who visited the battalion was not permitted to see the block-house. I was later informed that this was because he was a civilian and not an Official War Correspondent. Instead of the rank-less uniform of the War Correspondent, he wore a long camel hair overcoat. This was Charles Graves,* who like his brother Robert Graves, had a special affection for the Regiment. He was correspondent for the Daily Mail, based in Paris. He was a vital sort of man, full of life, and told a string of stories and anecdotes, some scandalous, but all very amusing. The article he wrote in the Overseas Edition of the Daily Mail was entitled "The Battalion with 85 Joneses".

Drafts of reinforcements arrived regularly, bringing the strength of the battalion on 30 November to twenty-two Officers and 704 N.C.Os and Fusiliers.[25] From late November 1939, there had been frequent air-raid alarms, none of which came to anything; and equally frequent divisional alarm exercises when the line was manned at short notice. On 2 December the battalion was withdrawn from the line for a period of divisional training at Beaurain Achicourt, two miles (3 kilometres) south of Arras, the first-line reinforcements taking over the line; following which the bulk of 4 Infantry Brigade moved to the Saar for a month's duty in the main Maginot defences.[26] While at Beaurain, the battalion provided a guard of honour for His Majesty King George VI, Colonel-in-Chief, at Bercu, under Captain Benyon, with Second Lieutenant Edwards as lieu-tenant of the guard and Second Lieutenant Kemp as ensign for the King's Colour.[27] J.L. King, who was the lieutenant of the guard, remembered that:

It had been a very cold day and we wore greatcoats. We travelled to Bachy in trucks, all standing up, to prevent any unsightly creases on our greatcoats. On debussing, we remained standing up, with Mr Sheriff, the Regimental Sergeant Major, watching us. Two hours later – maybe we were a bit early or lunch [with the Grenadier Guards] took longer than anticipated – we formed up. There was one embarrassing moment, when the King walked past the Guard without taking any notice of us. This was rectified and he came back, took the Royal Salute and inspected the Guard. This was a very tactless incident, as many of the Guard came from South Wales and had very strong views on the Abdication.[28]

*   Charles Ranke Patrick Graves (1899 –1971) was a journalist and writer, and brother of Robert Graves. He worked on the *Sunday Express, Daily Mail* and many other newspapers. He published forty-six books in all including *The Thin Blue Line or Adventures in the RAF.* He also wrote a continuation (more than a sequel) called *The Avengers.*

Given the King's record of taking care to meet and talk to the Regiment at every opportunity it was very likely not want of tact, but want of a proper briefing from the staff, that had caused the King to pass by thus: he was in all probability embarrassed and furious at the mistake.

On 18 December the first of a number of details left for leave, while the remainder of the battalion carried out training in the Beaurain area with 4th R.T.R. and No 2 Troop Carrying Company R.A.S.C. The battalion returned to Mouchin on 20 December and resumed work on the defences; D Company departed the next day to join 1st Battalion the Border Regiment for its spell in the Maginot Line, taking the place of one of the Borders' companies left behind to hold the line, at a strength of three Officers and 114 N.C.Os and Fusiliers.[29] The company had been given its Christmas dinner several days previously which was just as well, as Christmas Eve and Christmas Day were spent in a train.[30] The rest of the battalion had something of a holiday on 25 December, with dinners cooked in the bakers' ovens of Mouchin and entertainment by the popular singer Frances Day.[*] Work resumed on Boxing Day, however.

In early January there was something of a **January 1940** thaw in the cold weather, although it was still very cold at night. A draft of reinforcements under Lieutenant Stonehouse arrived on New Year's Eve – mostly transfers from the Cheshire Regiment – and another draft of attachments from the Regiment's T.A. battalions on 9 January; the latter remained

The King at Bachy, 2 December 1939. (Bundesarchiv O1785)

A group of reservists with 1 R.W.F. in France, 1940. (R.W.F. Mus 587)

The Carrier Platoon, 1939.

---

[*]   Frances Day (real name Frances Victoria Schenck) (1908–1984) was an American actress and singer who achieved great popularity in Britain in the 1930s. Her career began as a cabaret singer in New York City and then London. She toured the provinces in 1930 and made her London stage debut at the Hippodrome in 1932 in *Out of the Bottle*. In 1939 she was appearing in the stage play *Black and Blue* and in 1940 she starred in the film *Room for Two*.

until 22 February.[31] There was little or no warning of their arrival, but as the War Diary noted, this was quite usual. Cold weather returned with the War Diary noting that the roads were in a 'very dangerous condition.' On 26 January, a warning was received of another large draft of reinforcements totalling 108 men, or three per section; there is no strength return in the War Diary until 31 March when the total is recorded as twenty-four Officers and 709 W.Os, N.C.Os and Fusiliers.

On 14 February, Captain the Hon R.S. Best left to join the 5th Battalion Scots Guards, a ski battalion being raised from volunteers. He was the Regiment's only representative in this battalion, which was formed to assist the Finns in their fight against the Russians. Training was carried out in Chamonix, but the Finns made peace before the battalion could be committed. Best rejoined the 1st Line Reinforcements when 5th S.G. was disbanded at the end of March.[32]

February–March 1940

There was heavy snow during the second half of February which again curtailed both training and work on the defences. St David's Day was celebrated in almost peacetime fashion, 'according to Regimental tradition.' The Drums beat 'Reveille' and there was a holiday for all troops, with the Officers and senior N.C.Os serving the men's dinners and the youngest Fusiliers eating the leek. A football match was held in the afternoon in which 1 R.W.F. beat the rest of 6 Brigade 5-0. The Officers' Dinner took place in the evening and signals were exchanged with

Lieutenant Colonel Harrison and his French Liaison Officer, Sous-Chef Janvier, St David's Day 1940.
(R.W.F. Mus 4137)

Buckingham Palace. There had been considerable press interest in the celebrations which were recorded in the line on 28 February – including leek-eating in Blockhouse No 75 – so that pictures could appear in the Welsh newspapers on 1 March. That evening, however, a barn which was the Signal Platoon billet burnt down, destroying all the signal equipment and stores – including radios, batteries, and miles of copper cable – to the value of £1,000 (almost £50,000 at today's prices using a measure of purchasing power).[33]

So the winter passed, in conditions of cold and wet. The war somehow seemed more remote than ever, making it difficult to keep up the interest and enthusiasm of the men. Periods of front-line duty alternated with rest periods in the back areas, and one by one the monotonous days slid by. That the battalion's morale remained high throughout this difficult time was something of a triumph for all concerned.

Easter came early that year on 24 March, with the weather at last beginning to improve and with the coming of spring, the war sprang to life. On

April 1940

9 April 1940, a startled world learned that, moving with almost incredible swiftness, Germany had overrun Denmark in a single night, and that German troops had landed at many points along the Norwegian coast. From afar the men of the 1st Battalion followed the course of the fighting in Norway (see the chapter on the Independent Companies for full details). The days of 'the phoney war' were drawing to a close. The battalion was briefly moved from Mouchin on

1st Battalion Goat, St David's Day 1940. (R.W.F. Mus 4137); second picture gives a view of the village of Mouchin.

The men's dinners on St David's Day 1940. (R.W.F. Mus 4137)

12 April, to undertake guard duties, with Headquarters at Beaumont, six miles (9 kilometres) north-west of Douai; A Company at Fontaine, east of Arras, guarding ammunition and petrol dumps; B and C Companies at Quincy, just north of Douai, on similar duties; and D Company in reserve with Battalion Headquarters. J.L. King, the Signals Officer, remembered that:

> The village of Fontaine, which was between Arras and Douai, was in the middle of the line of [Great War] Cemeteries. There were war graves to the North and South of it. The village had been destroyed during the last War, being the scene of many battles. After the Armistice, the village had been rebuilt in the usual bright red bricks. On the 9th May 1940, the Headquarters and one infantry company of the 1st Battalion, the Royal Welch Fusiliers were billeted in this village.[34]

The battalion moved back to Mouchin on 14 April and concentrated there, although leave, which was suspended, resumed on 17 April.[35]

The strict neutrality of Belgium and the Netherlands, both standing in the path of any German move against Northern France, had presented severe constraints on the Allied command. To wait for an invasion of those two countries before a move forward could be made meant starting the battle at a grave disadvantage, leaving the initiative completely in German hands. Yet there was no alternative, for both Belgium and the Netherlands stood firm on their neutral status. In the end the Allied command adopted what was known as Plan D, which entailed an advance by British and French troops up to the River Dyle in the event of a German attack. This left half of Belgium and the whole of the Netherlands to be defended by their own forces, a task which even the most sanguine realised to be beyond their capabilities.[36] Yet no more could be done. Even Plan D meant the acceptance of grave risks, for not only did it mean leaving the prepared defences of the Gort Line on which the B.E.F. had spent so many months of labour; it meant also a hurried move up to a new line, to co-operate with new allies, with whom liaison was virtually non-existent. The activation of this plan had not been rehearsed in the 2nd Division to anything like the required degree, unlike, for example, as it had been in Montgomery's 3rd Infantry Division. Montgomery had:

> … trained the division for this task over a similar distance moving Westwards, i.e. back-wards into France. We became expert at a long night move, and then occupying a defensive position in the dark, and by dawn being fully deployed and in all respects ready to receive an attack.[37]

2nd Division did carry out training, as the battalion's War Diary makes clear, but over limited distances and usually for no more than twenty-four hours.*

---

*   The 1st Battalion War Diary for January to March 1940 inclusive is written in the hand of the Adjutant, Lieutenant J.E.C. Hood, except for the period 13 to 25 March when it was written by the Intelligence Officer and acting Adjutant, Captain J.E.T. Willes. The last page of the March diary also contains, in Lieutenant Hood's hand, the entries for 1 to 3 April. They are crossed out, indicating that a new page had then been started for April. There is, however, no detailed diary in Hood's hand for April, although the battalion remained at Mouchin and the German invasion of the Netherlands and

In the weeks that followed the outbreak of fighting in Norway, and unseen by the Allies, a total of 104 German infantry divisions, nine motorized divisions and ten *panzer* divisions were moving up to the west to implement the German plan for victory in the West. In the north, from the sea coast to Aachen (Aix-la-Chapelle), General Fedor von Boch's Army Group B would move into the Netherlands and then slowly into Belgium, drawing the French and British armies towards them. From Aachen to Sarreburg, General Gerd von Runstedt's Army Group A, containing the bulk of the German armour, would strike through the Ardennes into the Allied rear, splitting the Allied armies and driving the B.E.F. towards the coast. Subsequent operations would swing south, pushing the French back onto the Maginot defences, where General Wilhelm von Leeb's Army Group C was waiting. On the forward airfields the might of the *Luftwaffe* moved up – two air fleets with 3,500 high-level *Junkers* and *Dornier* bombers, *Stuka* dive bombers, and *Messerschmitt* fighters.

On 4 May, little realising that the storm was about to break, the battalion was again withdrawn to Douai for more guard duties at petrol and ammunition dumps; and as much training as the crops, the country, and the duty roster would allow. Battalion Headquarters with H.Q. and A Companies were at Fontaine, C and D Companies were at Beaumont and B Company was at Quincy.

May 1940

ii. The Advance to the Dyle

On 9 May there was little to herald the approaching storm. Over the rear area there was slightly more German air activity than usual, but not enough to warrant suspicion. That night all was quiet. In the early morning of 10 May, as usual, civilian wireless sets were switched on in billets to listen to the 07.00 hrs B.B.C. news bulletin.[38] It was the first intimation to the battalion that the enemy had struck, that his troops were flooding into the Low Countries. South of the B.E.F. sector, German armoured troops waited to debouch from the Ardennes in the direction of Sedan, into the Allied rear, when the moment was right.

Belgium was still a month in the future. The actual diary for April is preceded by a cover sheet (AF A3091) on which is typed
"1/R.Welch Fusiliers
APRIL & MAY 1940
    This diary received by C.7 on 26th September 1941 & assumed to be a re-written account."
    The diary has only three entries for the whole month, and is another hand. It must be assumed therefore that the original diary for April was lost during the chaotic circumstances surrounding the destruction of the battalion at St-Venant. The diary for May is in the same hand as April and is more detailed. It does, however, get dates wrong and some accounts of events are suspect. It covers the retreat to Dunkirk in some detail and was therefore probably compiled by someone who was in that part of the battalion which got away to Dunkirk.
    The War Diary from November 1940 to the end of 1941 is written in the same hand. The diary for September to December 1941 is also in the same format and on the same stamped paper as the 1940 pages. This substantiates the typewritten note on the cover sheet (see above), that the diary for April and May was not received by C.7 (Army Historical Branch) until September 1941. It is not understood why this happened, especially as the diary entry for 10 June 1940 states that 'The day spent in making up company war diaries'. It is reasonable to assume that a battalion diary would have been compiled at the same time. [R.W.F.\1-WD-40 RJMS 23 Sep 97]

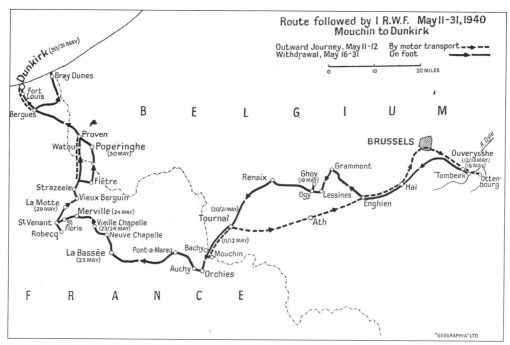

Map 16.2 Route followed by 1 R.W.F. May 11–31, 1940, Mouchin to Dunkirk. (Source: *The Red Dragon*)

Early on the 11th, however, J.L. King recalled that:

> I listened to a distant rumbling and intermittent droning overhead. They were not R.A.F. planes and therefore must be Luftwaffe. I dressed as quickly as possible and ran out of the billet. Overhead, flying Westwards, was a squadron of Dornier 'Flying Pencils' followed by a squadron of Heinkels… in the distance could be seen bursts of exploding A.A. shells and below, a dark cloud was rising … Arras was being bombed… John Hood, the Adjutant, met me. "The Boche are attacking all along the frontier. They've invaded Holland and Belgium. They're using parachute troops in Belgium and have bombed Rotterdam." The C.O. put the phone down. "Plan David is in operation. The B.E.F. is to take up positions on the River Dyle, between Louvain and Wavre, to the East of Brussels." The Colonel looked rather old as he made this statement. He had been through all this before and now it was happening again.[39]

The battalion was ordered to concentrate at Mouchin, before moving into Belgium in accordance with Plan D. As the companies reported their arrival, they brought with them stories of the chaotic conditions on the roads, with vehicles jammed nose to tail and progress at a rate of little more than one mile an hour. It was hardly a promising start to a campaign. Lieutenant Colonel Harrison ordered all companies to proceed separately with all possible speed. All three columns reached their destination between 17.00 and 19.00 hrs that evening.[40] Each reported confusion and near-gridlock on the roads. All trained troops who had been out at rest were making their way north to rejoin their divisions, whilst the partially-trained units which had relieved them were crowding Southwards down the road to rejoin their own formations. The traffic

Driving north into Belgium. (Author's collection)

streams heading north consisted of lines of vehicles, sometimes double banked, and often stationary. The rate of progress may be estimated by the fact that, using the by-pass route, it took a vehicle about an hour and a half to get past Douai, a distance of about a mile and a half (2.2 kilometres). A certain amount of enemy bombing of the route took place, particularly in Douai, but none of the three battalion columns were hit.[41]

There was little to be done on the last evening in Mouchin. The Commanding Officer knew by now that the battalion would not be required to move forward until late the following day. Except for the anti-aircraft L.M.Gs and for blankets and packs, the vehicles remained fully loaded. These comprised a section of the 53rd (Welsh) Division Troop Carrying Company under Major Roddy Swayne, of Denbigh, and were therefore old friends. The Commanding Officer decided to let the men have the evening to themselves. An exceptionally mild night brought many

1 R.W.F. digging in at Ottenbourg in Belgium, 12 May 1940. (R.W.F. Mus)

of the inhabitants to their doors to exchange remarks with the passing soldiers whilst most of the kitchens contained informal parties. During the night the Quartermaster, Lieutenant A.G. Bent, made a most welcome return from leave, several days early, having 'lorry-hopped' over half of France.

At 04.00 hrs on 11 May, the battalion recce party under Captain J.E.T Willes left to join the Brigade Commander in a forward reconnaissance **11 May 1940** into Belgium, followed at 09.00 hrs by a debussing-point party, under Captain R.O.F. Prichard. Neither the Commanding Officer nor the Senior Major went on the forward reconnaissance, as the former was to command the brigade on the night advance, whilst the latter commanded the battalion. On arrival at its destination in Belgium, the battalion was to occupy the brigade reserve position and was, therefore, allotted the rear position in the brigade column.

The day was passed by all ranks in giving a last overhaul to arms and equipment and in making final adjustments to transport loads. One of the main tasks was to organise the transport so that each of the battalion's sixty-six vehicles and twenty-five large R.A.S.C. troop-carrying lorries should pull out into its correct place in the column. Each platoon in its troop carriers had to be followed by the platoon baggage truck, the platoons and companies had to be in the right order and the Anti-Aircraft Platoon's trucks properly distributed along the column. The battalion's move forward into Belgium was timed to begin at 20.00 hrs and as that hour approached, the engines of the troop-carrying lorries were warmed up. Daylight was beginning to fade and, with folded arms and serious faces, the villagers of Mouchin stood at the doors of their cottages to wave goodbye. They had made many friends in the battalion, and there were feelings of genuine sorrow at this abrupt departure to the scene of the fighting. At one minute to the hour, all engines were started, and as the hour struck the leading vehicles moved off down the poplar-lined road. Only axle lights were permitted, but the march discipline was so good that no vehicle lost its way. The Belgian frontier was crossed to the East of Rumegies, and the battalion continued via Ath and Enghien to Hal without difficulty. Beyond Hal, however, driving conditions became more difficult since the route crossed the various main roads radiating Southward from Brussels. Just as dawn was breaking on the 12th, the battalion at last reached its destination at Tombeek, where it was met by Lieutenant Colonel Harrison and Captain J.E.T. Willes, the Intelligence Officer, who had gone on ahead.[42]

The Commanding Officer had been given orders to man the defensive line of the River Dyle. This was the last defensible position East of Brussels, **12 May 1940** and speed in manning it was made necessary by the German capture of a bridge over the Meuse at Maastricht, which had not only turned the main Belgian defence line along the Albert Canal, but had also opened up a line of advance into the Netherlands. The Belgian Army was in full retreat, crowding along the roads which led to Brussels. Here at Tombeek, there was no cover from aerial observation, but the debussing and the dispersal of vehicles was carried out quickly and smoothly. The battalion was dispersed by companies, each with its own first line transport, in a nearby wood on the side of a hill. The second line transport, together with the Quartermaster and his staff, were parked under brigade arrangements not far from Brussels. The cooks' lorries had been kept with the battalion and under the Master Cook – W.O. II Caldwell – the cooks rapidly prepared the battalion's breakfast. Before the meal was ready the Commanding Officer returned from making a further reconnaissance, and, after collecting the company commanders, gave out orders for the immediate occupation of a defensive position. Company commanders were allowed time to return to their companies and pass on their orders and were then taken forward by the Commanding Officer on a reconnaissance, leaving the battalion to follow within half an hour under the Senior Major.

The positions allocated to the battalion were at Ottenbourg, overlooking the Dyle North of Wavre, where it was placed, as expected, in brigade reserve; the forward battalions were in positions on the far side of the river. Ahead of them again was a covering force of armoured cars of the 4/7th Dragoon Guards.[43] The battalion was in position by 10.00 hrs, with A and C Companies detached forward, holding the left of the brigade position. The position was a bad one: the river was not a major obstacle and the companies were deployed on a forward slope. All frontages and distances were greatly in excess of those given in *Field Service Regulations* with the result that there was no mutual support between companies; in addition, the Commanding Officer's lay-down of platoons meant that there was no mutual support within the forward companies, whose platoons were oddly intermingled.[*] The remainder of the 12th, and the whole of the 13th, were spent in digging defences. The line of the river had previously been thought to have been prepared by the Belgians for defence, but apart from a few concrete blockhouses nothing had been done. Although considerable improvements were made, there was little time to do more than get the battalion command posts underground, while a shortage of barbed wire and anti-tank mines made it impossible to make the position a really strong one.

The river in front of the position was an anti-tank obstacle throughout the length of A Company's forward sector, but passable for dismounted troops. It was crossed by a stone bridge, covered by the company's right forward post, from which the road ran back Westwards through the position up a narrow steep valley at the head of which, more than a mile away, stood the village of Ottenbourg. On the south side of the valley, high ground was capped by woods, the edge of which was the inter-battalion boundary between 1 R.W.F. and 1 Royal Berkshires. The north side of the valley was framed by a spur, covered with thick bushes, which ran Eastward from near Ottenbourg and terminated, very steeply, about a quarter of a mile (400 metres) from the river. To the north of this spur was a large re-entrant with a gradual rise from the river. It was about half of a mile (800 metres) wide and absolutely devoid of any sort of cover. In the middle was a small mound or hillock. The northern or far side of the re-entrant was the rough line of the battalion, brigade and divisional left boundary – the troops beyond being 1st K.S.L.I. in the 3rd Division. Across the front of the position between the right and left battalion boundaries was a belt of flat ground between the spur and the river varying in breadth from a quarter to half a mile (400 to 800 metres). Along this belt ran a road about 300 yards from the river and parallel to it. Between the road and the river the country was fairly thick, marshy and scrubby, especially towards the southern end.[44] A section of Divisional M.G. battalion (2nd Manchesters) was placed under command, whose guns could sweep the low ground near the river from a position near A Company's right hand platoon; and a 2.5 cm anti-tank gun was also located in this area. A section of 2 pdr anti-tank guns was sited near the head of the big re-entrant. In the village itself, the defences had been more carefully sited in all-round defence, although mutual support was still lacking, and all approaches were covered by loop-holed posts with anti-tank rifles.

---

[*]   A reconnaissance of the position in late 2016 revealed the area little changed and the layout of the position hard to understand given the weapon ranges and the shape of the slopes.

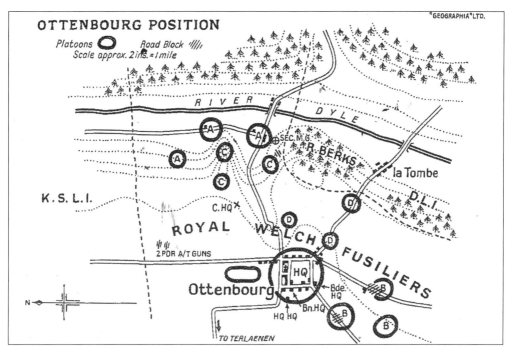

Map 16.3 the Ottenbourg Position. (Source: *The Red Dragon*)

The M.O. had discovered an ideal aid post in two connecting cellars of a strength and depth which were later to stand him in good stead. Battalion Headquarters moved to the vacated curé's house which boasted a well-built cellar. The priest had left early in the day with a wish that his large stock of wine was to be drunk by the English in case it fell into the hands of 'les Boches'. This benevolent intention was frustrated by the Commanding Officer who had the contents of the cellar transferred to one of the ground floor rooms and locked up, as J.L. King remembered:

> Being curé in Ottenburg must have been a convivial occupation. The curé had offered the contents of his cellar to the Colonel rather than let it fall into the hands of the Boche. But the Colonel who had very strong views on drink and battle, probably from some experience in the last war, ordered that every bottle be taken out of the cellar and locked in one of the ground floor rooms.[45]

The first line transport was sent back to join the second line hidden in the Forêt de Soignes. This decision, so much to be regretted later, was taken on account of the lack of cover. The cooks' lorries alone were left with companies.

iii. The Defence of Ottenbourg

In the early morning of 14 May came the news of the Dutch surrender, followed rapidly by signs of a serious Belgian collapse. Streams of refugees,

14 May 1940

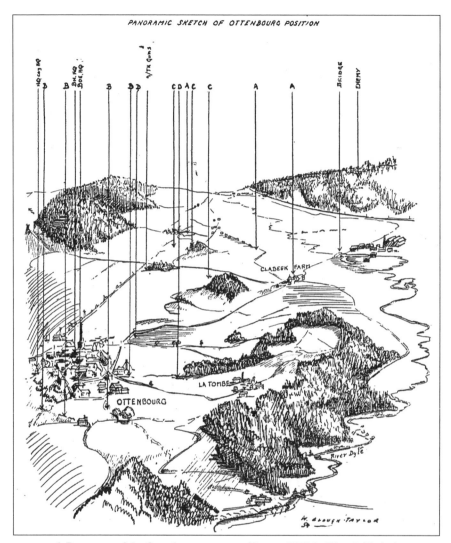

A Panorama of the Ottenbourg position. (Source: W.S.A. Clough-Taylor)

loaded with their few belongings, began moving back through the battalion area, completely blocking the road through Ottenbourg, as J.L. King remembered:

> Now ... came the refugees. Wooden farm carts, mostly four-wheeled, some two wheeled, on steel-rimmed wooden wheels, laden high with personal belongings and food for the humans and the animals. The carts drawn by cart horses, oxen, donkeys or a combination of any of them. On top of the load would sit the oldest members of the family and the smallest children. The older children would walk beside the carts or lead the horses or oxen.[46]

A remarkable photograph of the first contact with the Germans at Ottenbourg in May 1940 – probably B Company. (R.W.F. Mus)

Mingled with them were many Belgian soldiers, without arms and in total disorder. As the morning wore on the signs became even more ominous, with complete units struggling back among the refugees, again often without their arms. And by noon it was known that the main Belgian defence line had crumbled and that the enemy was across the Albert Canal.[47] Shortly before 13.00 hrs the armoured cars of the covering force withdrew across the bridge over the Dyle in A Company's sector, followed by a company of 1st Royal Berkshires, which had been manning the outpost line. The bridge was then blown on orders from Brigade Headquarters. It was later learned that the enemy was not yet in the vicinity, and the company of the Royal Berkshires was ordered back across the river, the Engineers constructing a footbridge for the purpose. One platoon of A Company also crossed to form a small bridgehead and to cover the advance and subsequent withdrawal of the outposts.

That evening the advancing enemy made contact and began to drive in the outposts. Major O.T.M. Raymont, commanding A Company, waiting for the Royal Berkshires and the covering platoon of his own company to cross, made plans to destroy the bridge, assisted by Engineers, and as soon as all were over, the footbridge was cut adrift with axes. It was just in time, for a few minutes later the leading German troops reached the eastern bank of the river.[48]

It was a noisy night, with the enemy probing across the river in an attempt to locate the forward British posts. There was a good deal of indiscriminate firing at first, for this was the first occasion on which most of the men had faced an active enemy, but as the night wore on the young soldiers settled down to their task well, and the fire discipline improved considerably. J.L. King recalled: 'It was natural, as the Colonel told John [Hood], for troops the first time in action to fire too much, but they would settle down. He was right.'[49] The forward companies put patrols out and, where possible, defence work went on uninterrupted under the old routine of two hours watching, two hours work, and two hours rest. In addition, C Company successfully laid a large anti-tank minefield in front of the position.

With the dawn of Wednesday 15 May the German IV Corps put in an attack along the whole of the brigade front.[50] The artillery S.O.S. signal sent up by A Company received a prompt response and this broke up the attack on their front without much difficulty.[51] The remainder of the battalion had little to do except to stand-to and

15 May 1940

to endure some light shelling. Towards the right of the brigade front some penetration over the river occurred in the D.L.I. area and, in consequence at about 10.00 hrs, D Company, under Captain A.J. Lewis, was ordered forward to take the place of the D.L.I.'s reserve company, whilst the D.L.I. put in a counter-attack. At the same time D Company's place was taken over by a company of the 1st Cameron Highlanders from 5 Brigade. On their arrival, D Company was ordered to take up a front line position well down on a forward slope and with very sparse cover. Enemy snipers were active and accurate and, although efforts were made to keep the fire down, the company suffered casualties during the hours of daylight.

A Company spent a most unpleasant morning. Their hastily dug positions on the forward slopes were overlooked by the enemy from the high ground on the far side of the river and, following the failure of his attack, the enemy systematically bombarded the company with artillery and mortars. The leading German troops were plentifully supplied with the 100 mm *Nebelwerfer* 35 mortar, which had a high rate of fire and great accuracy. They also had 10.5 cm FH 18 howitzers, the standard gun of the field artillery at this point, whose shells were capable of penetrating a cottage and coming out the other side when fired in the direct-fire role. These two German weapons were extremely hard to counter owing to the fact that after firing a few rounds, their well-drilled crews moved them to another position. Unless a gunner Forward Observation Officer (F.O.O.) had the luck to spot them firing, it was almost impossible to deal with them because of the length of time taken by a message to get back to the guns from the forward posts. For its part, the battalion had two 3-inch mortars with H.Q. Company. These were excellent weapons but too few in number, especially as one was destroyed in this action and could not be replaced. Each platoon in the rifle companies had a 2-inch mortar, making a total of twelve, but no H.E. bombs had been issued. The only recorded instance of the battalion having been able to fire these weapons was in training in November 1939, when three rounds per mortar had been expended.[52]

Enemy infantry, forming up for an attack in the shelter of an old factory on the far bank were dispersed by well-aimed rounds from the anti-tank gun directed by Major Raymont, but a few minutes later he was severely wounded when the gun received a direct hit. He managed to reach Battalion Headquarters and was evacuated to the advanced dressing station, but died from his wounds the same night. Captain A.H. Williams,* late of the 7th Battalion, succeeded him in command of the company.

The action quickened again in the evening when the enemy mounted a second attack across the river. The main weight fell on A Company, but, as in the morning engagement, it was soon broken up and the enemy driven back. It was followed by another heavy bombardment, both by guns and mortars, and there were further casualties both in A and C Companies. The stretcher-bearers rose to the occasion, making the long carry up the hill to the village with four bearers to each stretcher. As a result of this action, Sergeant T.J. Jones and Lance Sergeant L.D.P. Evans were later awarded the DCM.[53]

---

*   Later Lieutenant Colonel A. Humphrey Williams DSO OBE TD. He was commissioned into The Royal Welch Fusiliers (TA) in 1932. He commanded the 1st Battalion with distinction at Donbaik in Burma, during the first Arakan campaign, where he won a DSO, and later the 7th Battalion in Normandy, where he was badly wounded. He retired in 1947 and died after a long illness in 1983. See his obituary in *Y Ddraig Goch*, March 1984.

iv. The Withdrawal to the Escaut

That night, at about 22.00 hrs, orders reached Battalion Headquarters that the 3rd Division would relieve 2nd Division in place, and the 2nd Division was therefore to prepare for a withdrawal to the River Escaut.[54] As J.L. King remembered:

> The senior Officers sat around the table, the junior ones leant against the cellar walls, balancing their maps as best they could. As the Colonel took his seat and put on his spectacles, the only noise, apart from the bursting shells outside the curé's house, was the hissing of the two paraffin pressure lamps. "There has been a breakthrough to the South and some of our Allies have had to withdraw to new positions. In order to conform with these movements, the Brigade will withdraw."[55]

The successes of the day in holding the enemy to the east bank of the Dyle and in repulsing all attacks had not prepared the battalion for such an order, which came therefore as a considerable surprise.[56] But what was not known was the success of the enemy's break-through farther South from the forests of the Ardennes, into the Allied rear, in fulfilment of their plan. There the French defence had crumbled before the German armour, and through the gap had poured an unending stream of enemy tanks and motorized infantry. Even at this early date in operations the threat of encirclement was recognised, calling for a swift withdrawal to shorten and straighten the long Allied line.[57]

The task confronting Lieutenant Colonel Harrison, to be accomplished within the five hours of darkness available, was to withdraw a widely dispersed battalion from its present position and to occupy before daylight another position four miles (6 kilometres) in the rear in unknown and un-reconnoitred country. The enemy were closely pressing at least one and possibly two of his forward companies. In addition they were shelling the village and roads by which the battalion would have to withdraw. A Company was closely engaged and it was likely that enemy penetration had taken place between and behind the isolated forward posts. Harrison was at least half-an-hour behind time with his knowledge of the exact situation there and could expect to remain so. C Company was also an unknown quantity. Their relief by the Sherwood Foresters had been cancelled. The telephone line to their H.Q. was dead. The Commanding Officer could rely on being at least twenty minutes behind time with any news of D Company which was forward in the D.L.I. area and therefore for the moment not under command. Brigade Headquarters stated that they would rejoin at the village of Tombeek in time to take their place in the new position. H.Q. and B Companies were close at hand and could easily be controlled. Communication with A and C Companies would be by runner, since radios were not at this time issued below Battalion Headquarters level. The former, if reachable, would take thirty minutes and the latter twenty. A minimum of another half-hour would have to be allowed for both companies to get orders to their platoons. It will be remembered that all the first line transport, with the exception of two 8-cwt and two 15-cwt trucks, were twelve miles (19 kilometres) back in the Forêt de Soignes and even if they could have been brought up in time, they could not have come up the Terlaenen-Ottenbourg lane against the tide of the withdrawing brigade. Everything therefore had to be manhandled. The heavy *Boys* anti-tank rifles, the mortars, the reserve ammunition and bombs, the picks, shovels, and other tools would all have to be carried. This was a hard enough task for a full-strength unit but harder still for one reduced by casualties and already tired.

At about 22.30 hrs on 15 May, the Commanding Officer issued his orders. Major D.I. Owen, the Senior Major, was ordered back to reconnoitre the new position, lay out the battalion, and guide the companies into their places on arrival. He was to start at 23.00 hrs. The battalion was to withdraw on a timed programme by companies: H.Q. Company was to go first, followed by C at 01.00 hrs and A at 01.30 hrs. B was to await relief by a company of the Royal Berkshires. All personal kit was to be dumped and every man was to carry what he could of the reserve ammunition, mortar bombs and tools – priority being given to ammunition. The four available trucks at Battalion Headquarters were to leave with the Senior Major at 23.00 hrs, carrying as much as they could of the ammunition reserve. In view of the confused situation, the orders for the companies were delivered to them personally by Captain Willes, the I.O., described by J.L. King as 'probably the most active Officer in the battalion.'[58]

These arrangements were made, the orders drafted, lorries loaded, and troops concentrated, in an atmosphere of discomfort. Of the four trucks available for the transporting of the battalion's reserve ammunition, the drivers of two of them failed to carry out their orders and the trucks went back empty. The remaining two were hurriedly overloaded in the reflected glare of burning buildings, to the accompaniment of the thump of falling shells and the reply of the British artillery. The gunners had their ammunition limbers full and had, in addition, dumps beside each gun which they could not transport back. This surplus they were firing fast in order to get rid of it. The enemy replied vigorously and the noise of both gunfire and bursting shells was intense. The curé's house which sheltered Battalion Headquarters was hit three times and practically collapsed, thus rewarding the foresight in building a second cellar entrance which enabled business to be carried on as usual. On the other side of the narrow street the house above the Regimental Aid Post (R.A.P.) cellars blazed fiercely, but again the provision of a second entrance enabled the treatment of wounded to be continued underground though evacuation was hazardous.

Major D.I. Owen departed for the new position with the only two trucks which had remained, those of the cooks, carrying ammunition. B Company **16 May 1940** followed on foot. Captain Willes delivered the orders to A Company and it made a successful withdrawal, though without No. 2 Platoon, whose position had been overrun by the enemy. W.O. III (PSM) P. Anders, however, succeeded in getting his men out and managed to rejoin the battalion the following day. C Company also made a successful withdrawal, having also been reached by Captain Willes. By dawn on 16 May all companies had reached the rendezvous at the Tombeek cross-roads, and though all were tired and hungry they were still in good spirits, for in their view, they had had the better of the enemy. Without any rest they were led into their new positions, and as the sun rose the battalion began to dig in with the few tools it had. Tools were very scarce, as ammunition had been given priority in any extra load that the men could carry. There was no sight yet of any enemy on the skyline so the village in the valley in front of the position was hurriedly combed for picks and shovels, and also for hams and eggs, as Desmond Llewelyn's memoirs make clear, for breakfast had been left behind as had last night's supper, cooked and in containrs:

> … a couple of my chaps asked me if they should nip across to a nearby farm and see if they could scrounge some eggs. Momentarily I dithered, knowing I'd be court-martialled if I were caught sending soldiers to collect eggs. I turned to the sergeant for reassurance … "Up to you guv" came the reply. Weakened by the vision of fresh eggs, I gave my permission and

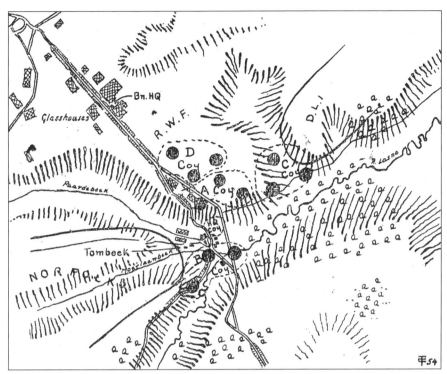

Map 16.4 The Tombeek position. (Source: 'The Story of the 1st Battalion, Royal Welch Fusiliers Friday, May 10th–Monday, May 27th, 1940')

off they scarpered to come back under sudden German fire … they arrived back unscathed, with the eggs unbroken.[59]

Major Owen – 'completely imperturbable and liked by everyone'[60] – was sent back to the transport lines in the Forêt de Soignes to obtain all the vehicle tools and any more that he could find en route, and also to bring up food.

The first stage of the withdrawal to the Escaut line was thus completed in remarkably good order and without loss by 16 May, the anniversary of the Battle of Albuhera in 1811. The opportunity was taken during the day to evacuate Captain Williams, O.C. A Company, who had been wounded in the previous day's fighting but had stayed at his post. His place was taken by Captain R.O.F. Prichard. Fortunately the enemy, delayed by the 3rd Infantry Division, had not been able to follow up the retirement of the brigade, and these

The River Escaut at Tournai. (Author's collection)

moves were made without interference. Meanwhile the Commanding Officer had been having a look at the position and found that, with a few minor adjustments, the dispositions stood the test of daylight. One of these adjustments was to bring forward all available men of H.Q. Company to take over some of the ground allotted to A Company, which had suffered such casualties as to be unable to man even a normal company frontage, let alone an extended one such as was the case at Tombeek.

The river in front of the position was not, in itself, an anti-tank obstacle, being narrower than the Dyle at Ottenbourg, but the ground rising up from it was steep and would render a tank advance difficult. The H.Q. Company forward position was in a market garden on a bluff overlooking the two destroyed viaducts. The garden contained about an acre of greenhouses: it would be a nasty place in which to be shelled. Battalion Headquarters had originally been sited in a small wood bordering the drive of a chateau and not far from D Company, which was in reserve. Headquarters was moved during the morning about 500 yards further back along the road on orders from Brigade Headquarters – the brigadier observing that a commander could better control a fight when not actually in it. Battalion Headquarters' new home was a farm which soon became known as 'Dead Cow Farm' – from the presence of a corpse outside its gates. It was more comfortable than the wood but very much under the eye of a German mobile observation balloon. At the Battalion Headquarters' farm some excellent hams were discovered and commandeered for issue to the troops, one being retained for the use of the Officers' Mess. This made its appearance on the wing of the Commanding Officer's *Humber*, having been placed there by Corporal Brown, the Officers' Mess Corporal, for some reason best known to himself. There it remained for several days of subsequent travel, being the *pièce de résistance* of many a hastily organised running buffet, until only a bone remained to tell the tale of a once proud ham.

It had been hoped that the night would be a quiet one, giving all ranks a chance to catch up on arrears of sleep – but it was not to be. The withdrawal to Tombeek was only the first stage of the full move back to the line of the Escaut, and shortly after 19.00 hrs, the Commanding Officer received orders to carry out the second stage of the withdrawal.[61] The stress laid on the importance of intelligent anticipation of orders while training at Blackdown during the previous year now bore fruit. The circumstances at Tombeek were typical of so many during this brief campaign and it should be remembered that no radio communications existed below battalion headquarters level. The time allowed to the battalion between the receipt of the message calling the Commanding Officer to Brigade Headquarters and the moment when the leading troops had to cross the start line was two hours. As has been seen, Battalion Headquarters, in passing the warning on, also automatically collected Company Commanders to await the Commanding Officer's return. Between the time that Lieutenant Colonel Harrison came back, and before he gave out his orders, to the moment when the leading troops passed the start line was one hour. Before leaving their companies, their commanders arranged for the platoon commanders to assemble and await their return. The section commanders warned their sections to be prepared to make a quick and quiet getaway. Within the hour allowed the Commanding Officer issued his orders, the company commanders digested them, got back to their companies and issued their own. The platoon commanders did the same, and the section commanders likewise. The battalion withdrew to a time-table and on time. H.Q. Company, having marched a mile, crossed the start line at the stipulated time, closely followed by the other companies in regular and quick succession.[62]

Under the withdrawal operation orders, the battalion and one machine-gun platoon of the 2nd Manchesters acted as rearguard to the brigade. This entailed taking up a temporary position in the area of a cross-roads about half a mile back from Dead Cow Farm. The area of the cross-roads was to be held until a stipulated time, by which hour the other two battalions would have come in from the left and be well on their way down the *Route Nationale*. One of these battalions was, however, late in clearing the brigade start line. The route of withdrawal followed the main road which, from the cross-roads position, ran down a steep cutting and across a bridge into the village of Overych, which lay in a hollow. The streets of the village were narrow and it lay within range of the enemy's artillery. It was safe to assume by now that the battalion had slipped away unnoticed, but it was also certain that, if the enemy knew the withdrawal was on, then the village might easily become a trap.

Eventually the order came for the battalion to pull out. One company of the D.L.I. had not yet come in but they were lucky and managed to rejoin later. The battalion had a pause in the cutting due to congestion ahead, but then crossed the bridge, where the Adjutant, Lieutenant J.E.C. Hood, was left to give the sappers orders when to blow the obstacle, and wound silently through the streets of the deserted village. After mounting the hill on the far side, all ranks gave a sigh of relief at the sight of the first line transport waiting at the outskirts of the village. L.M.Gs, ammunition, and tools were loaded and the transport then rolled out under the Senior Major for an R.V. in the Forêt de Soignes. The battalion covered the eight miles (12.8 kilometres) to the R.V. on foot, everyone being heartened by the promise of a hot meal and two-hour rest on arrival. En route they passed through another line of British troops who took over the duties of rearguard.[63] J.L. King remembered this time:

> After the first halt, a few men needed a shake to wake them up and get them back on the road, but otherwise it was a normal march. At the second halt, the usual order to remove packs before resting was relaxed. It wasted valuable resting time … There was a cheerful air about the infantry platoon, behind which I marched. They were puzzled by the reasons for the withdrawal, but they had complete confidence that they would cope with the Boche. They also knew that after a few more miles there would be food and transport, and transport meant a kip.[64]

The speed of the German advance in the north of Belgium now threatened Brussels, and at first light the following morning, 17 May, the battalion was once more on the move. The troop-carrying lorries which were to have made contact with the battalion in the Forêt de Soignes failed to arrive, and again the tired companies had to set out on foot. As the day wore on they reached Brussels, by now an almost deserted city, as J.L. King remembered: 'We were marching through the deserted suburbs of Brussels. There had been some bombing and the telephone or electricity wires had been broken and lay across the road…'[65] The battalion marched through the echoing streets towards a rendezvous on the Eastern outskirts where the lorries were to pick them up. Once again there was a disappointment in store, for there were no lorries at the rendezvous. The Commanding Officer ordered an hour's rest to give them a chance to turn up, but at the end of the period there was still no sign of them. There was nothing for it but to fall the companies in and continue to march on foot. On they went, subject to occasional attacks from the air. Though many were tired almost to the limit of exhaustion, discipline never wavered and no one fell out. Finally, as dusk was falling, orders were received

17 May 1940

for the battalion to lie up for the night in a farm near Gasillage, where a cow was slaughtered and a hot meal prepared, the first since the previous night. The battalion had marched twenty-eight miles (45 kilometres) that day. J.L. King remarked that: 'Under normal circumstances, the battalion being as fit as it was, twenty-five to twenty-eight miles was not an excessive distance but considering that there had been no proper rest for almost four days it was a very long distance.'[66] Interestingly, there seem to have been no complaints at all about sore feet throughout the march, reflecting the battalion's fitness, only about lack of seep.

At B.E.F. Headquarters the true picture of the German break-through in the south was becoming hourly more apparent. The enemy armour, racing through the gap,

The withdrawal to the Gort Line. (Author's collection)

was beginning to swing northwards, threatening the Channel ports. Already they had reached Amiens, and the B.E.F.'s communications to the rear had been cut. There were doubts, too, about the power of the Belgians to hold out in the north. They were the link between the British and the sea, and if they were to give way the situation would be perilous. It was this picture, as it unfolded itself on the campaign maps at Headquarters, which dictated the next order to the battalion. This came the same evening, an order to retire beyond the line of the River Dendre, fourteen miles (22.5 kilometres) to the west. There was still no transport for the tired troops, and as they fell in, there were many who doubted their ability to keep going. Yet there was nothing for it but to try, and at 20.30 hrs they left the farm at Gasillage where hopes of a full night's rest had been so high only three hours before.

Three factors governed this decision on retirement. First, the troop-carrying lorries had gone to the wrong brigade and were unavailable. Secondly, the forward line to the East of Brussels was being abandoned during the night. Last, in order to gain the shelter of the next defensive line it was necessary to reach Morbeck, which was about fourteen miles (22.5 kilometres) from Gassilage. With the prospect of a night march and bearing in mind the known inaccuracy of the small-scale maps as supplied, Brigade Headquarters made arrangements to picquet the route with small parties in order to prevent straggling. One Officer and ten men were called for from each battalion, the men whose feet were in the worst condition being chosen. The 1 R.W.F. party, however, failed to turn up on time and got left behind. This caused a shortage in the picqueting party and had a sequel later. A distance of 200 yards between battalions was laid down for the march and as a further precaution against losing touch, the Commanding Officer ordered one motorcyclist and three cyclists to go on ahead and contact the D.L.I. who were in front, the battalion being once more the rearmost of the brigade. With the approval of the Brigade Commander, the Commanding Officer also arranged that the first-line transport on reaching Morbeck was to off-load and return in order to pick up the worst cases of exhaustion.[67]

Almost at once the battalion ran into difficulties. The road was choked with refugees, through whom the troops had to make their way in the dark. Although the whole brigade was withdrawing along this road, there were no other British troops in sight, a fact which seemed to add to the loneliness and unreality of the scene. As the night wore on, it became more and more difficult to keep the men on the road. Many of them fell asleep while marching and veered off into the ditches, unable to keep a straight course. It became increasingly hard to wake them after the hourly ten-minute halt and to get them back on to the road for the next stage of the march. Yet somehow it was done – the Commanding Officer himself marching rather than using his *Humber*. What saved the day was singing:

> Fusilier Hopkins pulled back his shoulders and with his head held high started singing "There's a long, long trail a-winding ..." as the song ended and before the next one began I could hear from the company in front the same refrain. Fusilier Hopkins had given the battalion its second wind. The hour passed with Sospan Fach, When I grow too old to dream, It's a lovely day tomorrow, All through the night, My brother Sylvester, One black one, one white one, Guide me, O, thou great Jehovah, Men of Harlech. It was a wonderful sound and then the singers started to harmonise. For the first time, I had hopes that the battalion might reach its final destination without a straggler being left behind.[68]

As dawn was breaking on 18 May, the battalion was within a couple of miles of its destination, still together and still complete. After an hour's **18 May 1940** rest, the companies were again mustered for the last stage. A few passing lorries were able to take the men of A and D Companies to the new rendezvous at Morbeck, but B, C, and H.Q. Companies completed the journey on foot. They had now covered forty miles (64.3 kilometres) in thirty hours, and not a single straggler had been left behind – a rare event in any withdrawal but especially so during this operation.

In the main square of Morbeck was Lieutenant A.G. Bent, the Quartermaster, awaiting the arrival of the battalion with a hot meal and a store of new equipment. As they arrived, the men were collected, given their meal, and issued with replacements of their old and worn-out equipment. It was a wonderful tonic, though rest was even more necessary. But rest was the one commodity which could not be supplied. No sooner had the men eaten than the march was renewed, with Grammont as the battalion's next objective. There, at last, were the troop-carrying lorries. Gratefully the tired men piled in, to drive the last few miles to the village of Ogy, which they reached shortly before noon on 18 May. A hot meal and a few hours of sleep in billets made new men of everyone, so that they were ready for the move back that same night to Tournai. The lorries were ready for them at 22.00 hrs, but the great congestion on the roads made movement almost impossible. Dawn was breaking on 19 May before the city came into sight, and even then the last mile had **19 May 1940** to be covered on foot, since the vehicles were locked in a solid traffic jam. As the battalion marched into the city the men were subjected to a raid by about thirty bombers, which fortunately caused only a few minor casualties. So, at last, the line of the Escaut River was reached and the battalion at once moved into its defensive positions.

v. The Defence of the Escaut

The Brigade was to hold the line of the River Escaut, which ran roughly north and south, straight through the middle of the town. The frontage allotted to each battalion was some 1,400–1,500 yards (1,280–1,370 metres). The river was about thirty yards wide (27 metres) and appeared unfordable. The uncertain light from the burning houses revealed that it was canalised throughout the length of the battalion sector. For two-thirds of the length, from the northern or left-hand end, the banks on either side consisted of quay-like streets with a six-foot (2 metre) stone-fronted drop into the water. On both banks these quays or streets were about thirty feet broad (8 metres), with high houses, mostly shops or warehouses, which presented an unbroken frontage except where the façade was pierced by narrow streets or alleys which ran back into densely built-up areas behind. Towards the southern end of the sector, the buildings ceased and both banks showed park-like characteristics terminating at the gaol near the battalion right boundary. The river was spanned by four bridges and one footbridge. Of these, the ones on the right and left of the sector were the most substantial and important. The left-hand bridge used to carry the main road traffic through the town but it was now in the centre of the burning area and partially destroyed. The main road traffic had been diverted over the right-hand or gaol bridge which carried a continuous stream of withdrawing vehicles all through the night.

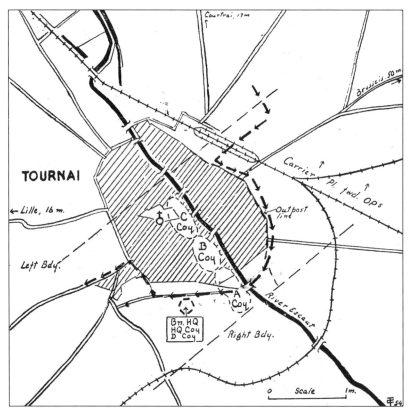

Map 16.5 The Tournai position. (Source: 'The Story of the 1st Battalion, Royal Welch Fusiliers Friday, May 10th–Monday, May 27th, 1940')

After a difficult reconnaissance in the dark, it had been decided that all three battalions were to be forward, 1 R.W.F in the middle holding the centre of the town and four bridgeheads, while the two flanking battalions held the line of the river on either side as far as the outskirts. There was to be an outpost line forward to the east of the river. Further in advance still, there were to be a series of observation posts manned by personnel of the Carrier Platoon, whose armoured vehicles would ensure them a good getaway on the arrival of the enemy. Tournai had already attracted the attention of the Luftwaffe, and many buildings were ablaze as the companies moved up into position on the line of the river. 1 R.W.F. covered its sector with three companies in line and the fourth holding the outpost line beyond the river. A Company was on the right of the battalion, where the river ran through park land; B, in the centre, had a long, built-up stretch to hold, while C on the left had a smaller area which was either still burning or burnt out. All the river bridges were blown except one in A Company's area, which was prepared for demolition but retained for the eventual withdrawal of D Company from the east bank. On withdrawing, D Company was to join H.Q. Company and Battalion Headquarters in the citadel. This was a kind of fortified barracks standing clear of buildings and on a small eminence some distance to the rear of the front line. The actual waterfront was to be held as lightly as possible consistent with effectively covering the river with fire. For this purpose half-sunk cellars were to be utilised, that part of their wall which was above ground being loop-holed.[69]

After a hot breakfast the companies began improving their defences by loop-holing cellars and building breastworks from the plentiful rubble available from bombed buildings. That there was little time for any extensive defence system was obvious to all, and the men worked with a will to do the best possible in the few hours available. Later in the day, C Company had a fortunate find of an ironmonger's warehouse with a good supply of tools. Even as it was, the work was carried out under heavy air attacks, which each time added to the fires sweeping across the city. The citadel, occupied by Battalion Headquarters, was sited on a small hill towards the western outskirts of the town. Inside a perimeter wall there was a large barracks built round spacious square. At the eastern, or business, end and outside the wall, there was an ancient earth rampart about fifty feet (16 metres) high and similarly broad at the base. Inside this earthwork were some good dugouts and the buildings were in an excellent state of repair. The whole place bore a depressing imprint of the haste with which it had been abandoned by the Belgian Army. Discarded clothing and equipment were lying everywhere in indescribable confusion. The craters of a stick of bombs which had dropped between one of the buildings and the perimeter wall pointed to a probable cause. In order to delude the enemy into thinking that the barracks were still deserted, the greatest possible care was taken in concealing vehicles and no-one was allowed to cross the square in daylight.[70]

In the afternoon of 19 May a brigadier from G.H.Q. B.E.F. arrived with authority to blow the last remaining bridge, near the gaol. This was still providing passage to detachments of withdrawing troops and to refugees. The brigadier had every intention of ordering the immediate destruction of the bridge in spite of the fact that D Company on outpost duty and the Carrier Platoon on observation duty were both still on the far side of the river and neither of them were as yet in contact with the enemy. In addition, elements of the division's rearguard were reported to be still east of the river.

The Commanding Officer was determined not to abandon D Company and the Carrier Platoon and, after some discussion with the brigadier, secured a period of grace to effect their withdrawal – 'providing they were quick about it.' Mistrusting the sound of those last words, Lieutenant Colonel Harrison sent the Senior Major onto the bridge, at the same time assuring him that 'the man would not be mad enough to blow the bridge with you sitting on the end of it.' After thirty minutes, the Carrier Platoon came in, closely followed by D Company in single file down each side of the road. Neither Captain Lewis of D Company, nor Second Lieutenant Garnett of the Carrier Platoon reported having seen any sign of the enemy up to the time that they left their positions at 16.00 hrs.

The arrival of the enemy was announced by machine-gun fire in the late afternoon of 20 May and at that point, the bridge was blown, with devastating effect. There was a report that two British battalions had failed to get across the Escaut before the last bridge was blown, and in an attempt to effect a means of rescue, Captain A.J. Lewis swam across the river with a long line attached to him. As he climbed the far bank he was seen by the enemy and shot dead. J.L. King remembered the news of this coming in: 'The Colonel was sitting at the table, looking absolutely dazed... "Tony [Lewis] has been killed", [Hood] said. I could not believe him. Tony, who commanded D Company, was the most liked Officer in the battalion, both by his fellow Officers and by all the Fusiliers who knew him.'[71] Lieutenant R.L. Boyle assumed command of A Company.[72]

20 May 1940

The bombing of Tournai continued throughout the 20th, but fortunately caused few casualties in the battalion. Work on the defences continued and two enemy positions on the far bank were destroyed. There was no attempt by the enemy to assault across the river and, apart from desultory rifle and machine-gun fire, he seemed content to remain on the east bank although building up his numbers. The battalion's position was improved further by the return of F.O.Os from 61st Medium Regiment R.A. The reason for the Germans' lack of haste in forcing the river was soon clear, for the attempt to stand on the Escaut was coming to its inevitable end as away to the West the German break-through gathered momentum and came within striking distance of the Channel coast at Boulogne. An attempt to cut through southwards on the flank of the German advance at Arras had not succeeded, and the B.E.F. was now facing complete encirclement. By the evening of the 20th the decision to abandon the Escaut line was taken and orders were received at Battalion Headquarters to withdraw under cover of darkness and occupy a position in the divisional reserve line. It was to be the first of a long series of moves over the next few days and nights with little chance of rest or recuperation.[73] News was received, with regret, that Brigadier Irwin had handed over command of 6 Infantry Brigade and had become G.O.C of the 2nd Division. He was a ruthless and extremely capable Officer in whom all had confidence. Lieutenant Colonel D.W. Furlong of the Royal Berkshires,* the senior Commanding Officer, assumed command of the brigade. He was to prove a poor substitute and his want of judgement in the final stages of the fighting withdrawal was to cost many lives.

vi. The Withdrawal to and Re-occupation of the Gort Line

Soon after dark on 20 May the companies concentrated around Battalion Headquarters and at midnight the battalion marched out through the deserted town. By the early hours of 21 May

---

*   Lieutenant Colonel Dennis Walter Furlong DSO OBE MC died on 5 September 1940, aged 43.

they had reached the new position, an exposed slope at Trien de Wailly which was under direct observation and fire from the enemy.[74] Here the battalion dug in, with orders to be prepared to mount a counter-attack in order to dislodge a party of the enemy who had crossed the river and occupied a sugar-beet factory in 4 Brigade's area. This position, on the divi-sional reserve line, was very strongly held, especially as regards machine-guns and anti-tank defences. Part of the battalion position had 1st Cameron Highlanders superimposed on it. Battalion Headquarters was in a small farm at a crossroads. It was the place where the last mail from home was received before the evacuation. Close to the farm a section of 18 pdrs was hidden in a small patch of sugar cane. They kept firing all day, attracting counter-battery fire from German 5.9 cm guns.[75] The proposed counter-attack was timed for 22.00 hrs, but was postponed for an hour and later cancelled completely. Instead, there were orders for the battalion to withdraw northwards to the village of Marmere, where it was to support 4 Infantry Brigade. Here, A and B Companies were temporarily detached under command of the D.L.I., and the 1/8th Lancashire Fusiliers in 4 Brigade, respectively.

21 May 1940

As the day wore on, the optimistic began to hope for a night's rest. Eleven nights had passed, a few with a couple of hours sleep and many with none at all. The days between, also, had been filled with toil or fighting. A real night's sleep, an undisturbed six hours, would have worked wonders with the tired men, but it was not to be, either on this night or on those which followed. The battalion reached the village of Marmere shortly after midnight, only to be met with orders to move a further three miles back to Willemeau. The rear positions were found to be already under heavy enemy shell fire on arrival, and it came as little surprise later in the day when further orders were received to continue the withdrawal under cover of darkness, this time back to the original Gort Line on the French frontier. This was the line into which the battalion had put so much effort during the first months of the war, and there were hopes that here, at last, a real stand could be made. The defences were known to be strong and well laid out. Yet even here, in the line so well remembered, things went wrong. The sector allotted to the battalion was around Bachy, no more than two miles from Mouchin where 1 R.W.F. had itself constructed so much of the defence and which it knew so well. Bachy, however, had been in the area of the neighbouring 1st Division, and the defensive plan on which it had been laid out was not known. Here the two detached companies rejoined.

Major Owen, who had preceded the battalion to make a reconnaissance of the area and to select the company areas, had his task made more diffi-cult for him by a thick fog which hung over the whole of the defence position. In spite of it he decided on the company areas, with A, C and D Companies up – since the frontage was exten-sive – and B Company in the second echelon. As the fog lifted, the company commanders took stock of their positions and manned them as best they could, but until the end the defensive lay-out as a whole remained something of a puzzle, not least because the firing positions had been constructed by Guardsmen, who were all over six feet tall, and sandbags had to be filled to raise the fire-steps so that the shorter members of 1 R.W.F. could see over the parapets or through the slits of the pill boxes.[76] Defence preparations went ahead and, after the arrival of the Carrier Platoon at about 10.00 hrs, a sharp lookout was kept for the enemy. The two bridges crossing a dyke which spanned the battalion front were blown and contact was established with troops on the flank. D Company, on the left, formed a junction point with the 2nd Norfolks which, like 1 R.W.F., was holding a wide front. At about midday a French Regiment started to arrive on the battalion position, coming up the lanes at the back of the area. They came in by

22 May 1940

twos and threes by car, motor-cycle and bicycle. One of the most impressive-looking cyclists was collared and introduced to Sous-Sergeant M. Janvier – the French *Officer-de-liaison* serving with the battalion. The outcome of a wordy tussle was to the effect that the Frenchmen had come to take over the line.

Sergeant Janvier was a notable athlete and secretary of the French Athletic Association. He now looked pleased for the first time in several days and said that the incoming unit was the 115th Regiment of Infantry. They had a fine fighting record and could be trusted to give a good account of themselves. In the early afternoon confirmation came through that the battalion was indeed to be relieved by the French with the added information that the 2nd Division was going into rest as G.H.Q. Reserve in the neighbourhood of La Bassée. The Commanding Officer, having read this message, smiled and said, 'We have heard that one before'. Such a message in the previous war generally indicated the reverse of what was written. The relief by the French troops was to be carried out during the day and the battalion was to be transported Westwards during the following night in troop-carrying lorries.[77] Once again Major Owen set off to reconnoitre the new positions, and arrived at La Bassée just after its second heavy air raid of the day. After some delay he reached Divisional Headquarters to learn that the situation had changed: 'The enemy were advancing from the west, the opposite direction to that which we had been fighting. They were on the La Bassée Canal near Merville. [6] Brigade would attack to prevent the Boche from advancing further eastwards.'[78] The Germans had got behind the B.E.F.: 1 R.W.F. was now to withdraw and clear the village of Vieille Chapelle.

vii. The Withdrawal to the River Lys and the Battles of St-Floris, Robecq and St-Venant

There were no maps available of the roads back to Vieille Chapelle, and a thick mist which came down with the coming of darkness made the task of the lorry drivers even more difficult. **23 May 1940** The battalion was due to start its move at 22.00 hrs, but it was not until 05.00 hrs on the 23rd that the lorries at last appeared. A wide detour was made round Lille, which was being heavily attacked from the air, and as the sun rose and dispersed the mist, the column was bombed as it was passing through the village of Anoelin; in spite of this, the whole convoy reached Vieille Chapelle in safety. The companies were quickly dispersed to billets and all ranks settled down to rest.[79] But once again it was not to be for long. Events now were moving rapidly, and it was from the west that the new attacks were coming. Boulogne had fallen, and Calais, attacked by two German divisions, was in the last throes. The new threat to the B.E.F. was mounted from the direction of the Channel ports, and a swift thrust from the west had taken the enemy across the La Bassée Canal in the vicinity of Calonne-sur-Lys. It was to be the task of 6 Infantry Brigade to re-establish the position; to 1 R.W.F. fell the duty of recapturing four bridges over the canal near Robecq and holding them until the Royal Engineers could blow them.

Two vital factors should be borne in mind when considering what followed. First, there were a limited number of daylight hours remaining for this attack. Secondly, and more important, for it covers the subsequent operations as well, there were only four maps available for the whole battalion which was operating in absolutely unknown country. This meant that some company commanders and all junior commanders had to fight their commands with no guide outside the limit of their own vision. It was useless to send a message which included a place name unless the originator was certain that the recipient could see the place named. Further, the recipient had not only to be able to see the place named but also to recognise it for what it was. Calling in artillery fire was also impossible without a map reference. The Commanding Officer could not go forward to explain matters with the map for this would leave his headquarters blind and unable to deal with any development which might arise in his absence. It is impossible to over-estimate the handicap thus imposed on the battalion.

The advance was thus a difficult one, and made even more so by the lack of any precise knowledge of the extent of the enemy's advance. The Carrier Platoon was to lead and if possible establish contact with the enemy. Riding in troop-carrying lorries, the battalion proceeded via La Fosse and Merville to Calonne, where the lorries left them. From Calonne the companies were to march forward to St-Floris, there to divide, with C Company's objective as St-Venant and the right-hand bridge, B Company's Robecq and the two centre bridges, and D Company's to the left of B and the left-hand bridge. A Company was to be held in reserve at St-Floris. The Carrier Platoon led the way to St-Floris, with C Company following on foot. A parallel advance was made by the Royal Berkshires to the north of the Bourne Canal.*

When the head of the convoy reached the village of Calonne, British troops on outpost duty were discovered, and also some French tanks. The outpost troops stated that there were no British troops in front of them. They were not in immediate contact with the enemy but that the latter were known to be about a mile away to the West. The French tanks were already headed for home and quickly vanished down the road up which the battalion was coming. C Company continued to advance and, at the cost of a few casualties, cleared the village and took several prisoners. Continuing along the road to St-Venant, the Carrier Platoon came under accurate fire from German anti-tank guns and the two leading carriers were knocked out with the loss of both their crews. Among those killed were the platoon commander, Second Lieutenant Garnett, and Sergeant Spilstead. Corporal M.D. McNeil took command of the platoon and successfully withdrew in contact, actions for which he was later awarded the MM.[80]

C Company was held up in the Western edge of St-Floris by heavy, accurate machine-gun fire from enemy positions on the Bourne Canal. In an attempt to dislodge them, Lieutenant Colonel Harrison sent B Company round the left flank of C. Near dusk, they came up against an enemy platoon, which they had little difficulty in removing and reached their objective, though with the three platoons strung out through lack of maps and out of touch with each other.[81] As a result of this action, Sergeant W. Morgan was later awarded the DCM.[82]

The River Dyle, looking towards the German advance.
(Author's collection)

---

*   The Bourne Canal is not noted on maps of the area and is probably a mis-transcription of the Bourre Canal, the Bourre being a tributary of the Lys which flows Southwards from Hazebrouk, joining the Lys at Merville, from where the Lys is canalised westwards through St-Venant.

The story of D Company was less happy. Again through lack of maps of the area, they had taken the wrong turning towards their objective, had run into an ambush in the dark, and had suffered heavy casualties, including Lieutenant R.L. Boyle, the company commander, who was killed.[83] His place was taken by Second Lieutenant M.J.B. Kemp. With no information of their fate or their whereabouts at Battalion Headquarters, the Commanding Officer sent Major Owen to discover what was happening. After a long search he found the remnants of the Company withdrawing from the scene of the ambush and led them back to Calonne.

By now darkness had fallen. The situation in the area was still very confused and any further attempt to advance towards the four bridges across unknown country seemed useless. Since little was known of the enemy's strength or dispositions, Lieutenant Colonel Harrison decided to concentrate what was left of the battalion at St-Floris for the night, and the four companies were brought back to form a defensive box around the village. Orders were issued for A Company to take up a position on the northern edge of the village. C Company was to continue to watch the west. B Company was to collect its missing platoons and guard the southern flank, while D Company, when it arrived, was to face rearwards towards the east. The transport was stowed away in orchards and lanes within the ring. Local patrolling was to be active, and at dawn, strong patrols were to be sent forward by B and C Companies to report on the progress of the enemy. Battalion Headquarters were moved forward to the western outskirts of the village and all was set for a further advance at first light.

The battalion was now, on the evening of 24 May, on the verge of its final action. For nearly a fortnight it had been withdrawing, often under conditions of great difficulty, in front of a rapidly advancing enemy. The days had been spent in fighting or digging and the nights in almost constant movement. During these thirteen days and nights, with the possible exception of one night at Tournai, few men had been able to achieve more than two consecutive hours of sleep. Several nights had passed with no sleep at all. Under these circumstances, the entire B.E.F had suffered a severe drain upon its physical resources, and 1 R.W.F. was no different. Mental alertness had also become dulled, in a campaign where quick thinking was essential. Morale remained high, as witness the rapid advance on St-Floris, which was stopped not by lack of the will to go forward, but by the hazard caused by darkness, lack of maps, and unknown country. It is astonishing that morale was as good as it was, given the factors which might have tended to weaken it. Since the beginning, rumours of disaster elsewhere had been a constant companion and these rumours had not been dispelled by the fact that the information received at Tournai concerning a stand there, had been followed so quickly by a further withdrawal. After the first few days, the enemy air superiority had been overwhelming. When the enemy aircraft were not overhead, their mobile observation balloons dominated the battlefield. The Germans possessed numerous mortars and high-velocity, low-trajectory, infantry light guns with a high degree of accuracy. The British Army possessed neither balloons nor infantry guns; also, so far, no H.E. ammunition had been issued for the 2-inch mortars.[84] These facts tended to give an impression that the enemy was superior in infantry equipment as well as in the air and in numbers of armoured fighting vehicles. With the exception of 115 Regiment at Bachy, the few French and Belgian Troops seen had obviously not been in fighting trim. However, it had been believed that all would be well when the Franco-Belgian frontier was reached and that a stand would certainly be made there on the Gort Line – to the fortification of which the battalion had devoted six arduous months of work. As has been related, the battalion was only in that line for a few hours before it was taken out and withdrawn towards the coast to fight an enemy advancing from the rear.

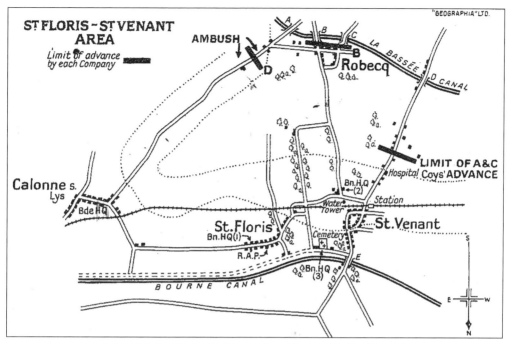

Map 16.6 St-Floris – St-Venant Area. (Source: *The Red Dragon*)

As dawn broke on 24 May, the battalion advanced once again towards
its objectives, the four bridges across the La Bassée Canal. A and C **24 May 1940**
Companies on the right made good progress, brushing aside the slight opposition they
met on the way. They reached the small town of St-Venant, found it to be clear of the
enemy, and proceeded on towards the bridge which was their objective. C Company
searched many houses, took prisoners and captured a large amount of road transport. This
transport included about eighteen huge lorries, with trailers attached, which were loaded
with motorboats and lighters for towing. They were an example of the thoroughness of
the German preparations and of the way they brought all their equipment well forward.
Second Lieutenant T.A.A. Jones with his platoon of A Company contacted a post of 1st
Royal Berkshires some distance to the other side of the canal. He reported that the Royal
Berkshires had been under very heavy fire, but, owing to the lack of maps, were only able to
give the vaguest of descriptions as to their position. They must, however at this time have
been lying very well back on the right flank of the battalion advance. A Company passed
through C and moved on up the road, but was soon held up by heavy machine-gun and
mortar fire about half a mile beyond the town and, because of the flatness and openness of
the country, was unable to work its way round the enemy's position. Unable to advance, and
taking casualties, the men dug themselves in.

B Company, on the left, was even less fortunate. The company's route led through the village
of Robecq to the remaining three bridges beyond. Casualties occurred, including Second
Lieutenant P.C.R. Carrington and Sergeant Harding wounded, but good progress was made
and, after an advance of about 400 yards, when the company was close to the village, the enemy

withdrew. It appears that these troops were from the SS *Verfügüngs* Division (later re-formed as *SS-Das Reich*)[85] and that this was the first time that an S.S. unit had been driven from its positions. Sergeant M. Lee later reported on these events, saying: 'When we were well inside the village, we encountered strong opposition from the enemy and we had great difficulty in dislodging them. We succeeded however by dusk.'[86] A house-to-house search revealed the place to be empty. The advance was then continued towards the bridges but, as soon as the leading troops were clear of the houses they came under intense hostile machine-gun fire against which no progress could be made. A careful reconnaissance by Captain J.R. Johnson, the company commander, confirmed him in his opinion that it was useless to try and advance further without support. Sergeant Lee again reported that:

> ... at a point South of St-Venant we successfully ambushed an enemy transport column numbering about nine trucks, a number of the enemy were killed and wounded, and we took about fifteen prisoners ... we then proceeded to push on but we encountered strong opposition from the enemy some 300 yards up the main road...[87]

In order to hold on to what had been gained, active preparations were at once put in hand to fortify the village. While these were going on, in the late morning and early afternoon, parties of the enemy could be observed infiltrating round the flanks. Unavailing attempts were made to obstruct this movement by the fire of L.M.Gs, but by 15.00 hrs the enemy had effectively surrounded B Company in the village and were digging a line of weapon pits across the return route to St-Floris.[88]

1 R.W.F. was in a perilous position. A and C Companies, unable to make any progress towards their final objectives and finding their position in the open untenable in the face of increasing machine-gun and mortar fire, began to withdraw in small parties. The original intention had been to retire on St-Venant and to form a strong defence line on the outskirts of the town, but many of the men, without maps and with no clear idea where they were, withdrew to St-Floris, from where they had started in the morning. Both companies suffered very heavy casualties: among them, Second Lieutenant A. Ll. Bowen was killed and Lieutenant W.P.D. Skillington severely wounded. Although most of the wounded were successfully evacuated, some had to be left behind at St-Venant, where they were placed in the care of the nuns of the local hospital[89]

In the meantime Lieutenant Colonel Harrison had brought Battalion Headquarters up to the outskirts of St-Venant, only to discover that the remnants of A and C Companies had passed through the town on their way back and were now at St-Floris. He at once sent the indefatigable Major Owen back to bring them up again and placed the reorganization of H.Q. and D Companies in the hands of Captain Willes, who had returned from a reconnaissance towards Robecq in a fruitless attempt to make contact with B Company. With the few men available, the Commanding Officer organized a new defence line, covering St-Venant and the bridge across the Bourne Canal, and as the various companies arrived, they were placed in the new line. All four companies were up, A on the right, then C, D, and H.Q. The left, or eastern, flank was known to be open, but it was thought that 1st Royal Berkshires were holding the area to the right. In the absence of any maps, however, it was impossible to know exactly where they were. Some artillery support was available, for on leaving Vieille Chapelle the battalion had been given the services of an F.O.O. complete with wireless Carrier, belonging to the 99th Field

German transport moving through St-Venant.

A German tank advances through St-Venant.

German infantry advancing on St-Venant.

An unidentified group on the banks of the
Lys looking towards the bridge at St-Venant.
(www.Delcampe.org)

The River Lys canal at
St-Floris.

The bridge at St-Venant,
badly damaged, with a
temporary German bridge
alongside.

Regiment, or Bucks & Berkshire Yeomanry. This was Captain Ambrose Awdry,* who went
with B Company to Robecq. Another F.O.O. from the same unit and also complete with wireless car, turned up during the morning. He was supposed to be with the Royal Berkshires, but
could not find them, so he settled down at Battalion Headquarters: this was Second Lieutenant
Peter Cave-Bigley.† His services were strictly limited, for he could only shoot his guns on occasions when he could borrow the one precious Battalion Headquarters map. The regiment was
equipped with Great War vintage 4.5-inch howitzers, rather than the modern 25 pdr, with a
maximum range of only 7,500 yards (6,800 metres).[90]

---

*   Ambrose Leonard Awdry was commissioned into the Territorial Army in June 1937 (*LG Supp* 3514,
     1 June 1937).
†   101033 Peter Jordayne Cave-Bigley was commissioned into the T.A. in October 1939 (*LG Supp*
     7170, 24 October 1939).

Casualties had been mounting across the battalion for although there had been no set piece attack, German guns and mortars had taken their toll. Casualties included W.O. III A.E. 'Buck' Evans, a former Pioneer Sergeant in both the 1st and 2nd Battalions, and Corporal Smithers, a well-known battalion character. But although the men were desperately tired after so long a succession of sleepless days and nights of continuous movement, and although they knew, too, that they were facing a desperate situation, the morale of the battalion remained remarkably high. With the coming of darkness, however, it was possible to take a better stock of the position. Contact was established with 1st Royal Berkshires on the right, though in doing so it became apparent that there was an ominously wide gap between the two battalions that could be covered neither by observation nor direct fire. During the night, too, 2nd D.L.I. was moved up on the battalion's left, covering the exposed flank. Although their arrival did not extend the line to the left, it gave some semblance of continuity to the thin defence around St-Venant, which alone stood between the enemy and the withdrawal route to Dunkirk over the Bourne Canal. This was the real significance of the position, even if the men there at the time did not realise it. Without the defence of the line by the 2nd Division, the fate of the troops at Dunkirk, waiting for evacuation, might well have been very different and the course of history changed.

Throughout the night the battalion continued to dig and to improve its defences. A shortage of tools and a complete lack of wire and anti-tank mines made it impossible, however, to do more than improvise. The work of digging went on steadily, but it was rather in the nature of a forlorn hope. It could be of little avail in the event of an attack by armour, and it was reasonably certain that it would be with the assistance of tanks that the final attack would come. B Company's defence at Robecq had certainly slowed the enemy and gave the battalion one more day in which to prepare for the inevitable. The day of 25 May passed slowly, for the men **25 May 1940** could do no more than sit and watch the German preparations. On the right the enemy worked an infantry gun and some heavy mortars close forward into the shelter of a large farm standing in a copse about 500 yards south-west of Battalion Headquarters. Opposite this farm, life was most unpleasant as the low trajectory shells came skimming along only a few feet above the ground. With the aid of the one map available, Cave-Bigley put a concentration into the farm using all available twelve field guns: 'I think the shelling had some effect', he reported later, 'though it was difficult to tell'.[91] Fortunately the German gunners, possibly suspecting an artillery O.P., turned their attention to the tank of a high water tower between Headquarters and the railway station, and thereafter life below became more normal. At this time, the battalion also lost the use of the second and last 3-inch mortar. In order to escape aerial observation, the crew went into action underneath a tree. However they went too far under and the first round struck a branch and the entire crew became casualties. On the whole, though, the day was ominously quiet, apart from the rumbling of enemy armour down to the south, obviously concentrating for the attack. The F.O.O. recalled later:

Two 2 pdr anti-tank guns were sited [just outside Bn HQ] facing to the left of the road to Robecq. The gun crews could see the German tanks that I was ranging 3–400 yards away, and they were itching to have a go themselves. The range was of course far too great but someone gave the order to engage. It was a bad decision because the 2 pdr shells at that distance had no effect, and within 5 minutes all Hell was let loose in our direction – German tank shells – machine guns and finally of course the inevitable mortar bombs.[92]

Continued but unsuccessful attempts were made to gain contact with the Royal Berkshires on the right flank and, as a precautionary measure, the Commanding Officer pushed out a platoon of C Company, to cover the southern end of the western outskirts of St-Venant.[93] It was all that could be done with the available men and the platoon sent out was no more than fifteen strong. Sergeant M. Lee of C Company later recalled that:

> ... We successfully ambushed an enemy column numbering about nine trucks, a number of the enemy were killed and wounded, and we took about 15 prisoners. We then proceeded to push on but we encountered strong opposition from the enemy some 300 yards up the main road leading to a place called Lillers... we were pinned down, and were subject to heavy small arms and mortar fire. After five hours it became obvious that the position could not be held much longer...[94]

At about 18.00 hrs, the Commanding Officer went to Brigade Headquarters for a conference. At this conference, the Brigade Commander stated that he was convinced that the enemy consisted of small and isolated detachments only. That was not the view held by the battalion, nor was it supported by the size and numbers of enemy movements already reported back. Brigade Headquarters therefore issued orders (later countermanded) for fighting patrols to go forward after dark along the roads to Robecq and the bridge there. Information was also given that the D.L.I. would move up after dark from brigade reserve and take up a position on the battalion's left flank.

As he had noted the ominous arrival of German tanks, Lieutenant Colonel Harrison asked permission to withdraw the battalion behind the Bourne Canal in order to use it as an effective tank obstacle. He was told by the brigade commander to stand firm in his present position, an order which made no sense at the time and makes even less with hindsight. At about 17.30 hrs on 25 May the enemy sent in an attack from the South-West which was repulsed. Two wireless messages were sent to Brigade Headquarters via the gunner O.P. wireless link; these messages described the situation in the village and a reply was received promising immediate help. Soon after the failure of their attack the Germans started accurate shelling and several direct hits were scored on buildings occupied by the battalion.

At dawn on Sunday morning, 26 May, following the arrival of the Brigade Commander at Battalion Headquarters, it was decided to send a **26 May 1940** strong patrol forward along the road to Robecq to try and re-establish contact with B Company. The acting brigadier, apparently, was still under the impression that there were only light mobile parties of the enemy in front and ordered the patrol to be motorised. Captain R.O.F. Prichard was placed in command of the patrol which consisted of a platoon in three 15-cwt trucks escorted by two *Bren* gun carriers. The patrol was hardly clear of the forward line when it came under heavy fire, including that of a German anti-tank gun firing straight down the road from a position near the road junction half-way to Robecq. The patrol withdrew in good order and was lucky to escape with light casualties.

Attention was now turned once more to the problem of the right flank. The Brigade Commander knew the location of the Royal Berkshires headquarters and took the Commanding Officer and the I.O. there in his car so that the two battalions could at last make contact. Both battalions, being short of maps, could only give a vague description as to their company locations. It seemed, however, that there was a considerable gap between the two units with the

Royal Berkshires lying back on 1 R.W.F.'s right. Either on this day or late on the previous one, an issue had been made of lithographed paper maps. These would have been excellent for a motor tour, but were of so small a scale and so lacking in detail that they were useless for tactical purposes.

While the Commanding Officer was away, Battalion Headquarters was heavily shelled. Headquarters was therefore temporarily moved to the shelter of a deep roadside ditch. Lieutenant Colonel Harrison, on his return, set out again to find a new position for the command post. This was established in a cemetery close to the Bourne Canal. The cemetery was an oblong enclosure with a gateway at the northern end from a metalled road running along the southern bank of the canal. About 100 yards to the east stood a farm, which was occupied by the D.L.I.'s battalion headquarters. To the west, about 150 yards away, the canal road joined a main road running north and south and which crossed the canal at a bridge; the Northernmost houses of St-Venant straggled on either side of the main road as far as this bridge. Between these houses and the cemetery there was a copse, the floor of which was chiefly swamp. It was clear that the enemy's observation over the whole St-Venant and St-Floris area was excellent and, in addition, they had the advantage of reconnaissance planes which droned undisturbed overhead, noting all the British dispositions and spotting for the artillery. The complete air supremacy of the enemy in this area had been emphasised earlier by the passage of ninety-two bombers, flying in formation, which had filled the western skyline before passing on.

During the morning enemy infantry was observed moving towards the La Bassée canal. They were engaged both by the *Vickers* guns of the attached Manchesters, and by the battalion's *Bren* guns. From early afternoon onwards, movement of enemy tanks could be seen to the front, crossing from the direction of Robecq village to an assembly area at the southern end of a long wood south-west of St Floris. This movement could not be seen by the crews of the 2.5 cm anti-tank guns down near the front line, but the tanks, as they crossed over in twos and threes, were fired on by the F.O.O. Two were knocked out, but the remainder got safely across to the shelter of the wood.

There was nothing now left for the depleted battalion to do but await the enemy attack which all knew was bound to develop. Attempts to establish communication with B Company were still without result, and the lack of knowledge of what was happening at Robecq was a depressing factor. In point of fact, B Company was approaching the end of its battle. Casualties had increased throughout the previous day, necessitating a continually contracting perimeter. In the evening Captain J.R. Johnson was seriously wounded in the throat and the command of the company devolved upon Second Lieutenant F.M. Edwards. With considerable skill and tenacity, he continued to organize the defence throughout the night, inflicting considerable casualties on the enemy whenever the opportunity occurred. But the end was in sight.

In the early hours of 26 May the Germans had put in an attack supported by one tank. It was held and driven back. An hour later a second attack was made with three tanks. Slowly B Company gave ground, but the enemy-dominated flat ground round the village offered no chance of an organized breakout. Calling the company together for the last time, Second Lieutenant Edwards split it up into small groups, each under the command of an N.C.O. or senior soldier. He showed the groups the general direction in which the battalion lines lay and ordered them to lie up for the rest of the day and to try to make their own way back individually under cover of darkness. What happened next was described later:

The company Sergeant-Major* was relieved of his command on the ground that he was drunk, and was replaced by a man who, through no fault of his own, had not been trained as a leader …† The first men had reached the line between the [German] posts [to the North of the village] which were about seventy-five yards apart, when the newly-appointed sergeant-major, believing they had already passed through the Germans, stood up suddenly and exclaimed: "This is a bloody waste of time!" What one man described as a "rabbit shoot" ensued. Most of the men were either killed or captured…"[95]

At 11.00 hrs on 26 May B Company, as a company, had ceased to exist.[96] Edwards was recommended for the Military Cross, but was recognised only by being later Mentioned in Despatches.[97]

None of this was known to the Commanding Officer, of course. During the afternoon a machine-gun platoon of 2nd Argyll & Sutherland Highlanders arrived and was attached to the D.L.I. to help with the left flank. The Commanding Officer also decided that St-Floris was too exposed for the Quartermaster, the R.A.P. and the transport and ordered them to cross over at dark via the bridge at St-Venant and find themselves a billet a short distance in rear. The night which followed passed without incident, Lieutenant Colonel Harrison going round the forward areas at about midnight

The battalion was by now in a very weakened state. A Company, for example, had been reduced to two platoons of fifteen men each, B Company **27 May 1940** no longer existed, and the other companies were in little better shape. Support came from two machine-gun platoons, five 2.5 cm anti-tank guns and one troop of three guns of the Bucks & Berkshire Hussars. Yet, even in this predicament, there was still one overriding consideration. Every hour that the enemy could be held from the bridge over the Bourne Canal meant one hour more of freedom to get the B.E.F. back along the road to Dunkirk. So the battalion stood firm with the rest of the 2nd Division in its precarious positions with, behind them, the Bourne Canal and the one remaining bridge over it.[98] At dawn on 27 May, therefore, everyone was on their toes. Captain Prichard of A Company sighted a large German patrol and, collecting a *Bren* gun and some men from the D.L.I., destroyed it. The German patrol consisted almost entirely of Officers and N.C.Os, of whom fifteen were killed. On the body of a dead Officer a map and complete orders for the intended enemy attack were found. These, together with a wounded prisoner, were sent back to Battalion Headquarters and by them, immediately forwarded on to the brigade commander. Further to the right of the line, D Company was also active and, a little later, captured a German Officer with a duplicate set of orders and another map. These were also sent on to Brigade Headquarters by despatch rider.

The Commanding Officer was now in possession of the complete enemy plans. 6 Infantry Brigade was facing the whole of the German 3rd *Panzer* Division, with two *S.S.* Divisions, one on either flank.[99] Zero hour was to be at 08.00 hrs. The attack was to be a frontal one by tanks, supported by infantry. The boundaries were known and also the avenues of approach. This knowledge was of little avail to the two battalions, however. Their final dispositions had been dug in, so far as possible, and could not be altered. Fortunately the enemy's intentions, in

---

*   W.O. II T.R. Cutler.
†   W.O. III G. Davies 49.

the main, followed on anticipated lines. Lieutenant Colonel Harrison was under no misapprehension as to the probable fate of his battalion, but he kept his own counsel. In a confidential talk with Major Owen, he expressed his confidence in the ability of the battalion to maintain its position against an infantry attack, but added that a heavy tank attack would be a different matter.[100] Owen was so affected that, as one witness recalled, he called the Commanding Officer 'Harry', something he would never normally have done even though they had known each other for many years. Harrison was right: a German *panzer* division in 1940, when at full strength, mustered 120 tanks of all types in its *panzer* brigade, fifteen mortars, twenty-two artillery pieces, a *Stuka* squadron, and 178 light and medium machine-guns mounted in vehicles or carried by the *panzergrenadier* brigade.[101]

A vicious concentration of shell fire at 08.00 hrs on the 27th heralded the attack. As it ceased, and the smoke and dust rolled away, the German armour could be seen approaching in waves. The first wave, of six tanks, was directed against A Company, which was covering the 2nd Argylls' machine-gun platoon. The few anti-tank rifles left to the battalion were knocked out early in the action, and the tanks rolled onward and over the forward positions, although the Argylls cut the German infantry down in swathes. For the next two hours the fighting was confused and piecemeal. A Company, after a most gallant fight against impossible odds which held up the enemy for over an hour, was finally surrounded in a small farm and taken prisoner, their O.C., Captain Prichard, with them. Prichard was subsequently awarded the Military Cross for bravery.[102] Captain E.C. Parker-Jervis, commanding C Company, was killed early on, and his company, which began the action no more than forty strong, overwhelmed. Further to the right D Company, crouching in their inadequate cover, were faced with annihilation or withdrawal. The Company Commander, Second Lieutenant Kemp, crossed over to C Company to ask Parker-Jervis's advice, but the latter was too busy fighting his own company to be of much help. On his return, Kemp found German tanks within 150 yards and decided to withdraw behind the railway embankment which he hoped might prove to be a tank obstacle. The withdrawal was effected with considerable casualties, Second Lieutenant F.A. Ewart-James being among those killed. The railway embankment as a tank obstacle proved ineffective, and Kemp decided to send what remained of the company back to Battalion Headquarters; he himself remaining to assist the wounded. Eventually, less than fifteen men of this company, including wounded, reached the canal area to take part in the subsequent fighting there. Amongst the wounded was W.O. III (PSM) H.J. Jenkins, who was trundled along in a wheelbarrow.

The canal bank position was held by the H.Q. Companies of 1 R.W.F and 2nd D.L.I., along with the machine-gun platoon of 2nd Manchesters. 1 R.W.F.'s anti-aircraft L.M.Gs had been dismounted and moved into a copse to the west of the cemetery so as to be able to play their part in the ground battle. Outside the cemetery on the south, west and east sides were roughly dug trenches held by perhaps a dozen men in each. On the road which ran between the North, or rear, end of the cemetery and the canal was Battalion Headquarters itself, consisting of about four Officers and some signallers, and clerks. On hundred and fifty yards along the road, to the east, the D.L.I.'s command post remained in its farm. On either side of the position, from the canal bridge on the right and the farm on the left, the canal bent slightly towards the rear, a factor which was to have an effect on the fighting.

After the forward companies had been overwhelmed, German armour rolled on towards the canal bank position. These tanks were armed with a small calibre quick-firing gun of great penetrative power, their shells easily piercing walls and, in some cases, emerging on the far side of the buildings. The canal bank position was defended by one 2 pdr anti-tank gun. This was sited in rear of the D.L.I. farm so as to cover the left flank. It shared the fate of the other guns in being knocked out soon after it got into action.

The D.L.I. Headquarters were early in trouble in this second phase of the fighting. From the cemetery, it could be seen that they were suffering many casualties and that enemy tanks had got behind them on the left flank and were shooting them up from the rear.[103] On returning from a visit to check on the anti-aircraft L.M.Gs, Major Owen was told by Lieutenant Colonel Harrison that some men had been seen crossing the canal bridge towards the rear. He was ordered to take the post at the head of the bridge and stop any further withdrawals. On arrival at the bridge, he found it to be under a close fire from an enemy machine-gun, situated 150 yards to the west, on the south bank of the canal. During the next ten minutes, one or two men came down the street from St-Venant, having got away after the forward position had been over-run by the enemy. They were positioned in a sort of trellis-work of heavy timber near the bridge, and did their best to suppress the machine-gun, the fire of which was in danger of making the bridge impassable.

At about 09.15 hrs the Brigade Commander came up from the rear and ran across the bridge. Major Owen briefed him on all that had happened and told him that a frontal tank attack was at that moment coming in. The Brigadier then went along the canal bank to 1 R.W.F.'s command post. After hearing the Commanding Officer's appreciation, he said, in substance: 'I leave it to you as to when you withdraw. D.L.I. to get out first, covered by the R.W.F. Afterwards cover the engineers whilst they demolish the bridge, and then get back to rear Brigade H.Q. where you will be put into a new position. Pass this information on to the D.L.I.'[104] The Brigade Commander then left. On passing Major Owen he told him the outline of the orders which he had given the Commanding Officer and ordered him to get what men he could across the bridge and put them into the huddle of cottages on the far bank of the canal, so as to cover the crossing of the remainder.

As soon as the Brigade Commander left, the Commanding Officer sent the gist of what the Brigadier had said to the D.L.I. by runner and radio. He next sent a runner for Captain Clough-Taylor, O.C. H.Q Company, from the cemetery and then ordered Corporal Jones to take the two remaining *Bren* carriers across the bridge and to position them near the cottages so as to help to keep the enemy fire down from the flanks. Meanwhile Major Owen at the bridge had started to send men across in twos and threes to establish themselves in the cottages and in the open nearby. Shortly afterwards, he crossed himself, to discover that both the cottages and the open ground around were under a heavy double enfilade machine-gun fire from enemy established on the canal banks on both flanks.

When Captain Clough-Taylor reported to Lieutenant Colonel Harrison, he was told to collect what remained of his men, take them down to the head of the bridge, and there try to subdue the fire from the German machine-gun on the canal bank further to the west. It was about this time that the Adjutant, Lieutenant J.E.C Hood, was killed whilst using an anti-tank rifle in the cemetery. The German tanks were now very close, almost within a stone's throw. Captain Clough-Taylor succeeded in collecting about fifteen men, including CSM G. Mantle and ORQMS H.G. Godfrey, and with them worked his way down a ditch to the head of the bridge.

The situation which confronted the remnant of the battalion was that the D.L.I. farm was surrounded by enemy tanks and it was obvious that the D.L.I. could not last long. 1 R.W.F was about thirty to forty strong. Of these, perhaps half were with the Commanding Officer at the southern, or enemy, end of the bridge, while the remainder were with Major Owen in the cottages at the northern end. Both these groups were subjected to tank gun fire and to intense machine-gun fire. The flat ground to the north, across which any withdrawal must take place, was also swept by enemy machine-gun fire.

At the bridgehead, after a short pause so as to allow any strays to turn up, the Commanding Officer ordered Clough-Taylor to get his men across the bridge in twos and threes. The bridge had no parapets and they did not escape without casualties. Amongst these was ORQMS Godfrey who subsequently died of his wounds. Lieutenant Colonel Harrison and Captain Clough-Taylor were the last to cross. Clough-Taylor later recalled what happened:

> I stood like some grim P.T. instructor in the middle of the road launching each man on his perilous journey with a shout of "Next, go!" They had to run the gauntlet over the bridge, which was being literally plastered with fire from stationary tanks down the road. I saw many stagger and fall as they ran. Martin, my trusty servant, had his arm blown off.
>
> At last it was my own turn. I summoned courage, waited for a burst of fire, and dashed forward. I was only a yard or so on the bridge when I was hit in the leg … I recoiled, and staggered crazily back to the culvert. As I stood thinking wildly how I would get across alive, I noticed there were girders, rising to about a foot in height in the centre, above the roadway. How I wished I had seen them before. I flung myself down, and caterpillaring madly along behind one of them arrived miraculously on the other side. I got up, and was at once hit again in the arm and hip. I staggered to the shelter of some houses.[105]

As the men had come back in twos and threes, they had been collected by Major Owen, formed into sections under an N.C.O., pushed into a roadside ditch, and set off on a long crawl across the fire-swept ground towards the R.V. given by the Brigade Commander.

When all were clear of the bridge, the enemy tanks had nearly reached the far end. The Commanding Officer then gave orders for the bridge to be blown, and it was found that the sapper demolition party was no longer there. The party had been seen about fifteen minutes earlier, but whether it had withdrawn or become casualties is not known. The one certain thing was that the bridge could not now be destroyed and that there was nothing to prevent the enemy tanks from following the remnant of the battalion over the canal. Clough-Taylor again:

> I heard Harry Harrison shouting: "Why the hell don't they blow the bridge?" I thought vaguely that if they did, they would undoubtedly blow me [up] too, as I was only 20 yards away. But I was past caring … The next thing I heard was an unmistakable German voice. I was horrified. [Then] I saw … the first of about two dozen tanks, which, after hesitating at the bridge, rolled triumphantly past.[106]

The leading German tank showed a strange hesitancy about crossing the bridge. Possibly the crew suspected a trap or perhaps were incredulous of the fact that the defenders now had no anti-tank weapons with which to oppose them. In any case, there was an appreciable pause which enabled another section to be despatched down the ditch. At last, the tank rolled forward across the bridge. Every weapon which the enemy could bring to bear was now firing on the cluster of cottages. The tanks, once over the canal, made short work of the few remaining defenders.[107] In the last flurry of disorganised fighting, Lieutenant Colonel Harrison met his death by a burst of machine-gun fire, fired at short range. Soon the enemy tanks were deployed on either flank, going forward across the open ground.[108] A letter from Captain Clough-Taylor said this of Harrison:

> He was extraordinarily cheerful during those endless marches back from Belgium, and when we stopped his first thought was always the comfort of others, however tired he was himself. He had a wonderful way of instilling fortitude into those around him. When the end was near, he stood in the road, outwardly calm, and with no thought for his own safety, under an absolute hail of bullets from tanks & M.G.s, directing the formation of a bridgehead. When I spoke to NCOs and Fusiliers in the hospital afterwards, our first words were always of the magnificent example which the Colonel showed during those last few minutes.[109]

When all resistance appeared to be over, Major Owen, with two runners and two men who were waiting to form the next section, dropped into the ditch and began a difficult passage to the north. They were the last to leave. German tanks were ranging the open ground on either side and one was firing up the road from the place they had just left at some stationery vehicles further up the road. These proved to be a blazing ammunition lorry of the Manchesters' machine-gun platoon, and a wrecked Carrier.

The farm turned out to be the R.A.P. It was filled with wounded soldiers on whom Lieutenant A.R. Lundie, the R.M.O, with some stretcher bearers and the Padre, the Reverend G.R. Miller, were working. The building had been under fire for some hours. The wrecked Carrier, one of the last two remaining with the battalion, had come back loaded up with wounded. While standing outside the farm it had been hit by an anti-tank shell: CSM Mantle, on the Carrier, had been killed and the R.M.O., who was talking to him, had a narrow escape. Captain Lundie was subsequently awarded the Military Cross and the Reverend Miller was mentioned in despatches.[110] Bandsman A.V. Bailey, a medical orderly, was awarded the MM.[111] Lieutenant Bent, the Quartermaster, who had managed to get clear with the first line transport, got his command back to Britain and was recommended for the MBE, but was recognised only by being later mentioned in despatches.[112]

Because the farm was under the protection of the Red Cross it could not be used as a fighting position. The second wave of the enemy tanks were now halted parallel with the farm and the voices of their crews could plainly be heard. It was hoped, by keeping quiet, to escape notice and that after dark such of the occupants as could move would have a chance of rejoining the British forces further north. However in the early afternoon, German infantry surrounded and entered the farm.

Those members of the battalion who were taken prisoner had a melancholy satisfaction in noting the state of the roads immediately behind the German leading troops, as detailed in the account of Captain J.E.T. Willes's experiences after his capture at St-Venant. Willes was recommended for the Military Cross for his many acts of bravery during the campaign, but was recognised only by being later mentioned in despatches:[113]

> I was with Mike Kemp (Second Lieutenant M.J.B. Kemp) when we were marched back through St-Venant. Some of the German tank crews spoke to us and relieved me of some of my cigarettes. They behaved very correctly and I was impressed by the number who could speak English. On the outskirts of St-Venant on a road leading South I saw on the side of the road a burnt-out 15-cwt truck and by the side of it my valise with my service

A German photograph showing a group of British prisoners captured around St-Venant and Robecq, including men of 1 R.W.F. (Author's collection)

A German photograph showing British prisoners being marched away at St-Venant.

British prisoners at St-Venant; the R.W.F. shoulder title is clearly visible.

dress jacket, greatcoat and blankets. I bent down to pick up my greatcoat and was smartly kicked up the backside by a German Warrant Officer and ordered to put it back as it was now German property. At this point it was noticed by the German that Mike Kemp was wearing a German pullover, and he was accused of taking it from a German prisoner. Somehow we managed to explain that it was taken from a German Quartermaster's lorry which we had captured. An ugly situation over, we were marched approximately 18 miles South. We were most impressed by the enormous amount of German equipment we passed – tanks, anti-aircraft guns, self-propelled guns and the like. At the end of the march we were put into lorries and driven all the way back from whence we came. We were billeted for the night in a château with a lot of French Officers. Here I met Robin Prichard (Capt R.O.F. Prichard) and other R.W.F. Officers who had been captured. It was a great relief to see them.

Next day we set off for a nearby station and were invited to help carry the French Officers' suitcases. Most of them had two, one filled with clothes, the other, as we subsequently discovered, was crammed with British compo rations. We politely declined. We were herded into cattle trucks which were already half filled with empty 4 gallon petrol cans. The fumes were intolerable; the French Officers were even more so. We had been given no rations for the journey, the destination being Mainz, and it was to take 24 hours. At meal times, out came the French suitcases, our rations were produced and, with a cloth placed over the suitcase, they had a most civilized meal. Nothing was offered to us. Later in the day we halted at a station, I think it was in Belgium, and the locals started passing loaves of bread through the small windows at the top of the trucks. Luckily we controlled the windows and, although the French Officers fought like maniacs to get to the window, not a loaf of bread did they get.

At Mainz we were put into an old prison where we were able to get a shower and a shave by a German. Two days rest, then into cattle trucks once again for a eight hour journey to Laufen in Bavaria. For this journey we were given a large sandwich which we consumed fairly quickly. The journey was punctuated by long stops in sidings and an unnecessary journey to another Laufen somewhere else in Germany. We eventually arrived at the correct Laufen, having take 48 hours with no food or water other than the original sandwich.

Exhausting and demoralising as these journeys were for those who were unwounded, the plight of those who were wounded was ten times worse, as the account by Captain Clough-Taylor outlines, following the moment when German tanks rolled past him as he lay wounded by the bridge in St-Venant:

… in a moment a German Officer was standing over me with his automatic close to my face. He appeared to be considering whether to finish me off, but decided against it and instead put a few questions to me in stilted English. "Why are you fighting us?" and then, "The English fought bravely". Having expressed these sentiments, he lit one of my cigarettes and walked off. Some time later I was bundled into an ambulance and taken to what I imagine was a Field Dressing Station where my wounds were roughly bandaged and I received an anti-tetanus injection. Then I was moved on to a temporary hospital in a school at St-Pol. This place was full to capacity with both English and French wounded, and when I arrived I was put into a small chapel with a thin layer of straw on the stone flags. There was a continuous chorus of cries and groans, and the smell was unbelievable. Food was very short. We got a small bowl of macaroni at midday, and a hunk of black bread and lard completed our ration for the day. I could not keep down either of these. Nights and days swam by. The only people who came near us were two nuns who extinguished the three candles when night fell. The dirty bowl of macaroni was filled once a day.

Jimmy Johnson [Captain J.R. Johnson] suddenly turned up one day and talked to me for a few minutes. He had been shot through the neck while commanding B Company South of St-Venant and he was now full of plans to escape. He succeeded, and was to become the only Officer in the Regiment who made his way back to England. He is an example to others of the proved maxim that the sooner you attempt an escape after capture the more likelihood of success there will be. For this escape he was awarded the MC.

I have many unpleasant memories of those early days of capture which are best forgotten. I had many operations and narrowly missed losing my leg. It was saved for me, as were the limbs of many others, by a magnificent French doctor who worked day and night amongst the hundreds of wounded (it was estimated that there were 900) with the assistance of one RAMC doctor, Major O'Meara. The latter was also a wonderful man who managed to make us all feel less sorry for ourselves by his splendid spirit and example. There were also several of the local inhabitants who worked ceaselessly and bravely amongst us. Three of them I remember particularly well. The Comtesse d'Hauteloque and her twelve-year-old daughter who came from the neighbouring château, and also a delightful cockney wife of a French soldier. The kindness of these three is another and pleasanter memory of those dark days.[114]

No 4188640 Bandsman K.W. Bateman had served as a medical orderly with the battalion and was taken prisoner on 25 May.* He later escaped and recalled in his debriefing, confirming what Captain Willes had said, that:

We ultimately de-trained [after four days] and had to march many miles until we arrived at Stalag XXA Prison Camp in Poland. On that march we were badly treated, many Officers and men were shot because they were unable to keep up, owing to hunger and fatigue. The French prisoners were always given preference to the English, and at halts when we had "food", the French were allowed always to go to the front, and the English were kept in the rear. At one halt, a Scottish Officer went up to the German Officer in charge, and asked if the English could not be put in front for a change. The German Officer remarked "insubordination", and shot the Scottish Officer on the spot.

… I escaped on 18th October 1940. It was a very small camp, and the latrines in the corner were higher than the barbed wire, and the lights were not shining on that particular part … I waited for the sentry to come close to where I was, when he did, I jumped on to his back, and with a brick, I bashed his head until he stopped twitching.[115]

---

* Bateman's escape is further chronicled in Annex Q.

viii. Dunkirk and After

A few of the men from A and C Companies, who had withdrawn beyond St-Venant, made their way back to Haverskerque, where 6 Brigade Headquarters was situated. Two days later some of the men whom Major Owen had sent back before the German tanks crossed the Bourne Canal joined them there. With what was left of the brigade they withdrew to La Motte,[116] being engaged by elements of enemy armour on their way. The remnants of B Company had split into three groups to try to get out as best they could. One group, which included Sergeant E. Jones 59, Corporal H. Wright, and Fusiliers B. Lloyd 86 and G. Owen 98, made for Douai. Lloyd was killed in an ambush but the others made it through, put on plain clothes and dispersed. Wright eventually reached Nice in Vichy France, where he was interned.[117]

Early on 28 May came the news of the surrender of the Belgian Army, which had been holding the left flank of the Allied line between Ypres and the sea, and its capitulation, after an unequal struggle, left an undefended gap which threatened with extinction the whole of the British and French forces in the north. By the great gallantry of a troop of British armour and with the aid of the guns of the Royal Navy, the advancing enemy was held up sufficiently for most of the British and French units engaged to withdraw within the defensive perimeter of Dunkirk and the neighbouring beaches.

The brigade column, containing the few remaining men of 1 R.W.F. who had escaped from the actions of the Bourne Canal, was attacked fiercely from the air during its withdrawal, which became a slow and painful process along roads blocked with abandoned transport, saved probably only by Hitler's order to halt offensive operations from 26 to 28 May. On the 28th it began a move to Poperinghe. En route, French artillery, horse transport and motor vehicles became intermingled with the column, blocking the road: 'The French eventually cut the traces of their horses and deserted their vehicles. All efforts now concentrated on clearing the route.'[118] Late on the 29th, the column reached Bergues and beyond there, the remaining motor vehicles were dumped in the Colne Canal and progress continued on foot. The brigade group finally reached the beaches at Bray Dunes on 30 May.[119] The situation in and around Dunkirk was recalled by one wounded veteran:

> I could see squadron after squadron of bombers dropping their loads on the town, the A.A. fire having little effect. Even the dockside seemed to shake as the bombs exploded … As the town received this attention, Stukas started to circle above the docks. One by one they peeled off from the circle and dived straight towards the docks, their fixed undercarriages like the talons of an eagle. As they came near the screams from the planes increased, then the bombs were let loose. The bombs could be seen coming nearer and nearer. At the end of the dive the plane would pull up … Seventy times they dived downwards … This was impossible, where the hell was the R.A.F. There were no German fighters in the skies, but there was not a British fighter to be seen.[120]

Sergeant J.C. Bennett, attached to the Brigade Headquarters, recalled of Dunkirk that:

> It was being shelled, strafed and bombed continuously. We joined the queue on the beach and after about four days wait, my group had reached the water's edge. After what seemed a very long wait in this spot, I was picked up in a small boat and put into a larger vessel

in the harbour ... When the boat docked [in England], the first passengers to leave were the wounded who were on stretchers followed by the walking wounded. Everything was done in an orderly and disciplined fashion.[121]

The remnants of the brigade were taken off during the next two days, but among them were pitifully few of 1 R.W.F. The majority either lay dead or wounded in the area of St-Venant, where their truly heroic defence had held up the enemy for two precious days and contributed in no small measure to the safe withdrawal of so many of their comrades in the B.E.F. Some were prisoners, even now on their way eastward, to face long years of frustration in prisoner-of-war camps:[122] the story of what happened to those taken prisoner is continued in the Annex on Prisoners of War. But their sacrifice had not been in vain: by the time

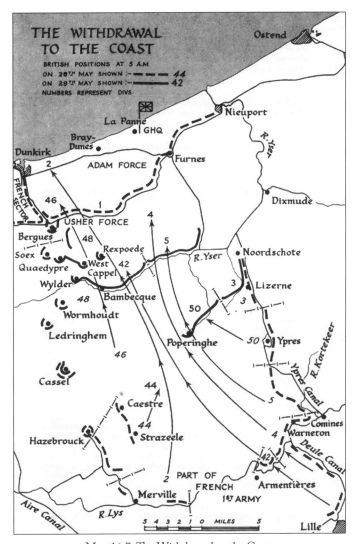

Map 16.7 The Withdrawal to the Coast.

that the battalion's positions had been over-run, more than 7,000 troops had already been evacuated from Dunkirk, twenty miles (32 kilometres) to the north and by the following day this figure had risen to more than 25,000. Four days later it was more than a quarter of a million.

* * *

There were members of the battalion not present at the final destruction of the St-Venant position. As well as those with B Echelon, there were returning leave details. During the period 17–20 May, all 2nd Division leave details were formed into a composite battalion under Major R.C.M. Barber of the Cameron Highlanders. No 3 Company, under Captain Bickford of the

Royal Berkshires, was formed chiefly from men of 6 Infantry Brigade, with one platoon of Royal Welch, one platoon of Royal Berkshires and one platoon of R.A.S.C. and other service corps.[123]

On the morning of 22 May, No 3 Company was sent to St-Omer to hold crossings over the Bergues – Furnes Canal and the Canal de Bergues. The Officer Commanding reported that he had 'No Bren guns or anti-tank rifles, 50 rounds of ammunition per man only … We had no picks or shovels, grenades, mines, wire, or medical appliances; nor had we any means of communication within the company in the form of wireless sets etc.'[124]

The R.W.F. platoon under an un-named Sergeant – probably Sergeant J. Gibbon – was ordered to defend the bridge over the Canal de Bergues at St-Momelin, just north of St-Omer; after it moved off, commu-nication was lost with the platoon.* On 24 May the Germans appeared in strength and Bickford reported hearing firing from St-Momelin, and later saw 'many

Fusilier George Griffiths and the 1st Battalion flag. (R.W.F. Mus 1396)

wheeled and track vehicles on the road to St-Momelin'. By the morning of 25 May, Bickford's company had been dispersed; he himself with a small party escaped the Germans, only to be arrested by the French, who robbed them and then took them to Bergues, where they joined a force under Lieutenant Colonel C.M. Ussher. Here, he reported meeting 'a number of Royal Welch Fusiliers, and also some of our party who had made their way back.' However, 'I never discovered what happened to the platoon of Royal Welch Fusiliers at St-Momelin, nor did I know the name of any one who was in that party'.[125]

Some joined a composite force formed at No 1 Infantry Base Depot in Rouen under Lieutenant Colonel L.E.C.M. Perowne *R.E.*, known as 'Vicforce', or 'Perowne's Rifles'.[126] These included Lieutenant St Clair Forde; after thirty-two days, this small force was evacuated with the 1st Armoured Division, having crossed the Somme at Neufchatel and moved south.

Another group under W.O. III Lewis attempted to get to the coast from No 1 Infantry Base Depot. They were captured by the Germans near St-Valery, but soon got away from their captors. One of these, Lance Corporal T. Owen 20, recalled the events:

> Somewhere North of Neufchatel the party in which I had been placed was approached by German tanks and motor-cyclists, and some of us were taken prisoner. We were rounded up by the motor-cyclists and taken in a Red Cross lorry to a field marked out as "Kriegsgefangenelage", where we were interrogated very informally by a German padre … His English was poor and I, acting as spokesman for the lot, gave no information … We marched for 2 days in the direction of Amiens, passing through Formerie and Poix. At

---

*   Some of the men were killed and buried in the C.W.C.G. cemetery at St-Omer. They were: Sgt J. Gibbon; Cpl J.L. Evans 10; Fus A. Evans 64; Fus H. Williams 29

this point LEWIS and myself, together with two others, decided to escape. There were no guards on the left hand side of the road, and when we were close to a village, which we believed to be SOUES, three of us (not Sgt. Maj. LEWIS) slipped through a gap in the hedge and ran down a small bank, where we lay hid until the column had passed by... [127]

Owen eventually slipped through the German lines to Paris and from there, with the help of the resistance to Marseilles, and then to Geneva. After many adventures he eventually reached England in March 1942.

* * *

Those of the battalion who came back from Dunkirk were concentrated in Yorkshire, with Headquarters set up in Huddersfield. In small parties, as they landed in England, they were sent north, arriving over the next few days. A battalion roll-call, held a week later, revealed that no more than five Officers and 263 Other Ranks had returned. Among them was Fusilier H. Griffiths, who somehow had managed to find and preserve the battalion's flag, which remains in the Regimental Museum's collections.[128] It should be recorded that in addition to the three DCMs and two MMs already noted, Fusilier J.R. Thomas was awarded the MM for his actions at Dunkirk;[129] and also that twelve Officers and men were mentioned in despatches.[130] These, who are recorded in the Annex dealing with honours and awards, included the Commanding Officer who was mentioned posthumously – the only award for bravery possible for a Lieutenant Colonel in command under the rules as then applied, apart from the Victoria Cross.

* * *

That Astonishing Infantry, first edition, by Michael Glover, states that by the end of the fighting in Belgium and France in May 1940 'the 1st Battalion had suffered 759 casualties'.[131] It is impossible to see how Glover was able to quote such a precise figure. He may have arrived at it by reference to *The Red Dragon*, subtracting those who returned to Britain from the numbers who fought with 1 R.W.F. This works out as follows:

Number who fought (*Red Dragon*)[132]	1000
Number returned to U.K. (War Diary)[133]	268
Estimated Casualties	732

The difference between Glover's 759 and the figure of 732 may have been twenty-seven Officer casualties. The total of 759 casualties cannot, however, be correct because, although the 268 who returned to the U.K. is, as far as can be verified, correct, the number who fought with 1 R.W.F. could not have been '1000-odd'. The strength returns in the war diary give the following:

Rank	Str	Date	Remarks
Officers	29	5 May 1940	
O.Rs	711	7 April 1940	The last O.Rs return in the diary
Total	740		

The original war diary for most of April did not survive the battles around Dunkirk, so the figure of 711 O.Rs may have increased by 10 May. It could not, however, have increased by over 250 to arrive at a total of about 1,000. Based on the last strength returns quoted above and the 13 June returned to U.K. figures, the 1st Battalion casualties would appear to be:

	Officers	ORs	Total
Strength	29	711	740
Returned to U.K.*	10	263	267
Casualties	19	448	473

This casualty total could have been made up as follows:

Killed	115	Accurate figure based on names
Wounded to U.K.	?25	An estimate. Most wounded men were probably taken prisoner
Prisoners	c.325	Numbers from depot nominal rolls
TOTAL	c.465	
Survivors	263	
GRAND TOTAL	728	

This figure of 465 is getting near to that quoted in the 1 R.W.F. war diary for 14 June 1940, which states that 'casualty list was compiled and sent to Records. 490 Other Ranks were reported missing'. It seems likely, therefore, that the total casualties were about 500, rather than the 759 given by Glover.[134]

There is inevitably a comparison to be drawn with the events of the opening months of the Great War in 1914. Then, the 1st Battalion, having shipped from Malta, landed on 7 October 1914 at Zeebrugge, at a strength of 1,150 men – of whom 342 were reservists – and joined the 7th Division.[135] During the First Battle of Ypres, 1 R.W. Fus had been ordered to advance eastwards from Ypres. In spite of reaching Dadizeele on 19 October it had to retreat to Zonnebeke with the loss of 177 men. No more than 400 men strong on the 20 October, it was almost annihilated by a German attack to the west of Zandvoorde where it was reduced by casualties to only ninety all ranks. Its Commanding Officer, Lieutenant Colonel H.O.S. ('Hal') Cadogan, was among those killed. By 31 October only thirty men and a Quartermaster Sergeant were still alive and unwounded in 1 R.W. Fus.[†] A final action took place at Zillebeke on 7 November.[136]

---

*   The War Diary and the Glover History totals include 10 Officers, some of whom were wounded:

Capt A.H. Williams	Lt O.H. Owens
Lt W.P.D. Skillington	2Lt J.D. Willans
Lt A.N.B. Sugden	2Lt A.C. Dolbey-Jones
Lt J.L. King	2Lt D.J.O. Thomas
Lt (QM) A.G. Bent MM	2Lt P.C.R. Carrington

Another seven Officers attached to different units also returned to Britain. They were:

Maj A.D.M. Lewis	Lt the Hon R.S. Best
Lt J. St Clair Ford	Lt A.G. ff Powell
Lt G.A. Tolhurst	2Lt D.J. Sidders
2Lt P.R. Glynne-Jones	

†   This was the official abbreviation used during the Great War, later amended to R.W.F.

The battalion's losses at this point amounted to thirty-seven Officers and 1,024 men, of whom twenty-two Officers and 796 men were either dead or had become prisoners of war.

Killed or PoW (incl wounded)	918
Wounded and evacuated	131
TOTAL	1,019
Survivors	31
GRAND TOTAL	1,150

A government report, published in 1922, summarised the losses of the B.E.F. in 1914.[137] The effect on the Army was dramatic, for in the opening months of the war, a huge number of professional Officers and N.C.Os were killed, badly wounded, or taken prisoner with the consequent effect on the efficiency of the Army. These losses were clearly felt in 1 R.W. Fus then, for the battalion had to be rebuilt almost from scratch. The same dramatic effect was again felt in 1940.

STAFF LIST, 1 R.W.F., FRANCE AND BELGIUM SEPTEMBER 1939–May 1940[138]

Appointment	Name	Remarks
Battalion HQ		
Commanding Officer	Lt Col H.F. Garnons-Williams	Killed in aircraft crash 10 Nov 39
	Lt Col H.B. Harrison MC	C.O. 11 Nov 39. Killed 27 May at St-Venant
Senior Major	Major H.B. Harrison MC	C.O., 11 Nov 39
	Major D.I. Owen	2IC 11 Nov 39; PoW 27 May at St-Venant
Adjutant	Lt W.L.R. Benyon	To I.T.C. Chester, 30 Nov 39
	Lt J.E.C. Hood	From 1 Dec 39. Killed 27 May at St-Venant
Intelligence Officer	Lt W.P.D. Skillington	From 14 Dec 39
	Capt J.E.T. Willes	PoW 27 May at St-Venant
Quartermaster	Lt A.G. Bent MM	Returned to U.K.
French Liaison Officer	Sgt Sous Chef M, Janvier	PoW 27 May at St-Venant
Medical Officer	Lt A.R. Lundie *R.A.M.C.*	PoW 27 May at St-Venant
Chaplain	Rev G.F. Miller *R.A.Ch.D.*	PoW 27 May at St-Venant
Regimental Sergeant Major	W.O.I S.M. Sherriff	PoW 27 May at St-Venant
R.Q.M.S.	R. Gendall	Returned to U.K.
O.R.Q.M.S.	CSgt H.G. Godfrey	Wounded 27 May at St-Venant. Died 28 May
	Sgt J. Walker *R.A.O.C.*	
Provost Sergeant	Sgt J. Gibbons	Killed 23 May
Headquarter Company (1–6 Pls)		
Officer Commanding	Capt W.S.A. Clough-Taylor	7 May 40. Wounded, PoW 27 May at St-Venant
Signal (No 1) Platoon	Capt Hon R.S. Best (later Lord Wynford)	To 5 S.G. 14 Feb 40.
	2Lt J.L. King	Wounded 25 May St-Venant. Returned to U.K.
A.A. (No 2) Platoon	2Lt J.L. King	To Signal Platoon 14 Feb 40.
	W.O. III Smith 05	

Mortar (No 3) Platoon	Capt R.O.F. Prichard	To O.C. A Coy 16 May 40.
	Sgt R.C. Farmer	
Carrier (No 4) Platoon	2Lt J.B. Garnett	From 10 Nov 39. Killed 24 May at St-Floris
	Sgt E. Jones 59	Missing
Platoon Sergeant	Sgt F.T. Spilstead	Killed 24 May at St-Floris
Pioneer (No 5) Platoon	W.O. III A.E. Evans 44	Killed 26 May near St-Venant
Admin (No 6 Platoon)	Lt J.E.T. Willes	M.T.O. to 1 Nov 39
	Lt A.G. ff Powell	M.T.O. from 1 Nov 39
	Lt O.H. Owens	M.T.O. c. Mar 40. Returned to U.K.
	W.O. II Caldwell	Master Cook.
Brigade Anti-tank Platoon*	Lt J.E.C. Hood	Adjt 1 Sep 39
	Lt A.N.B. Sugden	From 1 Sep 39. Wounded 27 May at St-Venant; returned to U.K.
	W.O. II R. Hayward	Returned to U.K.
Company Sergeant Major	W.O. II G. Mantle	Killed 27 May at St-Venant
C.Q.M.S.	CSgt Freeman	Returned to U.K.
Armourer Sergeant	Sgt H. Wells *R.A.O.C.*	Returned to U.K.

A Company (7, 8, 9 Pls)

Officers Commanding	Major O.T.M. Raymont	Wounded 15 May at Ottenburg. Died 16 May
	Capt A.H. Williams (7 R.W.F.)	O.C. 15 May. Wounded 15 May at Ottenburg. Returned to UK
	Capt R.O.F. Prichard	O.C. from 16 May. PoW 27 May at St-Venant
Second in Command	Capt A.H. Williams (7 R.W.F.)	O.C. 15 May
Platoon Commander	2 Lt T.A.A. Jones	PoW 27 May at St-Venant
Platoon Commander	2 Lt A. Ll. Bowen	Killed 25 May at St-Venant
Platoon Commander	2 Lt J.D. Willans	Returned to U.K.
Platoon Commander	W.O. III (PSM) W. Anders	From 15 Nov 39. Returned to U.K. K.i.A. Burma 18 Mar 43
Platoon Commander	W.O. III (PSM) Pepper	To I.T.C. 15 Nov 39
Company Sergeant Major	W.O. II Pritchard	Returned to U.K.
	W.O. II F. Wheeler	
Attached	Lt D.F. Jones	From 10 R.W.F., 4 Jan – 22 Feb 40.
	Lt R.L. Boyle	7 Mar 40.

B Company (10, 11, 12 Pls)

Officers Commanding	Capt J.R. Johnson	Wounded 25 May and PoW 26 May at Robecq; escaped to U.K.
	2 Lt F.M. Edwards	OC from 25 May. PoW 26 May at Robecq
Second in Command	2 Lt F.M. Edwards	O.C. 25 May
Platoon Commander	2 Lt P.C.R. Carrington	Wounded 25 May at St-Floris. Returned to U.K.

*   Anti-tank guns were not issued directly to the infantry battalion until later in the war. During the campaign in France, each infantry brigade included an anti-tank company of three platoons, each platoon equipped with three 22 mm guns – around 1 pdr – provided by the French, or in some cases British 2 pdrs; one such platoon was usually attached to each battalion, manned by personnel drawn from that battalion.

Platoon Commander	2 Lt D.W. Llewelyn*	PoW 26 May at Robecq
Platoon Commander	W.O. III (PSM) G. Davies 49	To CSM 25 May
Platoon Commander	W.O. III (PSM) E. Turvey	PoW
Platoon Sergeant	Sgt E. Harding	Missing
Platoon Sergeant	Sgt N. Lloyd 27	
Platoon Sergeant	Sgt A. Griffiths 46	Missing
Platoon Sergeant	Sgt H. Higgs	Missing
Platoon Sergeant	Sgt D. Hogan	Missing
Company Sergeant Major	W.O. II H. Cutler	dismissed June 1940
	A/W.O. II G. Davies 49	PoW 26 May at Robecq
C.Q.M.S.	Sgt J. Jones 22	Missing

C Company (13, 14, 15 Pls)

Officer Commanding	Capt E.C. Parker-Jervis	Killed 27 May at St-Venant
Second in Command	Capt R.O.F. Prichard	O.C. A Coy 16 May
Platoon Commander	2 Lt D.J.O. Thomas	Wounded 25 May at St-Venant. Returned to U.K.
Platoon Commander	2 Lt A.C. Dolbey-Jones	Returned to U.K.
Platoon Commander	Lt W.P.D. Skillington	To I.O. 14 Dec 39. Severely wounded 25 May at St-Venant. To U.K.
Platoon Commander	Lt A.H. Williams	14 Dec 39, from 7 R.W.F. To 2ic A Coy.
Platoon Commander	W.O.III T. Nash	PoW
Platoon Commander	W.O.III A. Jones 57	
Platoon Sergeant	Sgt M. Lee	Returned to U.K.
Platoon Sergeant	LSgt L.D.P. Evans DCM	
Platoon Sergeant	Sgt D. Griffiths 82	
Company Sergeant Major	W.O. II F. Whitley	Wounded 19 May at Tournai. Returned to U.K.

D Company (16, 17, 18 Pls)

Officers Commanding	Capt A.J. Lewis	Killed 19 May at Tournai
	Lt R.L. Boyle	O.C. from 19 May. Killed 24 May St-Floris area
	2 Lt M.J.B. Kemp	O.C. from 24 May. PoW 27 May at St-Venant
Second in Command	Lt R.L. Boyle	O.C. 19 May
Platoon Commander	2 Lt M.J.B. Kemp	O.C. 24 May
Platoon Commander	2 Lt F.A. Ewart-James	Killed 27 May at St-Venant
Platoon Commander	2Lt D.H. Sidders	Returned to U.K., on battalion strength return June 1940
Platoon Commander	W.O. III (PSM) H.J. Jenkins	Wounded and PoW 27 May at St-Venant
CSM	W.O. II C. Williams 01	?
CQMS	CSgt Durman	Returned to U.K.
Platoon Sergeant	Sgt Harding	
Platoon Sergeant	Sgt Stiff	To I.T.C. 15 Dec 39
Attached	Lt R.F. Beale	From 4 R.W.F., 4 Jan – 22 Feb 40.

---

*   Desmond Wilkinson Llewelyn (1914–1999) was later a successful actor. He is best remembered for having played 'Q' in seventeen of the *James Bond* films between 1963 and 1999. See his autobiography, *Q* ((Seaford, 1999).

Second Echelon/1st Line Reinforcements (Rouen)

No1 Base Depot Comdt	Capt G.N.H. Taunton-Collins	
	Lt the Hon R.S. Best	Waiting to rejoin. Returned to U.K. via Cherbourg
	Lt G.A. Tolhurst	Returned to U.K.
	Lt – Stonehurst *Cheshire*	31 Dec 39.
	W.O. II A. LePoideven	

Detached

Town Major	Maj A.D.M. Lewis MBE	Returned to U.K.
Bde Anti-Tank Officer	Capt R.F.A. David	Wounded 25 May at Calonne. Returned to U.K.
Bde M.T.O.	Capt W.S.A. Clough-Taylor	To 7 Mar 40.
	Capt A.G. ff Powell	7 Mar 40. Returned to U.K.
Regimental Band	B.M. H.G. Perdue	

Unplaced

Capt T.A.G. Pritchard	Special Reserve. Shown as det to I.T.C. 5 Feb 40.
Lt H.G. Brougham	To H.Q. 2 Inf Bde 20 Mar 40; PoW 26 May 40
Lt C. Griffiths	Evacuated sick 22 Jan 40; returned to U.K.
2Lt W.J. Griffiths	Tfr to R.A.S.C. 22 Apr 40
2Lt P.R. Glynne-Jones	Returned to U.K., on battalion strength return June 1940
2Lt J.R. St Clair Ford	From I.T.C. 9 Mar 40; joined Vicforce and returned to U.K.
W.O. III (PSM) J.A. Lewis	PoW
W.O. III (PSM) Whelan	
W.O. II A. Le Poideven	
Sgt J. Gibbon	Killed near St-Omer, 23 May
Sgt D. Griffiths	Killed near Calonne, 29 May
Sgt J.C. Neale	Killed 28 May 40
Sgt White	H.Q. Coy. To I.T.C. 15 Nov 39
Sgt T.J. Jones DCM	
Sgt W. Morgan DCM	
Sgt A.E. Sharpe	

Notes

1   Major L.F. Ellis, *The War in France and Flanders 1939–1940* (Official History of the Second World War, HMSO, London, 1954), p. 19.
2   *The Memoirs of Field Marshal the Viscount Montgomery of Alamein, K.G.* (London, 1958), p. 44.
3   *Memoirs of Field Marshal the Viscount Montgomery,* p. 45.
4   *A Short History of the Second Infantry Division 1809–1954* (Revised 1958) privately printed in B.A.O.R.; no page numbering.
5   T.N.A. WO 167/843, 1 R.W.F. War Diary 18 September 1939–30 June 1940.
6   J.L. King, F*arewell to Flanders* (unpublished memoir in R.W.F. Mus/Archives), p. 4.
7   T.N.A. WO 167/843.
8   *A Short History of the Second Infantry Division,* no page numbering.
9   1 R.W.F. Op Order No 1 dated 5 Oct 39 in T.N.A. WO 167/843.
10   T.N.A. WO 167/843.
11   King, p. 14.

12 1 R.W.F. Op Order No 1 dated 5 Oct 39 in T.N.A. WO 167/843.
13 T.N.A. WO 167/843.
14 Ellis, *Official History*, pp. 19–22.
15 1 R.W.F. Op Order No 1 dated 5 Oct 39 in T.N.A. WO 167/843.
16 Ellis, *Official History*, p. 21.
17 King, p. 4.
18 Notes by Lieutenant (later Lieutenant Colonel) P.C.R. Carrington, R.W.F. Mus L/2655/144.
19 King, p. 5.
20 T.N.A. WO 167/843.
21 Written by Fred Cliffe, George Formby and Harry Gifford; Lyrics © EMI Music Publishing.
22 T.N.A. WO 167/843.
23 *The Red Dragon*, p. 14.
24 King, pp. 9–11.
25 T.N.A. WO 167/843.
26 Ellis, *Official History*, p. 20; *A Short History of the Second Infantry Division*, no page numbering; *Memoirs of Field Marshal the Viscount Montgomery* p. 52.
27 T.N.A. WO 167/843.
28 King, p. 61.
29 T.N.A. WO 167/843; *A Short History of the Second Infantry Division*, no page numbering.
30 T.N.A. WO 167/843.
31 T.N.A. WO 167/843.
32 For more details on 5 S.G. see David Erskine, *The Scots Guards, 1919–1955* (London, 1956); and Jonathon Riley, *From Pole to Pole: the life of Quintin Riley* (Cambridge, 1998).
33 T.N.A. WO 167/843; www.measuringworth.com accessed 26 July 2015.
34 J.L. King, *Farewell to Flanders* (unpublished memoir, R.W.F. Mus, no date given), p. 1.
35 T.N.A. WO 167/843.
36 Ellis, *Official History*, p. 23.
37 *Memoirs of Field Marshal the Viscount Montgomery*, p. 52.
38 T.N.A. WO 167/843.
39 King, pp. 7–9.
40 T.N.A. WO 167/843.
41 'The Story of the 1st Battalion, Royal Welch Fusiliers Friday, May 10th – Monday, May 27th, 1940'.
42 *The Red Dragon*, p. 15.
43 Ellis, *Official History*, p. 36.
44 'The Story of the 1st Battalion, Royal Welch Fusiliers Friday, May 10th – Monday, May 27th, 1940'.
45 King, p. 25.
46 King, p. 21.
47 *The Red Dragon*, p. 15.
48 Ellis, *Official History*, pp. 39–42.
49 King, p. 25.
50 Ellis, *Official History*, p. 46.
51 'The Story of the 1st Battalion, Royal Welch Fusiliers Friday, May 10th – Monday, May 27th, 1940'; King, p. 25.
52 T.N.A. WO 167/843.
53 *LG* 22 October 1940, 3 September 1940.
54 *The Red Dragon*, p. 20.
55 King, p. 31.
56 Ellis, *Official History*, p. 60.
57 Ellis, *Official History*, pp. 59–62.
58 King, p. 24.
59 Desmond Llewelyn, *Q* (Seaford, 1999) p. 48.
60 King, p. 24.
61 Ellis, *Official History*, pp. 66–75.
62 'The Story of the 1st Battalion, Royal Welch Fusiliers Friday, May 10th – Monday, May 27th, 1940'.

63   'The Story of the 1st Battalion, Royal Welch Fusiliers Friday, May 10th – Monday, May 27th, 1940'.
64   King, p. 43.
65   King, p. 45.
66   King, p. 46.
67   'The Story of the 1st Battalion, Royal Welch Fusiliers Friday, May 10th – Monday, May 27th, 1940'.
68   King, p. 51.
69   'The Story of the 1st Battalion, Royal Welch Fusiliers Friday, May 10th – Monday, May 27th, 1940';
     T.N.A. WO 167/843, 1 R.W.F. War Diary May 1940.
70   'The Story of the 1st Battalion, Royal Welch Fusiliers Friday, May 10th – Monday, May 27th, 1940'.
71   King, p. 61.
72   T.N.A. WO 167/843, 1 R.W.F. War Diary May 1940.
73   *The Red Dragon*, p. 25.
74   T.N.A. WO 167/843, 1 R.W.F. War Diary May 1940.
75   'The Story of the 1st Battalion, Royal Welch Fusiliers Friday, May 10th – Monday, May 27th, 1940'.
76   King, p. 70.
77   'The Story of the 1st Battalion, Royal Welch Fusiliers Friday, May 10th – Monday, May 27th, 1940'.
78   King, p. 71.
79   T.N.A. WO 167/843, 1 R.W.F. War Diary May 1940.
80   *LG* 20 December 1940.
81   Statement by No 4178034 Cpl H. Wright in R.W.F. Mus/Archives/Dunkirk Missing.
82   *LG* 22 October 1940.
83   T.N.A. WO 167/843, 1 R.W.F. War Diary May 1940, amended by Capt J.E.T. Willes.
84   *Short History of the Second Infantry Division*, no page numbering.
85   Hugh Sebag-Montefiore, *Dunkirk. Fight to the last man* (London, 2006), p. 528; *German Order of
     Battle 1944: Directory, Prepared by Allied Intelligence* (London, 1994), p. F8.
86   MC/OR/14401 (Casualties) dated 25 January 1943 in R.W.F./Mus 42a.
87   MC/OR/14401 (Casualties) dated 25 January 1943 in R.W.F./Mus 42a.
88   'The Story of the 1st Battalion, Royal Welch Fusiliers Friday, May 10th – Monday, May 27th, 1940'.
89   *The Red Dragon*, p. 30.
90   Letter from Cave-Bigley dated 28 April 1987 [R.W.F. Mus 656].
91   Cave-Bigley, R.W.F. Mus 656.
92   Cave-Bigley, R.W.F. Mus 656.
93   T.N.A. WO 167/843, 1 R.W.F. War Diary May 1940.
94   Statement by Sergeant M. Lee in R.W.F. Mus/Archive/Dunkirk Missing.
95   Sebag-Montefiore, *Dunkirk*, pp. 293–294.
96   T.N.A. WO 167/843, 1 R.W.F. War Diary May 1940.
97   *LG* 29 November 1945.
98   Ellis, *Official History*, pp. 175–176.
99   Sebag-Montefiore, *Dunkirk*, p. 528.
100 'The Story of the 1st Battalion, Royal Welch Fusiliers Friday, May 10th – Monday, May 27th, 1940'.
101 www.niehorster.org, accessed 24 July 2015.
102 *LG* 29 November 1945.
103 T.N.A. WO 167/843, 1 R.W.F. War Diary May 1940.
104 'The Story of the 1st Battalion, Royal Welch Fusiliers Friday, May 10th – Monday, May 27th, 1940'.
105 Sebag-Montefiore, *Dunkirk*, pp. 294–295.
106 Sebag-Montefiore, *Dunkirk*, p. 295.
107 Ellis, *Official History*, pp. 188–189.
108 'The Story of the 1st Battalion, Royal Welch Fusiliers Friday, May 10th – Monday, May 27th, 1940'.
109 Letter from W.S.A. Clough-Taylor extracted from 2 R.W.F. War Diary, 15 July 1941. There is no
     indication as to whom the letter was addressed.
110 *LG* 29 November 1945.
111 *LG* 22 October 1940.
112 *LG* 29 November 1945.
113 *LG* 29 November 1945.

114 This document (R.W.F. Mus 2816) was compiled in the late 1950s with the intention of incorporating it into the regiment's World War II history, *The Red Dragon*. This did not, however, happen. There are two versions – the first is a manuscript, headed '2nd Rewrite' which is in two or three hands, one of which (pages 5–10) is that of Major F.M. Edwards. This narrative is an expanded version of a later (1959) typescript, which is headed in manuscript 'Appendix G'.

115 'My Experiences as a Prisoner of War, and my Escape from Germany by No 4188640 Bandsman Bateman K.W., Royal Welch Fusiliers.' in R.W.F. Mus/Archive.

116 T.N.A. WO 167/843, 1 R.W.F. War Diary May 1940.

117 Statement by No 4178034 Cpl H. Wright in R.W.F. Mus/Archives/Dunkirk Missing.

118 T.N.A. WO 167/843, 1 R.W.F. War Diary May 1940.

119 T.N.A. WO 167/843, 1 R.W.F. War Diary May 1940.

120 King, pp. 99–100.

121 J.C. Bennett, *Memoirs*, pp. 42–43.

122 *The Red Dragon*, p. 35.

123 R.C.M. Barber, 'Action of Leave Details, 2 Div, During the Period 17/30 May.' (R.W.F. Mus/Archive).

124 Bickford's report attached to 'Action of Leave Details, 2 Div'.

125 Bickford's report attached to 'Action of Leave Details, 2 Div'.

126 T.N.A. WO 167/1403.

127 Statement by No 197320 Lance Corporal Owen, Thomas, Royal Welch Fusiliers, 311 I.T.C., Chester.

128 'Henry Swam For It' (Griffiths' Obituary), *Warminster Journal* 15 August 1997, p. 13.

129 *LG* 3 September 1940.

130 *LG* 20 December 1940.

131 *That Astonishing Infantry*, 1st Edition, p. 191.

132 *The Red Dragon*, p. 35, states 'no more than five Officers and 263 Other Ranks had returned, all that remained out of the 1,000-odd who had fought in Belgium and France'.

133 This figure of 5 Officers and 263 Other Ranks comes from the war diary for 13 June 1940.

134 1st Bn The Royal Welch Fusiliers – Casualties 1940, A Note by Lieutenant Colonel R.J.M. Sinnett. See also the Roll on Honour compiled for this Volume.

135 C.H. Dudley Ward, *Regimental Records of the Royal Welch Fusiliers, Volume III, 1914–1918* (London, 1928).

136 See the account in Henry Cadogan, *The Road to Armageddon* (Wrexham, 2009).

137 *Statistics of the Military Effort of the British Empire during the Great War 1914–1920* (War Office, March 1922).

138 This list is based on one compiled by Captain J.E.T. Willes whilst a prisoner in Oflag VII C (R.W.F. Mus 2816). Additional information is taken from *The Story of the 1st Bn Royal Welch Fusiliers, Friday May 10th – Monday May 27th 1940*, published in *Y Ddraig Goch* Winter 1954, Summer 1955, Winter 1955 and Summer 1956. Data also from Major P.C.R. Carrington's notes on 1 R.W.F. 1939–1940 (R.W.F. Mus L/2655/144).

Chapter 17

101st Light Anti-Aircraft & Anti-Tank Regiment R.A. with the 1st Armoured Division in France, May–June 1940

Based on the accounts by Jonathan Ware, the regiment's War Diary and *The Red Dragon*

As the B.E.F. fell back from Belgium, German armoured columns raced for the coast, placing a wedge between the British Army and the bulk of French forces and threatening to surround the B.E.F. To reinforce French forces holding the line of the Somme, the 51st (Highland) Division was withdrawn from the Maginot Line and the 1st Armoured Division was ordered to France.[1]

The 1st Armoured Division, commanded by Major General R. Evans,[*] had two armoured brigades: 2 Armoured Brigade, consisting of the 2nd Dragoon Guards (Bays), 9th Lancers, and 10th Hussars; and 3 Armoured Brigade which consisted of the 1st, 2nd and

The badge of the 1st Armoured Division.

3rd Battalions of the Royal Tank Regiment. Although 2 Brigade was designated 'Light' and 3 Brigade as 'Heavy', both were identically equipped with a mix of light and cruiser tanks. 101st Regiment formed part of the Divisional Support Group under Brigadier F.E. Morgan.[†] This Group also contained two motorized infantry battalions, 1st K.R.R.C. and 1st R.B., and an engineer company. The division had no organic field artillery, no bridging equipment, few support units of any kind and a chronic lack of spare parts, ammunition and medical support. Insufficient shipping was available to transport the division all together, and 2 Brigade was moving inland while 3 Brigade was still at sea. It was never possible therefore for Major General Evans to fight his division *as a division*.

On 8 May 101st Regiment was ordered to mobilise and move to the continent for immediate service with the B.E.F. The advance party under Captain A.C. Bedborough moved to Southampton on 11 May, followed on 14 May by the M.T. party consisting of eleven Officers and 337 men, with twenty-four 2 pdr guns, 197 vehicles

8–16 May 1940

---

[*]   Major General Roger Evans CB MC (1886–1968).
[†]   Later Lieutenant General Sir Frederick Edgworth Morgan KCB (1894–1967), Chief of Staff C.O.S.S.A.C. 1943–1944 and Deputy C.O.S. Allied Expeditionary Force 1944–1945.

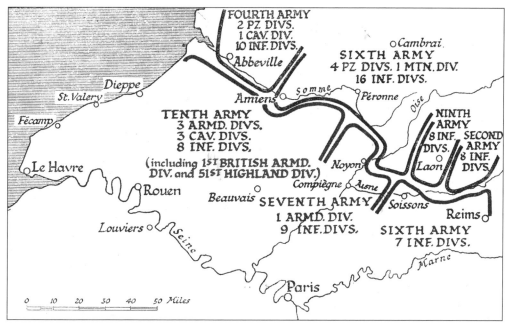

Map 17.1 1st Armoured Division Area of Operations, France, May–June 1940.

and forty-three motor-cycles, under Second Lieutenant N.D. Wardrop. At Southampton, they embarked on the M.T. *Tynwald*. The main body was inspected with the rest of the 1st Armoured Division's Support Group by The King and Queen at Blandford on 14 May; it then moved to Southampton on 16 May when the balance of eighteen Officers and 437 men embarked on the SS *Duke of Argyll*.[2]

The regiment assembled at Le Havre on 17 May and moved immediately thirteen miles (20 kilometres) north-east to Fauville-en-Caux; on the 21st it moved again to Les Andelys on the Seine, via Rouen, a distance of nearly sixty miles (100 kilometres). The B.E.F. was by now heading for Dunkirk and Guderian's *panzers* were driving westwards along the north bank of the Somme. North-south communication would therefore be lost unless vital crossing points over the Seine and then the Somme could be secured. The motor

8–14 May 1940

Major J.R.O. Charlton MC and Drum Major Jones, 101st L.A.A. & A.T. Regiment, 1940. (R.W.F. Mus)

battalions and 3rd R.T.R. had however been detached from the divi-   **24 May 1940**
sion to secure the port of Calais, leaving the division with few ground-
holding units. So it was that by 24 May, R.H.Q. 101st Regiment was deployed to defend five
road and rail bridges over the Seine. The deployment was as follows:

Bridge Site	Batteries responsible	Lewis A.A. guns	2 pdr anti-tank guns
Pont de l'Arche	44, 237	16	4
St-Pierre-la-Garenne	43, 237	12	4
Les Andelys	44, 237	16	6
Courcelles-sur-Seine	44, 239	12	4
Vernon	43, 239	16	4

The Germans had already, however, captured the key town of Abbeville further north on
the Somme and the plan was impracticable before it was launched. When 2 Armoured Brigade
crossed the Seine and moved north to attack the Germans on the Somme, they met well dug-in
infantry with plenty of tank support, and were repulsed with loss.

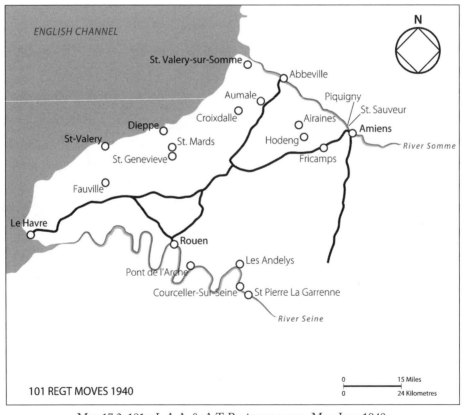

Map 17.2 101st L.A.A. & A.T. Regiment moves, May–June 1940.

On 25 May, with the situation changing rapidly, the regiment was moved **25 May 1940** north to a harbour area where it joined 2 Armoured Brigade. With the brigade, the regiment moved on later that day to Airaines where it was reinforced by an infantry battalion, 4th Battalion the Border Regiment. That night it was reported that the Germans had crossed the Somme at Picquigny and St-Saveur, just west of Amiens. 2 Armoured Brigade was ordered to counter-attack to secure an area in the suburbs of Amiens and thus contain the German bridgehead, a move which was to be supported by the two anti-tank batteries of the regiment.

All British formations south of the Somme were assigned to the Tenth French Army. These consisted of the 1st Armoured Division, which had already lost a third of its strength; 51st (Highland) Division, which was holding a sixteen-mile (25 kilometre) section of the front inland from the coast; and a scratch division of nine battalions scraped together from lines of communication and labour units, known as Beauman Force.

Over the next few days **26 May 1940** the regiment was increasingly redeployed as 1 Support Group was sent to assist 51st Highland Division, testing all ranks as they repeatedly dug in and sited the guns, only to redeploy hours later. On 26 May, Second Lieutenant B. MacGillycuddy was reported as the 101st Regiment's first fatality* and Second Lieutenant M. Martin was taken prisoner on the same day along with six Other Ranks. They were avenged in no short

Lieutenant Colonel B.D. Cameron DSO MC in France, 1940.
(Author's collection)

order the next day by 43 Battery which downed a *Dornier* bomber with *Lewis* gun fire – a remarkable feat of shooting.[3]

On 28 May, R.H.Q. was ordered to Fricamps with the batteries in the **28 May 1940** surrounding area. On the 29th the regiment moved again, to Hodeng and on the 30th to Croixdalle, on a circuitous route via Rouen, where contact was established with Brigadier F.E. Morgan and the rest of 1st Armoured Division Support Group. Here, the anti-tank batteries were deployed in all-round defence. Gunner A. Walsh later recalled that:

> We took up positions here, anti-tank guns dug in, and waited for the [enemy's advance.] During our two weeks here we were bombed heavily by dive-bombers; our guns made contact with forward German elements: our first fight. We knocked out some light armoured vehicles, but could not stop the heavy tanks with our light anti-tank guns."[4]

---

*   Although the War Diary clearly notes he died of wounds on 26 May, according to C.W.G.C. he died on 21 June.

Major L.H.H. Payne found it impossible to exercise operational control of his dispersed unit, but heard on 1 June that eleven 40 mm *Bofors* guns had **1 June 1940** landed in Cherbourg in Normandy; these he made immediate efforts to secure, successfully, and they were issued to Major Hardy's 44 Battery; however they came with no spare parts or ammunition. Hardy, by some means, obtained 1,500 rounds of 40 mm ammunition from 11 Anti-Aircraft Battery and at last engaged enemy aircraft with a good prospect of success.

On 4 June, while the regiment dug in, the evacuation from Dunkirk was wound up. On 5 June, Payne was succeeded by Lieutenant Colonel B.D. **5 June 1940** Cameron, and he became Second-in-Command of the regiment. With Chaplain H. Key, he repeatedly visited all the forward positions as best he could; Key was well known by the men and was motivated by unflagging zeal and concern for the welfare of the men of the regiment, taking cigarettes, mail and words of encouragement to those in the most exposed positions, often under fire. Key set a remarkable example for the men to follow, winning the Gunners' admiration.[6]

Major J.R.O. Charlton's 239 Battery first saw action against enemy armour at Aumale on 7 June. Charlton was pre-war Territorial from 5 R.W.F. and **7 June 1940** it was here that he first earned a reputation for going up into the thick of the fighting in order to support his gun detachments. A strong German attack developed on the battery's front and when enemy armour pressed too closely, Charlton oversaw the staged redeployment of the 2

Two photographs of a section of 4 Border, grouped with 101st Regiment in France, 1940. (King's Own Border Regiment)

An abandoned tank of the 1st Armoured Division in France, June 1940. (Author's collection)

A detachment of 43 L.A.A. Battery in France, 1940. (Author's collection)

pdrs and aided his detachments in the fight against enemy armour. Both batteries destroyed several tanks, but they were pushed back towards the coast and in this confused situation, both Cameron and Payne were captured. After deliberating with the other batteries, Major Charlton assumed de-facto command of the regiment and decided to withdraw towards St-Valery with the 51st Highland Division.[5]

10 June proved to be the decisive day of the campaign. After spending the night with 237 Battery near St-Mards and 239 Battery stationed around St Genevieve, Major Charlton received orders at 14.30 hrs to proceed to Fauville-en-Caux by 19.30 hrs. He sent out Captain Hardy and Second Lieutenant M.R.M. Steele-Mortimer to recce the route; both men were captured whilst doing so.[6] At 18.30 hrs, Major Charlton heard that enemy armour was advancing towards St Genevieve and at 18.45 hrs, Second Lieutenant H.W.E. Cleaver's Troop of 237 Battery made contact and engaged the enemy. Cleaver's men in effect sacrificed themselves to allow the rest of 1 Support Group to evacuate. Realising the likelihood of encountering enemy reconnaissance elements and having to fight their way through to St-Valery, Charlton placed 239 Battery at the head of the column, using their 2 pdrs to clear infantry positions blocking progress around key road junctions. He was, however, ultimately forced to split the column and allow smaller groups to try to infiltrate through the enemy positions.[7]

10 June 1940

During this action, Charlton instructed Second Lieutenant N.D. Wardrop to hold the rear with ten men from 237 Battery. Acting as infantry, they relied on two machine guns, a *Bren* and a *Lewis*, and Wardrop ordered them to turn their position into a strong point, hoping that Charlton would return. Until then they would hold their ground. After repelling a German infantry attack at 18.00 hrs that evening, the enemy having reached within 20 yards of their position, Wardrop acquired some more men and attempted to clear a path through a nearby wood:

> We were then heavily shelled and a direct hit killed 4 and all the rest wounded. Machine gun fire was very bad from the tanks on the other side … So we decided to shift them. Peter Walker led an attack along the front, but all the men were killed and he was taken prisoner.[8]

The regiment withdrew in a series of small packets, all of which encountered German opposition. Against all odds and fighting much of the way, the remnants of the regiment made it to St-Valery where Major Charlton deployed the handful of remaining 2 pdrs and then managed to arrange the evacuation of his men by sea. Major General Evans had realised that the situation was hopeless and there were strong rumours of an impending French surrender. 3 Armoured Brigade was able to withdraw to Cherbourg, where it loaded onto ships and was successfully evacuated. 2 Armoured Brigade made for Brest in Brittany where it too was evacuated, although much of its equipment had to be abandoned.

Some men from 101st Regiment were able to board vessels at St-Valery and set off for England: Charlton, who was subsequently awarded the Military Cross, was determined to save as many as possible, staying behind himself to ensure this happened.[9] Lieutenant Wardrop managed to bring fifty men from his earlier position and this group made its own way towards St-Valery, coming across Second Lieutenant R.W. Hinchcliffe who helped establish a roadblock with abandoned lorries. Wardrop was soon afterwards hit by a mortar bomb and Hinchcliffe was left in command. Eventually, as St-Valery burned, Hinchcliffe made contact with Major Charlton: the two fought a series of lively if one-sided actions against the advancing Germans. The two later became separated but Hinchcliffe was killed.[10]

After the surrender of the 51st Highland Division on 12 June, Lieutenant Wardrop managed to make his way down to the beach with four men and **12 June 1940** the *Lewis* gun. Here they boarded a grounded French gunboat, making a last stand against the Germans for some hours with the *Lewis* gun, until enemy fire hit the magazine and the vessel exploded. Only Wardrop and one man survived to be taken prisoner when they reached the shore.[11]

B Echelon, under the command of Lieutenant A.T. Currie, managed to reach Brest with 2 Armoured Brigade, where its remaining vehicles were destroyed in order to deny them to the enemy. During the period 15–18 June three Officers, including Chaplain Key, and 200 men embarked for Britain.[12] Although woefully short of equipment, 43 and 44 Batteries in total claimed forty-seven enemy aircraft destroyed with an additional sixty probable kills. Information on 237 and 239 Batteries' efforts remain sketchy but it is clear at the very least seven tanks were definitely destroyed,[13] but with the loss of all vehicles and equipment.[14]

B Echelon 101st L.A.A. & A.T. Regiment awaiting evacuation at Brest, June 1940. (Author's collection)

Thirty Officers and 780 men had embarked with the regiment for France; when the final accounting was made it was found that during the short campaign, twenty Officers and 365 men had been captured, including the Commanding Officer, the Second-in-Command, the Adjutant, three out of four battery commanders and all the battery captains. Two Officers and thirty-two men were killed or died of wounds; and one Officer and eighty men were missing: either dead, wounded or captured. When the regiment re-assembled in Britain, seven Officers and 303 men were found to have returned.[15]

The remnants of the regiment commenced re-formation at Longbridge Deverell in Wiltshire on 18 June 1940 under

B Echelon of 101st L.A.A. & A.T. Regiment embarks at Brest, June 1940. (Author's collection)

the command of Major J.R.O. Charlton. On 30 June it moved to Aldershot where on 6 July, Lieutenant Colonel J.D. Shapland MC took command. On the 26th, the regiment moved to a tented camp at Bramley, near Basingstoke, where it remained until it moved into billets for the winter on 28 September with R.H.Q. and 239 Battery in Godalming, Surrey; 237 Battery in Bramley; 43 Battery in Wonnersh, near Guildford; and 44 Battery in Blackwater, near Camberley.[16]

The task of re-forming and re-training the regiment was not made any easier by the very great shortages of equipment; for the first few weeks the regiment was issued with French 75 mm guns from the Great War.[17]

The composite nature of the regiment was brought to an end when separate anti-aircraft and anti-tank regiments were formed. R.H.Q. and the two R.W.F. anti-tank batteries were re-designated 76th (Royal Welch Fusiliers) Anti-Tank Regiment, R.A. at Godalming on 1 November 1940, 43 and 44 L.A.A. Batteries having been transferred elsewhere. The story of 76th (R.W.F.) Anti-Tank Regiment is continued in Part 2 of this Volume.

STAFF LIST, 101st L.A.A. & A.T. REGIMENT R.A., FEBRUARY–JULY 1940

Regimental Headquarters

Commanding Officer	Maj L.H.H. Payne	
	Lt Col B.D. Cameron DSO MC	5–7 Jun, PoW
	Maj J.R.O. Charlton MC (acting)	7 Jun
	Lt Col J.D. Shapland MC	6 Jul
Second-in-Command	Maj R.A. Hardy	PoW 26 May
	Maj L.H.H. Payne	PoW 7 Jun
Adjutant	Capt J.L. d'E. Darby	
Quartermaster	Lt A.T. Currie	to U.K.
R.Q.M.S.	W.O. II W. Cooper	kia 11 Jun
R.M.O.	Capt M.A. Eagan *R.A.M.C.*	
Chaplain	Rev H. Key *R.A.Ch.D.*	to U.K.
O.R.S.	Sgt K.M. Korke	

43 L.A.A. Battery

Officer Commanding	Maj G.G.W. Glazebrook	PoW 11 Jun
Battery Captain	Capt R.Q. Gurney	
R.O.	2Lt H.R. Herbert	
Troop Commander	2Lt M.H.A. Martin	PoW 26 May
Troop Commander	2Lt G.J.W. Bean	
Troop Commander	2Lt J.R. Miller	PoW
Troop Commander	2Lt C.A.C. Hamilton	
Troop Sergeant	Sgt G.H. Barrett	kia 24 May
Troop Sergeant	Sgt W.G.A. Draper	kia 12 Jun

44 L.A.A. Battery

Officer Commanding	Maj B. Davies	PoW 1 Jun
Battery Captain	Capt A.C. Bedborough	PoW 11 Jun
R.O.	2Lt J.A.M. Rutherford	PoW
Troop Commander	2Lt J.R. Lawrence	PoW
Troop Commander	2Lt D.H.M. Martin	PoW
Troop Commander	2Lt H.G. de G. Warter	
Troop Commander	2Lt N. Alexander	

237 (R.W.F.) A.T. Battery

Officer Commanding	Maj C.E. McCully	PoW 11 Jun
Battery Captain	Capt Sir James Hewitt Bt	PoW 11 Jun

R.O.	Lt H.W.E. Cleaver	PoW
Troop Commander	2Lt N.D. Wardrop	wia 11 Jun and PoW
Troop Commander	2 Lt R.W. Hinchcliffe	kia 11 Jun
B.Q.M.S.	Sgt P.B. Fox	

239 (R.W.F.) A.T. Battery

Officer Commanding	Maj J.R.O. Charlton	to U.K.
Battery Captain	Capt T. Owen	PoW 11 Jun
R.O.	2Lt B.O.J. Macgillycuddy	kia 26 May
Troop Commander	2Lt M.R.M. Steele-Mortimer	PoW 26 May
Troop Commander	2Lt P.A. Walker	PoW 10 Jun
Troop Commander	2Lt D.S. Unsworth	PoW
Troop Sergeant	Sgt G.F. Nethercott	kia 10 Jun
Troop Sergeant	Sgt E.W.A. Pierce	kia 7 Jun

Signals Section

| Officer Commanding | Lt L.A. Golding |

L.A.D. R.A.O.C.

| Officer Commanding | Capt H.N. Rogers *R.A.O.C.* |

Unplaced

Lt G.B. Siddall	
2Lt D.G.D. Dunlop	2Lt C.H.J. Corbett
W.O. II G. Norry	W.O. II W. Cooper
Sgt T.S. Pratt	Sgt F. Hughes

Notes

1   A summary of this part of the campaign in France can be found in Winston Churchill, *The Second World War, Volume II: Their Finest Hour* (London, 1949) pp. 130–135.
2   T.N.A. WO 167/654, 101 L.A.A. & Anti-Tank Regiment War Diary February–May 1940.
3   T.N.A. WO 167/1702, 101 L.A.A. & Anti-Tank Regiment War Diary February–June 1940.
4   Tony Walsh, *From Mold to St Valery, Egypt and Italy;* www.bbc.co.uk/history/ww2peopleswar accessed 29 November 2015
5   T.N.A. WO 373/16/45, citation for Charlton, John Roger Owen.
6   T.N.A. WO 167/654, 101 L.A.A. & Anti-Tank Regiment War Diary February–May 1940.
7   T.N.A. WO 167/1702, 101 L.A.A. & Anti-Tank Regiment War Diary February–June 1940.
8   T.N.A. WO 167/1702, 101 L.A.A. & Anti-Tank Regiment War Diary February–June 1940.
9   T.N.A. WO 167/1702, 101 L.A.A. & Anti-Tank Regiment War Diary February–June 1940.
10   Tony Walsh, *From Mold to St Valery, Egypt and Italy.*
11   T.N.A.WO 167/1702, 101 L.A.A. & Anti-Tank Regiment War Diary February–June 1940.
12   T.N.A. WO 167/1702, B Echelon 101 L.A.A. & Anti-Tank Regiment War Diary 15–18 June 1940.
13   T.N.A. WO 167/1702, 101 L.A.A. & Anti-Tank Regiment War Diary February–June 1940.
14   Tony Walsh, *From Mold to St Valery, Egypt and Italy.*
15   T.N.A. WO 167/654, 101 L.A.A. & Anti-Tank Regiment War Diary February–May 1940.
16   T.N.A. WO 166/1702, 101 L.A.A. & Anti-Tank Regiment War Diary June–September 1940.
17   *The Red Dragon*, p. 281.

Chapter 18

The Independent Companies

---

i. No 2 Independent Company, Norway, 1940

In the early months of the Second World War, Allied military planning was much concerned with Scandinavia. Europe's northern flank was enticing for two reasons: first, the German steel industry drew heavily on supplies of high-grade iron ore from the Gallivare district of Sweden. During the summer months the ore was shipped from the Baltic port of Lulea, but in winter this was ice-bound, so that the ore had to be railed to Narvik in Norway and from thence moved by sea through the Norwegian Leads. Allied plans therefore focused on the possibility of seizing Narvik in conjunction with naval activity, and then intervening directly in Sweden to deny the ore traffic to Germany and diverting it to the Allied cause. The second source of interest was the Russo-Finnish war. After the Molotov-Ribbentrop Pact in August 1939, the Soviet Union began to annex the small Baltic republics, and the Red Army attacked Finland on 30 November. To the Allies, this was a clear sign that Stalin intended to re-establish pre-revolutionary Russian control over Finland, and from there, seize either Narvik and eastern Norway, or the Swedish ore fields, or both. Whether or not Stalin and Hitler continued to co-operate, Soviet presence in the area was clearly undesirable. Of course both Norway and Sweden were neutral at this time, and both had a good deal more to lose than to gain by joining the Allies; moreover, although the Swedes had already assisted the Finns with men and weapons, neither Sweden nor Norway seemed in immediate danger of German attack so long as they remained neutral. Indeed, from the Scandinavian point of view, Germany represented a counterbalance to Soviet ambitions while the Allies, even to the Finns, gave little cause for hope.

By the beginning of 1940, the Allied governments had begun preparations for a military expedition into northern Norway, Sweden, and Finland. A wide-ranging series of operations was planned involving two British divisions with maritime and air support, with a brigade of French *Chasseurs Alpins*. The only British troops specifically prepared for arctic warfare were the 5th Battalion Scots Guards, a scratch battalion made up of individual volunteers.[1] Operations were due to begin on 20 March 1940,[2] and loading actually began on 14th. However matters were forestalled by the conclusion of an Armistice between the Finns and the Soviets, and most of the troops earmarked for the operation were sent to France. Two weeks later, however, the Allied Supreme War Council resurrected the idea of a campaign against Narvik and the ore mines as part of an intensified strategy of economic warfare against Germany. Allied mining of Norwegian waters was to begin on 14 April and when Lulea opened in May it too would be mined. It was also known that Germany, which had already divined Allied intentions, and which was further convinced after the Altmark incident that Norway was at least passively in the Allied camp, was preparing plans to invade Norway. Hitler had in fact decided that matters could not be left in their present state, and had given orders to Grossadmiral Erich Raeder on 26 March to launch Operation *Weserübung*, in order to occupy both Denmark and Norway, at the next new moon in early April.[3]

In parallel with German preparations, conducted in conditions of great secrecy, an Allied force of divisional size was prepared to land in Norway to forestall the Germans. In addition, the Military Intelligence (Research) Branch of the War Office General Staff under Lieutenant Colonel J.C.F. Holland,[*] known as MI(R), was directed to make plans for amphibious raids on the Norwegian coast. He at once summoned Lieutenant Colonel C. McV. Gubbins to take charge of this project.[†]

On 9 April 1940, German troops, assisted by total air superiority, invaded Norway by sea, and, assisted by Quislings, seizing Oslo, Narvik, Egersund, Bergen, Kristiansand and Trondheim. The Germans had won the race and in doing so launched the first large-scale combined operation in which all three components of a recognisably modern military organisation – land, maritime and air – were committed with equal weight under a unified command. Norwegian forces put up some opposition including sinking the German cruiser *Blücher* in Oslo fjord, but the Germans were everywhere successful. The Royal Navy and Royal Air Force joined the battle on the same day and there ensued a series of sea battles around Narvik, along with air attacks on German lines of communication. Although partly effective, these indirect means were insufficient to halt the German invasion and attention turned to impending land operations.

On 14 April, a British force – 'Avonforce' – under Major General Pierse Mackesy,[‡] G.O.C. 49th Infantry Division, was landed north of Narvik, and a second force was put ashore at Namsos on the 16th. Norway's long and rugged coastline could not be defended with the troops available and it was therefore decided to form a separate force to cover the coast between the defended areas at Namsos and Narvik, and prevent the Germans from setting up bases for air or U-boat operations. Gubbins had been working up the raiding force plans and had produced a draft proposal for special units known as Independent Companies,[4] smaller than a standard infantry battalion, but armed and equipped to operate in an independent role for up to a month. As time was pressing, the proposal was adopted. It was decided to raise these companies from volunteers drawn from the first and second line Territorial Army divisions still in Britain.

Formal orders for the formation of the Independent Companies were issued on 20 April. The scheme was that each company would have an establishment of twenty-one Officers and 268 men. Within each T.A. division, every brigade was to find a platoon, and every battalion a section. The high percentage of Officers meant that a subaltern would lead every section. Each

[*] Later Major General John Charles Francis Holland CB DFC (1897–1956). Holland had served with T.E. Lawrence as a pilot during the Great War, and then been badly wounded in Ireland. He had made several studies of irregular operations. *Who Was Who 1951–1960*, p. 532.

[†] Later Major General Sir Colin McVean Gubbins KCMG DSO MC DL (1896–1976). Served in the Great War on the Western Front, then in north Russia 1919. Director of Special Operations Executive 1940–1946. His biography *Gubbins and SOE* is cited in the footnotes to this chapter. See also *Who Was Who 1971–1980*, p. 323.

[‡] Major General Pierse Joseph Mackesy CB DSO MC (1883–1956). *Who Was Who 1951–1960*, p. 708.

company also included a section of Royal Engineers under an Officer, an ammunition section found by the Royal Army Service Corps, a medical section from the Royal Army Medical Corps, and an intelligence section. It was planned that each company would operate from a ship, which would act as a floating base, and because of this, the companies were not allocated any transport, nor were there any proper logistic arrangements other than about fifty tons of various stores, which were to be administered from Gubbins's headquarters.[5] The soldiers also carried up to five days' rations of pemmican.[6] Gubbins was very fortunate in the calibre of his company Officers: among them were T.H. Trevor, who later commanded No 1 Commando; A.C. Newman who later commanded No 2 Commando and won the Victoria Cross at St Nazaire, and R.J.F. Tod who subsequently commanded first No 9 Commando and later 2 Commando Brigade. His intelligence staff consisted of Captain N.A. Croft,[*] and Lieutenant Commander Q.T.P.M. Riley[†] R.N.V.R., both of whom were polar explorers and holders of the Polar Medal. Also going along with him was an American volunteer, Kermit Roosevelt, nephew of the late President Theodore Roosevelt.[‡]

The first company, No 1, was formed immediately on 20 April at Martock in Somerset, from 52nd Lowland Division. The remaining nine companies also began to form over the next ten days: No 3 at Ponteland under Major A.C. Newman,[§] from 54th East Anglian Division; No 4 at Sizewell in Westmoreland under Major J.R. Paterson, from 55th West Lancashire Division; No 5 at Lydd in Kent under Major J. Peddie, from 56th (1st London) Division; No 6 at Buddon Camp, Carnoustie in Fife, from 9th Scottish Division with Major R.J.F. Tod of the Argyll and Sutherland Highlanders in command;[¶] No 7 at Hawick under Major J.D.S. Young, from 15th Scottish Division; No 8 at Mundford in Norfolk under Major W.A. Rice, from 18th Eastern Division; No 9 at Ross-on-Wye in Herefordshire from 38th Welsh Division, under Major W. Siddons of the Royal Welch Fusiliers;[**] And No 10 from 66th East Lancashire Division under Major I. de C. Robertson.

Last but by no means least was No 2 Company, whose life began on Sunday 21 April 1940, when a conference of Brigadiers was called at H.Q. 53rd (Welsh) Division in Belfast, in order to pass out the orders for the formation of the divisional company, and begin the procedures for selecting the Officer Commanding, Officers and men of the company. Nominations from Commanding Officers to their brigade commanders came in at brigade conferences on 22 April.[7] Captain H.C. Stockwell, then Brigade Major of 158 (Royal Welch) Infantry Brigade was appointed to command the company.[8] The company began to form at Ballykinler Camp

---

[*]   Later Colonel Noel Andrew Cotton Croft DSO OBE FRGS (1906–1998). See his autobiography *A Talent for Adventure* (Worcester, 1991) and his obituary in *The Daily Telegraph*, 27 June 1998.

[†]   Lt Cdr Quintin Theodore Petroc Molesworth Riley FRGS *RNVR* (1905–1980), one of only five men to hold the Polar Medal with both Arctic and Antarctic clasps. Later C.O. of 30 Commando. His biography *From Pole to Pole* is cited in the endnotes to this chapter.

[‡]   Colonel Kermit Roosevelt (1889–1943). After his death, his widow instituted a series of exchange memorial lectures between the US and British armies, which still continue. *Who Was Who 1941–1950*, p. 997.

[§]   Later Lt Col Augustus Charles Newman VC OBE TD (1914–1972). *Who Was Who 1971–1980*, p. 580.

[¶]   Tod had joined the Nigeria Regiment R.W.A.F.F. in June 1935 (*Army List* 1937, p. 958); Pugh confirmed that Tod and Stockwell were great friends.

[**] Maj William Siddons DCM *R.W.F.* (1892–?)

the following day, although most of the men did not arrive until 25 April. Stockwell recalled the frantic course of events: 'Conferences with A and Q, everyone most helpful … Second-in-command appointed – I shall like him. Company starting to fill up with decent chaps. Went to Div HQ to fix up the Officers with GOC.'[9]

The Officers, N.C.Os and men of No 2 Independent Company were drawn from all battalions in the division, and organised into three platoons numbered 158, 159 and 160 after the three brigades of the division, along with a support section of *Bren* light machine guns, *Boys* anti-tank rifles, and 2-inch mortars, and the attachments already mentioned. Stockwell's second-in-command was Captain T.H. Trevor of the Welch Regiment,* and there were thirteen other infantry Officers, among them several Royal Welch Fusiliers. These included Lieutenant C.L. Wilding-Jones, who commanded 158 Platoon; 2nd Lieutenants N.J.H. Anderson, J. Fitton, T.H. Davies, who were all section commanders in 158 Platoon; Sir James Croft,† cousin of Captain N.A. Croft, who commanded 159 Platoon; Lieutenant J. Bradford of the Monmouthshires, who commanded 160 Platoon; and Lieutenant B.G.B. ('Puggie') Pugh, who commanded the support platoon‡. The Intelligence Officer was 2nd Lieutenant George Dilwyn-Venables-Llewellyn;§ the Medical Officer was Lieutenant S. Corry; and the Royal Engineer field section commander was 2nd Lieutenant L. Scott-Bowden.¶ There were in addition two gunner Officers, one General List Officer, and seven attached Officers from the Norwegian Army acting as interpreters and Liaison Officers.[10] After medical and dental inspections and some training tests, no less than fifty-six of the soldiers had to be returned to their units as unfit, and only thirty-two replacements could be persuaded to volunteer in the time available.[11] Persuaded, because as at least one account makes clear, a pretty liberal interpretation was put on the volunteer ethos. This from Sergeant (then Corporal) W.A. Jones of 6 R.W.F., from Caernarfon in North Wales:

> Very soon after our arrival in Lisburn … our names appeared on battalion orders informing us that we were selected to join a force for a special mission for service in an area that was not disclosed at that time, and we were ordered to appear before the C.O. at the Orderly Room where we were informed by the C.O. a little about the task before us, without disclosing the final destination. He emphasised that it was expected that we would be subject to very strong enemy aircraft attacks and he expressed the opinion that the Royal Air Force would not be able to give us any air support whatsoever owing to the distance to the target being beyond their range, and he finally asked us if anyone felt that he did not wish to go, and out of those assembled only one declared that he did not wish to go, so therefore the rest of us became volunteers. We were then ordered to report to the Quartermaster's stores to be kitted up … We would not be attending any parades, but [were] to wait for our moving orders. These came very soon after this, when we were loaded onto three-tonners, and left

---

*   Later Lt Col Thomas Houit Trevor OBE.

†   Sir James Herbert Croft, 11th Bt, of Croft Castle, Herefordshire (1907–1941). He was kia while serving with No 1 Special Service Battalion on 15 Aug 1941.

‡   Later Col Benjamin Gordon Pugh OBE TD *R.W.F.* (1917–2004), transferred in 1941 to Regular service in the Royal Welch Fusiliers.

§   Killed 26 May 1940 and buried in Saltdal main churchyard.

¶   Later Major General Logan Scott-Bowden CBE DSO MC *b*1920. *Who's Who 2001*, p. 1856.

with the good luck wishes of the Commanding Officer, and I must say we felt a little sad at leaving the Battalion.[12]

Even when volunteers were genuinely asked for, there was no mention of destination, nor arctic training, nor even winter sports of any kind, and usually men were asked for who were interested in unusual and adventurous training.

While the bulk of the force was forming up, Gubbins and his staff, with No 1 Company, was embarked at Rosyth on 27 April on HMS *Arethusa*. This advance guard sailed on 1 May for the Norwegian port of Mo, leaving Gubbins behind. On the same day, Stockwell was summoned to the War Office, where map packs were issued – although 'map packs' rather overstates a bundle of papers which consisted of illustrated holiday brochures, touring maps and the like.* Stockwell made notes on the series of briefings he received:

> … series of staff meetings, issue of pamphlets etc on irregular warfare. Not certain that all G1098 equipment could be provided in time especially: ice axes, alpine … sleeping bags, special boots, rucksacks, aluminium cooking utensils, *primus* stoves, kerosene containers, cap comforters, scarves, mittens, jerseys. Briefed on attacking railways, supply columns etc isolated en posts.[13]

He then set off to rejoin the assembling No 2 Company, where kit issue, inoculations, documentation and training had been in full swing:

> Briefing to Officers and then men and gave them a rough idea of what they were in for – guerrilla warfare in Norway. Will need to split coy up into self-contained packets, fast moving, everyone to pull his weight. Only a short time to get ready, explained tasks: organisation, admin, good discipline, fit out with kit, trg – physical fitness, PT cross country 20-25 miles on the flat 12-15 miles in the hills. Shooting. Snipers, Brens, Thompson machine carbines and revolvers. Night work. Compass. Map reading. Tactical exercises, Intelligence section, recce. Signal training. Verbal orders always. Mobility.[14]

Sergeant Jones described what had been happening during his absence:

> We finally unloaded at Ballykinler, an Army barracks, the Headquarters of an Irish Regiment, and we were placed in wooden huts. While we were there, more men were arriving from the 53rd Welsh Division … I could not help noticing what a tough looking bunch of men they were, and I began to wonder what I had let myself in for. We had not been told [who] our company commander was to be, only that we expected him to arrive from the War Office at any time now. And when he duly arrived I was glad to see that he was another Royal Welch Fusilier and a former Brigade Major of 158 Brigade, by the name of Major Hugh Stockwell. And a well-built formidable looking soldier, by the name of Captain Trevor, from the Welch Regiment, was to be his Second-in-Command. Very

---

* That said, Stockwell's papers from the campaign in King's College London contain a good quality Norwegian 1:100,000 map of Bodø and another of the Saltdal printed on linen. It is possible, of course, that he obtained these on arrival in Norway.

soon after his arrival we were ordered to assemble in the canteen so that he could introduce himself to us, and he went on to address us. He spoke in a very confident and jovial manner, and he [said] also [that he] had noticed that we were a tough looking bunch, and that it was what he had expected, and exactly what he wanted, and that he felt quite safe with [us] and went on to confirm that it was expected that we would encounter some heavy air attacks during the time after we had landed at our destination, and maybe before then, but he could not at that time tell us where this place was to be … he finally stated that he was more than confident that we would be able to cope, and give a good account of ourselves in these circumstances, and he wished us all the best of luck. Then he walked amongst the men talking to them individually as they moved about in the canteen. He spent a lot of time in the canteen with the men, which they greatly enjoyed.[15]

On 2 May, Gubbins himself was ordered to London for a briefing with Lieutenant General H.R.S. Massy,* commander of North-West Expeditionary Force, which included all troops and aircraft, except those at Narvik.[16] The fact that Massy and his headquarters never left London says much for how fast the campaign developed, and how much the British were left floundering by the tempo of the German advance. The orders were that Gubbins would form 'Scissorsforce', comprising initially of No 1, 3, 4, and 5 Companies, and to be followed by No 2 Company which had further to travel from Northern Ireland. The orders stated that:

> Your first task is to prevent the Germans occupying BODØ, MO and MOSJOEN. This they may try to do by small parties landed from the sea or dropped by parachute. Later, the Germans may be expected to advance Northwards on MOSJOEN from the TRONDHEIM area via GRONG. You will ensure that all possible steps are taken by demolition and harrying tactics to impede any German advance along this route.[17]

Gubbins was told not to attempt any full-scale engagement, since his troops lacked transport, training, heavy weapons and air support. Rather, he was to concentrate on harrying the enemy's flanks and his communications. He was also promised that eight Indian Army Officers with experience of mountain warfare would be attached to the force. Gubbins, with No 3, 4 and 5 Companies duly embarked at Gourock in the SS *Ulster Prince*, and on 5 May sailed for Bodø – which, with a population of about 5,000, was the only town of any size between Trondheim and Narvik.

From the end of April onwards, No 2 Independent Company was put through a rigorous programme of physical training, shooting and tactical schemes over the rugged terrain of the Mourne Mountains – more preparation than any other company had achieved, and which undoubtedly paid off later. The War Diary lists extensive kit issues, including 1937 pattern equipment – clearly the men, being Territorials, had still been in possession of the old pre-1908 pattern.[18] Quantities of new weapons arrived, on which men had to be trained: a sniper rifle per section; two *Thompson* sub-machine guns per section; three *Bren* guns and three *Boys* anti-tank rifles for the support section, one for each infantry section, and one for the company H.Q.; another two *Boys* anti-tank rifles for each platoon and one for company H.Q.[19] A large signal

---

*   Lieutenant General Hugh Royds Stokes Massy CB DSO MC (1884–1965).

section of twenty-eight men was also formed under 2nd Lieutenant G.W. Jenkins, with a wireless rear-link detachment equipped with the 18 set, maintenance detachment, flag and semaphore detachment, and a detachment for each platoon. Although Jenkins and twelve of the men were from the Royal Signals, the remainder were all infantry soldiers needing further training.

On 3 May, G.O.C. 53rd Division visited the Company, and on 8 May, it left Ballykinler and moved by ferry and train first to Glasgow, and then on to Leith. The soldiers' spirits were high. They were keen, eager, and fighting fit, and after a boisterous night on the town the Company embarked on 10 May on the MV *Royal Ulsterman*. Sergeant Jones recalled a few of the highlights:

> In the afternoon we were marched in full service marching order like pack mules to the waiting troopship … this boat had all the signs that it had been hastily converted from a passenger boat to a troopship, and there were double-decker barrack room beds placed in every available space. It was to prove most uncomfortable for this voyage … at last we were informed that our destination was Norway, and we were issued with some Norwegian currency, and since we had been repeatedly lectured to expect some heavy enemy air attacks we had no reason to believe we were going on a shopping expedition …
>
> … Each platoon took turns in providing anti-aircraft duties, with Bren guns mounted on tripods, and unexpected boat drill was called very often,* sometimes breaking up a game of cards. Soon walking on deck was becoming difficult, and many of the troops were starting to disappear down below where their bunks were situated, as the boat was now beginning to roll, and many of the men were suffering from sea sickness …[20]

Captain B.G.B. Pugh recalled that there had been a mix-up between government departments over who was to victual the ship, with the result that the Officers and men lived on compo and ships' biscuits, supplemented by pilchards![21] At 09.00 hrs on the 13th, the ship arrived at Bodø, the main port for reinforcement and supply of the expeditionary force.[22] Here they met up with the rest of Scissorsforce, which had had seventy-two hours of severe fighting, marching and countermarching. While No 3 Company had remained to secure Bodø, 4 and 5 had gone with Gubbins to Mosjoen on the 12th[23] to try to harry the Germans as they advanced. The troops performed well, but rapidly found they were no match for the Austrian ski troops they encountered, and on the 11th he had withdrawn the exhausted men in a Norwegian coastal ship.

In the wake of this withdrawal, Lieutenant General C.J.E. Auchinleck,[†] who assumed command of the Anglo-French military, and British air forces, in northern Norway on 3 June on the withdrawal of Massy and Headquarters 49th Division,[24] wrote to the Chief of the Imperial General Staff that he 'did not expect much of the Independent Companies. To be a successful guerrilla, you must, I think, be a *guerrilla* in your own country.'[25] Accordingly, Auchinleck issued orders from his H.Q. at Harstad on 14 May for the Independent Companies to be formed

---

*   This is confirmed by numerous entries in No 2 Independent Company War Diary.
†   Later Field Marshal Sir Claude John Eyre Auchinleck GCB GCIE CSI DSO OBE (1884–1981), C.-in-C. India 1940–1941 and 1943–1947, C.-in-C. Middle East 1941–1942. *Dictionary of National Biography 1981–1985*, pp. 15–18.

into a light force and placed under 24 (Guards) Infantry Brigade,* commanded by Brigadier the Hon. William Fraser,† this despite the fact that the Independent Companies had already been proved to have insufficient mobility, firepower and training for such a role. Already in 24 Brigade were the 1st Battalion Scots Guards, which with No 1 Independent Company was at Mo, the 1st Battalion Irish Guards and the 2nd Battalion South Wales Borderers, both of which were located with the Brigade H.Q. at Harstad. The specific task allocated to Gubbins was the denial of Bodø to the enemy while an airstrip there was completed. Gubbins therefore established his headquarters at Hopen, ten miles east of Bodø, along with No 5 Company, which needed time to rest and recuperate. No 1 Company was to remain at Mo, while No 3 Company was to hold Rognan at the head of the Saltfjord inland from Bodø until relieved by elements of 1st Irish Guards. No 4 Company was to guard the entrance to the Saltfjord at Straumen Island opposite Bodø.

No 2 Company was initially to remain at Bodø, and Stockwell therefore disposed his platoons around the town. 158 Platoon moved off to the south to occupy a large fish drying shed about two miles away, south-west of the harbour, at Langestranda, in which much salted fish was stored. From here, this platoon patrolled the town to control looting and look out for suspicious activity: Stockwell quickly came to the view that Quislings were active in the town and were somehow passing information to the Germans. With the assistance of an attached Norwegian Officer, Second Lieutenant Sönothagen, he interviewed a number of suspects, several of whom, including the chief of police, were placed under military arrest.[26] The other platoons worked at unloading the *Royal Ulsterman*, which proved to be difficult as the dock had no derricks. During this operation the ship was repeatedly attacked by German aircraft so that unloading could only be done at night, and the ship stood out to sea in daylight. Eventually, at about 02.00 hrs on 15 May the *Royal Ulsterman* had to sail, with about forty tons of No 2 Company's stores still on board.[27] These stores included all the magazines for the *Thompson* sub-machine guns, or 'Tommy guns', so that the company had the guns and the ammunition, but no means of introducing the one to the other![28]

Auchinleck's orders had also directed Brigadier Fraser to move with his H.Q. and the bulk of 1st Irish Guards to Mo. Fraser was uneasy at this, and a glance at the map does indeed show that Mo is at the head of a long, narrow fjord, exposed to enemy air attack, and difficult to supply or evacuate – especially as at this time of year, the one road northwards towards Rognan and Bodø was still blocked with snow. With Auchinleck's agreement, therefore, Fraser and his headquarters, and 1st Irish Guards, were to move to Bodø. The Irish Guards and the Brigade H.Q. were moved in small boats onto the Polish liner MV *Chobry*, while Fraser and some of his staff embarked on HMS *Somali*. Fraser stopped at Bodø to disembark his H.Q. and confer with Gubbins, before sailing up the fjord to brief No 1 Company. But the Germans now took a hand: HMS *Somali* was attacked from the air and badly damaged, and had to make for Scapa Flow to effect repairs – carrying with her Brigadier Fraser who had been injured and was therefore invalided home.[29]

---

*   One of the three brigades of 49th Infantry Division. See Patrick Delaforce, *The Polar Bears* (London, 1995) [a history of the 49th Division in the Second World War], pp. 4–5.

†   The Hon. William Fraser DSO MC late Grenadier Guards (1890–1964). *Who Was Who 1961–1970*, p. 419.

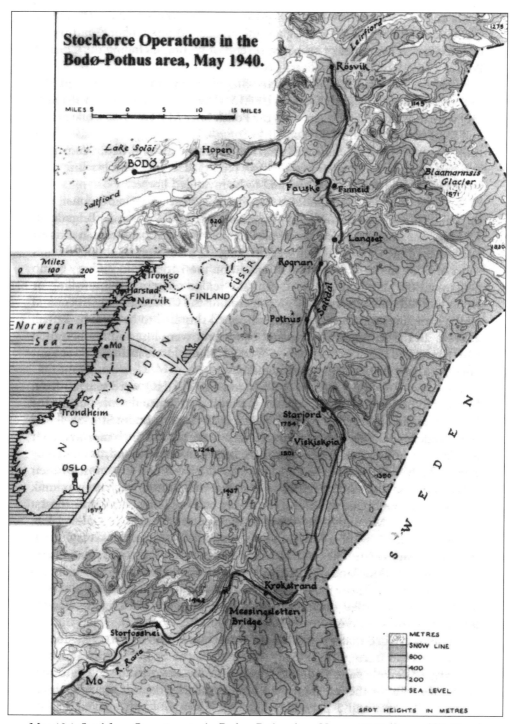

Stockforce Operations in the Bodø-Pothus area, May 1940.

Map 18.1 Stockforce Operations in the Bodø – Pothus Area, Norway 1940. (Source: T.K. Derry)

With the Brigade Commander gone, Gubbins, now an acting Colonel, was the senior Officer and accordingly took command of 24 (Guards) Brigade on 15 May. But disaster struck again. News came through that German aircraft had attacked the *Chobry*, which was carrying 1st Irish Guards, about thirty miles short of Bodø in the Westfjord at midnight on the 14th.[30] Later that night an incendiary bomb penetrated the ship and exploded near the senior Officers' cabins, killing and wounding eight Officers and 100 men, including the Commanding Officer and all the company commanders. Fire broke out on the ship, isolating the men, who could not lower the boats and, with ammunition blowing up, it seemed doomed. However the destroyer HMS *Wolverine* and the sloop *Stork* stood in, and managed to trans-ship 694 men in sixteen minutes[31] – a remarkable feat, and only possible due to the bravery of the ships' crews – both British and Polish – and the steadfastness of the guardsmen. But the abandoned ship had to be sunk by British aircraft, all the battalion's stores and equipment were lost and the battalion had to return to Harstad to re-equip. Worse still, the losses included three light tanks, the only British armour in Scandinavia. There was more to follow. That evening, news came through that German troops had landed around Hestnes[*] and No 2 Independent Company, tired and wet through as the men were, was ordered inland. Stockwell ordered 159 Platoon to a blocking position at Løp, where it was reinforced next day by the Support Platoon; 158 Platoon was to move to Storvellen;[†] and 160 Platoon to Vollen.[‡] The Company H.Q. moved into a garage near Rønvik, on the northern outskirts of Bødo. The Royal Engineer section was left at the fish factory to look after the stores, which were moved the next day.[32] The reported enemy landing turned out to be a false alarm, and the Company soon returned to security duties in and around Bødo, which continued to attract a great deal of attention from enemy aircraft.

Two days later – 17 May, which was Norway's Independence Day – 2nd S.W.B. along with Brigade H.Q. were sent up from Harstad to Bodø on HMS *Effingham*: taking an unusual route outside the Leads to avoid air attack the ship struck a rock close to Bodø.[33] Stockwell and No 2 Independent Company managed to salvage some 3-inch mortars and their ammunition, and vehicles, including three *Bren* gun carriers, and, as related by Captain Pugh, several cases of gin! However the S.W.B. had lost most of its equipment and it too had to return to Harstad while the *Effingham* had to be sunk by torpedoes. Gubbins, therefore, had available only one battalion – the 1st Scots Guards at Mo under the popular and respected Lieutenant Colonel T.B. Trappes-Lomax,[§] – and his Independent Companies, along with a troop of four 25 pdr field guns, a section of 37 mm *Bofors* light anti-aircraft guns, and an engineer field section: a total of only about 2,000 men.[34] Worse, the Scots Guards were 135 miles away. The Scots Guards had detached one company, but had been reinforced by another troop of field guns, a section of *Bofors* guns, and detachments of engineers and Royal Army Service Corps troops. No air support was available. The force at Mo was meant to protect the route northwards towards Bodø and its airstrip; German strength in area was estimated at a mountain brigade, possibly supported by light armour, and with air cover. As it turned out there was no armour, but the brigade was the advance guard of a division.

---

*   The war diary spells this as 'Esneset'.
†   The war diary spells this as 'Stover'.
‡   The war diary spells this as 'Volden'.
§   Later Brig Thomas Byrnand Trappes-Lomax CBE DL (1895–1964), commissioned 1915 into the Border Regiment, transferred to Scots Guards 1917.

Gubbins travelled south to Mo by road during 18 and 19 May. Meanwhile the Scots Guards and their Norwegian counterparts had withdrawn from their positions south of Mo into the town after the left flank of their position was turned by the advance of the German mountain troops, and a parachute landing. When Gubbins arrived, he and Trappes-Lomax clearly did not agree on the scheme of manoeuvre, but Gubbins at length gave way.

The road from Mo to Bodø ran for 135 miles (217 kilometres), of which twenty-three miles (37 kilometres) were over a treeless plateau. Trappes-Lomax decided that his main effort must be north of the plateau, and that he would offer only a guard action south of it. The Norwegians were sent north first, with instructions to send back all available civilian buses and trucks for a fast crossing of the vulnerable stretch on the plateau. This they duly did. At this stage, Trappes-Lomax received instructions from Auchinleck to stand and fight on the south side of the plateau. He replied direct by signal, that the best hope of stopping the Germans was north of the snow-bound plateau, where it would be harder for enemy to outflank. After a conversation with Lieutenant Colonel Arthur Dowler,* the G.S.O. I, Auchinleck's message was amended from defence to fighting withdrawal. Gubbins then wrote an order authorising Trappes-Lomax to withdraw 'from any position you hold if in your opinion there is serious danger to the safety of your force.'[35]

Trappes-Lomax had selected three delaying positions: an initial position at Krokstrand, south of the plateau; and firm blocking positions at Viskishoia and Storjord north of it. Contact with the enemy was made at 06.00 hrs on the 21st at Krokstarnd. Thereafter, the withdrawal did not go well. Three salvaged Carriers from No 2 Independent Company, which Stockwell had detached and sent forward under the command of 2nd Lieutenant N.J.H. Anderson, helped cover the withdrawal on 21 May with great skill. Two of the three Carriers were destroyed in the action, but the task was successfully accomplished. As a result of this, Anderson was awarded the Military Cross, the first won by a Royal Welch Fusilier during the Second World War.

At 19.00 hrs on the 22nd, Trappes-Lomax began embussing troops for the crossing of the plateau, and last vehicle began to move off at about midnight, just as the German main body began to appear. Gubbins ordered Trappes-Lomax to hold this position until the 27th; he subsequently ordered it abandoned on the 23rd when the danger of being outflanked and surrounded became apparent.

While this was going on, Auchinleck had sent reinforcements: H.Q. 24 Brigade and two companies of 2 S.W.B. arrived at Bodø on 20 May amid German bombing;[36] 1st Irish Guards were on their way in fishing boats and in on HMS *Firedrake* and *Walker*,[37] to oppose the Germans, who had now concentrated about 1,750 men to the south in the area of Mosjoen. All British troops were to be formed into 'Bodøforce' under Gubbins's command. When Gubbins became aware of the Scots Guards' withdrawal he moved the forward elements of 1st Irish Guards, along with No 2 Company, to a blocking position at Pothus, between Storjord and Rognan. As Stockwell's Company H.Q. was preparing to move, a German aircraft bombed the area, hitting the wireless tent, killing two soldiers and wounding another eight.[38]

Sergeant Jones recalled that the company travelled the thirty miles inland up the Saltdal fjord to Rognan in the fjord steamer *Bodin*, and from thence by a combination of route march, and

---

*   Later Lieutenant General Sir Arthur Arnhold Bullick Dowler KCB KBE DL (1895–1963). Then
       GSO 1 49th (West Riding) Infantry Division he later commanded 38th (Welsh) Division and was
       influential in the formation of Commando forces later in the war.

3-ton lorries which were repeatedly attacked by German aircraft
on the narrow road which follows
the Salt river as it flows into the
fjord from the south, the only prac-
ticable route from Mo, since the
country around was very mountainous, wooded and pitted with
lakes. The road was therefore the
natural focus for both the enemy
and the British.[39] The next day,
the Germans appeared in front
of 1st Scots Guards, and attacked
in strength, supported by aircraft
and mortar fire. The troops were
driven back and the main position
outflanked. Gubbins therefore
ordered the acting Commanding
Officer of the Scots Guards,
Major H.L. Graham,[40] to withdraw through Stockwell's position
at Pothus: Graham was acting
Commanding Officer because
earlier that day, Auchinleck had
signalled Gubbins, relieving
Trappes-Lomax of command.

Auchinleck meanwhile decided
to strengthen the position at
Bodø by building an airstrip, and

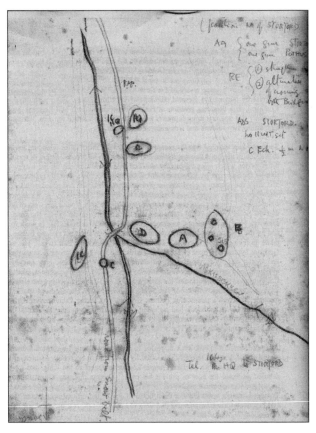

Map 18.2 The Viskishoia position, a sketch with notes from the
personal papers of Brigadier T.B. Trappes-Lomax.

bringing in more troops, including the remaining Independent Companies from Britain, and
some French *Chasseurs Alpins*, so as to develop a base for counter-offensive operations. It was
clear therefore that the force at Pothus, consisting of around 1,000 men with some vehicles and
heavy equipment from Nos 2 and 3 Independent Companies, and two companies of the 1st Irish
Guards, must now form a guard force, and to that end No 4 Independent Company was sent up
to reinforce the position. Stockwell, granted the local rank of Lieutenant Colonel, was directed
to form and take command of this grouping, which was to be known as 'Stockforce', and hand
over command of No 2 Independent Company to Captain T.H. Trevor.[41] Orders were issued
at 07.00 hrs on the 23rd, and Stockwell went forward with Captain H.C. McGildowny,* the
acting Commanding Officer of the Irish Guards, to have a look at the area. Opposite Pothus, a
thickly wooded razor-backed ridge stuck out from the mountains and behind it a small tributary
ran down into the Salt River. Stockwell decided to form his position at the hamlet around two

---

*   *The History of the Irish Guards in the Second World War* rather erratically lists him as either R. or H.C.
    McGildowney.

bridges over the Salt River, which was wide and deep, and swollen with melt water. The main road bridge was a substantial girder construction carrying the road from west to east, and it was prepared for demolition; a second bridge a few hundred yards downstream across the tributary, carrying a rough track over the ridge, was much smaller. This track continued along the eastern bank for about three miles (5 kilometres) until it too crossed the Salt by another small bridge. All in all, Stockwell decided that the position offered a good choke-point at which the advancing Germans could be held. 158 Platoon of No 2 Independent Company, about fifty-five men, along with its support platoon under Captain Pugh came up first at about 02.30 hrs on the 23rd,[42] and Stockwell placed these two platoons in positions on the west and east sides of the river. Pugh remembered that he '… had with me three *Bren* guns and a 3-inch mortar. We got into position at 11.00 in the morning, having had to climb a very steep mountain side, covered with trees.' Sergeant Jones, who was a section commander in 158 Platoon on the other side of the valley, recalled that:

> … there were also many piles of wooden logs scattered about in this area … The German Air Force seemed to be quite active, as many aircraft could be seen flying overhead, but alas it was always 'theirs' and not 'ours'.… we started off uphill in the woods to the high ground, and my section was positioned about 400 yards from platoon headquarters, we had ample supplies of Marmite* and cocoa, and very soon my position was being strafed by German aircraft, luckily with no casualties, and I moved my section slightly below the ridge, to where I found some crevices, that the men could use during air attack, as it was fairly obvious that our position was already known.[43]

They were followed by the Irish Guards who began to arrive at 10.00 hrs on the 24th, one of whose companies, No 1, covered the main bridge on the far side with a detached platoon from No 3 Company on the bridge itself with an Engineer N.C.O. who was responsible for preparing the bridge for demolition. Once the Scots Guards had passed through, this company and platoon were to be withdrawn and the bridge blown – but only on Stockwell's direct orders.[44] The only method of communication to this forward company was by runner, since there was insufficient cable available to lay a telephone line. A second company, No 3, covered the tributary and the river banks below the bridge, while No 4 Company on a plateau or terrace on the right of the position could command a long stretch of road and river. In support of the British troops, a Norwegian patrol detachment under Captain Pedersen took up a position four hundred yards west of the bridge, a machine gun detachment under Captain Ellinger, and a half-company from the 2nd Line Battalion, joined No 1 Company Irish Guards on the northern side of the bridge, with the other half company joining No 4 Company Irish Guards. A Norwegian mortar section deployed south-west of the bridge to cover the forward troops, while a troop of 25 pdr field guns, which had been brought up from Mo, also covered the main road.[45] As a backstop, Gubbins had ordered No 4 Independent Company to adopt an intermediate position in front

---

* As noted in the source notes, the Independent companies often carried up to five days supply of Pemmican. Quintin Riley said that the soldiers often refused to eat pemmican, but were quite content if it was called 'Special Bovril', or 'Oxo' or 'Marmite' (*From Pole to Pole*, Annex B). It may be this to which Sergeant Jones is referring.

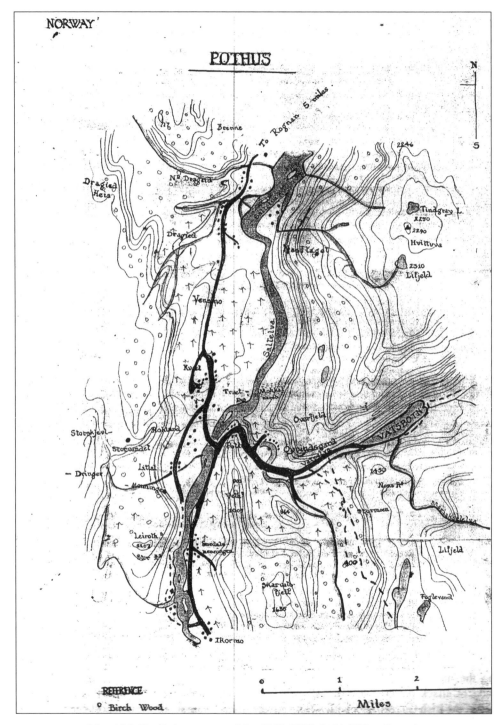

Map 18.3 The Pothus position, May 1940. (KCL Liddell Hart Centre)

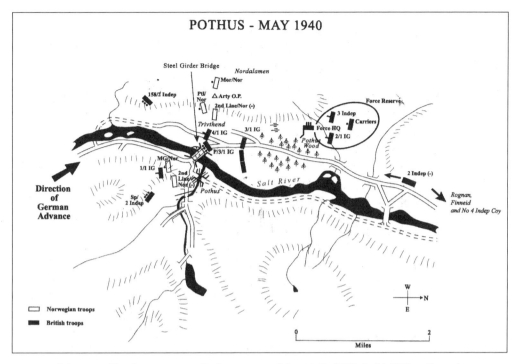

Map 18.4 The dispositions at Pothus position, May 1940. (KCL Liddell Hart Centre)

of Finneid to cover any subsequent withdrawal.* No 3 Independent Company, which came up at 20.00 hrs on the 24th, and the remaining company of the Irish Guards, No 2, formed Stockwell's reserve which was co-located with his H.Q. about a mile to the north in Pothus Wood. Here they were to be joined by the balance of No 2 Independent Company and the Carrier section as it moved forward.

Oral confirmatory orders were issued at noon.[46] It was a hot, clear summer's day, the sun thawed the frozen arctic soil and the men dug slit trenches with a will, 'smoking and chatting, beating off swarms of ants and midges, and quietly watching the German fighters overhead.'[47] Some civilians appeared, and several members of the force reinforced Stockwell's view that not all Norwegians were strong in the Allied cause. Riley noted that '… The whole country is riddled with Quislings and the Hun knows everything … Their equipment, training and speed are infinitely better than ours and they have complete control of the air …'[48] Sergeant Jones said that:

> … my section spotted a civilian moving uphill towards our position. I ordered the men not to fire at him, but keep him under observation and allow him to come into our position. He was then held until my interpreter could find out more about him. The Officer told me

*   Derry's official account does not mention No 4 Independent Company; however it is clear from Charles Messenger's interview with the Company Commander, Major J.R. Paterson, that the Company was indeed present.

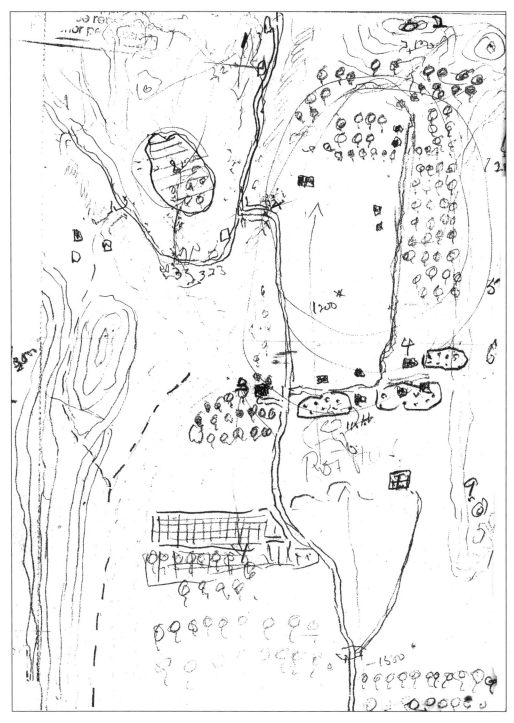

The position at Pothus, a sketch by Major H.C. Stockwell. (KCL Liddell Hart Centre)

that he was just an ordinary Norwegian looking for his wife, and that the German position was about two miles away. He was allowed to go on his way, and I soon realised that he was returning by the same route that he had taken to come into my position … so shouted at him to stop. On hearing me, he started running away. His action convinced me that he was not an ordinary civilian.[49]

As the men of Stockforce dug in, other British and Norwegian troops began to appear down the road from the direction of the front line. At first they came in twos and threes, many of them wounded. About 05.00 hrs, the advance party of the Scots Guards appeared. Pugh thought that they were 'marching very well, as though they were on parade.' Eventually the short arctic night fell, and the temperature dropped. The men wrapped themselves up in blankets, greatcoats and leather jerkins, and some welcome rations appeared, brought up by lorry from Rognan. By midnight on 24 May, reasonably effective defensive positions completed. Soon afterwards, the troops heard the unmistakable sound of tired men tramping slowly along the road, and as they watched through the gloom the Scots Guards passed silently through the position. There was now nothing between the main position and the Germans except No 1 Company Irish Guards and their Norwegian allies.[50] Then, without warning at 01.35 hrs, the girder bridge blew up, leaving the troops on the far side unsupported. This, it later turned out, had been done by the Engineer N.C.O. on information received from an unidentified Officer of the Scots Guards, in direct contravention of his orders.[51]

The enemy was now reported be closing up, and to muster about 4,500 men from the 2nd Mountain Division and 181 Infantry Division.[52] Captain B.G.B Pugh was the first to make contact. At about 08.00 hrs on 25 May his support platoon, now well positioned in the woods behind breastworks of rocks, stones and logs and with weapons sited to sweep the road, spotted a German motor-cycle patrol. The platoon let the Germans get well along the road to a stretch which was fairly straight and level and without cover except for the ditches on either side. 'Then' said Pugh, 'we opened up on them and I think got most of them.'

A fierce battle raged, often at close quarters, for the next thirty-six hours. It was the first taste of combat for most of the men of Stockforce – and they were not found wanting. By 11.00 hrs the support platoon had been outflanked and Stockwell ordered them to join the Irish Guards around the girder bridge, a move which took about an hour by a roundabout route. The last *Bren* gun carrier moved off the position 'a moment before a 4-inch mortar shell' fell on the spot.'[53] Around the bridge, the guardsmen of No 1 Company, who were well dug in and supported by artillery and machine-gun fire and the Norwegian mortars, held their ground strongly. In the early afternoon of the 25th, five *Heinkel* aircraft began to attack the position, including Stockwell's H.Q. which was burnt out by incendiaries, while German infantry put in an attack. They were driven back, but gradually managed to out-flank the position. Pugh remembered that:

I got my 3-inch mortar into action and we fought a desultory battle all that day until about 17.00 hours, when the Germans delivered a very determined attack and drove us off the hill on which we had established ourselves … it was very close country and my Bren guns had a very small field of fire. The Germans got within 50 yards of us before I saw any of them.'

---

*   The standard calibre of mortar in a German infantry division at this time was 81mm.

Eventually, Stockwell had to order a withdrawal. The men of No 2 Independent Company had to make their way along a track down the river to a small hanging footbridge about a mile below the reserve position. By about 08.00 hrs Stockwell had as clear an idea of the confused situation as was possible. He could see that the German attack was being held, but was worried about being outflanked. As he was also clear that his task was to hold the Germans here, he had no option but to commit his reserve. Two companies were ordered across the river to a blocking position at the northern angle of the river confluence, where cliffs afforded some protection. By 04.30 hrs on the 26th, Stockwell felt that the left, Southern, flank, was secure.

During the night, the Germans built a pontoon bridge upstream in order to switch the direction of attack onto the Northern bank. By about 09.00 hrs on the 26th, the Germans, using this pontoon, had pushed the platoon of No 2 Independent Company back onto the main position.[54] Seeing this, and recognising that the position was about to be penetrated, Stockwell personally led forward his only remaining reserve – the balance of No 2 Independent Company, which had joined the force at 03.00 hrs on the 25th.[55] The company moved uphill and managed for a time to prevent the Germans from pressing forward.

While this action was in progress early in the morning on 26 May, Gubbins had been warned by signal that the British government had decided to begin an evacuation. Stockwell was therefore given modified orders: he was to hold the Germans only for long enough to cover the withdrawal of Bodøforce, which was expected to evacuate between 1 and 3 June. The Germans kept pressing hard at Pothus, and at 11.30 hrs Gubbins therefore sent orders to Stockwell by wireless to carry out a withdrawal as far as Fauske, north of Rognan on the northern shore of the Saltfjord. This was to take place over severe, mountainous, and thickly wooded terrain, which, being within the Arctic Circle, was covered in places by belts of perpetual

Stockforce moves from Pothus to Rognan in Norway, 27 May 1940. (Imperial War Museum)

snow and ice. The fighting was so close, and his flanks were so threatened by German and Austrian ski troops, that it was not until the middle of the afternoon that Stockwell managed to organise a break of contact, and early evening before it could be effected.

From then onwards, Stockforce fought a vicious rearguard action – the most difficult operation of war – under continuous mortar fire and air attack. The move began just before 07.00 hrs with No 2 Independent Company concentrating in a covering position near the footbridge, from which it blocked the German advance in close fighting until 22.30 hrs that night. Captain Scott, with No 4 Company of the Irish Guards, was at his wits' end trying to find a way of breaking contact at the bridge, when two Gloster *Gladiator* aircraft from the strip at Bodø appeared, seemingly from nowhere, and machine-gunned the attacking Germans. This bought just enough time and space for the company to get away. But the respite was short-lived. Stockwell meanwhile had sent orders by runner to those companies he had not been able to see personally. No 2 Company Irish Guards was to move down and join the position at the footbridge, but the order never reached them – instead, it went to No 3 Independent Company.

Men of Stockforce embarked in a Puffer, Norway, 28–29 May 1940.
(Imperial War Museum)

But Captain A.C. Newman could not get clear of the Germans and had to withdraw down the eastern side of the river to the head of the fjord. A Norwegian Liaison Officer eventually contacted No 2 Company Irish Guards late that evening. With the Germans on the road, No 2 Company had no choice but to follow the same route as No 3 Independent Company.

The men of Stockforce now had to traverse ten miles (16 kilometres) of extremely rugged terrain from Pothus to Rognan. As they fought their way yard by yard slowly northwards along the line of the road, the men destroyed ammunition dumps, blew up bridges and jetties, and created as many ad hoc obstacles to impede the Germans as they could. The Germans for their part worked their way around the flanks and down to the road at several points, ambushing parties whenever they could. No 2 Independent Company was ambushed as it moved out of Pothus by Germans, who had infiltrated round their flanks, and the Company took casualties. A battle went on for most of the day with the Welsh soldiers giving as good as they got – 'Platoons 159 and 160 had a running fight with the Germans in which they wiped out a machine gun post.'[56] Losses were heavy during the fighting,* but all the casualties were either evacuated or carried by their comrades. Somehow, the companies, often broken up in the darkness and confusion into groups of individuals, made their way to the village of Nestby, about two miles (3 kilometres) from Rognan, where Stockwell had organised a blocking position from two platoons of No 4 Company Irish Guards and Captain Ellinger's Norwegian machine-gun detachment. Here, men sorted themselves out, found their comrades, and were moved off down the road in something approaching good order. To support the withdrawal, 1, 4 and 5 Independent Companies were all placed under command of Stockforce on the 27th.[57]

---

*   No 2 Independent Company War Diary, for example, lists three Officers and eight men killed, nineteen men missing – mostly Royal Welch Fusiliers from 158 Platoon which had been most heavily engaged – and another five men wounded between 26 and 29 May.

At Rognan, the road ended abruptly at the head of the fjord, providing a natural barrier to further German advance, although it picks up again at Langset on the north shore, and there is a rough track around the edge of the fjord. The force was to move the six miles (9 kilometres) from Rognan down to Finneid by small boats, a precarious run of an hour each way. To carry this out, Commander W.R. ('Tiny') Fell,* who was in charge of small boat operations, had assembled a flotilla consisting of a large ferry and ten armed fishing boats – known as 'Chuffers', or more often 'Puffers,' each around fifty feet long and powered by a single cylinder *Bollinder* engine. The engines were so temperamental that Fell had had to co-opt Norwegian engineers and seamen to work them; many of these men were most unwilling and took any opportunity to jump ship. Added to this, the boats had just returned from a walrus-hunting expedition, and stank to high heaven. The Puffers made repeated runs to and from Rognan, often under air attack,[58] and the task took longer than Gubbins and Stockwell had hoped. Inevitably, to get the men away, a lot of heavy equipment had to be left behind and destroyed, and demolition charges were laid under the wooden jetty at Rognan, timed to explode once the evacuation was complete. With things going slowly, there was only about a quarter of an hour left before the charges were due to blow, and the engine of the ferry, which Fell had flogged to get maximum speed, caught fire. At almost the last moment, Fell, manoeuvring his Puffer with great skill and bravery, managed to pull the ferry clear. The ferry was only fifty or sixty yards away from the jetty when the charge blew, showering the troops with burning debris. As the ferry was towed slowly away, German cyclists entered the town and began firing on the boats. All the troops were, however, safely extracted except for No 2 Company Irish Guards. Luckily for them, each Norwegian town and village owned a municipal motor bus.[59]

As the force passed through No 4 Independent Company, Stockwell ordered No 2 Independent Company to reinforce it and come under Major Paterson's command. Paterson recounted that:

> I had no sooner started talking about this than, BANG! Up went the bridge, the enemy were at our gates ... I gave orders [by runner] ... telling No 2 Coy to withdraw on their own but not to become involved, but before withdrawing to inform No 2 Platoon of my own Company what they were doing. In order to be sure this message was carried out I sent my Intelligence Officer with it. Actually by the time he got there, they had started their withdrawal ... We than sat and waited. After a short time the Boshe got a mortar going and a machine-gun which covered the road between Fauske and Finneid with long range fire. Copland† [Second-in-Command of the Company] came up in a car and got chased, also a lorry which turned up to get some explosives ... [60]

Stockforce consolidated that night at Fauske, with the Irish Guards and 2 Independent Company on a line north of Lakes Nedre and Övre, spread out to rest on the bleak terrain overlooking the village and covering the road which ran along the north side of the Saltfjord. The wounded were moved back by road to Bodø. The 27th dawned, dank and dreary, with plenty of attention

---

*   Later Captain William Richmond Fell CMG CBE DSC *RN* (1897–1981). Fell recorded his experiences in his autobiography *The Sea Our Shield* (London, 1966).

†   Captain W.O. Copland DSO *S. Lancs R.*, later commanded No 4 Company, and was Second-in-Command of No 2 Commando at St Nazaire.

from German aircraft. Stockwell and McGildowny set out to reconnoitre a holding position. At midnight the troops marched out to occupy a new position on the Valnes peninsula, about four miles further west, where it could block the roads and approaches into Bodø. 5 Independent Company was placed on the right, 4 Independent Company in the centre, the Irish Guards held the left, and No 2 Independent Company formed the force reserve.[61] Nos 1 and 3 Independent Companies meanwhile still held forward positions near Finneid. The men once again dug slit trenches, found what shelter they could in farms and barns, and relieved the Norwegian cows of their milk!.

During the 28th, the force consolidated the Fauske position. The Germans arrived early in the afternoon and engaged one of the platoons of 4 Independent Company. The company held on until dark and just before midnight, Stockwell ordered Paterson to adjust his position onto high ground overlooking Fauske. As they did so, Gubbins was working on the evacuation plan, which Auchinleck had ordered to begin on the night of 29/30 May. Destroyers would take off Bodøforce over that night and the two successive nights. The stubborn defence of Stockforce, and the destruction of jetties, Puffers and all small boats not in immediate use, had temporarily halted the German advance at Rognan so that Gubbins had a breathing space in which to issue his orders. On receiving these late on the morning of the 29th, Stockwell quickly made a plan. The force H.Q., No 1 and No 4 Independent Companies were ordered to move by truck and Puffer from Hopen to concentrate at Bodø, and there embark on 29 May. The Scots Guards, he knew, had been told to adopt a blocking position at Hopen, to allow Stockforce to move from Fauske on the 30th. No 2 Independent Company and 3 Company Irish Guards would adopt an intermediate position at Mjones, with No 5 Independent Company carrying out a delay action to give them the time to get into position. No 3 Independent Company would also come under command again and with the remainder of the Irish Guards, would move as quickly as possible to Hopen.[62]

At this point, the Germans were not pressing hard, and Nos 2 and 4 Independent Companies, which had begun to withdraw early, had been led back into position by Stockwell.[63] He then issued orders to the C.O. of the Irish Guards and the commanders of 1 and 5 Independent Companies, and sent a warning order to Paterson at about midday. The main body duly moved back on foot that night to Hopen, where Puffers picked the men up in relays and took them on to Bodø. As for No 2, 3 and 4 Independent Companies, a typewritten order was sent by dispatch rider, telling them to be on a destroyer at Bodø at midnight. This reached Paterson at about 18.30 hrs. Gathering up his platoons and loading them on to whatever transport he could find, Paterson made the rendezvous on time, blowing the Valnesfjord bridge on the way. There they joined Stockwell and his H.Q., just in time to hear the whispered message along the quayside: 'Destroyers *Firedrake, Fame* and *Vindictive* coming alongside. Five minutes to board.' So Stockforce was successfully evacuated and moved to Harstad.[64]

Stockforce was shipped from Norway back to Scapa Flow in the transport *Royal Scotsman*. It had lost two Officers and eight men killed, two Officers and eleven men taken prisoner, and two men wounded. With the other Independent Companies from Norway it remained for some time in Scotland. On 5 June, No 2 Company was transferred to the SS *Iris* in Scapa Flow from where it sailed for Aberdeen in convoy on the 10th. On the 11th, the Company moved by train to Kirkintilloch, north-east of Glasgow, where it remained undergoing refitting and training until it was merged into No 1 Commando in the autumn of 1940.[65]

ii. Home Defence: No 9 Independent Company, 1940

On his return from Norway, Major H.C. Stockwell, who was awarded a DSO for his bravery and leadership during the campaign, received a complimentary letter from the GOC 53rd Welsh Division. General Wilson wrote that:

> I am both proud and delighted at the success which has obviously been achieved by No 2 Coy and its gallant commander – go on to further glories always remembering to temper valour with discretion! I hope you will send me an account of your adventures without any too modest covering up of gallantry so that I can issue it as an inspiration to the division to go and do likewise. I have naturally asked for my Co[mpan]y back again. It was the carefully selected cream of the division.[66]

He did, not, however, get his men back. On 3 June, in the wake of the Dunkirk evacuation, Churchill had written to the Chiefs of Staff, directing that raiding forces were to be organised in order to keep the Germans tied down on the European coast.[67] The response from the War Office suggested guerrilla units which, from the start, should be called Commandos, after the Boer units of the South African War.[68] The Director of Military Operations and Plans, Major General Richard Dewing,[*] added to this by suggesting that Commandos should be billeted on seaside towns where they would live off the local economy and train, providing a pool of special troops able to undertake raiding operations at need, and which would be provided with specialist equipment and heavy weapons as required.[69] There would be ten Commandos, No 1 formed from the Independent Companies, and the rest formed from the United Kingdom Military Commands.[70] These units would be under the operational command of the newly designated commander, Offensive Operations, General Sir Alan Bourne.[†] In the short term the Independent Companies were not formed into No 1 Commando, but formed into two groups, and placed under the operational control of G.H.Q. Home Forces.

On 20 July 1940,[71] Major H.C. Stockwell was appointed to command one of these groups of Independent Companies. This comprised Nos 6, 7, 8 and 9 Companies[72] and his command formed the basis of the anti-invasion defences of the Land's End Zone, based at Carbiss Bay in Cornwall.[‡] The Land's End Zone was in the Cornwall Sub-Area of South-West Area, which in turn was part of Southern Command,[73] and was commanded by Colonel A.L. Symes.[§] The main tasks of the group were to protect the beaches, ports and harbours in the zone and in particular,

---

[*]   Major General Richard Henry Dewing CB DSO MC (1891–1981).
[†]   General Sir Alan George Barwys Bourne KCB DSO MVO (1882–1967) was Adjutant General, Royal Marines at the time of his appointment.
[‡]   G.F. Petty has stated in his autobiography *Mad Gerry – Welsh Wartime Medical Officer* (Newport, 1992), that Stockwell commanded No 11 Commando in the raid on Guernsey on 14/15 July 1940, and was subsequently reprimanded for its lack of success. This is not true. The raid was conducted by No 3 Commando under the command of John Durnford-Slater, and No 11 Commando under R.J.F. Tod. No personal reprimands were ever issued. See Charles Messenger, *The Commandos 1940–1946*, pp. 33–35 and Sally Dugan, *Commando*, pp. 16–23.
[§]   The other Sub-Areas were Plymouth (the responsibility of the Royal Marine Division), North Devon, and South Devon.

the towns of Penzance; St Just, which also boasted a small aerodrome; and Porthcurno, the terminal for the trans-Atlantic telegraph cable.[74]

No 9 Company had been formed at Ross-on-Wye from volunteers of the 38th (Welsh) Division, a large number of whom were drawn from 8 and 10 R.W.F. On 9 May it had moved to Bellahouston Park, Glasgow,[75] and on the following day it had actually embarked and sailed down the Clyde en route for Norway but returned immediately to Glasgow when news came in that the Germans had invaded the Low Countries that same day.

On joining Stockwell's command, No 9 Company, now under the command of Major W. Glendinning of the Welch Regiment, was immediately detached with No 6 Company to the Isles of Scilly, to forestall an invasion, support the Seigneur, Major Arthur Dorrien-Smith,* and to protect important, and highly secret, forward radar sites in the islands. Company headquarters was located on St Mary's Isle, with a platoon detached to each of Tresco, St Agnes and St Martin's.[76] The defence of the rest of the peninsula was left to Nos 7 and 8 Companies, the local anti-aircraft artillery and searchlight units, and the Local Defence Volunteers (L.D.V.), soon to become the Home Guard. Much time was spent by all companies working with the Royal Engineers, the Pioneer Corps, and civil labour constructing coastal obstacles and defences, cratering roads, building pill-boxes, trenches, bunkers, and observation posts for the Royal Observer Corps.[77] There was daily bombing by the *Luftwaffe*.[78] On 14 July, H.Q. Southern Command ordered that the ports and harbours of Looe, Par, Mevagissey, Charlestown, Porthleven, Portreath, Appledore, Barnstaple and Bideford should be prepared for immobilisation – a major task given the shortage of engineer assistance.[79]

As the Battle of Britain raged between June and September, and the Germans continued to build up their invasion fleet, tension mounted. On 7 September a serious invasion scare occurred when a large concentration of shipping was sighted south-west of the Isle of Wight: the codeword 'Cromwell' was received at 21.30 hrs, indicating that the Germans were landing, and the church bells were rung to sound the general alarm. Major Stockwell called an orders group where he passed on the information, received from above, that the Germans had landed at Plymouth with the intention of sealing off the peninsula as a bridgehead for further operations inland. Things rapidly returned to normal when the scare was exposed.[80]

Once the immediate threat of invasion had lifted, the Independent Companies were returned to the operational control of the Director of Combined Operations. On 17 October, Major Stockwell called a conference of his subordinate commanders and representatives of the small boat training centres, at Home Park, Plymouth. The tasks of the group were now over: Nos 1, 2, 3, 4, and 5 and 9 Independent Companies were to form No 1 Special Service Battalion.[81] In March 1941 this unit became No 1 Commando under Lieutenant Colonel W. Glendinning, and later Lieutenant Colonel T.H. Trevor, and because it contained a substantial contingent of Welsh soldiers from Nos 2 and 9 Independent Companies, this unit was known unofficially as 'The Welsh Commando.'

---

*   Major Arthur Algernon Dorrien-Smith DSO had served in the South African and Great Wars. He was a relative of the Great War General Smith-Dorrien.

STAFF LIST, INDEPENDENT COMPANIES 1940

	No 2 Company (53rd (Welsh) Division)	No 9 Company (38th (Welsh) Division)
Officer Commanding	Maj H.C. Stockwell DSO	Maj W. Siddons DCM[1]
Second-in-Command	Capt T.H. Trevor *Welch*	Maj W. Glendinning *Welch* (Jun 40)
Support Platoon Commander	Capt B.G.B. Pugh	Capt P. Hoffman
I.O.	Lt G. Venables-Llewellyn	2Lt J.C.K. Purdey
Platoon and Section Commanders	Capt Sir James Croft	
	Lt C.L. Wilding-Jones[2]	2Lt J.R.T. Waldron
	Lt J. Bradford *Mons*	2Lt T. Evill
	2Lt N.J.H. Anderson MC	2Lt G. Metcalfe
	2Lt J. Fitton[3]	2Lt R. Swain
	2Lt T.H. Davies[4]	2Lt D.T. Beddous
L.O.	2Lt Sönothagen, *Norwegian Army*	
Quartermaster	CQMS I.W. Lavender[5]	Lt & QM – Crookes
Medical Officer	Lt S. Corry *R.A.M.C.*	Lt G.F. Petty *R.A.M.C.*
R.E. attached	2Lt L. Scott-Bowden *R.E.*	Lt R. Holmes *R.E.*
		Sgt – Guy *R.E.*
Platoon and Section Sergeants	Sgt W.A. Jones	Sgt – Pritchard

Notes

1 Removed from command in June 1940 and returned to 8 R.W.F. in August. He was court-martialled and dismissed the service for misconduct.
2 Mentioned in Despatches.
3 PoW 26 May 1940.
4 Killed in action 26 May 1940.
5 Killed in action 26 May 1940.

iii. Subsequent History of No 1 Commando.[82]

In July 1941 the Commando joined Force 110 to prepare for the seizure of the Canary Islands, an operation which never took place. Thereafter the unit carried out some raids and also provided volunteers to No 2 Commando for the St Nazaire raid. In November 1942 the Commando took part in Operation *Torch*. Half the unit landed west of Algiers, capturing a fort at Cap Sidi Ferat and the airfield at Blida; the other half landed west of Algiers and captured Fort D'Estré. Thereafter the Commando took part in operations along the

CSM Andrew O'Marah with No 1 Commando.

Tunisian coast, raiding inland to disrupt the Axis lines of communication. In September 1943 the Commando returned home, to Winchester, where it joined No 1 Special Service Brigade under Lord Lovat. It landed on D-Day at Sword Beach and took part in operations in France and the Low Countries until late summer when it returned briefly to Britain. In September 1944 the Commando moved to Ceylon, joining No 3 Commando Brigade R.M. and from there to Burma where it came under the command of the 25th Indian Division. The Commando took part in the amphibious raid on Ramree Island, the capture of the Myebon Peninsula, south-east of Akyab, in January 1945 and then the attack on Kangdaw. At the close of the war the Commando moved to Hong Kong and was gradually reduced in strength, amalgamating with No 5 Commando in January 1946 and being disbanded in January 1947.

Notes

1   Their story is told in David Erskine, *The Scots Guards, 1919–1955* (London, 1956). See also J.P. Riley *From Pole to Pole*, (Cambridge, 1998) pp. 115–122.
2   Peter Wilkinson and Joan Bright Astley, *Gubbins and SOE* (London, 1997), p. 50.
3   *The German Campaign in Norway*. German Naval History Series BR 1840 (1) compiled by Tactical and Staff Duties Division of the Admiralty (27 November 1948) pp. 7–8. Full details of the German and Allied Plans and the conduct of the campaign can also be found in T.K. Derry *The Campaign in Norway*. *History of the Second World War, United Kingdom Military Series* (HMSO London, 1952).
4   They were first designated Guerrilla Companies, then Special Infantry Companies, and finally Independent Companies. T.N.A. WO 260/3 and 260/32. See also Messenger, pp. 19–20, and Wilkinson and Bright Astley, p. 51.
5   See the account by Trevor, O.C. No 2 Company, in T.N.A. DEFE 2/1 dated 1 June 1940.
6   Christopher Buckley *Norway, The Commandos, Dieppe* (HMSO, London, 1951), p. 138.
7   T.N.A. WO 166/1030–158 (Royal Welch) Infantry Brigade War Diary September 1939–April 1941.
8   KCL/Stockwell 2/1.
9   KCL/Stockwell 2/1.
10 *No 2 Independent Company – Account by Captain B.G.B. Pugh* dated 1st June 1940, Appendix 4. R.W.F. Museum 5439.
11 No 2 Independent Company War Diary, May 1940 (T.N.A. WO 168/106 folio 84227).
12 *No 2 Independent Company 1940*, account by Sergeant W.A. Jones 6 R.W.F., R.W.F. Mus 5168.
13 KCL/Stockwell/2/1.
14 KCL/Stockwell/2/1.
15 *No 2 Independent Company 1940*, account by Sergeant W.A. Jones.
16 Derry, p. 78.
17 HQ North-West Expeditionary Force Instructions dated 2 May 1940. T.N.A. WO 106/1944.
18 T.N.A. WO 168/106 folio 84337. No 2 Independent Company War Diary, May 1940.
19 KCL/Stockwell/2/1.
20 *No 2 Independent Company 1940*, account by Sergeant W.A. Jones.
21 Interview with Colonel B.G.B. Pugh, 3 April 2002.
22 Quintin Riley, *Personal Diary* held by Mrs N.A.C. Owen (daughter).
23 Quintin Riley, *Personal Diary*.
24 Auchinleck's instructions from the Secretary of State for War dated 5 May 1940 are cited in Derry, pp. 259–260.
25 Wilkinson and Bright Astley, pp. 53–54.
26 *No 2 Independent Company 1940*, account by Sjt WA Jones; *No 2 Independent Company – Account by Captain B.G.B. Pugh*.
27 T.N.A. WO 168/106.
28 *No 2 Independent Company – Account by Captain B.G.B. Pugh*.
29 Derry, p. 186.

30   *The German Campaign in Norway*, p. 66. See also the account in Major D.J.L. Fitzgerald MC, *History of the Irish Guards in the Second World War* (Aldershot, 1949), pp. 43–47.
31   See the obituary of Brigadier D.H. (Denis) FitzGerald DSO OBE (1911–2003), who survived the attack, in *The Daily Telegraph*, 8 August 2003.
32   T.N.A. WO 168/106.
33   Quintin Riley, *Personal Diary*.
34   Derry, p. 264 gives a figure of 4,000, which is too high. See also *The German Campaign in Norway*, p. 66.
35   Orders from Gubbins to Trappes-Lomax dated 20th May 1940 in Trappes-Lomax papers.
36   Quintin Riley, *Personal Diary*.
37   *History of the Irish Guards in the Second World War*, p. 55.
38   T.N.A. WO 168/106, Appendix 5.
39   *No 2 Independent Company 1940*, account by Sergeant W.A. Jones.
40   See the account in David Erskine, *The Scots Guards 1919–1955*.
41   Verney in *The Micks*, pp. 88–89, grossly misrepresents the true command relationship, giving the clear impression that the force was commanded by McGildowney. Neither Stockwell nor Stockforce are mentioned, and the Independent Companies receive no more than a passing reference.
42   T.N.A. WO 168/106.
43   *No 2 Independent Company 1940*, account by Sergeant W.A. Jones.
44   Stockforce War Diary in KCL/Stockwell/2/1.
45   Operation Order for Pothus. Annex A to Stockforce War Diary in KCL/Stockwell/2/1.
46   Stockforce War Diary in KCL/Stockwell/2/1.
47   *History of the Irish Guards in the Second World War*, p. 57.
48   *From Pole to Pole*, p. 127.
49   *No 2 Independent Company 1940*, account by Sergeant W.A. Jones.
50   Derry, p. 189; *History of the Irish Guards in the Second World War*, p. 58.
51   Annex B to Stockforce War Diary in KCL/Stockwell/2/1.
52   Derry, p. 189. For the German perspective on this and identification of formations and units see also *The German Campaign in Norway*, pp. 66–67.
53   *No 2 Independent Company – Account by Captain B.G.B. Pugh*.
54   T.N.A. WO 168/106.
55   KCL/Stockwell/2/1.
56   *No 2 Independent Company – Account by Captain B.G.B. Pugh*
57   Stockforce War Diary in KCL/Stockwell/2/1.
58   Quintin Riley, *Personal Diary*.
59   *History of the Irish Guards in the Second World War*, p. 65.
60   Major J.R. Paterson, cited in *The Commandos 1940–1946*, p. 24. T.N.A. WO 168/106 confirms his dispositions.
61   Appendix E to Stockforce War Diary in KCL/Stockwell/2/1.
62   Stockforce War Diary in KCL/Stockwell/2/1.
63   *The Commandos 1940–1946*, p. 25.
64   KCL/Stockwell/2/1; Quintin Riley, *Personal Diary*.
65   T.N.A. WO 168/106.
66   Letter from Maj Gen Wilson, G.O.C. 53rd Division, dated 20 June 1940 in KCL/Stockwell 2/6.
67   T.N.A. CAB 120/144.
68   Clarke's account is in T.N.A. DEFE 2/4.
69   Memo dated 13 June 1940 in T.N.A. WO 193/384.
70   Messenger, p. 30.
71   AB 439 in KCL/Stockwell/1/1.
72   Messenger, p. 33.
73   T.N.A. WO 166/578–48th (South Midland) Division Op Instruction No 14. This division was the Area reserve formation.
74   T.N.A. WO 199/1568 – Defence of aerodromes and landing grounds.

75 John Parker, *Commandos*, (London, 2000), p. 14; Gerald F. Petty, *Mad Gerry. Welsh Wartime Medical Officer* (Newport, 1982), p. 15.
76 *Mad Gerry,* p. 21.
77 Interview with Colonel B.G.B. Pugh, 3rd April 2002.
78 *Mad Gerry,* p. 23.
79 T.N.A. WO 199/1697 – Defence against invasion.
80 T.N.A. WO 166/578.
81 Messenger, p. 40; *From Pole to Pole*, p. 134.
82 Messenger, *The Commandos*; T.N.A. DEFE 2/31, No1 Commando War Diary, 1 November 1942–31 January 1945; A.G. 17 (A) 06/ 26.2.41 (AG Card).

Section V

Annexes

Annex A

Regimental Appointments, 1919–1940

Colonel-in-Chief
His Majesty King George V
His Majesty King George VI
Colonel of the Regiment
Lieutenant General Sir Francis Lloyd GCVO KCB DSO, 2 February 1915–26 February 1926
Lieutenant General Sir Charles Dobell KCB CMG DSO, 26 February 1926–26 October 1938
Major General J.R. Minshull-Ford CB DSO MC, 26 October 1938–3 March 1942
Brigadier E.O. Skaife OBE (acting), June 1940–3 March 1942*

REGULAR ARMY

THE REGIMENTAL DEPOT
Commanding Officers
Major E.R. Kearsley DSO, 27 May 1919
Major H.V. Venables Kyrke DSO, 27 May 1922
Major M.L. Lloyd-Mostyn, 27 May 1925
Major G.E.R. de Miremont DSO MC, 27 May 1928
Major Ll. A.A. Alston DSO MC, 21 October 1929
Major E. Wodehouse, 21 October 1932
Major A.M.G. Evans, 21 October 1935
Major H.C. Watkins MC, 21 October 1938
Adjutants
Captain D.M. Barchard, 1921
Lieutenant J.G. Bruxner-Randall, December 1922
Lieutenant D.I. Owen, 29 August 1923
Captain M.B. Dowse, 30 May 1927
Lieutenant Ll. Gwydyr-Jones, 30 May 1928
Lieutenant G.E. Braithwaite, 15 October 1930
Lieutenant C.H.V. Pritchard, 15 October 1933
Lieutenant R.C. Rose Price, March 1936

---

* Brigadier Skaife acted as Colonel of the Regiment as Major-General Minshull-Ford was ill following his escape from Guernsey where he was Lieutenant-Governor, just before the German occupation of the island.

Captain R.C.M. Kelly, 1939
Captain W.G. Daniel, 5 October 1940
Quartermasters
Captain H. Yates MC, 1921
Captain A.M. Watson MBE, 1925
Captain G.R. Whyley, 12 February 1930
Captain W.H. Albutt MBE DCM, February 1932
Regimental Sergeant Majors
Warrant Officer Class I A.M. Boreham MC, 2 May 1919
Warrant Officer Class I W. Heirene, 7 June 1922
Warrant Officer Class I A.G. Bent MM, 1930
Warrant Officer Class I A. Lungley DCM, 2 February 1932
Warrant Officer Class I J.T. Dale, 2 May 1937
Bandmaster
4178945 Warrant Officer Class I H.P.G. Purdue *(late Essex R.)*, 1932

1st BATTALION
Commanding Officers
Captain (Brevet Lieutenant Colonel) Ll. A.A. Alston DSO MC
Major E.L. Mills MC, 4 April 1919
Lieutenant Colonel J.B. Cockburn DSO, 10 June 1919
Lieutenant Colonel C.C. Norman CMG DSO, 7 April 1920
Lieutenant Colonel C.S. Owen CMG DSO, 23 September 1920 (acting until 10 September 1921)
Major E.O. Skaife (acting), 10 September 1923
Lieutenant Colonel C.S. Owen CMG DSO, 29 September 1923
Brevet Lieutenant Colonel P.R. Butler (acting), 23 April 1924
Lieutenant Colonel C.S. Owen CMG DSO, 29 July 1924
Lieutenant Colonel H.V. Venables Kyrke DSO, 10 September 1925
Lieutenant Colonel E.O. Skaife OBE, 4 September 1929
Major J.G. Bruxner-Randall (acting), 18 June 1930
Lieutenant Colonel E.O. Skaife OBE, 8 September 1930
Major J.G. Bruxner-Randall (acting), 16 September 1930
Lieutenant Colonel E.O. Skaife OBE, 25 December 1930
Major T.D. Daly MC (Acting), 19 July 1931
Lieutenant Colonel E.O. Skaife OBE, 29 September 1931
Lieutenant Colonel J.G. Bruxner-Randall, 18 May 1933
Lieutenant Colonel Ll. A.A. Alston DSO MC, 18 May 1937
Lieutenant Colonel H.F. Garnons-Williams, 19 July 1939*
Lieutenant Colonel H.B. Harrison MC, 11 November 1939†
Adjutants
Captain T. Bluck MC
Captain J.C. Wynne-Edwards, 1 April 1919
Captain (Brevet Lieutenant Colonel) W.G. Holmes DSO, 1 July 1919
Lieutenant M.B. Dowse, 1 July 1922
Lieutenant B.H. Hopkins, 1 July 1925

---

*   Killed in an air crash in France on 10 November 1939.
†   K.i.a. 27 May 1940 at St-Venant

Lieutenant M.H. ap Rhys Pryce, 1 July 1928
Lieutenant M.F.P. Lloyd, 1 September 1930
Lieutenant R.F.A. David, 1 December 1933
Lieutenant W.L.R. Benyon, 1 December 1936
Lieutenant J.E.C. Hood, 1 December 1939*

Quartermasters
Lieutenant A.J. Down
Captain D. Schofield MBE, 2 March 1919
Lieutenant G.R. Whyley, 12 February 1930
Captain A.G. Bent MM, 15 November 1934

Regimental Sergeant Majors
Warrant Officer Class I A. Smith
Warrant Officer Class I G.R. Whyley, 15 December 1921
Warrant Officer Class I R.W. Chambers, 1930
Warrant Officer Class I J.M. Kensett, 1933
Warrant Officer Class I S.M. Sherriff, 5 December 1939†

Bandmasters
4178899 Warrant Officer Class I S.V. Hays
4178945 Warrant Officer Class I H.P.G. Purdue (late *Essex R.*), 29 January 1925
Warrant Officer Class I W.J. Watkins, 1932
5172677 Warrant Officer Class I S. Hills ARCM (late *Railway Transport Corps*), 19 January 1935

2nd BATTALION

Commanding Officers
Lieutenant Colonel G.E.R. de Miremont DSO MC‡
Captain W.H. Fox (Cadre), 28 February 1919
Lieutenant Colonel (Brevet Colonel) O. de L. Williams CMG DSO, 21 August 1919
Major F.J. Walwyn DSO (acting), 29 October 1920
Lieutenant Colonel C.C. Norman CMG DSO, 30 October 1920
Lieutenant Colonel (Brevet Colonel) C.I. Stockwell CB CMG DSO, 12 May 1924
Major G.E.R. de Miremont DSO MC (acting), 22 August 1927
Lieutenant Colonel P.R. Butler DSO, 6 February 1928
Lieutenant Colonel C.C. Hewitt DSO MC, 20 January 1931
Lieutenant Colonel R.E. Hindson, 21 October 1934 (acting until 1 January 1935)
Major Ll. A.A. Alston DSO MC (acting), May 1936
Lieutenant Colonel D.M. Barchard, 2 November 1936
Lieutenant Colonel E. Wodehouse, 11 August 1939

Adjutants
Captain E. Howells MC
Lieutenant L. Coote, 16 July 1919
Captain (Brevet Lieutenant Colonel) G.E.R. de Miremont DSO MC, 18 February 1920
Captain D.M. Barchard, 18 February 1923
Lieutenant R.W.C. Martin, 18 February 1926
Captain M.B. Dowse, 4 September 1927

---

*   K.i.a. 27 May 1940 at St-Venant
†   Captured 27 May 1940 at St-Venant and PoW.
‡   Acting Lieutenant Colonel from 10 January 1919 (Personal documents).

Lieutenant Hon G.R. Clegg-Hill, 12 April 1929
Captain F.I. Gerrard MC, 20 October 1930
Captain (Brevet Major) H.A. Davies MBE MC, 20 October 1933
Lieutenant T.A.G. Pritchard, 21 January 1937
Lieutenant G.T.B.F. Dickson, November 1939
Quartermasters
Major H. Yates MC, 27 January 1912
Lieutenant C.J. Shea, 31 July 1919
Lieutenant W.H. Albutt DCM, 31 May 1924
Captain C. Jones DCM MM, 2 February 1932
Regimental Sergeant Majors
4178845 Warrant Officer Class I W.H. Albutt DCM, 1 May 1920 (acting from November 1919)
4178891 Warrant Officer Class I W. Gorham, 31 May 1924
4178914 Warrant Officer Class I C. Jones DCM MM,12 June 1930
4179190 Warrant Officer Class I A.G. Bent MM, 2 February 1932
4179052 Warrant Officer Class I N.T. Ridings, 15 November 1934
4027451 Warrant Officer Class I S. Metcalfe, 17 November 1937
Bandmasters
4178983 Warrant Officer Class I W.J. Clancy, 7 January 1912
533396 Warrant Officer Class I F. Burnett, 7 June 1932
Warrant Officer Class I S.E. Hills *(Late Glosters),* 19 January 1935

SPECIAL RESERVE (MILITIA)

3rd (SPECIAL RESERVE) BATTALION (ROYAL FLINT AND DENBIGH MILITIA)
Commanding Officer
Lieutenant Colonel A.R.P. Macartney-Filgate CBE, to October 1923
Adjutants
Lieutenant L. Coote
Lieutenant D.M. Barchard, 12 June 1919
Captain J.G. Bruxner-Randall, 18 August 1922
No further appointment from October 1923
Quartermaster
Lieutenant C.J. Shea

TERRITORIAL ARMY

4th (RESERVE) BATTALION (T.F.)
Lieutenant Colonel F.J. Gavin, to disbandment 23 September 1919

4th (DENBIGHSHIRE) BATTALION (T.A.)
Honorary Colonels
Colonel T.A. Wynne Edwards VD, 23 October 1919
Colonel E. Lloyd Edwards TD, 31 July 1926
Commanding Officers
Lieutenant Colonel J.H. Langton DSO, to disbandment 11 June 1919
Lieutenant Colonel J.R. Minshull-Ford DSO MC, 30 March 1920
Lieutenant Colonel C.H.R. Crawshay DSO, 3 May 1921

Lieutenant Colonel G.C.W. Westbrooke MC, 3 May 1924
Lieutenant Colonel G.R. Griffith OBE TD, 3 May 1929
Lieutenant Colonel R.G. Fenwick-Palmer, 1 November 1933
Lieutenant Colonel J.M. Davies MC, 1 November 1937
Lieutenant Colonel H. Allsebrook, 1 April 1939

Adjutants
Lieutenant C. Ellis, 10 April 1918
Captain M.L. Lloyd-Mostyn, 24 February 1920
Captain Hon G.R.B. Bingham, 1 March 1923
Captain H.A. Freeman MC, 1 September 1924
Lieutenant E.R. Freeman, 1 September 1927
Captain H.B. Harrison MC, 16 December 1931
Captain G.E. Braithwaite, 16 December 1935
Captain J.A.M. Rice-Evans, 23 December 1939

Quartermasters
Captain T. Mansfield, 1 July 1912
Lieutenant J.H. Randles, 3 July 1927

Regimental Sergeant Majors
Warrant Officer Class I H.E. Callus DCM, 1921
Warrant Officer Class I R. Leonard, July 1925
Warrant Officer Class I J.S. Mallett, December 1932
Warrant Officer Class I A. Lovell *W.G.*, December 1935
Warrant Officer Class I R. Gendall, December 1936
Warrant Officer Class I W.J. Hawkins, 1938

Bandmasters
Warrant Officer Class I – Kelly, 1921
Captain H. Delaney, December 1924

5th (FLINTSHIRE) BATTALION (T.A.)
Converted to 60th (R.W.F.) Anti-Tank Regiment R.A. on 28 November 1938

Honorary Colonels
Colonel J.S. Roberts VD TD, 15 July 1905
Colonel J. Sherrif Roberts VD TD DL JP, 1921 to March 1925
No appointment 1925–1933
Colonel E.H.W. Williams DSO, 23 April 1933
No appointment 1934–1936
Colonel Sir W.R.E. Mainwaring CB, 5 September 1936

Commanding Officers
Lieutenant Colonel F.H. Borthwick DSO, 9 June 1918
Lieutenant Colonel T.H. Parry DSO, 16 February 1920
Lieutenant Colonel R.C. Lloyd DSO MC TD, 1 September 1920
Lieutenant Colonel T. Freer Ash TD, 8 March 1921
Lieutenant Colonel E.H.W. Williams DSO, 20 June 1923*
Lieutenant Colonel H.M. Davies TD, 27 April 1933
Lieutenant Colonel S.H. Burton TD, 27 April 1938

---

*   Williams commanded the 5th Battalion for ten years, unusual even in the 1920s.

Adjutants
Captain K.B. Taylor MC
Major H.A. Jefferson DSO, 12 April 1920
Captain H. Alban Davies MBE MC, 12 April 1923
Captain D.I. Owen, 12 April 1927
Captain D.R. Evans, 1 November 1931
Lieutenant C.H.V. Pritchard, 1 November 1936
Quartermasters
Captain G. Claridge, 19 March 1920
Lieutenant E.F. Hollobon MM (Captain 1933), 30 April 1925
Regimental Sergeant Majors
Warrant Officer Class I G. White, 1921
Warrant Officer Class I H.W. Bloxham, June 1923
Warrant Officer Class I Clancey, June 1925
Warrant Officer Class I E. Davies, 1933
Warrant Officer Class I S. Sherriff, November 1935
Warrant Officer Class I Currie, November 1937
Bandmasters
Warrant Officer Class I H. Walsh, to 1935
Warrant Officer Class I Pratt, July 1935

6th (CAERNARVONSHIRE & ANGLESEY) BATTALION (T.A.)
Honorary Colonels
Colonel J.E. Greaves CBE TD, 16 November 1898
Colonel A.P.G. Gough CMG CBE DSO, 22 June 1929
No appointment 1930-32
Colonel the Lord Penrhyn, 5 October 1932
Commanding Officers
Lieutenant Colonel E.H. Evans MC
Lieutenant Colonel F. Mills DSO, 16 February 1920
Lieutenant Colonel F.J. Walwyn DSO, 31 December 1920
Lieutenant Colonel (Brevet Colonel) C.E. Vivian MC, 10 January 1923
Lieutenant Colonel A.M. Trustram Eve MC, 10 January 1927
Lieutenant Colonel M.L. Lloyd-Mostyn, 10 January 1931
Lieutenant Colonel J.M. Evans, 10 January 1937
Lieutenant Colonel A.M.G. Evans, 2 January 1940
Adjutants
Captain J.N. More, 12 March 1920
Captain (Brevet Lieutenant Colonel) W.G. Holmes DSO, 12 March 1923
Captain A.M.G. Evans, 12 September 1923
Captain H.F. Garnons-Williams, 12 September 1927
Captain D.H.W. Kirkby, 6 December 1930
Captain P.L. Bowers, 6 December 1934
Captain J.A.M. Rice-Evans, 1 July1938
Captain E.H. Cadogan, 1 November 1938
Quartermasters
Captain T. Deane, 24 June 1915
Lieutenant R.E. Griffiths, 1925
Lieutenant W.H. Kelly [later Captain], 29 January 1926

Lieutenant R.W. Howell MM, 20 December 1935
Regimental Sergeant Majors
Warrant Officer Class I H.A. Richards, 1921
Warrant Officer Class I Simpson, May 1924
Warrant Officer Class I H. Howell, 1927
Warrant Officer Class I G. Johnson, 1934
Warrant Officer Class I J. Brown, January 1938

5th/6th BATTALION (T.F.)
Commanding Officers
Lieutenant Colonel T.H. Parry DSO, 26 September 1918
Lieutenant Colonel H.A. Jefferson, 20 March 1919 to disbandment

7th (MERIONETH & MONTGOMERYSHIRE) BATTALION (T.A.)
Honorary Colonels
Colonel Sir E. Pryce-Jones Bt TD, 15 September 1908
Colonel Sir H.L. Watkin Williams Wynn Bt CB TD, 1 November 1907
Both re-appointed joint Honorary Colonels in 1923 on the disbandment of the Montgomeryshire
    Yeomanry of which Sir E. Pryce-Jones had been Honorary Colonel.
Commanding Officers
Lieutenant Colonel T.H. Harker DSO *K.R.R.C.*
Lieutenant Colonel R.O. Crewe-Read DSO *S.W.B.*, 16 February 1920
Lieutenant Colonel G.R.D. Harrison TD, 28 February 1925
Lieutenant Colonel C.S. Price Davies MC TD, 28 February 1929
Lieutenant Colonel W. Roberts MC, 28 February 1937
Lieutenant Colonel G.F. Watson DSO, 6 February 40
Adjutants
Captain T. Picton MC *Connaught Rangers*
Captain J.C. Wynne Edwards, 17 March 1920
Captain T. Picton MBE MC *Connaught Rangers [later Royal Sussex Regiment 1923]*, 1 October 1921
Captain G.F. Watson DSO, 16 October 1924
Lieutenant R.G. Davies-Jenkins, 14 November 1928
Lieutenant J.H. Liscombe, 14 November 1932
Captain R. de B. Hardie, 14 November 1936
Captain W.L. R Benyon, 17 February 1940
Quartermasters
Captain T.W. Grist, 22 March 1920
Captain R. Leonard, 13 November 1929
Regimental Sergeant Majors
Warrant Officer Class I F. Pepper, 1919
Warrant Officer Class I W.P. Allen, 1921
Warrant Officer Class I Dickenson DCM, October 1922
Warrant Officer Class I W. Martin, May 1923
Warrant Officer Class I N. Ridings, 1931
Warrant Officer Class I E. Davies, October 1934
Bandmaster
Warrant Officer Class I S.J. Jones, 1921

1/7th (MERIONETH & MONTGOMERYSHIRE) BATTALION (T.F.)
Disbanded 12 March 1920
Commanding Officer
Lieutenant Colonel E.W. Brighton Bedfs Herts, to 19 January 1920
Adjutant
Lieutenant F.D. Buchan, to 12 March 1920
Quartermaster
Lieutenant H. Delany, to 12 March 1920

8th (DENBIGHSHIRE) BATTALION (T.A.)
Commanding Officers
Lieutenant Colonel R.C. Lloyd, 5 May 1939
Captain W. Siddons DCM (acting), 21 December 1939
Major Sir Henry Tate Bt (acting), 2 January 1940
Lieutenant Colonel R.G. Fenwick-Palmer, 25 March 1940
Adjutant
Captain S.V. Misa, September 1939
Quartermaster
Captain E. Davies MBE, 24 May 1939
Regimental Sergeant Major
Warrant Officer Class I J. Bacon

9th (CAERNARVONSHIRE & ANGLESEY) BATTALION (T.A.)
Commanding Officers
Lieutenant Colonel R.R. Davies, 27 May 1939
Lieutenant Colonel G.E. Malcolm MC *Gordons*, 6 February 1940
Adjutants
Captain C.V. Whiting, September 1939
Captain N.R.G. Bosanquet, February 1940
Regimental Sergeant Major
Warrant Officer Class I W. Howells, 1938

10th (MERIONETH & MONTGOMERYSHIRE) BATTALION (T.A.)
Commanding Officers
Lieutenant Colonel W.W. Kirkby DSO, 27 May 1939
Lieutenant Colonel D.W.H. Kirkby, 6 February 1940
Adjutant
Captain H. Phibbs, 27 May 1939
Quartermaster
Lieutenant W. Gorham, 1 July 1939
Regimental Sergeant Major
Warrant Officer Class I N.T. Ridings

23rd BATTALION (T.F.)
Lieutenant Colonel G.F. Tod, to disbandment, 21 March 1919

24th (DENBIGHSHIRE YEOMANRY) BATTALION (T.F.)
Commanding Officer
Lieutenant Colonel H.N.M. Clegg DSO, to disbandment 28 March 1919

25th (MONTGOMERYSHIRE YEOMANRY AND WELSH HORSE) BATTALION (T.F.)
Commanding Officer
Lieutenant Colonel J.G. Rees DSO, to disbandment 29 June 1919
Adjutant
Captain F.E. Beavan, 22 June 1918 to disbandment
Quartermaster
Lieutenant T.H. Knowles
Regimental Sergeant Major
Warrant Officer Class I E. Branch DCM

NATIONAL DEFENCE COMPANIES, 1936–1940
Commanding Officers
Denbighshire
Major V.C. Roberts MC
Flintshire
Captain R. Hyde-Linaker
Caernarvonshire & Anglesey
Captain T.A. MacMillan
Merioneth & Montgomeryshire
Captain E.W. Edwards

INDEPENDENT COMPANIES, 1940–1941
Officers Commanding
No 2 Independent Company
Maj H.C. Stockwell DSO, 21 April 1940
Capt T.H. Trevor *Welch*, 20 July 1940

No 9 Independent Company
Maj W. Siddons DCM, 20 April 1940
Maj W. Glendinning *Welch*, June 1940

115 (Royal Welch) Brigade Anti-Tank Company
Captain A.F. Jones, May 1940–1 February 1941

158 (Royal Welch) Brigade Anti-Tank Company
Major A.S.D. Graesser, May 1940–1 February 1941

SERVICE BATTALIONS

8th (SERVICE) BATTALION
Commanding Officer
Lieutenant Colonel E.A. Stretch DSO DCM, to disbandment 16 August 1919
Regimental Sergeant Major
Warrant Officer Class I A. Haycock

9th (SERVICE) BATTALION
Commanding Officer
Lieutenant Colonel C.E. Davies DSO *R. War. R.*, to disbandment 2 June 1919

11th (SERVICE) BATTALION
Commanding Officer
Lieutenant Colonel A.H. Yatman DSO, to disbandment 14 October 1919

13th (SERVICE) BATTALION
Commanding Officer
Lieutenant Colonel J.F. Leman DSO, to disbandment 4 June 1919

14th (SERVICE) BATTALION
Commanding Officer
Lieutenant Colonel B.W. Collier DSO *S.W.B.*, 5 November 1918
Lieutenant Colonel C.C. Norman CMG DSO, 11 November 1918 to disbandment 4 June 1919

16th (SERVICE) BATTALION
Commanding Officer
Lieutenant Colonel E.J. de Pentheny-O'Kelly DSO, to December 1918
Lieutenant Colonel C.E. Davies, to disbandment 6 June 1919

17th (SERVICE) BATTALION
Commanding Officer
Lieutenant Colonel R.L. Beasley, 11 November 1918 to disbandment 7 June 1919

26th (SERVICE) BATTALION
Commanding Officer
Lieutenant Colonel E.H. Thurston, to 11 November 1918
Lieutenant Colonel H.H. Lee, to disbandment 6 January 1920

1st GARRISON BATTALION
Commanding Officer
Lieutenant Colonel A.J. Arnold CBE DSO, to disbandment 14 February 1920

2nd GARRISON BATTALION
Commanding Officer
Lieutenant Colonel W.H, Hussey-Walsh, to November 1918
Lieutenant Colonel W.R. Howell, to disbandment 17 September 1919

6th GARRISON BATTALION
Commanding Officer
Lieutenant Colonel E.C.M. Lushington, to 16 June 1919

3rd RESERVE GARRISON BATTALION
Commanding Officer
Lieutenant Colonel C.E. Willes CMG, to disbandment 16 May 1919

VOLUNTEER BATTALIONS
1918–1919

1st VOLUNTEER BATTALION (ANGLESEY VOLUNTEER REGIMENT)
County Commandant
Lieutenant Colonel T.E.J. Lloyd
Commandant
Lieutenant Colonel Sir John Neave Bt
Adjutant
Captain H.F. Harries *Welch*
Quartermaster
Lieutenant J.E. Jones

2nd VOLUNTEER BATTALION (FLINTSHIRE & DENBIGHSHIRE VOLUNTEER REGIMENT)
County Commandants
Lieutenant Colonel H.R.L. Howard *Cheshire* (Flint)
Brevet Lieutenant Colonel Lieutenant Colonel The Lord Trevor (Denbigh)
Commandant
Lieutenant Colonel The Lord Colwyn
Adjutant
Captain G.T. Royle *Gen List*
Quartermasters
Lieutenant E.R. Hughes
Lieutenant F.L. Jones

3rd VOLUNTEER BATTALION (CAERNARVONSHIRE VOLUNTEER REGIMENT)
County Commandant
Colonel J.E. Greaves
Commandant
Major the Lord Mostyn
County Adjutant
Captain R.S. Ransome
Adjutant
Captain A.O. Roberts
Quartermasters
Lieutenant B.P. Gunn
Lieutenant R. Williams

4th VOLUNTEER BATTALION (MERIONETHSHIRE VOLUNTEER REGIMENT)
County Commandant
Lieutenant Colonel A.E.R. Jelf-Revely
Commandant
Hon Colonel Sir A.O. Williams Bt
Adjutant
Lieutenant R.S. Allen
Quartermaster
Lieutenant F.H. Pryce

5th VOLUNTEER BATTALION (MONTGOMERYSHIRE VOLUNTEER REGIMENT)
County Commandant
Lieutenant Colonel Sir H.L.W. Williams-Wynn Bt CB
Commandant
Captain Lord H.L.H. Vane-Tempest KCVO (acting)
Adjutant
Captain G.M.S. McAlister *W.I.R.*
Quartermaster
Lieutenant J.W. Davies

ARTILLERY REGIMENTS
1938–1940

60th (R.W.F.) ANTI-TANK REGIMENT R.A., 1939–1940
Honorary Colonel
Colonel Sir W.R.E. Mainwaring CB, 28 November 1938
Commanding Officer
Lieutenant Colonel S.H. Burton TD, 28 November 1938
Lieutenant Colonel H. Sheriff Roberts, July 1939
Adjutant
Captain C.H.V. Pritchard
Quartermasters
Captain E.F. Hollobon MM, 28 November 1938
Lieutenant A.T. Currie, May 1940
Regimental Sergeant Major
Warrant Officer Class I A.T. Currie, 28 November 1938
Bandmaster
Warrant Officer Class II S. Jones

70th (R.W.F.) ANTI-TANK REGIMENT R.A., 1939–1940
Commanding Officers
Lieutenant Colonel H.M. Davies OBE TD, 1 September 1939
Lieutenant Colonel J.H. Colbourn, 22 April 1940
Adjutant
Captain J.J. Borthwick
Quartermaster
Lieutenant C.A. Barnes

101st LIGHT ANTI-AIRCRAFT & ANTI-TANK REGIMENT R.A., 1940
Commanding Officers
Lieutenant Colonel H. Sheriff Roberts
Major L.H. H. Payne, April 1940
Lieutenant Colonel B.D. Cameron, 5–7 June 1940
Major J.R.O. Charlton MC (acting), 7 June 1940
Lieutenant Colonel J.D. Shapland MC, 6 July 1940
Adjutant
Captain J.L. d'E. Darby
Quartermaster
Lieutenant A.T. Currie

RUTHIN SCHOOL CADET CORPS
Officer Commanding
Captain J. Lloyd-Jones, 1922–1932
Permanent Staff Instructor
Warrant Officer Class I – Mallet, to December 1929
Sergeant – Roberts, January 1930–December 1932

REGIMENTAL INSTITUTIONS

Chairman of the Officers' Association
Lieutenant Colonel C.H.R. Crawshay DSO, 1920–1934
Major L.N. Vincent Evans CB, 1934–1946
Secretary of the Officers' Association
Captain P.F. Knightley DSO, 1920–1946

Chairman of the Old Comrades' Association
Lieutenant Colonel C.H.R. Crawshay DSO, 1921–1934
Major E.R. Kearsley DSO, 1934–1946

Secretary of the Old Comrades' Association
Mr F. O'Neil, 1921–1928
Mr S.B. Lord, 1928–1956

Annex B

Biographies of the Colonels of the Regiment, 1915–1946

---

i. Lieutenant General Sir Francis Lloyd GCVO KCB DSO (1915–1926)

Sir Francis Lloyd was commissioned into the 33rd Foot, later the Duke of Wellington's Regiment, in 1875, but transferred within a few months to his father's old regiment, the Grenadier Guards. He served in the Suakin Expedition in 1885 and was mentioned in despatches. He served in Egypt in 1898 and was awarded the DSO and again mentioned in despatches. He commanded the 2nd Battalion Grenadier Guards during the South African War and was badly wounded at Biddulphsberg. He commanded 1 Guards Brigade from 1904 to 1908 and 53rd (Welsh) Division from 1909 to 1912. In 1913 he was appointed to command London District in the rank of Lieutenant General, a command he held for five years throughout the Great War. He was ordered by Lord Kitchener to raise the Welsh Guards on 1 March 1915 and it was this, coupled with his appointment to

Lieutenant General Sir Francis Lloyd
GCVO KCB DSO. (R.W.F. Mus)

the Colonelcy of The Royal Welsh Fusiliers after the death of Sir Luke O'Connor on 2 February 1915 that probably gave rise to the unfounded rumour that the Royal Welsh Fusiliers declined the honour of becoming the Welsh Guards. He retired in 1920 and remained Colonel until his death in 1926.[1]

ii. Lieutenant General Sir Charles Dobell KCB CMG DSO ADC (1926–1938)

Charles Macpherson Dobell was born in Canada and entered the R.M.C. Kingston, from where he was commissioned into The Royal Welsh Fusiliers in 1890. He joined the 1st Battalion just in time for the Hazara Expedition of 1891. By 1899 he was a Brevet Major and was appointed to command the 2nd Battalion Mounted Infantry in South Africa, where he won a DSO and was mentioned in despatches. He then joined 2 R.W. Fus in China for the Pekin Expedition of 1900. From 1905 to 1906 he saw further active service in West Africa where he was again mentioned in despatches and made Brevet Lieutenant Colonel. He attended the Staff College, Camberley, in 1907 and then went to the War Office. In May 1912 he was appointed to command the 1st Battalion Bedfordshire Regiment but after only a year in command he was appointed Inspector General of the Royal West African Frontier Force as a Brevet Colonel and temporary Brigadier General. When war broke out in August 1914 he was given the task of capturing the German colony of Cameroon. This he did with conspicuous success and small casualties, for which he was made both CMG and KCB. He became a Major General in June 1915 and given command of the Western Frontier Force in Egypt under Sir Archibald Murray, after which he commanded a sector of the Suez Canal defences. He held the temporary rank of Lieutenant General from September 1916 to April 1917 and was responsible for the 1st and 2nd Battles of Gaza, both of which ended badly. He was replaced in Palestine by Lieutenant General Sir Edmund Allenby and given command of the 2nd (Rawalpindi) Division in India. In

Lieutenant General Sir Charles Dobell KCB CMG DSO ADC. (R.W.F. Mus)

1919 he took part in the 3rd Afghan War and was twice mentioned in despatches. He retired in 1923. He was appointed Colonel of the Regiment on 26 February 1926 and held the appointment until 26 October 1938 when he resigned the Colonelcy in favour of Major General Minshull-Ford. He was thus the first Colonel since General Sir William Codrington who had not died while Colonel of the Regiment. Lieutenant General Dobell died in 1958.[2]

iii. Major General J.R. Minshull-Ford CB DSO MC (1938–1940)

John Randle Minshull-Ford ('Scatter') was commissioned into The Royal Welsh Fusiliers in

1900 and joined 2 R.W. Fus in Hong Kong. He qualified as an interpreter in French and was promoted to Captain in 1911. He served as Adjutant of the 4th Battalion from 1912 to November 1914 when in the aftermath of the disaster of First Ypres, he assumed the post of Adjutant 1 R.W. Fus and for a short time commanded the battalion. He was then staff captain and afterwards Brigade Major 115 (Royal Welch) Infantry Brigade in France. He was wounded at the Battle of Neuve Chapelle in March 1915. As a Temporary Lieutenant Colonel, he commanded the 1st Battalion from October 1915 until February 1916. He then commanded a brigade in the Home Forces and then in France until 1919. He was wounded in all four times, won a MC and a DSO and was mentioned in despatches six times.

Major General J.R. Minshull-Ford CB DSO MC. (R.W.F. Mus)

After the War he was briefly a Brigade Commander in the British Army of the Rhine in 1919 but with the post-war reductions in the size of the Army, he reverted to his substantive rank and then served as Commanding Officer of the 4th Battalion South Staffordshire Regiment from 1920 to 1921. He was placed on half pay from 1929 but returned to active duty as Commander 5 Infantry Brigade in the 3rd Division, Aldershot Command, from 1930 to 1932, and was appointed General Officer Commanding 44th (Home Counties) Infantry Division in 1932. In all, he had commanded four different battalions and seven different brigades. He was appointed CB in 1933, before retiring in 1938. He was briefly Lieutenant Governor of Guernsey and its dependencies, Sark and Alderney, in 1940, and was lucky to escape just before the Germans arrived. Being ordered to abandon the people of Guernsey to their fate had a huge effect on him, both personally and professionally, after his distinguished service in the Great War, for he knew just what living under German occupation did to people. He was Colonel of the Regiment from 26 October 1938 until 3 March 1942, although ill health caused him to hand over the acting Colonelcy to Brigadier Eric Skaife in 1940. He died on 1 April 1948.[3]

iv. Brigadier Sir Eric Skaife CB OBE DL (Acting Colonel, 1940–1942)

Brigadier Sir Eric Skaife CB OBE DL. (R.W.F. Mus)

Eric Ommaney Skaife was commissioned into The Royal Welsh Fusiliers in 1903 and joined the 1st Battalion, which had just returned from South Africa. He served with the 1st Battalion until 1908 when he became Signal Officer 17 Infantry Brigade at Cork, and then Signal Officer 6th Infantry Division also at Cork. He also, in 1907, passed the qualifying exam in Russian, spent two months in Moscow in 1908, and later that year qualified as an interpreter. He rejoined 1 R.W. Fus. in October 1909 and served with the battalion until the outbreak of war in 1914, in Ireland, at home and in Malta. In 1911 he again spent two months in Moscow. In August 1914 he crossed with the 1st Battalion to France where, during the First Battle of Ypres, he was wounded in the face, head and arm, and taken prisoner. He was at first reported killed, and was also mentioned in despatches. He spent the remaining war years in prison camps in Germany and interned in the Netherlands, using his enforced leisure to improve his Russian and also to learn Welsh. After his release in 1918 he was posted to the War Office and was made OBE. He attended the Staff College, Camberley, in 1920. He joined 2 R.W.F. as a company commander in Limerick in 1921 during the campaign in Ireland and later that year was posted back to 1 R.W.F. as Senior Major during the campaign in Waziristan, where he was again mentioned in despatches. After a further spell at the War Office from 1924 to 1928, during which time he published a revised edition of an earlier work, *A Short History of The Royal Welch Fusiliers*, he again joined 2 R.W.F., this time in Germany, for a year, after which he was promoted to Lieutenant Colonel. In 1929 he took command of 1 R.W.F., holding the command in India, the Sudan and Tidworth, until 1933. He was then promoted Brevet Colonel and became Assistant Adjutant General at H.Q. Eastern Command in Colchester. In 1934, his proficiency in Russian led to his appointment as Military Attaché at the British Embassy in Bolshevist Moscow. He remained there until 1937 when he returned home and assumed command of 158 (Royal Welch) Infantry Brigade (T.A.) at Wrexham. Shortly after the outbreak of war he was badly injured in a car crash. After his recovery he commanded 15 and 215 Infantry Brigades, and was an Area Commander in London. In 1941 he was appointed to the Foreign Office for special duties in the political intelligence department. He retired in 1944. He was later County Commandant of the Merioneth and Montgomeryshire Army Cadet Force and Honorary Colonel 636 (Royal Welch) L.A.A. Regiment R.A. (T.A.). He became acting Colonel of the Regiment from 1940 to 1942, during the illness of Major General Minshull-Ford. He was again Colonel of the Regiment from 1948 to 1952, when he was appointed CB.

In addition to his military career, Skaife, an Englishman, is remembered for his devotion to matters of Welsh language and culture. As early as 1933 he became a member of the *Gorsedd Beirdd ynys Prydain*, and was a Day President of the Wrexham *Eisteddfod*. From 1943 to 1955 he was Vice-President of the Welsh League of Youth, or *Urdd*. In 1945 he was initiated as a *Gorsedd Bard Gwas Derfel* at the Rhosllanerchrugog *Eisteddfod*. He was appointed a Deputy Lord Lieutenant of Merioneth in 1950, and High Sheriff in 1956. He became Vice-President of the Honourable Society of Cymmrodorion in 1953 and in 1956 was promoted to the Druidic Order of the *Gorsedd*. He also served as a member of the Governing Body and of the Representative Body of the Anglican Church in Wales. In January 1956 he was knighted, but died suddenly on 2 October of that year. After his death, he left a generous bequest, which became the Skaife Fund, to the Regiment, which continues to benefit serving Officers and men to this day.[4]

v. Major General N. Maitland Wilson CB DSO OBE (1942–1946)

Nigel Maitland Wilson was commissioned into The Royal Welsh Fusiliers in 1904, transferring four years later to the 10th Gurkhas. He served in Europe during the Great War, where he won the DSO and was mentioned in despatches. He was made OBE for his service in Waziristan in 1922 and 1923. After commanding the 1/10th Gurkhas he was promoted to Colonel in 1933 and appointed Assistant Adjutant & Quartermaster General for Rawalpindi District. In 1935 he was promoted to Brigadier and appointed to command the Sind Independent Brigade Area. In 1936 he became Director Personal Services at Army H.Q., India. In 1938 he was promoted to Major General, made CB, and appointed Deputy Adjutant General & Director of Organisation at Army H.Q., India. He retired in 1941. He then held the appointment of Secretary to the Lord Great Chamberlain from 1945 to 1948. He was

Major General N. Maitland Wilson
CB DSO OBE. (R.W.F. Mus)

appointed Colonel of the Regiment on 3 March 1942. He held the appointment for the rest of the war years and the first eighteen months of peace, until poor health obliged him to retire on 31 December 1946. He died on 24 February 1950.[5]

Notes

1   *Regimental Records*, Volume IV, p. 275.
2   E.L. Kirby, *Officers of The Royal Welch Fusiliers, 1689–1914.*
3   E.L. Kirby, *Officers of The Royal Welch Fusiliers, 1689–1914.*
4   *Y Ddraig Goch*, Winter 1956, pp. 12–14; *Who Was Who*, Volume 5, 1951–1960; *News Chronicle*, 13 October 1956; *Wrexham Leader*, 5 October 1956; *The Daily Post* (Liverpool), 6 October 1956; *The Times*, 6 October 1956.
5   *Y Ddraig Goch*, Summer 1950, p. 5; *Who Was Who*, Volume 4, 1941–1950.

Annex C[1]

Honours, Awards and Decorations, 1919–1940[*]

Readers should note that this annex is not indexed

Rank & Name	No.	Unit	Place & Date	London Gazette
Orders of Chivalry				
Companion of the Most Honourable Order of the Bath (CB)				
Maj Gen W.G. Holmes DSO	4613	Staff	UK	1938
Maj Gen N. Maitland Wilson DSO		Staff	India	1938
Maj Gen J.R. Minshull-Ford DSO		Staff	UK	1938
Commander of the Order of the British Empire (CBE)				
Lt Col A.R.P. Macartney-Filgate		3 R.W.F.	U.K.	3 June 1919
Bt Col R.G. Fenwick-Palmer		4 R.W.F.	U.K.	9 June 1938
Companion of the Distinguised Service Order (DSO)				
Maj H.C. Stockwell	23894	2 Indep Coy	Norway, 1940	6 June 1940
Officer of the Order of the British Empire (OBE)				
Capt H.A. Freeman MC	13564	1 R.W.F.	Cyprus, Oct 1931	3 Jun 1932
Bt Col Davies H. Maldwyn		5 R.W.F.	U.K.	9 Jun 1938
Lt Col S.O. Jones	8995	H.Q. Orkney Is	U.K., 1939–1940	11 July 1940
Maj M.B. Dowse	6418	H.Q. 3rd Division	B.E.F.	11 July 1940
Member of the Order of the British Empire (MBE)				
Lt H.A. Davies MC				1 Jan 1923

---

[*] These lists do not include any awards made in 1919 or after which relate to service in the Great War up to the Armistices with Turkey, Austria and Germany. Lists of awards relating to the Great War, including foreign awards, continued to appear in *The London Gazette* until 1921.

Rank & Name	No.	Unit	Place & Date	London Gazette
Capt (QM) G.M. Scofield		1 R.W.F.		3 Jun 1927
Lt (QM) W.H. Albutt DCM		Depot	U.K.	3 Jun 1932
W.O. II F. Wilson		7 R.W.F.	U.K.	3 Jun 1937

British Empire Medal (BEM)

Sgt C. Clemence	4180608	1 R.W.F.	Cyprus, Oct 1931	3 Jun 1932

Awards for Bravery and Distinguished Conduct

Bar to the Military Cross

Capt G.E.R. de Miremont DSO MC	3969	att 46 R.F.	Gorodock, North Russia, 1919	21 Jan 1920
Lt L.W. Jones MC		att 45 R.F.	Seltso, North Russia, 1919	21 Jan 1920

Military Cross (MC)

Lt A. Matson		att 46 R.F.	Borok, North Russia, 1919	21 Jan 1920
Lt N.J.M. Anderson		2 Indep Coy	Norway, May 1940	6 Aug 1940
Capt R.O.F. Prichard	64603	1 R.W.F.	Belgium and France, May 40	29 Nov 1945
Capt A.R.T. Lundie *R.A.M.C.*	94926	att 1 R.W.F.	Belgium and France, May 40	29 Nov 1945
Capt J.R. Johnson	44928	1 R.W.F.	France and Spain, Jun – Oct 40	31 Jan 1941
T/Maj J.R.O. Charlton *R.A.*	39814	101st L.A.A. & A.T. Regt R.A.	France, May 40	27 Sep 1940

Distinguished Conduct Medal (DCM)

LSgt D.P. Evans	4189858	1 R.W.F.	Ottenburg, Belgium	22 Oct 1940
Sgt T.J. Jones	4076321	1 R.W.F.	France and Belgium	3 Sept 1940
Sgt W. Morgan	4188023	1 R.W.F.	Calonne sur Lys, France	22 Oct 1940
Gnr W.G. Robinson *R.A.*	1456235	101st L.A.A. & A.T. Regt R.A.	France, May 1940	27 Sep 1940
A/Sgt W. Welburn *R.A.*	816620	101st L.A.A. & A.T. Regt R.A.	France and Belgium, May 1940	20 Dec 1940

Bar to the Military Medal

Pte J. Jones MM	235425		Archangel Command, North Russia	22 Jan 1920

Military Medal (MM)

Fus P. Jackson	4181397	1 R.W.F.	Split Hill, Waziristan, 5 Feb 1923	18 Sep 1923

Rank & Name	No.	Unit	Place & Date	London Gazette
Fus A. Jones	4179528	1 R.W.F.	Split Hill, Waziristan, 5 Feb 1923	18 Sep 1923
Fus W.H. Owens	4180533	1 R.W.F.	Split Hill, Waziristan, 5 Feb 1923	18 Sep 1923
Fus R.J. Williams	4179475	1 R.W.F.	Split Hill, Waziristan, 5 Feb 1923	18 Sep 1923
Cpl M.D. McNeil	4192216	1 R.W.F.	Merville Nord, France	20 Dec 1940
Bdsm A.V. Bailey	4209918	1 R.W.F.	St Venant, France	22 Oct 1940
Fus J.R. Thomas	4191217	1 R.W.F.	Dunkirk	3 Sep 1940
Bdr M.L. Fox *R.A.*	1431402	101st L.A.A. & A.T. Regt R.A.	France, May 1940	27 Sep 1940

Mention in Despatches (MiD)

Rank & Name	No.	Unit	Place & Date	London Gazette
Maj J.C. Cuthbert MC	46365	N.R.E.F.	Archangel Command, North Russia, 1919	3 Feb 1920
Capt R.E. Hindson		N.R.E.F. (Inf)	Murmansk Command, North Russia, 1919	30 Jan 1920
Capt R.E. Hindson (Second Award)		N.R.E.F. (Staff)	Murmansk Command, North Russia	3 Feb 1920
Maj E.O. Skaife OBE	3903	1 R.W.F.	Waziristan 1922-23	30 May1924
Capt H.D'O. Lyle	15330	1 R.W.F.	Waziristan 1922-23	30 May1924
RSM G.R. Whyley	4178899	1 R.W.F.	Waziristan 1922-23	30 May1924
Sgt H.F. Bradstreet	4179129	1 R.W.F.	Waziristan 1922-23	30 May1924
Sgt J. Soane	4179938	1 R.W.F.	Waziristan 1922-23	30 May1924
Lt Col H.B. Harrison MC	12194	1 R.W.F.	France and Belgium	20 Dec 1940
Maj R.C.K. Allen	6183	H.Q. 23rd Division	France and Belgium	20 Dec 1940
Capt A.G. ff Powell	53714	1 R.W.F.	France and Belgium	20 Dec 1940
Lt A.N.B. Sugden		1 R.W.F.	France and Belgium	20 Dec 1940
2Lt B.G.B. Pugh	75575	2 Indep Coy	Norway	25 Dec 1940
2Lt C.L. Wilding-Jones		2 Indep Coy	Norway	20 Dec 1940
WO II A. Cheetham	4180510	A.M.P.C.	France and Belgium	26 Jul 1940
Sgt A.E. Sharpe	4186740	1 R.W.F.	France and Belgium	20 Dec 1940
LCpl A.H. Ball	4209918	1 R.W.F.	France and Belgium	20 Dec 1940
Fus W. Davies	4189660	1 R.W.F.	France and Belgium	20 Dec 1940
Fus G. Lewis	4196065	1 R.W.F.	France and Belgium	20 Dec 1940
Fus J. Madden	4189210	1 R.W.F.	France and Belgium	20 Dec 1940

Imperial Russian Awards[1]

Rank & Name	No.	Unit	Place & Date	London Gazette
Capt R.E. Hindson		Order of St Anne, 2nd Class, with Swords	Murmansk Command, North Russia 1919	16 Jul 1921

Rank & Name	No.	Unit	Place & Date	London Gazette
Lt M.K. Shaw		Order of St Stanislaus, 3rd Class	Murmansk Command, North Russia1919	16 Jul 1921
CSM J.E. Bowen	4847	Medal of St George, 4th Class	Murmansk Command, North Russia1919	16 Jul 1921

Order of the Nile (Egypt)[*]

Maj E.A.T. Bayley DSO			8 Apr 1919
Capt R. Hall MBE MC	3rd Class		12 Jan 1920
Lt Col W.H. Hussey-Walsh		Commandant Beirut	16 Jan 1920
Lt Col W.R.K. Mainwaring CBE			16 Jan 1920
Maj T.H. Parry DSO			26 Nov 1919
Capt J.D. Porter OBE			16 Jan 1920

Brevet Rank[†]

Name	No.	Brevet	Date
Maj W.G. Holmes DSO	4613	Lt Col	1 Jan 1919
Maj P.R. Butler DSO	6958	Lt Col	3 Jun 1919
Maj & Bt Lt Col C.I. Stockwell CB CMG DSO		Col	1 Jan 1923
Capt T.D. Daly MC	9491	Maj	1 Jan 1929
Capt & Bt Maj T.D. Daly MC	9491	Lt Col	1 Jan 1932
Lt Col E.O. Skaife OBE	3903	Col	18 May 1932
Capt H.A. Freeman OBE MC[3]	13564	Maj	1 Jan 1934
Capt M.B. Dowse	6418	Maj	1 Jan 1936
Capt S.O. Jones MC	8995	Maj	1 Jul 1936
Capt G.F. Watson DSO		Maj	1 Jan 1937
Capt & Bt Maj H.A. Freeman-Attwood OBE MC	13564	Lt Col	1 Jul 1938
Capt M.H. ap Rhys Pryce	701	Maj	1 Jul 1938
Capt & Bt Maj G.F. Watson DSO		Lt Col	1 Jul 1939

---

[*]   The Order of the Nile (*Kiladat El Nil*) is Egypt's highest state honour. The award was instituted in 1915 by Sultan Hussein Kamel to be awarded by Egypt for exceptional services to the nation.

[†]   Various Imperial Awards continued to be made after the revolution by various Grand Dukes and Duchesses, in the Tsar's name.

Awards for Meritorious and Long Service

Meritorious Service Medal (MSM)

Name	Number	Authority
WOII R.W. Chambers	10115	LG 12 Dec 1919
BM T.W. Bennett		AO 397/1921 (Annuity)
CSgt J. Carpenter	1951	AO 430/1924
Sgt S. Evans		AO 397/1921 (Annuity)
CSgt G.L.A. McCully		AO 231/1925
Mil SM C.S. McGregor		AO 397/1921 (Annuity); Medal 1893
CSgt F.R. Mellor	1055	AO 127/1932
CSgt D. Morris	327	AO 205/1929
CSgt J. Russell		AO 248/1920 (Annuity)
CSgt G.J. Vale	763	AO 163/1932
BM G. Walsh	5276	AO 430/1924
CSM F.A.R. Webb		AO 10/1933

Long Service & Good Conduct Medal (LSGC)[4]

Name	Number	Authority
Sgt T.W. Adams	4179351	AO 224/1937
WO I G. Alabaster	38037	AO Oct 1921
CSM W.P. Allen	6170	AO Sep 1919
WO II E. Austin	4178930	AO Oct 1926
CSgt J.R. Austin	4178864	AO Apr 1921
Sgt J.H.B. Bacon	4178964	AO 73/1931
Fus R. Balaam	2179228	AO Apr 1924
Dmr A.W. Baston	11181	AO Mar 1920
Sgt J. Bean	4179609	AO 222/1934
Sgt J. Bean	4179609	AO 222/1934
Fus O. Beard	1042728	AO 17/1933
WO II H. Beardmore	3903042	AO Nov 1923
Cpl T.G. Beck	4183567	AO 193/1940
Fus C.E. Beddowes	4178906	AO Oct 1924
WO A.G. Bent MM	4179190	AO 104/1934
Sgt A.V.H. Bevan	6569	AO Sep 1919
WO II H.W. Bloxham	4178935	AO Oct 1926
WO II E.B. Box	4180772	AO Oct 1930
WO II H.F. Bradstreet	4179129	AO 17/1933
Sgt D. Brannan	4179393	AO 62/1940
Pte R.J. Bunnett	5670	AO Oct 1920
WO II J. Burns	7109103	AO Oct 1926
WO II C. Burton	4179747	AO 198/1935
Sgt W. Byles	4178876	AO Apr 1921
Sgt C.W.M. Cahill	4179227	AO Nov 1923
Fus J. Campbell	4179193	AO 62/1940
Sgt F. Cashmere	7110610	AO Apr 1928
Pte G. Cassidy	4178889	AO 443/1922
Sgt G.E. Challoner	11089	AO Sep 1919
WO II R.W. Chambers	4178945	AO Oct 1927
CQMS P. Chard	4178967	AO Oct 1929
WO II A. Cheetham	4180510	AO 231/1938
Sgt J.J. Cheley	4179928	AO 231/1938

Sgt A.H. Chesters	4179558	AO 62/1940
Cpl B. Clark	4183335	AO 195/1936
WO II B.F. Clancy	4178988	AO 17/1933
Fus F. Coathupe	4180674	AO 75/1939
CQMS P. Condon	7109236	AO Oct 1929
Cpl W. Coton	3761346	AO Oct 1928
WO II A.H. Cumberland DCM	4178904	AO Apr 1924
Sgt T.R. Cutler	4180501	AO 231/1938
Cpl F. Dann	4178880	AO Oct 1921
Pte A. Davies	4178875	AO 1921
WO II E. Davies	4179678	AO 17/1933
WO II E. Davies	1480317	AO 198/1935
Sgt G. Davies	4179449	AO 224/1937
Cpl R.H. Davies	7129	AO Oct 1920
CSM E.F. Dealing	5881	AO Mar 1920
WO II W.H. Dickinson DCM	4179641	AO Apr 1926
CSgt J. Dodd	4179842	AO 224/1937
Sgt E. Eagar	7109098	AO Oct 1927
Sgt W. Edwards	4178926	AO Oct 1926
Sgt A.E. Evans	4180444	AO 79/1938
Fus M.M. Evans	4183537	AO193/1940
Sgt P. Evans	3949680	AO198/1935
Fus T.R. Evans	4180588	AO 231/1938
WO II C. Fell	417644?	AO Oct 1927
Pte T. Ferriday	5386	AO Sep 1919
WO II E. Fisher	15790	AO Oct 1929
Sgt J. Flanagan	4179274	AO 195/1936
Sgt Shoemkr W. Forrest	11396	AO Sep 1919
LCpl L. Fountaine	5580	AO Sep 1919
Sgt H. Fox	6543	AO Sep 1919
Sgt V.R. Fraser	4179128	AO 641/1933
Sgt A. Galbraith	4179266	AO 81/1936
Sgt R.W. George	4180458	AO 75/1939
WO II W. Gorham	4178891	AO 222/1922
WO II J.H. Green	4813460	AO 62/1940
Sgt E. Griffiths	4180791	AO 74/1931
WO II T.W.J. Grinham	4179398	AO 224/1937
Sgt J.J. Hall	4178910	AO Oct 1924
WO II T. Hannon MC DCM	4178892	AO Apr 1923
WO II J.R. Harrison	4179324	AO 224/1937
Cpl H.F. Hatton	4181697	AO 81/1936
WO I W.J. Hawkins	4183833	AO 193/1940
Sgt W. Hellier	4181597	AO 218/1939
Sgt P.H. Hewer	4178915	AO May 1925
Fus I. Higgs	4183336	AO 81/1936
Cpl R. Hill	4180647	AO Apr 1928
WO I S. Hills	5172677	AO 198/1935
Sgt H.G. Holderness	4178954	AO Apr 1928
WO II H. Howell	4180688	AO Oct 1929
WO II R.W. Howell	4178992	AO 208/1931
WO II W. Howells	4179135	AO 104/1934
WO II I. Hughes	4180021	AO 17/1933
WO II J. Hughes DCM	4178909	AO Oct 1924
Fus W.H. Hutchins	4178901	AO Oct 1924

Fus H.H.B. Ing	4179135	AO 104/1934
CSgt P. Ireland	7109081	AO Oct 1929
CSgt G. Johnson	4179039	AO 17/1933
Sgt A.R. James	4180524	AO 231/1938
Fus A. Jones	4179440	AO 224/1937
Cpl G.H. Jones	4179420	AO 76/1937
WO II H.C. Jones DCM MM	4178914	AO Oct 1925
Fus J. Jones	4178940	AO Apr 1927
CSgt J.E. Jones	1366	AO Apr 1919
CSgt L. Jones	4179094	AO 641/1937
Sgt O. Jones	4178999	AO 208/1931
Cpl S.H. Jones	4179353	AO 224/1937
CSM T. Jones	14239	AO Apr 1919
Sgt J.W. Jordon	7144624	AO Nov 1923
Sgt B.J. Kelly	4114233	AO Oct 1925
Fus C. Kelly	4179109	AO 17/1933
WO II W.H. Kelly	4179623	AO Apr 1924
WO II J. Kensett	4179004	AO 64/1932
CSgt H. Kidgell	4181610	AO 218/1939
CSgt J. Kirby	4178933	AO Oct 1926
Sgt B.E. Kitching	4181715	AO 218/1939
WO II F.T. Langford	4180480	AO 79/1938
CQMS T. Leddington DCM	4178905	AO Nov 1923
Fus G.H. Lee	4180618	AO 218/1938
CSgt W. Leicester	4179367	AO 224/1937
WO II R. Leonard	4180574	AO Apr 1926
Sgt A. Le Poidevin	6192175	AO 224/1937
Fus E. Lewis	4178911	AO May 1925
Sgt J.R. Ling	11332	AO Sep 1919
WO II S. Lord	4178887	AO Oct 1922
Sgt J. Lowe	4183334	AO 62/1940
WO I A. Lungley	7808890	AO Apr 1933
WO II J. Mallett	4179637	AO Apr 1933
Sgt M. Malley	5806	AO Oct 1924
Sgt W. Maloney	62588	AO Oct 1921
WO II W. Martin	7807200	AO Apr 1924
Sgt A.A. Marvin	4181840	AO 62/1940
Sgt P.J.H. McCourt	5097679	AO 218/1939
Cpl W.H. McGuinness	4179012	AO 64/1932
WO II S. Metcalfe	4027451	AO 17/1933
Sgt O. Miles	7109086	AO Nov 1923
Fus F. Millward	4179653	AO 104/1934
Cpl G. Moreland	4178919	AO Oct 1925
WO II G.R. Morris	4179451	AO 224/1937
WO II C. Morrissey	4180550	AO 222/1934
WO II E.T. Morse	4179111	AO Apr 1933
Fus W. Neal	4179278	AO 81/1936
Sgt F. Newbold	4178979	AO 195/1930
Sgt R.R.G. Newman	8500	AO Apr 1922
Sgt J.D. O'Brien	7075119	AO Oct 1926
Sgt W. Oliver MM	4179017	AO 18/1932
Sgt A.G. Otton	7177388	AO Oct 1929
Sgt F.J. Pepper	4179295	AO 195/1936
WO I H.P.G. Perdue	5998094	AO Oct 1929

WO II W.H. Poole	4179640	AO Apr 1927
WO II F. Powell	4178895	AO Apr 1923
WO II B.C. Pratt	7109233	AO Oct 1929
WO II R.J. Price	4182073	AO 218/1939
Sgt A.H. Quinn	4178902	AO Nov 1923
CSgt A.D. Randall	4182009	AO 79/1938
WO III R.A. Raynor	418341?	AO 62/1940
Cpl W. Read	38239	AO Sep 1919
QMS J. Reeves	6775	AO Mar 1920
Fus J. Reynolds	4180871	AO 74/1930
Sgt A.C. Richards DCM	4182074	AO Apr 1926
WO II N.T. Ridings	4179052	AO 18/1932
Sgt L. Roberts	4179735	AO 195/1936
CSgt M. Roberts	4179414	AO Oct 1927
CSgt W.H. Robinson	4180203	AO Apr 1933
CSgt P.B. Roderick DCM	4178903	AO Apr 1922
Fus D.H. Salisbury	4179337	AO 62/1940
Sgt J. Salisbury	4179154	AO 198/1935
WO III W.T. Scammells	4071248	AO 62/1940
Fus J. Scott	7143597	AO 62/1940
Cpl A.E. Sheldon	4178868	AO Oct 1921
WO II S. Sherriff	4179131	AO 75/1939
Cpl A.J. Silk	4178986	AO 193/1930
Sgt J.W. Simkins	4178893	AO Apr 1923
WO II A. Simpson MC	4178949	AO Apr 1927
WO II G.I. Smalldon	4179835	AO 195/1936
WO I E.J. Smith	6891	AO Oct 1920
WO II J. Smith	4178859	AO Oct 1921
Fus W. Smith	4179264	AO 231/1938
WO II J. Soane	4179938	AO 17/1933
Cpl A.E. Soanes	4178990	AO 18/1932
CSgt O.J. Stanley	4179085	AO 62/1940
WO II A. Steele	4179021	AO Oct 1929
WO II J.W. Storer	4179335	AO 224/1937
Sgt P. Sullivan	4178884	AO 443/1922
Bdsmn A. Taylor	6974	AO Mar 1920
Fus W. Taylor	4184570	AO 79/1938
Sgt J.L. Thatcher	419005	AO 18/1932
WO II R. Thomas	4179378	AO 75/199
Sgt G.W. Timmins	4179336	AO 224/1937
Sgt A.A. Tompson	4178873	AO Apr 1921
Sgt R. Townley	71465	AO Sep 1919
CSgt W. Tubby	4179153	AO 17/1933
Fus D.G. Urquhart MM	4178952	AO Apr 1928
CQMS M. Walshe	7109073	AO Oct 1924
CSM V.W. Ward	6047	AO Apr 1919
Sgt F. Watkins	4179761	AO 198/1935
Sgt A.P. Weeks	4180113	AO Apr 1926
Sgt J. Whalley	4179320	AO 231/1938
WO II G. White	1478809	AO Apr 1923
Fus A.G. Whitehead	4179001	AO 208/1931
WO I G.R. Whyley	4178899	AO Nov 1923
Sgt J.C. Widenbar	9347	AO Sep 1919
Sgt J.T. Wilde	4178896	AO Apr 1923

Sgt J.H. Williams	4183467	AO 62/1940	
Sgt J.M. Williams	4179419	AO 218/1939	
Pte R.L. Williams	5891	AO Sep 1919	
Sgt F.F. Wilson	4180602	AO Apr 1927	
Sgt F. Witts	4180448	AO Oct 1922	
Sgt A.M. Wonnacott	4026305	AO Oct 1926	
WO II M. Wood	4178890	AO Oct 1922	
Fus A. Woods	4179123	AO 17/1933	
Farr H. Woodfield	4179035	AO 18/1932	
CQMS W.J. Woolman	6516	AO Apr 1919	
Sgt A. Wright	4181592	AO 75/1939	
Sgt B.V. Wright	4178894	AO Apr 1923	
Fus G. Wyldbore	4797263	AO 75/1939	
WO II J.J. Wylie	7109074	AO Oct 1924	

Special Reserve Long Service & Good Conduct Medal, 1919–1936

Pte T. Gray	2595	3 R.W.F.	AO Jan 1921
Pte R. Powell	3219	3 R.W.F.	AO Jul 1920
Pte T. Read	1950	3 R.W.F.	AO Sep 1924
Pte H. Roberts	2786	3 R.W.F.	AO Jul 1926

Efficiency Medal (Militia) 1930–1940

Fus I. Richards	4194018	3 R.W.F.

Territorial Decoration, 1919–1940[5]

Name	Rank	Battalion	Authority
Borthwick, F.H. CMG DSO	Lt Col	5 R.W.F.	6 May 1920
Brisco, Robert John Arbuthnot	Maj	7 R.W.F.	8 May 1928
Bury, Thomas O.	Lt Col	4 R.W.F.	31 December 1920
Burton, Edgar Oliver	Maj	5 R.W.F.	20 September 1938
Burton, Sydney Howard	Maj	5 R.W.F.	1 December 1933
Claridge, George	Capt (QM)	5 R.W.F.	3 January 1925
Davies, Harold Maldwyn	Maj	5 R.W.F.	27 July 1928
Davies, John C.	Maj	4 R.W.F.	17 May 1919
Davies-Jenkins, John G.	Lt Col	R of O, att 7 R.W.F.	13 March 1919
Edwards, Edward Lloyd	Hon Col	R.W.F.	23 February 1932
Gilbert, Noel MC	Maj	6 R.W.F.	15 November 1935
Greaves, J.E. CBE	Hon Col	6 R.W.F.	2 January 1923
Griffith, Goronwy Robert OBE	Maj	4 R.W.F.	1 March 1929
Jenkins, Herbert T.	Maj	6 R.W.F.	30 May 1919
Llewellyn, R.G. MC	Lt Col	R.W.F.	3 May 1938
Makey, Victor	Maj	7 R.W.F.	24 September 1937
Manfield, Thomas MBE	Capt (QM)	4 R.W.F.	3 May 1927
Mayes, George R.	Maj	4 R.W.F.	30 May 1919
Mayger, James L.	Capt	6 R.W.F.	4 November 1919
McManus, Francis Patrick	Capt	R of O, att 5 R.W.F.	18 September 1936
Mostyn, John MC	Maj	5 R.W.F.	3 May 1935
Mottram, Thomas Wilfred MC	Capt	4 R.W.F.	6 November 1934
Phillips, Gordon T.	Capt	6 R.W.F.	4 November 1919
Price, Edward Powell MC	Maj	7th Bn	26 October 1928
Pryce-Jones, Albert W.	Maj	R of O, att 7 R.W.F.	30 May 1919
Pryce-Jones, Sir Edward	Hon Col	7 R.W.F.	2 January 1919

Roberts, John Sheriff VD	Hon Col	5 R.W.F.		30 December 1921
Trustram Eve, Arthur Malcolm (Lord Silsoe)	Col	Staff		28 August 1934
Tuxford, William A.		6 R.W.F.		15 July 1919
Borthwick, F.H. CMG DSO	Lt Col	5 R.W.F.		6 May 1920

Territorial Force Efficiency Medal, 1919–1921[6]

H. Austin	A/Sgt	200046	4 R.W.F.	AO 23/Feb 1920
F. Brown MM	Sgt	235031	10 R.W.F.	AO 275/ Aug 1919
J.E. Dakin	Pte	290116	7 R.W.F.	AO Nov 1920
A.N. Davies	LCpl	265045	6 R.W.F.	AO 178/May 1919
D. Davies	Sgt	4182268	5 R.W.F.	AO Nov 1928
J. Davies	Pte	290114	7 R.W.F.	AO Aug 1922
J.C. Davies	Sgt	315042	4 R.W.F.	AO 65/ Feb 1921 (1st Clasp)*
J.T. Davies	Sgt	240031	5 R.W.F.	AO 178/May 1919
T. Davies	Pte	200164	4 R.W.F.	AO Nov 1920
T. Davies	Sgt	290380	7 R.W.F.	AO 148/Apr 1920
W. Davies	Sgt	240138	5 R.W.F.	AO 23/Feb 1920
W. Davies	WO II	290372	7 R.W.F.	AO 369/Aug 1920
W. Davies	Cpl	355019	25 R.W.F.	AO 23/Feb 1920
W.G. Davies	A/Sgt	1011	5 R.W.F.	AO 369/Aug 1920
W.L. Davies	Sgt	240148	5 R.W.F.	AO Nov 1920
W.R. Davies	Sgt	200043	4 R.W.F.	AO 23/Feb 1920
D.L. Dykins	Pte	240113	5 R.W.F.	AO 178/May 1919
R. Edwards	Pte	265083	6 R.W.F.	AO 380/Oct 1919
R. Edwards	Pte	316658	23 R.W.F.	AO 23/Feb 1920
E. Ellis	LCpl	767	5 R.W.F.	AO 23/Feb 1920
J. Ellis	LSgt	240025	5 R.W.F.	AO 275/Aug 1919
D.H. Evand	Sgt	240147	5 R.W.F.	AO 148/Apr 1920†
B. Evans	LCpl	4178520	6 R.W.F.	AO May 1921
C. Evans	Sgt	345047	24 R.W.F.	AO Aug 1921‡
C.H. Evans	Sgt	290014	7 R.W.F.	AO May 1921
E. Evans	Sgt	290363	7 R.W.F.	AO 178/ May 1919
G. Evans	Pte	343718	5 R.W.F.	AO 275/Aug 1919
G. Evans	Pte	290403	7 R.W.F.	AO Nov 1921
H. Evans	Sgt	240234	5 R.W.F.	AO 380/Oct 1919
J.E. Evans	CSM	265010	6 R.W.F.	AO 178/May 1919
L. Evans	Pte	2062	5 R.W.F.	AO Nov 1921§
O.J. Evans	Pte	345005	24 R.W.F.	AO 369/Aug 1920
R. Evans	Sgt	240028	5 R.W.F.	AO 178/May 1919
R.D. Evans	LCpl	240071	5 R.W.F.	AO 178/May 1919
R.J. Evans	Pte	240096	5 R.W.F.	AO 275/Aug 1919
R.T, Evans	Sgt	265039	6 R.W.F.	AO 178/May 1919
W.A. Evans	Sgt	5519	4 R.W.F.	AO 275/Aug 1919
W.B. Evans	Cpl	290117	7 R.W.F.	AO Nov 1920
F. Ferrington	Pte	240179	5 R.W.F.	AO 275/Aug 1919
G. Forsyth	Pte	240177	5 R.W.F.	AO 275/Aug 1919
A. Frimstone	Pte	240070	5 R.W.F.	AO 369/Aug 1920
R.J. Frimstone	LCpl	240067	5 R.W.F.	AO 178/May 1919

*   Medal as 2797 in 1909.
†   Later 362675 *Labour Corps*
‡   Late 636 *Denbighs Yeo.*
§   Later 195829 *R.E.*

H. Frost	Pte	293221	7 R.W.F.	AO Aug 1920
T. Gale	Pte	240184	5 R.W.F.	AO 275/Aug 1919
J. Gerrard	Pte	265748	6 R.W.F.	AO 275/Aug 1919
J. Green	LCpl	200072	4 R.W.F.	AO 369/Aug 1920
D.T. Griffiths	LCpl	240015	5 R.W.F.	AO 175/May 1919
E.C. Griffiths	Pte	4178290	4 R.W.F.	AO Nov 1921
J.B. Griffiths	Cpl	4178599	6 R.W.F.	AO 65/Feb 1921
W.R. Griffiths	Sgt	204151		AO 134/Aug 1946
J. Grundy	Sgt	8668	5 R.W.F.	AO 23/Feb 1920*
A. Haines	Sgt	240143	5 R.W.F.	AO 178/Aug 1919
S.J. Halman	Pte	200274	4 R.W.F.	AO May 1921
H. Hamlington	Pte	4178125	4 R.W.F.	AO Nov 1921
W.E. Harker	Pte	292971	7 R.W.F.	AO Aug 1921
A. Harrington	Pte	290058	7 R.W.F.	AO 275/Aug 1919
W. Hatton	Pte	200075	4 R.W.F.	AO 380/Oct 1919
T.P. Hayden	Sgt	240087	5 R.W.F.	AO 178/Mar 1919
Hayes	Pte	240183	5 R.W.F.	AO 275/Aug 1919
A. Heany	LCpl	243348	5 R.W.F.	AO Nov 1920
W. Herring	Sgt	5476	7 R.W.F.	AO 23/Feb 1920
W.J. Heym	Pte	200112	4 R.W.F.	AO 23/Feb 1920
R.G. Hickson	Pte	267362	6 R.W.F.	AO 178/May 1919
F. Hill	Pte	235216	4 R.W.F.	AO Nov 1920
B. Hodgkinson	Pte	6091	4 R.W.F.	AO 380/Oct 1919
J. Holman	Sgt	6406	4 R.W.F.	AO 380/Oct 1919
J. Holmes	Pte	200082	4 R.W.F.	AO Nov 1920
G. Homer	Pte	240069	5 R.W.F.	AO 178/May 1919
J. Horrocks	CQMS	345018	24 R.W.F.	AO 275/Aug 1919
A. Hughes	Pte	4178646	6 R.W.F.	AO May 1921
A.E. Hughes	Sgt	200107	4 R.W.F.	AO 178/May 1919†
A.E. Hughes	WO II	4178189	4 R.W.F.	AO May 1930 (1st Clasp)‡
C.J. Hughes	Cpl	316650	23 R.W.F.	AO Nov 1920
H. Hughes	Pte	571	6 R.W.F.	AO 369/Aug 1920
J. Hughes	Pte	240078	5 R.W.F.	AO 178/May 1919
J. Hughes	Sgt	204313	6 R.W.F.	AO 369/Aug 1920
J. Hughes	Sgt	265047	6 R.W.F.	AO 275/Aug 1919
J. Hughes	Cpl	265181	6 R.W.F.	AO Nov 1920§
R.T. Hughes	CQMS	200123	4 R.W.F.	AO 275/Aug 1919
T. Hughes	CQMS	5111	4 R.W.F.	AO 65/Feb 1921
T. Hughes MM	CSM	240109	5 R.W.F.	AO 380/Oct 1919
W. Hughes	LCpl	240110	5 R.W.F.	AO 178/May 1919
W. Hughes	CQMS	265095	6 R.W.F.	AO 275/Aug 1919
W.C. Hughes	Fus	4181622	6 R.W.F.	AO May 1932
W.E. Hughes MM	Cpl	290031	7 R.W.F.	AO 380/Oct 1919
L. Humphreys	Pte	290061	7 R.W.F.	AO Nov 1920
R. Iball	Pte	5132	4 R.W.F.	AO 275/Aug 1919
R. James	Pte	203409	4 R.W.F.	AO 23/Feb 1920
J. Jarvis	Cpl	200141	4 R.W.F.	AO 178/May 1919
A. Jenkins	Pte	200077	4 R.W.F.	AO Nov 1920

* Later 542404 *Labour Corps.*
† Later 4178179.
‡ Late 200107.
§ Later 4178518

A.W. Jenkins	Sgt	165	5 R.W.F.	AO Nov 1920*
R.E. Jenkins	Pte	356026	25 R.W.F.	AO Nov 1920
W.R. Jenkins	CSgt	290398	7 R.W.F.	AO 178/May 1919
A. Jenks	Cpl	315074	4 R.W.F.	AO 148/Apr 1920
T. Johnson	Pte	4178347	4 R.W.F.	AO Nov 1921
A. Jones	Pte	240075	5 R.W.F.	AO 178/May 1919
A.E. Jones	WO II	200060	4 R.W.F.	AO 65/Feb 1921
C. Jones	Pte	290416	7 R.W.F.	AO Feb 1921
C.H. Jones	Pte	809	7 R.W.F.	AO 369/Aug 1920
D. Jones	Pte	200094	4 R.W.F.	AO Nov 1920
D. Jones	Pte	265131	6 R.W.F.	AO 369/Aug 1920
D. Jones	Pte	265005	6 R.W.F.	AO Nov 1920
D.J. Jones	Pte	290366	7 R.W.F.	AO 65/Feb 1921
D.T. Jones	Pte	510	6 R.W.F.	AO 369/Aug 1921†
E. Jones	Sgt	265056	6 R.W.F.	AO 178/May 1919
E. Jones MM	Cpl	265075	6 R.W.F.	AO 178/May 1919‡
E. Jones	Cpl	4178579	6 R.W.F.	AO Feb 1931 (1st Clasp)
E. Jones	LCpl	290083	7 R.W.F.	AO 380/Oct 1919
E. Jones	Pte	265758	6 R.W.F.	AO 178/May 1919
E.O. Jones	Sgt	265013	6 R.W.F.	AO 380/Oct 1919
E.R. Jones	Sgt	2004	6 R.W.F.	AO 103/Apr 1919
E.R. Jones	Pte	260039	7 R.W.F.	AO 275/Aug 1919
E.W. Jones	Pte	2574	7 R.W.F.	AO 275/Aug 1919
H. Jones	Pte	2420	7 R.W.F.	AO 369/Aug 1920
H. Jones	QMS	355009	25 R.W.F.	AO 380/Oct 1919
H.D. Jones	Pte	6841	4 R.W.F.	AO Nov 1921
H.T. Jones	Pte	243565	5 R.W.F.	AO 148/Apr 1920
I. Jones	Sgt	5097	4 R.W.F.	AO 23/Feb 1920§
I. Jones	Sgt	4178003	4 R.W.F.	AO May 1932 (1st Clasp)
J. Jones	Pte	200125	4 R.W.F.	AO 23/Feb 1920
J. Jones	LCpl	240108	5 R.W.F.	AO 369/Aug 1920
J. Jones	Pte	265102	6 R.W.F.	AO 178/May 1919
J.P. Jones	Cpl	240141	5 R.W.F.	AO May 1922
J.R. Jones	Pte	3033	4 R.W.F.	AO Nov 1920
J.T. Jones	WO II	290369	7 R.W.F.	AO May 1922
L. Jones	LCpl	4178557	6 R.W.F.	AO May 1921
P. Jones	Pte	240059	5 R.W.F.	AO 178/May 1919
R.W. Jones	Pte	200027	4 R.W.F.	AO 178/May 1919
T.E. Jones	Pte	200065	7 R.W.F.	AO 23/Feb 1920
T.H. Jones	Sgt	265078	6 R.W.F.	AO 148/Apr 1920
T.J. Jones	Pte	2216	6 R.W.F.	AO 313/1925¶
T.J. Jones	WO II	4183144	6 R.W.F.	AO May 1934(1st Clasp)
W. Jones	Cpl	240044	5 R.W.F.	AO 178/May 1919
W. Jones	Pte	2123	5 R.W.F.	AO 369/Aug 1920
W. Jones	Pte	265043	6 R.W.F.	AO 178/May 1919
W. Jones	Pte	290092	7 R.W.F.	AO Nov 1921
W.H. Jones	CSgt	4178632	4 R.W.F.	AO 437/1926 (1st Clasp)

*	Later 38068 *R. Norfolk.*
†	Also *R.W.F.* 913, 2035, 3715 and *M.G.C.*
‡	Later 4178579 D/Maj.
§	Later 4178003.
¶	Later 4183144.

W.M. Jones	Sgt	240045	5 R.W.F.	AO 23/Feb 1920
H. Kershaw	Sgt	345378	24 R.W.F.	AO 23/Feb 1920
H. King	LCpl	292978	7 R.W.F.	AO Nov 1922
E.J. Lake	Sgt	205184	4 R.W.F.	AO 380/Oct 1919
J.T. Liddy	Sgt	845	6 R.W.F.	AO 380/Oct 1919
W.P. Lines	RSM	265035	6 R.W.F.	AO 380/Oct 1919
D.T. Lloyd	Pte	265067	6 R.W.F.	AO 178/May 1919
E. Lloyd	Sgt	200138	4 R.W.F.	AO 65/Apr 1921
J. Lloyd	Pte	240061	5 R.W.F.	AO 275/Aug 1919
R.J. Lloyd	Pte	667	5 R.W.F.	AO Nov 1920
H. Martin	Pte	292381	7 R.W.F.	AO Nov 1920
J.E. Mathews	Pte	484	5 R.W.F.	AO 369/Aug 1920
W. McCoy	Sgt	34548	24 R.W.F.	AO 23/Feb 1920
C. Milligan	Sgt	200215	4 R.W.F.	AO 380/Oct 1919
E. Minton	Pte	243201	5 R.W.F.	AO 375/Aug 1919
J. Mitchell	Pte	200059	4 R.W.F.	AO 178/May 1919
W.E. Morgan	Pte	240168	5 R.W.F.	AO 275/Aug 1919
A. Morris	Cpl	200173	4 R.W.F.	AO 23/Feb 1920
J. Morris	LCpl	5329	4 R.W.F.	AO 380/Oct 1919
R.C. Morris	Sgt	4178488	5 R.W.F.	AO May 1923
S.H. Morris	Pte	773	7 R.W.F.	AO Aug 1921
T. Morris	Pte	2023	7 R.W.F.	AO 23/Feb 1920
F. Moulder	Pte	238142	4 R.W.F.	AO 23/Feb 1920
H. Negus	CSM	200093	4 R.W.F.	AO 23/Feb 1920
G. Owen	WO II	4181285	6 R.W.F.	AO May 1932
H.M. Owen	Pte	265765	6 R.W.F.	AO 380/Oct 1919
J. Owen	Sgt	200003	4 R.W.F.	AO Nov 1921 (1st Clasp)
J. Owen	Sgt	265011	6 R.W.F.	AO 178/May 1919
J. Owen	Sgt	290361	7 R.W.F.	AO 178/May 1919
J. Owens	Sgt	4178404	4 R.W.F.	AO Nov 1921
F. Palmer	LCpl	200159	4 R.W.F.	AO Nov 1920
E.G. Parry	Pte	4178228	4 R.W.F.	AO Nov 1921
J. Parry	Pte	290307	7 R.W.F.	AO Nov 1920
R. Parry	CSM	240043	5 R.W.F.	AO 380/Oct 1919
R. Parry	CSM	256003	6 R.W.F.	AO 178/May 1919
R.J. Parry	Pte	765	7 R.W.F.	AO 23/Feb 1920
T.R. Parry	Pte	2002	5 R.W.F.	AO 275/Oct 1919
R. Pearch	Pte	293104	7 R.W.F.	AO 148/Apr 1920
T.E. Pennington	Cpl	11673	7 R.W.F.	AO 380/Oct 1919
E.H. Phillips	Pte	240172	5 R.W.F.	AO Nov 1920
J. Phillips	LCpl	240006	5 R.W.F.	AO 178/May 1919
E.J.J. Pierce	Sgt	4178039	5 R.W.F.	AO Aug 1935 (1st Clasp)*
J.H. Popple	Pte	4180710	7 R.W.F.	AO Feb 1931
E. Price	Pte	240001	5 R.W.F.	AO 192/May 1922
E. Price	Pte	240001	5 R.W.F.	AO May 1934 (1st Clasp)†
H. Price	Pte	942	5 R.W.F.	AO 369/Aug 1920
J. Pritchard	Pte	265876	6 R.W.F.	AO 178/May 1919
W.H. Pritchard	Pte	290384	7 R.W.F.	AO 369/Aug 1920
J. Randles	Sgt	4178031	4 R.W.F.	AO 65/Feb 1921
T. Ratcliffe	Sgt	240034	5 R.W.F.	AO 178/May 1919

*   Late 3483.
†   Later 4182331.

R.J.H. Reese	QMS	290118	7 R.W.F.	AO 380/Oct 1919
E. Reynolds	QMS	200124	4 R.W.F.	AO 178/May 1919
H.H. Richards	Pte	290439	7 R.W.F.	AO 369/Aug 1920
T. Richards	Pte	240068	5 R.W.F.	AO 178/May 1919
W.J. Richards	Pte	290122	7 R.W.F.	AO Nov 1920
A. Roberts	Pte	200103	4 R.W.F.	AO 65/Feb 1921
C. Roberts	Pte	200161	4 R.W.F.	AO 65/Feb 1921
D. Roberts	Cpl	14788656	6 R.W.F.	AO May 1921
D. Roberts	LCpl	265029	6 R.W.F.	AO 178/May 1919
E.E. Roberts	CQMS	265224	6 R.W.F.	AO Nov 1920
H. Roberts	Pte	710	5 R.W.F.	AO 148/ Apr 1920
I. Roberts	Pte	4178482	5 R.W.F.	AO Aug 1921
J. Roberts	Pte	200200	4 R.W.F.	AO 148/Apr 1920
J. Roberts	Pte	265051	6 R.W.F.	AO 178/May 1919
J. Roberts	Sgt	240140	5 R.W.F.	AO 23/Feb 1920
J. Roberts	WO II	265025	6 R.W.F.	AO Aug 1922*
J. Roberts	Sgt	345379	24 R.W.F.	AO Feb 1923
R. Roberts	Sgt	264	5 R.W.F.	AO Jul 1922
R. Roberts	Fus	4178106	4 R.W.F.	AO May 1929
R. Roberts	Pte	200143	4 R.W.F.	AO 23/Feb 1920
R.B. Roberts	Cpl	34539	24 R.W.F.	AO Feb 1923
S. Roberts	LSgt	240085	5 R.W.F.	AO 178/May 1919
W. Roberts	Pte	240046	5 R.W.F.	AO 178/May 1919
W. Roberts	LCpl	240098	5 R.W.F.	AO 178/May 1919
W.D. Roberts	Cpl	345008	24 R.W.F.	AO 23/Feb 1920
Z. Roberts	Sgt	290382	7 R.W.F.	AO 178/May 1919
A.C. Rose	Sgt	293099	7 R.W.F.	AO 178/May 1919
W.A. Rose	Pte	200346	4 R.W.F.	AO 148/Apr 1920
P.H. Rowell	Cpl	240076	5 R.W.F.	AO 148/Apr 1920
E. Rowland	CQMS	2010	7 R.W.F.	AO 380/Oct 1919
J.R. Rowlands	Pte	4178524	6 R.W.F.	AO May 1921
R. Rowlands	Pte	265760	6 R.W.F.	AO 178/May 1919
W.E. Rowlands	Pte	240156	5 R.W.F.	AO 23/Feb 1920
W.G. Sanrey	Pte	355041	25 R.W.F.	AO148/Apr 1920
J.F. Saunders	Pte	240040	5 R.W.F.	AO 178/May 1919
L. Schwarz	QMS	240079	5 R.W.F.	AO 148/Apr 1920
A.B.O. Scott	Cpl	290159	7 R.W.F.	AO Nov 1921
J. Seillo	QMS	3098	4 R.W.F.	AO 23/Feb 1920
S, Sheady	Pte	938	5 R.W.F.	AO 369/Aug 1920
J.R. Simon	Pte	240118	5 R.W.F.	AO 148/Apr 1920
J. Singleton	LCpl	240004	5 R.W.F.	AO 275/Aug 1919
R.W. Taylor	Sgt	265007	6 R.W.F.	AO 380/Oct 1919
E. Thomas	Pte	243229	5 R.W.F.	AO Aug 1921
J. Thomas	Sgt	265762	6 R.W.F.	AO 507/Nov 1920
J. Thomas	Sgt	4178606	6 R.W.F.	AO May 1921
J.A. Thomas	Sgt	886	6 R.W.F.	AO 507/Nov 1920
J.O Thomas	Sgt	200001	4 R.W.F.	AO 507/Nov 1920
O. Thomas	CSM	265749	6 R.W.F.	AO 275/Aug 1919
R.E. Thomas DCM	CSM	240014	5 R.W.F.	AO 275/Aug 1919
R.J. Thomas	Sgt	2165	6 R.W.F.	AO 178/May 1919
H.E. Tovey	Sgt	205159	4 R.W.F.	AO 380/Oct 1919

*   Later 4182352.

T.A. Tudor	Pte	3350	4 R.W.F.	AO Nov 1921
F.G. Turner	Cpl	200311	4 R.W.F.	AO Nov 1921
A. Vaughan	Pte	240055	5 R.W.F.	AO 275/Aug 1919
J.H. Vaughan	Cpl	776	7 R.W.F.	AO Nov 1920
P. Vaughan	Pte	202898	4 R.W.F.	AO 380/Oct 1919
S. Vaughan	Pte	290010	7 R.W.F.	AO 178/May 1919
W. Vaughan	Sgt	4178820	7 R.W.F.	AO Nov 1934 (1st Clasp)
A.J. Wadsworth	CSM	240080	5 R.W.F.	AO 178/May 1919
A. Wainwright	Pte	240122	5 R.W.F.	AO 178/May 1919
G.W. Wainwright	CSM	5503	4 R.W.F.	AO 65/Jul 1921
H.E. Watson	CQMS	290417	7 R.W.F.	AO 178/May 1919
H. Webb	Pte	200104	4 R.W.F.	AO 380/Oct 1919
H. Webb	Sgt	4178200	4 R.W.F.	AO Feb 1934 (1st Clasp)*
L.P. White	Pte	292409	7 R.W.F.	AO Aug 1921
R.H. White	CSM	265082	6 R.W.F.	AO 178/May 1919
W. Whittington	Pte	290037	7 R.W.F.	AO Nov 1920
B. Williams	LCpl	240112	5 R.W.F.	AO 178/May 1919
E. Williams	Sgt	4178362	4 R.W.F.	AO Nov 1921
E. Williams	Pte	630	6 R.W.F.	AO 369/Aug 1920
E.J. Williams	Pte	392	6 R.W.F.	AO 23/Feb 1920
E.L. Williams	Pte	988	6 R.W.F.	AO May 1921
J. Williams	Pte	265108	6 R.W.F.	AO 380/Oct 1919
J.H. Williams	Fus	4183198	6 R.W.F.	AO May 1932
J.W. Williams	Pte	200174	4 R.W.F.	AO Nov 1921
L. Williams	Sgt	240126	5 R.W.F.	AO 23/Feb 1920
O. Williams	CQMS	345049	24 R.W.F.	AO Nov 1922
O.R. Williams	Sgt	345009	24 R.W.F.	AO Aug 1922
P. Williams	Sgt	4178148	4 R.W.F.	AO Nov 1922
R.D. Williams	Cpl	345041	24 R.W.F.	AO 507/Nov 1920
R.O. Williams	Fus	4182882	6 R.W.F.	AO Aug 1928
T. E. Williams	Sgt	200098	4 R.W.F.	AO Aug 1922
T.E. Williams	Sgt	345017	24 R.W.F.	AO Feb 1923
T.E. Williams	Cpl	924	5 R.W.F.	AO Nov 1920
W. Williams	Fus	4183157	6 R.W.F.	AO May 1932
C.A. Wilson	CSM	292396	7 R.W.F.	AO Feb 1923
F. Wilson	Sgt	4741	4 R.W.F.	AO Nov 1920
F.L. Wilson	CQMS	290066	7 R.W.F.	AO 175/May 1919†
F.L. Wilson	CSgt	4181754	7 R.W.F.	AO Nov 1930 (1st Clasp)
H.J. Wilson	Pte	390	6 R.W.F.	AO 380/Oct 1919
C. Wood	Sgt	290397	7 R.W.F.	AO23/Feb 1920
J.A. Wood	Sgt	290089	5 R.W.F.	AO 65/Feb 1919
A. Woolley	Sgt	4178704	7 R.W.F.	AO May 1930
F.T. Woolley	WO II	4178703	7 R.W.F.	AO 354/1924 (1st Clasp)‡
F.T. Woolley	WO II	4178703	7 R.W.F.	AO Aug 1934 (2nd Clasp)
W. Worley	Cpl	265072	6 R.W.F.	AO 178/May 1919
T, Wynne	LCpl	290362	7 R.W.F.	AO Nov 1920
J.E. Yarnell	Pte	240171	5 R.W.F.	AO 275/Aug 1919
R.J. Yarnell	Pte	1482037	5 R.W.F.	AO May 1923

*   Late 200104.
†   Later 4181754.
‡   Late 65, medal awarded in 1911.

Territorial Efficiency Medal, 1921–1930

J. Bellis	Fus	1142	5 R.W.F.	AO Aug 1931
C. Bryan	Fus	4180693	4 R.W.F.	AO Feb 1925
J. Bulkely	WO II	265767	6 R.W.F.	AO 162/Aug 1935
S. Carpenter	Fus	290028	7 R.W.F.	AO Feb 1932
W. Chamberlain	Pte	315423	7 R.W.F.	AO May 1928
W.G. Clutton	Sgt	345390	24 R.W.F.	AO Nov 1922
W. Collier	Bdsm	4178597	6 R.W.F.	AO May 1928
T, Cummings	Fus	4178198	4 R.W.F.	AO Aug 1929
C. Davey	Pte	293235	7 R.W.F.	AO Feb 1922
A. Davies	Fus	4178179	4 R.W.F.	AO 33/Feb 1935
A. Davies	Fus	200171	4 R.W.F.	AO Feb 1927
C. Davies	Pte	4180707	6 R.W.F.	AO Aug 1922
D. Davies	Fus	4183532	5 R.W.F.	AO Nov 1928
E. Davies	Cpl	4178632	6 R.W.F.	AO Aug 1928
F.R. Davies	WO II	200055	5 R.W.F.	AO Feb 1922
H. Davies	CSgt	355023	25 R.W.F.	AO Feb 1923
J. Davies	Pte	290114	7 R.W.F.	AO Aug 1922
W.O. Davies	Pte	265089	6 R.W.F.	AO May 1923
E. Eagles	Fus	4178811	7 R.W.F.	AO Aug 1928
R. Edwards	Pte	293133	7 R.W.F.	AO Jul 1922
R. Ellis	Fus	4178603	6 R.W.F.	AO May 1932
J.A. Evans	Fus	290121	7 R.W.F.	AO Feb 1931
T. Evans	Fus	247		AO May 1933
T.M. Evans	WO II	4182275	7 R.W.F.	AO May 1930
W. Evans	Fus	4182671	4 R.W.F.	AO 177/1924
W. Evans	Fus	4182671	4 R.W.F.	AO May 1934 (1st Clasp)
E.H. Gascoigne	Sgt	202830	4 R.W.F.	AO 162/Aug 1935
E. Gratton	Pte	4183762	5 R.W.F.	AO May 1923
C.V. Griffiths	Pte	355010	25 R.W.F.	AO May 1923
D. Griffiths	WO II	290373	7 R.W.F.	AO Aug 1922
E. Griffiths	Sgt	4181224	5 R.W.F.	AO May 1923
P. Guest	Sgt	4178152	4 R.W.F.	AO Nov 1922
J. Hawkes	Fus	240077	5 R.W.F.	AO 177/Aug 1937
W. Herbert	Sgt	200096	4 R.W.F.	AO 39/Feb 1936
F. Hobson	Cpl	4181354	5 R.W.F.	AO 27/Feb 1939
F. Hoddinott	Sgt	3904229	5 R.W.F.	AO 1935
P. Hogan	Pte	200071	4 R.W.F.	AO Feb 1923
E. Hough	Sgt	4181993	5 R.W.F.	AO Feb 1933
P. Hough	Pte	240197	5 R.W.F.	AO Feb 1923
T. Hughes	Cpl	4178518	6 R.W.F.	No date (1st Clasp)*
R. Hughes	Cpl	4182940	6 R.W.F.	May 1932
W.W. Hughes	WO II	265164	6 R.W.F.	AO 97/May 1936
J.D. Ingman	Sgt	200054	4 R.W.F.	AO Jul 1922
J.H. Jackson	Cpl	265032	6 R.W.F.	AO Feb 1923
L. Jackson	Fus	773	6 R.W.F.	AO May 1932
J.W. Jenkins	WO II	240011	5 R.W.F.	AO Feb 1922
B. Jones	Fus	4183500	7 R.W.F.	AO Feb 1928
E. Jones	Fus	4185777		AO 53/1927
E.M. Jones	Pte	2585	7 R.W.F.	AO Aug 1922
G.T. Jones	Cpl	478209	4 R.W.F.	AO May 1933

*   TFEM as 265181 in Nov 1920

I. Jones	Fus	4178445	4 R.W.F.	AO May 1933
J. Jones	Sgt	345065	24 R.W.F.	AO Feb 1923
J.J. Jones	WO II	3	6 R.W.F.	AO May 1922
J.T. Jones	Fus	1151	6 R.W.F.	AO 177/Aug 1937
T. Jones	Sgt	200095	4 R.W.F.	AO Feb 1929
T. Jones	Pte	355027	25 R.W.F.	AO Nov 1922
T.E. Jones	WO II	4178828	7 R.W.F.	AO Aug 1928
T.J. Jones	WO II	4183144	6 R.W.F.	AO May 1934
T.P. Jones	Cpl	5085	5 R.W.F.	AO Jul 1922
W/H. Jones	CSgt	4178632	4 R.W.F.	AO May 1932
A.J. Linzey	Fus	4178159	4 R.W.F.	AO May 1932
T. Lloyd	Pte	240169	5 R.W.F.	AO May 1922
W.S. Martin	WO II	315829	23 R.W.F.	AO 34/Feb 1938
G. Maybury	Pte	200153	4 R.W.F.	AO May 1923
J.E. Morgan	Sgt	41788070	4 R.W.F.	AO May 1929
R.E. Morgan	LSgt	290078	7 R.W.F.	AO Feb 1923
F. Morris	LSgt	345013	24 R.W.F.	AO Feb 1923
J.E. Morris	Pte	290045	7 R.W.F.	AO Feb 1922
W. Morris	Fus	200168	4 R.W.F.	AO 222/Nov 1936
F. Morrish	LSgt	345013	24 R.W.F.	AO Feb 1923
P. Murphy	Fus	2204	6 R.W.F.	AO May 1936
L.S. Newcombe	Pte	293187	7 R.W.F.	AO Feb 1923
S.J. O'Hare	CSgt	4182164	7 R.W.F.	AO 437/1926
J. Owen	Sgt	4178613	6 R.W.F.	AO May 1932
W.A. Owen	CQMS	4178689	6 R.W.F.	AO May 1930
A.E. Owens	Fus	200111	4 R.W.F.	AO 33/Feb 1935
E. Parkinson	WO II	131	5 R.W.F.	AO 106/May 1935 (1st Clasp)*
J.E. Parry	WO II	4178206	4 R.W.F.	AO May 1929
J.T. Parry	Sgt	200191	4 R.W.F.	AO Feb 1922
R.J. Phillips	Fus	2156		AO May 1928
E.J.J. Pierce	Sgt	478039	5 R.W.F.	AO 162/Aug 1935 (1st Clasp)†
T. Pierce	Pte	20061	4 R.W.F.	AO Aug 1922
W. Roberts	Pte	290475	7 R.W.F.	AO Feb 1923
W.H. Roberts	Sgt	265031	6 R.W.F.	AO May 1928
H.T. Rose	CQMS	2010	24 R.W.F.	AO Jul 1922
R.G. Sissons	Cpl	315642	7 R.W.F.	AO Aug 1922
R. Smith	Pte	200170	4 R.W.F.	AO Aug 1922
W. Soden	Fus	200140	4 R.W.F.	AO May 1929
G. Tatum	Fus	4178183	4 R.W.F.	AO Aug 1932
E. Taylor	Sgt	352	4 R.W.F.	AO Nov 1922
J.A. Taylor	Sgt	345030	24 R.W.F.	AO 33/Feb 1937
R. Taylor MM	Sgt	345386	24 R.W.F.	AO 224/Nov 1935
R. Thomas	Fus	265766	6 R.W.F.	AO 224/1935
R. Thomas	Fus	4183107	6 R.W.F.	AO Aug 1928
E. Tippett	WO II	4182476	7 R.W.F.	AO May 1929
E.H. Vaughan	Sgt	4181544	5 R.W.F.	AO Aug 1929
J. Vaughan	Cpl	4181190	7 R.W.F.	AO Feb 1933
W.H. Vaughan	Pte	345020	24 R.W.F.	AO Feb 1923
W.J. Walden	Pte	293029	7 R.W.F.	AO Feb 1922
J.P. Watkins	Sgt	590	7 R.W.F.	AO Aug 1931

*   TFEM AO 186/1909).
†   TFEM AO 107/1912).

R. White MM	Sgt	4181694	7 R.W.F.	AO May 1933
G. Whitley	Fus	240013	5 R.W.F.	AO Feb 1932
A. Williams	Fus	4178036	4 R.W.F.	AO Aug 1932
C.E. Williams	Pte	345035	24 R.W.F.	AO Feb 1923
E. Williams MM	Pte	200284	4 R.W.F.	AO Jul 1923

Efficiency Medal (Territorial) (GRI), 1936–1940

W.L. Eagles	Cpl	4193976
A. Hall	CSgt	4027058
D.T. Jones	Sgt	4194936
J. Jones	Fus	4195718
J.J. Murphy	Fus	3773228
A.V. Owen	Fus	4195604
T.L. Pritchard	Fus	4195405
D. Williams	Fus	4188152
D. Williams	Fus	4188152 (1st Clasp)

Efficiency Medal (Territorial), 1930–1940

W. Astbury	Fus	4184979	5 R.W.F.	AO 39/Feb 1936
S. Bailey MSM	Sgt	4178100	4 R.W.F.	AO 33/Feb 1936
W. Barber	Bdsm	4186230	4 R.W.F.	AO 177/Aug 1937
E. Bartley	Fus	4186269	4 R.W.F.	AO 177/Aug 1937
G. Bennett	Cpl	4187512	4 R.W.F.	AO 98/May 1939
E.D. Bithell	Fus	4178270	4 R.W.F.	AO 33/Feb 1936
C. Bowler	WO II	4184040	5 R.W.F.	AO 33/Feb 1935
P. Boyce	WO II	4178141	4 R.W.F.	AO 84/May 1940
G. Brereton	WO II	4184794	6 R.W.F.	AO 224/Nov 1935
A. Bright	Sgt	4185127	7 R.W.F.	AO 224/Nov 1935
J. Brownley	Fus	4186124	6 R.W.F.	AO 107/May 1938
J.J. Burke	Dmr	4185624	4 R.W.F.	AO 154/Aug 1936
E. Cartwright	Cpl	4188290	4 R.W.F.	AO 156/Aug 1940
S. Challinor	Fus	4185216	4 R.W.F.	AO 33/Feb 1937
W.H. Challoner	Sgt	4178006	4 R.W.F.	AO 98/May 1939
W. Colegate	Sgt	4186363	5 R.W.F.	AO 177/Aug 1937
T.R. Cornwall	Dmr	4183662	4 R.W.F.	AO 177/Aug 1937
E.R. Cox	Fus	4185163	6 R.W.F.	AO 224/Nov 1935
C.O. Davies	Fus	4184698	4 R.W.F.	AO 106/May 1936
G.S. Davies	Bdsm	4185699	4 R.W.F.	AO 110/May 1937
H. Davies	Sgt	4184989	7 R.W.F.	AO 224/Nov 1935
J.F.F. Davies	Fus	4181770	7 R.W.F.	AO 27/Feb 1939
J.H. Davies	Fus	4184923	6 R.W.F.	AO 224/Nov 1935
R.P. Davies	Sgt	4184713	4 R.W.F.	AO 162/Aug 1935
T. Davies	Fus	4182569	4 R.W.F.	AO 33/Feb 1935
T.H. Davies	Sgt	4184641	5 R.W.F.	AO 162/Aug 1935
W.H. Davies	Sgt	4181800	5 R.W.F.	AO 177/Aug 1937
P. Duckers	Fus	4187034	60th A.T. (R.W.F.)	AO 252/Nov 1938
R. Edwards	Cpl	4187220	6 R.W.F.	AO 252/Nov 1938
J. Ellis	Fus	4185579	4 R.W.F.	AO 154/Aug 1936
D.E. Evans	Cpl	4187219	7 R.W.F.	AO 27/Aug 1939
G. Evans	Fus	4185000	4 R.W.F.	AO 162/Aug 1935
J. Evans	Cpl	4186546	6 R.W.F.	AO 107/May 1938
M. Evans	Fus	4185765	4 R.W.F.	AO 33/Feb 1937
R.T. Evans	Fus	4186957	5 R.W.F.	AO 190/Aug 1938
T. Evans	Fus	4187166	6 R.W.F.	AO 252/Nov 1938

W. Evans	Sgt	4185871	7 R.W.F.	AO 27/Feb 1939
A.E. Gabriel	Cpl	4188007	4 R.W.F.	AO 154/Aug 1936
W. Garrigan	Fus	4184648	4 R.W.F.	AO 162/Aug 1935
W.H. Gentle	Cpl	4186588	7 R.W.F.	AO 107/May 1938
H.E.G. Goodwin	Fus	4186507	7 R.W.F.	AO 107/May 1938
R.H. Gough	Fus	4184997	4 R.W.F.	AO 162/Aug 1935
D. Green	Cpl	4186965	6 R.W.F.	AO 190/Aug 1938
A. Griffiths	CSgt	4178144	4 R.W.F.	AO 33/Feb 1937
H. Griffiths	Fus	4182072	4 R.W.F.	AO 39/Feb 1936
J. Griffiths	WO II	4194548	4 R.W.F.	AO 84/May 1940
J.A. Griffiths	Sgt	4178108	4 R.W.F.	AO 84/May 1940 (1st Clasp)
J.R. Griffiths	Sgt	7809430	4 R.W.F.	AO 162/Aug 1935
J.R.A. Griffiths	Fus	4185175	6 R.W.F.	AO 224/Nov 1935
W.T. Gwilliam	Sgt	4183874	7 R.W.F.	AO 224/Nov 1935
G. Hannan	Fus	4178133	4 R.W.F.	AO 84/May 1940 (1st Clasp)
O. Hannon	Fus	4186408	7 R.W.F.	AO 107/May 1938
A.J. Hardman	Fus	4186397	7 R.W.F.	AO 107/May 1938
T. Harrison	Fus	4184961	7 R.W.F.	AO 154/Aug 1936
K. Haynes	Fus	4185547	4 R.W.F.	AO 154/Aug 1936
D. Hayward	Fus	4185630	4 R.W.F.	AO 33/Feb 1937
E. Heyward	Cpl	4184912	4 R.W.F.	AO 162/Aug 1935
A. Hodson	Sgt	4181652	5 R.W.F.	AO 33/Feb 1937
J. Holland	Fus	3949216	4 R.W.F.	AO 34/Feb 1938
R. Holland	Fus	4178318	4 R.W.F.	AO 156/Aug 1940
J.D. Holt	Fus	4187437	7 R.W.F.	AO 98/May 1939
N. Hopwood	Bdsm	4188694	60th A.T. (R.W.F.)	AO 252/Nov 1938
A.H. Hughes	Fus	4184865	4 R.W.F.	AO 162/Aug 1935
C. Hughes	Cpl	4178355	4 R.W.F.	AO 27/Feb 1939 (1st Clasp)*
F. Hughes	Sgt	4181356	60th A.T. (R.W.F.)	AO 27/Feb 1939
F.L. Hughes	Fus	4187223	7 R.W.F.	AO 27/Feb 1939
J.O. Hughes	Sgt	4186103	4 R.W.F.	AO 177/Aug 1937
J.R. Hughes	Fus	4185101	6 R.W.F.	AO 162/Aug 1935
N. Hughes	Cpl	4187067	6 R.W.F.	AO 252/Nov 1938
R. Hughes	Sgt	4185206	6 R.W.F.	AO 224/Nov 1935
T.J. Hughes	Cpl	4187116	6 R.W.F.	AO 252/Nov 1938
W.E. Hughes	Fus	4185168	6 R.W.F.	AO 224/Nov 1935
W.H. Hughes	Fus	4184242	6 R.W.F.	AO 224/Nov 1935
A. Humphreys	Sgt	4187602	4 R.W.F.	AO 84/May 1940
H. Humphries	Fus	4182145	4 R.W.F.	AO 156/Aug 1940 (1st Clasp)
J. Jarvis	Cpl	4178197	4 R.W.F.	AO 84/Aug 1940 (1st Clasp)
R.W. Johnson	Fus	4183775	5 R.W.F.	AO 33/Feb 1935
B.E. Jones	Cpl	4183453	7 R.W.F.	AO 107/May 1938
B.W. Jones	Fus	4185154	4 R.W.F.	AO 39/Feb 1936
C.R. Jones	Fus	4185328	7 R.W.F.	AO 154/Aug 1936
E.E. Jones	CSgt	4186502	5 R.W.F.	AO 243/Nov 1937
F.E. Jones	Fus	4187006	4 R.W.F.	AO 190/Aug 1938
G. Jones	Cpl	4185051	4 R.W.F.	AO 33/Feb 1935
G.E. Jones	Fus	4184508	7 R.W.F.	AO 154/Aug 1936
G.T. Jones	Cpl	478209	4 R.W.F.	AO May 1933
H. Jones	Sgt	4186300	4 R.W.F.	AO 34/Feb 1938
H. Jones	Fus	4178281	4 R.W.F.	AO 27/Feb 1939 (1st Clasp)

*   Medal as 200107.

H.L. Jones	Fus	4186035	7 R.W.F.	AO 107/May 1938
I.E. Jones	Fus	4182181	4 R.W.F.	AO 27/Feb 1939
J. Jones	Fus	4186086	5 R.W.F.	AO 110/May 1937
M. Jones	Sgt	4185543	6 R.W.F.	AO 177/Aug 1937
O.H. Jones	Fus	4185880	6 R.W.F.	AO 107/May 1938
P. Jones	Fus	4185707	4 R.W.F.	AO 33/Feb 1935
T. Jones	Fus	4186443	5 R.W.F.	AO 243/Nov 1937
T.H. Jones	Fus	4178354	4 R.W.F.	AO 27/Feb 1939
T.J. Jones	Sgt	4184944	6 R.W.F.	AO162/Aug 1935
W. Jones	Fus	4186814	5 R.W.F.	AO 34/Feb 1938
J. Kelsall	Fus	4187009	4 R.W.F.	AO 190/Aug 1938
G. Kendrick	Fus	4182556	4 R.W.F.	AO 33/Feb 1935
P. Lancaster	Fus	4186328	6 R.W.F.	AO 177/Aug 1938
R.T. Langford	Sgt	4182470	4 R.W.F.	AO 27/Feb 1939
J. Lawlor	Sgt	4178013	4 R.W.F.	AO 156/Aug 1940
D. Lewis	Fus	4183902	6 R.W.F.	AO 224/Nov 1935
R. Lloyd	Sgt	4185509	6 R.W.F.	AO 177/Aug 1937
W. Lloyd	Sgt	4180976	7 R.W.F.	AO 110/May 1937
S. Marland	Sgt	4184143	5 R.W.F.	AO 33/Feb 1935
E.C. Mason	WO II	723084	7 R.W.F.	AO 224/Nov 1935
R. Matthias	Fus	4185067	4 R.W.F.	AO 39/Feb 1936
D. McAllister	Sgt	4187351	5 R.W.F.	AO 27/Feb 1939
T. McManus	Cpl	4182199	60th A.T. (R.W.F.)	AO 252/Nov 1938
F.E. Mesham	Fus	4185685	5 R.W.F.	AO 33/Feb 1937
R.H. Meyrick	Fus	4183933	7 R.W.F.	AO 224/Nov 1935
A. Morris	Fus	4185123	4 R.W.F.	AO 39/Feb 1936
D.C. Morris	Fus	4186656	7 R.W.F.	AO 107/May 1938
E.S. Morris	Fus	4182165	7 R.W.F.	AO 224/Nov 1935
H. Morris	CSgt	4187298	6 R.W.F.	AO 252/Nov 1938
J.D. Morris	Fus	23915	4 R.W.F.	AO 110/May 1937
W.E. Morris	Fus	4186490	7 R.W.F.	AO 107/May 1938
W.H. Morris	Fus	4186972	4 R.W.F.	AO 156/Aug 1940
W.R. Morris	Cpl	4186455	7 R.W.F.	AO 107/May 1938
B. Mullen	Fus	4185712	4 R.W.F.	AO 110/May 1937
A. Nicholls	CSgt	4178024	4 R.W.F.	AO 190/Aug 1938 (1st Clasp)[*]
R. Nicholson	Sgt	1842455	6 R.W.F.	AO 29/Feb 1940
G. Norry	WO II	4186615	60th A.T. (R.W.F.)	AO 29/Feb 1940
H. Norry	WO II	4184088	5 R.W.F.	AO 33/Feb 1935
R. Norry	CSgt	4186660	5 R.W.F.	AO 243/Feb 1937
T. Owen	Fus	4185178	6 R.W.F.	AO 224/Nov 1935
E. Parker	Fus	4185736	7 R.W.F.	AO 27/Feb 1939
A.W. Parkinson	Fus	4186429	5 R.W.F.	AO 177/Aug 1937
E.S. Parry	Fus	4185181	6 R.W.F.	AO 224/Nov 1935
G.T. Parry	Fus	4185900	7 R.W.F.	AO 110/May 1937
R. Parry	Fus	3949808	6 R.W.F.	AO107/May 1938
R.C. Parry	WO II	4188316	4 R.W.F.	AO 156/Aug 1940
W. Pennington	Sgt	4184707	4 R.W.F.	AO 106/May 1935
E.J.J. Pierce	Sgt	4178039	5 R.W.F.	AO 162/Aug 1935
T.W. Powell	Cpl	4185087	4 R.W.F.	AO 39/Feb 1936
A. Pratt	Sgt	4184105	6 R.W.F.	AO 162/Aug 1935
T.S. Pratt	Sgt	4186307	60th A.T. (R.W.F.)	AO 27/Feb 1939

[*]   TFEM AO 148/1932.

J.E. Pritchard	Bdsm	4178330	4 R.W.F.	AO 34/Feb 1938
T.H. Pritchard	CSgt	4178325	4 R.W.F.	AO 33/Feb 1935
W.F. Pritchard	WO II	4178260	4 R.W.F.	AO 27/Feb 1939 (1st Clasp)*
P. Pryce	Sgt	4181856	7 R.W.F.	AO 107/May 1938
H. Pugh	CSgt	4185050	7 R.W.F.	AO 154/Aug 1936
W. Pugh	Fus	4185941	7 R.W.F.	AO 107/May 1938
W. Rathbone	Sgt	4186625	4 R.W.F.	AO 34/Feb 1938
C.L. Rees	Sgt	4181215	7 R.W.F.	AO 107/May 1938
H. Reynolds	Fus	482186	4 R.W.F.	AO 33/Feb 1935
G. Rhydwen	WO II	4185065	4 R.W.F.	AO 39/Feb 1936
J.H. Ricketts	Fus	4183790	5 R.W.F.	AO 33/Feb 1935
G. Roberts	Fus	4187243	6 R.W.F.	AO 252/Nov 1938
H.P. Roberts	Bdsm	4178143	4 R.W.F.	AO 110/May 1937
J. Roberts	Fus	4183035	6 R.W.F.	AO 98/May 1939
J.H. Roberts	Sgt	4183315	7 R.W.F.	AO 27/Feb 1939
J.L. Roberts	Fus	4187490	4 R.W.F.	AO 98/May 1939
J.T. Roberts	Fus	4187085	4 R.W.F.	AO 27/Feb 1939
R.T. Roberts	Fus	4178267	4 R.W.F.	AO 27/Feb 1939
Z. Roberts	Fus	4185111	4 R.W.F.	AO 39/Feb 1936
W.J. Rowlands	CSgt	4187236	7 R.W.F.	AO 27/Feb 1939
W. Salisbury	Cpl	4178370	4 R.W.F.	AO 39/Feb 1936
W.H. Sankey	Sgt	4185840	7 R.W.F.	AO 110/Feb 1937
B. Slawson	Cpl	4182304	4 R.W.F.	AO 33/Feb 1935
B.J. Sodin	Fus	4185719	4 R.W.F.	AO 110/Feb 1935
H. Stanton	Sgt	4186370	5 R.W.F.	AO 177/Aug 1937
E.J. Starling	Fus	4185671	6 R.W.F.	AO 177/Aug 1937
T.W. Stevens	Bdsm	4187231	7 R.W.F.	AO 27/Feb 1939
J. Sweeney	Fus	4184949	6 R.W.F.	AO 162/Aug 1935
T. Tattum	Cpl	4178216	4 R.W.F.	AO 238/Nov 1939
H. Thomas	Sgt	4181516	7 R.W.F.	AO 107/May 1936
H.V. Thomas	Fus	4185008	5 R.W.F.	AO 162/Aug 1935
I. Thomas	WO II	4182219	7 R.W.F.	AO 107/May 1938
R.J. Thomas	Sgt	4185215	6 R.W.F.	AO 224/May 1935
W.J. Tomkins	Fus	4184015	5 R.W.F.	AO 33/Feb 1935
A.A. Tompson	Sgt	4178873	7 R.W.F.	AO 224/Nov 1935
A. Toy	Sgt	4178821	7 R.W.F.	AO 107/May 1938
H.G. Underhill	Cpl	4185753	5 R.W.F.	AO 222/Nov 1936
P.F. Waters	Cpl	4187203	7 R.W.F.	AO 27/Feb 1939
J.F. Welsh	Cpl	543728	5 R.W.F.	AO 154/Aug 1936
G. Whitley	Fus	4184126	5 R.W.F.	AO Feb 1932
A.B. Williams	Fus	4185592	4 R.W.F.	AO 154/Aug 1936
A.L. Williams	Sgt	4185306	6 R.W.F.	AO 252/Nov 1938
E.N. Williams	Sgt	4186789	5 R.W.F.	AO 34/Feb 1938
H. Williams	Sgt	4178017	4 R.W.F.	AO 33/Feb 1935
H. Williams	Fus	4186651	6 R.W.F.	AO 107/May 1938
J. Williams	Fus	4185726	4 R.W.F.	AO110/May 1937
L. Williams	Sgt	4183897	6 R.W.F.	AO 162/Aug 1935
L.A. Williams	Cpl	4185623	4 R.W.F.	AO 154/Aug 1936
R.O. Williams	Fus	4179967	6 R.W.F.	AO 162/Aug 1935
T.J. Williams	Fus	4184110	6 R.W.F.	AO 162/Aug 1935
W. Williams	Sgt	4178265	4 R.W.F.	AO 33/Feb 1935

*   TFEM AO 125/1934.

A. Woodhall	Fus	4187514	4 R.W.F.	AO 98/May 1939
W.B. Wright	Sgt	4185605	5 R.W.F.	AO 222/Nov 1936

Commemorative Medals

King's Silver Jubilee Medal, 1935

Lt (QM) A.G. Bent MM	1 R.W.F.	Capt (QM) W.H. Kelly	6 R.W.F.
Lt Col J.G. Bruxner-Randall	1 R.W.F.	Lt (QM) R. Leonard	7 R.W.F.
Bt Lt Col T.D. Daly MC	MA Belgrade	Col T.E.J. Lloyd TD DL	Chmn TA Assoc Anglesey
Lt Col H.M. Davies MC	5 R.W.F.	Bt Col M.L. Lloyd-Mostyn	6 R.W.F.
Lt Gen Sir C. Dobell KCB CMG DSO	Col R.W.F.	Lt Col Sir W.R.K. Mainwaring CBE JP DL	Chmn T.A. Assoc Flint
Col E.L. Edwards TD	Hon Col 4 R.W.F.	Maj Gen J.R. Minshull-Ford CB DSO MC	Staff
Bt Col R.G. Fenwick-Palmer	4 R.W.F.	Bt Col C.S. Price-Davies MC	7 R.W.F.
Bt Maj H.A. Freeman OBE MC	1 R.W.F.	Lt (QM) J.H. Randles	4 R.W.F.
Col C.C. Hewitt DSO MC	Staff	Col E.O. Skaife OBE	M.A. Moscow
Lt Col R.E. Hindson	2 R.W.F.	Col A.M. Trustram Eve MC	R.W.F. T.A.
Capt (QM) E.F. Hollobon MM	5 R.W.F.	Capt G.F. Watson DSO	Staff
Col W.G. Holmes DSO	Staff	Lt (QM) G.R. Whyley	Depot R.W.F.
Bt Col W.H. Hughes CBE TD JP	Chmn T.A. Assoc Caerns	Maj E. Wodehouse	Depot R.W.F.
Lt (QM) C. Jones DCM MM	2 R.W.F.		
4181303 WO II F.W. Arnold MM	5 R.W.F.	4179653 LCpl E. Millward	1 R.W.F.
4180772 WO II E. Box	2 R.W.F.	4184088 WO II H. Norry	5 R.W.F.
4178472 Fus J.E. Davies	5 R.W.F.	4178260 Sgt W.F. Pritchard	4 R.W.F.
4183120 CSgt N.T. Doughty	6 R.W.F.	4179052 WO I N.T. Ridings	2 R.W.F.
4182671 Fus W. Evans	4 R.W.F.	4178786 WO II R. Riley	7 R.W.F.
4178144 CSgt A. Griffiths	4 R.W.F.	4178821 Sgt A. Toy	7 R.W.F.
4183336 Fus I. Higgs	Depot R.W.F.	4182159 Dmr H. Tudor	7 R.W.F.
4180309 Bdsmn W. Humphries	1 R.W.F.	4179001 Fus G. Whitehead	2 R.W.F.
4179004 WO I J.M. Kensett	1 R.W.F.	4181680 Sgt H.J. Williams	6 R.W.F.
7808890 WO I A. Lungley	Depot R.W.F.	4182882 Fus R.O. Williams	6 R.W.F.

Coronation Medal 1937

Lt Col D.M. Barchard	2 R.W.F.	Lt (QM) C. Jones DCM MM	2 R.W.F.
Lt (QM) A.G. Bent MM	1 R.W.F.	Maj S.O. Jones MC	Staff
Lt W.L.R. Benyon	1 R.W.F.	Capt J.H. Liscombe	1 R.W.F.
Capt P.L. Bowers	6 R.W.F.	Capt D.R. Llewellyn	6 R.W.F.

Capt E.O. Burton	5 R.W.F.	Col Sir W.R.K. Mainwaring CBE DL JP	Hon Col 5 R.W.F.
Bt Lt Col H.M. Davies TD	5 R.W.F.	Maj V. Makey	7 R.W.F.
Bt Lt Col J.M. Davies MC	4 R.W.F.	Maj Gen J.R. Minshull-Ford CB DSO MC	Staff
Maj R.S. Davies	7 R.W.F.	Maj H.D.T. Morris	Staff
Capt A.E. Davis	4 R.W.F.	Bt Col R.G. Fenwick-Palmer	4 R.W.F.
Capt (Hon BM) H. Delaney	4 R.W.F.	Col M.D. Gambier-Parry MC	Staff
Lt Gen Sir C. Dobell KCB CMG DSO	Col R.W.F.	Capt M.H. ap Rhys Pryce	2 R.W.F.
Maj W.M. Dugdale DSO MC	Chmn T.A. Assoc Monts	Lt Col J.G. Bruxner-Randall	1 R.W.F.
Maj H.M. Richards OBE DL	Chmn T.A. Assoc Mer'th		
Col E.L. Edwards TD	Hon Col 4 R.W.F.	Lt Col W. Roberts MC	7 R.W.F.
Maj A.M.G. Evans	Depot R.W.F.	Lt R.J.F. Snead-Cox	1 R.W.F.
Lt Col J.M. Evans	6 R.W.F.	Col A.M. Trustram Eve MC	R.W.F. T.A.
Maj H.A. Freeman OBE MC	1 R.W.F.	Lt F.D. Williams	4 R.W.F.
Col C.C. Hewitt DSO MC	Staff		
Col W.G. Holmes DSO	Staff		
Lt (QM) E.W. Howell	6 R.W.F.		
Bt Col W.H. Hughes CBE TD JP	Chmn T.A. Assoc Caerns		

Mr F. Barter VC MC   Mr J. Collins VC DCM
Mr J. Davies VC   Mr H. Weale VC
Mr A. Hill VC

4179747 WO II C. Burton	2 R.W.F.	4027451 WO I S. Metcalfe	2 R.W.F.
4179289 WO II A.T. Currie	1 R.W.F.	4178691 Sgt G.P. Mills	1 R.W.F.
4182734 Sgt H. Edwards	5 R.W.F.	4186010 Cpl G.L. Muzzelle	1 R.W.F.
5103836 LCpl W.E. Evans	1 R.W.F.	4179278 Bdsmn W. Neal	1 R.W.F.
4185401 Cpl G.H. Forbes	1 R.W.F.	4182164 WO II S.J. O'Hare	7 R.W.F.
4183833 WO II W.J. Hawkins	1 R.W.F.	4185840 Sgt W.H. Sankey	7 R.W.F.
4189616 Fus W.A. Hoffman	1 R.W.F.	4185719 Fus B.J. Soden	4 R.W.F.
4181622 Fus W.C. Hughes	6 R.W.F.	4184570 Fus W. Taylor	2 R.W.F.
4188106 Fus D. Hurley	1 R.W.F.	4182219 WO II I. Thomas	7 R.W.F.
4183775 Fus R.W. Johnson	5 R.W.F.	4185753 Cpl H.G. Underhill	5 R.W.F.
4182365 Sgt J.E. Jones	6 R.W.F.	4179520 Sgt J. Whalley	Depot R.W.F.
4181952 Fus J.W. Jones	7 R.W.F.	4181358 WO II D.R. Williams	5 R.W.F.
4178278 WO II P.W. Jones	4 R.W.F.	4186789 Sgt E.N. Williams	5 R.W.F.
4179004 WO I J.M. Kensett	1 R.W.F.	4183897 Sgt L. Williams	6 R.W.F.
4178253 CSgt J.L. Kent	4 R.W.F.	4183213 LCpl R.H. Williams	6 R.W.F.
4186066 Fus G.H. Melvin	Depot R.W.F.		

Life-Saving Awards

Royal Humane Society Medal

Capt M.L. Lloyd-Mostyn   2 R.W.F.   attempting to save 41809054 Fus A. Harwood
                                                   from drowning at Freshwater West, Pembrokeshire,
                                                   5 Jul 1923.[7]

Royal Life Saving Society Medallion of Merit

Boy J.J. Meade   2 R.W.F.   No records found.[8]   4183786

Notes

1   Lt Col R.J.M. Sinnett, *R.W.F. Awards 1919–1939* (unpublished, 4 November 2001).
2   The rules regarding Brevet Promotion as laid down in King's Regulations 1935, para 179:
    a) The object of brevet promotion is to ensure the advancement of selected Officers, in order that they may be able to reach the higher ranks of the army at the most suitable ages.
    b) Distinguished service in the field or meritorious or distinguished service of an exceptional nature other than in the field, both at regimental duty and on the staff, may be recognized by the grant of brevet promotion to the next higher rank.
    c) Recommendations for brevet promotion are considered by the Army Council half yearly. They will be submitted by commands at home and abroad (in the case of India through the Commander-in-Chief in India) and forwarded to reach the War Office by 1st May and 1st November in each year.
3   He changed his name to Freeman-Attwood on 20 October 1937, *London Gazette* 12 November 1937.
4   Compiled by John Tyler.
5   Compiled by Richard Ward.
6   The large number of awards is accounted for by the fact that war service counted double in terms of the qualifying period.
7   *Y Ddraig Goch*, October 1923, p. 194.
8   *Y Ddraig Goch*, October 1922, p. 51; Letter Royal Life Saving Society – Lt Col P.A. Crocker dated 26 November 2001.

Annex D

Campaign Medals, 1919–1940

The Territorial Force War Medal, 1914–1919
This is the least commonly issued campaign medal. It was instituted in 1920 and only applicable to men or women who had served in a unit of the Territorial Force. To qualify, the soldier must have completed four years or more service prior to 4 August 1914, and if not still serving must have rejoined by 30 September 1914; they must have agreed to serve overseas by the same date; they must have served overseas at some point up to and including 11 November 1918; and they must not have otherwise qualified for a 1914 or 1914-15 Star. Only 33,944 of this medal were issued, to members of the T.F. and the T.F. Nursing Service. At least fourteen Officers and 413 Other Ranks from the Regiment received this medal.

The Territorial Force War Medal

British War Medal, 1914–1920
The British War Medal 1914-1920, authorised in 1919, was awarded to eligible service personnel and civilians. Qualifications for the award varied slightly according to service. The basic requirement for army personnel and civilians was that they either entered a theatre of war, or rendered approved service overseas between 5 August 1914 and 11 November 1918. Service in Russia in 1919 and 1920 also qualified for the award. Individuals from the Regiment who served in those theatres, but had not qualified through service before 11 November 1918, therefore received this medal.

The British War Medal.
(*Medals Year Book*)

The Victory Medal, 1914–1919

This medal was awarded to all those who entered a theatre of war. It follows that every recipient of the Victory Medal also qualified for the British War Medal, but not the other way round. For example if a soldier served in a garrison in India he would get the B.W.M. but not the Victory Medal. In all, 300,000 fewer Victory Medals were required than British War Medals. Victory Medals continued to be awarded after the Armistice, for the British forces who saw action in North Russia (up to 12 October, 1919) and Trans-Caspia (up to 17 April 1919) also qualified. Individuals from the Regiment who served in those theatres, but had not qualified through service before 11 November 1918, therefore received this medal.

The Victory Medal.
(*Medals Year Book*)

Indian General Service Medal (1908–1935)

Clasp: Afghanistan N.W.F. 1919

12558	Pte	R.J.	Barker
49301	Pte	A.G.T.	Bartle
4179929	Pte	H.A.	Burgis
30440	Pte	H.	Clegg
4179176	Pte	J.	Compton
13492	Pte	T.J.	Davies
4179151	Sgt	J.N.	Dufty
30319	Pte	T.	Duffy
30210	Pte	J.	Fanthorpe
4180005	Pte	W.A.H.	Farrington
70051	Pte	F.	Fisher
69465	Pte	A.J.	Gooday
30025	Pte	G.	Hardwick
30372	Pte	C.P.	Herd
37936	Pte	T.B.	Hicks
49830	Pte	D.E.	Hughes
19007	Cpl	D.R.	James
4182403	Cpl.	W.	Jones
43705	Pte	H.	King
44189	Pte	F.G.	Lunt
30345	Pte	F.	Martin
4182090	A/Sgt	F.	McKay
59832	Pte	S.	Parker
4179710	Pte	R.	Pughe
4179082	Pte	F.	Richards

The Indian General Service Medal.
(*Medals Year Book*)

61597	Pte	D.J.	Roberts
4179935	Pte	G.F.	Rowland
41780	Pte	F.	Saunderson
49846	Pte	C.	Slawson
4179709	Pte	R	Smith
4178955	Pte	W.	Smith
315787	Pte	C.H.	Symmons
12168	Pte	H.G.	Thomas
9799	Pte	L.G.	Tysall
69975	Pte	C.V.	Williams
4179630	Pte	D.O.	Williams
200554	Pte	F.	Williams

Clasp: Waziristan, 1919-21[1]
Awarded for punitive operations – 6th May 1919 to January 1921 – against the Tochi and Wana Wazirs and Mahsuds who had caused considerable depredations since the end of the Third Afghan War. A total of 18 Officers and 625 members of the Regiment appear in the roll.

Clasp: Waziristan, 1921-24
For operations against the Mahsuds in North and South Waziristan, Bannu and Dera Ismail Khan Civil Districts from 21 December 1921 to 31 March 1924.

1 R.W.F. received this clasp, with 32 Officers and 1,058 Other Ranks on the roll.

Clasp: North West Frontier 1930-31
This clasp was awarded for services in Kohat, Waziristan and the Peshawar Districts between 23 April 1930 and 22 March 1931. Only one member of the Regiment appears in the roll:

4179735 Sgt L. Roberts, A/QMS Rest Camp, Razani, Waziristan

Clasp: Burma 1930-32
Awarded for service in Burma 22 December 1930 to 25 March 1932. Only two members of the Regiment appear in the roll:

1038999 CQMS W. Potter, 4th Indian Division Signals
2319885 Fus J. Stanton, 4th Indian Division Signals

General Service Medal (1918–1962)

Clasp: Kurdistan (1919)
For service in the areas of Kirkuk, Dohok, and near Akra and Amadia from 23 May to 6 December 1919 in what is now Iraq. Most, if not all the Royal Welchmen who were awarded this clasp had been serving in Mesopotamia. 8 R.W.F. left Mesopotamia for India in April 1919.[2]

Capt H.C. Wanke, 8 R.W.F.
56605 T/RSM A. Haycock R.W.F. attached 6 Loyals[3]
40985 Sgt R.F. Jones 8 R.W.F. attached 6 Loyals
59808 Cpl R. Edwards 8 R.W.F. attached 6 Loyals
69104 Cpl T.E. Jones 8 R.W.F. attached 1/5th East Surreys[4]
44817 Cpl G.T. Neal 8 R.W.F. attached 6 Loyals
30105 Pte P.A. Cooper R.W.F. attached 1/5th East Surreys
59803 Pte E. Dyer 8 R.W.F. attached 1/5th East Surreys
39211 Pte C.E. Ellington 8 R.W.F. attached 6 Loyals
61329 Pte T. Green 8 R.W.F. attached 6 Loyals
30222 Pte W.A. Harrison 8 R.W.F. attached 1/5th East Surreys
204343 Pte H.C. Hughes R.W.F. attached 1/5th East Surreys

The General Service Medal 1918.
(*Medals Year Book*)

204446 Pte H. Jones 8 R.W.F. attached 6 Loyals
61591 Pte W.C. Jones 8 R.W.F. attached 6 Loyals
61581 Pte P. Mather 8 R.W.F. attached 6 Loyals
30242 Pte W. Moore 8 R.W.F. attached 6 Loyals
30278 Pte P.F. Olliff 8 R.W.F. attached 6 Loyals
69103 Pte W.G. Page 8 R.W.F. attached 6 Loyals
30123 Pte P. Saines 8 R.W.F. attached 6 Loyals
69111 Pte R. Sargeaunt 8 R.W.F. attached 6 Loyals
30145 Pte A.E. Stroud 8 R.W.F. attached 6 Loyals
30174 Pte A.A. Tipper 8 R.W.F. attached 6 Loyals
55139 Pte H. Whitham 8 R.W.F. attached 6 Loyals
60835 Pte R.R. Williams 8 R.W.F. attached 6 Loyals

Clasp: Iraq (1919-20)

For service at Ramadi and north of it between 10 December 1919 and 13 June 1920; and for those who were on the strength of an establishment within the boundaries of Iraq from 1 July to 17 November 1920.

Capt E.E. Ford
Lt H.E. Hughes-Davies
4178882 Sgt T. Mullins, formerly 7819
4179073 Pte R. Blakeman, formerly 12546
4179685 Pte T. Broadhurst, formerly 57736
4180239 Pte E.N. Davies, formerly 100851
4180247 Pte H.J. Ellis, formerly 100862
4179955 Pte T. Hall, formerly 92738
4180285 Pte R.W. Jones, formerly 101230 and 292302
3513761 Pte F. Williams, attached 2 Manchesters[5]

Clasp: N.W. Persia (1920)

Awarded for service with NORPERFORCE (North Persia Force) between 10th August and 31st December 1920. Only one member of the Regiment appears in the roll:

240138 Sgt W. Davies

Clasp: Palestine (1936–39)

For service in Palestine between 19th April 1936 and 3rd September 1939 following the Arab uprising to demand an end to Jewish immigration and land purchase in Palestine. The members of the Regiment below who received the clasp were Section A Reservists who served with the 2nd East Yorkshire Regiment. How long they served in Palestine is not known. The Regimental Journal lists thirty-six men who served in Palestine, and includes a photograph of thirty-two of them on their return. The Medal Roll, however, lists only twenty-three. All but one of the names which appear on the Medal Roll are also in the *Journal*; the name that does not is Fusilier R. Gardner.[6]

23 names included in the Medal Roll:
4188591 LCpl F.E. Dowding
4188479 LCpl T. Moloney
4188581 LCpl A. Smith
4187025 Fus J. Alcock
4188428 Fus C. Bailey
3650501 Fus J. Birchall
4187627 Fus P.M. Butler
4188530 Fus L.E. Cook
4188127 Fus F.A. Coote
4188451 Fus J.R. Crompton
4188522 Fus R.T. Davis
3955136 Fus S. Evans
4121517 Fus R. Gardner
4186928 Fus A.D. Handley
4187767 Fus R.H. Harvey
4074605 Fus T.D. Jones
37712 Fus W.J. Morgan
754247 Fus D.J. Parry
4188526 Fus J. Priestley
4187777 Fus W.C. Redler
4188014 Fus T. Ryan
4188318 Fus E. Smith
4188015 Fus C. Stockley

14 names not on the Medal Roll, most if not all are on the roll of other Regiments.
4188096 Fus A.W. Bedson
775992 Fus E.J. Carne
4188484 Fus G. Evans

4188187 Fus T.C. Gaughran
4188596 Fus R.O. Hughes
4188531 Fus G.H. Johnson
4188391 Fus H. Jones
4188063 Fus L. Jones
4188073 Fus J. Leonard
4188592 Fus A.J. Moore
4188077 Fus E. Pearce
4188047 Fus W.J. Price
4188053 Fus R. Simmonds
4188378 Fus E. Watts

1939–1943 Star

Originally designated the 1939–1943 Star, but later known as the 1939–45 Star, this medal, the commonest of all the Second World War stars and the senior in the order in which worn, was instituted on 8 July 1943 for services in a number of theatres of operations from the declaration of war in September 1939 to the surrender of Japan in August 1945. The usual qualifying period was six months, however this did not apply to Dunkirk, Norway or airborne and Commando operations. This medal was awarded to members of 1 R.W.F. and 101st (R.W.) L.A.A. & A.T. Regiment serving in France and Belgium from September 1939 to May 1940; and to those members of the Regiment serving with No 2 Independent Company in Norway, from April to May 1940.[7]

The 1939–1943 Star. (*Medals Year Book*)

Notes

1   Major L.L. Gordon, *British Battles and Medals* (London, 1979). On p. 317, the article concludes with the words, 'The following regiments which took part in the later stages of the campaign also received the award: R. W. Fusiliers…' This cannot be correct as 1 R.W.F. did not leave Lucknow for Waziristan until 2 December 1921.
2   8 R.W.F. War Diary.
3   The Loyals' full title was the Loyal North Lancashire Regiment. The 6th Battalion was serving in Mesopotamia at the end of the war, as was 8 R.W. Fus. Brigadier E.A. James, *British Regiments 1914–1918* (London 1978).
4   The battalion was serving in India at the end of the war. James, *British Regiments*.
5   2nd Manchesters were serving in Iraq in 53 Infantry Brigade, 18th Division.
6   *Y Ddraig Goch*, January 1937, pp. 78–79; the medal information was extracted from the Roll in the Army Medal Office at Droitwich before it moved to Innsworth.
7   *Medals Year Book* (London, 1999) p. 90.

Annex E

Dress, 1919–1945

1919–1938

Full dress, although not abolished, was not re-issued to most of the Army and its use was confined to the Brigade of Guards; Officers attending levées at Court; bands, corps of fifes and drums, bugles and pipes; and special occasions such as the Aldershot Tattoo. Within the Regiment, St David's Day was a day when full dress usually made an appearance, with, for example, the Quarter Guard turned out in red coats and fur caps.

For most line and territorial battalions, including those of the Regiment, Service Dress was the norm. It was, however, smartened up. Caps regained their pre-war stiffness. Tunics and breeches were better tailored. The web equipment is described in Chapter 3.

Officers' Service Dress remained much as before the war, along with the Sam Browne belt, although the wearing of rank badges was returned to the shoulder straps rather than the sleeve. Mounted field Officers and adjutants continued to wear breeches and field boots, while subalterns and captains adopted looser breeches similar to civilian Oxford trousers or plus-fours.

To preserve the serge uniform, soldiers were usually issued with a suit of brown canvas fatigues. These were worn for fatigues or for training and drill in barracks.

For the Coronation of 1937, all ranks on parade were issued with a suit of Coronation Blues, essentially pre-war blue patrols which could be purchased by individual Officers and men for walking-out. Field Officers wore these with strapped trousers. The red and blue forage cap was worn but the overall effect was marred by the wearing of khaki web and Sam Browne belts, rather than white buff for the men and sashes for the Officers.

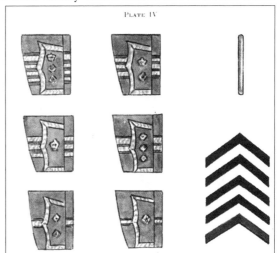

Officers' rank as worn at the close of the Great War

Officers continued to wear mess dress according to the pre-war pattern. In the tropics or the Mediterranean, the scarlet woollen jacket was replaced with a white drill jacket.

1924

The wearing of the Flash was extended to non-commissioned ranks in Service Dress, as described under Regimental Matters.

1927

6 January, buff wash leather gloves were taken into wear by all Officers and the RSM on all occasions when Review Order was worn. [1 R.W.F. Digest of Service]

4 June, medals were taken into wear with walking-out dress. [1 R.W.F. Digest of Service]

14 July, 'The main buckle of the topi chin-strap buckle will in future be worn on the left and not on the right as heretofore... .' [1 R.W.F. Digest of Service]

13 December, 'The length of Officers' sword knots when hanging loose will be 7 inches from the points at which the actual hanging portion joins the hilts to the ends of the knots'.

August, a sealed pattern cane for all Officers was decided upon.

1928

Blue Patrol was taken into wear for walking out. [1 R.W.F. Digest of Service]. N.B., blue patrol had to be purchased by each individual regardless of rank.

1933

An experimental field uniform was issued for trials. The hat resembled a deer-stalker; the tunic resembled a Norfolk jacket with four pockets, closely buttoned cuffs and an open collar. Leg-wear was either shorts with puttees, or trousers with canvas gaiters. This clothing was abandoned after the trials.

The Experimental Uniform of 1933. (*Journal of The Queen's Royal Regiment,* May 1933)

SHORT-SIGHTED GENTLEMAN: "PARDON ME, BUT HOW DO YOU FIND THE NEW REGIMENTAL UNIFORM—NICE AND COMFORTABLE ?"

A cartoon showing the general view of the experimental uniform of 1933.
(*The Humourist* Magazine, May 1934)

1935
The wearing of blue patrol was extended to the T.A.

1938
The introduction of Battledress (B.D.) in 1938 broke away from all previous forms, resembling a suit of workman's overalls. The tunic was a belted blouse with two breast pockets, attached to the trousers at the back by two buttons. The trousers were generously cut with two hip and one side pocket, and a pleated front pocket for the field dressing. Short canvas gaiters were issued to join the trousers to the boot tops. The web equipment is described in Chapter 3. Head-dress took the form of the 1890 pattern side-hat, but in khaki; the blue side hat was retained for Officers, bandsmen and drummers, pioneers and the Goat Major. Except for the cap badge, all metal shoulder titles and rank badges were abolished in favour of cloth versions. Officers' B.D. was identical to the men's except that shirts and ties were worn and the collar left open; the field service cap continued to be worn. In January 1941, however, it was ordered that Officers should wear collar badges on B.D. [T.N.A. WO 166/4630].

The 1916 pattern steel helmet continued in service until 1944.

The old brown canvas fatigues were abolished and replaced by cotton denims, of the same cut as B.D.

1941
Parachute and glider-borne battalions adopted a maroon beret and a round brimless steel helmet with reinforced chin-strap that would not impede the control of the parachute harness when the arms were raised above the head.

1942
With the opening of the campaign in Burma, infantry battalions were issued with green light-weight uniforms suitable for the climate and the cover. These consisted of a bush jacket, trousers, light boots, puttees or gaiters, and a broad-brimmed felt campaign hat.

1943
The khaki side-hat was replaced by an even more unsightly form of head-gear, the Cap G.S.: a round, pancake-like object with a wide brow-band, somewhere between a tam o'shanter and a Basque beret.

1944
A new pattern of steel helmet was introduced. This helmet sloped more gently towards the back than the front and the brim was only slightly curved at the sides, in contrast to the medieval 'salet' appearance of the 1916 helmet.

1945
Soldiers were permitted to wear the B.D. blouse open with a shirt and tie when walking-out.

Badges

Hackles and Plumes
As a Fusilier Regiment, a white plume (as the hackle was then called) was worn in the Wolseley helmet when on formal parades in place of a badge. Plumes for Officers, W.O.s and Sergeants were made from cut feather mounted in a gilt socket. The length of the plume was laid down in *Army Dress Regulations* as 4½ inches. Other Ranks wore a shorter version made from horsehair, 5 inches high and bound at the base

Full Dress
Pre-war versions of the metal grenade badge for the sealskin and bearskin caps were continued; the distinction between Regular and Volunteer units (the latter wearing white metal) was discontinued. The soldiers' badge was brass only, the Officers bi-metal: a gilt grenade and white metal PoW feathers.

Embroidered badges
The embroidered cap badge was worn on the forage cap and side hat – both blue and khaki – by all Officers during the period, in spite of the stated requirement in *Army Dress Regulations* 1911 and 1934 for a gilt and silver badge to be worn. Embroidered collar badges were worn on the lapels of mess dress and on the collar of the blue patrol. The backing colour varied: blue for cap badges and the Officers' collar badges; red for the W.O.s' and Sergeants' collar badges.

The Officers' embroidered cap badge as worn on the side hat.

The Officers' bronze cap and collar badges.

Metal cap and collar badges

The bi-metal pre-war cap badge for the peaked forage cap, both khaki and blue, and later the cap, G.S., was continued for non-commissioned ranks; badges with the spelling of 'Welsh' continued to be issued until stocks were exhausted and thereafter, the spelling of 'Welch' was restored. The pre-war brass grenade collar badge was continued unchanged.

An all-brass economy version was issued early in the Second World War, similar to that issued during the Great War, but with the spelling 'Welch' on the title scroll.

The all-brass economy badge was replaced by a brown Bakelite (plastic) version c. 1943; variations in the colour exist.

With the issue of the khaki side-hat in 1938, a brass grenade collar badge was worn in the cap by non-commissioned ranks and a left-facing bronze collar badge by Officers and Warrant Officers.

The Officers' gun-metal cap badge, a slightly different shape flame from that of the O.R.'s badge, continued to be worn in the field service cap, with the same change in spelling noted above. This was also worn in the cap, G.S. and in the beret by the 6th (R.W.) Parachute Battalion until the adoption of the Parachute Regiment badge in 1943. The pre-war gun-metal collar badges, with the dragons facing inwards, were maintained unchanged.

The O.R.s' bi-metal cap badge.

From 1920 to 1939, Territorial Officers wore a brass letter T under their collar badges; in 1939, the T was abolished, emphasising the Army Council's wish to integrate fully Territorial formations into the field army.

In the bush hat or slouch hat, a left-facing gun-metal collar badge was worn as a cap badge by the Officers of the 2nd Battalion in Madagascar, India and Burma. In both Regular battalions, non-commissioned ranks wore the divisional sign on the slouch hat (2nd Division for the 1st Battalion, 36th Division by the 2nd); this was also worn by the Officers of the 1st Battalion.

Shrapnel helmet

The red dragon rampant above the title R.W.F. in old English script was painted on the front of the helmet during the 2nd Battalion's tour in Shanghai, 1937.

Cloth badge

The 2 R.W.F. slouch hat embroidered badge.

The red dragon embroidered on a dark blue square backing was worn on the pith helmet and later the bush hat or slouch hat by the 1st Battalion in India and Burma, 1942–1945.

Shoulder titles

No shoulder title was worn by Officers before the introduction of Battledress in 1938.

For Regular Other Ranks, the pre-war brass shoulder title grenade/R.W.F. continued to be worn in service dress and khaki drill. Territorial N.C.O.s and Fusiliers wore a brass shoulder title T/4/ grenade/R.W.F. – or whichever number was appropriate.

The Regiment's shoulder title as worn on Battledress. (R.W.F. Mus)

With the introduction of battledress, cloth shoulder titles were adopted and the T for territorial units was abolished, emphasizing the Army Council's wish to integrate fully Territorial formations into the field army. Cloth shoulder titles were red, with ROYAL WELCH FUSILIERS in white lettering. These were manufactured in felt and later in a more hard-wearing canvas cloth. There was also a shoulder title 'sleeve' which was worn on the shoulder strap, R.W.F. embroidered in black on khaki.

Sleeve and rank badges

When Officers' rank badges returned from the lower sleeve to the shoulder strap of the Service Dress, gun-metal stars and crowns were taken back into use. In 1939, Infantry Officers' cloth rank badges were also introduced for wear on Battledress, edged in red.

N.C.Os' rank badges and good conduct badges continued unchanged from the Great War and pre-war period.

Divisional and independent brigade patches were also worn on the B.D. sleeve.

In 1943, Arm of Service flashes, narrow strips of coloured felt, were introduced on the sleeve; for the infantry, this was red.

Home Guard badges

The Home Guard wore the same uniform and badges as the rest of the Regiment, with the exception of shoulder titles and sleeve patches.

The shoulder title was in khaki cloth with the words HOME GUARD printed in yellow.

Beneath the shoulder title a letter designation patch was worn, with black letters on khaki cloth, the letters representing the county. For R.W.F. Home Guard battalions, these were as follows:

A Anglesey
CC Caernarvonshire
DEN Denbighshire
F&D Flint and Denbighshire
FT Flintshire
M Merionethshire and Montgomeryshire

Below or beside the letter designation was the battalion number, also black on khaki.

M.T. companies wore the letters MT below the county designation

A Proficiency badge was also worn, described in Chapter 46.

Annex F

The Colours and the Battle Honours for the Great War

---

i. The Regular Battalions

1. The 1st Battalion

New Colours were presented to the 1st Battalion by H.R.H. the Prince of Wales (later H.M. King Edward VII) on 16 August 1880 at Portsmouth. The size of these Colours was much smaller than those of 1849 for in September 1858, a new regulation reduced the size from 6 feet flying and 5 feet 6 inches deep – which had been laid down on 6 November 1855 – to only 4 feet flying and 4 feet six inches on the pike. The ancient spear-head was also abolished and replaced with a gilt crown and lion; cords and tassels of gold and crimson were made richer; in 1868 a gold fringe was added to increase the appearance of size as the smallness of Colours after 1858 had attracted a great deal of unfavourable comment. In 1868, the length of the pike was also reduced for the same reason, from 118 inches to 105 inches including the finial.

In design, the King's (or Queen's) Colour remained unaltered. The Regimental Colour received new Battle Honours awarded retrospectively in 1910: 'NAMUR' from the Nine Year's War in 1695 under William III; and honours for the campaigns of the Duke of Marlborough between 1704 and 1714: 'BLENHEIM', 'RAMILLIES', 'OUDENARDE' and 'MALPLAQUET'.[1] Also added as they were gained on operations were 'ASHANTEE' awarded in 1876 for the campaign in West Africa, to which the dates '1873–4' were added in 1914; 'BURMA 1885–87' in 1890;[2] 'RELIEF OF LADYSMITH', 'SOUTH AFRICA 1899–1902' and 'PEKIN 1900' (won by the 2nd Battalion),[3] all in 1904. After the Great War, new Battle Honours were added to the King's Colour, as described below. An illustration of the Colours forms part of the frontispiece of Part One of this Volume.

2. The 2nd Battalion

Following the expansion of the Army after the disbandment of the Army of the East India Company and with it, the need to garrison India, the first twenty-five regiments of foot were ordered to recruit a 2nd Battalion. 2 R.W. Fus began to form on 3 March 1858. It received its Colours on 21 December 1859 at Valetta from His Excellency Sir John Gaspard Le Marchant, Governor of Malta. The Colours were blessed by the Venerable Archdeacon Le Mesurier.[4] These Colours should have conformed in size to the Regulation of September 1858, i.e. four feet flying and four feet six inches on the pike; however they were much larger and were the same in design as the Crimea Colours of the 1st Battalion, presented in 1849. Major Peter Kirby, curator of the

Regimental Museum, wrote in his notes on Colours that: 'The 2nd Battalion Colours are the old 6 ft. fringeless type which was superseded on 11 May 1858. As the 2nd Battalion had been formed on 3 March 1858 and work on the new colours having been put in hand shortly after this date, the battalion was presented with the obsolete pattern colours in 1859.'

New Battle Honours were added to these Colours at the same times as already described for the 1st Battalion. These Colours remained in service for close on a century. An illustration of the Colours forms part of the frontispiece of Part Two of this Volume.

ii. The 3rd (Special Reserve) Battalion (Denbigh and Flint Militia)

On its formation in 1908, the battalion took on the Colours of the 3rd (Royal Denbigh and Flint Militia) which had been presented at Wrexham in 1885. These followed the 1858 regulations, four feet on the pike and four feet six inches flying and were of the same design as those presented to the 1st Battalion in 1880 except for the battalion number. The battalion received the Battle Honour 'SOUTH AFRICA 1899–1902' for its role in providing men to the 1st Battalion in that war. The battalion was re-designated as the 3rd (Special Reserve) Battalion of The Royal Welsh Fusiliers in 1908. The ten selected Great War Battle Honours were added to the King's Colour in 1925. The battalion was placed in suspended animation in 1919, and disbanded in 1953. The Colours were retained in the Regimental Depot at Hightown Barracks, Wrexham.

The Regimental Colour of the 3rd (Special Reserve) Battalion.

iii. The Territorial Battalions

1. General
After the Great War, in 1921, the Territorial Force became the Territorial Army and in 1925 its battalions were granted the privilege of bearing all the Regimental Battle Honours and the Flash, in recognition of their war service which had earned many of the honours awarded. Thus for the first time, the Volunteers had the same status as the rest of their regiments. The King's Colours were therefore emblazoned with the union wreath and the same ten Battle Honours as the 1st, 2nd and 3rd Battalions; a golden wreath of laurel was added to the Regimental Colours, emblazoned with the pre-1914 Battle Honours of the Regiment.

2. The 4th (Denbighshire) Battalion
The battalion received its first stand of Colours, the gift of the ladies of Denbighshire, with the 5th and 7th Battalions, from H.M. King Edward VII at Windsor on 19 June 1909. These Colours conformed to the Regulations of 1881, modified in 1900, three feet nine inches flying and three feet on the pike. The King's Colour was the Union with a red roundel in the centre

bearing the title '4th (DENBIGHSHIRE) BATTALION', surrounded by a gold-bordered red strap with the regimental title 'THE ROYAL WELSH FUSILIERS' and surmounted by a King's crown. The Regimental Colour was a blue sheet with the rising sun in the top left and bottom right corners, the red dragon on a white ground in the top right corner and the white horse of Hannover with the motto 'NEC ASPERA TERRENT' in the bottom left corner. Also in the top left corner, below the rising sun, was the Roman numeral IV. In the centre of the Colour was a red roundel bearing the coronet, plumes and motto of the Prince of Wales, surrounded by a gold-bordered red strap with the regimental title 'THE ROYAL WELSH FUSILIERS' and surmounted by a King's crown. This was in turn surrounded by a union wreath with, across its base, the title 'DENBIGHSHIRE BATTALION' on a gold scroll. Below this was the Battle Honour 'SOUTH AFRICA 1900–1902'. After the Great War, these Colours were re-emblazoned as described below.

3. The 5th (Flintshire) Battalion

The battalion received its only stand of Colours with the 4th and 7th Battalions from H.M. King Edward VII at Windsor on 19 June 1909. These Colours were identical to those of the 4th Battalion except for the distinguishing numeral and title. After the Great War, these Colours were re-emblazoned as described below. The battalion was converted to the anti-tank role and re-badged to the Royal Artillery in 1938, although retaining the R.W.F. title and Flash; it therefore ceased to carry Colours. However, the Colours remained with the unit until they were laid upon 12 March 1967 at St Asaph Cathedral, where they remain.

4. The 6th (Caernarvonshire & Anglesey) Battalion

The battalion received its first stand of Colours in 1908 at Abergavenny from the Lord Lieutenant and Honorary Colonel of the Battalion, Colonel J.E. Greaves. These Colours were identical to those of the 4th Battalion except for the distinguishing numeral and title. These Colours were taken out of service in 1939 but not laid up until 25 July 1959 when they were deposited in St Cybi's Church, Holyhead, Anglesey.

The battalion received its second stand of Colours on 6 August 1939 at Caernarfon Castle. They were presented by Sir Richard Williams-Bulkeley, Lord Lieutenant of Anglesey, who served as Lord Lieutenant from 30 November 1896 until 7 July 1942. These Colours were of the same design as the previous stand, with the addition of the Regiment's Battle Honours described below.

The Regimental Colour of the 6th Battalion (Caernarvonshire & Anglesey) Battalion, 1939–1946.

5. The 7th (Merioneth & Montgomeryshire) Battalion

The battalion received its only stand of Colours with the 4th and 5th Battalions from H.M. King Edward VII at Windsor on 19 June 1909. The King's Colour was the gift of a former Commanding Officer, Colonel Sir E.V. Pryce-Jones, and the Regimental Colour was the gift of the counties of Montgomery and Merioneth. These Colours were identical to those of the 4th Battalion except for the distinguishing numeral and title, as shown. The Regiment's Battle Honours were added after the Great War as described below.

The Regimental Colour of the 7th (Merioneth & Montgomeryshire) Battalion.

iv. The Service and Garrison Battalions and War-Raised Territorial Force Battalions

1. General

At the end of the Great War, His Majesty King George V instigated the award of a King's Colour to every Service, Young Soldiers, Graduated and Garrison battalion of the Army that had served overseas; and also to second and third line Territorial Force battalions, T.F. units serving as infantry and battalions of overseas troops also serving as infantry on active service. The details were promulgated in General Routine Orders and later in Army Council Instructions,[5] which described these Colours as 'silk union flags' although it was stated in the G.R.O. and the A.C.I. that 'His Majesty has been further pleased to command that these Flags, which will represent the King's Colour, are to be consecrated and are to be granted all the salutes and compliments authorised to be paid to Colours.'[6] In most cases, the battalions had been disbanded or reduced to cadre by the time of the actual presentation, so that the Colours were sent almost directly to their laying-up.

For the Royal Welsh Fusiliers, this applied to the 8th, 9th, 10th, 11th, 13th (1st North Wales Pals), 14th (Anglesey and Caernarvon Pals), 15th (1st London Welsh), 16th, 17th (2nd North Wales Pals), 19th (Bantam) and 26th (Service) Battalions; the 24th (Denbighshire Yeomanry) and 25th (Montgomery & Welsh Horse Yeomanry) Battalions (T.F.); and the 1st, 2nd and 6th Garrison Battalions. In the centre of each Colour was a red roundel edged in gold bearing the Regimental title and surmounted by a royal crown. In the centre of the roundel was the battalion numeral. Although the issue of these Colours pre-dated the award of Battle Honours for the war, some had honours or distinguishing marks on them as described below and all used the spelling 'Welch' which was not officially approved until 1920.[7]

2. The Yeomanry Battalions (T.F.)

The Colour of the 24th (Denbighshire Yeomanry) Battalion bore no numeral. It was presented at Hondeghem staging camp, twelve miles (20 km) east of St Omer, by Brigadier General the Hon L.J.P. Butler Commanding 94 (Yeomanry) Brigade, on 19 February 1919,[8] at the same time as that of the 26th Battalion, and before the final disbandment of the battalion. The subsequent fate and current whereabouts of this Colour are not known, in spite of extensive enquiries.

The Colour of the 25th (Montgomery & Welsh Horse Yeomanry) Battalion bore the title 'Montgomery & Welsh Horse Yeomanry' inside the roundel in place of a numeral, with XXV in the top left corner next to the pike; it also, like the 15th, bore the ten selected Great War Battle Honours which must have been added at a later date. There are no details available of any presentation before the final disbandment of the battalion on 29 June 1919;[9] indeed it seems that no such presentation occurred, for the account of the laying-up on 25 September 1920 in St Mary's Church, Welshpool, said that 'The King's Colours of the Yeomanry and Welsh Horse, as the 25th Royal Welsh Fusiliers, have remained at the War Office till sent down to Welshpool as the headquarters of the combined regiments, to be laid up with the guidon.'[10]

3. The Service Battalions

The Colour of the 8th (Service) Battalion bore the numeral VIII in the centre of the roundel. It was presented at Wrexham Barracks on 9 August 1921 by Lieutenant General Sir Francis Lloyd, Colonel of the Regiment, and laid up the same day in the Regimental Chapel in St Giles's Church, Wrexham at the same time as the 9th, 10th, 11th, 19th, and 26th (Service) Battalions and the three Garrison battalions.

The Colour of the 9th (Service) Battalion bore the numeral IX in the centre of the roundel. It was presented at Berteaucourt-les-Dames, about twelve miles (20 km) north-west of Amiens, on 12 January 1919 by Major General G.D. Jefferies, G.O.C. 19th Infantry Division,[11] before the final disbandment of the battalion on 8 June 1919 and laid up in the Regimental Chapel in St Giles's Church, Wrexham,

The Union Flag presented to the 9th (Service) Battalion.

on 9 August 1921 at the same time as the 8th, 10th, 11th, 19th and 26th (Service) Battalions and the three Garrison battalions.

The Colour of the 10th (Service) Battalion bore the numeral X in the centre of the roundel. The battalion was one of those disbanded in February 1918 to make good shortages of manpower. The Colour was presented at Wrexham Barracks on 9 August 1921 by Lieutenant General Sir Francis Lloyd, Colonel of the Regiment, and laid up the same day in the Regimental Chapel in St Giles's Church, Wrexham,[12] at the same time as the 8th, 9th, 11th, 19th and 26th (Service) Battalions and the three Garrison battalions.

The Colour of the 11th (Service) Battalion bore the numeral XI in the centre of the roundel. It was presented at Wrexham Barracks on 9 August 1921 by Lieutenant General Sir Francis Lloyd, Colonel of the Regiment, and laid up the same day in the Regimental Chapel in St Giles's Church, Wrexham at the same time as the 8th, 9th, 10th, 19th and 26th (Service) Battalions and the three Garrison battalions.

The Colour of the 13th (1st North Wales) (Service) Battalion bore the numeral XIII on the pike, but not in the centre of the roundel. It was presented at Allonville, four miles (6 km) north-east of Amiens by Major-General T. Astley Cubitt, G.O.C. 38th (Welsh) Division, on 16 January 1919 before the final disbandment of the battalion.[13] It was laid up with that of the 17th Battalion on 6 June 1919 at Trinity Church, Llandudno, recalling the origins of the battalion as North Wales Pals.

The Colour of the 14th (Service) Battalion bore no numeral and was a plain Union as issued.[14] It was presented at Allonville, four miles (6 km) north-east of Amiens by Major General T. Astley Cubitt, G.O.C. 38th (Welsh) Division, on 16 January 1919 before the final disbandment of the battalion.[15] It was laid up on 31 May 1919 at Bangor Cathedral, where 250 men of the battalion were present,[16] recalling the origins of the battalion as Anglesey & Caernarvon Pals. It remained in Bangor Cathedral until it was removed by Major Merfyn Thomas, in very poor condition, in July 2015 and taken into the Museum collections for conservation.

The Colour of the 15th (Service) Battalion was unusual in several respects. It bore the numeral XV in the top left-hand corner next to the pike; it bore the title '1st London Welsh' in the centre of the roundel; and it bore the Regiment's ten selected Battle Honours, which must have been added at a later date, since the battalion was one of those disbanded in February 1918 to make good shortages of manpower; although it had for many years a very active Association. The Colour was presented at Wrexham Barracks on 9 August 1921 by Lieutenant General Sir Francis Lloyd, Colonel of the Regiment and laid up in County Hall, London, on 25 October 1921 where 200 men of the battalion were present.[17] On the demise of the Greater London Council in 1985 it was removed to the Regimental Museum, where it remains.

The Union flag presented to the 15th Battalion (1st London Welsh).

The Colour of the 16th (Service) Battalion bore no numeral and was a plain union as issued.[18] It was presented at Allonville, six kilometres north-east of Amiens by Major General T.A. Cubitt, G.O.C. 38th (Welsh) Division, on 16 January 1919 before the final disbandment of the battalion.[19] It was laid up on 4 June 1919 at St Asaph Cathedral.

The Colour of the 17th (2nd North Wales) (Service) Battalion was a plain Union as issued;[20] it bore the numeral XVII painted on the pike but not on the Colour. It was presented at Allonville, four miles (6 km) north-east of Amiens by Major General T.A. Cubitt, G.O.C. 38th (Welsh) Division, on 16 January 1919 before the final disbandment of the battalion.[21] It was laid up with that of the 10th Battalion on 6 June 1919 at Trinity Church, Llandudno.

The Colour of the 19th (Bantam) Battalion bore no numeral and was a plain Union as issued.[22] It was presented at Wrexham Barracks on 9 August 1921 by Lieutenant General Sir Francis Lloyd, Colonel of the Regiment, and laid up the same day in the Regimental Chapel in St Giles's Church, Wrexham at the same time as the 8th, 9th, 10th, 11th and 26th (Service) Battalions and the three Garrison battalions.

The Colour of the 26th (Service) Battalion – originally the 4th (Garrison) Battalion – bore no numeral and was a plain Union as issued. It was presented at Hondeghem staging camp, twelve miles (20 km) east of St Omer by Major General N.M. Smyth, G.O.C. 59th (2nd North Midland) Division, on 17 January 1919 along with the 24th Battalion, before the final disbandment of the battalion. It was laid up on 9 August 1921 in the Regimental Chapel in St Giles's Church, Wrexham at the same time as the 8th, 9th, 10th, 11th, 19th (Service) Battalions and the three Garrison battalions.

4. The Garrison Battalions

The Colours of the three Garrison battalions were all Union flags. Only the 1st had its title in the centre of a red roundel surmounted by a royal crown, with the Regimental title on the roundel. The 2nd and 6th were plain unions, as issued. All three Colours were presented at Wrexham Barracks on 9 August 1921 by Lieutenant General Sir Francis Lloyd, Colonel of the Regiment, and laid up the same day in the Regimental Chapel in St Giles's Church, Wrexham at the same time as the 8th, 9th, 10th, 11th 19th and 26th (Service) Battalions.

The Union flag presented to the 1st Garrison Battalion.

v. The Battle Honours for the Great War

1. General

In August 1919 the Battle Honours Nomenclature Committee was appointed to tabulate the actions fought during the Great War and to define the geographical and chronological limits of each action. The committee produced its report in July 1920. To qualify for a battle honour, an infantry battalion or cavalry regiment had to have its headquarters and at least 50% of its effective strength present in the given area and within the prescribed time limits.[23]

Regimental committees were then ordered to be formed in 1922 to put forward recommendations for Battle Honours to the War Office, where a second committee, the Battle Honours Committee, would allot Battle Honours to Regiments.[24] Regiments were required to put forward a list of honours, with the battalions claiming them and these were then verified against the master lists and if there was doubt, the War Office Historical Section would carry out a further check against the War Diaries of the unit and its parent formation. As a result, eighty-eight honours were awarded to reflect the service of the Regiment's forty battalions in all theatres of war. There were some surprises: the 2nd Battalion gained 'MONS', 'LE CATEAU' and 'RETREAT FROM MONS' without suffering a single fatal casualty; the 9th Battalion claimed, and was awarded 'VALENCIENNES' (1/2 November 1918) even though it was not engaged and only just within the geographical area; the 6th Battalion received 'EL MUGHAR' (13/14 November 1917) even though it was, with the other battalions of the Regiment in the 53rd (Welsh) Division, nearly forty miles away. Other dubious awards include 'MORVAL' (1/4th Battalion), 'LANGEMARCK 1917' (17th); 'SCHERPENBERG' (9th); 'St QUENTIN CANAL' (2nd and 17th); and 'SCIMITAR HILL' at Gallipoli (1/5th and 1/6th).

2. Battle Honours Awarded

The full list of Battle Honours awarded to the Regiment, by battalions, is as follows:

Regular Battalions.

1st

Ypres 1914, Langemarck 1914, Gheluvelt, Neuve Chapelle, Aubers, Festubert 1915, Loos, Somme 1916, Albert 1916, Bazentin, Delville Wood, Guillemont, Bullecourt, Ypres 1917, Polygon Wood, Broodseinde, Poelcappelle, Passchendaele, France & Flanders 1914-17, Piave, Vittorio Veneto, Italy 1917-18

2nd

Mons, Le Cateau, Retreat from Mons, Marne 1914, Aisne 1914, La Bassée 1914, Messines 1914, Armentières 1914, Loos, Somme 1916, Bazentin, Arras 1917, Scarpe 1917, Ypres 1917, Menin Road, Polygon Wood, Somme 1918, Albert 1918, Bapaume 1918, Hindenburg Line, Havrincourt, Epéhy, St Quentin Canal, Beaurevoir, Cambrai 1918, Selle, Sambre, France & Flanders 1914-18

Territorial Force Battalions

1/4th

Givenchy 1914, Aubers, Loos, Somme 1916, Flers-Courcelette, Morval, Le Transloy, Messines 1917, Ypres 1917, Cambrai 1917, Somme 1918, St Quentin, Bapaume 1918, Ancre 1918, Albert 1918, France & Flanders 1914-18

1/5th

Suvla, Landing at Suvla, Scimitar Hill, Gallipoli 1915, Rumani, Egypt 1915-17, Gaza, Jerusalem, Tell Asur, Palestine 1917-18

1/6th

Suvla, Landing at Suvla, Scimitar Hill, Gallipoli 1915, Rumani, Egypt 1915-17, Gaza, El Mughar, Tell Asur, Palestine 1917-18

5th/6th

Megiddo, Nablus, Palestine 1918

1/7th

Suvla, Landing at Suvla, Gallipoli, 1915, Gaza, Nablus, Palestine 1917-18

24th

Egypt 1916-17, Gaza, Jerusalem, Jericho, Tell Asur, Palestine 1917-18, Ypres 1918, France & Flanders 1918

25th

Egypt 1916-17, Gaza, Jerusalem, Jericho, Tell Asur, Palestine 1916-17, Somme 1918, Bapaume 1918, Hindenburg Line, Epéhy, France & Flanders 1918

Service Battalions

8th

Suvla, Sari Bair, Gallipoli 1915-16, Tigris 1916, Kut al Amara, Baghdad, Mesopotamia 1916-18

9th

Loos, Somme 1916, Albert 1916, Pozières, Ancre Heights, Ancre, Messines 1917, Ypres 1917, Menin Road, Polygon Wood, Broodseinde, Poelcappelle, Passchendaele, Somme 1918, St Quentin, Bapaume 1918, Lys, Messines 1918, Bailleul, Kemmel, Scherpenberg, Aisne 1918, Selle, Valenciennes, Sambre, France & Flanders 1915-18

10th
Somme 1916, Albert 1916, Bazentin, Delville Wood, Ancre, Arras 1917, Scarpe 1917, Arleux, Ypres 1917, Polygon Wood, France & Flanders 1915-18

11th
Doiran 1917, Doiran 1918, Macedonia 1915-18

13th (1st North Wales)
Somme 1916, Albert 1916, Ypres 1917, Pilckem, Somme 1918, Albert 1918, Hindenburg Line, Epéhy, Beaurevoir, Cambrai 1918, Selle, Sambre, France & Flanders 1915-18

14th
Somme 1916, Albert 1916, Ypres 1917, Pilckem, Somme 1918, Albert 1918, Hindenburg Line, Epéhy, Cambrai 1918, Selle, Sambre, France & Flanders 1915-18

15th (1st London Welsh)
Somme 1916, Albert 1916, Ypres 1917, Pilckem, France & Flanders 1915-18

16th
Somme 1916, Albert 1916, Ypres 1917, Pilckem, Somme 1918, Albert 1918, Cambrai 1918, Selle, Sambre, France & Flanders 1915-18

17th (2nd North Wales)
Somme 1916, Albert 1916, Ypres 1917, Pilckem, Langemarck 1917, Somme 1918, Albert 1918, Bapaume 1918, Hindenburg Line, Epéhy, St Quentin Canal, Beaurevoir, Cambrai 1918, Selle, Sambre, France & Flanders 1915-18

19th (Bantam)
Cambrai 1917, France & Flanders 1916-18

26th
Somme 1918, Albert 1918, Ypres 1918, France & Flanders 1918

3. Battle Honours Borne on the Colours
From the total Battle Honours awarded, ten were selected to be borne on the Colours: from France and Flanders, 'MARNE 1914', 'YPRES 1914, 17, 18', 'SOMME 1916, 18' and 'HINDENBURG LINE'; from Italy, 'VITTORIO VENETO'; from Macedonia 'DOIRAN 1917, 18'; in Turkey 'GALLIPOLI 1915–16'; in the Middle East 'EGYPT 1915–17', 'GAZA' and 'BAGHDAD'.[25]

These Honours were to be added to the King's Colour, returning to a practice abandoned in 1844, since when Honours had only been borne on the Regimental Colour. They were physically in place by St David's Day 1926.

vi. Flags and Company Colours

1. Regimental Flag
The Regimental flag was a blue sheet bearing the red dragon above the letters 'R.W.F.' in Old English type. This device was also used on the flags of 115 and 158 (Royal Welch) Infantry Brigades, with the addition of a scroll bearing the brigade title. From 1881 to 1921 a gryphon was imposed by the War Office in place of the dragon on flags and badges, although the term 'dragon' was always used. No distinguishing battalion numerals are known to have been used.

The Red Dragon and the Griffon used on the Regimental Flag.

2. Company Colours and flags

Each company flew a flag and carried a small Colour with its distinguishing badge on parade, held by the right marker. These flags and Colours were all blue and the company badges were as follows:

A – The Rising Sun.

The Rising Sun.

B – The Prince of Wales's Feathers, coronet and motto 'ICH DIEN'; two variants used are shown.

The Prince of Wales's feathers.

C – The White Horse of Hannover, with the motto 'NEC ASPERA TERRENT'; two variants used are shown, although on the Regimental Colours, 'NEC ASPERA TERRENT' was always in superscript.

The White Horse of Hanover.

D – The Sphinx over a wreath of laurels and myrtle, superscribed 'EGYPT'.

The Sphinx superscribed 'Egypt'.

E – Support – The Minden Rose.

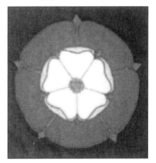

The Minden Rose.

HQ – The Red Dragon as on the regimental flag but without the letters 'R.W.F.'.

Each company also used a distinguishing colour for sports kit, signs and the marking of baggage:

A – Green;
B – Orange;
C – Red;
D – Yellow;
Support – Red and White;
HQ – Blue.[26]

Notes

1   A.O. 45 of 1910.
2   A.O. 392 of 1890.
3   A.O. 21 December 1904.
4   A detailed account of the ceremony is in *Regimental Records, Vol II*, pp. 125–129.
5   A.C.I. 444 dated 21 July 1919; General Routine Order (G.R.O.) 5734 of 1918.
6   For more details see James D. Geddes, *Colours of British Regiments, Volume II*, (privately published, 2000), pp. 69–73.
7   A.O. 56 of 1920.
8   Geddes, p. 118.
9   Bryn Owen, *Owen Roscomyl and the Welsh Horse* (Caernarfon, 1990), p. 35.
10   *County Times*, 25 September 1920.
11   "The 9th (Service) battalion in the War. A Short History" in *The Cheshire Observer*, 18 October 1930.
12   Lieutenant Colonel F.N. Burton and Lieutenant A.P. Comyns (ed), *The War Diary (1914–1918) of 10th (Service) Battalion Royal Welch Fusiliers* (Plymouth, 1926), p. 98.
13   Lieutenant Colonel J.E. Munby (ed), *A History of the 38th (Welsh) Division* (London, 1920), p. 84.
14   Geddes, p. 117.
15   Munby, p. 84.
16   14th (Service) Battalion Royal Welch Fusiliers War Diary (R.W.F. Museum).
17   *A Concise History of the 15th R.W.F. (1st London Welsh)* (15h R.W.F. Association, London, 1925), p. 15.
18   Geddes, p. 118.
19   Munby, p. 84.
20   Geddes, p. 118.
21   Munby, p. 84.
22   Geddes, p. 118.
23   Major T.J. Edwards, 'Battle Honours. The History of their Award' in *R.U.S.I. Journal*, Vol LXXIX (May 1934), no 514, pp. 357–366.
24   A.O. 338 and C.C.I. 1922.
25   Major C.H. Dudley Ward, *Regimental Records of The Royal Welch Fusiliers (Formerly 23rd Foot) Vol IV 1915–1918* (London, 1929), p. 406.
26   R.W.F. Regimental Standing Orders, p. 7.

Annex G

Roll of Honour, 1919–1939

All deaths during the Second World War are recorded in the Roll of Honour in Part Two

Part One, 1919–1922

This section records those members of the Regiment who died as a result of wounds received, or other causes, during the Great War. They are recorded in the C.W.G.C. Registers but because they died after 1 January 1919, they are not included in the Roll of Honour in *Regimental Records*, Volume IV. Their names are now recorded, in rank order and by date, up to the cut-off point laid down by the C.W.G.C. on 31 August 1921.

Readers should note that this annex is not indexed.

Regtl No.	Rank	Name	Battalion	Date of Death
	Maj	Cleave, James F.	General List	6.2.19
	Maj	Aubertin, W.A.	2 Garrison	20.2.19
	Maj	Battersby, G.L.	2/6	29.10.19
	Maj	Brocklehurst, William S.	10	15.5.20
	Maj	Cooper, E.S.	11	27.11.20
	Capt	Jones, Arthur V.	Att. GHQ Staff	16.2.19
	Capt	Croke Morgan, Richard	Att. Third Army HQ	18.2.19
	Capt	Tobias, Leslie M.	2 Garrison	25.2.19
	Capt	Rosher, John R.	23	19.3.19
	Capt	Higginson, John V.	26	23.9.19
	Capt	Hughes, Arthur P.	17	31.3.21
	Lt	Crosland, John H.	3 Garrison	13.4.19
	Lt	Boucher, Basil E.C.	1	10.5.19
	Lt	Evans, J. Harold	7	12.12.19
	Lt	Parry, G.O.		14.4.20
	2Lt	Rowland, William H.	26	22.9.19
	2Lt	Williams, J.J.		6.6.21
	Lt & QM	Thomas, Joseph H.	14	25.6.19

Regtl No.	Rank	Name	Battalion	Date of Death
47215	WO II	Ashton, G.H.	4 Garrison	12.3.19
315097	WO II RQMS	Miles, Frederick	3	6.7.19
3540	WO II	Banner, F.J.		4.12.19
345716	WO II	Jones, John K		24.6.20
355725	WO II	Morris, John DCM	25 (M & WH Yeo)	5.10.20
24703	CQMS	Jones, John	1	27.3.21
14032	CSgt	Gilham, Evan R.	11	4.3.19
8751	CSgt	Down, Sidney	1	20.6.20
290517	Sgt	Jones, William S.	1/7	2.1.19
240101	Sgt	Williams, David M.	5	20.1.19
200325	Sgt	Jones, Alfred	4	30.1.19
33450	Sgt	Lee, Harry	3	6.2.19
39089	Sgt	Maddocks, Joseph	17	26.2.19
21649	Sgt	Mills, Arthur	9	20.3.19
39972	Sgt	Evans, Peter		26.3.19
16358	Sgt	Cole, Arthur W.	13	22.4.19
235366	Sgt	Davies, Thomas J.	2	19.6.19
5611	Sgt	Kelly, James	8	14.8.19
73259	Sgt	Evans, Reginald E.	26	19.9.19
49945	Sgt	Evans, Edward I.	9	1.11.19
69989	Sgt	Clement, William G.	8	6.11.19
215067	Sgt	Callow, J.R.	24 (Denbigh Yeo)	2.5.20
14915	Sgt	Parry, S.P.		14.5.20
46144	Sgt	Eustis, Thomas I. MM	17	16.5.20
10375	Sgt	Evans, Harold	1	14.6.20
63702	Sgt	Hardaker, William		6.9.20
8396	Sgt	Slater, Charles S.		12.11.20
208611	Sgt	Jones,G.	3	27.4.21
56756	Sgt	Williams, T.	10	14.5.21
9437	LSgt	Peate, John	2	1.2.19
15065	LSgt	Hewitt, W.	11	29.8.21
201052	Cpl	Jones, Thomas	17	3.1.19
241211	Cpl	Welch, R.O.		11.2.19
266790	Cpl	Newton Williams, J.	Depot	19.4.19
40415	Cpl	Phillips, R.E.	2	24.6.19
5967	Cpl	West, W.		29.12.19
315522	Cpl	Hughes, Richard		28.1.20
4071	Cpl	Jones, R.E.		5.3.20
70208	Cpl	Barker, Thomas.	3	19.2.20
4091	Cpl	Lilley, H.		22.12.20
8065	Cpl	Rollason, George R.[1]		26.4.21
60580	Cpl	Lavelle, M.O.	9	12.6.21
10564	LCpl	Claffey, Bertie[2]	2	26.2.21

Regtl No.	Rank	Name	Battalion	Date of Death
9060	LCpl	Dwyer, John	2	3.1.19
74848	LCpl	Hier, William G.	8	11.1.19
9433	LCpl	Llewellyn, Albert E.	2	16.1.19
39652	LCpl	Foot, Reginald R.		7.2.19
3005	LCpl	Davies, William E.	8	13.2.19
46318	LCpl	Warrington, Ernest	13	17.2.19
11026	LCpl	Stokes, Walter	9	21.2.19
40147	LCpl	Griffith, W.J.	3	23.2.19
30245	LCpl	Parker, George H.	3	23.2.19
203108	LCpl	Pleavin, Charles	1/4	2.3.19
9322	LCpl	Neal, John H.	3	10.3.19
16119	LCpl	Lord, David	10	18.10.19
291867	LCpl	Beever, Bernard	7	20.10.19
315569	LCpl	Roberts, Richard S.	6, att 2	10.1.20
5457	LCpl	Evans, Thomas	9	28.1.20
5457	LCpl	Evans, Thomas	9	28.1.20
16683	LCpl	Scott, David	13	20.2.20
18784	LCpl	Veale, J.	1/7th	22.3.20
26099	LCpl	E.A. Jones	Depot	14.5.20
18691	LCpl	Morris, Charles R.	16	24.6.20
4179189	LCpl	Jones, J.A.	2	16.9.20
26772	LCpl	Storey, C.		6.8.21
1184	Pte	Hughes, Thomas		1.1.19
355128	Pte	Evans, Ernest	23	2.1.19
39705	Pte	Noall, Ernest B.	11	4.1.19
96909	Pte	Taylor, Albert J.	Signal Training Depot	4.1.19
11409	Pte	Griffiths, Jesse	2	5.1.19
57479	Pte	Burridge, Frederick	9	6.1.19
25789	Pte	Lewis, Henry	9	7.1.19
37931	Pte	Howells, Frederick	8	8.1.19
240835	Pte	Bowley, Charles E.	5/6	10.1.19
204124	Pte	Rogers, John M.	14	12.1.19
49699	Pte	Williams, Evan R.	2 Garrison	12.1.19
27191	Pte	Bailey, Arthur C.	2 Garrison	13.1.19
9071	Pte	Jones, William F.	4 Reserve	13.1.19
40600	Pte	Myers, Edwin	8	13.1.19
46199	Pte	West, Herbert	17	15.1.19
26887	Pte	Coutts, Alfred	9	19.1.19
11737	Pte	Devlin, Robert	6	23.1.19
39527	Pte	Sykes, Harry[3]		24.1.19
73932	Pte	Owens, Owen		26.1.19
46132	Pte	Johnstone, William B.	11	31.1.19
74696	Pte	Kenefick, George C.	5 Reserve	31.1.19

Regtl No.	Rank	Name	Battalion	Date of Death
202433	Pte	Walker, W.		1.2.19
316908	Pte	Garbutt, Joseph		2.2.19
266245	Pte	Jones, R.W.	5/6	2.2.19
200499	Pte	Roberts, George	1/4	2.2.19
135304	Pte	Everitt, C.J.		4.2.19
2831	Pte	Williams, Isaac	1/5	4.2.19
4427	Pte	Jones, Edward W.	7	5.2.19
78428	Pte	Price, E.A.	4	5.2.19
38951	Pte	Teague, C.H.	2 Garrison	6.2.19
87957	Pte	Gawith, Alfred J.	3	7.2.19
266459	Pte	Roberts, David[4]		7.2.19
7706	Pte	Edwards, Douglas F.	4	8.2.19
13957	Pte	Emery, Harry	11	8.2.19
14499	Pte	Knight, Harry	11	8.2.19
21317	Pte	Roberts, William	14	9.2.19
91172	Pte	Brown, S.E.	3	11.2.19
73719	Pte	Davies, Edwin	9	11.2.19
66985	Pte	Hatcher, A.R.		11.2.19
200729	Pte	Griffiths, William	4	12.2.19
57333	Pte	Storey, Mason	Depot	12.2.19
96375	Pte	Wallington, W,H,	4	13.2.19
345640	Pte	Wegg, Frank	24	14.2.19
36140	Pte	Jarvis, George		15.2.19
6725	Pte	Roberts, William	4	15.2.19
90558	Pte	Jones, D.	3	16.2.19
98207	Pte	Russell, J.	3	16.2.19
95514	Pte	Gowland, W.H.	4	17.2.19
265185	Pte	Jones, Robert O.	6	17.2.19
488	Pte	Griffiths, John	6	18.2.19
40243	Pte	Jones, J.E.		18.2.19
18988	Pte	Hague, William A.		19.2.19
67143	Pte	Harwood, William		19.2.19
33968	Pte	Kennedy, Thomas	2	19.2.19
36783	Pte	Williams, John		19.2.19
58178	Pte	Wills, Norton	13	19.2.19
6482	Pte	Biggins, S.	3	20.2.19
227456	Pte	Cope, Charles R.	17	20.2.19
60300	Pte	Gill, Edward	1	20.2.19
73580	Pte	Herd, Hugh	26	21.2.19
47158	Pte	Robinson, John	26	21.2.19
12482	Pte	Gordon, James A.	8	22.2.19
69511	Pte	Rowlands, Thomas		22.2.19
76159	Pte	Gibbon, Arthur H.	4	23.2.19
9359	Pte	Hughes, D.W.	23	23.2.19

Regtl No.	Rank	Name	Battalion	Date of Death
10692	Pte	Tomlinson, Robert[5]	1	23.2.19
53835	Pte	Taylor, Thomas J.	2	24.2.19
46842	Pte	Morgan, William	4 Garrison	25.2.19
95484	Pte	Cash, J.	2	25.2.19
72216	Pte	Clifton, John J.	26	26.2.19
9525	Pte	James, Leonard	2	26.2.19
72136	Pte	Thompson, Frederick	1 Garrison	27.2.19
67181	Pte	Curnow, Herbert J.		28.2.19
22973	Pte	Hobbs, Richard W.	13	28.2.19
12148	Pte	Jones, Robert W.	5 Reserve	28.2.19
82230	Pte	Marchant, Henry	10	28.2.19
317069	Pte	Jenkins, George	23	1.3.19
39823	Pte	Gray, Leonard	20	2.3.19
72829	Pte	Pugh, Gwyn	17	2.3.19
21587	Pte	Wells, Bernard	15 (1st London W.)	2.3.19
36747	Pte	Bury, David B.[6]		3.3.19
57202	Pte	McCullogh, Samuel		3.3.19
91074	Pte	Coulton, H.	3	4.3.19
5167	Pte	Thomas, R.W.	6	4.3.19
18005	Pte	Bell, William	1	5.3.19
98133	Pte	Turner, Francis	3 Garrison	5.3.19
202832	Pte	Ashley, Alfred	Depot	6.3.19
46166	Pte	McDermott, Walter	8	6.3.19
59982	Pte	White, William	24	8.3.19
67518	Pte	Loveless, William	1/7	11.3.19
	Pte	Rowlands, William[7]		11.3.19
205176	Pte	Ecclestone, A.	3	13.3.19
291462	Pte	Morgan, Evan	8	13.3.19
204483	Pte	Hammond, E.	4 Reserve	19.3.19
97408	Pte	Kyffin, W.H.	23	20.3.19
204467	Pte	Jones, J.T.	Depot	22.3.19
38690	Pte	Whittle, Thomas	2 Garrison	22.3.19
15277	Pte	Thomas, Joseph	10	28.3.19
18125	Pte	Perkins, David J.	7	29.3.19
567	Pte	Jellicoe, H.[8]	24	31.3.19
200243	Pte	Johnson, Richard		3.4.19
315580	Pte	Williams, Henry R.	1/7	5.4.19
267319	Pte	Goodwin, J.		8.4.19
53101	Pte	Jones, W.	8	10.4.19
30112	Pte	Jesson, Frederick R.	8	12.4.19
4872	Pte	Pithers, S.	Depot	15.4.19
204318	Pte	Hughes, Evan	14	16.4.19
1474	Pte	Preece, George		18.4.19
51717	Pte	Thomas, Richard	4 Garrison	25.4.19

Regtl No.	Rank	Name	Battalion	Date of Death
78065	Pte	Roberts, H.H.	4 Reserve	29.4.19
90236	Pte	Jones, Thomas		2.5.19
69614	Pte	Podgar, J.C.		4.5.19
26031	Pte	Cartwright, Theophilus	17	8.5.19
796	Pte	Edwards, Thomas J.	7	9.5.19
8643	Pte	Slater, George		10.5.19
8111	Pte	Brennan, Robert	2	16.5.19
291640	Pte	Howland, William A.	14	16.5.19
292958	Pte	Wright, Walter C.	1/7	25.5.19
62118	Pte	Cleary, Thomas	6	28.5.19
39297	Pte	Moores, Albert	3	29.5.19
58933	Pte	Carr, Thomas A.	3	30.5.19
7663	Pte	Poole, Joseph A.	4	31.5.19
88703	Pte	Walker, Charles	3	3.6.19
58002	Pte	Rutter, Alfred H.	13	4.6.19
5538	Pte	Bush, William J.	26	8.6.19
72175	Pte	Canvin, William B.	26	15.6.19
35000	Pte	Holmes, Henry C.	2	15.6.19
57001	Pte	Kell, Robert		19.6.19
73099	Pte	Noon, John	1/7	22.6.19
77938	Pte	Horngold, Frederick H.		25.6.19
10023	Pte	Green, Alfred A.	11	26.6.19
28408	Pte	Evans, Edwards	19	30.6.19
34148	Pte	Scully, Bartholomew	1 Garrison	30.6.19
67061	Pte	Dickinson, George		3.7.17
60584	Pte	Oldfield, Walter	17	3.7.19
37354	Pte	Bell, L.	8	7.7.19
242427	Pte	Burns, Daniel		7.7.19
70700	Pte	Crompton, James I.	1/7	7.7.19
35291	Pte	Harvey, Bertie		13.7.19
26023	Pte	Morris, John J.	25	15.7.19
7793	Pte	Evans, Francis W.	3	17.7.19
240682	Pte	Griffiths, Thomas	1/5	23.7.19
242173	Pte	Tompkins, Jacob	2 Garrison	1.8.19
58468	Pte	Fraser, Alexander		7.8.19
3251	Pte	Peach, Albert[9]		8.8.19
203570	Pte	Roberts, Evan	9	12.8.19
64190	Pte	Morton, W.A.		15.8.19
87531	Pte	King, Edward	2	17.8.19
25113	Pte	Davies, William H.	17	18.8.19
241458	Pte	Morris, Robert	2	21.8.19
92213	Pte	Davies, David W.	11	22.8.19
291515	Pte	Roberts, Hugh	24	27.8.19
69218	Pte	Windsor, Richard E.	17	7.9.19

Regtl No.	Rank	Name	Battalion	Date of Death
315087	Pte	Jones, John	9	8.9.19
37566	Pte	Davies, Arthur	6	9.9.19
4100	Pte	Roberts, W.R.	7	13.9.19
47076	Pte	Johnson, Tom	4	16.9.19
86673	Pte	Anderson, W.H.	Depot	21.9.19
55559	Pte	Jones, David R.	2	23.9.19
7038	Pte	Peters, John H.[10]		24.9.19
94731	Pte	Ravenhill, Ernest W.	26	25.9.19
24300	Pte	Clarke, Hugh	4	27.9.19
265668	Pte	Williams, Owen	5/6	1.10.19
25714	Pte	Roberts, Thomas	17	6.10.19
315503	Pte	Boyce, S.C.	23	19.10.19
34624	Pte	Watts, John C.		13.10.19
241995	Pte	Hulme, Edward	Depot	20.10.19
266297	Pte	Williams, Morris	6	21. 10.19
93103	Pte	Stafford, Norman H.	1/7	25.10.19
100142	Pte	Walters, Harold S.	11	26.10.19
731194	Pte	Redmore, Frederick J.	9	30.10.19
58393	Pte	Coxon, Harold V.	16	4.11.19
97248	Pte	Watkins, Enoch	1//7	9.11.19
52712	Pte	Roberts, Albert E.	3 Reserve	10.11.19
78051	Pte	Spray, J.H.[11]		11.11.19
3323	Pte	Jones, W.C.	7	15.11.19
242590	Pte	Allen, Frederick J.	1/7	25.11.19
89195	Pte	Vickery, William	13	28.11.19
26219	Pte	Morris, Phillip	Depot	10.12.19
22653	Pte	Creesey, William A.[12]		12.12.19
23342	Pte	Jones, Lewis S.	16	12.12.19
14565	Pte	Thomas, Ivor W.	8	18.12.19
21206	Pte	Hughes, Samuel	14	23.12.19
89535	Pte	Griffiths, G.	1	24.12.19
15282	Pte	Maddison, William	1	26.12.19
202934	Pte	Evans, Edward	4	3.1.20
3228	Pte	Jones, David R.	7	4.1.20
92579	Pte	Brown, M.	2	12.1.20
63556	Pte	Murray, Stephen	3	17.1.20
39219	Pte	Aston, Samuel A.	3	22.1.20
38128	Pte	Jones, David C.	2	2.2.20
201210	Pte	Edwards, Herbert	1/4th	16.2.20
25953	Pte	Roberts, John[13]	17	17.2.20
38048	Pte	Andrews, H.		22.2.20
55347	Pte	Gittens, Rhys P.	14	25.2.20
91122	Pte	Roberts Jones, William	3	7.3.20
1870	Pte	Jones, T.	24th (Denbigh Yeo)	11.3.20

Regtl No.	Rank	Name	Battalion	Date of Death
205038	Pte	Collins, Edward	No 4 (T.F.) Depot	17.3.20
290540	Pte	Pugh, William	1/7th	18.3.20
30071	Pte	Moon, H.	Depot	24.3.20
202170	Pte	Pinches, A.		25.3.20
27086	Pte	Duncan, William T.		27.3.20
240937	Pte	Clarke, J.	4 Reserve	30.3.20
57294	Pte	Sharkey, V.	4	5.4.20
241343	Pte	Roberts, R.J.	3/5th	15.4.20
60905	Pte	Humphreys, William	10	18.4.20
291318	Pte	Jones, W.H.	1/7th	22.4.20
203047	Pte	Griffiths, J.K.	4	23.4.20
9418	Pte	Westwood, S.		25.4.20
9592	Pte	Whyte, John C.		26.4.20
6984	Pte	Shaw, James		27.4.20
36247	Pte	Morgans, John		9.5.20
91842	Pte	Hughes, J.P.		10.5.20
63724	Pte	Evans, Caradoc	24	15.5.20
203395	Pte	Williams, W.	4	21.5.20
291963	Pte	Daniel, H.D.	Depot	25.5.20
34177	Pte	Morgan, David W.	1	31.5.20
34633	Pte	Mansfield, Albert E.	10	3.6.20
17129	Pte	Salisbury, Herbert	13	5.6.20
202607	Pte	Thomas, Cedric L.	2	9.6.20
200209	Pte	Gallagher, J.J.	1/4th	11.6.20
238058	Pte	Bower, H.	4	16.6.20
63802	Pte	Edmondson, H.	3 Garrison	19.6.20
20425	Pte	Evans, John	14	19.6.20
17235	Pte	James, J.	13	23.6.20
315469	Pte	Wellings, E.P.	25 (M & WH Yeo)	25.6.20
33883	Pte	Heehan, P.	3	28.6.20
51815	Pte	Chapman, William		1.7.20
55997	Pte	Mountjoy, A.		7.7.20
345674	Pte	Davies, E.		12.7.20
66388	Pte	Fiddler, Timothy	Depot	12.7.20
98170	Pte	Hollywell, Robert	3	16.7.20
75588	Pte	Wozencroft, A.	23	21.7.20
42494	Pte	Gregory, Thomas		22.7.20
20549	Pte	Thomas, R.	3/6th	25.7.20
45546	Pte	Trenholm, F.	Depot	27.7.20
31610	Pte	Wilkinson, J.R.		10.8.20
3009	Pte	Owen, T.		12.8.20
73591	Pte	Holdeon, Thomas		21.8.20
37765	Pte	Hodgson, H.	14	24.8.20
37071	Pte	Lovatt, Percy W.		26.8.20

Regtl No.	Rank	Name	Battalion	Date of Death
23830	Pte	Thomas, R.D.		1.9.20
21948	Pte	Harniman, James H.	3	10.9.20
73589	Pte	Holden, Lewis V.	15 (London Welsh)	22.9.20
20426	Pte	Thomas, Thomas	2/6th	22.9.20
10752	Pte	Llewellyn, William S.		26.9.20
3389	Pte	Mcleod, D.	3/5th	1.10.20
265030	Pte	Jones, Robert O.	1/6th	16.10.20
266267	Pte	Jones, W.	6 Garrison	8.11.20
97235	Pte	Evans, F.	1/7th	9.11.20
61797	Pte	Oliver, Mathias	6	10.11.20
203788	Pte	Jones, J.T.	4	10.11.20
60638	Pte	Jones, J.H.		17.11.20
30482	Pte	Weaver, J.H.		24.11.20
98044	Pte	Horan, James	2	25.11.20
51403	Pte	Ball, John		28.11.20
69311	Pte	Thomas, W.W.	Depot	2.12.20
9498	Pte	Jones, Thomas	1	12.12.20
97382	Pte	Kirkpatrick, J.T.	2	28.12.20
33612	Pte	Keilly, S.	Depot	12.1.21
240127	Pte	Griffiths, Richard		28.1.21
17074	Pte	Doyle, Edward		29.1.21
265484	Pte	Griffith, L.L.	5th/6th	3.2.21
21203	Pte	Williams, L.H.		12.2.21
443917	Pte	Schultz, Edward		13.2.21
26514	Pte	Little, Horace S.	16	16.2.21
5826	Pte	Buckley, R.		20.2.21
33539	Pte	Hopkinson, J.		16.3.21
55658	Pte	Barnfield, R.		19.3.21
5698	Pte	Robinson, Edmund		8.4.21
21399	Pte	Owen, William		11.4.21
3453	Pte	Platt, Frederick	Depot	24.4.21
51596	Pte	Evans, W.	3	26.4.21
45129	Pte	Roberts, R.M.	3	30.4.21
21695	Pte	Wyatt, Albion J.	15 (London Welsh)	6.5.21
54586	Pte	Williams, G.	Depot	7.5.21
268200	Pte	Isles, H.		10.5.21
19522	Pte	Davies, John W.	1	17.5.21
57938	Pte	Ward, H.	9	19.5.21
57383	Pte	Longhorn, C.W.		12.6.21
4484	Pte	Williams, James	2	15.6.21
90276	Pte	Jones, William	25 (M & WH Yeo)	22.6.21
256	Pte	Burke, Peter	5	23.6.21
201605	Pte	Roberts, W.		24.6.21
345236	Pte	Mapp, W.H.	24 (Denbigh Yeo)	11.7.21

Regtl No.	Rank	Name	Battalion	Date of Death
65341	Pte	Hodges, W.	7 Garrison	17.7.21
20519	Pte	Crippin, Lester S.	14	26.7.21
201220	Pte	Hughes, W.	4	28.7.21
38205	Pte	Jones, C.	2	10.8.21
35586	Bdsm	Williams, H.	2	26.4.19

Part Two, 1919–1939

This section records, in rank order and by date, those members of the Regiment who died while serving from 1 January 1919 to 3 September 1939, where their deaths are not attributable to their service in the Great War unless this is after 31 August 1921 – there are only two cases (noted) of this being so.

Legend:

B.M.H.	British Military Hospital
Gsw	Gunshot wound
Kia	Killed in action
Rta	Road traffic accident

Regtl No.	Rank	Name	Battalion	Date of Death	Cause	Died at/in
	Hon Col	Williams, E.H.W. DSO	5	8.34	Natural causes	U.K.
	Lt Col	Parry, Thomas H. MP DL	Staff (late 5)	8.10.39	Pneumonia	Wrexham
	Maj	Compton-Smith, Geoffrey L. DSO	2	c.30.4.21	Murder by the I.R.A.	Co. Cork
	Capt	Williams, Thomas R. MC	4	26.4.21		U.K.
	Capt	Brunditt, Percy W.	4	11.11.22		U.K.
	Capt	Griffith, R.E.	6	9.6.35	Not known	U.K.
	Capt	Williams, R.S.	5	21.12.35	Not known	U.K.
	Capt	Courtney, Myles B.	3/16th Punjabis	9.4.37	Enemy fire	Waziristan
	Capt	Whitaker, Marmaduke W.	2	5.6.38	Cerebral malaria	Torit, Sudan
	Flt Lt	Parry	RAF, late 6	4.22	Air accident	Ireland
	Lt	Martin, Richard W.C.	2	18.7.27	Rta	Germany
	Lt	Parker, D.M.S.	6	6.11.38		Portmadoc
	WO I (BM)	Burnett, F.	2	?18.1.35	Post operative	Hong Kong
4178898	CSM	Rush, C. DCM	1	11.12.21	Sniper	Sararogha, Waziristan
4179610	CSM	Grindley, G. MM	1			Waziristan
4178931	CSgt (ORS)	Evans	1	31.7.23		India. *En route* to Dagshai
4187241	CSM	Cush, P.C.	6	16.11.26	Not known	Holyhead
4183474	CSM	Evans, T.	6	5.31	Not known	Caernarfon

Regtl No.	Rank	Name	Battalion	Date of Death	Cause	Died at/in
	CSM	Evans, T.M.	7	3.11.33	Not known	U.K.
4184579	D Maj	Williams, William P.	1	27.4.37	Rta	Woking
10375	Sgt	Evans, Harry	1	14.6.20		India
8751	Sgt	Down, Sidney	1	29.6.20	Typhoid	India
5375875	Sgt	Jones, E. DCM *Oxf & Bucks L.I.*	Att 5	22		U.K.
	Sgt	Hanscombe, David	1	19.2.22	Sniper	Kldana, Waziristan
4178932	Sgt	Bracken, G	1	5.22	Pneumonia	Lucknow
4180003	Sgt	Rhodes, G.	1	12.22		Hospital, India
4179857	Sgt	Crowley, J.	2	28.3.23	Malaria	Netley
7809991	Sgt	Barkley	?Depot	4.8.23	Typhoid	Wrexham
4178926	Sgt	Edwards, W.	1	12.10.27	Pneumonia	Nasirabad
4182851	Sgt	Jackson, L.	6	1.33	Not known	Caernarfon
	Sgt	Meades, A.	4	1.34	Not known	Wrexham
	Sgt	Setterfield, William H.	2	21.10.35	Bronchial pneumonia	Hong Kong
	Sgt-I	Wills, George	7	11.37		U.K.
4183323	Sgt	Wills, G.	Att. 7	1.1.38	Pneumonia	Welshpool
	Sgt	Roberts, T.S.	4	21.10.38		U.K.
3849134	LSgt	Nedderman, William	1	10.9.37	Rta	Newmarket
3903651	Cpl	Roberts, Alfred E.	2	19.2.22	Suicide	Dublin
	Cpl	Huges, A.S.	6	6.31	Not known	Caernarfon
4185894	Cpl	Williams, G.H.	6	8.36	Car crash	U.K.
	Cpl	Jones, W.T.	4	37	Cancer?	U.K.
4185474	Cpl	Green, S.J.	1	5.11.38		Aldershot
4182580	LCpl	O'Brien, W.P.	4	23.3.22		U.K.
4182682	LCpl	Hughes, C.J.	4	27.3.24		U.K.
4184478	L Cpl	Walsh, D.	1	5.10.27		Nasirabad
4185436	LCpl	Guthrie, Alexander	1	21.4.32	Pneumonia	S'hampton
4189960	L Cpl	Hammersley, Harold	1	27.1.37	Pneumonia	Aldershot
4189474	LCpl	DeLacey, J.	1	23.5.38		M. Tydfil
91172	Pte	Brown, S.E.	3	11.2.19	Rta	?Limerick
88703	Pte	Walker, Charles	3	3.6.19		?Limerick
87531	Pte	King, Edward	2	17.8.19	'Accidentally killed'	?Limerick
241458	Pte	Morris, Robert	2	21.8.19		Ireland
96819	Pte	Williams, J.	1	5.3.20	Murder	India
24698	Pte	Quinn, F.H.	2	27.4.20		Dublin
35802	Pte	Wallworth, F.P.	1	14.5.20		India
35776	Pte	Martin, Henry	2	14.6.20	Kidney stone	Cork
100437	Pte	Rowlands, W.	1	14.6.20		India
101349	Pte	Williams, R.E.	1	21.6.20		India
89343	Pte	Jones, Thomas	1	11.7.20		India

Regtl No.	Rank	Name	Battalion	Date of Death	Cause	Died at/in
93149	Pte	Scaife, Jospeh	1	24.7.20		India
100381	Pte	Ferriday, Ernest F.	1	29.7.20		India
4179349	Pte	Shorey, W. T.	1	15.8.20		India
4180426	Pte	Owen, Harry	2	20.9.20	Acc.shot	Ireland
4180415	Pte	Hunt, B.W.	1	6.6.21	Drowning?	India
4179638	Pte	East, H.	1	6.6.21	Drowning?	India
4180549	Pte	Excell, Francis J.	1	6.6.21	Drowning?	India
4179390	Pte	Williams, Reginald W. or William R. [14]	2	10.7.21	Gsw	Bunratty Bridge, Co. Clare
4181234	Pte	Murphy, M.	2	14.8.21		?Limerick
4182677	Pte	Bowen, J.E.	4	30.10.21		U.K.
4178045	Pte	Jones, J.	4	4.11.21		U.K.
		Nyk	1	29.11.21		?Lucknow
4178995	Pte	Carr, R.H.	5	22.12.21		U.K.
4180491	Pte	Lamb, B.	1	1.22	Tubercular peritonitis	Hospital, India
53966	Pte	Lewis, John[15]		19.2.22	Wounds rec'd in WW1	U.K.
4183101	Pte	Evans, T.	5	1.3.22		U.K.
4180483	Pte	Hughes, J,	1	5.22	C'bral haemorr-hage	India
4180235	Pte	Longfellow, E. H.	1	5.22		India
4183010	Pte	Parry, A.O.	5	19.5.22		U.K.
4182037	Pte	Carter, E.	4	30.5.22		U.K.
4182011	Pte	Bowen, L.	1	29.7.22	kiA	Windy Snip Waziristan
4180560	Pte	Lloyd, C.	1	29.7.22	DoW	Windy Snip Waziristan
4179366	Pte	Tevendale, F.	1	29.7.22	Sniper	Prospect Picquet Waziristan
12463	Pte	Moses, Evan	8	15.12.22	Wounds rec'd in WW1	U.K
4179902	Pte	Owen(s), J.	1	12.22	Football injury	Hospital, India
4181806	Pte	Stealey, R.J.	5	23.11.22		U.K.
5097437	Pte	Heath, H.	1	6.2.23	kia	Waziristan
4114088	Pte	Jones, F.	1	6.2.23	kia	Waziristan
273111	Pte	Murphy, B.	1	6.2.23	kia	Waziristan
4181586	Pte	Sherriff, H.	1	6.2.23	kia	Waxiristan
4180473	Pte	West, G.	1	6.2.23	kia	Waziristan
4179204	Pte	Freegrove, J.	1	11.3.23	sniper	Waziristan
347089	Fus	Barton, J.	1	1.7.23	Drowned	India
4180904	Fus	Harwood, A	2	5.7.23	Heat stroke	Freshwater West
4180055	Fus	Hope	1	19.10.23		Multan, India

Regtl No.	Rank	Name	Battalion	Date of Death	Cause	Died at/in
4180536	Fus	Chance	1	11.2.24	Pneumonia	India
4184381	Fus	Worthington, J.	1	4.7.24	Pneumonia	India
4181948	Fus	Jordan, W.	1	8.8.24	Pneumonia	India
4170079	Fus	Holcombe, W.H.	1	19.8.24	Pneumonia	Lahore, India
7577435	Fus	Omerod	1	29.4.25	Heart failure	Multan
4181315	Fus	Miller	1	27.5.25	Pneumonia	India
2731256	Fus	Lunt	1	27.5.25	Drowning	Bhandar Ghat
4184499	Fus	Cooke, T.	1	24.5.26	Tubercular peritonitis	Ahm'bad, India
4185252	Fus	Durbin, R,	1	27.8.26	Appendicitis	Nasirabad
3434967	Fus	Howard	1	31.10.27		Quetta
4179472	Fus	Cullen E.	1	27.1.28	Carbon monoxide poisoning	India
4185518	Fus	Ross, W.P.	2	2.31	Rta	U.K.
4189034	Fus	Parry, E.R.	6	8.5.31	Not known	Cwm-y-Glo
	Fus	Walters, Richard	1	29.5.31	Struck by lightning	Gebeit, Sudan
	Fus	Johnson	6	7.31	Railway accident	U.K.
4186883	Fus	Varmin, Vivian T.	1	22.7.31	In hospital	Atbara, Sudan
4187334	Fus	Boaler, Lawson	2	19.4.32	Bronchial pneumonia	Gibraltar
4188826	Fus	Williams, T.	6	21.1.33	Fire	Cwm-y-Glo
4190974	Fus	Williams, H.	6	16.11.33	Not known	Holyhead
4187395	Fus	Manning, F.J.	1	3.8.33	Rta	Andover
4179109	Fus	Kelly, Charles	1	10.10.33	Bronchial pneumonia	Tidworth
	Fus	Fox, W.H.	2	24.10.33	In hospital	Gibraltar
	Fus	Humphreys, David	2	7.3.34	Drowned	Gibraltar
4189970	Fus	Wills, P.	1	16.4.34	Cerebro-spinal meningitis	Tidworth
4190321	Fus	Young, H.B.	6	27.7.34	rta	Conway
	Fus	Griffiths, R.	7	11.10.34	Not known	Wrexham
4190467	Fus	Strange, Frederick	4	14.10.34	Nat causes	Wrexham
	Fus	Lawton, T.	2	34		Hong Kong
4190321	Fus	Pritchard, R.S.	6	10.2.35	Not known	Conway
4179936	Fus	Turner, Ll.	6	27.7.35	Not known	Portmadoc
	Fus	Turner, Llewellyn	6	8.35	After prolonged illness	Bangor
11	Fus	Roberts	2	4.36		Hong Kong
	Fus	Roberts, E.T.	7	11.35	After prolonged illness	Llanidloes
4191757	Fus	Davies, James	1	16.7.36	Drowned	Shillinglea Park, Sussex

Regtl No.	Rank	Name	Battalion	Date of Death	Cause	Died at/in
4190635	Fus	Jones, W.M.	5	11.11.36		St Asaph
4191475	Fus	Platt, B.M.	2	20.4.37	In hospital	Hong Kong
	Fus	Evans, B.E.	4	37		U.K.
4189534	Fus	Evans, G	2	5.9.37	Accident	Shanghai
4192410	Fus	Lloyd, Douglas	2	13.9.37	Appendix abcess	B.M.H. Shanghai
4189957	Fus	Francis, John M.	2	2.38		Shanghai
	Fus	Ebrey	2	2.38		Shanghai
	Fus	Jones	4	5.38		Gwersyllt
	Fus	Jones, E.H.	6	5.6.38		U.K.
4189862	Fus	Davies, W.G.	1	28.6.38		Aldershot
4191821	Fus	Parry, J.H.	6	11.9.38		I.O.W.
4191693	Fus	Parry, Edward	6	15.10.38		Caernarfon
4185474	Fus	Green, S.J.	1	5.11.38	Carc'ma of the stomach	U.K.
	Bdsm	Walker	1	27.12.28	In hospital	India
	Bdsm	Buck, P.	6	11.37		Llanberis
4180437	Boy	Matthews, F.	1	5.22	kiA	Waziristan
	Boy	Carrs	Depot 1 R.W.F.	2.22		Dalhousie, Punjab

Part Three, Gresford Colliery, 22 September 1934

This section records twenty-seven serving and former members of the Regiment who are known to have died, the majority being Territorials from the 4th Battalion, who died in the explosion at Gresford Colliery near Wrexham, on 22 September 1934. The explosion and its aftermath killed a total of 266 men and boys.

Regtl No.	Rank	Name	Decorations	Unit/Coy
4178003	Sgt	Jones, Iorwerth		4 R.W.F./A
	Sgt	Rowlands, John	MM	4 R.W.F./A
4187087	Sgt	Tittle, Ralph E.		4 R.W.F./M
4183662	Dmr	Cornwell, Thomas R.		4 R.W.F./H.Q.
4183216	Sgt	Archibald, Joseph		4 R.W.F./Pro
4183969		Bew, Arthur		4 R.W.F.
4188103		Cartwright, Albert Edward		4 R.W.F.
4190685	Fus	Clutton, George Albert.		4 R.W.F./H.Q.
4182570	Fus	Davies, Arthur		4 R.W.F./H.Q.
4188348	Fus	Davies, Mathias		4 R.W.F./A
4183750		Dodd, Thomas		4 R.W.F.
	Fus	Ellis, George Edward		4 R.W.F.
200512		Jarvis, Ernest		4 R.W.F.
		Kelsall, Harry		4 R.W.F.
		Nicholls, Harry		4 R.W.F.
		Nicholls, William Henry		4 R.W.F.
20066		Owens, Evan Henry		4 R.W.F.
4191282	Fus	Parry, John Richard		4 R.W.F./A
25332		Prince, Mark		4 R.W.F.
4186286		Roberts, William H.		4 R.W.F.
		Rogers, Edward Llewellyn		4 R.W.F.
4179329		Ross, Albert H,		4 R.W.F.
4190774	Fus	Stevens, Richard T.		4 R.W.F./B
4187086		Strange, Albert		4 R.W.F.
69288		Taylor, William Henry		4 R.W.F.
8690		Wynneyard, William Walter		4 R.W.F.
4186383	Bdsm	Hampson, Frank		4 R.W.F./H.Q.

The Gresford Disaster

THE Colonel of the Regiment informed His Majesty The King, through his Private Secretary, of the loss The Royal Welch Fusiliers had sustained by this disaster.

The King's Private Secretary replied that :

"*The King greatly regrets to learn that twenty-seven serving men and old comrades of The Royal Welch Fusiliers were killed in the disaster at Gresford Colliery, and His Majesty sends his sincere condolences to the Regiment for the loss they have sustained.*"

Notes

1 After transfer to Labour Corps as 331861.
2 Given new number 4180821, PoW 1914–1918.
3 After transfer to 1/1st Herefordshire Regt as 33411.
4 After transfer to Labour Corps as 452571.
5 Served as Robert Wilson.
6 After transfer to Army Service Corps as M/376202.
7 After transfer to 2 Welsh as 47901.
8 After transfer to 805 A.E. Coy, Labour Corps, as 361742.
9 After transfer to 4 S.W.B. as 28441.
10 After transfer to S.W.B. as 30730.
11 Served as Williams.
12 After transfer to M.G.C. as 24912.
13 After transfer to Labour Corps as 659157.
14 2 R.W.F. Digest of Service has W.R., C.W.G.C. has R.W.; Digest of Service also says that 'Neither the body or cycle were recovered'.
15 After transfer to R. Defence Corps as 75113.

Annex H

Major G.L. Compton-Smith DSO (1889–1921)
This Annex is the work of Major Glyn Hughes MBE

Geoffrey Lee Compton-Smith was born on 19 August 1889. His father was William Compton Compton-Smith (b. 1860), a barrister of 1 Paper Buildings, Temple, London[1] who had been educated at Westminster and Cambridge. His mother was Henrietta Beatrix Lee (b. 1862), one of eight children and the eldest of three daughters of Sir Joseph Cocksey Lee of Parkgate, Altrincham, Cheshire.[2] Following her marriage in 1888 to William they lived at Sumner Place not far from Kensington Palace. Geoffrey was baptised at the church of St Mary Magdalene on 30 August 1889. When he was eight the family moved to a new and larger house in fashionable Campden Hill.[3]

In April 1903, at the age of thirteen, Geoffrey was sent to school at Radley College, Abingdon where he joined Wharton's Social, one of the boarding houses. He

Major G.L. Compton-Smith DSO, an oil painting in the possession of the Regiment. (R.W.F. Mus)

showed potential at rowing and was stroke in the Junior Fours. It is recorded in November 1904 that, 'Among the juniors, decidedly promising form was shown: Day, Snelling, Compton-Smith … being specially noticeable.' At the time he weighed only 9st 11½ lb. He remained at the school for just two years after which he went to Heidelberg, where he completed his education in 1908.[4] He joined the Royal Military College, Sandhurst in 1909 and was commissioned into Alexandra, Princess of Wales's Own (Yorkshire Regiment) as a Second Lieutenant on 20 April 1910. Whilst at Sandhurst he represented the College at athletics against the Royal Military Academy Woolwich.

His early career was spent in Egypt, the Sudan, and India; the 1st Battalion of the Regiment arrived in India in August 1914 and there it remained until the end of the Great War. He had been forced to leave a lady behind in Hartley Witney because Officers were not permitted to marry before they were thirty. His enthusiasm for athletics continued and he won the cross-country in Sudan and had similar success at the mile and a half on a number of occasions in India. He also won a military history competition in 1913.[5] On 19 July 1911 he was promoted to Lieutenant. On 29 May 1915, his younger brother, Roger, a Second Lieutenant in the Manchesters, was killed at Gallipoli aged 20.[6] On 10 June 1915 Geoffrey was promoted to Captain and at about the same time he transferred to the 3rd (Special Reserve) Battalion The Royal Welch Fusiliers at Litherland, in Liverpool. What made him join the Royal Welch Fusiliers in 1915 is unknown, but it may have been because he felt he was missing out and wanted to get into the action. He could, however, have joined the 2nd Green Howards in France. Possibly he wanted to get back to Europe in order to be closer to his lady friend. He did not, however, remain in England for long. On 1 October 1915 he joined the 1st Battalion in the line at Cambrin, France, during the battle of Loos, where it suffered 454 casualties. At the end of the month he assumed the appointment of Senior Major (in other Regiments the second-in-command). For a time in February 1916 he was in acting command of the battalion. On 1 July 1916 the battle of the Somme began, remembered chiefly for the small gain at enormous cost – 60,000 casualties on the first day alone – and the amazing courage of all those engaged. On the 14th, 1 R.W.F. was involved in an attack on the ridge behind the village of Bazentin. It was on this day that Compton-Smith was wounded.[7] During sick leave in England he married his lady, Gladys Mary Lloyd, at the parish church at Hartley Witney. On 23 October he joined the 10th (Service) Battalion in billets at Bus (les Artois) and assumed command as a local Lieutenant Colonel. During the first battle of the Scarpe 9–11 April 1917) he was slightly wounded but remained with the battalion, which suffered over 200 casualties. Two weeks later the battalion returned to the line at Monchy and in eight days sustained another 113 casualties, followed by 161 between 13 and 19 June. In July he was awarded the DSO and the French *Légion d'Honneur*. The citation for the former read as follows:

> For conspicuous gallantry and devotion to duty. He commanded his battalion with great skill and determination, immediately the objective was gained he moved forward to supervise consolidation and cover the advance of the brigade. Although wounded he remained in the position, and his personal example was of utmost value to all.[8]

On 26 September 1917, the first day of the battle of Polygon Wood, Compton-Smith was evacuated with shell-shock.[9] He was temporarily employed as Deputy Assistant Adjutant General at an Officer Cadet battalion in Aldershot.[10] In 1918 he joined the 12th Battalion of the King's Liverpool Regiment in France.[11]

He returned to the Royal Welch in late 1918 and went with the re-formed 2nd Battalion to Ireland in August 1919. Here he was stationed at New Barracks, Limerick. For a while he was accompanied by his wife until he felt it was too dangerous and sent her home to England.[12] A daughter, Anne Cecilia Beatrix, was born in 1919. He was posted from the battalion and arrived at Ballyvonaire Camp, near Buttevant in Co. Cork early in February 1920 where he was employed as an intelligence Officer.[13]

Although Compton-Smith was a loyal soldier he was uneasy about some of the measures introduced in the hope they would help in the defeat of the I.R.A. He disapproved of the atrocities carried out by the Black and Tans and Royal Irish Constabulary Auxiliaries, and less frequently and on a smaller scale by the army. He disliked the policy of 'Official Reprisals' which was introduced in January 1921, which led to the destruction of hundreds of private houses and shops, leaving families without homes and their menfolk without jobs.[14]

Compton-Smith's orderly from December 1920 was Private Tom Preedy of the Royal Warwicks. He liked to flirt with the Irish girls, but they were unresponsive as they risked ostracism for fraternisation. The I.R.A., however, saw that such tendencies were exploitable and encouraged trusted women to respond positively for intelligence purposes. Although this was tried with Preedy it failed, because Compton-Smith, aware of the need for security, did not talk about his job nor leave sensitive material lying around.[15]

Compton-Smith loved architecture and sketching, the latter probably developed whilst at Sandhurst where 'field-sketching' was part of the curriculum. In the beautiful countryside of Southern Ireland there were many places, from stately homes to medieval castles, where he could indulge his interests. This had not gone unnoticed by the I.R.A., which viewed with suspicion the motives of a British Officer, sometimes in uniform and at others in civilian clothes, reportedly engaged in sketching. Amazingly, no attempt ever appears at this point to have been made to kidnap or kill him.

The worst defeat suffered by the I.R.A. during the War of Independence occurred on 20 February 1921 at Clonmult. Acting on intelligence, 2nd Hampshires searched properties where members of a rebel flying column were thought to be staying. Shooting broke out and the engagement lasted for nearly two hours; at the end of it, thirteen rebels were dead and four who were wounded were taken prisoner. Three of the latter – the other was too badly injured to stand trial – were tried by court martial at Cork and sentenced to be hanged. In April, at an I.R.A. brigade conference, the need to obtain the reprieve of their comrades was agreed. It was decided that the best course of action was to capture a high-ranking British Officer who could be used as a bargaining counter. It was thought that the resolve of General Strickland, G.O.C. 6th Division at Cork, would weaken if the life of one of his own Officers was at stake. He had not been moved earlier, though, after the I.R.A. had captured Mrs Lindsay and her chauffeur in January and she had written to the General begging for the lives of other I.R.A. men awaiting execution.[16]

Compton-Smith decided to go on a sketching trip to the ruins of the fifteenth century castle at Blarney.[17] On the evening of 15 April he telephoned Smith's Hotel in Blarney to reserve a room. The hotel, which was attached to the R.I.C. barracks next door, was a favourite watering-hole for Officers from Ballincollig and from Victoria Barracks in Cork. It is possible that he was also planning to look for indications of the whereabouts of Mrs Lindsay of whom he would have been aware, although it was not known that she had already been murdered. The telephone call to the hotel was heard at the I.R.A. listening post outside Blarney and early the following morning the information was passed to Frank Busteed, second-in-command of the 6th I.R.A. Battalion, whose mother lived at Blarney.

On the 16th, Compton-Smith caught the midday train from Buttevant to Cork via Blarney. Busteed was waiting at the station which was about a mile from the village. Compton-Smith, who was pointed out to him, set off on foot for the village carrying his suitcase. After walking a short distance he was confronted by two I.R.A. men armed with pistols, relieved of his suitcase, and taken into a field where there were two more rebels armed with rifles. His hands were tied and within an hour a pony and trap appeared and he was taken to a temporary prison in a farm at Knocknasuff. Busteed departed to a hastily convened battalion meeting at Donoughmore. Because of the presence of troops searching for Mrs Lindsay it was decided to move Compton-Smith to a house at Courtbrack where he could be interrogated.[18] He was put in a loft and fed by the mothers and sisters of I.R.A. men. He was well treated. Jackie O'Leary, the 26 year old commanding Officer of the 6th Battalion, arrived to undertake the interrogation. Compton-Smith admitted he was an intelligence Officer and that his suitcase contained the tools of his trade, including binoculars, maps and notes in code. O'Leary told him that he was being held hostage for the lives of I.R.A. men awaiting execution in Cork, and that a letter to that effect was being sent to General Strickland from the I.R.A. brigade commander. He added that he hoped that Compton-Smith's good relations with the General would save his life. On the next day Compton-Smith was allowed to write a letter to his wife, concluding, 'I have no doubt that I shall get out of this scrape as I have got out of others. There is nothing to worry about.'[19]

By now the disappearance of Compton-Smith was known to his colleagues and military activity in the Blarney area intensified. O'Leary decided that he had to be moved to a safer location without delay. A Rolls Royce was commandeered from a loyalist and in this he was moved at night to an empty house at Donoughmore, previously owned by an English Protestant family. After only one night he was moved again a short distance to an isolated house owned by the Moynihans at Barrachauring. He got on well with his guards with whom he had long discussions about the situation in Ireland.[20] He wrote another letter to Gladys which she did not receive until 3 June in which he said, 'they treat me most fairly.'[21] On the 29th, ten days after he had arrived at the Moynihan's house, he noticed that the guards were more reserved and less communicative. The next morning O'Leary arrived accompanied by an elderly man who, judging by the respect with which he was treated, was a senior I.R.A. Officer. The latter, having ascertained that Compton-Smith had been well treated, informed him that as Strickland had gone ahead with the executions on the previous day he, Compton-Smith, was to be executed immediately. He was permitted to write a letter to his wife, but a request to be allowed to see a priest was refused on the grounds that the nearest Church of Ireland vicar had served in the Great War and been decorated. He was then led to a spot near a freshly dug grave. Whilst waiting he recited some prayers. O'Leary summoned four men to form the firing squad. After Compton-Smith refused a blindfold, the order to fire was given. He died with the words 'I love you, Alice' on his lips.[22]

According to Maurice Brew,[23] Compton-Smith, to whom he referred as Chief British Intelligence Officer for Munster, wrote three letters before his execution: to his wife, to his father, and to his Regiment. He went on to record that, 'When removed to the place of execution, he placed his cigarette case in the breast pocket of his tunic and asked that, after his death, it should be sent to his regiment. He then lighted a cigarette and said that when he dropped the cigarette it could be taken as a signal by the execution squad to open fire.' The final letters written by Compton-Smith were:

> My own darling little wife,
> I am to be shot in an hour's time. Dearest your hubby will die with your name on his lips, your face before his eyes, and he will die like an Englishman and a Soldier. I cannot tell you sweetheart how much it is to me to leave you alone – nor how little to me personally to die – I have no fear, only the utmost, greatest tenderest love to you, and my sweet little Anne. I leave my cigarette case to the Regiment, my miniature medals to my father – whom I have implored to befriend you in everything – and my watch to the Officer who is executing me because I believe him to be a gentleman and to mark the fact that I bear him no malice for carrying out what he sincerely believes to be his duty. Goodbye, my darling, my own. Choose from among my things some object you would particularly keep in memory of me, and I believe that my spirit will be in it to love and comfort you.
> Tender, tender farewells and kisses –
> Your own
> Geof

Dear Father,

I had the misfortune to be made prisoner by the Sinn Feiners on Saturday. I am however quite safe and sound and have been most kindly treated. Exactly what is likely to happen to me I don't know. But whatever happens, it will have been a most interesting experience. I am at present engaged in growing a beard.

> Your affectionate son
> Geoffrey

This letter does not appear to have been written on the day of his execution. It is clearly the letter to Strickland (below) which was written shortly before the execution.

Dear Royal Welch Fusiliers,

I am to be shot in an hour's time. I should like you fellows to know that this sentence has been passed on me and that I intend to die like a Welch Fusilier with a laugh and forgiveness for those who are carrying out the deed.

I should like my death to lessen rather than increase the bitterness which exists between England and Ireland.

I have been treated with great kindness and, during my short captivity, have learned to regard Sinn Feiners rather as mistaken idealists than as a 'Murder Gang'.

My cigarette case I leave to the Mess. I carried it with the Regiment throughout the war and I shall die with it in my pocket.

> God bless you all, Comrades.
> GL C-S

Finally there is a letter which he appears to have written shortly before he was shot, to General Strickland:

Dear General,

As a result of my disobeying your orders and wandering about alone I have been captured by Sinn Feiners, and am to be shot in a few minutes time. May I ask you to make it known that it is my last wish there should be no reprisals on my behalf. I am sure the feeling is bitter enough already without our adding fuel to the fire. I believe these fellows are idealists who are doing what they earnestly believe to be right. For our part let us try to forgive, which is more salutary and far more difficult than to revenge ourselves.

> Yours sincerely,
> GL Compton-Smith[24]

He was murdered only ten weeks before a truce was announced on 8 July, which came into effect three days later. It was to be nearly another five years before Compton-Smith's body was formally interred. The first intimation that he was missing reached his family on 25 April when his father, William, received a letter from the 2nd Battalion at Limerick. The letter, from Captain Venables Kyrke, was dated the 22nd, six days after the kidnap. In it, Venables Kyrke wrote that:

… we are most anxious about your son. He left Ballyvonaire Camp last Saturday with the intention of returning the same afternoon, was traced to Blarney where he took a jaunting car. Nothing has been heard of him since… . He was unarmed I think at the time and in mufti, and alone so I don't think there is the least chance of any harm having come to him… it is most unfortunate altogether… . As far as I can gather he was going to have tea with a friend at Blarney but the friend apparently knows nothing of his intended visit.[25]

It seems strange that this information should have come from 2 R.W.F. rather than from the unit in which he worked. Had this been too secret to disclose the letter could have been sent from the Garrison H.Q. or some such organisation.

A month later William Compton-Smith received another letter from Venables Kyrke, dated 18 May, in which he said:

I am afraid I have nothing further to tell you … . We hoped that by the end of the week he would be released. We had had information to this effect. I don't know why he is being kept now unless he may know too much about them and they don't care to let him go until things are settled. Of course every effort is being made to get his release. We don't know where he is but he was seen by an individual last week and was then very fit… . It is of course only a matter of time before his release is effected either by his being released by the S.F.'s [Sinn Feiners] themselves which I believe they will or else we shall hear where he is and get him.[26]

This letter was written almost exactly a month after Compton-Smith disappeared and no body had been found. He had been dead for nearly a fortnight before he was alleged to have been seen and 'was very fit.' It was probably meant to allay fears until some definite information was available, rather than any deliberate obfuscation, but doubts must remain. The information, however, very soon surfaced. A letter from General Headquarters in Dublin on 27 May informed William of his son's death:

I write to informed you that as a result of a raid which took place yesterday in Dublin, on one of the Rebel Headquarters [one of Michael Collins'' offices] the following letters were discovered written by your son … :
1 addressed to yourself;
2 and 3 addressed to Mrs Compton-Smith
4 addressed to Major General Sir Peter Strickland
5 addressed to the Adjutant, Royal Welch Fusiliers

Numbers 1, 2 and 3 are enclosed herewith, with the request that you be good enough to break the sad news to Mrs Compton-Smith. Numbers 4 and 5 have been despatched to the addressees… . Your son's silver cigarette case was also recovered and this he directs should be left to the Officers' Mess.

---

*   Michael Collins was the main driving force behind the independence movement. He was the I.R.A.'s Director of Intelligence and actively involved in providing funds and weapons for I.R.A. units.

General Sir Nevil Macready desires me to say how much he sympathises with you and your family in the loss which you have sustained.[27]

On 7 June William wrote to Major Jamieson* as follows:

I think I ought to send you this addition to my former letter of today's day.
   After leaving the draft with you on 3rd June I heard from Major Kyrke.
   He did not know that they had threatened to shoot my son. When he knew I do not know.
   The dates are of importance as bearing on my action in the matter.

16th April. My son kidnapped.
18th April. Major Kyrke knew it.
21st April. Mrs Compton-Smith received a letter from her husband saying he was in Sinn Fein hands but was well treated.
21st April. [I] called at the W.O. and they knew nothing at all.
25th April. I received a letter from Major Kyrke dated 22nd saying no need for anxiety. Upon receiving this I thought it best to remain quiescent.
18th May. Major Kyrke advised me to continue this attitude saying my son had been seen "last week" and that he expected "on good authority" that he would have been by that time released.
28th May. I received the "Shot in an hour" letter written by my son to his wife.
1st June. At the House of Commons I first heard of the threat to shoot if the rebels were executed on 28th April.[28]

I have had two letters from G.H.Q. Dublin but the threat is not mentioned. They say they "know no reason why he should have been shot". I have been in communication with Colonel Norman† – he does not mention the threat. This is a vital matter which I had a right to know at the earliest possible moment. It will be to me as long as I live a cause of the bitterest regret that because the information which was given to me was so tardy and misleading I was induced to remain inactive and to let my boy perish if indeed he has been shot without stirring a hand to try to save him.
   Yours faithfully,
   Wm Compton-Smith[29]

This is a poignant letter which clearly shows his great indignation at the way he had been treated by the military authorities. At about this time Sir J. Harmood-Banner M.P. asked in the Commons for particulars of the murder of Major Compton-Smith 'who left his home in mufti to meet the monthly nurse who was coming to attend on his wife … .' To attend on a wife who had been sent to England when it was deemed too dangerous to continue living in Ireland!

---

*   The position held by Major Jamieson is not known. He was not serving the 2 R.W.F., but he could have been an Officer on the staff at G.H.Q. Dublin.
†   Commanding Officer 2 R.W.F.

William decided, with the agreement of G.H.Q. Ireland, to advertise a reward in the newspapers for information leading to the conviction of the murderers. The *Irish Times* published his advertisement but all other newspapers approached refused to do so. There was no response.

The family next directed its attention to finding Geoffrey's body. Gladys took up the cudgels supported by her cousin Captain Hastings. She wrote to Michael Collins on 22 February 1922:

> Dear Sir,
> My cousin Captain Hastings has sent me your letter in which you say you are able to inform us that it is possible to locate the burial place of my husband Major Compton-Smith. I should be very much obliged if you will let me know the exact place as I have been trying for months to find out with no success… . if you know any other particulars … I should be most grateful as you will understand what a lot it means to me.
> Yours faithfully,
> GM Compton-Smith[30]

In his response Collins informed her that the matter was in hand. On the same day he wrote to General Tobin at the H.Q. of the Irish Army in Dublin telling him to ask General Cullen, Commanding First Southern Army, to make a definite inquiry about the place of burial and if the remains could be removed if requested by the relatives. As Cullen's response was unhelpful Collins again pressed Tobin for the place of burial. Using bereavement paper, Gladys wrote to Michael Collins from the Isle of Wight on 21 April 1922:

> Sir,
> As it is nearly 2 months since you wrote last to me promising to let me know the burial place of my husband I am writing again to remind you as I am so very anxious to know because I am thinking of going over to Ireland to visit the spot as soon as I hear of it from you. Hoping you will let me know as soon as possible.
> Yours truly,
> Gladys M Compton-Smith.[31]

Michael Collins' part in the search for the body ended on 22 August 1922 when he was shot and killed during the Irish Civil War which raged from June 1922 until mid-1923. On 19 May 1924, *Hansard* reported that a parliamentary question elicited the fact that his body, at that date, had not been recovered. It confirmed that £10,000 had been paid to his wife and daughter together with interest of £385, and £68 in costs and expenses.

Nothing more was heard until Friday 5 March 1926 when a headline in the *Irish Independent* announced, 'Major's body found in a bog.' The article went on to report that on the previous Wednesday evening a party from the *Gardai Siochana** had disinterred the remains, which were not so badly decomposed to render identification impossible. They were removed to Collins barracks, Cork pending arrangements by the British Government to transfer the body to England for burial. A telegram was sent immediately to Gladys informing her that the body had

*   The Civil Guard, i.e. the Police.

been found. It was received by her mother who wrote to William telling him of the discovery, and also informing him that Gladys was travelling in Italy. On the 12th, William, who had only recently returned from the Canaries, sent a telegram to the *Gardai*, 'If my son's body identified with certainty please incur all necessary expenses on my behalf'. He followed this up with a letter confirming that if the remains could be identified to his satisfaction he wished them to be sent to England, but only if identification was possible. On the 18th, he received a letter from the Deputy Commissioner of the *Gardai* saying that 'the local police have no doubt as to the identity of the body.' On the 19th and 20th he wrote respectively to the War Office and the Deputy Commissioner in the following terms:

> Sir,
> ... In the correspondence there is nothing which can be described as evidence establishing the identity of the remains alleged to have been found with those of my son who was alleged to have been murdered.
> The correspondence is of course indicative of some evidence and my daughter-in-law, when I get in touch with her may be able to throw additional light upon the matter.
> I will consult her upon the subject of exhumation and transport to this country.
> So far as I am personally concerned as at present advised the body may as well rest in the British Military Cemetery at Cork since, from my experience it would appear that in England the mental complexity of the Episcopacy is of too politic and time serving a character to permit any epitaph over my son's alleged remains which would, except very remotely, represent the truth.
> Yours faithfully,
> W Compton-Smith[32]

He also sent a most critical letter on the 20th to Gladys' mother:

> Dear Mrs Lloyd,
> I am sending you a copy of the correspondence up to date that you may know exactly what is the present position.
> I do not know where Gladys is. Although there is technically no evidence before me of the identity of the remains, I have little doubt but that the body is that of my son. I think myself that it would be idle to exhume it.
> It is very sad to think that the engagements of Gladys abroad should have prevented her having made arrangements, which might have admitted of her being present with Anne at her husband's funeral.
> Yours sincerely,
> W Compton-Smith[33]

On 24 March the remains of Major Compton-Smith were taken from Collins Barracks, Cork at 08.00 hrs and escorted to Penrose Quay by a party of fifty Non-Commissioned Officers and men of the Irish Army. When the cortege halted the guard of honour turned inwards and rested on arms reversed. At 08.20 hrs a British launch from Spike Island, one of the fortifications of the Treaty Ports, arrived with one Officer, one N.C.O. and twelve men. Six pall-bearers from the British detachment took the coffin from the hearse, passed through the guard of honour, and took the body on board. When the launch finally steamed out, the guard of honour presented arms and sounded the Last Post. Compton-Smith was buried in Fort Carlisle Military Cemetery, on a cliff at the entrance to Cork Harbour.[*]

The depth of William Compton-Smith's bitterness can be seen from the inscription attached to the frame in which Geoffrey's decorations and medals are displayed:

> They concealed from the War office, the Army, his Regiment, his Father and his Wife, his peril and his fate. They fraternized with his murderers, denied justice, and stifled all enquiry into the circumstances of the crime.

Gladys remarried in 1926, a retired Canadian Officer, Colonel Peter Petersen, in Hong Kong. They had one child, a son called Peter. As a result of the marriage William cut her out of his will.[34]

His mother's eldest brother, Lennox Bertram Lee, acquired How Caple Court, a country house near Ross-on-Wye in Herefordshire, in 1900. Here, in the small church, William placed a memorial on the north wall of the nave:

to the memory of
Geoffrey Lee Compton-Smith
D.S.O. Legion d'Honneur
Major Royal Welsh Fusiliers
born 19th Aug. 1889
shot when a defenceless prisoner in
the hands of the Irish Sinn Fein party
as an act of reprisal
about April 30th 1921 County Cork

There is also a memorial in the Regimental Chapel, St Giles's Church, Wrexham.

Notes

1   Letter from Radley College, 28 Feb 2011.
2   Burke's *Landed Gentry* (London, 1937) p. 1343.
3   Tim Sheehan, *Execute Hostage Compton-Smith* (Dripsey, 1993) pp. 26–28.
4   Radley.
5   Sheehan, p. 29.
6   From a memorial in How Caple Church, Herefordshire.
7   *Regimental Records* Volume IV, pp. 153–154.
8   *London Gazette*, 18 July 1917.
9   In Siegfried Sassoon's *Memoirs of an Infantry Officer* (London, 1930) he features as 'Major Robson.'
10   Research by Major E.G. Hughes MBE.
11   John Tyler, *Officers of the Royal Welch Fusiliers 1914–1920* (unpublished).
12   Major E.G. Hughes.
13   During a relaxed interrogation by Jackie O'Leary after the kidnap, when asked, 'Is this an admission that you are an intelligence Officer?' Compton-Smith replied, 'Yes.' Sheehan, pp. 85–86.
14   Sheehan, pp. 34–35.
15   Sheehan, pp. 36–37.

*   Fort Carlisle was re-named Davis Fort in 1980.

16   Sheehan, pp. 57–58.
17   Major E.G. Hughes.
18   Sheehan, pp. 79–81.
19   Sheehan, pp. 85–88.
20   Sheehan, pp. 92–97.
21   Sheehan, pp. 101.
22   Sheehan, pp. 102–110.
23   Witness Statement 1695 recorded on 14 November 1957 and noted by Major E.G. Hughes.
24   The letter to his brother Officers, together with his silver cigarette case, is in the Royal Welch
      Fusiliers Museum at Caernarfon. The other letters were noted by Major E.G. Hughes.
25   Major E.G. Hughes.
26   Major E.G. Hughes.
27   Major E.G. Hughes.
28   This was during a meeting with Sir Hamar Greenwood M.P. at the House of Commons. Major E.G.
      Hughes.
29   Major E.G. Hughes.
30   Major E.G. Hughes.
31   Major E.G. Hughes.
32   Major E.G. Hughes.
33   Major E.G. Hughes.
34   Major E.G. Hughes.

Annex I

General Officers, 1919–1945

This Annex records those Officers of the Regiment who attained the ranks of Brigadier, Major General and Lieutenant General during the years under review.

Rank	Name	Appointments
Lieutenant General	Sir Charles Dobell KCB CMG DSO ADC	G.O.C. 2nd Indian Division, 1919–1923
Lieutenant General	Sir William Holmes KBE CB DSO *OP* (Greece)	G.O.C. 42nd (East Lancs) Division, 1938–1940; G.O.C. VII Corps, 1940–1941; G.O.C. X Corps, 1941; G.O.C.-in-C. Ninth Army, 1942–1943; British Military Mission in Athens, 1945
Major General	H.A. Freeman-Attwood DSO OBE MC *L de H* LoM (US)[1]	Commander 5 (London) Infantry Brigade, 1940; Commander 141 Infantry Brigade, 1941; G.O.C. 46th Infantry Division, 1942–1943
Major General	N. Maitland Wilson CB DSO OBE	Commander Sind Independent Infantry Brigade, 1935; D.P.S. India, 1936; D.A.G. India, 1938–1941
Major General	J.R. Minshull-Ford CB DSO MC	Commander 5 Infantry Brigade, 1930–1932; G.O.C. 44th (Home Counties) Infantry Division, 1932–1938; Lieutenant-Governor of Guernsey, 1940
Major General	G.W. Richards CB CBE DSO MC	Transferred to R.T.C. in 1923
Major General	H.C. Stockwell CB DSO[2]	Commander 29 Infantry Brigade, 1943–1945; G.O.C. 82nd (West African) Division, 1945
Major General	G.F. Watson CB DSO OBE	Director Manpower Planning, War Office.
Brigadier	Ll. A.A. Alston CBE DSO MC LoM (US)	Commander 113 Infantry Brigade, 1940; Area Commander Home Forces, 1941; Commander Base Area, Florence, Italy, 1944–1945
Brigadier	D.M. Barchard	Commander 21 (East African) Infantry Brigade, 1941–1945

Rank	Name	Appointments
Brigadier	J.G. Bruxner-Randall CBE MoF (U.S.)	Commander 159 (Welsh Border) Infantry Brigade, 1937–1941; Commandant R.M.C. O.C.T.U. 1941–1943; 57 (Naples) Area, C.M.F., 1943–1944
Brigadier	T.D. Daly CBE MC MA *C de G, L d'H.* OWE (Serbia) OStJ	H.Q. Caribbean Area; British Military Attaché, Athens, 1945
Brigadier	H.A. Davies MBE MC	Commander 52 (Indian) Infantry Brigade
Brigadier	M.B. Dowse CBE[3]	B.G.S. H.Q. A.L.F.S.E.A.
Brigadier	J.M.J. Evans MC	Deputy Assistant Director T.A., 1919–1923
Brigadier	R. Gambier-Parry CMG[4]	Air Ministry, 1919–1921; MI6 1931; F.O. 1938–1939; Special Operations, 1939–1945
Brigadier	Ll. Gwydyr-Jones DSO OBE	Commander 26 Infantry Brigade 1945
Brigadier	C.C. Hewitt DSO MC	National Fire Service College 1944–1945
Brigadier	S.O. Jones OBE MC	Commander 158 (Royal Welch) Infantry Brigade, 1941–1942 and 1943–1944; Army Staff College Camberley, 1944; D.M.S. War Office 1945
Brigadier	H.S.K. Mainwaring CB CBE DSO TD DL LoM (U.S.)	B.G.S. H.Q. S.A.C. Italy, 1944–1945
Brigadier	C.H.V. Pritchard DSO *CROG* (Greece)	Commander 2 Independent Parachute Brigade, 1943–1945
Brigadier	E.O. Skaife CB OBE[5]	Commander 158 (Royal Welch) Infantry Brigade, 1939; Commander 15 Infantry brigade, 1940; Commander 215 Infantry Brigade, 1941–1942; Special Projects Foreign Office, 1943–1944
Brigadier	C.I. Stockwell CB CMG DSO *C de G*	Group Commander Shetlands Area 1941–1942
Brigadier	E. Wodehouse CBE	Commander 217 Infantry Brigade, 1940–1942; Military Attaché Dublin, 1943–1945

Notes

1 Formerly H.A. Freeman.
2 Later General Sir Hugh Stockwell GCB KBE DSO.
3 Later Major General Sir Maurice Dowse KCVO CB CBE.
4 Later Sir Richard Gambier-Perry KCMG.
5 Later Brigadier Sir Eric Skaife Kt CB OBE DL.

Annex J

Bibliography and Sources

Interviews

Major Nigel Anderson, 12 December 2004: Stockforce, Norway, 1940

Lieutenant Colonel Neville Bosanquet, 19 July 2002: 158 Infantry Brigade, 1938–1940

Professor Nick Bosanquet, 5 June 2003

Colonel M.A. Demetriadi, May 2000

Lieutenant Colonel L.J. Egan, 1 May 2002: Royal Welch Fusilier Officer 1941–1969

General Sir Anthony Farrar-Hockley, 16 May 2003; 12 February 2004; 6th (RW) Para

Rear Admiral E.F. Gueritz, 10 June 2002; 26 June 2002; 29 October 2002; 28 January 2004: Madagascar 1942

Major H.J.E. Jones, 28 May 2002: Madagascar and Burma 1942–1944

Lord Parry of Neyland, 14 June 2002

Colonel B.G.B. Pugh, 3 September 2003: Stockforce, Norway, 1940

R.F.F. Simmonds, 21 February 2003: Burma

Max Arthur with Sir Anthony Farrar-Hockley in *Men of the Red Beret: Airborne Forces 1940 – 1990* (London, 1990) (Italy, the South of France and Greece)

Peter Liddle of the WW2 Experience Centre, Leeds, with Sir Anthony Farrar-Hockley in July 2001

Francesco di Cinito with Major Paddy Deacon and Major Richard Hargreaves of 4 Para, August 2013

Fusilier Jack Ellis, 13 November 2014.

Major Glyn Hughes on behalf of the author with Sergeant, later Major, Cliff Meredith, 29 December 2014

14759162 Fus Bruce McCay, 13 January 2016

14659192 Fus Huw Jones, 16 June 2016

Recorded interviews by Lieutenant Colonel L.J. Egan in the R.W.F./Mus 42821:

Major P.C. Kenyon

Colonel R.O.F. Pritchard

Brigadier M.H. ap Rhys Pryce

Lieutenant Colonel J.G. Vyvyan

Colonel J.E.T. Willes

Lieutenant Colonel W.S.A. Clough-Taylor

Colonel C.E. Hill

National Archive Papers

1919–1921, General
WO 380/17 Register of Formations, Amalgamations and Disbandments 1914–1920
WO 90/8 G.C.M.s Abroad, 1917–1943

Formation Headquarters 1939–1945
WO 172/2059, H.Q. 6 Infantry Brigade Group War Diary 1943
WO 172/4288, H.Q. 6 Infantry Brigade War Diary 1944
WO 230/53 29 Independent Infantry Brigade War Diary, January–December 1942
WO 172/2078, 29 Independent Infantry Brigade War Diary, January–December 1943
WO 172/4404, 29 Brigade War Diary January–December 1944
WO 166/974 H.Q. 115 (Royal Welch) Infantry Brigade, January–December 1941
WO 166/6592 H.Q. 115 (Royal Welch) Infantry Brigade, January–December 1942
WO 166/10771, H.Q. 115 (Royal Welch) Infantry Brigade, January–December 1943
WO 166/14341, H.Q. 115 (Royal Welch) Infantry Brigade, January–December 1944
WO 171/4387, H.Q. 115 Independent Brigade War Diary 1–28 February 1945
WO 166/1030, 158 (Royal Welch) Infantry Brigade War Diary September 1939–April 1941
WO 171/689, 158 (Royal Welch) Infantry Brigade War Diary, 1 January–31 December 1944
WO 169/1185, 7th Armoured Division War Diary, 1 January–31 December 1941

1 R.W.F., 1918–1939
WO 73/110, 1 R.W. Fus War Diary 1918–1919
WO 73/111–115 and 120–141, 1 R.W. Fus. Digest of Service, compiled annually
WO 73/116–117, 1 R.W. Fus War Diary Waziristan

1 R.W.F., France, Belgium and the United Kingdom, 1939–1942
WO 167/843, 1 R.W.F. War Diary September 1939–June 1940
WO 166/4624, 1 R.W.F. War Diary June 1940–December 1941
WO 166/8927, 1 R.W.F. War Diary January–April 1942
WO 166/892, 1 R.W.F. War Diary May 1942

1 R.W.F. India and Burma, 1942–1945
WO 172/892, 1 R.W.F. War Diary 1942
WO 172/2552, 1 R.W.F. War Diary 1943
WO 172/4925, 1 R.W.F. War Diary 1944
WO 172/7671, 1 R.W.F. War Diary January–June 1945
WO 172/7672, 1 R.W.F. War Diary June–December 1945

2 R.W.F. 1918–1939
2 R.W. Fus Digest of Service, compiled annually

2 R.W.F. Madagsacar
CAB 120/44
CAFO 2491

COS (41) 629
DEFE 2/312; 2/314; 3/314
WO 166/4625, 2 R.W.F. War Diary 1 July–31 December 1941
WO 166/8928, 174/36, 2 R.W.F. War Diary 1 January–31 August 1942

2 R.W.F. India and Burma
WO 166/4625, 2 R.W.F. War Diary 4 June 1940–31 December 1941
WO 166/8928, 2 R.W.F. War Diary 1 January–31 August 1942
WO 172/2553, 2 R.W.F. War Diary 6 January–27 February 1943
WO 172/4926, 2 R.W.F. War Diary I Jan–31 December 1944
WO 172/7673, 2 R.W.F. War Diary 1 January–31 May 1945

6th (RW) Para Britain, North Africa, Italy, France and Greece, 1941–1945
WO 166/8557, WO169/10348, WO175/530: 6th (RW) Para War Diary 1942–1943
WO 170/1343, 6th (RW) Para War Diary 1 Jan–31 December 1944
WO 170/4973, 6th (RW) Para War Diary 1 Jan–29 June 1945
WO 169/20083, 6th (RW) Para War Diary 1 October 1945–31 December 1945
WO 169/20083, 23227 and 261/404: 6th (RW) Para War Diary 1 October 1945–31 December
    1946

TA Battalions, 1919–1939
WO 95/1280 and WO 95/2721, 4 and 1/4th R.W. Fus. 1919–1920.
WO 95/4323, WO 95/4626 and WO 95/4627, 5 and 1/5th R.W. Fus. 1919–1920
WO 95/4323, WO 95/4626 and WO 95/4627, 6 and 1/6th R.W. Fus. 1919–1920
WO 95/4627, 5th/6th R.W. Fus. 1919–1920
WO 95/4679 and WO 95/2366, 24 R.W. Fus. 1919
WO 95/4679 and WO 95/3154, 25 R.W. Fus. 1919

TA Battalions, United Kingdom 1939–1944
WO 166/4626, 4 R.W.F. War Diary September 1939–April 1941
WO 166/8929, 4 R.W.F. War Diary 1 January–31 December 1942
WO 166/2784, 4 R.W.F. War Diary 1 January–31 December 1943
WO 171/1389, 4 R.W.F. War Diary 1 January–31 December 1944
WO 166/4627, 6 R.W.F. War Diary September 1939–April 1941
WO 166/8930, 6 R.W.F. War Diary, 1 January–31 December 1942
WO 166/12765, 6 R.W.F. War Diary, 1 January–31 December 1943
WO 171/1390, 6 R.W.F. War Diary, 1 January–31 December 1944
WO 166/4628, 7 R.W.F. War Diary September 1939–April 1941
WO 166/8931, 7 R.W.F. War Diary 1 January–31 December 1942
WO 166/12766, 7 R.W.F. War Diary 1 January–31 December 1943
WO 171/1391, 7 R.W.F. War Diary 1 January–30 June 1944
WO 166/4629, 8 R.W.F. War Diary 1 January–31 December 1940
WO 166/8932, 8 R.W.F. War Diary 1 January–31 December 1941
WO 166/12767, 8 R.W.F. War Diary 1 January–31 December 1942
WO 166/15157, 8 R.W.F. War Diary 1 January 1943–12 September 1944

WO 166/4630, 9 R.W.F. War Diary 30 October 1940–31 December 1941
WO 166/8933, 9 R.W.F. War Diary 1 January–31 December 1942
WO 166/12768, 9 R.W.F. War Diary 1 January–31 December 1943
WO 166/15158, 9 R.W.F. War Diary 1 January–31 May 1944
WO 166/4631, 10 R.W.F. War Diary 1 January–31 December 1940
WO 166/8934, 10 R.W.F. War Diary 1 January 1941–9 July 1942
WO 166/8935, 13 R.W.F. War Diary 1 January 1942–31 December 1942
WO 166/12769, 13 R.W.F War Diary, I January–31 December 1943
WO 166/15159, 13 R.W.F War Diary, I January–31 December 1944

T.A. Battalions, North-West Europe 1944–1945
WO 171/1389, 4 R.W.F. War Diary 1 January–31 December 1944
WO 171/5281, 4 R.W.F. War Diary 1 January–30 April 1945
WO 171/5282, 4 R.W.F. War Diary 1 May–31 December 1945
WO 171/9289, 4 R.W.F. War Diary, 1 January–7 July 1946
WO 171/190, 6 R.W.F. War Diary, 1 January–31 August 1944
WO 171/1390, 6 R.W.F. War Diary, 1 September–31 December 1944
WO 171/5283, 6 R.W.F. War Diary 1 January–31 March 1945
WO 171/5283, 6 R.W.F. War Diary 1 April–31 December 1945
WO 171/9290, 6 R.W.F. War Diary 1 January–31 June 1946
WO 171/1392, 7 R.W.F. War Diary 1 July–30 September 1944
WO 171/1393, 7 R.W.F. War Diary 1 October–31 December 1944
WO 171/5284, 7 R.W.F. War Diary 1 January–31 March 1945
WO 171/5285, 7 R.W.F. War Diary 1 May–31 December 1945
WO 171/5285, 7 R.W.F. War Diary 1 January–28 February 1946

Service Battalions, 1918–1920
WO 95/5162 and WO 95/4303, 8 R.W. Fus. 1919–1920
WO 95/2092, 9 R.W. Fus. 1919–1920
WO 95/4922, 11 R.W. Fus. 1919–1920
WO 95/2555, 13 R.W. Fus. 1919
WO 380/17, 16 R.W. Fus. 1919
WO 95/2561, 17 R.W. Fus. 1919
WO 380/17, 18 R.W. Fus. 1919
WO 95/409 and WO 95/3021, 26 R.W. Fus. 1919–1920

Artillery Regiments, 1938–1945
WO 170/1036, 60th (R.W.F.) Anti-Tank Regiment R.A. War Diary, 1 April–31 December 1944
WO 166/1642, 70th (R.W.F.) Anti-Tank Regiment War Diary 1 September 1939–31 December 1940
WO 166/1642, 70th (R.W.F.) Anti-Tank Regiment War Diary 1 January–31 December 1941
WO 166/7099, 70th (R.W.F.) Anti-Tank Regiment War Diary 1 January–31 December 1942
WO 166/11341, 70th (R.W.F.) Anti-Tank Regiment War Diary 1 January–31 December 1943
WO 166/4927, 70th (R.W.F.) Anti-Tank Regiment War Diary 1 January–31 December 1944

WO 166/16830, 70th (R.W.F.) A.T. Regiment War Diary 1 January–31 December 1945
WO 166/1643, 71st (R.W.F.) A.T. Regiment War Diary September 1940–December 1941
WO 166/7100, 71st (R.W.F.) A.T. Regiment R.A. War Diary 1 January–31 December 1942
WO 166/11341, 71st (R.W.F.) A.T. Regiment R.A. War Diary 1 January–31 December 1943
WO 171/923, 71st (R.W.F.) A.T. Regiment R.A. War Diary 1 January–31 December 1944
WO 171/4775, 71st (R.W.F.) A.T. Regiment R.A. War Diary 1 January–31 October 1945
WO 166/1648, 76th (R.W.F.) A.T. Regiment War Diary 1 November 1940–31 August 1941
WO 166/1523, 76th (R.W.F.) A.T. Regiment War Diary 1 September–31 December 1941
WO 169/4725, 76th (R.W.F.) A.T. Regiment War Diary 1 January–20 April and 5 September–31 December 1942
WO 169/9626, 76th (R.W.F.) A.T. Regiment R.A. War Diary, 1 January–31 December 1943
WO 170/1040, 76th (R.W.F.) A.T. Regiment R.A. War Diary, 1 January–31 March 1944
WO 167/654, 101st L.A.A. & A.T. Regiment War Diary February–May 1940
WO 166/1702, 101st L.A.A. & A.T. Regiment War Diary June–September 1940
WO 166/7702, 116th L.A.A. Regiment R.A. (R.W.) War Diary, 1 January–31 December 1942
WO 166/11735, 116th L.A.A. Regiment R.A. (R.W.) War Diary, 1 January–31 December 1943
WO 171/1133, 116th L.A.A. Regiment R.A. (R.W.) War Diary, 1 January–31 December 1944
WO 170/4703, 237 (R.W.F.) Independent Anti-Tank Battery R.A. War Diary, 13 March–30 September 1945
WO 169/4577, 9471, 11th (H.A.C.) Field Regiment R.A. War Diaries, 1943–1944
WO 169/9636, 106th A.T. Regiment R.A. War Diary, 1 January–31 March 1945

Independent Companies and Commandos
DEFE2/1; DEFE2/4.
WO 106/1944. H.Q. North-West Expeditionary Force Instructions dated 2 May 1940
WO 168/106 folio 84277, No 2 Independent Company War Diary, May 1940
WO 166/578; WO 193/384; WO 199/1568; WO 199/1697
CAB 120/14

Service Battalions 1939–1946
WO 166/4632, 11 R.W.F. War Diary 1 January 1940–31 December 1941
WO 166/4635, 2/11th R.W.F. War Diary 25 September–30 November 1940
WO 166/4633, 12 R.W.F. War Diary, 4 July 1940–31 December 1941
WO 166/4534, 13 R.W.F. War Diary 9 October 1940–31 December 1941
WO 166/8935, 13 R.W.F. War Diary 1 January–31 December 1942
WO 166/4635, 14 R.W.F. War Diary 24 September 1940–31 December 1941
WO 166/4632, 30 R.W.F. War Diary 10–31 December 1941
WO 166/8936, 30 R.W.F. War Diary 1 January 1942–20 January 1943
WO 166/12770, 30 R.W.F. War Diary 1–31 January 1943
WO 166/4635, 31 R.W.F. War Diary 18 November–31 December 1941
WO 166/8937, 31 R.W.F. War Diary 1 January–31 December 1942
WO 166/12771, 31 R.W.F. War Diary 1 January–31 December 1943
WO 166/15160, 31 R.W.F. War Diary 1 January–31 December 1944
WO 166/17216, 31 R.W.F. War Diary 1 January–31 December 1945

WO 166/4656, 70 R.W.F. War Diary, September 1940–31 December 1941
WO 166/8938, 70 R.W.F. War Diary 1942
WO 166/12772, 70 R.W.F. War Diary January–June 1943

Training Organisations
WOUM 1/720; B/1644; B 1950; WO UPT R/2540; UPT 1/148; WO/L/20/Infy/3114
WO 163/92

Home Guard
WO 199/3274, Strength of the Home Guard
WO 199/1866, Home Guard Battalions
WO 199/1878, Chain of Command for Home Guard Sectors
WO 199/2932, H.G. Defence of South Queensferry
WO 199/3201, 3317, 7 Denflint H.G. War Diary, 1940–1944
WO 199/3311, 3314, 2 Anglesey H.G. War Diary, 1940–1944

Imperial War Museum

British Army of the Rhine, 1919–1930
Thwaites collection, IWM 416.311 – the Occupation of the Rhineland (photographs)

India and Burma
'Inquiry on Whether the Japanese Ever Contemplated an Invasion of India', in IWM Japanese
    Interrogation Reports, Box 8, AS 5002
IWM 82/15/1 The Life and Times of Sir Philip Christison Bt

Sound Archive
4383 – H.C.Stockwell's interview on service in Burma

Liddell Hart Centre (King's College London) Papers

Independent Companies and Commandos
KCL/Stockwell 2/1; KCL/Stockwell/3/1

2 R.W.F., 1919–1930
KCL/Stockwell/1/1 and 1/4
KCL/Clarke 1/9 1968: Chapter IX of *The Memoirs of a Professional Soldier in War and Peace*, by
    Brigadier F.A.S. Clarke
KCL/Clarke/2/2
KCL Clarke/2/5

1 and 2 R.W.F. India and Burma
KCL/Stockwell/3/1; 5/3; 5/7/5; 5/8; 10/12

National Library of Wales, Aberystwyth

Home Guard
Collection Services P1/11, 6th Denbighshire
Derrick Pratt, 'Wrexham Home Guard Part 1' in *Clwyd Historian* No 28, Spring 1992; Part 2
    in No 37, Autumn 1996; Flint in No 35, Autumn 1995
Plas Power Estate Records, 6th Denbighshire

Royal Welch Fusiliers Archive (Caernarfon) Papers

1 R.W.F. 1919–1939
1 R.W.Fus. Digest of Service 1 June 1919–31 August 1939

2 R.W.F. 1919–1939
2 R.W. Fus. Digest of Service 1 June 1919–31 March 1939 (R.W.F. Mus 294).
*Memoirs of Valentine Frederick Loos Grevitt, Royal Welch Fusiliers, Shanghai 14th Aug 1937 Jan
    1938.*

1 R.W.F. France and Belgium 1939–1940
J.L. King, *Farewell to Flanders* (unpublished MS)
L/2655/144, Notes by Lt (later Lt Col) P.C.R. Carrington
'The Story of the 1st Battalion, Royal Welch Fusiliers Friday, May 10th–Monday, May 27th,
    1940'
MC/OR/14401 (Casualties) dated 25 January 1943 in Mus 42a 2816, account of 1 R.W.F.
    1939–1940 by Major F.M. Edwards and others
1st Bn The Royal Welch Fusiliers – Casualties 1940, A Note by Lieutenant Colonel R.J.M.
    Sinnett
2816, Captain J.E.T. Willes, account written in Oflag VII C
R.C.M. Barber, 'Action of Leave Details, 2 Div, During the Period 17/30 May'

1 R.W.F. United Kingdom 1940–1942
L/2655/146, notes by Lieutenant Colonel C.O. Hilditch
L/2655/136, notes by Colonel M.A. Demetriadi

1 R.W.F. India and Burma 1942–1945
Lieutenant Colonel N.R.G. Bosanquet dated 29 Oct 1987, *TAI* files, Vol 2, f.157
Lieutenant Colonel G. Braithwaite's comments on *The Red Dragon*
Fusilier G.H. Davies dated 8 Nov 1987, *TAI* files Vol 2, f.166 and account of Donbaik, TAI
    file ff 166, 181
Captain M.A. Demetriadi, L/2655/136
Major C.O. Hilditch, L/2655/14
Sergeant A. (Albert) Jones 64 comments on *TAI*, TAI file f. 183
Fusilier J.R. (John) Jones 73, *Repulse in Arakan, 1943*
Captain M.H. Lloyd-Davies, *TAI* file f.185

Sergeant F. (Fred) Simmonds's account of Donbaik
Lieutenant Colonel A.J. Stocker, L/2655/160
Lieutenant Colonel A.H. Williams's Diary, 3722e and 3722f in Arch 24/4

Independent Companies and Commandos

5439 – No 2 Independent Company – Account by Captain BGB Pugh dated 1st June 1940
5168 – No 2 Independent Company 1940, account by Sjt WA Jones

2 R.W.F. Madagascar

L/2655/190 (A) – Brian Cotton *A Short War History of 2 R.W.F.*

2 R.W.F. India and Burma

Gordon Milne (late 236 Field Company RE, 29 Brigade), *Reminiscences on General Sir Hugh Stockwell and Brigadier Ll Gwydyr-Jones.*

T.A. Battalions 1939–1945

L2655/262, 263264. 269, 275, 279, 115 (R.W.) Infantry Brigade (8, 9, 10, R.W.F.) 1940–1945, letters
    from G.A.F. Mostyn, E. Powell-Price, Brigadier A.E. Robinson, and Sir Henry Tate Bt
L2655/217, 6 R.W.F., K.G. Exham
238–260, 4, 6 and 7 R.W.F., A.H. Williams, F. Rutten, R.J. Snead-Cox, H.W. Tyler, B.G.
    Wennink and H.R. Roberts
Major N.P. Cutcliffe's illustrated diary, 1940–August 1944

Training Organisations

245, Depot
245, War Diary 7 Infantry Holding Battalion 2 Jan–6 June 1940
245, War Diary 50th (Holding) Battalion R.W.F. 6 June–9 October 1940

Home Guard

History of the 10th Denbigh Home Guard Battalion, unpublished MS, L/2655/332

Farrar-Hockley Papers

R.J.M Sinnett, 6 (R.W.) Para Summary
Letter Ian Chatham to R.J.M. Sinnett dated 27 June 2007 (6 (R.W.) Para)
Letter Cliff Meredith to R.J.M. Sinnett (undated) (6 (R.W.) Para)

Merionydd County Archives

GB 0220 ZDDW 5, 6, 11, 12 14, 24, 27, 50 (Home Guard)

Denbighshire Record Office

DD/DM 311/8; 815/1-2; 874/1-6, 913/1; 1546/1-2 (Home Guard)
TA/D/6–7 Minutes of the Denbighshire T.A.A. General Meetings, 1922–1938

Flint Record Office

TA/F/6–8, Minutes of the Flintshire T.A.A. General Meetings 1913–1938

Gwynedd Archives
XD/115/1/10 Minutes of General Meetings of the Caernarvonshire and Anglesey T.A.A., 1925–1932
XM 1301; XC/12/1/47; XC 12/1/94–99 (Home Guard)

Private Papers

Independent Companies and Commandos
Andrew Croft private letters and papers held by the Croft family
Quintin Riley *Personal Diary* held by Mrs N.A.C. Owen (daughter)
Papers and Diaries of Brigadier T.B. Trappes-Lomax, held by Tessa Trappes-Lomax (daughter)

6th (R.W.) Para
1944 Diary of Major D. Fleming Jones, 6th (Royal Welch) Para, transcribed by and with the permission of his family

Books

R.W.F. Regimental Histories and General Memoirs
W.J.P. Aggett, *The Bloody Eleventh: History of the Devonshire Regiment*, Vol III, 1914–1969 (Exeter, 1995)
A. Babington, *The Devil to Pay: the mutiny of the Connaught Rangers, India, July 1920* (Barnsley, 1991)
Veronica Bamfield, *Cornucopia* (London, 2006)
Veronica Bamfield, *On the Strength. The Story of the British Army Wife* (London, 1974)
G. Blight, *History of the Royal Berkshire Regiment 1920–1947* (London, 1953)
A.D.L. Carey & Stoupe McCance, *Regimental Records of the Royal Welch Fusiliers (Late 23rd Foot), Vol II 1816–1914* (London, 1923)
H. Maldwyn Davies, ed Dilys Glover, *A Flintshire Territorial at War, 1914–18* (Wrexham, 2016).
J.C. Dunn, *The War the Infantry Knew* (London, 1938)
Michael Glover and Jonathon Riley, *That Astonishing Infantry. The History of The Royal Welch Fusiliers 1689–2006* (Barnsley, 2007)
Anything for A Quiet Life. The Autobiography of Jack Hawkins (London, 1973)
Fusilier W.H. Jones 85, *A Soldier Reminisces* (privately printed)
Lieutenant Commander P.K. Kemp and John Graves, *The Red Dragon; the Story of the Royal Welch Fusiliers 1919–1945* (Aldershot, 1960)
David Langley, *Duty Done: 2 R.W.F. in the Great War* (Privately published, 2002)
K.W. Parkhurst, *Padre Pastor and Poet* (Privately published *c*.1988)
Frank Richards, *Old Soldiers Never Die*, (London,1933)
Frank Richards, *Old Soldier Sahib*, (London,1936)
Fus W.C. (Cyril) Smith 55, *The Unsung Heroes* (June 1995)
Fus R.G. (Ron) Thomas 25, *Memoirs 1939–1945: The Burma Campaign* (John Watson, Wirksworth, Derbyshire, 2000)

Kyffin Williams, *Across the Straits* (London, 1973)

Reference Books

*Burke's Peerage and Baronet*age (London, 1921, 1930, 1953, 1956, 1999, 2003)
Burke's Landed Gentry (London, 1937)
Cambridge Biographical Encyclopaedia (1994)
Field Marshal Lord Carver, *Britain's Army in the 20th Century* (London, 1998)
David Chandler and Ian Beckett (ed), *The Oxford History of the British Army* (OUP, 1996)
H.C. Darby and H. Fullard, *Modern History Atlas* (Cambridge, 1979)
Debrett's People of Today, various years as cited in endnotes, 2000–2005
Dictionary of National Biography, various volumes and editions as cited in endnotes
Peter Dietz (ed), *Garrison: Ten British Military Towns* (London, 1986)
Carlo D'Este, *Decision in Normandy* (London, 1983)
James Douet, *British Barracks, 1600–1914* (English Heritage, 1997)
Encyclopaedia Britannica, Supplement Vol III, 1926
J. Gardiner and N. Wenborn, *History Today Companion to British History* (London, 1995)
Martin Gilbert, *World in Torment: Winston Churchill, Volume IV, 1917–1922* (London, 1975)
George Gill, *British Coloneis and Dependencies* (London, c. 1920)
J.A.S. Grenville and Bernard Wasserstein, *The Major International Treaties of the Twentieth Century* (London, 2001)
Alistair Horne, *Harold Macmillan* (2 Vols, London 1988–1989)
Brigadier E.A. James, *British Regiments, 1914–1918* (London, 1978)
Lt-Col H.F. Joslen, *Orders of Battle: Second World War, 1939–1945* (Uckfield, 2003)
Keesing's Contemporary Archives, various years 1920–1945
Major EL Kirby, *Officers of The Royal Welch Fusiliers, 1689–1914* (Privately Published, 1997)
Robin McNish, *Iron Division: The History of the 3rd Division 1809–1989* (Revised Edition, H.M.S.O., 1990)
Charles Messenger, *For Love of Regiment. A History of British Infantry Vol II 1915–1994* (London, 1996)
Clive Parry and Charity Hopkins, *Index to British Treaties, Vol III* (H.M.S.O., 1970)
Pear's Cyclopaedia, 51st Edition, 1940
Philip's *University Atlas* (London, 1975)
H.C.B. Rogers, *Troopships and their History* (London, 1963)
H.C.B. Rogers, *Weapons of the British Soldier,* (London, 1968)
Dudley Ward, *Regimental Records of the Royal Welch Fusiliers (23rd Foot), Vol III 1914 1918 France and Flanders* (London, 1928) and *Vol IV, Turkey, Bulgaria, Austria* (London, 1929)
Who's Who and *Who Was Who*, various years as cited in endnotes 1900–1945

General Histories

Field Marshal Lord Alanbrooke, *Diaries 1939–1945* ed Danchev and Todman (London, 2001)
Max Arthur, *Men of the Red Beret: Airborne Forces 1940–1990* (London, 1990)
Veronica Bamfield, *On the Strength: The Story of the British Army Wife* (London, 1974)
Correlli Barnet, *Britain and Her Army 1509–1970* (London, 1970)
Thomas Bartlett and Keith Jeffery (ed), *A Military History of Ireland* (C.U.P., 1996)
G Best and A Wheatcroft (ed), *War Economy and the Military Mind* (London, 1976)

Omar Bradley, *A General's Life* (New York, 1983)

J.M. Brereton, *The British Soldier: A Social History, 1661 to the Present Day*, (London, 1986)

Mike Chappell, *British Infantry Equipments 1908–1980*, Men-at-Arms Series 108

Anthony Clayton, *The British Empire as a Superpower, 1919–1930* (University of Georgia Press, 1986)

Jeremy Crang, *The British Army and the People's War 1939–1945* (MUP, 2000)

Martin van Crefeld, *Command in War* (Cambridge, Mass, USA, 1985)

Martin van Crefeld, *Supplying War* (Cambridge, Mass, USA, 1977)

Norman Dixon, *On the Psychology of Military Incompetence* (London, 1976)

Norman Dixon, *Our Own Worst Enemy* (London, 1987)

Michael Evans and Alan Ryan (ed), *The Human Face of Warfare. Killing, Fear and Chaos in Battle* (St Leonard's, Australia, 2000)

Lt Gen Sir Geoffrey Evans, *The Desert and the Jungle: An Account of the Campaign in Africa and Burma* (London, 1959)

Niall Ferguson, Empire: How Britain made the Modern World (London, 2003)

David French, *Military Identities. The Regimental System, the British Army, & the British People c. 1870–2000 (O.U.P., 2005)*

David French and Brian Holden Reid (ed), *The British General Staff. Reform and Innovation 1890–1939* (London, 2001)

Sir John Fortescue, *History of the British Army* (13 Vols, London.1909–1930)

J.F.C. Fuller, *Generalship: The Disease and Its Cure* (Harrisburg, Pennsylvania, 1936)

General Sir Richard Gale, *Call to Arms: An Autobiography* (London, 1968)

Brevet-Major AR Godwin-Austen, *The Staff and the Staff College* (London, 1927)

A.J. Grant & H. Temperley, *Europe in the Nineteenth and Twentieth Centuries (1789–1950)* (London, 1953)

Sir William Jackson and Lord Bramall, *The Chiefs. The Story of the United Kingdom Chiefs of Staff* (London, 1992)

Lawrence James, *Mutiny in the British and Commonwealth Forces 1797–1956* (London, 1987)

P. Kennedy, *The Rise and Fall of the Great Powers* (London, 1988)

B.H. Liddell Hart, *The British Way in Warfare* (London, 1934)

Timothy Lupfer, *The Dynamics of Doctrine: The Changes in German Tactical Doctrine during the First World War* (Combat Studies Institute, U.S. Army Command and General Staff College, 1981)

Jay Luvaas, The Education of an Army. British Military Thought, 1815–1940 (University of Chicago Press, 1964)

Robin McNish, *Iron Division. The History of the 3rd Division, 1809–1989* (Privately published, 1989)

F.O. Miksche, *Blitzkrieg* (London, 1941)

Lord Moran (C. MacM. Wilson), *The Anatomy of Courage* (London, 1945)

Field Marshal Viscount Montgomery of Alamein, *Memoirs* (London, 1958)

Timothy Harrison Place, *Military Training in the British Army 1940–1944* (London, 2000)

Jonathon Riley, *Decisive Battles. From Yorktown to Operation Desert Storm* (London, 2000)

G.R. Searle, *A New England? Peace and War 1886–1918* (Oxford, 2005)

Richard Simpkin, *Deep Battle: The Brainchild of Marshal Tukhachevsky* (London, 1987)

Wilfred I. Smith, *Codeword CANLOAN* (Toronto, 1992)

A.J.P. Taylor, *English History 1914–1945* (Oxford, 1986)

Lyall Wilkes, *Festing – Field Marshal* (Lewes, 1991)

Harold Winton, *To Change an Army. General Sir John Burdett-Stuart and British Armoured Doctrine, 1927–1938* (University of Kansas PhD thesis, 1988)

The British Army, 1919–1945

A Short History of the Second Infantry Division 1809–1954 (Revised 1958) privately printed in B.A.O.R.; no page numbering

W.S. Bainbridge, *A Report on the present conditions in the Ruhr and Rhineland* (New York, 1923)

Major A.F. Becke, *Order of Battle of Divisions* (Newport, 1989)

Shelford Bidwell and Dominick Graham, *Fire-power. British Army Weapons and Theories of War 1904–1945* (London, 1982)

Brian Bond, *British Military Policy Between the Two World Wars* (Oxford, 1980)

Brian Bond, 'The Army Between The Two World Wars 1918–1939' in *The Oxford Illustrated History of the British Army* (O.U.P., 1994)

Brian Bond, *The Victorian Army and the Staff College* (London, 1972)

Lord Butler, *The Art of the Possible* (London, 1971)

Joseph T. Carroll, *Ireland in the War Years 1939–1945* (Newton Abbot, 1975)

Jeremy A. Crang, *The British Army and the People's War, 1939–1945* (MUP, 1995)

Peter Dennis, *The Territorial Army 1907–1940* (RHS, 1987)

David Erskine, *The Scots Guards, 1919–1955* (London, 1956)

James Anderson Findlay, *A Handbook of Pembroke Dock* (Haverfordwest, 1885)

Robert Fisk *In Time of War. Ireland, Ulster and the price of neutrality 1939-45* (London, 1983)

George Forty, *British Army Handbook 1939–1945* (Sutton, 1998)

David Fraser, *And We Shall Shock Them. The British Army in the Second World War* (London, 1983)

David French, *Raising Churchill's Army* (London, 2000)

Robert Graves and Alan Hodge, *The Long Week-End. A Social History of Great Britain 1918–1939* (London, 1940)

Sir Charles W. Gwynn, *Imperial Policing* (London, 1936)

J.P. Harris, *Men, Ideas and Tanks. British Military Thought and Armoured Forces, 1905–1939* (MUP, 1995)

J.P. Harris, 'The British General Staff and the Coming of War, 1933–1939' in *The British General Staff: Reform and Innovation1890–1939* ed. David French and Brian Holden Reid (London, 2002)

Major James Hawkes, *Private to Major* (London, 1938)

Robin Higham, *Armed Forces in Peacetime. Britain, 1918–1940, a case study* (Hamden, CT, U.S.A., 1962)

General Sir William Jackson and Field Marshal Lord Bramall, *The Chiefs. The Story of the United Kingdom Chiefs of Staff* (London, 1992)

Keith Jeffery, The Military Correspondence of Field Marshal Sir Henry Wilson 1918–1922 (Army Records Society, 1985)

A.C. Kennett, *Life is What You Make It* (Durham, 1992)

John Masters, *Bugles and a Tiger* (London, 1956)

The Memoirs of Field Marshal the Viscount Montgomery of Alamein (London, 1958)

Sara Moore, *Peace Without Victory for the Allies 1918–1932* (Oxford, 1994)

Official History of Operations on the N.W. Frontier of India, 1920–1935 (New Delhi, 1945)

Anne Perkins, *A Very British Strike: The General Strike 1926* (London, 2006)

Field Marshal Viscount Slim, *Defeat Into Victory* (London, 1956)

Julian Thompson, *The War in Burma, 1942–1945* (IWM, 2002)

Timothy Travers, *The Killing Ground. The British Army, the Western Front and the Emergence of Modern Warfare 1900–1918* (London, 1987)

David G Williamson, *The British in Germany, 1918–1930* (Oxford, 1991)

Tom Wintringham, *New Ways of War* (London, 1940)

1 R.W.F. France and Belgium, 1939–1940

Henry Cadogan, *The Road to Armageddon* (Wrexham, 2009)

Major L.F. Ellis, *The War in France and Flanders 1939–1940* (Official History of the Second World War, H.M.S.O., London, 1954)

German Order of Battle 1944: Directory Prepared by Allied Intelligence (London, 1994).

Desmond Llewelyn, *Q* (Seaford, 1999)

The Memoirs of Field Marshal the Viscount Montgomery of Alamein (London, 1958)

Hugh Sebag-Montefiore, *Dunkirk. Fight to the last man* (London, 2006)

1 R.W.F. United Kingdom 1940–1942

A Soldier Reminisces, by Fusilier W.H. Jones, 4193285, Signaller, 1st Battalion Royal Welch Fusiliers

1939–1945 The Unsung Heroes. A personal account by 5186455 Fusilier W.C. Smith 1st Battalion Royal Welch Fusiliers

Independent Companies and Commandos

Brigadier C.N. Barclay, *The History of the 53rd (Welsh) Division in the Second World War* (London, 1956)

The German Campaign in Norway. German Naval History Series BR 1840 (1) compiled by Tactical and Staff Duties Division of the Admiralty (27 November 1948)

Andrew Croft, *A Talent for Adventure* (Worcester, 1991)

Christopher Buckley, *Norway, The Commandos, Dieppe* (HMSO, London, 1951)

T.K. Derry, *The Campaign in Norway. History of the Second World War, United Kingdom Military Series* (HMSO London, 1952)

James Dunning, *It Had To Be Tough* (Durham, 2000)

Sally Dugan, *Commando* (London, 2001)

John Durnford-Slater, *Commando* (London, 1953)

W.R. Fell, *The Sea our Shield* (London, 1966)

Major D.J.L. Fitzgerald MC, *History of the Irish Guards in the Second World War* (Aldershot, 1949)

Charles Messenger, *The Commandos 1940–1946* (London, 1985)

F.O. Miksche, *Blitzkrieg* (English edition, London, 1940)

J.P. Riley, *From Pole to Pole: The Life of Quintin Riley (Cambridge, 1988 and 1999)*

F. Spencer Chapman, *Northern Lights* (London, 1932)

Peter Verney, *The Micks* (London, 1970)

Peter Wilkinson and Joan Bright Astley, *Gubbins and SOE* (London, 1997)

2 R.W.F. Madagascar

History of the Combined Operations Organisation 1940–1945 (Amphibious Warfare Headquarters, London, 1956)

Christopher Buckley, *Five Ventures* (HMSO, 1977)

Winston Churchill, *The Second World War, Volume IV: The Hinge of Fate* (London, 1951).

Anthony Mockler, *Our Enemies The French* (London, 1976)

G.F. Petty, *Mad Gerry – Welsh Wartime Medical Officer* (Newport, 1992)

Warren Tute, *The Reluctant Enemies: The story of the last war between Britain and France 1940–1942* (London, 1990)

Jean-Noel Vincent, *Les Forces Françaises dans la Lutte Contre l'Axe en Afrique* (Vincennes, 1984)

1 and 2 R.W.F., India and Burma

C.J. Argyle, *Japan At War 1937–1945* (London, 1976)

Christopher Bayly and Tim Harper, *Forgotten Wars. The End of Britain's Asian Empire* (London, 2007)

Captain J.C. Bennett, *Memoirs Of A Very Fortunate Man* (Royston, nd).

Mike Calvert, *Slim* (London, 1973)

Michael Carver, *Out of Step. The Memoirs of Field Marshal Lord Carver* (London, 1989)

John Colvin, *No Ordinary Men. The Battle for Kohima Reassessed* (London, 1994)

J.P. Cross, *Jungle Warfare: Experiences and Encounters* (London, 1989)

Geoffry Foster, *36th Division, The Campaign in North Burma 1944–45* (Privately Printed, 1946)

George Macdonald Fraser, *Quartered Safe Out Here* (London, 1992)

J.C. Kemp, *The Royal Scots Fusiliers 1919–1959* (Glasgow, 1963)

B.H. Liddell Hart, *History of the Second World War* (London, 1973)

A Soldier Reminisces, by Fusilier W.H. Jones, 4193285, Signaller, 1st Battalion Royal Welch Fusiliers

H.F. Joslen, *Orders of Battle, Second World War, Vol I* (HMSO, 1960)

John Masters, *The Road Past Mandalay* (London, 1961).

Daniel Marston (ed), *The Pacific War Companion. From Pearl Harbour to Hiroshima* (Osprey, 2005)

Bryan Perrett, *Tank Tracks to Rangoon* (London, 1978)

F. Romanus and Riley Sunderland, *The United States Army in World War II. The Burma China-India Theater; Stillwell's Mission to China* (Department of the Army, Washington, U.S.A., 1970)

D. Rooney, *Burma Victory* (London, 1992)

Hugh Skillen, *Spies of the Airwaves* (Privately published, 1989)

Field Marshal Viscount Slim, *Defeat into Victory* (London 1999)

Martin J. Smith, *Burma: insurgency and the politics of ethnicity* (London, 1999)

Captain D.C. Rissik, 2 D.L.I, *The History of the Durham Light Infantry, 1939–1945* (Brancepeth Castle, 1953)

1939–1945 The Unsung Heroes. A personal account by 5186455 Fusilier W.C. Smith 1st Battalion Royal Welch Fusiliers

Julian Thompson, *War in Burma* (IWM, 2002)

Patrick Turnbull, *The Battle of the Box* (London, 1979)

S. Woodburn Kirby, *The War Against Japan, Vol III* (Official History of the Second World War, H.M.S.O., 1961)

S. Woodburn Kirby, *The War Against Japan, Volume IV: The Reconquest of Burma* (Official History of the Second World War, HMSO, London, 1965)

The Personal Diary of Admiral the Lord Louis Mountbatten, Supreme Allied Commander South-East Asia 1943–1946. Ed Philip Ziegler (London, 1988)

6th (R.W.) Para, 1941–1945

Kevin Jefferys, *Anthony Crosland* (London, 1997)

Brigadier C.J.C. Molony with Captain F.C. Flynn *RN*, Major-General H.L. Davies & Group Captain T.P. Gleave, *The Mediterranean and Middle East, Volume V: The Campaign in Sicily 1943 and The Campaign in Italy 3rd September 1943 to 31st March 1944.* History of the Second World War, United Kingdom Military Series, (H.M.S.O., 1973)

United States Army in World War Two: The Mediterranean Theater of Operations, *Cassino to the Alps* by Ernest F. Fisher, Jr. (Center of Military History, United States Army, Washington D.C., 1977)

Fifth Army at the Winter Line 15 November 1943–15 January 1944, (United States Army Center of Military History Publication 100-9, Washington DC, 1945)

4, 6 and 7 R.W.F. North-West Europe, 1944–1945

(Anon), *History of the 6th Battalion The Royal Welch Fusiliers, Europe 1944–45* (Privately published and printed, 1946)

Noel Annan, *Changing Enemies. The Defeat and Regeneration of Germany* (London, 1995)

C.N. Barclay, *The History of the 53rd (Welsh) Division in the Second World War* (London, 1955)

Martin Blumenson, *Breakout and Pursuit* (U.S. Army in World War II, Center of Military History, Washington D.C., 1993)

Bob Carruthers and Simon Drew, *The Normandy Battles* (London, 2000).

Hugh M. Cole, *The Ardennes: Battle of the Bulge* (U.S. Army in World War II, Center of Military History, Washington D.C., 1993)

Major R.B.S. Davies, *The Seventh. A Territorial Battalion 1908–1946* (Llanidloes, 1950)

Patrick Delaforce, *Red Crown and Dragon* – 53rd Welsh Division in North-West Europe, 1944–1945 (Brighton, 1996)

T.C.C. Dumas, *Lucky Tim.* (unpublished memoir) in R.W.F. Mus/Archives

Luc van Gent, *October 1944, Den Bosch – Bevochten en bevrijd* (Privately published, 1984)

Donald E. Graves, *Blood and Steel: The Wehrmacht Archives Vol I, Normandy 1944* (London, 2013)

Donald E. Graves, *Blood and Steel: The Wehrmacht Archives Vol 2, Retreat to the Reich, September to December 1944* (London, 2015)

Donald E. Graves, *Blood and Steel: The Wehrmacht Archives Vol 3, The Ardennes Offensive, December 1944–January 1945* (London, 2015)

Gordon A. Harrison, *Cross-Channel Attack* (U.S. Army in World War II, Center of Military History, Washington D.C., 2004)

Stephen Hart, *Colossal Cracks: Montgomery's 21st Army Group in Northwest Europe, 1944–1945* (Mechanicsburg, U.S.A., 2000).

Charles B. MacDonald, *The Last Offensive* (U.S. Army in World War II, Center of Military History, Washington D.C., 1993)

Charles B. MacDonald, *The Siegfried Line Campaign* (U.S. Army in World War II, Center of
Military History, Washington D.C., 1993)

John Ottewell, *A Cry from the Heart* (Privately published and printed)

John Russell, *No Triumphant Procession. The Forgotten Battles of April 1945* (London 1994)

Charles Whiting, *Hitler's Werewolves* (London, 1983)

C. 'Wally' Williams, *The Rain, the Mud and the Blood* (Privately published and printed, Wells,
date unknown)

Service Battalions, 1919–1945

Lt Col F.N. Burton (ed), *The War Diary of 10th (Service) Battalion Royal Welch Fusiliers* (Plymouth,
1926)

Artillery Regiments, 1939–1945

'The Story of D Troop 381/116 (R.W.) L.A.A. Regiment R.A. at 's-Hertogenbosch, 27th–30th
October 1944.' Account compiled by E.H. Williams and others and privately printed

The First Division 1809–1985. A Short Illustrated History (Verden, 1985)

Home Guard Battalions

Les Darbyshire, *Our Backyard War. West Merioneth in World War II* (Talybont, 2015)

S.P. Mackenzie, *The Home Guard. The Real Story of 'Dad's Army'* (OUP, 1996)

Henry Smith, *Bureaucrats in Battledress. The History of the Ministry of Food Home Guard* (Conway,
1945)

A.G. Veysey, *Clwyd at War 1939–45* (Clwyd Record Office, 1989)

John R. Williams, *A Record of the 1st Denbighshire Home Guard* (R.E. Jones, 1943)

Lieutenant H.L. Wilson, *Four Years. The Story of the Fifth Batt. Caerns. Home Guard* (Conway,
1944)

Articles in Newspapers and Periodicals

General

Sir Arthur Bryant, 'The Fate of the Regiment', *The Times*, 4 April 1948

Field Marshal Montgomery, 'Morale in Battle' in *British Medical Journal* No 2 (1946), p 704

The Wish Stream, (R.M.A. Sandhurst) 1948, 1949, 1950, 1951

Y Ddraig Goch – The Journal of The Royal Welch Fusiliers: various issues from Series I, May 1922–
June 1925; Series II, March 1931–December 1933; Series III, March 1933–Spring 1940;
Spring 1946 and Winter 1946 as cited in endnotes

R.W.F. Regimental Newsletter, one issue in May 1941 and five issues from August 1943–
August 1945

Life before the Second World War

Peter Caddick-Adams, 'The Territorial Army before The Second World War' *British Army
Review,* Number 121

Army Quarterly 14/131 (1931); 2/268–280 (1933); 37/150 (1938)

China Post, 1 March 1937

The *Cologne Post and Wiesbaden Times* Christmas souvenir number 1926

'The Irish Rebellion in the 6th Divisional Area. From after the 1916 Rebellion to December, 1921' in *The Irish Sword, The Journal of the Military History Society of Ireland*, Vol XXVII, Spring 2010, No 107

J.C. Rowley 'Education on Active Service (Waziristan, 1921–1923)', *Journal of the Army Educational Corps*, Vol II No 1, March 1925

History Today: Martin Pugh 'The General Strike', May 2006

Hansard (House of Commons) C2298, 20 March 1928

Hong Kong Naturalist, March 1938

Historical Journal, 1972

R.U.S.I Journal, LXIV (1919), No LXVII, (1922), LXXV (1930), LXXVI (1931), LXXIX (1934), LXXX (1935), No LXXXI (1936), No LXXXII (1937)

The Times, 16 December 1922

The Daily Express, 5 September 1938 (leader)

Peter Silverman, 'The Ten Year Rule', *RUSI Journal* No 116, March 1971

Shanghai Evening Post, 19 October 1937

Time Magazine, Monday 10 September 1937

1 R.W.F. France and Belgium, 1939–1940

'Henry Swam For It', *Warminster Journal*, 15 August 1997

Independent Companies and Commandos

The Daily Mail, 5 June 1940

2 R.W.F. Madagascar

British Army Review: Jim Stockman 'Madagascar 1942. Part1: Prelude to Assault', April 1986; Jim Stockman 'Madagascar 1942: Part 2 – The Battle', August 1986

Sunday Graphic, 20 September 1942

1 and 2 R.W.F. India and Burma

Army Quarterly: Lieutenant Colonel J.R.L. Rumsey, 'Air Supply in Burma,' Vol LV, October 1947–January 1948; Captain F.W.E. Fursdon, 'Draft Conductor to Togoland', Vol LVII, No 1, October 1948

The Monsoon (29 Infantry Brigade), 1943

The Times, 23 November 1944

6th (R.W.) Para

Y Ddraig Goch, Journal of the Royal Welch Fusiliers: Cliff Meredith, 'The Sinking of HMS Abdiel–9th/10th September 1943', March 1994, p. 88

Lt Col John Pearson OBE, 'The Tragedy of HMS Abdiel 1943', *Y Ddraig Goch*, March 1995, p. 91–92

British Army Review: Review of Camilla Whitby Films, 'A Summer in Provence: The Story of Operation Dragoon (1944)', No. 110, p. 105

T.A. Battalions in the U.K., 1919–1945
After the Battle, No 49 (1985)

T.A. Battalions in North-West Europe, 1944–1945
The Red Dragon [53rd Welsh Division News Letter]
Victor Thompson, 'They Fought Non-Stop for a Month', *Daily Herald* 12 March 1945
The Flash, 6th Battalion Newspaper (fortnightly) from October 1945–June 1946

Websites and Internet Material

www.itnsource.com/en/partners/gaumont-graphic
www.measuringwroth.com
www.niehorster.org

Military Publications, Studies and Pamphlets

'A Parachute Battalion', X/127/2 in Army Council Instructions 3 June 1942 (Establishment table for 1942–1943)
Royal Warrant for the Pay of the Army, 1931, 1940
J.E. Edmunds, *The Occupation of the Rhineland* (H.M.S.O., 1944)
Kevin Abraham, Chip Chapman, and Brian Plenty H.C.S.C. *Campaign Case Study, Suez.* (Joint Services Command and Staff College, 2003)
Major J.B. Higham and E.A. Knighton *The Second World War 1939–1945 Army Movements* (War Office Official Publication, 1955)
Field Service Regulations, Volume I (Organisation and Administration) 1930. WO 26/Regs/1849
Field Service Regulations, December 1939. WO 26/GS Publications/176.
Field Service Pocket Book 1926. WO 26/863
Field Service Pocket Book (WO 1939)
Field Service Pocket Book (WO 1940)
Field Service Pocket Book Part I – Pamphlet No 3, Abbreviations (WO 26 GS 1275, 1944)
Infantry Training Volume I (WO 1926)
Infantry Training 1937 (WO26/1447)
Field Service Manual, 1930, *Infantry Battalion*
A. Kennet and C.H.T. Clayton, H.C.S.C. *Campaign Case Study, Madagascar* (Joint Services Command and Staff College, 2003)
Japanese Weapons Illustrated (WO, 1944)
Signal Training All Arms, 1938
Operations – Military Training Pamphlet 23 Part I. WO 26/GS Publications/602 (1942)
Periodical Notes on the Japanese Army, Nos 1, 7. WO 26/GS Publications/1285
Regulations for the Territorial Army 1936
Report to the Combined Chiefs of Staff by the Supreme Allied Commander South-East Asia 1943–1945 (H.M.S.O., 1951)
Welsh Army Corps, 1914–1919. Report of the Executive Committee (Cardiff, 1921)

Other Official Publications

Parliament Command Papers
Cmnd 2528, *Memorandum of the Secretary of State for War relating to the Army Estimates for 1926*, 1 March 1926
Army Orders
382 of 1914; 388 of 1914; 399 of 1914; 366 of 1925
Army Council Instructions
103 of 1914; 768 of 1916; 212 of 1916; 276 of 1916; 421 of 1916; 818 of 1916; 225 of 1916; 1024 of 1916; 1528 of 1916; 208 of 1918
London Gazette
13–18 September 1923; 3 June 1932; 3 September 1940; 22 October 1940; 20 December 1940; 29 November 1945

Lectures

Major M. Everett DSO *R.E.*, *The Destruction of Makin – February 1923*. (A lecture given at the Staff College, Quetta)

Broadcasts

Frank Gillard, *Combat Diary* broadcast, B.B.C. Home and Forces Programme, Saturday 20 January 1945

Annex K

Index

Index of People

Alexander, Major-General H.R.L.G 60, 281, 440, 444

Allen, Seymour 233, 236

Allenby, General Lord 89–91

Allsebrook, Lieutenant Colonel H. 318, 366

Alston, Major Ll. A.A. ('Woolly') 101, 120, 131, 175, 190, 272

Anderson, 2nd Lieutenant N.J.H. 512, 519

Ap Rhys Pryce, Lieutenant M.H. ('Ap') 132, 135–136, 139, 152–154, 166, 183, 193, 203, 222, 225, 227, 231, 237, 240, 269, 271, 275

Armitage, Brigadier C.C. 167, 256, 259

Auchinleck, Lieutenant General C.J.E. 515–516, 519–520, 529, 533

Bainbridge, W.S. 245, 254

Barchard, Lieutenant Colonel D.M. 184, 193, 231, 240, 253, 272, 275, 282, 294, 301, 401, 405, 407

Beauvoir de Lisle, Lieutenant General Sir Henry 232, 313, 323, 343, 401

Bennett, Sergeant J.C. 198, 488

Bent, Lieutenant A.G. 184, 194, 202, 405, 427–428, 453, 465, 484, 492–493

Benyon, Captain W.L.R. ('Winkie') 59, 166, 169, 172, 174, 182, 184–186, 189, 191, 194, 202, 204–205, 260, 373, 375, 428, 445, 493

Bingham, Captain the Honourable G.R.B. 104, 116

Birdwood, Field Marshal Sir William 116, 127, 133, 138

Bosanquet, Lieutenant Colonel N.R.G. 169, 171, 184, 194, 204, 269, 275, 294, 301, 364, 381, 398, 408

Boyle, R.L. Lieutenant 194, 201, 204, 275, 294, 301, 468, 472, 494–495

Braithwaite, Major G.E. 184, 190, 241, 247, 253, 260, 319–320, 367, 373, 375, 405–406, 429

Brougham, Second Lieutenant H.G. 192–193, 428

Bruxner-Randall, Lieutenant Colonel J.G. 137, 139, 149, 152, 166, 174–177, 183, 189–190, 193, 203, 221, 241, 259–260, 268, 275, 294, 301, 312, 315, 405–407, 419

Butler, Lieutenant Colonel P.R. 127, 129, 131, 248, 252, 257, 259, 425

Butler, Brigadier S.S. 156, 158

Cadogan, Captain Edward H. 59, 171, 175–176, 179, 185, 336, 370

Caldwell, W.O. II 453, 494

Cameron, Brigadier General A.R. 216, 219

Cameron, Lieutenant Colonel B.D. 503–505

Cave-Bigley, Second Lieutenant Peter 476–477, 498

Chambers, RSM R.W. 152, 166, 175, 184

Charlton, Major J.R.O. 327, 390, 501, 504–506

Churchill, Sir Winston 55–57, 75, 80, 84, 98, 254, 303, 357, 388, 408, 442, 508, 530

Clements, Sergeant 164–165

Clough-Taylor, Captain 327, 482–484, 486

Cockburn, Lieutenant Colonel J.B. 102, 108, 208–209, 422

Colleton, Brigadier General Sir Robert A.W. 259, 415

Condon, CQMS P. 241, 259

Cooper, Duff 309, 362

Crauford, Colonel Commandant G.S.C. 135, 137

Crawshay, Lieutenant Colonel C.H.R. 313–315

Crewe-Read, Lieutenant Colonel R.O. 343–345

Croft, Sir James 512, 532

Croft, Captain N.A. 511–512

Index of Places

Index of Military Units & Formations

6th (Reserve) Battalion (T.F.) 95, 97
6th Garrison Battalion 89, 94, 413–414
6th (Caernarvonshire & Anglesey) Battalion
    (T.F.) 83, 85, 95, 305, 330, 336, 368, 370
7 R.W.F 89–90, 93–94, 196, 304–305, 308,
    319, 343–345, 350, 361–363, 376, 421, 425,
    428–429, 433–434, 458
7th Holding Battalion 379, 382
7th (Merioneth & Montgomeryshire) Battalion
    (T.F.) 83, 92, 94–95, 305, 343, 349, 351, 372,
    374
8th (Service) Battalion, R.W.F. 86, 110, 299, 361,
    366, 376–377, 381, 389, 392, 413, 531–532
8th Entrenching Battalion 87, 89, 97
9th (Service) Battalion, R.W.F. 86, 361, 368–369,
    392, 414, 423, 433
10th (Service) Battalion, R.W.F. 87, 89, 361,
    372–373, 382, 384, 392, 413, 494, 531
11th (Service) Battalion, R.W.F. 87, 390
13th (Service) Battalion, R.W.F. 86–88, 96, 116,
    122, 146, 148, 183, 239, 278, 332, 413–415,
    433, 454, 515
14th (Service) Battalion, R.W.F. 86, 88, 96,
    413–415, 420, 432–433
15th (1st London Welsh) (Service) Battalion 88,
    229, 240, 413–414, 420, 432
16th (Service) Battalion, R.W.F. 86, 88, 96,
    413–415, 420
17th (Service) Battalion, R.W.F. 86, 88, 96, 208,
    332, 413–414, 420, 433
18th (Reserve) Battalion (2nd London Welsh),
    R.W.F. 95–96, 420, 432
19th (Service) Battalion, R.W.F. 86–88, 89, 413
24 R.W.F. 94, 303
24th (Denbighshire Yeomanry) Battalion
    (T.F.) 89, 414, 420
25th (Montgomeryshire & Welsh Horse
    Yeomanry) Battalion 89, 414
26th (Service) Battalion, R.W.F. 89, 93–94, 209,
    413–414, 434
62nd Training Reserve Battalion 95–97
63rd Training Reserve Battalion 95–97
64th Training Reserve Battalion 95–97
Buckinghamshire Battalion 349–350

Batteries
43 Battery 391, 506–507

44 Battery 504, 507
237 Battery 386, 388, 390, 505–506
239 Battery 386, 389–390, 504–506
240 Battery 386, 389

Companies
No 1 Independent Company 514, 516, 527, 529,
    531
No 2 Independent Company 367, 370, 374,
    376, 509, 511–516, 518–521, 523, 526–529,
    531–534
No 3 Independent Company 511, 514–516,
    520–521, 523, 526–527, 529–530, 531, 533
No 4 Independent Company 514–516, 520–521,
    523, 526–529, 531
No 5 Independent Company 514–516, 527, 529,
    531
No 6 Independent Company 530–531
No 7 Independent Company 530–531
No 8 Independent Company 530–531
No 9 Independent Company 379, 381, 383,
    529–532

Other Forces and Formations
Army Reserve 69, 79
Black and Tans 217, 219, 227
Bodøforce 519, 526, 529
Home Service battalions 66, 83, 94, 362
National Defence Companies 356, 362, 364
North Russia Relief Force 208, 440
North-West Expeditionary Force 514, 533, 638
Royal West African Frontier Force 65, 229
Scissorsforce 514–515
Stockforce 517, 520, 525–529, 534
Supplementary Reserve 79, 407
Vicforce 490, 496
Volunteer Force 84, 97–98, 100, 303, 418
Waziristan Field Force 109, 126

Other Services
Royal Navy 163–164, 228, 233, 239, 260,
    270–271, 274, 488, 510
Royal Marines 68, 174, 270, 530
Royal Air Force (R.A.F.) 55–56, 59, 121, 139,
    141, 155, 158–159, 165, 174, 214, 222, 233,
    240, 253, 258, 260, 268, 275, 295, 323, 381,
    406, 451, 488, 510, 512

Index of Materiel

Index of General & Miscellaneous Terms